Surveys in Econometrics

Surveys in Econometrics

Edited by

Les Oxley, Donald A. R. George,
Colin J. Roberts and Stuart Sayer

BLACKWELL
Oxford UK & Cambridge USA

Copyright © Basil Blackwell Ltd 1995

First published 1995

Blackwell Publishers, the publishing imprint of
Basil Blackwell Ltd
108 Cowley Road
Oxford OX4 1JF
UK

Basil Blackwell Inc.
238 Main Street
Cambridge, Massachusetts 02142
USA

British Library Cataloguing in Publication Data

A CIP catalogue record for this book is available from the British Library.

Library of Congress Cataloging-in-Publication Data
Surveys in econometrics / edited by Les Oxley . . . [et al.].
    p. cm.
    Selected articles from the Journal of economic surveys from its inception in 1987, with an update of Adrian Pagan's original 1987 article.
    Includes bibliographical references and index.
    ISBN 0–631–19065–1 (pbk).
    1. Econometrics. I. Oxley, Les.
HB 139.S874   1994   93–29369
330′.01′5195—dc20   CIP

Typeset in 10 1/2 on 12 pt Times by Pure Tech Corporation, Pondicherry, India

This book is printed on acid-free paper

Contents

Preface

The *Journal of Economic Surveys* was conceived in 1985 as a reaction to the growing balkanization of economics and the increasing barriers to entry to specialist subject matter raised against non-specialists. The first issue was produced in 1987 with the lead article being Adrian Pagan's 'Three econometric methodologies: A critical appraisal', a paper much used and referenced. Clearly there was a need for such papers and just as importantly a hungry market. A steady stream of high quality papers have continued to be published and the *Journal* is now entering its seventh year.

From its inception it was hoped that collections of recent contributions from the *Journal* could be arranged to reflect particular themes. *Surveys in Econometrics* is the first such volume comprising nine recent or forthcoming surveys of important developments in econometrics, plus an update to the original Pagan (1987) article. The contributions are extensive and broadly self-contained surveys of the literature with full bibliographic references and, where possible, data used as illustration are reproduced with the text. As such, many articles will have an obvious teaching use. The surveys have been written to be accessible to a wide range of readers from advanced undergraduates, through technically competent non-specialist economists from a wide range of environments to specialists in the area. However, *Surveys in Econometrics* should not be seen as a textbook or an advanced monograph on econometrics, but as an up-to-date and readable adjunct to modern econometrics textbooks and specialist books of readings. Many of the published contributions have a proven track record as both cited seminal contributions and teaching adjuncts. The book provides a unique single-volume collection of many useful surveys of recent developments in econometrics.

Producing such a book has obviously accumulated a list of thankyou's, acknowledgements and future favours! First, thanks to the authors and referees who have produced carefully constructed surveys (and comments) and responded to editors' requests to appeal to the non-specialist. Thanks also to Basil Blackwell Ltd and particularly Mark Allin, Judith Harvey and Sally Davies for steering the book through inception and production. A major vote of thanks, however, must go to Mike Grover of Tieto Ltd who had the vision to see that the *Journal of Economic Surveys* was a venture worth backing.

1 Introduction

Les Oxley and Colin Roberts

The last 15 years have been witness to many influential developments in econometrics. In addition, there has been a revolution in the growth and particularly the accessibility of computer power and sophisticated computer software. Furthermore, the accessibility and frequency of economic data, particularly financial, has broadened enormously the opportunities for prospective applied econometricians. However, one consequence of such developments has been a growing gap between those with modern econometric skills and those without. Many economists would like to undertake applied research but either feel intimidated by the set-up costs or simply do not know where to start with regard to the relevant literature. A further consequence has been a growth in the specialization of certain areas of econometrics, making it difficult even for trained econometricians to keep in touch with all recent developments in the discipline.

The aim of this collection of papers, drawn from recent or forthcoming articles in the *Journal of Economic Surveys*, is to present a number of important recent influential developments in econometrics in such a way as to act both as an introduction to the area for non-specialists and as an up-to-date review of the topic. A particular emphasis has been placed on developments with an applied content or implication as it is here where we feel most interest from non-specialists is likely to lie. Because of the number and extent of developments such a selection will, by necessity, be restricted. However, readers will notice a concentration on contributions which either support or follow the 'LSE tradition' of econometric modelling. This emphasis reflects a number of features. First, the majority of econometric articles submitted to the *Journal* follow such a line. Second, the paradigm appears to be both the dominant UK view and one gaining support worldwide, particularly in Australasia and the Far East. Finally, it reflects, to some extent, the inevitable biases created by the editors' own views. However, it must be stressed that this book is not an econometrics textbook nor a book of reading on a particular narrow field. Furthermore, the contributions are not intended to survey all recent developments in econometrics. Readers wishing to consider such overviews may wish to consult Pagan and Wickens (1989) or Giles (1991). As a consequence any connections between contributions in this book will almost inevitably be fairly loose ones.

Outline of the contents

Overview

The contributions in the book can be loosely grouped into three sections. The first four contributions, by Pagan (two), Giles and Giles, and McAleer, consider aspects of modern econometric methodologies with a particular emphasis on the 'LSE methodology' most often associated with the ideas of David Hendry. These first four contributions can be usefully read by those wishing to gain insights into one of the major approaches to econometric modelling.

The second set of contributions by Alogoskoufis and Smith and by Muscatelli and Hurn concentrate on the issue of error correction mechanism (ECM) formulations of short-run and long-run relationships and the implications of cointegrated data. The former piece provides a thorough review of the alternative rationales for the ECM formulation including associations with the notion of cointegration. This leads naturally into Muscatelli and Hurn's paper, a rewritten version of their original *Journal* contribution, where considerable effort has been made to consider the practical aspects of the estimation of cointegrated relationships with explicit examples based on a data set presented in the article. As a readable introduction to ECMs and cointegration this section is highly recommended with more specialized contributions to be found in Engle and Granger (1991).

The contributions by Bera and Higgins, Mills, Oxley and McAleer, and Delgado and Robinson consider various developments in estimation methods which have attracted recent attention. Such attention has materialized for a number of reasons; for example, the growth of interest in the implications of testing the rational expectations hypothesis (REH) has created a need to estimate models with unobserved variables. These issues are discussed in Oxley and McAleer. A growing interest in financial economics and the availability of high frequency data have led to considerable interest in autoregressive conditional heteroskedasticity (ARCH) processes, reviewed in Bera and Higgins. The increased frequency of data has also accelerated the development of many semi-parametric and nonparametric methods discussed in Delgado and Robinson as well as developments in time series methods, some of which are considered in Mills.

Detailed contents

The opening contribution of the book was the lead article in *Journal of Economic Surveys*, volume 1, issue 1. This seminal piece by Adrian Pagan was one of the first papers to consider the growing debate on econometric methodology. The debate continues (see Granger, 1990; Dharmapala, 1993). However, the issues raised by Pagan had a considerable impact on the way applied econometricians thought about research methods. The dichotomies he discussed, focusing upon the work of Hendry, Leamer and Sims, put econometric methodology into the domain of an active research area. In his second contribution Pagan has updated some of his views expressed in 1987. In particular, Pagan discusses the progress made within his original three classifications of econometric methodology, although they have been de-personalized as the 'LSE methodology' (LSM), the Bayesian methodology (BM) and the VAR methodology (VM). He also identifies two important areas of recent developments within theoretical econometrics, namely cointegration and nonparametrics, two of the chosen areas of emphasis in this volume. Cointegration has had a major impact on the LSM approach, adding another 'step', an order of integration and analysis of cointegration pre-test, to the four-step process identified in Pagan (1987). Pagan discusses some of the consequences of this 'marriage of cointegration techniques and the LSM', noting the curious mixture of reduced form and structural analysis. Using the example of the superficial similarities of the ECM formulation from the cointegration and the LSM tradition, he adds to the cautionary tone of Alogoskoufis and Smith. Pagan also identifies the coming together of the LSM and VM methodologies demonstrated by the work of Hendry and Mizon (1993). The VM approach has also witnessed considerable growth since Pagan (1987) not least because of the developments from the cointegration literature. As Pagan postulates, 'it is not too fanciful to suggest that a synthesis of these two approaches (LSM and VM), is likely to be achieved'. What of the Leamer or BM approach? If the proof of the pudding is in the eating then the BM has stayed on the shelf. Hampered by the lack of computer software, sensitivity analysis has not attracted much more than lip-service. Developments in the unit root literature have given the BM a necessary shot of adrenalin spurred by the development of the Gibbs sampler (see Koop, 1994). However, developments in the BM approach have not matched those from the LSM or VM schools.

An issue often raised in criticism of the LSM approach is the lack of understanding of the effects of pre-test strategies. This important topic is the substance of the third contribution, by Judith and David Giles. This area is attracting considerable attention and the Giles's present a thorough review of the state of theoretical knowledge on the subject. They start with a distinction between pre-test estimators and pre-test tests which is often not made explicit by casual users of the terms. Their extensive survey includes analysis of pre-test strategies under model mis-specification and generalized regression errors with some exact sampling distribution results being presented. As part of our explicit intention to emphasize applied aspects of the recent developments, practical advice is offered to assist applied econometricians and some warnings are issued about the current state of knowledge on the effects of pre-test strategies.

Pre-test strategies are a part of the wider issue of specification searches and the role of diagnostics. Michael McAleer is at the forefront of the development, application and dissemination of diagnostic tests and his thorough critical review entitled 'Sherlock Holmes and the search for truth: a diagnostic tale' reflects his current views on the subject. Drawing upon his broad intellectual background, McAleer asks the question: 'can applied econometricians learn anything from the master of detection?' – Sherlock Holmes. McAleer isolates the problem solving; theorizing; reconciliation with the data; and testing phases of Holmesian techniques and relates them to model specification and testing in econometrics. However, the main substance of the paper is a thorough analysis of the role of diagnostic tests of the auxiliary assumptions of the regression model where such assumptions include correct functional form; no heteroskedasticity; no serial correlation; normality of the errors; and robustness. In addition he considers the need to test for the order of integration and cointegration of variables basically as a pre-test strategy. Diagnostic testing procedures are not without their critics and McAleer raises a number of questions related to their use. In particular, how many tests should be used; are the tests independent; what ordering of tests is optimal; are the tests powerful; and are they robust? Some answers are offered in relation to specific tests, for example the lack of power of the Box–Pierce (1970) test, and issues related to pre-test estimation and testing are discussed in Giles and Giles. McAleer concentrates on several alternative methods of developing RESET-type tests of functional form in an attempt to encourage applied economists to test such assumptions, something many seem reluctant to do. The combination of a totally clear expository style and theoretical rigour makes the McAleer contribution a 'must be read' paper for all applied econometricans. Furthermore, its links with the two Pagan pieces and the papers by Giles and Giles and Bera and Higgins strengthen the emphasis of this section of the book which addresses issues of model selection procedures.

The second section of the book relates to ECM models and cointegration. George Alogoskoufis and Ron Smith present a unique discussion of the various origins of ECM models – their common elements and main differences. In particular they identify four variants of the approach which is often used as an economic hypothesis about the nature of adjustment in dynamic models. The origins of the ECM approach are identified with Phillips's (1954) and (1957) contributions on feedback control mechanisms for stabilization policies, through Sargan's much cited (1964) Colston paper to its most extensive expositor David Hendry and the latest twist in the ECM saga coming from Granger and his associates. The contribution represents a careful critical discussion of the uses and abuses of the ECM approach and identifies a number of previously over-looked explicit modelling restrictions which must be addressed if the approach is to be used correctly. In particular, estimation of certain formulations of the ECM explicitly involves nonlinear restrictions on parameters which need to be satisfied if the modelling approach is to have empirical validity. Furthermore, they distinguish the work of Granger and his colleagues, which is explicitly multivariate and atheoretical, from the other three approaches. This is important in relation to the association of Granger (type) ECM models and cointegration and the now-common blanket association of such models with cointegrated relationships. Many readers will be aware of the Granger representation theorem which states that 'if a set of variables is cointegrated of order 1,1 [CI(1,1)], then there exists a valid error correction representation of the data'. One implication of the theorem is that in the Granger case the argument is invertible; however, this property does not carry over to all versions of the ECM approach. Alogoskoufis and Smith support their theoretical discussion with a number of empirical examples which can be easily replicated with proven robustness.

This element of empirical illustration is a feature of the partner to Alogoskoufis and Smith in this section – Muscatelli and Hurn. With a recent update to include results derived from Phillips and Hansen (1990) estimation methods, Muscatelli and Hurn present an applied economist's view of the recent literature on cointegration including a discussion of the effects of seasonal differencing. Using a data set on the UK demand for money, reproduced in the book, they present a step-by-step approach to the testing and identification of the order of integration and cointegration of the data. They contrast these results with those from more traditional methods of estimating such models. Reinforcing the warnings issued by Alogoskoufis and Smith, Muscatelli and Hurn caution about the unthinking use of cointegration methods. Following such procedures, even carefully, does not guarantee the discovery of an unambiguously powerful empirical model. Furthermore, they highlight some of the statistical weaknesses of current unit root tests, particularly their power, and warn of the use of such tests as pre-tests in econometric model building – an issue to consider in relation to the survey by Giles and Giles.

The final group of contributions is led by Anil Bera and Matt Higgins's extensive review of the literature on ARCH processes. The current interest in ARCH processes originated in the work of Engle (1982), since which the developments and extensions have mushroomed, in part because of its success in accounting for many observed volatility properties of asset prices. ARCH, GARCH, EGARCH, IGARCH, QTARCH, ... AARCH,!! Bera and Higgins present a clear theoretical discussion of the various variants of the original formulation (together with a glossary of terms!). Moreover, they illustrate, using both simulated and financial data, some of the properties of ARCH processes and the estimation and testing of ARCH models. Many state-of-the-art developments are discussed including nonlinear ARCH processes, utilizing the techniques associated with Box and Cox (1964) and the effects of non-normal error structures which often necessitate the use of nonparametric estimation methods. In addition to the empirical illustrations, Bera and Higgins provide an extensive discussion of many of the empirical applications of the ARCH model and its extensions and provide an extensive bibliography. The product of such a thorough theoretical and empirical discussion is a serious primer on most aspects of ARCH modelling. Some of the developments of the original model discussed by the authors, including the joint presence of ARCH and bilinearity and nonparametric estimation, are complemented by the contributions of Terry Mills and of Miguel Delgado and Peter Robinson.

Recently there has been a resurgence of interest in nonlinear modelling of economic relationships in general and macroeconomics in particular. This interest has been mirrored by a greater interest in developing nonlinear extensions to the basic autoregressive integrated moving average (ARIMA) models of Box and Jenkins (1976). Following a brief introduction to ARIMA models, Mills considers the effects of various transformations of data, particularly the effects on estimation. Fractional integration, leading to ARFIMA (AR fractionally IMA) models, is developed. ARFIMA models would seem to have implications for the development of new tests of stationarity in the tradition of Dickey and Fuller (1979). The links between the bilinear model and ARCH processes are discussed, as are other conditional variance models, including those of Hsu (1977, 1979) and Clark (1973). Establishing the existence of nonlinear relationships is addressed through a discussion of some tests of nonlinearity, including the Brock, Dechert and Scheinkman (1987) (BDS) statistic, which is based on the concept of the correlation integral. An important feature of the Mills paper is its emphasis on developing the relationships between different nonlinear model formulations in an attempt to establish overlaps between the time series data literature associated with ARIMA modelling and that of the time series modellers discussed in Bera and Higgins. As such it provides a useful cross-fertilization of ideas, to be considered in conjunction with the previous contribution.

The REH has undoubtedly revolutionized many areas of economics and formed the cornerstone of the New Classical macroeconomics (NCM) of Barro, Lucas and Sargent. Following the theoretical developments, numerous attempts were (and still are) made to test models with (unobserved) expectational variables. Oxley and McAleer, in an extended version of their earlier paper for the *Journal*, present a detailed discussion of macroeconomic models with unobserved (generated) variables in general and NCM models of monetary neutrality in particular. The paper considers the econometric implications of models with generated regressors and the testable implications of the REH in general and NCM models in particular, and discusses issues of estimation. The discussion is extensive and utilizes a common generic model to aid understanding. The properties of different estimation methods are discussed and the important question of when two-step estimation is efficient is raised and answered. In addition to the theoretical discussion, Oxley and McAleer critically review some 60 published papers which test versions of the NCM monetary neutrality hypothesis. The paper complements texts such as Pesaran (1987), presenting the material in a readable self-contained format. The review of tests of the NCM monetary neutrality hypothesis is extensive and up to date and contains a full bibliography and tables of results.

The final contribution to the book departs from many of the estimation procedures used, either implicitly or explicitly, by many of the previous contributors. Most econometric models have a parametric underpinning, which is utilized in estimation and when drawing statistical inferences. However, the choice of parametric model is crucial if the desirable properties of estimation and inference are to be achieved. Economic theory may, in some limited cases, determine the underlying parametric representation, but generally this is not the case with arbitrary (or convenient) assumptions made on, for example, functional form. Nonparametric models allow the data to 'speak for themselves' and provide a more robust approach to statistical inference. These are the messages of Miguel Delgado and Peter Robinson's contribution on nonparametric and semiparametric methods for economic research. Starting from first principles, Delgado and Robinson develop some of the necessary techniques of nonparametric models, including the crucial concept of the kernel and kernel estimation. The development is, at times, demanding given the very general nature of the parametric representation under discussion. However, the discussion of the relative strengths and weaknesses of different estimators is thorough and self-contained. In many practical circumstances, for example estimation via N-KERNEL or XploRe (see Lee, 1992), only a familiarity with such issues will be required. However, those wishing to know the exact properties of different estimators will find many answers in the chapter by Delgado and Robinson. Finally, some discussion of the estimation of such semiparametric and nonparametric models is raised, including the availability of software. An extensive bibliography should allow interested readers to delve deeper into this growing field.

Epilogue

Understanding recent developments in econometric theory is an important requirement for many applied economists. Another barrier to entry has been created by the growth of powerful and sophisticated econometric software. Many of the surveys reproduced in this book either use explicitly or refer tangentially to a selection of software packages including Microfit 3.0, RATS, PC-GIVE and SHAZAM. To some such acronyms are as foreign as ARCH, ECM and DF. As a consequence some readers may wish to consult recent software reviews published in the *Journal of Economic Surveys* including Byers (1992), Lee (1992) and Psaradakis (1993).

These, and other reviews in the *Journal*, present the main salient features of the package(s) concerned, including hardware requirements, data handling facilities and estimation capabilities. They provide a useful review facility to allow novice and expert alike to choose the best software package for their own needs. Not only is there a need for an introduction to the relevant econometric theory, there is a need for an introduction to the software to produce the results to analyse.

Software reviews have not been reproduced in this book because of space constraints and the inevitable rapid dating of their content. However, new versions of existing packages and new developments will continue to be published in the *Journal* to which your attention is drawn.

References

Box, G. and Cox, D. (1964) An analysis of transformations. *Journal of the Royal Statistical Society Series B*, 26, 211–43.

—— and Jenkins, G. (1976) *Time Series Analysis: Forecasting and Control*. San Francisco, CA: Holden Day.

—— and Pierce, D. (1970) Distribution of the residual autocorrelations in autoregressive-integrated-moving average time series models. *Journal of the American Statistical Association*, 65, 1509–26.

Brock, W., Dechert, W. and Scheinkman, J. (1987) A test for independence based on the correlation dimension. Mimeo, University of Wisconsin-Madison.

Byers, D. (1992) Microfit 3.0. *Journal of Economic Surveys*, 6, 287–97.

Clark, P. K. (1973) A subordinated stochastic process model with finite variance for speculative prices. *Econometrica*, 41, 135–55.

Dharmapala, D. (1993) On the history and methodology of econometrics. *Journal of Economic Surveys*, 7, 85–104.

Dickey, D. and Fuller, W. (1979) Distribution of the estimators for autoregressive series with a unit root. *Journal of the American Statistical Association*, 74, 427–31.

Engle, R. F. (1982) Autoregressive conditional heteroscedasticity with estimates of the variance of UK inflation. *Econometrica*, 50, 987–1008.

—— and Granger, C. W. J. (eds) (1991) *Long Run Economic Relations: Readings in Cointegration*. Oxford: Oxford University Press.

Giles, D. E. A. (1991) Some recent developments in econometrics: lessons for applied economists. In K. W. Clements, R. G. Gregory and T. Takayama (eds), *International Economics Postgraduate Research Conference Volume* (Supplement to the *Economic Record*), 3–19.

Granger, C. W. J. (ed.) (1990) *Modelling Economic Time Series: Readings in Econometric Methodology*. Oxford: Blackwell.

Hendry, D. F. and Mizon, G. M. (1993) Evaluating dynamic econometric models by encompassing the VAR. In P. C. B. Phillips and V. B. Hall (eds), *Models, Methods and Applications of Econometrics: Essays in Honor of Rex Bergstrom*, Oxford: Oxford University Press.

Hsu, D. A. (1977) Tests for variance shift at an unknown time point. *Applied Statistics*, 26, 279–84.

—— (1979) Detecting shifts of parameter in gamma sequences with applications to stock price and air traffic flow analysis. *Journal of the American Statistical Association*, 74, 31–40.

Koop, G. (1994) Recent progress in applied Bayesian econometrics. *Journal of Economic Surveys*, 8, 1–34.

Lee, D. K. C. (1992) N-KERNEL and XploRe. *Journal of Economic Surveys*, 6, 89–105.

Pagan, A. R. (1987) Three econometric methodologies: a critical appraisal. *Journal of Economic Surveys*, 1, 3–24.

—— and Wickens, M. (1989) A survey of some recent methods for estimation and testing in econometrics. *Economic Journal*, 99, 962–1025.

Pesaran, M. H. (1987) *The Limits to Rational Expectations*. Oxford: Basil Blackwell.

Phillips, A. W. (1954) Stabilization policy in a closed economy. *Economic Journal*, 64, 290–323.

—— (1957) Stabilization policy and the time form of lagged responses. *Economic Journal*, 67, 265–77.

Phillips, P. and Hansen, B. (1990) Statistical inference in instrumental variables regression with I(1) processes. *Review of Economic Studies*, 57, 99–125.

Psaradakis, Z. (1993) PcGive version 7: a review. *Journal of Economic Surveys*, 7, 399–.

Sargan, J. D. (1964) Wages and prices in the United Kingdom: a study in econometric methodology. *Proceedings of the Sixteenth Symposium of the Colston Research Society 1964*, vol. XVI, London: Butterworths.

2 Three econometric methodologies: a critical appraisal

Adrian Pagan
University of Rochester

Methodological debate in economics is almost as long-standing as the discipline itself. Probably the first important piece was written by John Stuart Mill (1967), and his conclusions seem as pertinent today as when they were written in the nineteenth century. He observed that many practitioners of political economy actually held faulty conceptions of what their science covered and the methods used. At the same time he emphasized that, in many instances, it was easier to practise a science than to describe how one was doing it. He finally concluded that a better understanding of scope and method would facilitate the progress of economics as a science, but that sound methodology was *not* a necessary condition for the practice of sound methods. 'Get on with the job' seems the appropriate message.

It is interesting that it was not until the Fifth World Congress of the Econometric Society in 1985 that a session was devoted to methodological issues. There are good reasons for this. Until the mid-1970s it would have been difficult to find a comprehensive statement of the principles guiding econometric research, and it is hard to escape the conclusion that econometricians had taken to Mill's injunction with a vengeance. Even the debate between 'frequentists' and 'subjectivists' that prevailed in statistics was much more muted in econometrics. It is true that there was a vigorous attempt to convert econometricians to a Bayesian approach by Zellner (1971) and the 'Belgian connection' at CORE (see Drèze and Richard, 1983). But this attempt did not seem to have a great impact upon applied research.

All of this changed after 1975. Causes are always harder to isolate than effects, but it is difficult to escape the impression that the proximate cause was the predictive failure of large-scale models just when they were most needed. In retrospect it seems likely that the gunpowder had been there for some time, and that these events just set it off. Most, for example, will know Ed Leamer's (1978, p. vi) account of his dissatisfaction with the gap between what he had been taught in books and the way practitioners acted, and it seems likely that many others had felt the same way about the type of econometrics then prevalent. But these misgivings were unlikely to have any impact until there was evidence that there was something to complain about.

Since 1975 we have seen a concerted attempt by a number of authors to build methodologies for econometric analysis. Implicit in these actions has been the notion that work along the prescribed lines would 'better' econometrics in at least three ways. First, the methodology would (and should) provide a set of principles to guide work *in all its facets*. Second, by codifying this body of knowledge it should greatly facilitate the transmission of such knowledge. Finally, a style of reporting should naturally arise from the methodology that is informative, succinct and readily understood.

In this paper we look at the current state of the debate over methodology. Three major contenders for the 'best methodology' title may be distinguished. I will refer to these as the 'Hendry', 'Leamer' and 'Sims' methodologies, after those individuals most closely *identified* with the approach. Generally, each procedure has its origins a good deal further back in time, and is the outcome of a research programme that has had many contributors apart from the named authors above. But the references – Hendry and Richard (1982), Leamer (1978) and Sims (1980a) – are the most accessible and succinct summaries of the material, and therefore it seems appropriate to use the chosen appellations. Inevitably, there has been some convergence in the views, but it will be most useful to present them in polar fashion, so as to isolate their distinct features.

1   The 'Hendry' methodology

Perhaps the closest of all the methods to the 'old style' of investigation is the Hendry methodology. It owes a lot to Sargan's seminal (1964) paper, but it also reflects an oral tradition developed largely at the London School of Economics over the past two decades. Essentially it comprises four steps.

1   Formulate a general model that is consistent with what economic theory postulates are the variables entering any equilibrium relationship and which restricts the dynamics of the process as little as possible.
2   Reparameterize the model to obtain explanatory variables that are near orthogonal and which are 'interpretable' in terms of the final equilibrium.
3   Simplify the model to the smallest version that is compatible with the data ('congruent').
4   Evaluate the resulting model by extensive analysis of residuals and predictive performance, aiming to find the weaknesses of the model designed in the previous step.

Steps 1 and 2

Theory and data continually interplay in this methodology. Unless there are good reasons for believing otherwise, it is normally assumed that theory suggests which variables should enter a relationship, and the data are left to determine whether this relationship is static or dynamic (in the sense that once disturbed from equilibrium it takes time to re-establish it).

It may help to understand the various steps of Hendry's methodology if a particular example is studied. Suppose that the investigator is interested in the determinants of the velocity of circulation of money. Let m_t be the log of the money supply, p_t be the log of the price level and y_t be the log of the real income. Theoretical reasoning suggests that, for appropriately defined money, $m_t - p_t - y_t$ should be a function of the nominal interest rate (I_t) along any steady state growth path. With $i_t = \log(I_t)$, we might therefore write $m_t^* - p_t^* - y_t^* = \delta i_t^*$ where the starred quantities indicate equilibrium values.

Of course equilibrium quantities are not normally observed, leading to the need to relate these to actual values. For time series data it is natural to do this by allowing the relations between the variables m_t, p_t, y_t and i_t to be governed by a dynamic equation of the form

$$m_t = \sum_{j=1}^{p} a_j m_{t-j} + \sum_{j=0}^{q} b_j p_{t-j} + \sum_{j=0}^{r} c_j y_{t-j} + \sum_{j=0}^{s} d_j i_{t-j}. \tag{1}$$

The first step in Hendry's methodology sets p, q, r and s to be as large as practicable in view of the type of data (generally $p = q = r = s = 5$ for quarterly data), and then to estimate (1). This model, the general model, serves as a vehicle against which all other models are ultimately compared.

Now (1) could be written in many different ways, all of which would yield the same estimates of the unknown parameters, but each of which packages the information differently and consequently may be easier to interpret and understand. Generally, Hendry prefers to rewrite the dynamics in (1) as an 'error correction mechanism' (ECM). To illustrate this point, the simple relation

$$x_t = a x_{t-1} + b_0 x_t^* + b_1 x_{t-1}^*, \tag{2a}$$

where x_t^* is the equilibrium value of x_t, has the ECM

$$\begin{aligned} \Delta x_t &= (a - 1)(x_{t-1} - x_{t-1}^*) + b_0 \Delta x_t^* + (a - 1 + b_0 + b_1) x_{t-1}^* \\ &= (a - 1)(x_{t-1} - x_{t-1}^*) + b_0 \Delta x_t^* \end{aligned} \tag{2b}$$

since steady state equilibrium in (2a) implies $x = ax + b_0 x + b_1 x$ or $a + b_0 + b_1 = 1$. Although (2b) is no different from (2a), Hendry prefers it since Δx_t^* and $x_{t-1} - x_{t-1}^*$ are closer to being orthogonal and he is able to interpret its elements as equilibrium (Δx_t^*) and disequilibrium ($x_{t-1} - x_{t-1}^*$) responses.

Moving away from this simple representation we can get some feeling for the type of equation Hendry would replace (1) with by assuming that m_t adjusts within the period to p_t, making the log of real money $m_t - p_t$ the natural analogue of x_t in (2a). The equilibrium value is then $x_t^* = y_t + \delta i_t$, and by appeal to (2b) it is clear that a re-formatted version of (1) would involve terms such as Δy_t, Δi_t and $x_{t-1} - x_{t-1}^* = m_{t-1} - p_{t-1} - y_{t-1} - \delta i_{t-1} = (m_{t-1} - p_{t-1} - y_{t-1}) - \delta i_{t-1}$. Since $(m - p - y)_{t-1}$ is related to the lagged velocity of circulation, it may be easier to interpret this re-formulated equation. Terms such as $(m - p - y)_{t-1}$ frequently appear in studies of the demand for money by Hendry and his followers. For example, in Hendry and Mizon (1978) the following equation appears:

$$\begin{aligned} \Delta(m - p)_t = {}&1.61 + 0.21\Delta y_t - 0.81\Delta i_t + 0.26\Delta(m - p)_{t-1} \\ &- 0.40\Delta p_t - 0.23(m - p - y)_{t-1} + 0.61 i_{t-4} + 0.14 y_{t-4} \end{aligned}$$

where I have replaced $\log(1 + i_t)$ with $-i_t$.

Thus, steps 1 and 2 demand a clear statement of what the variables in the equilibrium relation should be, as well as a choice of parameterization. Hendry (1986) provides what is currently the most detailed explanation of his second step, but even a perusal of that source leaves an impression of the step being more of an art than a science, and consequently difficult to codify. To some extent the problem arises since Hendry tends to blur steps 2 and 3 in his applied work, with the re-formatted equation sometimes seeming to derive from an inspection of the parameter estimates in (1). In those cases (1) is both simplified and rearranged at the same time.

The idea of beginning with a general model as the benchmark against which others might be compared seems only commonsense, but there is little doubt in my mind that it was a minority view in the 1960s (and may still be). One frequently saw (and sees) explicit rejection of this step on the grounds that it was impossible to do because economic variables were too 'collinear', with no attempt made to discover if there was even any truth in that assertion for the particular data set being used.[1] Over many years of looking at my own and students' empirical studies, I have found the rule of starting with a general model of fundamental importance for eventually drawing any conclusions about the nature of a relationship, and cannot imagine an econometric methodology that did not have this as its primary precept. As will be seen, all the methodologies analysed in this paper ascribe to that proposition.

Step 3

The first two steps in the methodology therefore seem unexceptionable. It is in the third that difficulties arise. These relate to the decision to simplify (1) and the reporting of this decision, i.e. how to go from the large model implicit in (1) to one that is easier to comprehend but which represents the data just as well. Normally, in Hendry's methodology this step involves the deletion of variables from (1), but it could also involve choosing to set combinations of parameters to particular values. For convenience our discussion will centre upon model reduction via variable deletion. To simplify at all requires a *criterion function* and a *decision rule*; how to use and report inferences from such information are the difficult issues in this third step.

First, the decision stage. It is rare to find a criterion that is not based upon the log likelihood (or its alter ego, in regression models, the sum of squares). Frequently, it is something equivalent to the likelihood ratio test statistic $-2\log(L_S/L_G)$, where L_S and L_G are the likelihoods of simplified and general models respectively. For regression models this is approximately the product of the sample size and the proportional change in the residual variance in moving from the general to simplified model. To know what is a 'big' change in the likelihood, it is common to select critical values from a table of the χ^2 distribution by specifying a desired probability of type I error. As is well known, one can think of this probability as indicating the fraction of times the simplified model would be rejected when it is true, given that the general model is re-estimated with data from many experiments differing solely by random shocks. Many see this myth as implausible in a non-experimental science such as economics, but myths such as this form the basis of many disciplines, e.g. perfect competition in economics. What is important is that any framework within which analysis is conducted lead to useful results. If reliance upon the 'story' regularly causes error, it is then time to change it for something else.

On the whole, I believe that these concepts have served us well, but there are some suggestions of alternative decision rules that may prove to be more useful. Thus Akaike (1973) and Mallows (1973) derive decision rules that opt for the deletion of a variable in a linear model if the change in the residual variance is less than $\sqrt{2}$ times the inverse of the sample size.[2] Rissanen (1983), looking at the likelihood as an efficient way to summarize all the information in the data, formulates a decision rule that the change in residual variance must be less than a function of the sample size and difference in model dimensions. None of these is incompatible with the 'Hendry' methodology; to date they have not been used much, but that is a matter of choice rather than necessity.

Having made a decision what should be reported? My own attitude, summarized in McAleer et al. (1985), is that an exact description of the decisions taken in moving from a general to a simplified model is imperative in any application of the methodology. Rarely does this involve a single decision, although it would be possible to act as if it did by just comparing the finally chosen simplified model and the original one, thereby ignoring the path followed to the simplified version. This is what Hendry seems to do in various applied studies; he normally only provides the value of a test statistic comparing the two models at each end of the path, with very little discussion (if any) of the route followed from one end to the other.

There seem to me to be some arguments against this stance. First, it is hard to have much confidence in a model if little is explained about its origin. Hendry's attitude seems to be that how a final model is derived is largely irrelevant; it is either useful or not useful, and that characteristic is independent of whether it comes purely from whimsy, some precise theory, or a very structured search (Hendry and Mizon, 1985). In a sense this is true, but it is cold comfort to those who are implementing the methodology or who are learning it for the first time. Reading Hendry's applied papers frequently leaves only puzzlement about how he actually did the simplification. In Hendry (1986), for example, the transition from a model with thirty-one parameters to one with only fourteen is explained in the following way (p. 29):

> These equations ... were then transformed to a more interpretable parameterisation and redundant functions were deleted; the resulting parsimonious models were tested against the initial unrestricted forms by the overall F-test.

It is true that confidence in the simplified model is partly a function of the value of the F-test, but by its very nature this evidence can only mean that *some* of the deleted variables do not matter. To see why, consider a general model with three regressors x_1, x_2 and x_3, all of which are orthogonal. Suppose the F statistic for the deletion of x_3 is 5 and that for x_2 is 0.5. Then the F statistic for the joint deletion of x_2 and x_3 is 2.75, and joint deletion is likely, even though it is dubious if x_3 should be deleted at all. Thus an adequate documentation of the path followed in any simplification process is desirable, rather than just accompanying any simplification with a vague statement about it. More than that, I do believe in the possibility of situations in which simplification may be done in a systematic way, e.g. in choosing dynamics via COMFAC (as in Hendry and Mizon, 1978, or McAleer et al., 1985), polynomial orders within Almon procedures and various types of demand and production restrictions that form a nested hierarchy. As far as possible I am in favour of exploiting such well-developed strategies for simplification.

Research should also be encouraged with the aim of developing new procedures or methods that require fewer assumptions.

Knowledge of the path may be important for another reason. As discussed above the critical value used in the decision rule is taken from the tables of the χ^2 or F distribution. But under the conditions of the story being used, this is only true if the simplification path consists of a single step. When there has been more than one step, the critical values cannot normally be taken from a χ^2 distribution, and it may be misleading if one proceeds as if they can. Some, for example Hill (1986), see this as a major flaw in the methodology, and others feel that the decision rule needs to be modified quite substantially in the presence of such 'data mining'. When the move from a general to a simplified model can be formulated as a nested sequence, adjustments can be made to obtain the requisite critical value (Mizon (1977) gives an account of this), but in the more common case where this is not possible theoretical analysis has made little progress. Nevertheless, numerical methods of type I error evaluation, such as the bootstrap, do enable the tracing of type I error for *any* sequence of tests and specified decision rules. Veall (1986) provides an application of this idea.

I am not certain that it is worthwhile computing exact type I errors. Ignoring the sequence entirely produces a bias against the simplified model, but that does not seem such a bad thing. Moreover, the ultimate change in the criterion function is independent of the path followed. It is frequently the change in the criterion itself which is of interest, in that it displays the sensitivity of (say) the log likelihood to variation in parameter value for the deleted variables as these range from zero to the point estimates of the general model.

Step 4

Excellent accounts are available of the necessity of this step (Hendry and Richard, 1982) and the techniques for doing it (Engle, 1984). Essentially, these procedures check whether sample moments involving the product of specified variables with functions of the data (typically residuals) are zero. Very general treatments of diagnostic tests from this viewpoint have recently been given by Tauchen (1985) and Newey (1985).[3] These procedures fulfil a number of roles within the methodology. They are important within a modelling cycle for the detection of inadequate models, but they are also important in the reporting phase, where they provide evidence that the conventions underlying almost any modelling exercise are not violated by the chosen model. Routine examination of such items as the autocorrelation function and recursive estimation of parameters have proved to be indispensable both to my own modelling (Anstie et al., 1983; Pagan and Volker, 1981) and to those of a large number of students studying applied econometrics at the Australian National University over the past decade (Harper, 1980; Kirby, 1981, for example). More than anything else, it is step 4 which differentiates Hendry's methodology from that which was standard practice in the 1960s.

2   The 'Leamer' methodology

Providing a succinct description of Leamer's methodology is a good deal more difficult than doing so for the Hendry variant. Basically, the problem lies in a lack of applications of the ideas; consequently it is hard to infer the general principles of the approach from any classic studies of how it is to work in practice. Despite this qualification, I have reduced Leamer's methodology to four distinct steps.

1   Formulate a general family of models.
2   Decide what inferences are of interest, express these in terms of parameters, and form 'tentative' prior distributions that summarize the information not contained in the given data set.
3   Consider the sensitivity of inferences to a particular choice of prior distributions, namely those that are diffuse for a specified subset of the parameters and arbitrary for the remainder. This is the extreme bounds analysis (EBA) of Leamer (1983) and Leamer and Leonard (1983). Sometimes step 3 terminates the process, but when it appears that inferences are sensitive to the prior specification this step is only a warm-up for the next one.
4   Try to obtain a narrower range for the inferences. In some places this seems to involve an explicit Bayesian approach, but in others it seems just to involve fixing a prior mean and interval for prior covariance matrices. If the restrictions in the latter step needed to get a narrow range are too 'implausible', one concludes that any inference based on these data is fragile.

Collected as in 1–4, Leamer's methodology seems to be just another sect in the Bayesian religion, and there is little point in my going over the debate in statistics concerning Bayesian procedures. Much of this is epistemological and I doubt if it will ever be resolved. In practice, the limited appeal of Bayesian methods to econometricians seems to have been based on the difficulties coming from a need to formulate high-dimensional priors in any realistic model, nagging doubts about the need to have precise distributional forms to generate posterior distributions, and the fact that many dubious auxiliary assumptions are frequently employed (e.g. lack of serial correlation and heteroskedasticity in the errors). In theory, all these doubts could be laid to rest, but the computational burden becomes increasingly heavy.

Viewed as basically an exercise in Bayesian econometrics, I have therefore very little to say about Leamer's method. It is not to my taste, but it may well be to others'. However, in attempting to sell his ideas, Leamer has produced, particularly in step 3, an approach that can be interpreted in a 'classical' rather than a Bayesian way, and it is this which one tends to think of as the Leamer methodology. The reasons for such a belief lie in the advocacy of such ideas in Leamer's two most widely read articles, Leamer (1983) and Leamer and Leonard (1983), although it is clear from Leamer (1985, 1986) that he now sees the fourth step as the important part of his analysis. Nevertheless, applications tend to be of step 3, and we will therefore analyse it before proceeding to 4.

Returning to steps 1 and 2, it is apparent that they do not differ greatly from Hendry's methodology (HM); the main distinction is that in HM the emphasis is on building a model from which inferences will later be drawn, whereas Leamer focuses upon the desired inference from the beginning. Because of this concern about a particular parameter (or, more correctly, a linear combination of parameters), it is not clear whether Leamer has a counterpart to the simplification step in Hendry's methodology. In published applications he always retains the complete model for inferences, but he has suggested to me that some simplification may be practised as an aid to communication or in the interest of efficient prediction.

Thus, cast in terms of (1) the essential distinction between the two methodologies in these early steps is that Leamer would want a clear definition of what the issues in modelling money demand are at the beginning. Suppose it was the question of the impact of interest rate variations on money demand, the question raised by Cooley and LeRoy (1981) in one of the best known applications of Leamer's ideas. Then either the size of individual d_js or $(1 - \Sigma a_j)^{-1}\Sigma d_j$ (the long-run response) would be the items of interest, and the model would be re-parameterized to reflect these concerns. In Hendry's case it is rare to find a particular set of coefficients being the centre of attention; it is variable interrelationships as a whole that seem to dominate. As in McAleer et al. (1985), questions about the magnitude of the interest rate response in (1) are answered after the final model is chosen.

Step 3

To gain a better appreciation of what is involved in step 3, particularly as a contrast to HM, it is necessary to expose the link between them. Accordingly, take the general model

$$y_t = x_t\beta + z_t\gamma + e_t \tag{3}$$

where z_t are a set of doubtful variables and interest centres upon the point estimate of the first coefficient in the β vector, β_1. In terms of the variables in (1), x_t would relate to the interest rate variables while z_t would be the remainder. In step 3 Leamer examines the extreme values of the point estimates of β_1 as all possible linear combinations of z_t are entered into regressions that always contain x_t (this being formally equivalent to diffuse priors upon β and arbitrary priors on γ). In McAleer et al. (1983, Appendix) it is shown that the absolute difference between these bounds, scaled by the standard deviation of the ordinary least squares (OLS) estimate of β_1 from (3), is given by[4]

$$\mathrm{SD}(\hat{\beta}_1)^{-1}|\hat{\beta}_{1,\max} - \hat{\beta}_{1,\min}| = \phi\chi_D^2 \tag{4}$$

where $0 \leqslant \phi \leqslant 1$ and χ_D^2 is the χ^2 statistic for testing if γ is zero.

Leamer refers to the left-hand side of (4) as 'specification uncertainty'. Let us first take the extreme case that $\phi = 1$ and ask what extra information is provided by an EBA that is not available to someone following HM. In the latter, if χ_D^2 was small, the recommended point estimate of β_1 for someone following HM would be that from the model deleting z_t. From (4) an exactly equivalent statement would be that the 'specification uncertainty' is very small, and the point estimate of β_1 would not change very much as one moved from the general to the simplified model. This is to be expected since, following Hausman (1978), a large difference between $\hat{\beta}_1$ for the simplified and general models must mean evidence against any simplification. Thus the two approaches provide a different packaging of the same information, and share exactly the same set of difficulties. In particular, all the problems of nominating a critical value for χ_D^2 have their counterpart in Leamer's methodology as providing critical values for specification uncertainty. As observed in McAleer et al. (1985), there has been no agreement on the latter question by users of the EBA method, with a range of definitions being proposed. Another interesting concomitant of (4) is that, if $\gamma \neq 0$ in (3), $\chi_D^2 \to \infty$ as the sample size grows, and so, when $\phi \neq 0$, the range between the bounds tends to infinity. Thus Leamer's complaints about classical hypothesis testing apply also to his own methodology!

Now, in HM it is an *insignificant* χ_D^2 that is important, but this need not be *numerically small* if the dimension of z_t is large. Taking the previously cited example from Hendry (1986), where seventeen parameters were set to zero, $\chi^2(17, 0.05) = 27.59$, allowing a potentially enormous gap between $\hat{\beta}_{1,\min}$ and $\hat{\beta}_{1,\max}$; point estimates of the simplified model might therefore depart substantially from those based upon other ways of combining the z_t. *If it is point estimates of* β_1 *that are desired,* it becomes very informative to perform an EBA (i.e. to compute ϕ); knowledge of χ_D^2 only sets an upper limit to the specification uncertainty, as it is the collinearity between regressors, reflected in ϕ, that determines the exact value of the 'specification uncertainty'.[5] Whenever a large number of variables are deleted in a simplification exercise, the provision of extreme bounds for any coefficients of interest seems desirable.

Where the two methodologies really part company is over the interpretation of a large χ_D^2. Followers of HM would argue that one should take point estimates of β_1 from the general model, concluding it would be an error to take them from the simplified model as the data clearly indicate that the z_t appear in the relationship.[6] Leamer would presumably conclude that 'Because there are many models which could serve as a basis for a data analysis, there are many conflicting inferences which could be drawn from a given data set' and therefore 'inferences from these data are too fragile to be useful' (Leamer and Leonard, 1983, p. 306). I confess that I cannot be convinced that our response to a situation where the data are clearly indicating that valid point estimates of β_1 will not be found by deleting z_t from (1) should be to conclude that the data are not informative about β_1!

There is no denying that there would be comfort in narrow bounds, as any conclusions that depend upon the precise value of β_1 would then be unchanged by variation in specifications. Some, for example Feldstein (1982), even see this as a desirable characteristic. But I think it hard to argue that the majority of modelling exercises can be formulated in terms of interest in the value of a single coefficient (or a linear combination of them). It is perhaps no accident that the examples Leamer provides in his articles do feature situations where single parameter inference is paramount, whereas Hendry's examples – money demand, consumption – are more concerned with the model as a whole. If equation (3) was being developed as part of a policy model, or even to provide predictions, knowledge of χ_D^2 is important, as a large value would presumably imply that models which retained z_t would out-perform those that did not. Any model should be judged on all its dimensions and not just a few of them. One might argue for an extension of Leamer's methodology that chose 'β_1' as representative of many characteristics of a model. Since prediction errors can be estimated as the coefficients of dummy variables (Salkever, 1976) these might be taken as $\hat{\beta}_1$. Alternatively, why not look at the extreme bounds for the residual variance? But these must be the two estimates of σ^2 obtained by including and deleting all the z_t in (1), and so one is essentially reproducing the χ_D^2 statistics. Accordingly, once attention shifts from a single parameter to overall model performance EBA begins to look like a version of step 2 of HM.

Step 4

The fourth step constitutes the clearest expression of Bayesian philosophy in Leamers work. Until this step it is not mandatory to formulate a prior distribution, but now at least the mean and variance of it must be provided (only two moments are needed given the type of prior assumed in his SEARCH program). A proper Bayesian would then proceed to combine this prior knowledge with a likelihood, reporting the posterior distribution for the coefficient. If forced to give a point estimate of the coefficient, such an individual would probably give the mode, median or mean of the posterior distribution. That would then be the end of the exercise, the data and prior beliefs having been optimally combined to provide the best information possible about the parameter value. Consequently, when modelling money demand as in (1), a Bayesian would need to formulate a $(p + q + r + s)$-dimensional prior distribution upon the parameters of this model – a daunting task, although some progress has been made in automating the process of prior elicitation in recent years, and Leamer (1986) gives an excellent example of how to do this in a context similar to that in (1).

What differentiates Leamer from a standard Bayesian is his reluctance to follow the above prescription rigidly. Rather, he prefers to study how the mean of the posterior distribution changes as the prior variances change. In Leamer (1986) he stipulates a prior covariance matrix A, but then modifies it to V obeying the following constraint:

$$(1 - \lambda)A \leqslant V \leqslant [1/(1 - \lambda)]A \qquad (0 < \lambda < 1).$$

As λ ranges from zero to unity the precision of the prior information diminishes and, for any given value of λ, bounds for the posterior mean can be computed corresponding to each side of the inequality. What is of primary interest to Leamer is how these bounds change in response to variations in λ, rather than just the values at $\lambda = 0$. As he says in Leamer (1985), what he is concerned with is *sensitivity analysis*, and it is the question of sensitivity of inferences to variation in assumptions which should preoccupy the econometrician.

If step 4 is thought of as a tool to provide a Bayesian analyst with evidence of how important prior assumptions are for conclusions based on the posterior, it seems unexceptionable and useful. Is this also true for an investigator not operating within the Bayesian paradigm? What is of concern to that individual is the shape of the likelihood. Step 4 can provide some information on this aspect. On the one hand, if the likelihood is completely flat the posterior and prior means would always coincide. On the other hand, if the likelihood was sharply defined around a particular point in the parameter space, changing λ would cause the posterior mean to shift from the prior mean to this point. Unfortunately, it is not entirely reliable as a guide to the characteristics of the likelihood, as can be seen in the case of the linear model. With the prior mean set to $\hat{\beta}_{OLS}$ and A proportional to $(X'X)^{-1}$, the posterior and prior means always coincide, so nothing is learnt about the likelihood as λ is varied.

From the above, the intention of step 4 seems good, even if in execution it may leave something to be desired. I think it certainly true that workers in the HM tradition do not pay enough attention to the shape of the likelihood (see note 6). The provision of second derivatives of the log likelihood (standard errors) gives some feel for it, but they can be very unreliable if problems are nonlinear. Whether Leamer's procedure is the best response is a moot point; at the moment it is one of the few methods we have of discovering information about curvature in the likelihood, and its strategy to overcome the problems caused by a high-dimensional parameter space (index it by a single parameter λ) may well be the best way to proceed. Certainly, we can use all the help we can get when it comes to the analysis of data.

My main reservation about step 4, however, is that it does not do *enough* sensitivity analysis, being restricted to the parameters of the prior distribution. As exemplified in his SEARCH program, there are many conventions underlying the methodology (just as there were in HM), but those applying it have made very little attempt to query the validity of such conventions for the data set being analysed. This is odd since, in principle, there should be few difficulties in mimicking step 4 of HM. Since most diagnostic tests can be formulated as measuring the sensitivity of the log likelihood to the addition of variables designed to detect departures from the conventions (Pagan, 1984) they should be readily adapted to Leamer's framework.[7] It seems imperative that this become part of the methodology. Leamer has indicated to me that he does see the need to examine the data for anomalies that suggest revision of the model space or of the initial prior distributions, the tools in this task ranging from unexpected parameter estimates and peculiar residual patterns to (possibly) goodness-of-fit statistics. But he emphasizes that adjustments must be made for any data-instigated revision of the model or prior. Because such adjustments are difficult his first preference is for an initial selection of prior and model extensive enough as to make any such revision unlikely. Nevertheless, when theory is rudimentary and underdeveloped, commitment to the original model and prior is likely to be low, and the need for revision correspondingly high.

3   The 'Sims' methodology

Interdependence of actions is one of the characteristics of economic studies. Hence, it might be argued that the evaluation of policy will normally need to be done within a framework that allows for such interdependence. In fact, a good deal of analysis, and the econometrics supporting it, is done in a partial rather than a general equilibrium way – see Feldstein (1982) for example, where the impact of taxes upon investment is assessed in a series of single-equation studies. Traditionally, such questions were analysed with the aid of a system of structural equations:

$$By_t - Cx_t = e_t \tag{5}$$

where y_t is a vector of endogenous variables, x_t is a vector of predetermined variables and e_t is the disturbance term. In (5), following the lead of the Cowles Commission researchers, both B and C were taken to be relatively sparse, so as to 'identify' the separate relations, i.e. it was assumed that an investigator could decide which variables appeared in which equations.

Both of the two previous methodologies would probably subscribe to this framework, aiming to calibrate the non-zero elements in B and C (Leamer might regard the exclusion restrictions as only approximately correct, but I know of nowhere that he has explicitly stated his preferred procedure). By contrast, the third methodology jettisons it. Sims

(1980a) dissented vigorously from the Cowles Commission tradition, resurrecting an old article by Liu (1960) which insisted that it was 'incredible' to regard B and C as sparse. The argument touches a chord with anyone involved in the construction of computable general equilibrium models. If decisions on consumption, labour supply, portfolio allocations etc. were all determined by individuals maximizing lifetime utility subject to a budget constraint, each relationship would be determined by the same set of variables. Consequently, theoretical considerations would predict no difference in the menu of variables entering different equations, although the quantitative importance of individual variables is likely to vary with the type of decision.[8] Prescription of the zero elements in B and C therefore involves excluding variables with coefficients 'close' to zero. In this respect, the action is little different from what is done in any attempt to model reality by capturing the major influences at work. This was Fisher's (1961) reply to Liu, and I find it as pertinent now as when it was written.

Much more could be said about this issue of identifiability, but this is not the place to do so. One cannot help wondering, however, if it is as serious as Sims suggests. There do not seem many instances in applied work where identification is the likely suspect when accounting for poor results. Despite the large amount of attention paid to it in early econometrics, it is hard to escape the impression that issues of specification and data quality are of far greater importance.

Nevertheless, it would be silly to ignore these arguments if it was indeed possible to do analysis without such assumptions. Sims claims that it is. In the Cowles Commission methodology, 'structure-free' conclusions would have been derived from the reduced form

$$y_t = B^{-1}Cr_t + B^{-1}\varrho_t - \Pi x_t + v_{ts} \tag{6}$$

but Sims chooses instead to work with a vector autoregressive representation (VAR) for the endogenous and exogenous variables. Defining $z_t' = (y_t'\bar{x}_t')$, where $\bar{x}_t$ includes all members of x_t that are not lagged values of variables, this has the form

$$z_t = \sum_{j=1}^{p} B_j z_{t-j} + e_t. \tag{7}$$

Although it is (7) that is estimated, two further manipulations are made for use in later stages of the methodology. First, (7) is inverted to give the innovations (or moving average) form:

$$z_t = \sum_{j=0}^{\infty} A_j e_{t-j} \tag{8}$$

where $\bar{A}_0 = \text{cov}(e_t)$. Since $\bar{A}_0$ is a positive definite matrix there exists a non-singular lower triangular matrix P such that $PA_0P' = I$, allowing the definition $\eta_t - Pe_t$, where η_t has zero mean and covariance matrix I. Equation (8) may then be rewritten in terms of η_t as

$$z_t = \sum_{j=0}^{\infty} A_j P^{-1} P e_{t-j} = \sum_{j=0}^{\infty} D_j \eta_{t-j} \tag{9}$$

where the η_t are the *orthogonalized innovations*.

Having dispatched the preliminaries it is possible to summarize Sims's methodology in four steps.

1 Transform data to such a form that a VAR can be fitted to it.
2 Choose as large a value of p and of $\dim(z_t)$ as is compatible with the size of the data set available and then fit the resulting VAR.
3 Try to simplify the VAR by reducing p or by imposing some arbitrary 'smoothness' restrictions upon the coefficients.
4 Use the *orthogonalized* innovations representation to address the question of interest.

Step 1

This is an important step. The idea that z_t can be expressed as a VAR has its origins in the theory of stationary processes, particularly in the Wold decomposition theorem. But that justification is not essential until the last step; until then the VAR might well have unstable roots. However, stable roots are indispensable to step 4, as the coefficients $\bar{A}_j$ only damp out for a stable VAR, i.e. $z_t = az_{t-1} + e_t$ (z_t a scalar) becomes

$$z_t = \sum_{j=0}^{\infty} a^j e_{t-j}$$

and $a^j \to 0\,(j \to \infty)$ only if $|a| < 1$. If step 4 is to be regarded as an essential part of the methodology, the question of the appropriate transformation to render z_t stationary must be faced at an early stage.

In Sims (1980a) and Doan et al. (1984), as well as most applications, this seems to be done by including time trends in each equation of the VAR. In the latter article the attitude seems to be that most economic time series are best thought of as a stationary autoregression around a deterministic trend: after setting up the prior that the series follow a random walk with drift (equation (3), p. 7) they then say:

> While we recognise that a more accurate representation of generally held prior beliefs would give less weight to systems with explosive roots . . . .

It is not apparent to me that this is a 'generally held prior belief', particularly given the incidence of random walks with drift in the investigation of Nelson and Plosser (1982) into the behaviour of economic time series. If the series are of the random walk type, placing deterministic trends into a regression does not suffice to induce stationarity, and an innovations form will not exist for the series in question. Of course, the sensible response to this objection would be to focus upon growth rates rather than levels for variables that are best regarded as autoregressive integrated moving average processes. I suspect that this makes somewhat more sense in many contexts anyway. In macroeconomic policy questions, for example, interest typically centres upon rates of growth of output and prices rather than levels, and it therefore seems appropriate to formulate the VAR in this way. Consequently, the difficulties raised by the type of non-stationarity exhibited by many economic time series is not insurmountable, but it does suggest that much more care needs to be taken in identifying the format of the variables to be modelled than has been characteristic of past studies employing Sims's methodology.

Step 2

Both p and the number of variables in z_t need to be specified. The first parameter will need to be fairly large (the decomposition theorem sets it to infinity), and most applications of Sims's methodology have put p between 4 and 10. Doan et al. (1984, fn. 3) indicate that, at least for prediction performance, conclusions might be sensitive to the choice of lag length. Stronger evidence is available that the selection of variables to appear in z_t is an important one – Sims's conclusions about the role of money in Sims (1980a) were severely modified in Sims (1980b) by expanding z_t to include an interest rate. Essentially step 2 is the analogue of step 1 in the previous two methodologies, and the need to begin with a model that is general enough haunts all the methodologies. Perhaps the difficulties are greater in Sims's case, as he wants to model the reduced form rather than a single structural equation. To adopt such a position it would be necessary to respond to Sims's contention that structural equations should also contain a large number of variables, although what is really at issue is whether they are quantitatively more important to the reduced form analysis.

Step 3

Step 3 is required precisely because of the fact that both p and $\dim(z_t)$ need to be large, and so the number of unknown parameters, $p \times \dim(z_t)$, can easily become too large to be estimated from the available data. In his original article Sims chose p via a series of modified likelihood ratio tests in exactly the same way as was done in step 2 of Hendry's methodology. Because there are few degrees of freedom available in the most general model, this may not be a good way to select p. Accordingly, in Doan et al. (1984) a different approach was promoted that was 'Bayesian in spirit'. In this variant the B_j were allowed to vary over time as

$$\text{vec}(B_{j,t}^i) = \pi_8 \, \text{vec}(B_{j,t-1}^i) + (1 - \pi_8) \, \text{vec}(B_j^i) + v_{j,t}^i \tag{10}$$

where the i indicates the ith equation and $v_{j,t}$ is a normally distributed random variable with covariance matrix V that is a function of $\pi_1, \ldots, \pi_7$. Fixing the B_j^i in (10) (at either unity, if the coefficient corresponds to the first lag of the dependent variable of the equation, or zero), there remain eight unknown parameters. Equation (10) describes an 'evolving coefficient model'. The likelihood for (9) and (10) was derived by Schweppe (1965) and can be written down with the aid of the Kalman filtering equations. Two of the π parameters were then eliminated by maximizing this likelihood conditional upon the fixed values of the others.

One might well ask what the rationale for (10) is; Doan et al. claim (p. 6):

> What we do thus has antecedents in the literature on shrinkage estimation and its Bayesian interpretation (for example, the works by... Shiller (1973) ....

I would dispute this connection. In the Bayesian formulation of shrinkage estimators, shrinkage occurs only in a finite sample, since the prior information is dominated by the sample information as the sample size grows, i.e. changes in (say) the prior variance have a negligible effect upon the posterior distribution in large samples. This is not true for (10); changes in π always have an effect upon the likelihood, since the variance of the innovations is always a function of the π (see equation (10) of Doan et al.). Reference to Shiller's work seems even more misleading. Shiller allows the coefficients to be 'random' *across the lag distributions, not across time*, i.e. he would have

$$\text{vec}(B^i_{j,t}) = \pi_8 \text{vec}(B^i_{j-1,t}) + (1 - \pi_8) \text{vec}(B^i_j)$$

and not

$$\text{vec}(B^i_{j,t}) = \pi_8 \text{vec}(B^i_{j,t-1}) + (1 - \pi_8) \text{vec}(B^i_j).$$

Thus, as (10) is a model for coefficient evolution, and not the imposition of prior information, it is hard to see why this procedure is any less objectionable than that followed by the Cowles Commission; Malinvaud's (1984) reaction to the idea is easy to sympathize with.

Step 4

As step 4 has been the subject of a number of excellent critiques, particularly that by Cooley and LeRoy (1985), little will be said about it. There are two major objections. First, the move from innovations to orthogonal innovations raises questions. With the exception of the first variable in z_t, the orthogonal innovations are hard to give any sensible meaning to; resort is frequently made to expressions such as 'that part of the innovation in money not correlated with the innovations in other variables'. In many ways the difficulty is akin to that in factor analysis; the mathematics is clear but the economics is not. Unfortunately, many users of the technique tend to blur the two concepts in discussion, e.g. in Litterman and Weiss (1985) the 'orthogonalized' soubriquet is dropped.

A second query arises over the *use* of the orthogonalized innovations representation. As Cooley and LeRoy (1985) point out, to ascribe any meaning to impulse responses for these innovations, it is necessary that the latter be treated as exogenous variables, and this requires the imposition of prior restrictions upon the causal structure of the system in exactly the same fashion as was done by the Cowles Commission. The strong claims the methodology makes to being free of prior information therefore seem to be largely illusory.

As an aid to understanding the issues raised above it may help to return to (1) and the question of the response of money to interest rate variations. Sims would first choose a lag length and a set of variables to form the VAR. A minimal subset would be the variables m_t, p_t, i_t and y_t in (1), but because one is attempting to capture economy-wide interactions rather than just a money demand relation, extra variables that may need to be included could be world activity, the exchange rate and fiscal policy variables. A lot of thought has to go into this choice. Making the set too small can seriously bias the answers, whereas making it too large renders the method intractable unless other restrictions are imposed upon the VAR coefficients as in step 3. Once the latter strategy is followed the 'clean-skin' appeal of VARs begins to dissipate.

Granted that steps 1–3 have provided a satisfactory VAR for m_t as in (7), it is then inverted to give the innovations representation (8) that expresses m_t as a linear function of the innovations in the interest rate $e_{i,t}$ and the other variables in the VAR: $e_{p,t}$, $e_{m,t}$, $e_{y,t}$ etc. The equation corresponding to m_t in (8) would be of the form

$$m_t = \bar{a}_{0,mm}e_{m,t} + \bar{a}_{0,mp}e_{p,t} + \bar{a}_{0,mi}e_{i,t} + \bar{a}_{0,my}e_{y,t} + \cdots$$

and the response of m_t to a unit innovation in the interest rate would be $\bar{a}_{0,mi}$. This is to be contrasted with the response of m_t to a unit innovation in the interest rate provided by (1) $(d_0\bar{a}_{0,ii})$ obtained by replacing i_t in (1) by $i_t = \bar{a}_{0,ii}e_{i,t} + \cdots$ (the interest rate equation in (8)). Therefore different answers to the question of the response of m_t to variations in i_t would be obtained from methodologies concentrating upon (1) alone than from those that incorporate system responses; in (1) the response is estimated by holding prices and income constant, whereas Sims seeks the effects on the quantity of money without such *ceteris paribus* assumptions. To some extent the methodologies are not competitive, as they frequently seek to answer different questions.

Sims aims to analyse a much broader set of issues than Hendry or Leamer normally do, but there are difficulties commensurate with this breadth. Making the set of variables to appear in the VAR large enough is one of these, and his fourth step illustrates another. To speak of the response of m_t to a unit innovation in the interest rate It must be possible to carry out that experiment without disturbing current prices, incomes etc. But that means that the innovations $e_{i,t}$ must be uncorrelated with all the other innovations. When they are not, Sims invokes artificial constructs, the orthogonal innovations, $v_{i,t}$, $v_{p,t}$, $v_{y,t}$ etc. These are linear combinations of $e_{i,t}$, $e_{p,t}$, $e_{y,t}$ designed to be orthogonal to one another, and hence capable of being varied independently of each other. Just like principal components, it is uncertain what meaning should be attached to these entities, leading to the controversy recounted above in the discussion of step 4.

4   Summing up

Our review of the methodologies now being complete, it is time to sum up. Ignoring the criticisms of details that have been offered, how effective are the methodologies in meeting the three criteria of 'goodness' listed at the beginning of this essay, namely the provision of general research tools, the codification and transmission of principles, and the reporting of results?

None of the methodologies claims to be completely general. Sims explicitly deals only with time series, while many of Hendry's concerns are specific to such series as well. Leamer's techniques are heavily based upon the OLS estimator. All have the common deficiency of a failure to address explicitly the burgeoning field of micro-econometrics. Whilst it is true that the philosophies underlying Hendry's and Leamer's work transfers (see, for example, Cameron and Trivedi, 1986), the actual techniques employed would need extensive modification, particularly in the light of the very large data sets that make traditional model selection methods inappropriate. There is clearly a lot to be done before any of the three methodologies provides a complete set of techniques for data analysis.

Part of the objective of this paper has been to try to set out the general principles of each methodology so as to assist in the communication and teaching roles. But this was done at a high level of abstraction. When it comes to application many questions arise which currently seem to be resolved only by 'sitting at the feet of the master'. Hendry, for example, is very vague about how he manages to simplify his models, so little is learnt about how this is to be done by a reading of his articles. Leamer recommends formulating multidimensional priors, but provides little practical guidance on how (say) the covariance matrices featuring in them are to be selected. Sims's methodology seems clearest when it is applied to the big issues of macroeconomics such as the neutrality of money, but altogether vaguer when the question is of the much more prosaic kind such as the impact of a quota upon import demand. No doubt Sims would be able to handle such queries, but the personal ingenuity required seems a stumbling block to the transmission of knowledge.

What about reporting? Hendry's methodology seems to provide useful information in a concise form, although it is sometimes possible to be overwhelmed with the detail on the statistics presented when judging the adequacy of a model. Perhaps this just reflects a lack of familiarity and an early stage in learning about what are the most useful tests. Leamer's extreme bounds are easy to understand; however, the extensions in which prior variances are restricted become much harder to interpret. To my mind, it is Sims's methodology which is the worst when it comes to the reporting role, with pages of graphs and impulse responses being provided. Whether this reflects a transition stage, or the problems mentioned previously about step 4, is still unclear, but a more concise method of reporting does seem to be needed.

Granted that no methodology has managed to obtain a perfect score, what have we learnt from all of this debate? First, a substantial clarification of the procedures of model selection and auxiliary concepts such as 'exogeneity'. Second, a pronounced recognition of the limits of modelling. Any reading of (say) Marschak (1953) makes it evident that the Cowles Commission researchers were not deficient in this respect (doubters might note the amount of space Marschak denotes to discussing the 'Lucas critique'), but somehow it got lost in the euphoria of the 1960s. The much more critical attitude towards econometrics that prevails today is generally a good thing, although there is a danger that the emergence of differing methodologies will be interpreted as a tacit admission of a complete failure of econometrics, rather than as constructive attempts to improve it.

What about the future? Constructing 'systematic theologies' for econometrics can well stifle creativity, and some evidence of this has already become apparent. Few would deny that in the hands of the masters the methodologies perform impressively, but in the hands of their disciples it is all much less convincing. It will be important to rid econometrics of the 'black box' mentality that always besets it. A poor modelling strategy is unlikely to give useful results, but a good one cannot rescue a project by rigidly following any methodology if it was badly conceived from the very beginning. What I see as needed is a greater integration of the different methodologies. Although it is convenient to draw demarcation lines between them in discussion, this should not blind a researcher to the fact that each methodology can provide insights that the others lack. EBA is an important adjunct to Hendry's methodology if large numbers of parameters have been omitted in any simplification. Examining the residuals for model deficiencies should be as automatic in Leamer's and Sims's methodologies as it is in Hendry's. Checking if the restrictions imposed on the VAR parameters by a model selected by Hendry's or Leamer's methodologies are compatible with the data should be part of any analysis involving time series. Our data are such that we cannot ignore the fact that the information therein may need to be extracted by a wide range of techniques borrowed from many different approaches.

Notes

Much of this paper was presented in the symposium on econometric methodology at the World Econometric Congress at Boston in August 1985. I am grateful to Ed Leamer for his extensive comments on it.

1   As is well known the importance of collinearity is a function of the parameterization used. Thus the data may be very informative about certain parameters, e.g. long-run responses, but not others, e.g. dynamics. It is not useful (or valid) to claim it is uninformative about everything.

2   Problems emerge if a decision rule is employed based on keeping type I errors constant – see Berkson (1938). As the test statistic is the product of the sample size and the proportional change in variance, even very small changes in the latter become large changes in the criterion when the sample size is large. Decision rules such as those in Rissanen (1983) and Schwartz (1978) overcome this, but it might be better to model formally the underlying conflict between type I and type II error as in Quandt (1980).

3   Both papers treat only the case where the observations making up the sample moments are independent and identically distributed, but it is clear that the analysis extends to the case where the 'orthogonality' relations follow a martingale difference process. This covers most cases of interest in econometrics. Note, however, that Tauchen's results require that the maintained model be estimated by maximum likelihood.

4   Breusch (1985) gives an elegant proof of this.

5   This division shows that interpretations which see the differences between the methodologies as due to different attitudes to collinearity are incorrect. Bounds can be wide even if collinearity is weak (ϕ small).

6   We have not dealt with the question of what inferences about β_1 might then be drawn from $\hat{\beta}_1$. Unfortunately, it is not uncommon in econometrics to see sharp conclusions drawn about the value of β_1 on the basis of a test of a sharp hypothesis such as $\beta_1 = 1$ or $\beta_1 = 0$ (Hall, 1978; Barro, 1977). All that can be concluded, however, is that a range of possible values for β_1 is compatible with $\hat{\beta}_1$, and this range is frequently found by examining $k\text{SD}(\hat{\beta}_1)$, where k is some selected constant. Traditionally, k was set by stipulating the type I error to be sustained, but Don Andrews (1986) has recently suggested a way of incorporating power requirements into the determination of k.

7   In Pagan (1978) I used CORE's Bayesian Regression Program to check for serial correlation. Lagged residuals were added to the model and the posterior distribution for the coefficient of that variable was then calculated.

8   Even within these models the existence of governments means that (say) prices entering demand relations will be different from those in supply relations by the presence of indirect taxes, and this gives an external source of variation. It should be noted that Sims gives a number of other arguments against identifiability, some relating to expectations and others about our inability to specify the exact order of dynamics.

References

Akaike, H. (1973) Information theory and the extension of the maximum likelihood principle. In B. N. Petrov and F. Csaki (eds), *2nd International Symposium on Information Theory*, Budapest: Akademiai-Kiado, 227–81.

Andrews D. W. K. (1986) Power in econometric application. Mimeo, Yale University.

Anstie, R., Gray, M. R. and Pagan, A. R. (1983) Inflation and the consumption ratio. In P. K. Trivedi and A. R. Pagan (eds), *The Effects of Inflation: Theoretical Investigations and Australian Evidence*, Canberra: Centre for Economic Policy Research.

Barro, R. J. (1977) Unanticipated money growth and unemployment in the United States. *American Economic Review*, 67, 101–15.

Berkson, J. (1938) Some difficulties of interpretation encountered in the application of the chi-square test. *Journal of the American Statistical Association*, 33, 526–42.

Breusch, T. S. (1985) Simplified extreme bounds. Discussion Paper 8515, University of Southampton.

Cameron, A. C. and Trivedi, P. K. (1986) Econometric models based on count data: comparisons and applications of some estimators and tests. *Journal of Applied Econometrics*, 1, 29–54.

Cooley, T. F. and LeRoy, S. F. (1981) Identification and estimation of money demand. *American Economic Review*, 71, 825–44.

—— and —— (1985) Atheoretical macroeconometrics: a critique. *Journal of Monetary Economics*, 16, 283–308.

Doan, T., Litterman, R. and Sims, C. (1984) Forecasting and conditional projection using realistic prior distributions. *Econometric Reviews*, 3, 1–100.

Drèze, J. H. and Richard, J. F. (1983) Bayesian analysis of simultaneous equation systems. In Z. Griliches and M. D. Intriligator (eds), *Handbook of Econometrics*, Amsterdam: North-Holland.

Engle, R. F. (1984) Likelihood ratio, Lagrange multiplier and Wald tests in econometrics. In Z. Griliches and M. D. Intriligator (eds), *Handbook of Econometrics*, Amsterdam: North-Holland.

Feldstein, M. (1982) Inflation, tax rules and investment: some econometric evidence. *Econometrica*, 50, 825–62.

Fisher, F. M. (1961) On the cost of approximate specification in simultaneous-equation estimation. *Econometrica*, 29, 139–70.

Hall, R. E. (1978) Stochastic implications of the life cycle – permanent income hypothesis: theory and evidence. *Journal of Political Economy*, 86, 971–1007.

Harper, I. R. (1980) The relationship between unemployment and unfilled vacancies in Australia: 1951–1978. *Economic Record*, 56, 231–43.

Hausman, J. A. (1978) Specification tests in econometrics. *Econometrica*, 46, 1251–72.

Hendry, D. F. (1986) Empirical modelling in dynamic econometrics. Applied Economics Discussion Paper 1, University of Oxford.

—— and Mizon, G. E. (1978) Serial correlation as a convenient simplification, not a nuisance: a comment on a study of the demand for money by the Bank of England. *Economic Journal*, 88, 549–63.

—— and —— (1985) Procrustean econometrics. Discussion Paper, University of Southampton.

—— and Richard, J. F. (1982) On the formulation of empirical models in dynamic econometrics. *Journal of Econometrics*, 20, 3–33.

Hill, B. (1986) Some subjective Bayesian considerations in the selection of models. *Econometric Reviews*, 4, 191–246.

Kirby, M. G. (1981) An investigation of the specification and stability of the Australian aggregate wage equation. *Economic Record*, 57, 35–46.

Leamer, E. E. (1978) *Specification Searches*. New York: Wiley.

—— (1983) Let's take the con out of econometrics. *American Economic Review*, 73, 31–44.

—— (1985) Sensitivity analysis would help. *American Economic Review*, 75, 308–13.

—— (1986) A Bayesian analysis of the determinants of inflation. In D. A. Belsley and E. Kuh (eds), *Model Reliability*, Cambridge, MA: MIT Press.

—— and Leonard, H. (1983) Reporting the fragility of regression estimates. *Review of Economics and Statistics*, 65, 306–17.

Litterman, R. and Weiss, L. (1985) Money, real interest rates and output: a re-interpretation of postwar U.S. data. *Econometrica*, 53, 129–56.

Liu, T. C. (1960) Underidentification, structural estimation, and forecasting. *Econometrica*, 28, 855–65.

Malinvaud, E. (1984) Comment to forecasting and conditional projection using realistic prior distributions. *Econometric Reviews*, 3, 113–18.

Mallows, C. L. (1973) Some comments on C_p. *Technometrics*, 15, 661–75.

Marschak, J. (1953) Economic measurements for policy and prediction. In W. C. Hood and T. C. Koopmans (eds), *Studies in Econometric Method*, Cowles Commission Research Monograph 14, New Haven, CT: Yale University Press, 1–26.

McAleer, M., Pagan, A. R. and Volker, P. A. (1983) Straw-man econometrics. Working Paper in Econometrics 097, Australian National University.

——, —— and —— (1985) What will take the con out of econometrics? *American Economic Review*, 75, 293–307.

Mill, J. S. (1967) On the definition of political economy and on the method of investigation proper to it. *Collected Works*, vol. 4. Toronto: University of Toronto Press.

Mizon, G. E. (1977) Model selection procedures. In M. J. Artis and A. R. Nobay (eds), *Studies in Modern Economic Analysis*, Oxford: Basil Blackwell.

Nelson, C. R. and Plosser, C. I. (1982) Trends and random walks in macroeconomic time series: some evidence and implications. *Journal of Monetary Economics*, 10, 139–62.

Newey, W. (1985) Maximum likelihood specification testing and conditional moment tests. *Econometrica*, 53, 1047–70.

Pagan, A. R. (1978) Detecting autocorrelation after Bayesian regression. CORE Discussion Paper 7825.

—— (1984) Model evaluation by variable addition. In D. F. Hendry and K. F. Wallis (eds), *Econometrics and Quantitative Economics*, Oxford: Basil Blackwell.

—— and Volker, P. A. (1981) The short-run demand for transactions balances in Australia. *Economica*, 48, 381–95.

Quandt, R. E. (1980) Classical and Bayesian hypothesis testing: a compromise. *Metroeconomica*, 32, 173–80.

Rissanen, J. (1983) A universal prior for integers and estimation by minimum description length. *Annals of Statistics*, 11, 416–31.

Salkever, D. S. (1976) The use of dummy variables to compute predictions, prediction errors and confidence intervals. *Journal of Econometrics*, 4, 393–7.

Sargan, J. D. (1964) Wages and prices in the United Kingdom: a study in econometric methodology. In P. E. Hart, G. Mills and J. K. Whitaker (eds), *Econometric Analysis for National Economic Planning*, London: Butterworth.

Schwarz, G. (1978) Estimating the dimension of a model. *Annals of Statistics*, 6, 461–4.

Schweppe, F. C. (1965) Evaluation of likelihood functions for Gaussian signals. *IEEE Transactions on Information Theory*, 11, 61–70.

Shiller, R. J. (1973) A distributed lag estimator derived from smoothness priors. *Econometrica*, 41, 775–88.

Sims, C. A. (1980a) Macroeconomics and reality. *Econometrica*, 48, 1–47.

—— (1980b) Comparison of interwar and postwar cycles: monetarism reconsidered. *American Economic Review*, 70, 250–7.

Tauchen, G. (1985) Diagnostic testing and evaluation of maximum likelihood models. *Journal of Econometrics*, 30, 415–43.

Veall, M. R. (1986) Inferences on the deterrent effect of capital punishment: bootstrapping the process of model selection. Mimeo, University of Western Ontario.

Zellner, A. (1971) *An Introduction to Bayesian Inference in Econometrics*. New York: Wiley.

3 Three econometric methodologies: an update

Adrian Pagan
Australian National University

1 Introduction

In the 1950s visitors driving into Sydney over the Razorback Mountain would have soon a gnarled eucalyptus tree proclaiming the philosophy of one of Sydney's major retail merchants: 'While I live I grow'. One could easily have felt that the converse was equally valid and that growth was perhaps the surest way of demonstrating the continued vitality of an organism. So it is with methodologies. Those that grow remain central to econometric investigation. Those that stagnate are ignored. In this spirit the present paper sets out to look at the state of econometric methodologies some eight years after 'Three econometric methodologies: a critical appraisal' (3EM) (Pagan, 1987) was written. The three methodologies distinguished in the previous work are now examined for their vital signs, with the paper being ordered in the same way as the original, section 2 dealing with the 'LSE methodology' (LSM), section 3 with the Bayesian methodology (BM) and section 4 with the vector autoregressive representation (VAR) methodology (VM).[1] Section 5 provides concluding remarks.

2 The LSE methodology

Theoretical work in econometrics during the past eight years has been concentrated into two major areas: cointegration and nonparametrics. The yield from the latter in terms of assistance to applied work is still meagre and none of the methodologies mentioned here has shown much interest in absorbing the ideas thrown up by it. In contrast, the methods stemming from the former area have become pervasive in applied work. Indeed, the impact has been so extensive that Darnell and Evans (1990) have even referred to a 'cointegration methodology'. The LSM has probably been the most successful in absorbing the techniques of cointegration analysis into its structure, partly because of correspondences between some of the basic concepts and partly because much of the work originated in or was promoted by those who had some affiliation with the LSM. It is interesting to observe that my earlier paper did not mention cointegration in connection with the LSM, but now the 'four steps' given in 3EM would almost certainly be preceded by an analysis of the integration and cointegration properties of the set of variables being modelled. Studies working with the LSM approach and making this the first step are now legion, e.g. Fisher and Park (1991), Driver and Moreton (1991) and Alogoskoufis and Smith (1991). Whether this step would be recommended by the principal creators of the LSM is unclear, but certainly it has become a standard in many applied works in this tradition.

To appreciate why the LSM has grown in this direction, and to understand some of the reservations one might have about it, it is useful to begin by assuming that the n I(1) variables z_t being modelled have a VAR(1) structure[2]

$$z_t = A z_{t-1} + e_t \tag{1}$$

where e_t will be assumed to be independently and identically distributed (IID) with zero mean and constant covariance matrix. Equation (1) may be reparameterized as

$$\Delta z_t = \Pi z_{t-1} + e_t \tag{2}$$

It is well established (Engle and Granger, 1987) that cointegration among the n variables means that there are r linear combinations of the I(1) variables z_t that are I(0), i.e. there exists an $n \times r$ matrix α such that $\alpha' z_t$ is I(0) and $\Pi = \gamma \alpha'$. Thus a cointegrating restriction reduces (2) to

$$\Delta z_t = \gamma(\alpha' z_{t-1}) + e_t \tag{3}$$

where $\alpha' z_t$ are the 'cointegrating errors'. In the special case of $r = 1$ we might put $z_t' = (y_t\; x_t')$ and $\alpha' z_t = \alpha_0 y_t + x_t' \alpha_1 = y_t - x_t' \beta$, if it is sensible to normalize upon y_t. Then the equation for Δy_t in (3) becomes

$$\Delta y_t = \gamma_1(y_{t-1} - x_{t-1}' \beta) + e_{1t}, \tag{4}$$

producing an 'error correction mechanism' (ECM).

Equation (4) makes it clear why LSM followers took to cointegration like ducks to water. The ECM model was a centrepiece of the LSM and therefore a partial 'justification' seemed available from the fact that an ECM model was necessary to ensure that y_t and x_t tracked together. Actually, the connection is superficial. A traditional ECM has the format

$$\Delta y_t = \delta \Delta x_t' \beta + \phi(y_{t-1} - x_{t-1}' \beta) + u_t, \tag{5}$$

where $y_t^* = x_t' \beta$ is the target or equilibrium value of y_t, and a comparison of (4) with (5) shows up a missing term Δx_t. This is no slip; it reflects fundamentally different ideas about the nature of the modelling to be done. The traditional ECM model (5) is a *structural* model; that in (4) is the *closed reduced form* corresponding to a structure, i.e. if we look at the equations for Δx_t in (3) they would have the form $\gamma_2(y_{t-1} - x_{t-1}' \beta) + e_{2t}$ and would be used to eliminate Δx_t from (5).[3]

The new step in the LSM is first to ascertain which variables are I(1) and then to estimate the cointegrating vectors α by some procedure. With this estimate in hand, say $1 - \hat{\beta}$ if $r = 1$, the ECM in (5) is estimated by replacing β with $\hat{\beta}$ and then getting estimates of δ and ϕ. In many instances β is found by ordinary least squares (OLS) regression of y_t on x_t, in which case the strategy is referred to as the Engle–Granger two-step method, but it is now increasingly common to see α being estimated by Johansen's (1988) procedure.

Why would one want to do this step rather than directly estimating (5) as the older tradition would dictate? I think that three reasons probably underlie it. First, there is the fact that, if x_t is of dimension $q > 1$, it reduces the number of parameters in the 'ECM estimation' step from $q+2$ down to 2 (δ and ϕ). Second, in general, imposing the ECM structure in (5) entails restrictions, as there are $2q + 1$ variables on the right-hand side of (5) but only $q + 2$ parameters; moreover these restrictions are nonlinear, as all the regressors in x_{t-1} and Δx_t have coefficients in the same ratio, δ/ϕ. Many times I have set the task of estimating ECMs to students and, almost invariably, they resort to nonlinear estimation. Yet most of the illustrations of LSM modelling either set β to known values (say unity) or ignore the nonlinear constraints, redefining $\delta\beta$ as δ^* and then treating δ^* as an unrestricted set of parameters to be estimated. Alogoskoufis and Smith (1991) complain about this fact, arguing that it is these very restrictions that are important to allow interpretation of a dynamic regression as an ECM. Finally, I think that there is a feeling that one might want to test the validity of long-run information before imposing it, i.e. even if we feel that β has a value like -1 (if $q = 1$), it might be desirable to test whether this is true before going ahead and inserting that value into the ECM. Here the cointegration literature proved enticing, arguing that one could estimate and test hypotheses about β of the form $\beta = \beta^*$ without needing to know anything about the structural ECM model, except that all the I(1) variables in the relation were captured by y_t and x_t; free lunches are always hard to resist!

The three reasons given above for being interested in cointegration have different requirements about the ability to estimate β. For the first two, only a consistent estimate is needed, while the last demands some knowledge of the distributional properties of whatever estimator of β is adopted. The latter information must be of suspect quality given the sample sizes available to us, but achieving the former goal might seem feasible provided the R^2 of the cointegrating regression was high. However, whether it is even possible to estimate β (or more generally α) depends upon the nature of our problem. Cointegrating vectors derived from the VAR are not unique since $\gamma\alpha' = \gamma BB^{-1}\alpha' = \gamma^*\alpha^{*\prime}$, i.e. linear combinations of α also serve as vectors that are statistically indistinguishable, in the sense of having the same reduced form. Anyone using Johansen's estimator will have experienced this problem; sometimes one obtains quite strange cointegrating vector estimates as one is looking at linear combinations of the basic set, but this feature can also occur for estimators of α such as OLS although, as explained shortly, for a different reason.

To emphasize this last point I conducted a simple simulation experiment of a demand–supply system driven by a single stochastic trend, income Y_t. The equations used in the experiment were

$$q_t = -p_t + 0.5Y_t + \xi_t \tag{6a}$$

$$q_t = 2p_t + \varepsilon_t \tag{6b}$$

$$Y_t = Y_{t-1} + v_t \tag{6c}$$

where q_t is quantity, p_t is price and v_t, ξ_t and e_t are all N(0, 1) IID random variables. A very large sample size, $T = 2500$, was used for estimation, although the same outcome is evident when $T = 100$.[4] Emulating the Granger–Engle two-step idea, q_t is regressed against p_t and Y_t, producing $q_t = 0.5009p_t + 0.2503Y_t$, which clearly does not provide the correct values of (6a). What has happened? The true cointegrating vectors are [1 1 −0.5] and [1 −2 0]. Adding these together gives [2 −1 −0.5] which, after normalization, leaves [1 −0.5 −0.25], i.e. what was obtained by OLS regression. Thus the 'estimates' obtained are of a linear combination of the two cointegrating vectors and not of any single one. Lest it be thought that this fickle behaviour is a product of OLS estimation, Johansen's estimator gives estimates of the two cointegrating vectors as [1 −0.596 −0.233] and [1 20.87 −3.82]. Making these [1 −0.5 −0.25] and [1 22 −4] we see that the first is the same as the OLS results while the second can be derived by taking eight times [1 1 −0.5] less seven times [1 −2 0]. Since we actually know the true cointegrating vectors in this experiment it would be possible to reconstruct the 'correct' ones from the 'estimates', but in practice this information is unlikely to be available. If it was, it is unclear why we would be performing a cointegration analysis. Certainly we might feel more comfortable if we can find a cointegrating vector that is 'close' to what we expect, but this seems to give only a very minor role to such analysis.

Why does the OLS estimator fail in this experiment? The answer is that it is not possible to *identify* the parameters in the demand equation (6a) as the reduced form for p_t is $p_t = 0.16Y_t + 0.33e_t − 0.33\varepsilon_t + 0.66\xi_t$, meaning that there are no excluded exogenous variables in the structural equation (6a). Because OLS is estimating a *structural* equation, rank and order conditions for identification associated with the simultaneous equations literature must also hold in the presence of integrated processes, as those results concern the relationships between reduced form and structural parameters and are independent of the nature of the data. This point has been emphasized by Park (1990) and Phillips and Park (1992). To illustrate this fact, (6b) might be modified by the addition of an I(1) variable, 'wages' (w_t), thereby identifying the parameters of both (6a) and (6b) and allowing them to be estimated.[5] Moreover, OLS is known to be consistent, even though p_t is correlated with the errors in each equation (Engle and Granger, 1987). This consistency is observed, with the fitted equations being $q_t = −0.97p_t + 0.50Y_t$ and $q_t = 1.95p_t + 0.99w_t$ respectively. The critical feature in this outcome is that OLS was applied to a *just identified structural equation*. Johansen's estimator, because it only works with a closed reduced form and a stipulation of the number of cointegrating vectors, cannot estimate the cointegrating vectors consistently, a fact borne out by the estimates obtained: [1 −0.61 −0.23 −0.53] and [1 18.9 −3.49 6.01], instead of [1 1 −0.5 0] and [1 −2 0 1] (assigning weights to the true cointegrating vectors of [0.5 −0.5] and [−5 6] gives values approximately equal to the two estimated vectors).[6] The moral of this story is that, when cointegrating vectors are structural parameters, to estimate them it is necessary to determine their identification status, and this inevitably means some attention has to be paid to the specification of the remainder of the system. Free lunches have a habit of disappearing!

Does it matter that α may not be consistently estimated? Since α and α^* are indistinguishable it is of no concern to any conclusions that rely simply on the VAR, such as tests that α have known values or for forecasts of y_t. However, it must be of concern if one is using such 'estimates' as preliminary inputs into the estimation of the parameters of a structural ECM, which is what the LSM is all about. It is simple to see why. Suppose that one had decided to fit an ECM to the quantity and price data in the numerical example: the true cointegrating error for the demand function is $v_t = q_t + p_t - 0.5Y_t$, whereas the 'Engle–Granger' estimate would be $v_t + (q_t - 2p_t)$, and we would get different estimates of δ and ϕ as a result of using quite different regressors when estimating an ECM model for demand. A numerical example based on the *identified* case can be constructed to illustrate this.[7] I replaced (6a) by an ECM

$$\Delta q_t = -\Delta p_t + \Delta y_t - 0.5^*(q_{t-1} + p_{t-1} - 0.5y_{t-1}) \tag{6a}'$$

and then proceeded to estimate this using the lagged cointegrating errors from different methods as the values for $q_{t-1} + p_{t-1} - 0.5y_{t-1}$. Choosing the true lagged cointegrating error and applying an instrumental variables estimator with Δw_t as an instrument for Δp_t, the estimates of the coefficients of Δp_t, Δy_t and the ECM term were $(-1.1\ 1.1\ -0.55)$ respectively. However, if the true lagged cointegrating error is replaced by the two estimates of this quantity yielded by Johansen's estimator, we get $(-1.1\ 1.0\ 0.1)$ and $(-1.1\ 1.1\ -0.57)$. Therefore, if the first cointegrating error from Johansen had been selected as the ECM term in (6a)', it would have been concluded that the ECM coefficient was zero, as its t value was 1.82, whereas adopting the second would give us the right outcome (with a t ratio of 22). In conclusion, if it is desired to utilize two-step methods for the estimation of structural ECMs, it is necessary to be quite precise about the identifying information.

The upshot of all of this is that the marriage of cointegration techniques and the LSM must be an unhappy one as it involves a curious mixture of reduced form and structural analysis. Because it basically works with a reduced form perspective *cointegration analysis is best thought of as another form of data analysis*. Provided that we treat it in this way it is a useful adjunct to the LSM, since it can perform some tests for specific hypotheses and it may highlight many puzzles about the nature of interrelationships in the data, resolution of which may guide us towards selecting good specifications for structural models. But it is not a substitute for structural models and has to be treated with great caution. In my opinion the emphasis accorded to it in recent work in the LSM tradition is entirely misplaced.

The central problem just discussed was the inability of the VAR to give information about an unidentified structure. However, it does not preclude the VAR from being effectively used to assess an over-identified structure. As the Cowles Commission researchers recognized, structures impose restrictions on reduced forms, and so they may be evaluated in that way. In my earlier paper I argued that the 'modern' reduced form, the VAR, could profitably be used for this purpose, and papers have appeared on this theme (Monfort and Rabemananjara, 1990; Hendry and Mizon, 1993; Clements and Mizon, 1991).[8] The idea is to take the structural equation estimates and derive the parameter values implied by the structure for the VAR. These values are then compared with those found by fitting the VAR directly to the data. This trend represents an extension of the 'fourth step' of the LSM towards the evaluation of complete systems rather than a single equation.

3   The Bayesian methodology

In my 1987 paper Leamer's work was presented as having provided a variant of the BM that had the potential for greatly influencing applied econometric work, owing to his recognition that, as prior knowledge was inaccurate, one might prefer to report bounds on the posterior modes for a wide range of prior beliefs rather than giving a single outcome. 'Sensitivity analysis' was his battle cry. An important factor militating for success was his provision of a simple to use computer program that performed the analysis. All of this was in contrast to traditional Bayesian methods which had fixed priors and were computationally quite clumsy.

Eight years later some things are the same and some radically different. Application of Leamer's methods has been rare – Levine and Renelt (1992) being a noticeable exception – whereas 'mainstream' Bayesian ideas have gained many adherents. It is worth canvassing the reasons for this success. It is certainly not due to any resolution of the question of settling on a prior. Any reader of the *Journal of Applied Econometrics* special issue on 'Classical and Bayesian methods of testing for unit roots' (October 1991) is struck by how almost all the argument is over what the prior distribution should look like, and how an enormous range of outcomes can be generated by the selection of different priors. Some of the resurgence, at least among macroeconometricians, is to be explained by the growth of the literature about asymptotic theory in the presence of unit roots, where the bewildering diversity of outcomes was perceived to be incredibly complex and confusing. Trying to learn all the different outcomes, or even to read most of the literature, with their integrals of Brownian motion etc., was enough to make anyone long for the simplicity of the prior/likelihood/Bayes theorem approach of the BM. As Sims and Uhlig (1991) pointed out so forcefully, the Bayesian philosophy of conditioning upon the data meant that it did not matter whether processes are integrated or not.[9]

Actually this contrast is exaggerated; almost all the complexity of the unit root literature derives from its agenda, which sets out to estimate parameters with minimal assumptions on the nature of the data. To illustrate this claim consider

$$y_t = x_t\beta + u_t \tag{7}$$

where y_t and x_t are I(1) and are cointegrated. If we could condition upon x_t, as in the BM, the t ratio for testing hypotheses about β would be asymptotically normal (Park and Phillips, 1989).[10] Hence any differences must reside in the fact that we are not willing to condition upon x_t. One case where this action is dubious is if x_t is contemporaneously correlated with u_t, i.e. it is endogenous. Then the distribution of $\hat{\beta}_{OLS}$ is non-symmetric, and the t ratio for testing restrictions on β, whilst asymptotically normal, is not centred on zero, even under the null hypothesis. Fortunately, in this situation it is easy to find a simple transformation that centres the t ratio at zero, thereby allowing one to conduct asymptotic inference with the normal distribution (see Phillips and Hansen, 1990; Park, 1992). But the unit root literature goes further than just wishing to take account of a contemporaneous correlation between x_t and u_t, its ultimate objective being to allow x_t to have correlation with u_{t+j}, $j = 1, 2, \ldots$, and for u_{t+j} and Δx_t to have general (unknown) serial correlation. These last demands are far beyond that envisaged in most Bayesian work. Traditionally, the BM has Δx_t and u_t being normally and independently distributed and requires a precise specification for the correlation structures in order to be able to write down a likelihood. Consequently, it does not seem profitable to contrast the simplicity of the BM approach with the complexities of the unit root literature, as they are making an entirely different set of assumptions about what is known to an investigator. If one really wanted the generality of the models studied in the frequentist approach – a dubious proposition in my view – then the BM would be hard pressed to come up with a solution.

Although I feel that the gains made by the BM, due to difficulties with unit root theory, may well be wrongly motivated, there is no denying that the computational difficulties have been greatly relaxed in the past decade. Numerical integration methods have been increasingly replaced by evaluation of posterior densities by simulation techniques (see Geweke, 1989). This has enabled much greater flexibility in prior construction and the concomitant analysis of much more realistic models. Moreover, simulation methods have become far more efficient, with methods such as Gibbs sampling – a quick way of drawing random numbers from joint densities – emerging as particularly appealing, owing to the fact that many econometric models have structures that enable the technique to be employed (see Gelfand et al., 1992; Albert and Chib, 1992).

4   The VAR methodology

Growth in the VM has been very impressive and the account given in 3EM is an inadequate summary of the rich analyses that are now performed in this framework. To understand these developments, consider the structural relations that underpin (1):

$$B_0 z_t = B_1 z_{t-1} + \varepsilon_t. \tag{8}$$

If the covariance matrix for ε_t is diagonal and B_0 has unity on its main diagonal, each member of z_t is thereby assigned its own structural equation, which ensures that the shocks can be given an economic interpretation, i.e. ε_{jt} is the 'money demand' shock if z_{jt} is the dependent variable of the money demand equation. Now, by definition, $A = B_0^{-1} B_1$, $V = \text{cov}(e_t) = \text{cov}(B_0^{-1}\varepsilon_t)$ and A, V can be estimated by applying OLS to (1). If B_1 is unrestricted it is impossible to estimate B_0 from $A = B_0^{-1}B_1$, as there are n^2 unknowns in B_1 and only n^2 known values in A. Therefore recourse must be had to solving for both B_0 and the $\text{var}(\varepsilon_t)$ from $V = \text{cov}(B_0^{-1}\varepsilon_t) = B_0^{-1}\text{cov}(\varepsilon_t)(B_0^{-1})'$. As there are $n(n + 1)/2$ knowns on the left-hand side of this equation (due to symmetry) and $\text{cov}(\varepsilon_t)$ contains n elements, from the diagonality assumption, $n(n + 1)/2 - n$ members of B_0 can be recovered in this way.[11] Many ways of effecting this recovery exist and it is the multiplicity of solutions which accounts for the vitality of the VM in recent years.

The account of the VM in 3EM assumes that B_0 is made lower triangular, i.e. it is possible to order the endogenous variables so that they are determined recursively. Given such an ordering the resulting $n(n + 1)/2 - n$ elements in B_0 are recoverable from V, and impulse response analysis can proceed as the ε_t are uncorrelated, i.e. they are orthogonalized innovations. Such a triangular structure was Sims's original selection. Subsequently, Sims (1986), Bernanke (1986) and Blanchard and Watson (1986) pointed out that one might prefer a different pattern to B_0, with the aim of providing a more accurate description of how the economy was thought to operate. Provided the number of unknowns in B_0 remains the same, any such alternative patterns will be observationally equivalent, as they give rise to the same VAR, i.e. A and V, and any choice between them must be made on grounds other than data. As an example of a non-triangular pattern set $n = 3, z_t' = (y_t \ i_t \ m_t)$, where y_t is output, m_t is real money and i_t is an interest rate, and postulate an economy governed by IS–LM relations with a money supply rule:[12]

$$y_t = b_1 i_t + \varepsilon_{\text{IS},t} \qquad \text{(IS curve)} \qquad (9a)$$
$$i_t = b_2 y_t + b_3 m_t + \varepsilon_{\text{LM},t} \qquad \text{(inverse LM curve)} \qquad (9b)$$
$$m_t = \varepsilon_{\text{ms},t} \qquad \text{(money supply rule)} \qquad (9c)$$

This simple model has the structure

$$B_0 = \begin{bmatrix} 1 & -b_1 & 0 \\ -b_2 & 1 & -b_3 \\ 0 & 0 & 1 \end{bmatrix}$$

which possesses the same number of unknown parameters as a triangular representation, i.e. 3, but seems to have a better theoretical base than the assumption that there is a recursive structure.

Cointegration ideas have also had their impact upon the VM. On a negative note, impulse response analysis has to be adapted to the singularity of Π, as inversion of the VAR to produce the moving average structure needed to compute impulse responses is now no longer possible. Nevertheless, it is possible to adjust for this difficulty (see Lutkepohl and Reimers, 1992; Mellander et al., 1992). On a positive note, cointegration opens the way for an alternative style of data analysis. As shown in Stock and Watson (1988), the existence of r cointegrating vectors among the n variables in z_t means that each z_t is driven by $n - r$ stochastic trends τ_t possessing the form $\tau_t = \tau_{t-1} + \zeta_t$. The shocks ζ_t have a *permanent* effect upon z_t, and this points to the possibility of replacing the n shocks e_t by linear combinations of $n - r$ permanent (ζ_t) and r transitory (η_t) shocks, i.e.

$$e_t = F \begin{bmatrix} \zeta_t \\ \eta_t \end{bmatrix}$$

where F is some non-singular matrix.[13] Making the permanent and transitory shocks uncorrelated allows a separate consideration of each of the impulse responses. This decomposition is an alternative to the traditional labelling of shocks as 'supply-side', 'money' and may be more appropriate for certain types of policy analysis.

Another way to allow more than $n(n+1)/2 - n$ parameters to be free in B_0 is to force a known relationship between B_0 and B_1. The most popular way of doing this, introduced by Blanchard and Quah (1989), is to restrict to zero the long-run responses of some of the z_t to certain shocks. Because the long-run responses are $(I - A)^{-1} = (I - B_0^{-1} B_1)^{-1}$, fixing some of these introduces restrictions between B_0 and B_1, which are substitutes for the restrictions that B_0 has zero elements. In Blanchard and Quah's example the long-run response of output to demand shocks is taken to be zero.

The emergence of 'structural VARs' represents a much more satisfactory mode of analysis than the recursive assumptions imposed in early VAR work, and has had the effect of moving the VM back towards structural ideas. In doing so the differences between the Cowles Commission philosophy and the VM have become more sharply etched. The *modus operandi* of the Cowles Commission was to leave $\text{cov}(\varepsilon_t)$ unrestricted but to allow B_0 and B_1 to have no more than n^2 elements, thereby enabling those parameters to be recovered from the n^2 elements in A. In contrast the VM restricts $\text{cov}(\varepsilon_t)$ and B_0 but leaves B_1 unrestricted. Which of these approaches is preferable? One cannot escape the feeling that a combination of the ideas would be best. It seems ridiculous to assume we know something about contemporaneous relations (B_0 and $\text{cov}(\varepsilon_t)$) and nothing about dynamics (B_1) as in the VM; equally silly is the idea that we would wish to leave $\text{cov}(\varepsilon_t)$ unrestricted at the expense of saying something about dynamics and contemporaneous relations. In fact it now seems very strange that traditional simultaneous equations work should have made this assumption, as nothing was gained from this level of generality owing to the fact that all attention was centred on the impact of exogenous upon endogenous variables and therefore the pattern of the covariance matrix of ε_t was irrelevant. Polar cases are striking, but compromise is probably the best solution for empirical work. Thus there seems to be no reason why one would not want to use ideas from both approaches, with restrictions placed upon both B_1 and $\text{cov}(\varepsilon_t)$.[14]

5 Conclusion

Of the three methodologies surveyed in this paper, two have moved towards one another; the LSM has increasingly used the VAR to assess the quality of fit of structural models while the VM has adopted structural ideas. It is not too fanciful to suggest that a synthesis of these two approaches is likely to be achieved, with researchers selecting whichever method of investigation is best suited to their purpose, rather than behaving as if one must always subscribe to a single tradition. The same cannot be said of the third methodology; it is hard to be a Bayesian one day and a non-Bayesian the next. There can be little doubt that the time is coming when the BM will be a serious competitor to the other methodologies. At present the BM is still hampered by the lack of good computer programs for implementing its ideas, and this means it is still hard to find applications which can be regarded as serious pieces of applied research. Within the next decade this feature is likely to change, and it will be interesting to observe whether the attraction of conditioning upon the data when making inferences is strong enough to convince applied workers of the merits of the BM. Although there are circumstances where the argument for such conditioning is compelling, there are also cases, such as with censored data, where it is not so clear that one wishes to restrict the estimation horizon in this way.

Discussion has been avoided of whether there are other methodologies followed by econometricians. To some extent there always have been; microeconometric work and large-scale modellers seem to have evolved approaches that sit uneasily with all the methodologies mentioned. But, most importantly, we have ignored the rise of the 'calibration' school, which places heavy emphasis upon the role of neoclassical theory in delivering tightly specified models. Whether this school has a methodology is unclear, although there exist attempts to put it on such a footing (Kydland and Prescott, 1991). My reservations about providing a description of these developments derive from the fact that there seem to be great variations in how it is practised, probably because it is in its infancy. Only in maturity, after it has been put to the test as a method of delivering insights into the working of actual economies, will we know how to provide a succinct summary of its operating characteristics.

Notes

Thanks are due to Trevor Breusch, Colin Hargreaves, Hashem Pesaran and John Robertson for their careful reading of an earlier version and the suggestions they made for its improvement.

1 After the earlier paper was published I received a number of complaints about my personification of the methodologies. These writers wanted me to be more neutral (and more accurate) by not attributing methodologies to any one individual. I agreed with this point, but the earlier paper had its origins in the World Congress symposium where the representatives of the methodologies were Hendry, Leamer and Sims. In this I have renamed the methodologies. One reason for doing this is that it is uncertain where some of the participants in the 1985 debate would now locate themselves. However, even then I encounter problems, as developments in the 'LSE methodology' owe as much to Yale, San Diego and Copenhagen as to the London School of Economics. Still, I think there is a 'spiritual' heritage among these centres that justifies the nomenclature.

2 Generalizing to a VAR(p) does not change the essentials of the argument.

3 We need to distinguish between open and closed reduced forms. Let z_t be composed of two sets of variables z_{1t} and z_{2t}. In an *open* reduced form the z_{1t} are expressed as functions of z_{t-1} and z_{2t}, i.e. $z_{1t} = Dz_{t-1} + Gz_{2t}$, while in a *closed* reduced form both z_{1t} and z_{2t} are determined by z_{t-1} alone. The traditional Cowles reduced form is an open one as it makes no assumption about how the 'exogenous' variables z_{2t} are generated. VAR models are obviously closed systems as they make no distinction between which variables are exogenous and which endogenous, unless some restrictions are put upon the A matrix.

4 Those wishing to duplicate the results given below should use the 386 version of Microfit (Pesaran and Pesaran, 1991), setting V = NORMAL(123), EPS = NORMAL(456) and E = NORMAL(789), to find realizations for v_t, ε_t and ξ_t respectively. To generate Y_t I set $Y_1 = 1$ and used the SIM command.

5 $w_t = w_{t-1} + u_t$ where u_t is N(0, 1) and independent of the other errors. u_t was generated by the U = NORMAL(678) command.

6 In some versions of Johansen's program it is possible to use structural information, e.g. by assigning values of elements in the cointegrating vector. Identification might be achieved in that way. In the example pursued here we are referring to those computer programs which implement the estimator by only requiring that the user set the *number* of cointegrating vectors.

7 Thus the supply equation has w_t in it. Exact details of the experiment are available on request.

8 The VAR is not the only type of 'reduced form' appropriate for time series. Vector ARMA or ARMAX processes are obvious alternatives, but these have tended to be too hard to estimate. Moreover it is not clear that all series can be profitably modelled as an autoregression. Incidents such as tax rate changes, financial deregulation etc. are probably better handled as dummy variables, so that most LSM studies pursuing this theme have used a combination of a reduced form and a VAR. In the jargon, the attempt is to characterize the 'Haavelmo density' (Spanos, 1989), i.e. the joint density of the variables of interest, and this may best be done as conditional upon a set of

fixed quantities such as dummy variables as well as the past history of the variables of interest.

9   Sims and Uhlig (1991) were concerned with the case of the estimator of ρ in $y_t = \rho y_{t-1} + e_t$ and not the regression case dealt with later, but the implications of their analysis would be the same.

10   Notice that no y_{t-1} appears in (7). This comes from the fact that the z_{t-1} in (1) only appear as $\alpha' z_{t-1}$ in a cointegrating relation and, being I(0), such terms would become part of u_t.

11   This is a necessary condition but not sufficient. The caveat is ignored in what follows to keep the exposition simple.

12   The example is inspired by Gali (1992). All dynamics are omitted for clarity.

13   Details on how to construct F are available in Mellander et al. (1992) and King et al. (1991).

14   The interpretation given here to the Cowles Commission philosophy applies only to exactly identified systems, i.e. the number of parameters in the reduced form equals the number in the structure, so that all estimation is being done with the reduced form and we are just re-interpreting these estimates in a structural way. This appears to be a sensible way to effect a comparison between the methodologies, although it should be borne in mind that the Cowles Commission went much further and concentrated upon *over-identifying* restrictions, albeit recommending that these be tested. Moreover, the Cowles Commission did not use the VAR as they invoked exogeneity assumptions.

References

Albert, J. and Chib, S. (1992) Bayes inference via Gibbs sampling of autoregressive time series subject to Markov mean and variance shifts. Mimeo, Washington University, St Louis.

Alogoskoufis, G. and Smith, R. (1991) Error correction models. *Journal of Economic Surveys*, 5, 95–128.

Bernanke, B. (1986) Alternative explanations of the money–income correlation. *Carnegie-Rochester Conference in Public Policy*, 25, 49–100.

Blanchard, O. and Quah, D. (1989) The dynamic effects of aggregate demand and supply disturbances. *American Economic Review*, 79, 655–73.

—— and Watson, M. W. (1986) Are business cycles all alike. In R. A. Gordon (ed.), *The American Business Cycle*, Chicago, IL: University of Chicago Press.

Clements, M. P. and Mizon, G. E. (1991) Empirical analysis of macroeconomic time series: VAR and structural models. *European Economic Review*, 35, 887–917.

Darnell, H. and Evans, J. L. (1990) *The Limits of Econometrics*. Aldershot: Edward Elgar.

Driver, C. and Moreton, D. (1991) The influence of uncertainty on U.K. manufacturing investment. *Economic Journal*, 101, 1452–9.

Engle, R. F. and Granger, C. W. J. (1987) Cointegration and error correction: representation, estimation and testing. *Econometrica*, 55, 251–76.

Fisher, E. O'N and Park, J. Y. (1991) Testing purchasing power parity under the null hypothesis of co-integration. *Economic Journal*, 101, 1476–84.

Gali, J. (1992) How well does the IS–LM model fit postwar U.S. data. *Quarterly Journal of Economics*, 709 38.

Gelfand, A. E., Smith, A. F. M. and Lee, T. M. (1992) Bayesian analysis of constrained parameter and truncated data problems using Gibbs sampling. *Journal of the American Statistical Association*, 87, 523–32.

Geweke, J. (1989) Bayesian inference in econometric models using Monte Carlo integration. *Econometrica*, 57, 1317–39.

Hendry, D. F. and Mizon, G. M. (1993) Evaluating dynamic econometric models by encompassing the VAR. In P. C. B. Phillips and V. B. Hall (eds), *Models, Methods and Applications of Econometrics: Essays in Honor of Rex Bergstrom*, Oxford: Oxford University Press.

Johansen, S. (1988) Statistical analysis of cointegrating vectors. *Journal of Economic Dynamics and Control*, 12, 231–54.

King, R. G., Plosser, C. I., Stock, J. H. and Watson, M. W. (1991) Stochastic trends and economic fluctuations. *American Economic Review*, 81, 819–40.

Kydland, F. E. and Prescott, E. C. (1991) The econometrics of the general equilibrium approach to business cycles. *Scandinavian Journal of Economics*, 93, 161–78.

Levine, R. and Renelt, D. (1992) A sensitivity analysis of cross-country growth regressions. *American Economic Review*, 82, 942–63.

Lutkepohl, H. and Reimers, H. G. (1992) Impulse response analysis of co-integrated systems. *Journal of Economic Dynamics and Control*, 16, 53–78.

Mellander, E., Vredin A. and Warne, A. (1992) Stochastic trends and economic fluctuations in a small open economy. *Journal of Applied Econometrics*, 7, 369–94.

Monfort, A. and Rabemananjara, R. (1990) From a VAR model to a structural model with an application to the wage–price spiral. *Journal of Applied Econometrics*, 5, 203–27.

Pagan, A. R. (1987) Three econometric methodologies: a critical appraisal. *Journal of Economic Surveys*, 1, 3–24.

Park, J. Y. (1990) Maximum likelihood estimation of simultaneous cointegrated models. Discussion Paper 1990–18, University of Aarhus.

—— (1992) Canonical co-integrating regressions. *Econometrica*, 60, 119–43.

—— and Phillips, P. C. B. (1989) Statistical inference in regressions with integrated processes: Part 2. *Econometric Theory*, 5, 95–131.

Pesaran, M. H. and Pesaran, B. (1991) *Microfit 3.0: An interactive econometric software package*. Oxford: Oxford University Press.

Phillips, P. C. B. and Hansen, B. E. (1990) Statistical inference in instrumental variables regression with I(1) processes. *Review of Economic Studies*, 57, 99–126.

—— and Park, J. Y. (1992) Unidentified components in reduced rank regression estimation of ECM's. Mimeo, Cowles Foundation, Yale University.

Sims, C. A. (1986) Are forecasting models usable for policy analysis. *Quarterly Review of the Federal Reserve Bank of Minneapolis*, 10, 2–16.

—— and Uhlig, H. (1991) Understanding unit rooters: a helicopter tour. *Econometrica*, 59, 1591–9.

Spanos, A. (1989) On re-reading Haavelmo: a retrospective view of econometric modelling. *Econometric Theory*, 5, 405–29.

Stock, J. H. and Watson, M. W. (1988) Testing for common trends. *Journal of the American Statistical Association*, 83, 1097–1107.

4 Pre-test estimation and testing in econometrics: recent developments

Judith A. Giles and David E. A. Giles
University of Canterbury, New Zealand

1 Introduction

1.1 Background discussion

In applied econometrics it is generally apparent that the researcher has undertaken a 'search' for the preferred specification of the model, or for the appropriate estimator to use. Sometimes this strategy is made explicit and it may have been undertaken in a systematic way. In other cases there is only a vague impression that the final results are not the only ones that were generated during the course of the analysis. Most economists who use econometric tools are aware that 'mining' the data may be distortive in some sense and that the end results may not be what they appear to be.

Consider some simple but common examples of this sort of sequential econometric analysis. First, suppose that the following regression model has been fitted to the data by ordinary least squares (OLS):

$$y_i = \beta_0 + \beta_1 x_{1i} + \beta_2 x_{2i} + e_i. \tag{1}$$

Then, to determine the 'significance' of x_2 in the model, a t test is conducted. If the usual t ratio exceeds the tabulated critical value (for the chosen significance level) then x_2 is deemed to be a 'significant' regressor and it is retained in the model. On the other hand, if x_2 is 'insignificant' it is deleted from the model, which is then re-estimated (effectively by restricted least squares (RLS)). So, the final specification of the model depends on the outcome of a prior test and the estimates of the coefficients of the other variables in the model also depend on the outcome of this test. In addition, the properties of any further tests that may be conducted are affected by the way in which the model's specification was determined.

As a second example, consider the estimation of (1) by OLS. Then, suppose the Durbin–Watson statistic is computed to test whether or not the model's errors are serially independent. If this hypothesis cannot be rejected, the OLS estimates of the coefficients are retained. However, if serial independence is rejected the model is re-estimated (perhaps using the Cochrane–Orcutt estimator), and different coefficient estimates are obtained. Again, the estimates that are finally reported depend on the outcome of a 'preliminary test', and if (for example) one then tests the significance of a regressor in the usual way, the '*t* statistic' is no longer *t* distributed.

Both of these examples are realistic, though they over-simplify the situation because in practice a sequence of such tests might be adopted. However, they capture the essential feature of 'pre-test' strategies in econometrics – the choice of estimator, and the final estimates, depend on the outcome of a *random event*. The probability of choosing OLS or RLS estimation in the first example, or of choosing OLS or Cochrane–Orcutt estimation in the second example, depends on the significance level for the pre-test, as well as on the test's power. In effect, the estimator that generates the reported estimates is a stochastic mixture of two (in these examples) 'component' estimators. In general this pre-test estimator (PTE) will differ from each of its components in the sense that it will have a different sampling distribution, and so generally its bias and precision will also differ. Pre-testing generally affects the sampling properties of the estimators that we use. For instance, in the first example given above the PTE is biased unless $\beta_2 = 0$. These effects are often complicated and depend on the unknown parameters in the model.

Pre-test *testing* is also widely practised in econometrics, and the consequences of such strategies are of considerable interest. In certain rather special cases, two successive econometric tests may be independent. Then, the effect of the first test on the properties of the second can be controlled, and this may have implications of the extent of which there is a pre-test testing 'problem'. Two further examples may be helpful.

Consider a sequence of 'nested' models or hypotheses, such as when we take a multiple regression model and successively delete regressors in such a way that each model in the sequence can be obtained from its predecessor by the deletion of one or more regressors, and we attempt to find the most parsimonious 'significant' model specification. It is well known (e.g. Mizon, 1977) that, with such a nesting, the size of the test of restrictions on the coefficients at any stage can be controlled (against the overall maintained hypothesis) if each null is tested against the previously accepted null in the sequence. Without such nesting, size control is not generally possible, and the resulting size distortion is due to the inherent pre-test nature of the analysis. Similarly, if the hypotheses are nested but the researcher tests each successive null against any alternative other than the immediately preceding null, then a pre-test problem arises.

Finally, consider the familiar Chow test for the structural stability of a regression coefficient vector. It is well known that the validity of the standard form of this test relies, among other things, on the homoskedasticity of the error variance across the two subsamples. When this assumption is violated, we have a form of the famous Behrens–Fisher problem and alternative approximate tests are available. So, there is a strong motivation to pre-test for homogeneity of the variance prior to conducting the test of primary interest (the test for structural stability). In contrast to the preceding example, however, in this case the form of the second test depends on the outcome of the pre-test. The standard pre-test statistic in this case is an F ratio, and it is readily shown (e.g. Phillips and McCabe, 1983) that this statistic is independent of the Chow test statistic. Consequently, the *true* size of the second stage Chow test is the product of the *nominal* sizes chosen for this test and for the pre-test. Judicious choices of these nominal sizes can be used to control the true second stage size for the Chow test itself, as desired. However, even with this independence there remains a pre-test testing issue as an alternative test would be used only if the pre-test null was rejected. We explain this further in section 6.1.

Typically non-independence of successive test statistics is the norm in sequential hypothesis testing in econometrics, and in these cases there are pre-test testing issues to be addressed, as we shall see in section 6. Specifically, how are the (true) size and the power of a second test affected by the presence of a pre-test?

Although sequential inference alters the properties of estimators and tests, the commonly held view, that pre-testing is intrinsically 'bad', need not be true, as we shall see. It should also be emphasized that these effects arise purely because of the introduction of a randomization process, and not because the same data are being used more than once. Indeed, even if the sample is split and one part is used for preliminary testing and the other part for subsequent estimation, the pre-test effects that we have described still arise.[1] Also, if a sequence of pre-tests is used, the randomization process becomes increasingly complicated, especially if the various tests are not independent of each other. In such cases it becomes difficult to determine the properties of the resulting estimators.

The above examples will be familiar to anyone who has undertaken applied econometric research. Indeed, pre-testing is probably the norm, rather than the exception, in applied econometrics and so it not surprising that a sizable literature on this topic has developed. While much of this literature does not attempt to offer *prescriptions* about what researchers should or should not do in their empirical work, it does provide a considerable amount of information about the likely consequences of pre-testing in econometrics. Accordingly, the recent contributions in this field are of practical interest to many economists, and the purpose of this paper is to highlight some of the major themes that have emerged recently in the pre-testing literature, at least with respect to econometric (as distinct from purely statistical) analysis. We also attempt to extract practical recommendations as far as possible to assist applied workers.

1.2   Historical setting

The seminal contribution of Bancroft (1944) can be taken as the starting point for the analysis of pre-testing problems that are of direct interest to economists. Motivated in part by the earlier remarks of Berkson (1942) that there was a need to investigate the statistical properties of sequential estimation strategies, Bancroft analysed two pre-testing problems which set the scene for much of the subsequent work in this field.

The first is as follows. Suppose that we draw two independent samples from two normal populations, each with possibly different variances. These variances can be estimated separately from the respective samples. We can also test for variance homogeneity, and if this hypothesis is accepted then there is good reason to 'pool' the two samples and estimate the (common) population variance from the combined data. In particular this 'pooled' estimator may be more efficient than one based on a single sample. This suggests a pre-test strategy: test for variance homogeneity and either pool the data or not according to the outcome of the prior test. Bancroft derived exact analytic expressions for the bias and variance (and hence mean squared error (MSE)) of this PTE, for the case where the pre-test involves a one-sided alternative. For economists, the interest in this result is that it can be translated into a regression problem where one is testing for a specific type of heteroskedasticity of the errors and pooling sub-samples of data prior to estimating the error variance only if the errors are thought to be homoskedastic. This in turn suggests another related pre-test problem to which we return later: after pre-testing for this type of homoskedasticity, what are the sampling properties of the regression coefficient estimator?

The second problem considered by Bancroft was explicitly regression oriented, and was essentially that discussed above in relation to equation (1). To reiterate, suppose a regression model with two regressors has been fitted by OLS, and the model is either retained or simplified by deleting one of the regressors, depending on the outcome of a *t* test. Bancroft derived an exact analytic expression for the bias of this PTE. Subsequent authors considered the estimator's second moment, and extended the analysis to the more realistic case of the multiple regression model.

Much of the basic work on pre-test problems of this type, or problems of 'inference based on conditional specification', as it was referred to, was undertaken by Bancroft in collaboration with his colleagues and students. Bancroft and Han (1977) provide an annotated bibliography of this early work, though many of the problems considered are not of direct interest to econometricians. A second bibliography is given by Han et al. (1988).

Pre-test problems with an explicit econometric content were taken up subsequently by a series of researchers. In particular, work by Dudley Wallace and a series of graduate students at the University of North Carolina led to several seminal developments, and helped to raise interest in this field among a number of Japanese researchers. Other path-breaking contributions came from George Judge, Thomas Yancey, Mary Ellen Bock and their associates and students at the University of Illinois, Purdue University and later at Berkeley. The range of econometric pre-test problems that has now been analysed is extensive, but in many cases they are essentially variants of those first considered by Bancroft (1944).

In the next section the key results from the econometrics pre-testing literature are stated and summarized briefly, as a background to a more systematic discussion of the major themes that have emerged recently in research in this field. These are taken up in sections 3–7, and some concluding remarks appear in section 8. Each subsection includes some summary comments to assist the reader who is concerned primarily with the practical implications of the results under discussion.

2   Principal results

2.1   Pre-testing linear restrictions in regression

As in the rest of this paper, we concentrate here on 'conventional' PTEs, i.e. those whose components are the traditional ones that have been used in applied econometrics. In particular, while recognizing their interest and importance, we do not consider Bayesian or Stein-like PTEs. For a discussion of these, the reader is referred to Judge and Bock (1978, 1983), Vinod and Ullah (1981) and Judge et al. (1985).

Much of the econometrics pre-test literature is based on a natural generalization of Bancroft's second problem. This involves the linear multiple regression model

$$y = X\beta + e \qquad e \sim \mathrm{N}(0, \sigma^2 I) \tag{2}$$

where y and e are $T \times 1$; X is $T \times k$, non-stochastic and of rank k; and β is $k \times 1$. In addition, prior information suggests m ($< k$) exact independent linear constraints on the regression coefficients

$$R\beta = r \tag{3}$$

where R is $m \times k$, r is $m \times 1$, and both are known and non-stochastic. We will consider the estimation of both β and σ^2. Let $\delta = R\beta - r$ be the error in the prior information. This situation is commonly encountered in applied econometrics, except usually the researcher is uncertain of the accuracy of the prior beliefs. Accordingly, the procedure usually followed in practice is to (pre-)test the validity of the restrictions and if the outcome of the pre-test suggests that they are correct then the model's parameters are estimated incorporating the restrictions. If the pre-test rejects the prior information then the parameters are estimated from the sample information alone. Prior to considering the properties of such PTEs of β and σ^2 we will briefly review the estimators which ignore the restrictions (the 'unrestricted' estimators) and those which assume that the restrictions are correct (the 'restricted' estimators).

The unrestricted OLS (and maximum likelihood) estimator of β is well known to be $b = S^{-1}X'y$, where $S = (X'X)$ and $b \sim \mathrm{N}(\beta, \sigma^2 S^{-1})$. Consequently its risk under squared error loss (the sum of the MSEs of each individual element of b) is $\rho(\beta, b) = E\left[(b - \beta)'(b - \beta)\right] = \sigma^2 \mathrm{tr}(S^{-1})$. From the Gauss–Markov theorem we know that b is the best linear unbiased estimator (BLUE). It is minimax and, among the class of unbiased estimators, minimizes risk under quadratic loss.

A best (minimum variance) quadratic unbiased estimator of σ^2 is the usual least squares estimator, given by $\tilde{\sigma}_{\mathrm{L}}^2 = (y - Xb)'(y - Xb)/v$, where $v = T - k$ and $\rho(\sigma^2, \tilde{\sigma}_{\mathrm{L}}^2) = 2\sigma^4/v$. If we allow the estimator of σ^2 to be biased then the estimator of σ^2 with smallest MSE is $\tilde{\sigma}_{\mathrm{M}}^2 = (y - Xb)'(y - Xb)/(v + 2)$, and as long as the OLS residuals are used its risk is $\rho(\sigma^2, \tilde{\sigma}_{\mathrm{M}}^2) = 2\sigma^4/(v + 2)$. The maximum likelihood estimator of σ^2 is $\tilde{\sigma}_{\mathrm{ML}}^2 = (y - Xb)'(y - Xb)/T$ and $\rho(\sigma^2, \tilde{\sigma}_{\mathrm{ML}}^2) = (2v + k^2)\sigma^4/T^2$.

Imposing the restrictions in (3), we estimate β by $b^* = b + S^{-1}R'[RS^{-1}R']^{-1}(r - Rb)$, which, with $D = S^{-1}R'[RS^{-1}R']^{-1}RS^{-1}$, has a risk under squared error loss of $\rho(\beta, b^*) = \sigma^2 \mathrm{tr}(S^{-1} - D) + \mathrm{tr}(S^{-1}R'[RS^{-1}R']^{-1}\delta\delta'[RS^{-1}R']^{-1}RS^{-1})$. b^* is unbiased if and only if the restrictions are correct ($\delta = 0$). Further, as D is at least positive semi-definite, $\mathrm{var}(b_i^*) \leqslant \mathrm{var}(b_i)$, $i = 1, 2, \ldots, k$, and within the class of linear estimators of β, b^* is the BLUE in this case.

The corresponding restricted estimators of σ^2 are $\sigma_{\mathrm{L}}^{*2} = (y - Xb^*)'(y - Xb^*)/(v + m)$, $\sigma_{\mathrm{M}}^{*2} = (y - Xb^*)'(y - Xb^*)/(v + m + 2)$ and $\sigma_{\mathrm{ML}}^{*2} = (y - Xb^*)'(y - Xb^*)/T$. Now $(y - Xb^*)'(y - Xb^*)/\sigma^2 \sim \chi_{v+m;\lambda}^2$ where the non-centrality parameter λ, defined by $\lambda = \delta'[RS^{-1}R']^{-1}\delta/2\sigma^2$, is a measure of the validity of the linear restrictions. If the restrictions are true, $\delta = 0$ and so $\lambda = 0$. It is straightforward to show that $\rho(\sigma^2, \sigma_{\mathrm{L}}^{*2}) = 2(2\lambda^2 + 4\lambda + v + m)\sigma^4/(v + m)^2$, $\rho(\sigma^2, \sigma_{\mathrm{M}}^{*2}) = 2(2\lambda^2 + v + m + 2)\sigma^4/(v + m + 2)^2$ and $\rho(\sigma^2, \sigma_{\mathrm{ML}}^{*2}) = \left[2(m + v + 4\lambda) + (m - k + 2\lambda)^2\right]\sigma^4/T^2$.

Several studies[2] have considered the conditions under which the risk of b dominates that of b^* and vice versa. These conditions are generally data specific, as the risks depend on X. This limits the generality of any comparisons based on quadratic risk, and so to avoid this complication we shall concentrate, as others have, on the conditional forecast of y rather than on β itself. This is equivalent to assuming orthonormal regressors (i.e.

$X'X = I_k$) in the β space. So, though similar conclusions are drawn from comparing the risk functions, the mapping from the conditional mean (or orthonormal regressors) case to that of considering the unweighted risk of estimators of β (i.e. non-orthonormal regressors) is *not* direct and is significantly more complicated.[3] The risk of Xb, the unrestricted estimator of $E(y)$, is

$$\rho\,[E(y), Xb] = E\left[(Xb - X\beta)'(Xb - X\beta)\right]$$
$$= E\left[(b - \beta)'X'X(b - \beta)\right]$$
$$= \sigma^2 k, \tag{4}$$

while that of the restricted estimator Xb^* is

$$\rho\left[E(y), Xb^*\right] = \sigma^2(k - m + 2\lambda). \tag{5}$$

Comparing (4) and (5) we see that the risk of Xb^* is less than or equal to that of Xb if $\lambda \leqslant m/2$, as is depicted in figure 1.

Similarly, there is a λ range over which the risk of the restricted estimator of σ^2 is less than or equal to that of the unrestricted estimator, as is seen in figure 2. The values of λ, λ_j^* ($j \equiv L, M, ML$) for which the risks are equal depend on the estimation method, but it is readily shown that $\lambda_j^* \neq m/2$ and so, if the researcher desired the minimum risk estimators of $E(y)$ and σ^2, there will be some λ range over which his strategy should be to use the restricted estimator of σ^2 but the unrestricted estimator of $E(y)$. This suggests considering a joint risk function for $E(y)$ and σ^2, something which has not been pursued in the literature.

We now consider the situation where the researcher undertakes a pre-test of the validity of the restrictions. Traditionally,

$$H_0: \delta = 0 \text{ versus } H_1: \delta \neq 0$$

is tested using the Wald statistic

$$\mathfrak{f} = \frac{(Rb - r)'[RS^{-1}R']^{-1}(Rb - r)v}{m(y - Xb)'(y - Xb)}.$$

If H_0 is correct, the test statistic $\mathfrak{f}$ has a central F distribution with m and v degrees of freedom, $F_{(m,v)}$. If one or more of the restrictions are invalid, $\mathfrak{f}$ has a non-central F distribution with m and v degrees of freedom and non-centrality parameter λ. We reject H_0 if $\mathfrak{f} > F_{(m,v)}^{\alpha} = c$, where the critical value c is determined for a given significance level of the test α by

$$\int_0^c dF_{(m,v)} = \Pr\left[F_{(m,v)} \leqslant c\right] = 1 - \alpha.$$

This is a uniformly most powerful invariant (UMPI) size-α test of the validity of the restrictions. If H_0 is rejected we use the unrestricted estimators of $E(y)$ and σ^2. If $\mathfrak{f} \leqslant c$, we assume the restrictions are correct and use the restricted estimators of $E(y)$ and σ^2. So, the estimators of $E(y)$ and σ^2 actually reported are the PTEs

$$X\hat{b} = \begin{cases} Xb & \text{if} \quad \mathfrak{f} > c \\ Xb^* & \text{if} \quad \mathfrak{f} \leqslant c \end{cases} \tag{6}$$

and

$$\hat{\sigma}_j^2 = \begin{cases} \tilde{\sigma}_j^2 & \text{if} \quad \mathfrak{f} > c \\ \sigma_j^{*2} & \text{if} \quad \mathfrak{f} \leqslant c \end{cases} \tag{7}$$

$j \equiv (L, M, ML)$. It is useful to rewrite (6) and (7) as

$$X\hat{b} = I_{[0,c]}(\mathfrak{f})Xb^* + I_{(c,\infty)}(\mathfrak{f})Xb \tag{8}$$

and

$$\hat{\sigma}_j^2 = I_{[0,c]}(\mathfrak{f})\sigma_j^{*2} + I_{(c,\infty)}(\mathfrak{f})\tilde{\sigma}_j^2 \tag{9}$$

where $I_{[.,.]}(\mathfrak{f})$ is an indicator function which takes the value unity if $\mathfrak{f}$ falls within the subscripted range and zero otherwise. From (8) and (9), it is clear that the PTEs are functions of the data, the hypothesis and the significance level of the test. Representing a PTE in this way highlights the difficulty of deriving its sampling properties; it is the sum of two parts, both of which are composed of products of non-independent random variables.

Bancroft's second problem is a special case of the above – he considers a single 'zero' restriction when $k = 2$, and derives the bias of $\hat{b}_1$. Toro-Vizcarrondo (1968) derives the MSE of $\hat{b}_1$ for this estimator, and Brook (1972, 1976) generalizes these results by deriving the unweighted risks of the PTEs of β and $E(y)$ for the general multiple restrictions problem, as outlined here. Sclove et al. (1972) also derive the risk of the PTE of β in the orthonormal regressor model and Bock et al. (1973) extend their analysis to the non-orthonormal case.[4]

The risk of $X\hat{b}$, under squared error loss, is

$$\rho[E(y), X\hat{b}] = \sigma^2 [k + (4\lambda - m)P_{20} - 2\lambda P_{40}] \tag{10}$$

where[5]

$$P_{ij} = \Pr\left[F'_{(m+i,v+j;\lambda)} \leqslant cm(v+j)v(m+i)\right] \qquad i, j = 0, 1, \ldots . \tag{11}$$

Figure 1 illustrates typical risk functions of Xb, Xb^* and $X\hat{b}$ (for $c \in (0, \infty)$). Some features are as follows.

1   If the restrictions are valid the pre-test risk is less than that of the unrestricted estimator but higher than that of the restricted estimator. Intuitively, if $\lambda = 0$, the PTE will lead us to use the restricted estimator $100(1 - \alpha)$ per cent of occasions but 100α per cent of the time we will erroneously ignore the prior information.

2   $\rho[E(y), Xb] = \rho[E(y), X\hat{b} \mid c \in (0, \infty)]$ occurs for a value of λ, $\lambda_1 \in [m/4, m/2]$. So, for $\lambda \in [0, \lambda_1]$ the risk of the PTE, $X\hat{b}$, is less than that of the unrestricted estimator, Xb, but higher than that of the restricted estimator, Xb^*, while for $\lambda \in (\lambda_2, \infty)$, $X\hat{b}$ has smaller risk than that of Xb^* but is dominated by Xb, where λ_2 is the value of λ such that $\rho[E(y), Xb^*] = \rho[E(y), X\hat{b}]$. For $\lambda \in (\lambda_1, \lambda_2)$, $X\hat{b}$ has

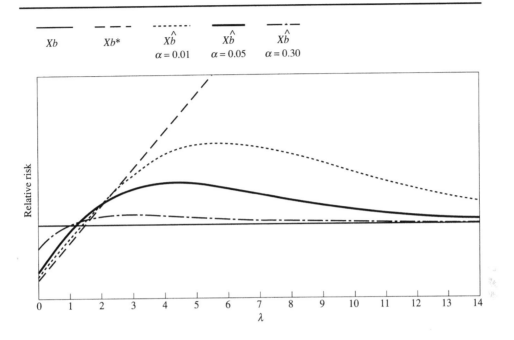

Figure 1 Relative risk functions for Xb, Xb^* and $X\hat{b}$.

higher risk than that of *both* Xb and Xb^*. Thus, pre-testing is *never* the preferable strategy.

3 For finite c, as δ increases, the risk of $X\hat{b}$ monotonically increases to a maximum, which occurs at a value of $\lambda > \lambda_2$; it then monotonically decreases and, as $\lambda \to \infty$, $\rho[E(y), X\hat{b}] \to \rho[E(y), Xb]$. Intuitively, when the prior information is so wrong that λ is very large, then pre-testing will lead us to do the right thing: to ignore the restrictions.

4 The smaller α is (the larger c is), the closer $\rho[E(y), X\hat{b}]$ is to $\rho[E(y), Xb^*]$ as a smaller test size increases the probability of accepting the null hypothesis. This results in a risk gain in the region to the left of λ_1 but at the cost of a (possibly) much higher risk for relatively large λ. An analogous argument can be made for large α. Clearly, from (8), if c is chosen to be zero (infinity), we always reject (accept) the hypothesis, and the PTE degenerates to the unrestricted (restricted) estimator.

5 Of the estimators considered, no one strictly dominates any of the others. Cohen (1965) proves, under certain assumptions and a squared error loss function, that the PTE is inadmissible. Basically, this is because the estimator is a discontinuous function of the test statistic $\mathfrak{f}$, with a single jump at $\mathfrak{f} = c$. Nevertheless, practitioners continue to report the conventional PTE and so, given the lack of dominance of either $X\hat{b}$, Xb or Xb^* and the fact that λ is rarely known, the next obvious question to ask is 'is there an "optimal" pre-test estimator?'. The answer will certainly depend on the definition of 'optimal' but, more importantly, it will be linked to the choice of test size. This question is taken up below.[6]

We now consider the PTE of σ^2, which has received less attention in the literature than have the PTEs of β and $E(y)$. As σ^2 is often regarded as a nuisance parameter, this is perhaps not surprising. However, an estimator of σ^2 is often used as a measure of the model's 'goodness of fit' and, if one is interested in forming standard errors, prediction or confidence intervals or undertaking certain hypothesis tests after pre-testing, then the PTE of σ^2 needs to be investigated. The risk functions of $\hat{\sigma}_j^2$ are derived by Clarke et al. (1987a, b). They depend on the data only through T, k, m and λ. Figure 2 depicts typical risk functions for $\hat{\sigma}_{ML}^2$, σ_{ML}^{*2} and $\hat{\sigma}_{ML}^2$. The following points may be noted:

1   As the pre-test size increases, we reject the hypothesis more frequently, and so the risk of the PTE approaches that of the unrestricted estimator. This has the effect of decreasing the maximum risk of $\hat{\sigma}_j^2$ but at the expense of increasing its minimal risk value. A converse argument can be given for a decrease in the test size.
2   When using the maximum likelihood components pre-testing is never the preferred strategy, and it can be the worst alternative.
3   Among the component estimators of σ^2 considered, under a minimax criterion with respect to risk, those based on the principle of minimum MSE are preferable when constructing the PTE of σ^2. Clarke et al. (1987b) show that the PTE $\hat{\sigma}_M^2$, though composed of the minimum MSE unrestricted and restricted (when H_0 is true) estimators of σ^2, is not itself best invariant.
4   The risk of the restricted estimator is smaller than that of the unrestricted estimator and of the PTE when the restrictions are true. The restricted estimator continues to dominate the pre-test and unrestricted estimators for $\lambda \in [0, \lambda_j^*)$. However, as the hypothesis error grows and approaches infinity, the risk of the restricted estimator is unbounded, while the pre-test risk approaches that of the unrestricted estimator.

For certain values of c the risks of $\hat{\sigma}_L^2$ and $\hat{\sigma}_M^2$ approach that of the unrestricted estimator from below. That is, the PTE can strictly dominate the unrestricted estimator. This feature, which is noted by Ohtani (1988a), contrasts with the results found when estimating $E(y)$ (or β) after a pre-test for linear restrictions. It does also occur, however, when estimating the error variance after a pre-test for homogeneity in the two-sample model, as we shall see below. Ohtani (1988a) extends the work of Clarke et al. (1987b) by deriving the improved estimator of the variance proposed by Stein (1964), which dominates the unrestricted estimator $\hat{\sigma}_M^2$. He shows that this estimator, say $\hat{\sigma}_S^2$, is in fact a PTE with a critical value equal to $v/(v+2)$. Using numerical evaluations Ohtani proposes that $\hat{\sigma}_S^2$ has the minimum risk among the pre-test estimators which dominate the unrestricted estimator. This result is proved by Gelfand and Dey (1988a).[7]

Giles (1991a) shows that a similar result holds when using the least squares component estimators. Then there exists a family of PTEs with $c \in (0, 1]$ which strictly dominate the unrestricted estimator, and it is optimal to use $c - 1$. She also suggests, from her numerical evaluations, that when $m \leqslant 2$ the PTE which uses $c = 1$ strictly dominates *both* of its component estimators. Giles (1990) shows that there is no corresponding case when using the maximum likelihood estimators. Then the smallest risk results from either using the unrestricted or the restricted estimator.

Clarke (1986, 1990) derives and analyses the PTE of the 'standard error of estimate', σ, after a preliminary test of linear restrictions on the coefficients; this PTE, say $\hat{\sigma}$, is

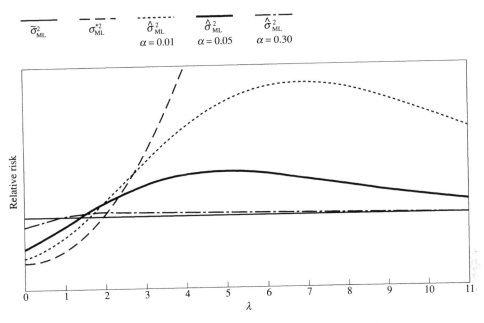

Figure 2 Relative risk functions for $\tilde{\sigma}^2_{\text{ML}}$, σ^{*2}_{ML} and $\hat{\sigma}^2_{\text{ML}}$.

not equal to $(\hat{\sigma}^2)^{1/2}$. We shall not discuss this research here; it suffices to say that the results are found to be *qualitatively* similar whether one is estimating σ^2 or σ.

From a practical viewpoint, applied researchers should be aware that pre-test estimation of the regression coefficients, after a test of restrictions on the coefficient vector, is *never* better than estimating the model without a prior test. Indeed, from an MSE viewpoint it may be the *worst* of the three basic strategies that can be adopted. The same is true if the maximum likelihood estimator of the error variance is obtained after the pre-test, and there is some advantage in using the minimum MSE estimator instead. Finally, when using the least squares PTE of the error variance, it is best to set the pre-test critical value to unity, especially if only one or two restrictions are being tested.

2.2 Homoskedasticity pre-test regression estimators

Frequently we wish to estimate models for which we suspect that the assumption of a scalar error covariance matrix is invalid. For example, the errors may be autocorrelated or the observations may be drawn from different populations, which may result in different error variances. Then, least squares is generally an unbiased but inefficient estimator of the coefficient vector; the generalized least squares (GLS) estimator is minimum variance unbiased. So, we might test for the presence of a non-spherical error covariance matrix prior to estimating the model. Here we consider one such case, that of pre-testing for homogeneity of the error variances in the two-sample linear model. This is a natural extension of Bancroft's first problem. The other obvious case of pre-testing for autocorrelated errors is discussed in section 7.1. So, we assume that model (2) involves two samples, with T_1 and T_2 observations ($T_1 + T_2 = T$) respectively:

$$
\begin{bmatrix} y_1 \\ y_2 \end{bmatrix} = \begin{bmatrix} X_1 & 0 \\ 0 & X_2 \end{bmatrix} \begin{bmatrix} \beta_1 \\ \beta_2 \end{bmatrix} + \begin{bmatrix} e_1 \\ e_2 \end{bmatrix} \qquad \begin{bmatrix} e_1 \\ e_2 \end{bmatrix} \sim \mathrm{N}\left(0, \begin{bmatrix} \sigma_1^2 I_{T_1} & 0 \\ 0 & \sigma_2^2 I_{T_2} \end{bmatrix}\right) \tag{12}
$$

where y_i and e_i are $T_i \times 1$, X_i is $T_i \times k_i$, β_i is $k_i \times 1$ and $k_i < T_i$, $i = 1, 2$. In section 2.2.1 we consider the estimation of σ_1^2, given the uncertainty about whether the second sample comes from the same population as the first. We examine the estimation of the coefficient vector, assuming that $\beta_1 = \beta_2 = \beta$, in section 2.2.2.

2.2.1   Estimation of the scale parameter

If the variances are equal then the two samples may be pooled and an unbiased estimator of σ_1^2 is $s_A^2 = (v_1 s_1^2 + v_2 s_2^2)/(v_1 + v_2)$ where $v_i = T_i - k_i$, $s_i^2 = (y_i - X_i b_i)'(y_i - X_i b_i)/v_i$, $b_i = S_i^{-1} X_i' y_i$, $S_i = (X_i' X_i)$, $i = 1, 2$. We call s_A^2 the always-pool estimator of σ_1^2. Conversely, if the variances are unequal, an unbiased estimator of σ_1^2 is $s_N^2 = s_1^2$. We call s_N^2 the never-pool estimator.

The usual procedure for deciding which estimator of σ_1^2 to use is to undertake a preliminary test of the hypothesis

$$
H_0: \ \sigma_1^2 = \sigma_2^2 \quad \text{versus} \quad H_1: \ H_0 \text{ not true.}
$$

The alternative hypothesis can be one or two sided depending on the researcher's prior beliefs. A test statistic for homoskedasticity is $J = s_2^2/s_1^2$ (or $J^* = s_1^2/s_2^2$, depending on H_1), with $f(J) = \phi^{-1} f\left[F_{(v_2, v_1)}\right]$, where $F_{(v_2, v_1)}$ is a central F variate with v_2 and v_1 degrees of freedom and $\phi = \sigma_1^2/\sigma_2^2$ is a measure of the hypothesis error. Assuming for simplicity the one-sided alternative $H_1: \ \sigma_1^2 < \sigma_2^2$, we accept H_0 if $J \leqslant F_{(v_2, v_1)}^{\alpha} = c$ where the critical value of the test, c, satisfies

$$
\int_0^c dF_{(v_2, v_1)} = \Pr\left[F_{(v_2, v_1)} \leqslant c\right] = 1 - \alpha
$$

for a size-α test.

If the outcome of the pre-test suggests that the variances are equal ($J \leqslant c$) then we estimate σ_1^2 using the always-pool estimator s_A^2, while we employ the never-pool estimator s_N^2 if $J > c$, i.e. when we reject H_0. After such a (pre-)testing procedure, the estimator of σ_1^2 actually reported is the PTE

$$
s_P^2 = \begin{cases} s_N^2 & \text{if } J > c \\ s_A^2 & \text{if } J \leqslant c. \end{cases} \tag{13}
$$

The risks of s_N^2, s_A^2 and s_P^2 are[8]

$$
\rho(\sigma_1^2, s_N^2) = \frac{2\sigma_2^4 \phi^2}{v_1} \tag{14}
$$

$$
\rho(\sigma_1^2, s_A^2) = \frac{\sigma_2^4 \left[\phi^2(2v_1 + v_2^2) - 2v_2^2 \phi + v_2(v_2 + 2)\right]}{(v_1 + v_2)^2} \tag{15}
$$

$$
\rho(\sigma_1^2, s_P^2) = \rho(\sigma_1^2, s_N^2) + \sigma_2^4 \left\{\phi^2 v_2 \left[2v_1(v_1 + v_2)Q_{02} - (v_1 + 2)(v_2 + 2v_1)Q_{04}\right]\right.
$$

$$
\left. + 2v_1 v_2 \phi \left[v_1 Q_{22} - (v_1 + v_2)Q_{20}\right] + v_1 v_2(v_2 + 2)Q_{40}\right\} \left[v_1(v_1 + v_2)^2\right]^{-1} \tag{16}
$$

where, for $i, j = 0, 1, 2, \ldots,$

$$Q_{ij} = \Pr \left[F_{(v_2+i,\,v_1+j)} < \frac{v_2(v_1+j)c}{v_1(v_2+i)} \right]. \tag{17}$$

Bancroft's first problem is equivalent to the one described here with an appropriate redefinition of the degrees of freedom. He derives the bias and variance of s_P^2 and finds that the bias of s_P^2 is smaller than that of s_A^2 when ϕ is close to zero: that range of ϕ where the bias of s_A^2 is highest. We recall that the always-pool estimator is only unbiased when the variances are equal. Intuitively, the pre-test is leading us to follow the correct path when ϕ is small – reject the null. From the MSE comparisons Bancroft finds that the pre-test which uses $c = 1$ results in an MSE equal to or smaller than that of s_N^2 for all possible values of ϕ, i.e. this PTE *strictly dominates* the never-pool estimator. These estimators are considered further by Toyoda and Wallace (1975).

Figure 3 illustrates typical risk functions for s_N^2, s_A^2 and s_P^2, for various values of $c \in (0, \infty)$. Note that when $c = 0$ we always reject the hypothesis and so $\rho(\sigma_1^2, s_P^2) = \rho(\sigma_1^2, s_N^2)$. Conversely, $\rho(\sigma_1^2, s_P^2) = \rho(\sigma_1^2, s_A^2)$ when $c = \infty$, so that we always accept the hypothesis. This figure highlights the following points.

1 Comparing equations (14) and (15), there are two possible values of ϕ, ϕ_1 and ϕ_2, for which $\rho(\sigma_1^2, s_A^2)$ and $\rho(\sigma_1^2, s_N^2)$ intersect, provided that $v_1 v_2 - 4 v_1 - 2 v_2 \neq 0$ (see Toyoda and Wallace, 1975). In any particular case only one of these values, say ϕ_1, will lie in the interval $(0, 1]$. If $0 < \phi < \phi_1$ then s_N^2 dominates s_A^2. Intuitively, the variances are so different that the gain in sampling error from the extra degrees of freedom is outweighed by the bias from pooling the (unequal) variances. Alternatively, s_A^2 has smaller risk than s_N^2 when $\phi_1 < \phi < 1$.

2 There exist values of $c \in (0, 2)$ such that s_P^2 strictly dominates s_N^2 for all possible values of $\phi, 0 < \phi \leqslant 1$. Though these particular PTEs do not dominate s_A^2 for all ϕ, they do so over a wide range of ϕ. It is only within the neighbourhood of $\phi = 1$ that the risk of s_A^2 is smaller. Ohtani and Toyoda (1978) prove, for a given value of ϕ and $c \in [0, 1]$, that the minimum pre-test risk occurs when $c = 1$; so s_N^2 is inadmissible and, specifically, is dominated (at least) by the PTE with $c = 1$. These features raise the question of an optimal pre-test critical value – we return to this issue in section 2.3.

2.2.2 Estimation of the coefficient vector

Assume that $\beta_1 = \beta_2 = \beta$, model (12) is

$$\begin{bmatrix} y_1 \\ y_2 \end{bmatrix} = \begin{bmatrix} X_1 \\ X_2 \end{bmatrix} \beta + \begin{bmatrix} e_1 \\ e_2 \end{bmatrix} \qquad \begin{bmatrix} e_1 \\ e_2 \end{bmatrix} \sim \mathrm{N}\left(0, \begin{bmatrix} \sigma_1^2 I_{T_1} & 0 \\ 0 & \sigma_2^2 I_{T_2} \end{bmatrix}\right) \tag{18}$$

or

$$y = X\beta + e \qquad e \sim \mathrm{N}(0, \Sigma). \tag{19}$$

If the variances are equal we estimate β from the $T_1 + T_2$ observations and $b_A = S^{-1} X' y$, which is the usual least squares (and maximum likelihood) estimator of β, is the BLUE. b_A is the always-pool estimator of β. However, if the variances are unequal, a feasible GLS estimator of β is the 'two-step' Aitken estimator (2SAE)

$$b_N = \left(\frac{S_1}{s_1^2} + \frac{S_2}{s_2^2} \right)^{-1} \left(\frac{X_1' y_1}{s_1^2} + \frac{X_2' y_2}{s_2^2} \right).$$

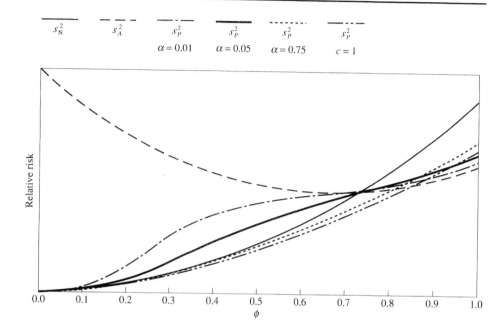

Figure 3   Relative risk functions for s_N^2, s_A^2, and s_P^2.

b_N is the never-pool estimator of β. The PTE of β is

$$b_P = \begin{cases} b_N & \text{if } J > c \\ b_A & \text{if } J \leqslant c. \end{cases} \qquad (20)$$

The research on this particular pre-test problem has worked within either the framework of the orthonormal model[9] or a reparameterized version of the model[10] given by

$$y = X^*\beta^* + e \qquad (21)$$

where $X^* = XP$, $\beta^* = P^{-1}\beta$ and $P = T \times \text{diag}\left[(1 + \mu_i)^{-1/2}\right]$ is a non-singular matrix, and μ_i are the roots of the polynomial $|X_2'X_2/\sigma_2^2 - \mu X_1'X_1/\sigma_1^2| = 0$ $(i = 1,\dots,k)$. The matrix T is chosen so as to diagonalize $X_1'X_1$ and $X_2'X_2$ simultaneously.

Taylor (1978) establishes the finite sample moments of the ith element of the 2SAE within the context of (21). Let this estimator be β_{Ni}^*, $i = 1, 2, \dots, k$. He shows that β_{Ni}^* is an unbiased estimator of β_i^* and that under appropriate conditions the 2SAE is consistent and asymptotically efficient. The least squares estimator of β^* is also unbiased, and Taylor shows that neither estimator dominates, in terms of risk, though he concludes that substantial gains can result from using the 2SAE, depending on the values of v_1, v_2, ϕ and μ_i.[11]

Greenberg (1980) follows Taylor's approach and derives the risk of the two-sided pre-test estimator $\beta_{Pi}^{*\prime}$, corresponding to the ith element of b_P', for the reparameterized model and where the test statistic is J^* rather than J. He shows that $\beta_{Pi}^{*\prime}$ is an unbiased estimator of β_i^*, and that no one estimator, of those evaluated, strictly dominates the others. Nevertheless, the results would seem to favour the 2SAE unless one had a very strong belief that the variances were equal.

Ohtani and Toyoda (1980) derive the risk of the PTE, for the orthonormal model, when the alternative hypothesis is H_1: $\sigma_1^2 > \sigma_2^2$. They show that in this situation the 2SAE is inadmissible as it is dominated by the PTE when the critical value is chosen appropriately. In particular, if one adopts the criterion of minimizing average risk, then the optimal critical value is unity. Mandy (1984) generalizes Ohtani and Toyoda's analysis to the non-orthonormal case. He shows that if the direction of the alternative hypothesis is correct then the (inequality) PTE that takes this directional information into account is superior, in terms of risk, to the two-sided (equality) PTE analysed by Greenberg (1980). However, of course, if the alternative hypothesis should be H_1: $\sigma_1^2 < \sigma_2^2$ then the inequality PTE is risk inferior to the equality PTE.

Finally, Adjibolosoo (1989, 1990a) suggests that this traditional pre-test procedure may lead the researcher to use the 2SAE when in fact the degree of heteroskedasticity may be such that it is still preferable to use OLS. Consequently, he considers a PTE (the 'probabilistic heteroskedasticity PTE') which chooses between b_A and b_N according to a measure of the degree of severity of the heteroskedasticity rather than according to the Goldfeld–Quandt J test. Using a Monte Carlo experiment, Adjibolosoo shows first that this new test is generally more powerful than the J test, and second he shows that the probabilistic heteroskedasticity PTE is typically preferable, in terms of MSE, to its traditional Goldfeld-Quandt counterpart.

Some of the most important practical implications for the applied researcher who pre-tests for error variance homogeneity in the two-sample case are the following. First, if estimation of the error variance is of direct interest, then there are advantages in pre-testing with a critical value of unity rather than using simply the 'never-pool' or 'always-pool' estimators. Second, as far as estimation of the coefficient vector is concerned, the preferred strategy may depend on the form of the alternative hypothesis for the pre-test itself. If this alternative is that the subsample variances are unequal, then the use of the 2SAE (without pre-testing) seems advisable. On the other hand, if the alternative hypothesis is one-sided then pre-testing with a critical value of unity is again a good strategy.

2.3 Another homoskedasticity pre-test estimator of the error variance

Several studies examine the problem of estimating the error variance in the classical linear regression model $y = X\beta + e$, $e \sim N(0, \sigma^2 I_T)$, after a preliminary test of H_0: $\sigma^2 = \sigma_0^2$, where σ_0^2 is some known value available from previous experience. The alternative hypothesis H_A can be one or two sided. If we accept H_0 then we use σ_0^2 as our 'estimator' of σ^2, while we use $\hat{\sigma}^2 = (y - Xb)'(y - Xb)/v$, the usual least squares estimator of σ^2, if we reject H_0. The PTE is then

$$\sigma_P^2 = \begin{cases} \sigma_0^2 & \text{if accept } H_0 \\ \hat{\sigma}^2 & \text{if reject } H_0. \end{cases}$$

Assuming orthonormal regressors, Yancey et al. (1983) (see also Srivastava, 1976) derive the risk, under squared error loss, of σ_P^2 assuming H_A: $\sigma^2 \geq \sigma_0^2$; and also the risk of the PTE, say $\overset{*}{\sigma}{}^2$, which would arise after testing H_0: $\sigma^2 \geqslant \sigma_0^2$ versus H_A: $\sigma^2 < \sigma_0^2$. They numerically evaluate their exact risk expressions for a 5 per cent significance level and find, of the estimators investigated, that there is no strictly dominating estimator, though when the direction of the hypothesis is correct the risk of $\overset{*}{\sigma}{}^2$ is always equal to or less than the risk of $\hat{\sigma}^2$. Comparing the risks of $\overset{*}{\sigma}{}^2$ and σ_P^2 their results suggest that if $\sigma^2/\sigma_0^2 \in [0.75, 1.25]$ then $\overset{*}{\sigma}{}^2$ has smaller risk than σ_P^2, while the converse is typically the case for other values of σ^2/σ_0^2.

Inada (1989) considers the problem of estimating the variance of a normal variate after a pre-test that the variance lies in the neighbourhood of a known value; i.e. H_0: $\sigma_0^2/c_0 \leqslant \sigma^2 \leqslant \sigma_0^2 c_0$, where c_0 is a known positive constant. He considers two PTEs, say PT_1 and PT_2, where

$$PT_1 = \begin{cases} \sigma_0^2 & \text{if } c_1^{-1} < u/\sigma_0^2 < c_1 \\ wu & \text{if } u/\sigma_0^2 \geqslant c_1 \\ w^{-1}u & \text{if } u/\sigma_0^2 \leqslant c_1^{-1} \end{cases}$$

and

$$PT_2 = \begin{cases} wu & \text{if } u/\sigma_0^2 > 1 \\ w^{-1}u & \text{if } u/\sigma_0^2 \leqslant 1 \end{cases}$$

where

$$u = \sum_{i=1}^{n} \frac{(X_i - \overline{X})^2}{n-1},$$

the weight w is a constant such that $0 < w \leqslant 1$, and c_1 is an appropriate critical value. Inada derives the risks of PT_1 and PT_2, and solves for the values of w such that PT_1 and PT_2 are minimax estimators, given the value of c_0. He compares these PTEs with the traditional PTE σ_P^2 and shows that it is preferable to use PT_1, in small or moderate samples, when H_0 is in the neighbourhood of being true, but in large samples the risks of PT_1, PT_2 and u are virtually indistinguishable.

Ohtani (1991b) (see also Ohtani, 1991a) considers the PTE $\overset{+}{\sigma}{}^2$, which arises after testing H_0: $\sigma^2 = \sigma_0^2$ versus H_A: $\sigma^2 > \sigma_0^2$, when we use the Stein (1964) estimator of σ^2, say σ_S^2, rather than $\hat{\sigma}^2$ if we reject H_0. Recall from the discussion in section 2.1 that σ_S^2 is itself a PTE, so $\overset{+}{\sigma}{}^2$ is a special type of multistage PTE. We discuss this further in section 7.2. Ohtani shows that if the direction of the prior information is valid, and the size of the pre-test on σ^2 is chosen appropriately, then $\overset{+}{\sigma}{}^2$ strictly dominates σ_S^2.

2.4 The choice of significance level

One feature of the pre-test risk functions considered so far is their dependence on the choice of significance level. If the test size is varied, the pre-test risk function changes, and so too do the differences between the risk of the PTE and the risks of its component estimators. A second feature is that for any particular problem there exists no dominating estimator; in general, the risks of the PTE and its component estimators cross somewhere in the hypothesis error space.

As the extent to which the non-sample information is true or false is unknown, these features raise the question: is there an optimal choice of test size such that the pre-test risk is as close as possible to the smallest that could be achieved? Several studies have addressed this issue. Among other things, the answer depends on the pre-test under investigation and the chosen optimality criterion.

First, we review those studies which have considered the optimal choice of test size after a pre-test for linear restrictions. From figure 1, the minimum risk that could conceivably be achieved, for all λ, is given by the boundary traced out by the risk of the restricted estimator for $\lambda \in [0, m/2]$, and for $\lambda \in [m/2, \infty)$ by the risk of the unrestricted estimator.[12] So we desire a choice of test size which results in the risk of the PTE being as close as possible to this boundary. As α increases, the risk of the PTE moves down (up) toward the risk of the unrestricted estimator to the right (left) of $\lambda = m/2$, and there is a tradeoff between the proximities of the pre-test risk and the minimum risk boundary. There are various ways of measuring this distance.

One possibility is the criterion of minimax regret. For a given test size, we determine the maximum regret of $\rho[E(y), X\hat{b}]$ from the boundary for all λ and then solve for the value of the critical value c which minimizes the maximum regret. This value of c is the optimal critical value. For the case of a single hypothesis involving a t test, Sawa and Hiromatsu (1973) use this criterion and find an optimum value of c of about 1.8 (see also Farebrother, 1975). For the situation of multiple restrictions, Brook (1972, 1976) chooses values of c, say c^*, that minimize the maximum regret on either side of $\lambda = m/2$. This is a slight modification of the Sawa and Hiromatsu criterion.

For the conditional mean forecast problem (or when the regressors are orthonormal), Brook finds that c^* is generally very close to 2, regardless of the degrees of freedom. This result gives *some* comfort to researchers who traditionally use the 5 per cent significance level: 2 is an *approximate* critical value when the degrees of freedom are moderate to high, say greater than 25, and $m > 4$. The robustness of this result to model mis-specification is considered in section 3.

Another way of defining the optimal critical value is as follows. Instead of searching for the maximum regret for each level of α, we could take into account the regret for each value of λ and search for the value of α which minimizes their sum or average, i.e. we could minimize the area between the pre-test risk and the minimum possible risk boundary. This criterion is considered by Toyoda and Wallace (1976), who find that it leads to a critical value of zero (i.e. use the least squares estimator) if the number of restrictions is less than five. For $m \leqslant 5 < 60$, they find that the (non-constant) optimal critical value is smaller than that observed by Brook (1976), and approximately equal to Brook's values for $m \geqslant 60$.

Brook (1976) and Toyoda and Wallace (1976) effectively assume a diffuse (non-informative) prior for λ. This may be giving too little weight to small λ, as the investigator must believe λ is in the neighbourhood of zero to be pre-testing at all.[13] Wallace (1977) postulates that with a strong prior on λ weighted towards zero, the minimum average risk critical value would be increased. Toyoda and Ohtani (1978) extend the analysis of Toyoda and Wallace (1976) to include prior knowledge about λ, by assuming a gamma prior density on λ which allows one to weight the likely values of the hypothesis error. They find that if more weight is given to values of λ around the null hypothesis then the optimal critical values do increase from those proposed by Toyoda and Wallace. Nevertheless, typically, their results support the use of test sizes which are larger than the commonly used ones of 1 per cent and 5 per cent.

Brook and Fletcher (1981) extend the analyses of Toyoda and Wallace (1976) and Brook (1976) to the case of multicollinear (non-orthonormal) regressors. Then the optimal critical value depends on the level of multicollinearity. They consider testing H_0: $\beta_2 = 0$ in $y = X_1\beta_1 + X_2\beta_2 + e$, under the usual classical assumptions, where β_1 is $(k - m) \times 1$ and β_2 is $m \times 1$, and show that the optimal critical value of the pre-test according to the Toyoda and Wallace average risk criterion can be well approximated by $c^*_{TW} = v(m + t - 4)/m(v + 2)$, where $v = T - k$, $t = \text{tr}(C_{22})$ and C_{22} is the $m \times m$ submatrix of the (standardized) matrix

$$(X'X)^{-1} = \begin{bmatrix} C_{11} & C_{12} \\ C_{21} & C_{22} \end{bmatrix}.$$

When the regressors are orthonormal $C_{22} = I_m$ and $t = m$, but as the columns of X exhibit higher degrees of collinearity then t increases. Brook and Fletcher find c^*_{TW} to be very accurate, especially for large m and v values, and they show that the optimal critical value of the prior F test for $t \leqslant 4$ is 0; i.e. it is preferable to ignore the prior information. This is analogous to the result found by Toyoda and Wallace (1976). For $t \geqslant 4$, c^*_{TW} increases with m and v, and it increases as t increases for a given m and v, implying a higher probability of choosing the restricted estimator.

Under a minimax regret criterion Brook and Fletcher show that the optimal critical value, for multicollinear X, is well approximated by $c^*_B = 1 + t/m$. Recall that for orthonormal regressors $t = m$ and so $c^*_B \approx 2$, as found by Brook (1976). c^*_B depends only on t/m, and not on v, and increases as the relative degree of multicollinearity (t/m) increases. Typically these optimal critical values are still substantially higher than those implied by the traditional 1 per cent and 5 per cent significance levels, and c^*_B is close to c^*_{TW} for reasonably large m and v.

Until recently there has been no research into the choice of an optimal critical value when estimating the error variance after a pre-test for exact linear restrictions. Then, when using the least squares component estimators, the PTE which uses $c = 1$ strictly dominates the unrestricted estimator and can also strictly dominate the restricted estimator for $m \leqslant 2$. For the latter case there is then no optimal size problem – it is always optimal to pre-test using $c = 1$ *even if the restrictions are valid*. When using the minimum MSE component estimators Ohtani (1988a) shows that the PTE using $c = v/(v+2)$ strictly dominates the unrestricted estimator but that there is still a range in the neighbourhood of the null hypothesis where the restricted estimator has smaller risk. Finally, Giles (1990) shows that it is never better to pre-test when using the maximum likelihood components.

Giles and Lieberman (1991) consider the choice of optimal critical value for a pre-test of exact linear restrictions when estimating the regression error variance. They calculate the critical value c^* according to a minimax regret criterion and show that regardless of which component estimators are used c^* is not constant. This contrasts with Brook's general finding. However, for a given m, k and estimation procedure, c^* is relatively constant as v varies. Giles and Lieberman also compare the risk functions of the PTE which uses c^* and that which uses the critical value which minimizes the pre-test risk function ($c = 1$ for the L estimators, $c = v/(v + 2)$ for the M estimators and $c = 0$ for the ML estimators). They find that generally the risk of the PTE which uses the latter (easier to apply) critical values is smaller than that which uses the critical value derived from the minimax regret criterion.

We now consider the question of the optimal size for a pre-test for homogeneity. Toyoda and Wallace (1975), Hirano (1978), Ohtani and Toyoda (1978) and Bancroft and Han (1983) each investigate this problem when the parameter being estimated is the error variance σ_1^2, while Ohtani and Toyoda (1980) seek an optimal critical value for the PTE of the location vector in the orthonormal model.

Toyoda and Wallace base their choice of optimal critical value on the minimum average risk criterion, with a diffuse prior. They prove that the necessary condition for the minimum is attained when $c = 1$ and they numerically check the sufficiency and the uniqueness of this minimum. They show that this optimal critical value typically implies a type I error ranging from 40 to 60 per cent. Relatively high optimal levels of significance are also reported by Hirano (1978). He considers the choice of significance level one should adopt for the pre-test on the basis of minimizing Akaike's information criterion.

A minimax regret criterion is employed by Ohtani and Toyoda (1978). When the alternative hypothesis is one-sided they find that the optimal critical value depends on the degrees of freedom and varies from about 1.7 to 2.8. This contrasts with the results of Toyoda and Wallace (1975).

Bancroft and Han (1983) investigate yet another criterion: relative efficiency of the PTE to the never-pool estimator. For given values of v_1, v_2 and α, and a one-sided alternative hypothesis, they numerically solve for the maximum and minimum values of this efficiency. For certain values of α, the PTE strictly dominates the never-pool estimator; and so they suggest selecting a test size such that maximum efficiency is the largest and minimum efficiency is no less than unity. This procedure should ensure the largest gain in efficiency. Bancroft and Han find that this criterion results in optimal significance levels in the region of 30–50 per cent.

Ohtani and Toyoda (1980) adopt the criterion of minimizing average relative risk when they seek the optimal critical value of the pre-test for homogeneity, prior to estimating the location vector in the orthonormal model. They consider a one-sided alternative hypothesis and show that the 2SAE is inadmissible as it is strictly dominated by the PTE with a critical value of unity. Ohtani and Toyoda derive the extrema of the average relative risk function and conclude that the optimal critical value for the pre-test is $c^* = 1$.

From these studies we see the influence of the chosen criterion on the proposed optimal test size. Nevertheless, the results suggest optimal values of α that are substantially larger than those traditionally used in practice. Further, depending on the criterion adopted, the optimal critical values may vary with the degrees of freedom.

There are some clear prescriptions here for the applied economist who adopts pre-test estimation strategies. If the pre-test relates to linear restrictions on the coefficients then one should apply the F test with a critical value of 2 if low predictive risk is desired. If attention focuses on estimation of the coefficient vector itself, then the c_{TW}^* and c_{β}^* critical value formulae of Brook and Fletcher provide clear guidelines. On the other hand, when estimating the error variance after this same pre-test, it is generally advisable to use a critical value of unity, $v/(v+2)$, or zero, depending on whether one uses the OLS, minimum MSE or maximum likelihood variants of the scale parameter estimator. Finally, if the pre-test is one for variance homogeneity, a critical value of unity seems advisable when estimating the coefficient vector, assuming a one-sided alternative hypothesis.

3   Robustness of pre-test estimators

In any econometric application there is some chance of mis-specifying the model. The errors may not obey the usual 'ideal' assumptions; some irrelevant regressors may be included in the model, or relevant ones excluded; the error term may be non-normal, serially correlated or heteroskedastic; or the functional form of the model may be mis-represented.

The traditional pre-testing literature in econometrics is based on the premise that there are no such mis-specifications. No other 'complications' are allowed for. Recently, this situation has been rectified, and several studies have considered some of the consequences of pre-testing in the context of models that are already mis-specified in some way. Specifically, models which are incorrectly specified in terms of the regressors or with respect to the error term assumptions have now been analysed. Pre-testing in the context of a model whose functional form is mis-specified has yet to be researched explicitly, though to some extent it is covered implicitly by the omitted-regressors case.

3.1   Mis-specification of the regressors

Mis-specification of the regressor matrix in a linear regression model is a common situation. Extraneous regressors may be included in the model but it is more likely that relevant regressors will be omitted. The latter situation may arise either because of the researcher's lack of understanding of the underlying theory, or because certain data are unavailable. In the latter case, another type of mis-specification may also arise – a proxy variable may be substituted for the 'real' regressor.

With this in mind, several authors have reappraised some of the standard pre-test estimation strategies, allowing for such model mis-specification. The inclusion of extraneous regressors is easily dealt with. Giles (1986) shows that in this case the risks of the OLS, RLS and pre-test estimators of the regression coefficient vector, after a test of exact linear restrictions on this vector, are the same as in the properly specified model except for a simple scaling of the results. Accordingly, there are the usual regions in the parameter space over which the relative dominance of one of these estimators over the others arises, as in figure 1. In particular, such pre-testing is never the best of these three strategies, and can be worst. Moreover, the results relating to the optimal choice of pre-test size are unaffected by such a mis-specification.

This situation changes fundamentally if relevant regressors are excluded from the regression. Effectively, this possibility and that of including extraneous regressors was first studied by Ohtani (1983). He considered a pre-test for exact restrictions on the regression coefficients when the model includes proxy variables, i.e. effectively, relevant regressors are omitted and irrelevant ones are also included in the model. Unaware of this work, Mittelhammer (1984) dealt with the more extreme case of pre-testing in the context of omitted regressors. Measuring performance in terms of squared error predictive risk, he showed that imposing *valid* restrictions no longer guarantees dominance of RLS over OLS, or of the PTE over OLS! This should be contrasted with result (1) noted in connection with figure 1. Further, referring to result (2) associated with that diagram, the region in which the pre-test and OLS predictive risks must cross is unaltered if the model is mis-specified in this way. Finally, as the degree of model mis-specification increases, the OLS, RLS and pre-test predictive risks are all unbounded, for a given level of hypothesis error.

When the model is mis-specified in this way, it is also natural to ask whether or not the optimal choice of pre-test size is affected. Intuitively, one would expect that the omission of relevant regressors would generally affect this choice, given the preceding comments about the effects on the risk functions themselves. Giles et al. (1992c) reconsider Brook's (1976) result relating to a preliminary test of linear restrictions on the coefficient vector when the regressors are orthonormal.

They find that Brook's minimax regret criterion no longer leads to an optimal critical F value of approximately 2 when the model is mis-specified. In fact, the optimal critical value is then sensitive to the degrees of freedom in the problem, and can differ substantially from Brook's value. Further, for a given number of restrictions and regression degrees of freedom, the optimal choice of pre-test critical value declines, and the optimal pre-test size increases monotonically as the model becomes increasingly mis-specified. This has the effect of accentuating the other strong result from Brook's analysis – the optimal choice of pre-test size in this problem is often much greater than the commonly assigned values such as 5 or 1 per cent – when relevant regressors are omitted from the model.

Giles and Clarke (1989) study the estimation of the regression scale parameter after the same pre-test in the same mis-specified model. Qualitatively, they come to the same conclusions as Mittelhammer in the case of predictive risk. In particular, imposing valid restrictions need not lead to lower risk than if the prior information is ignored or if a pre-test is undertaken. Clearly, there can be serious costs in omitting relevant regressors. Giles (1991b) extends the analyses of Mittelhammer (1984) and Giles and Clarke (1989) to cases in which the disturbances are incorrectly assumed to be normal and we have simultaneously omitted relevant regressors. We discuss this study further in the next section.

Estimation of the scale parameter in the context of omitted regressors is also considered by Ohtani (1987a), but for a different preliminary test, namely H_0: $\sigma^2 = \sigma_0^2$ versus H_A: $\sigma^2 \neq \sigma_0^2$ or H_A: $\sigma^2 > \sigma_0^2$. He finds that under the one-sided alternative (but not under the two-sided one), there exists a family of PTEs for σ^2 which strictly dominate the unrestricted estimator. This dominance is robust to mis-specification through the omission of regressors. He considers a numerical example with $v = 20$ degrees of freedom, and conjectures that the PTE based on a size of 45 per cent has minimum risk in this dominating family. It is straightforward to show, using the approach of J. A. Giles (1991a, b, 1992), that the optimal such critical value is $c = v$ (regardless of model mis-specification). This implies a pre-test size of 45.8 per cent if $v = 20$.

Assuming a one-sided alternative, Giles (1993) extends Ohtani's (1987a) and her own (1992) analyses to the testing of homogeneity in the two-sample linear heteroskedasticity model when relevant regressors are omitted from the models for each sample (possibly different regressors) and the disturbances are spherically symmetric. Then the J test for homogeneity is invalid under the null, as its distribution depends on all aspects of the problem, including the degree of mis-specification and the variance mixing distribution. She also shows that the critical values, identified in the (1992) paper (see the next section), which minimize the pre-test risk in the correctly specified model also hold this property for the mis-specified model. Analogous to Ohtani's results, there is a family of PTEs which strictly dominate the never-pool estimator, and also in some cases the always-pool estimator. It is never preferable to always-pool the samples without testing the validity of the null hypothesis, nor is it optimal to ignore the prior information.

Ohtani's (1983) contribution focuses on predictive risk in the context of proxy variables, when the pre-test involves coefficient restrictions. Implicitly, it subsumes the essential pre-test results of Mittelhammer (1984) and Giles (1986). One of Ohtani's most important results is that the pre-test strategy can have lower risk than *both* of its component estimators. This is contrary to the situation in the properly specified regression model, as depicted in figure 1, and it again underscores the point that, once we move away from the make-believe world of a properly specified model to the real-life situation of invalid models, our standard textbook results need to be reassessed. In this context, perhaps the most important lesson for applied econometricians is that extreme care must be taken over the model's specification. With a mis-specified model it is difficult to offer many helpful prescriptions.

3.2   Non-normal regression errors

Our discussion so far has assumed that the regression disturbances are normally distributed, but there is a large literature which suggests that this assumption is sometimes unrealistic. In particular, many economic data series exhibit more kurtosis (and hence fatter tails) than the normal distribution.[14] This has obvious implications for the distribution of the regression disturbance term, and accordingly there has been increasing interest in the sampling properties of estimators and test statistics for non-normal disturbances. Many studies have considered this issue and various distributions have been investigated (see, for example, Judge et al., 1985). Two general forms of non-normality are usually analysed. The first assumes that the errors are dependent but are uncorrelated (for example, multivariate Student-t errors), while the second assumes that the non-normal errors are identically and independently distributed (for example, univariate Student-t).

Little work has been undertaken on the investigation of the properties of PTEs with non-normal disturbances. Assuming particular non-normal distributions, Mehta (1972) and J. A. Giles (1992, 1993) consider the risk, under squared error loss, of estimators of the error variance after a pre-test for homogeneity of the variances in the two-sample linear regression model, while Giles (1991a, b) derives the risk of PTEs of the prediction vector and of the error variance after a pre-test for exact linear restrictions.

Mehta (1972) considers a family of symmetric distributions given by

$$f(x \mid \theta_1, \sigma_1^2, \beta) = \left[\Gamma\left(\frac{\beta+3}{2}\right) 2^{(\beta+3)/2} \sigma_1^2 \right]^{-1} \exp\left(-\frac{1}{2}\left|\frac{x-\theta_1}{\sigma_1^2}\right|^{2/(1+\beta)}\right)$$

which includes the normal, double exponential and rectangular distributions as special cases. Mehta considers the problem of estimating the scale parameter from a random sample which follows this distribution when we also have a second, independent, random sample which follows the same distribution but with σ_1^2 different from σ_2^2. The interest in this problem to economists was outlined in section 1.2.

Mehta derives the MSE of two PTEs of σ_1^2. The first is analogous to the PTE for this problem that was discussed in section 2.2 – this PTE is a discontinuous function of the test statistic. He also derives the MSE of a PTE which is a continuous function of the test statistic, and he compares the MSEs of the estimators. For the cases investigated, the qualitative results are the same for all values of β, the non-normality parameter. He suggests that a test size of between 25 and 50 per cent be used.

The remaining pre-test literature in this area considers that the departure from normality is to the spherically symmetric family of distributions, which includes the multivariate Student-t (Mt) and normal as special cases. Aside from the normal distribution, this family results in dependent uncorrelated disturbances. One particularly strong motivation for considering this family is that a particular subclass, the so-called compound normal family, can be expressed as a variance mixture of normals. That is, $f(e) = \int_0^\infty f_N(e)f(\tau)\,d\tau$, where $f(e)$ is the probability density function (pdf) of e, $f_N(e)$ is the pdf of e when $e \sim N(0, \tau^2 I)$ and $f(\tau)$ is the pdf of τ supported on $[0, \infty)$. Non-normal regression disturbances can arise, even if each e_i ($i = 1, \ldots, T$) is normally distributed, when the variance of e_i is itself a random variable.[15] For example, the Mt distribution arises if τ is an inverted gamma variate.

Many studies have investigated linear regression models with spherically symmetric disturbances.[16] Of particular relevance to this paper, Box (1952) shows that the null distribution of $\mathfrak{f}$, the test statistic for exact linear restrictions, is the same for all members of the spherically symmetric family.[17] Thomas (1970) derives the non-null distribution of $\mathfrak{f}$ and shows that it depends on the specific form of the variance mixing distribution. King (1979) extends many of Thomas's results. In particular, he shows that if a test has an optimal power property for normal disturbances over all possible values of τ^2 then it maintains this property when the errors are compound normal. Consequently, $\mathfrak{f}$ is a UMPI size-α test for compound normal disturbances. King also proves that if any function of y (be it a test statistic or an estimator) is invariant to the values taken by τ^2 when $e \sim N(0, \tau^2 I_T)$ then the function has the same distribution for the wider class of spherically symmetric distributions (in fact, elliptically symmetric). So, assuming a correctly specified design matrix, the test statistic for homoskedasticity, J, has the same null and non-null distributions under the wider error term assumption (see also Chmielewski, 1981b).

J. A. Giles (1992) considers the same pre-test problem as Mehta (1972) (and, for instance, Bancroft (1944) and Toyoda and Wallace (1975) under normal errors) when the disturbances follow the compound normal family of elliptically symmetric distributions but are wrongly assumed to be normal. She derives the risk of the PTE and also broadens the standard assumption that the never-pool variance estimators are based on the least squares principle. Two families of variance mixing distributions are considered for specific illustrations – the inverted gamma density and the gamma density. The former mixture results in the Mt family of densities, while Teichroew (1957) derives the density and distribution functions of a random variable generated from the latter member of the spherically symmetric family. Giles shows that the results are qualitatively invariant to which of these mixing distributions is used and to the choice of estimation method used to form the never-pool estimator.

The key results from the J. A. Giles (1992) study are, first, that the PTE can strictly dominate *both* of its component estimators for sufficiently non-normal disturbances. Second, it may be preferable to use the maximum likelihood principle rather than the least squares principle to form the never-pool estimators for non-normal disturbances. Finally, she shows that the risk function of the pre-test estimator has a minimum when $c^* = 1$ for the least squares component estimators, $c^* = v_1 T_2 / v_2 T_1$ for the (usual) maximum likelihood component estimators and $c^* = v_1(v_2+2)/v_2(v_1+2)$ for the (usual) minimum MSE component estimators.[18] Giles (1993) extends this analysis to the simultaneous possibility of omitted regressors, as discussed in the previous section.

Assuming a correctly specified design matrix, Giles (1991a) derives the risk of PTEs of the prediction vector and of the error variance after a pre-test for linear restrictions when the disturbances are compound normal. Her study suggests that the risk properties of the PTE of the prediction vector are qualitatively the same for all members of the compound normal family as presented in section 2.1 for normal disturbances. In particular, pre-testing is never the preferable strategy. This is incorrect. Wong and Giles (1991) show that it is possible for the PTE to dominate both of its component estimators over some of the λ range. The investigations of Wong and Giles for Mt disturbances suggest first that the existence and magnitude of the dominating region for the PTE depends on the values of m and v, the degrees of freedom parameter of the Mt distribution.[19] Second, their results show that there is no strictly dominating PTE.

Giles (1991a) also shows that the wider error distribution assumption can have a substantial impact on the risk function of the estimators of the error variance. She considers the least squares estimators of the error variance[20] and she shows that the pre-test risk function has extrema when $c = 0, c = \infty$ and $c = 1$, so that the PTE can dominate both of its component estimators. In fact, using the Mt distribution to illustrate, she shows that there exists a family of PTEs with $c \in (0, 1]$ which strictly dominate the unrestricted estimator for all λ, and the PTE using a critical value of unity has the smallest risk of those PTEs with $c \in [0, 1]$ for all λ.

This family of PTEs also dominates the restricted estimator over part of the λ range, and the numerical evaluations suggest that this will be strict dominance for small values of v, say $v < 15$. The results also suggest that this may occur for normal disturbances if m is small, say equal to unity. Thus, when estimating the error variance using the least squares estimators, it is never preferable to ignore any linear restrictions on the coefficients. Pre-testing is always preferable, and the optimal pre-test critical value is unity. Further, it is better to pre-test using $c = 1$ than to impose the restrictions without testing, unless there is a strong belief that the restrictions are valid. Then pre-testing is better only if v is small (i.e. the tails of the marginal distribution of the disturbances are 'fat' in relation to normality) or m is small.

Giles (1991b) extends the Giles (1991a) study to the omitted-variables model. She finds that the results of Mittelhammer (1984) and Giles and Clarke (1989) assuming normal errors carry over to the wider error term assumption. In particular, imposing valid restrictions does not guarantee a reduction in risk if we have omitted relevant regressors.

The question of the optimal size of a pre-test for linear restrictions with non-normal disturbances has received little attention. The evaluations of Giles (1991a) show that Brook's optimal critical value of 2 does not extend to all members of the compound normal family, though she offers no alternative critical value. Wong and Giles (1991) consider the extension of the Brook minimax regret criterion to Mt disturbances. They show first that the optimal critical values are not constant for all values of ν. Second, for a given value of ν, the optimal critical values are relatively invariant to the degrees of freedom and the number of restrictions. For instance, the optimal critical value is approximately 2.4 for $\nu = 5$, approximately 2.1 when $\nu = 10$, and the optimal critical value of 2 suggested by Brook for normal errors holds reasonably well for the case of Mt errors when $\nu \geqslant 20$. Wong and Giles also suggest, if ν is unknown, that a researcher could be (practically) content to continue to use Brook's optimal critical value prescribed for normal errors.

Further research is obviously required on deriving the properties of PTEs under non-normal disturbances. In particular, it would be of interest to know whether the observed results extend to the situation of non-normal but identically and independently distributed disturbances. However, from a practical viewpoint it is clear that, in the likely event of non-normal disturbances, the prescriptions offered so far may have to be re-examined.

3.3   Other forms of model mis-specification

Recent studies of the effects of model mis-specification on the properties of standard pre-test strategies have proved to be most enlightening, in the sense of overturning a number of apparently strong results which in fact rely on a correct model specification for their validity. A final form of mis-specification that has been considered in this context is that of a non-scalar covariance matrix for the regression errors. Given the likelihood of autocorrelated or heteroskedastic errors in practice, it is natural to ask what effects these may have on some of the standard pre-testing results.

The only two contributions to date which respond to this question are those of Albertson (1991) and D. E. A. Giles et al. (1992b). Albertson considers the estimation of the regression coefficient vector after a pre-test of linear restrictions on the coefficients, and where the researcher fails to take account of the fact that the errors have an arbitrary non-scalar covariance matrix. Exact analytic results are derived for the OLS, RLS and PTE risks under quadratic loss, and these are evaluated for various data sets and for the cases of AR(1), MA(1), AR(4) and heteroskedastic errors.

The form of the regressor variables appears to have some bearing on the results, and several interesting points emerge. First, in the case of trended data and positive AR(1) errors, the usual PTE can be strictly dominated by OLS. Second, MA(1) errors have little or no effect on the relative dominance of the estimators. Third, in the case of non-trended data, or negative autocorrelation, pre-testing becomes more attractive relative to OLS estimation as the degree of model mis-specification increases. Accordingly, prior information about the error process is helpful in prescribing an overall strategy, though it should be noted that autocorrelation pre-test testing raises other considerations, as is discussed in section 6.4. Fourth, AR(4) and heteroskedastic errors affect the properties of the PTE in a less systematic way, though again it is possible for this strategy to be strictly dominated by OLS, something which cannot occur if the model is properly specified.

Other work in progress in this area considers the consequences of this type of mis-specification for optimal pre-test size and pre-test estimation of the regression scale parameter, and investigates the implications of simultaneously mis-specifying the error term properties and omitting relevant regressors.

D. E. A. Giles et al. (1992b) consider the robustness of the exact restrictions PTE for the prediction vector in the multiple regression model to the presence of autoregressive conditionally heteroskedastic (ARCH) or generalized ARCH (GARCH) errors. As such an error distribution is typically more leptokurtic than under normality, it is not surprising that the results are qualitatively somewhat similar to those reported by J. A. Giles (1991a) in the case of errors which follow multivariate Student-t and certain other compound normal distributions. In particular, D. E. A. Giles et al. find that when the conventional pre-test is applied (based on the assumption of normal errors), but the disturbances actually follow a sufficiently strong GARCH process, it is possible for the PTE to strictly dominate *both* the OLS and RLS estimators in terms of quadratic risk.

Again, the intention of both the latter study and that undertaken by Albertson is to base the analysis of pre-test strategies in a more realistic environment, thus making the results more useful to applied econometricians.

4   Pre-testing with inequality restrictions

Frequently, we may wish to test the validity of inequality restrictions on the coefficients of a regression model, as opposed to testing exact equality restrictions as we have discussed so far. For example, after the estimation of a consumption equation we may test whether the marginal propensity to consume is less than unity. Suppose, in the classical linear regression model $y = X\beta + e$, that we have prior information on the coefficient vector which we express as a *single* inequality constraint, $C'\beta \geqslant r$, where C' is a $1 \times k$ known vector and r is a known scalar. The estimator of β which ignores the prior constraint is simply the OLS estimator b, while the estimator which includes the non-sample information is the so-called inequality restricted estimator b^{**}. Rather like a PTE, b^{**} comprises two components: if b satisfies the inequality constraint then $b^{**} = b$, but if $C'b < r$ then $b^{**} = b^*$, the equality restricted estimator: $b^* = b - (X'X)^{-1}C[C'(X'X)^{-1}C]^{-1}(C'b - r)$.

The sampling properties of b^{**} are well known. Zellner (1961) shows that b^{**} is biased and that it has a truncated normal distribution (see also Judge and Takayama, 1966). This implies, for instance, that a standard t test based on b^{**} can be misleading (Lovell and Prescott, 1970). The superiority of b^{**} relative to b is considered by, for example, Lovell and Prescott (1970), Liew (1976), Judge et al. (1980), Judge and Yancey (1981, 1986), Thomson (1982) and Thomson and Schmidt (1982). They find that when the direction of the inequality constraint is correct it is preferable, in terms of quadratic risk, to use b^{**} rather than b. Further, if the direction of the constraint is in fact incorrect then it is still preferable to use b^{**} rather than b in the neighbourhood of H_0, but b has smaller risk than b^{**} for a sufficiently large hypothesis error. These features are evident in figure 4, which illustrates typical risk functions for this problem.

The sampling properties of the estimator of the model's parameters which results after a pre-test for the validity of H_0: $C'\beta \geqslant r$ versus H_A: $C'\beta < r$ have not received as much attention. Assuming that σ^2 is known, Judge et al. (1980) and Judge and Yancey (1981, 1986) derive the exact risk of the PTE defined by

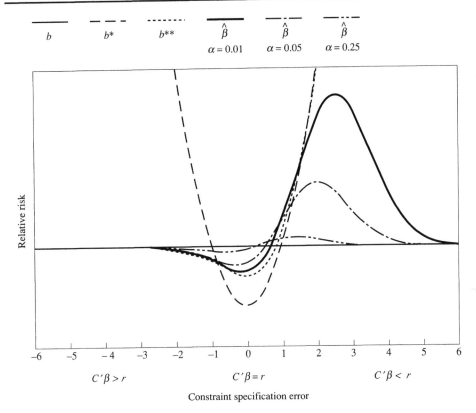

Figure 4 Relative risk functions for b, b^*, b^{**} and $\hat{\beta}$.

$$\hat{\beta} = \begin{cases} b & \text{if we reject H}_0 \\ b^{**} & \text{if we cannot reject H}_0; \end{cases} \quad b^{**} = \begin{cases} b & \text{if } C'b \geqslant r \\ b^* & \text{if } C'b < r. \end{cases}$$

So, $\hat{\beta}$ is the unrestricted OLS estimator of β, b, if we reject the validity of the constraint, while it is the inequality restricted estimator of β, b^{**}, if we cannot reject H$_0$. Figure 4 depicts a typical risk result (under quadratic loss) and shows, in particular, that it is never preferable to pre-test. In fact, pre-testing is sometimes the worst strategy. These results are qualitatively the same as those that we discussed in section 2.1 with reference to the pre-test for exact linear restrictions. Hasegawa (1989) considers the unknown σ^2 case and shows that qualitatively there is no change in the results. He also considers some Bayesian estimators and shows that these can be preferable to the classical estimators, in a risk sense.

Yancey et al. (1989) and Judge et al. (1990) extend this literature to the multi-parameter hypothesis case (see also Judge and Yancey, 1986). They consider the case of two inequality constraints and investigate a number of potential PTEs. Yancey et al. (1989) examine two multivariate inequality PTEs, the first after a pre-test of H$_0$: $R\beta = r$ versus H$_A$: $R\beta > r$ and the second after a pre-test of H$_0$: $R\beta \geqslant r$ versus H$'_A$: not H$'_0$. They show that neither of the inequality PTEs strictly dominates the other.

The pre-tests examined by Judge et al. (1990) are similar although, unlike Yancey et al. (1989), they consider the same test statistic for each of the hypothesis tests. Judge et al. (1990) find that no one PTE strictly dominates any other and over some parts of the hypothesis error space the equality restricted PTE has smaller risk than the inequality PTEs.

The current literature on inequality pre-testing has considered only the unrealistic situation of a properly specified model. The effects of model mis-specifications on the above results have only recently begun to receive attention. Wan (1992) extends the analyses of Judge et al. (1980), Judge and Yancey (1981, 1986), and Hasegawa (1989) to the case of a researcher who unwittingly omits relevant regressors from the design matrix.[21] Wan shows that the use of valid prior information in an underfitted model does not necessarily guarantee a reduction in risk. This is consistent with the results found for the exact linear restrictions pre-test which we discussed in section 3.1. He also shows that many of the results of Judge and Yancey carry over qualitatively to the mis-specified case. An exception is the dominance of b by $\hat{\beta}$ when the direction of the constraint is valid. This need not occur when we have omitted relevant regressors.

Given these results there is an obvious question of the choice of an optimal critical value for the pre-test of inequality constraints. Wan (1992) investigates this issue using the Toyoda and Wallace (1976) criterion of minimizing the average relative risk. His results suggest that for the case of testing *one* inequality restriction we should simply ignore the prior information and use b. This result is analogous to that obtained by Toyoda and Wallace (1976) for the pre-test of exact linear restrictions.

We can also define a corresponding inequality PTE of the scale parameter. Wan (1992) derives the exact risk of this estimator for both the correctly specified and the omitted-variables models. He finds that qualitatively many of the results noted in sections 2.1 and 3.1 for the estimation of σ^2 after a pre-test for exact linear restrictions carry over to the pre-test of inequality constraints on the coefficient vector. In particular, he shows that the choices of c which result in stationary points of the risk function of the PTE are identical to those reported by Giles (1990, 1991a, b).

Hasegawa (1991) considers the PTE of the coefficient vector when the pre-test relates to the validity of an interval constraint H_0: $r_1 \leqslant C'\beta \leqslant r_2$, where r_1 and r_2 are known scalars. He assumes that the testing procedure is undertaken in two steps. First, we test H_{01}: $C'\beta \geqslant r_1$ versus H_{A1}: $C'\beta < r_1$ using the usual standard normal test statistic (assuming σ^2 is known). If H_{01} is rejected we use the OLS estimator b as our estimator of β.

If, on the other hand, we cannot reject H_{01} we proceed to the second test, H_{02}: $C'\beta \leqslant r_2$ versus H_{A2}: $C'\beta > r_2$. If H_{02} is rejected then b is used as the estimator of β, while we use the so-called interval-constrained least squares estimator b^+ if we cannot reject H_{02}. The latter estimator is given by

$$b^+ = \begin{cases} r_1 & \text{if } b < r_1 \\ b & \text{if } r_1 \leqslant b \leqslant r_2 \\ r_2 & \text{if } b > r_2. \end{cases}$$

The properties of this estimator are examined by, for example, Escobar and Skarpness (1986, 1987) and Ohtani (1987d). So, the PTE is

$$\hat{\beta}^+ = \begin{cases} b & \text{if we reject } H_{01} \text{ or we accept } H_{01} \text{ and reject } H_{02} \\ b^+ & \text{if we accept } H_{01} \text{ and accept } H_{02}. \end{cases}$$

Hasegawa derives the risk, under quadratic loss, of $\hat{\beta}^+$ and he also solves for the critical value of the second-stage test, given that this test depends on the outcome of the first-stage test. He compares the risks of b^+ and $\hat{\beta}^+$, finding first that neither strictly dominates the other, and second that the preference for one estimator over the other depends on the relative width of the interval constraint. In particular, when the distance of the interval constraint increases, b^+ dominates $\hat{\beta}^+$ over a wider range.

5   Exact distributions of pre-test estimators

As will be apparent from the discussion so far, the main emphasis in the pre-test literature has been on the first two moments of PTEs. In particular, the literature emphasizes the use of risk under quadratic loss as a measure of estimator performance, and so it focuses on MSE and the associated tradeoff between estimator bias and precision. Accordingly, the emphasis is on the consequences of pre-testing for *point estimation* rather than *interval estimation*.

To deal with the latter important topic we need more information. For example, to determine the effects of pre-testing on the probability content of a confidence interval we need knowledge of the full sampling distribution of the PTE. Given the additional demands that this places on the analysis, it is not surprising that the econometrics literature was virtually silent on this point until quite recently.

To date, there appear to be only two exact results and one simulation experiment relating to the full sampling distribution of PTEs which are of direct interest to econometricians. Fittingly, the exact results relate to the two problems first studied by Bancroft (1944), as discussed in section 1.2. D. E. A. Giles (1992a) considers the sampling distribution of the estimator of a variance parameter after a preliminary test of variance homogeneity across two normal populations; and Giles and Srivastava (1993) derive the sampling distribution of the OLS estimator of a coefficient in a two-regressor model after a preliminary t test of the significance of the other regressor.

The first of these problems has an econometric interpretation in terms of the estimation of the error term's scale after a pre-test for homoskedasticity in a regression model which may be subject to structural change. So, it relates directly to the earlier discussion in section 2.2.1. D. E. A. Giles (1992a) considers two random samples, $\{x_{ij}\} \sum_{i=1}^{N_j} \sim N(\mu_j, \sigma_j^2), j = 1, 2$. The usual unbiased estimator of σ_j^2 is

$$s_j^2 = \frac{1}{n_j} \sum_{i=1}^{N_j} (x_{ij} - \bar{x}_j)^2$$

where

$$\bar{x}_j = \frac{1}{N_j} \sum_{i=1}^{N_j} x_{ij}$$

and $n_j = N_j - 1; j = 1, 2$.

The hypothesis under test is H_0: $\sigma_1^2 = \sigma_2^2$ versus H_A: $\sigma_1^2 > \sigma_2^2$. As is well known, the statistic s_1^2/s_2^2 is F distributed with n_1 and n_2 degrees of freedom if H_0 is true. If H_0 is accepted there is an incentive to pool the samples and estimate σ_1^2 by $s^2 = (n_1 s_1^2 + n_2 s_2^2)/(n_1 + n_2)$, which leads to the following PTE of σ_1^2:

$$\hat{\sigma}_1^2 = \begin{cases} s_1^2 ; & \text{if } s_1^2/s_2^2 > F_c \\ s^2; & \text{if } s_1^2/s_2^2 \leqslant F_c \end{cases}$$

where $F_c = F_c(\alpha)$ is the critical F value for a significance level α.

The sampling properties of $\hat{\sigma}_1^2$ differ from those of the 'never-pool' estimator s_1^2 and the 'always-pool' estimator s^2. In particular, $\hat{\sigma}_1^2$ is *biased* in finite samples. Clearly, misleading inferences may be drawn if one constructs confidence intervals centred on $\hat{\sigma}_1^2$ but with limits chosen as if no pre-testing had occured. To analyse this situation fully, D. E. A. Giles (1992a) derives the full cdf of $\hat{\sigma}_1^2$, which is shown to be a rather complicated function of the various parameters of the problem, *but it does not depend on the sample values* and is easily evaluated numerically. Given such evaluations, the pdf for the pre-test estimator is readily obtained by numerical differentiation, and is found to be uni-modal.

Extending earlier related work by Bennett (1956), D. E. A. Giles (1992a) uses these results to examine the extent to which confidence intervals for σ_1^2 are distorted when they are based on $\hat{\sigma}_1^2$ but with the confidence limits (wrongly) determined from the $\chi_{n_1}^2$ distribution of s_1^2 or the $\chi_{n_1+n_2}^2$ distribution of s^2. It transpires that as long as H_0 is not too false, confidence intervals based on pre-testing have higher probability content than those based on s_1^2, while they have lower probability content than those based on s^2. The converse applies for large departures from the null hypothesis. Substantial departures from the assumed confidence level can arise in practice, so extreme care must be taken in applied work.

As with point estimation, the choice of critical value, F_c, can crucially affect the results. Interestingly, when the optimal values suggested by Toyoda and Wallace (1975) and Bancroft and Han (1983) are chosen, there are regions of the parameter space for which the pre-test confidence interval for σ_1^2 has higher probability content than do *either* of the intervals based on s_1^2 or s^2.

Broadly speaking, similar conclusions emerge with the problem analysed by Giles and Srivastava (1992). They consider the estimation of β_1 in the model

$$y_t = \beta_1 x_{1t} + \beta_2 x_{2t} + u_t \qquad t = 1, \ldots, T$$

where the u_t are independent and identically distributed $N(0, \sigma^2)$, after a pre-test of H_0: $\beta_2 = 0$ versus H_A: $\beta_2 \neq 0$. Their result extends earlier related work for normal means by Bennett (1952). The cdf of the PTE $\hat{\beta}_1$ is readily evaluated, and its (uni-modal) pdf is again obtained numerically. Using these results to assist in the evaluation of confidence limits, results corresponding to those of D. E. A. Giles (1992a) above emerge. It is clear that while pre-testing may affect the true confidence level of an interval estimate either adversely or favourably, only by applying the unrestricted estimator without any prior testing can we be sure that the true and nominal levels coincide.

Monte Carlo simulation results reported by Basmann and Hwang (1988) focus on the effect of certain pre-tests on the location and shape of the sampling distributions of estimators of a simultaneous structural model. More specifically, the pre-testing situation that is considered relates to the application of a likelihood ratio test of the over-identifying restrictions on the parameters prior to estimation of the latter by two-stage least squares (2SLS) or three-stage least squares (3SLS).

The Monte Carlo experiment is based on Klein's Model I of the US economy. Using the Kolmogorov–Smirnov goodness-of-fit test, the authors conclude that the sampling distributions of the PTEs under consideration are not particularly sensitive to the size of the pre-test itself. The same goodness-of-fit test and the first four moments of the estimators are used to compare the conditional and marginal distributions of the 2SLS and 3SLS estimators.

On the basis of such a limited study it is difficult to offer strong practical recommendations, but one conclusion that emerges is that the pre-test 2SLS estimator is generally superior to the pre-test 3SLS estimator in terms of bias and MSE, but the latter exhibits less skewness than the former. Also, as it seems that the identifiability test statistic is *not* distributed independently of the restricted structural coefficient estimators, the usual diagnostic statistics such as t ratios and R^2 may be extremely misleading, and one should be aware of this in applied work.

6 Pre-test testing

6.1 Introduction

The econometrics pre-testing literature has emphasized pre-test *estimation* much more than pre-test *testing*, resulting in something of an imbalance. However, work in progress may soon alter this situation. To some degree, this imbalance has arisen because the properties of many of the PTEs that we have considered can be established analytically and without resorting to asymptotic approximations, while the properties of their pre-test test counterparts are generally somewhat less tractable. So, there has been a tendency to focus attention on those problems for which exact results are more readily forthcoming.

The two pre-test testing examples cited in section 1.1 exposed the importance of the independence of successive tests if a controllable pre-test situation is to be attained. For instance, the researcher's ability to control the overall test size in the context of 'nested' hypotheses relies on the independence of such tests, if appropriately formulated, and can be established by appealing to Basu's (1955) independence theorem. Moreover, Anderson (1971, pp. 34–43, 116–34, 270–6) shows, for the case of normal linear models, that such a nested testing procedure is UMP in the class of procedures which fix the probabilities of accepting a less restrictive hypothesis than the true one. Seber (1964) provides some asymptotic justification when nested testing is conducted in the context of nonlinear models. Here, there is no substantive pre-test testing 'problem'. Parenthetically it is worth noting that this result provides strong justification for testing from the 'general' to the 'specific' when deciding on a regression specification, and underscores Leamer's (1988) point that most 'stepwise regression' routines are probably better described as 'step UNWISE'.

The second pre-test testing example given in section 1.1 also involves an independence issue, but one of a different sort. Extensions of that independence result to a range of other interesting testing situations involving statistics based on quadratic forms in normal random vectors are considered by Phillips and McCabe (1989). However, even with this independence there remains a pre-testing issue. The Chow test would be used only if the null for the pre-test could not be rejected. Otherwise an alternative test, such as a Wald test, for structural stability would be used. So, even with the advantage of statistical independence there remains a pre-test effect of substance in this case – the true size of the two-part test for structural change will differ from the nominal sizes assigned to the Chow test and its alternative, because of the prior test for variance homogeneity.

Furthermore, pre-test testing generally involves an element of non-independence between the 'component' test statistics. In such cases, there are immediate effects on the true (as opposed to nominal) sizes of the second and subsequent tests, as well as on their powers. These issues have been considered primarily in the context of three testing situations in the econometrics literature, each of which is considered in turn below. The properties of certain estimators after more than one preliminary test are discussed briefly in section 7.2 under the title of 'Multistage pre-testing'. If several tests are undertaken simultaneously, rather than sequentially, then one can consider the global or multiple significance level for the collection of tests. A good discussion of this situation is given by Krämer and Sonnberger (1986, pp. 147–54), and we do not pursue it further here.

6.2   Testing the coefficient vector after a pre-test of the error variance

Several studies have used exact analytic methods to consider the properties of the test for linear restrictions on the regression model's coefficient vector, after a pre-test of some hypothesis relating in one way or another to the variance of the error term. In this class of problems, the form of the test for linear restrictions depends on the outcome of the pre-test. For instance, Ohtani and Toyoda (1985) consider a pre-test of the form $H_0: \sigma^2 = \sigma_0^2$ versus $H_A: \sigma^2 \neq \sigma_0^2$, where σ^2 is the regression error variance and σ_0^2 is a fixed value, supposedly known on the basis of previous experience or analysis. In this case, the test of primary interest (that of linear restrictions on the coefficient vector) is based on the usual F statistic if the pre-test null is rejected, and otherwise on a χ^2 statistic. Ohtani (1987b) extends this analysis to the case where σ_0^2 is unknown and is estimated from an 'auxiliary' regression; and Ohtani (1987c) considers a closely related problem, one where the model includes a 'proxy' regressor and the main test of linear restrictions is simply one of the significance of the unobservable regressor which is being proxied. In each of these studies, similar results emerge. The true size of the second-stage test can differ substantially from the nominal size of the main test, especially for small degrees of freedom, but this can be corrected by assigning a 25–30 per cent significance level to the pre-test. Further, the two-stage test can often be more powerful than the single main test, once size correction has been taken into account. Both of these results have obvious implications for applied researchers.

Toyoda and Ohtani (1986) and Ohtani and Toyoda (1988) generalize earlier work by Gurland and McCullough (1962) by considering a more familiar testing problem of the type discussed in the second example cited in section 6.1. Specifically, the pre-test is for variance homogeneity (against either a one-sided or a two-sided alternative) in a two-sample linear regression situation, followed by a Chow test or an alternative test for the structural stability of the coefficient vector across the two samples, depending on whether the first null is accepted or rejected. The first of these two studies employs a modified (approximate) F test as the alternative to the Chow test, while the second study uses the Wald test. Consistent with the results noted above, it is found that a pre-test size of up to 80 per cent may be advisable in order to avoid size distortion in the test for structural change. Then, the two-stage test is generally more powerful than the single-stage test suggested by Jayatissa (1977) and the Wald test, though typically less powerful than the size-corrected variant of the latter suggested by Rothenberg (1984). Again, there are some clear implications here for applied econometricians.

6.3   Testing the error variance after a pre-test on the coefficient vector

A pre-test testing strategy which is essentially the reverse of the ones just discussed is considered by Ohtani (1988b). Specifically, his pre-test relates to exact linear restrictions on the regression coefficient vector, while the main test of interest is of H_0: $\sigma^2 = \sigma_0^2$ against H_A: $\sigma^2 \neq \sigma_0^2$, where σ_0^2 is known.

As before, the size of the two-stage test can be controlled to that of the main test if the nominal pre-test size is much larger than would commonly be chosen. Specifically, a size of the order of 30 per cent is recommended. Again, with such a choice, pre-test testing can be more powerful than applying the main test by itself.

6.4   Autocorrelation pre-test testing

In the next section we consider the properties of various estimators involving a preliminary test for the serial independence of the regression errors. However, autocorrelation pre-testing also gives rise to some important pre-test testing situations. Primarily, attention has focused here on the following problem: what are the properties of the usual *t*-test for the significance of a regression coefficient after a prior Durbin–Watson (or similar) test for autocorrelation? In this case, the form of the *t* test varies according to the outcome of the pre-test – if the null of independent errors is accepted then the *t* test is based on OLS estimates; but if the errors are found to be autocorrelated then the second test is based on Cochrane–Orcutt or full maximum likelihood estimates, for example. Attention has centred on tests of single linear restrictions at the second stage, and the nature of the problem has necessitated Monte Carlo simulation rather than exact analytical treatment.

Nakamura and Nakamura (1978) and King and Giles (1984) have studied this problem. The former study is the more limited, being based on a model with a single trended regressor and considering only the Durbin–Watson and Geary autocorrelation tests. A much wider range of tests and design matrices are examined by King and Giles, and (following the findings of Fomby and Guilkey, 1978) both 5 per cent and 50 per cent sizes are considered for the pre-tests. Nakamura and Nakamura find that the size of the pre-test *t* test exceeds its nominal size, increasingly so as the degree of positive first-order autocorrelation in the errors increases. They also suggest that simply adjusting for autocorrelation and then testing is preferable to either pre-test testing or *t* testing on the basis of OLS estimation in this context. This preference is based on the degree of size distortion.

King and Giles find that their results are somewhat sensitive to the regressor data, and that trended regressors can produce extreme results, so this raises some questions as to the strength of the results just cited. Generally, they find that the size of the pre-test *t* test is distorted less than those of the two component *t* tests, especially if a 50 per cent pre-test size is used. Further, once size distortion is taken into account, the powers of the pre-test *t* test and the *t* test conducted after an automatic allowance for

AR(1) errors are found to be similar, and greater than that of the simple OLS-based *t* test. *These results are quite supportive of autocorrelation pre-testing, especially if a larger than usual pre-test size is adopted*, and they are broadly consistent with the principal results discussed in the last two subsections. The converse autocorrelation pre-testing problem is discussed by Giles and Lieberman (1992). That is, they consider the size and power of the (exact) Durbin–Watson test after a preliminary *t* test. Their results are based on a mixture of analytical and Monte Carlo results. When there is no pre-testing the exact power properties of the Durbin–Watson test are easily computed for any regressor data, but a simulation experiment is needed to analyse the pre-test strategy.

Working with a range of data sets, different sample sizes and pre-test sizes of 5 and 50 per cent, Giles and Lieberman find that pre-testing distorts the true size of the Durbin–Watson test above its nominal value unless the restriction under test is true. This distortion can be reduced in percentage terms by choosing a large nominal size (say, 50 per cent) for the Durbin–Watson test. The results with respect to power are less clear, but there are situations in which pre-testing can result in increased power of the Durbin–Watson test. These results suggest that autocorrelation pre-testing, defined in either of the above ways, is not necessarily a 'bad' thing. Moreover, they lend considerable support to the case made by Fomby and Guilkey (1978) for assigning much larger sizes than usual to tests for autocorrelation, and this should be borne in mind by applied econometricians.

7   Other developments

There are several other important pre-test problems which have attracted attention in the more recent econometrics literature. Some of these are discussed briefly next.

7.1   Autocorrelation pre-testing estimation

The second motivating example given in section 1.1 serves as an introduction to an interesting pre-test situation that arises frequently in applied econometrics. That example relates to the use of the Durbin–Watson test for serial independence of the regression errors, as a basis for choosing between least squares estimation and Cochrane–Orcutt estimation of the regression coefficients. Pre-test strategies of this general type have been analysed to some degree.

Judge and Bock (1978, pp. 143–64) consider the empirical risks of such autocorrelation PTEs based on both the Durbin–Watson and Berenblutt and Webb tests, with various component estimators. Specifically, the Durbin, Cochrane–Orcutt and Prais–Winsten estimators are considered when a positive AR(1) error process is detected by one of the tests. A limited Monte Carlo experiment, based on a model with four orthonormal regressors, forms the basis of their analysis, and estimator performance is measured in terms of risk under squared error loss. Only positive autocorrelation is considered. The risks of the component estimators and of the various PTEs increase with the degree of autocorrelation.

This study suggests, among other things, that it is the choice of estimators rather than the choice of test which determines the risk consequences of autocorrelation pre-testing.

Strategies which incorporate the Durbin estimator when serial correlation is detected are especially favoured. It also indicates that autocorrelation pre-testing does not incur particularly large risk losses (relative to no pre-testing), even when there is slight serial correlation, and for moderate to large degrees of serial correlation there can be substantial gains from pre-testing.

These conclusions are corroborated in recent work by Chen and Saleh (1991). Their experimental design is virtually identical to that of Judge and Bock, but they emphasize the performance of autocorrelation pre-test strategies based on shrinkage estimators of the type proposed by Sen and Saleh (1985) and Saleh and Sen (1985). In particular, they find that autocorrelation PTEs of this type uniformly dominate their conventional autocorrelation pre-test counterparts. This illustrates the (known) inadmissibility of standard autocorrelation pre-test strategies, in the same way that Judge and Bock (1978, pp. 189–95) illustrate the inadmissibility of the conventional linear restrictions PTE for the regression coefficients. (Of course, the autocorrelation PTEs suggested by Chen and Saleh are themselves inadmissible, being discontinuous functions of the random data.)

King and Giles (1984) extend the results of Judge and Bock in several directions by considering additional tests for serial independence as well as the full maximum likelihood estimator to allow for AR(1) errors. They also consider the effects of autocorrelation pre-testing on the power of the test for regressor significance, as was discussed in section 6 above, and on predictive performance. Their Monte Carlo experiment is more comprehensive than those discussed above, with an allowance for different (non-orthogonal) design matrices with three to six regressors, different sample sizes, and both the 5 per cent and 50 per cent pre-test significance levels. The latter size reflects results obtained by Fomby and Guilkey (1978) and extended recently by Kennedy and Simons (1991). Fomby and Guilkey showed that, in terms of maximizing the (MSE) efficiency of the PTE relative to that of OLS, after a preliminary Durbin–Watson test, the size of the latter test should be of the order of 50 per cent rather than the conventional 1 or 5 per cent.

One of the most important findings from the study by King and Giles is that the form of the regressor matrix is crucial in determining the risks of autocorrelation PTEs. This implies that other related results based on more limited studies should be interpreted cautiously. This study also finds that PTEs which incorporate the full maximum likelihood estimator to allow for autocorrelation are preferable to those which involve the Durbin estimator, except for problems involving relatively small degrees of freedom. At conventional significance levels, and especially with small sample sizes, the results also suggest a slight preference for the Berenblutt and Webb test or King's point optimal test as the pre-test. The choice of pre-test is generally less consequential if a 50 per cent significance level is used.

Griffiths and Beesley (1984) extend the earlier Judge–Bock analysis in a different direction. In a Monte Carlo experiment limited to a single regressor model, but considering both trended and stationary data, they analyse the autocorrelation PTE based on the (two-sided) Durbin–Watson test and either OLS or maximum likelihood estimation. They also consider what is effectively a multistep PTE (further examples of which appear in the next section). In particular, they analyse the consequences of using the Durbin–Watson test to discriminate between serial independence and autocorrelation of the errors, and Akaike's information criterion to select between AR(1) and MA(1) disturbances in the latter case. In terms of reasonably uniform point estimation relative efficiency over the entire parameter space, the multistep PTE is found to be quite successful. However, in the case of interval estimation, the OLS AR(1) PTE of the form considered by the other authors is found to be preferable to multistage pre-testing, at least in terms of the tests considered by Griffiths and Beesley. As with the results of King and Giles, the type of regressor data is found to be an important determinant of the estimators' relative performances.

Folmer (1988) provides a more complete summary of the studies discussed above, and provides Monte Carlo and bootstrap approximations to the full distribution of the autocorrelation PTE based on the Durbin–Watson test and the OLS and Durbin estimators. His results accord with those noted already, and he concludes that (wrongly) applying standard results when autocorrelation pre-testing has taken place can be very misleading. This is especially so in the case of confidence intervals, a result which accords with the conclusions reached in section 5 above.

Autocorrelation pre-testing in the context of models which include a lagged dependent variable as a regressor is considered by Giles and Beattie (1987). Again, given the nature of the problem, this study is based on Monte Carlo analysis. The risks of nine PTEs are evaluated and are found to exhibit similar shapes to those encountered in the fixed-regressor studies discussed already. Consistent with those other results, this study also finds that autocorrelation pre-testing can lead to significant reductions in risk over large parts of the parameter space, and that the choice of component estimators is generally more important than the choice of preliminary test. PTEs which incorporate Wallis's (1967) three-step procedure and Durbin's (1970) '*m* test' are found to be advantageous from a risk viewpoint.

In summary, autocorrelation pre-testing is generally preferable to simply applying OLS. In terms of both point estimation and interval estimation, pre-testing is also preferable to simply estimating under the assumption of AR(1) errors when the degree of autocorrelation is small, and for high degrees of autocorrelation pre-testing is no worse than this alternative approach. Finally, significance levels much higher than those conventionally assigned in econometric work deserve serious consideration in this context.

7.2 Multistage pre-testing

Though the majority of the pre-test literature concentrates on the properties of PTEs after a single pre-test, the analysis of multistage PTEs has recently received attention. This is, of course, closer to the procedure actually undertaken by applied researchers, who would typically undertake a series of pre-tests prior to deciding the 'final' version of the model. For instance, a researcher may test for autocorrelation, and on the basis of this test decide whether to use OLS or some feasible GLS estimator. After this decision, he may then undertake a test for heteroskedasticity, with the test used being dependent on the outcome of the prior pre-test for autocorrelation. The outcome of the second pre-test – the heteroskedasticity test – will determine whether he keeps the 'current' version of the model or whether some modification is undertaken and so on.

Clearly, given that each step in this sequential testing procedure is dependent on the outcome of the previous pre-test, and that, typically, the tests are not independent of each other, it is difficult to derive the properties of multistage PTEs analytically. To date, as far as we are aware, only four studies have attempted to consider some finite sample properties of various multistage PTEs – Shukla (1979), Adjibolosoo (1990b), Özcam and Judge (1991) and Ohtani (1991a).

Shukla (1979) considers the estimation of the slope coefficients in the two-sample simple linear regression model

$$y_{ij} = \gamma_j + \beta_j x_{ij} + e_{ij} \qquad j = 1, 2; \; i = 1, 2, \dots, T_j$$

where $e_{ij} \sim N(0, \sigma^2)$, after two preliminary tests of significance. The first pre-test is of H_{01}: $\sigma^2 = \sigma_0^2$, where σ_0^2 is a known constant, and this test is undertaken using a χ^2 statistic. The second pre-test is of H_{02}: $\beta_2 = \beta_1$, for which a z test is used if we do not reject H_{01}, while if we reject H_{01} a t test is undertaken. Shukla derives the bias and MSE of the PTE of β_1. Unfortunately, though he notes that the expressions are too complicated for comparisons to be made, he does not undertake any numerical evaluations of them.

Özcam and Judge (1991) extend Shukla's investigation to the multiple regression case and possibly heteroskedastic error variances. The first pre-test is of H_{01}: $\sigma_1^2 = \sigma_2^2$ (versus H_{A1}: $\sigma_1^2 > \sigma_2^2$) followed by a second pre-test of H_{02}: $\beta_1 = \beta_2$ (versus H_{A2}: $\beta_1 \neq \beta_2$) in

$$y = \begin{bmatrix} y_1 \\ y_2 \end{bmatrix} = \begin{bmatrix} X_1 & 0 \\ 0 & X_2 \end{bmatrix} \begin{bmatrix} \beta_1 \\ \beta_2 \end{bmatrix} + \begin{bmatrix} e_1 \\ e_2 \end{bmatrix}$$

where $e_i \sim N(0, \sigma_i^2 I_{T_i})$ and the usual assumptions on X_i are satisfied; $i = 1, 2$.

The two-stage pre-test estimator (2SPE) of β_1, assuming orthonormal regressors, comprises the least squares estimator $(\text{LSE} = (X_1' y_1 + X_2' y_2)/2)$, the two-step Aitken estimator $(2\text{SAE} = \theta X_1' y_1 + (1 - \theta) X_2' y_2$, where $\theta = s_2^2/(s_1^2 + s_2^2)$ and s_i^2 is the usual unbiased estimator of σ_i^2) and the Gauss–Markov estimator $(\text{GME} = X_1' y_1)$. H_{01} is tested using the Goldfeld–Quandt test, while H_{02} is tested using the Chow test if we accept that the error variances are homoskedastic but using the Wald test if we reject homoskedasticity. Özcam and Judge derive the risk, under quadratic loss, of the 2SPE and using numerical evaluations of these exact expressions they compare the estimators assuming that each test is undertaken at the (nominal) 5 per cent level. For a given value of σ_1^2/σ_2^2 they find that the 2SPE is preferable to the GME, regardless of whether β_1 and β_2 are equal. Further, their results suggest that the risk advantages of the 2SAE and the LSE over the 2SPE under H_{01} disappears as the difference between β_1 and β_2 disappears.

Adjibolosoo (1990b) also considers a two-step estimator of the coefficients in the two-sample heteroskedastic linear regression model. Following the lines of Adjibolosoo (1989, 1990a) he considers the possibility that one may still prefer to use the LSE, even if H_{01} is rejected, if the degree of heteroskedasticity is not severe, and suggests that a second step should be incorporated if we reject H_{01} to compare the relative efficiency (strong MSE) of the LSE and the 2SAE. If the LSE is relatively more efficient we use this estimator even though we have rejected homoskedasticity. Using a Monte Carlo experiment, he shows that the risk of the two-step PTE is typically better than that of the traditional PTE discussed in section 2.2.2.

Ohtani (1991a) investigates the sampling properties of a PTE for the variance of the classical linear regression model, $\overset{+}{\sigma}{}^2$, after a pre-test for homogeneity H_{02}: $\sigma^2 = \sigma_0^2$, where σ_0^2 is known (versus H_{A1}: $\sigma^2 > \sigma_0^2$), when the estimator we use if we reject the null hypothesis is Stein's (1964) estimator σ_S^2. We mentioned Ohtani's study in section 2.3 and we recall that σ_S^2 is itself a PTE with its components being the restricted (σ_M^{*2}) and unrestricted ($\tilde{\sigma}_M^2$) minimum MSE estimators of the error variance when the test critical value is $v/(v+2)$. The pre-test is for exact linear restrictions, H_{01}: $R\beta = r$ versus H_{A1}: $R\beta \neq r$. So, we first test H_{01} using a critical value of $v/(v+2)$; if we reject this hypothesis we use $\tilde{\sigma}_M^2$, while we use σ_M^{*2} if we accept H_{01}. Thus, the estimator actually used is σ_S^2. We then test H_{02}; if we accept H_{02} we use σ_0^2, while we continue to use σ_S^2 if we reject H_{02}. Ohtani derives the MSE of this two-stage PTE and compares it with that of σ_S^2 using numerical evaluations. He shows that if the size of the test for H_{02} is chosen appropriately (say, 25 per cent) then the two-stage PTE strictly dominates the Stein estimator, assuming that the direction of H_{A2} is valid, and that it is only around the neighbourhood of H_{02} being true that other choices of test size may be more appropriate.

Given these studies, it is apparent that further research is required into the properties of multistage PTEs. Nevertheless, the papers discussed in this section suggest that multistep pre-testing may be a preferable option to naively imposing or ignoring prior information.

7.3   Alternative loss functions

All of the above discussion reflects the emphasis in the econometrics pre-testing literature on the use of a quadratic loss function. The appeal of this type of loss, of course, is that it leads to risk measures which are in the form of the matrix MSE (or its trace) and so incorporate the familiar bias–variance tradeoff when assessing estimator performance. However, an interesting question that naturally arises is to what extent the various results in the pre-testing literature are robust to departures from the quadratic loss assumption.

There is only scant evidence in answer to this question, though this is an important topic currently under research. One feature of a quadratic loss function is that it is symmetric – underestimation and overestimation are equally penalized. Accordingly, it would be interesting to know whether the standard pre-testing results are sensitive to choices of loss functions which are non-quadratic but still symmetric, as opposed to ones which are asymmetric. With respect to the former, there is apparently no published evidence. Work by Giles (1992b) reconsiders the first of Bancroft's (1944) problems in terms of risk based on an absolute error loss function. The results suggest that, except in one respect, the known results under quadratic loss apply qualitatively under absolute error loss. In particular, when estimating a single regression coefficient after a preliminary t test of the significance of the second regressor, the risk of the unrestricted estimator is still independent of the test statistic's non-centrality parameter; the pre-test estimator's risk has the same shape properties as in figure 1; but the risk of the restricted estimator is mildly concave to the origin. The same types of regions of estimator dominance hold as for the quadratic loss function. So, pre-testing can be the worst strategy, it is never best, and the same question of the optimal choice of pre-test size arises.

Any symmetric loss function is unduly restrictive in certain estimation situations. For example, underprediction and overprediction of the future exchange rate are unlikely to be equally costly mistakes. Underestimating the error variance in a regression model will lead to calculated *t* statistics which make the regressors appear to be more 'significant' than is warranted. A conservative researcher may prefer to err in the opposite direction.

Work in progress by D. E. A. Giles et al. (1992a) considers the former problem, using the asymmetric LINEX loss function proposed by Varian (1975) and subsequently adopted by Zellner (1986) and Srivastava and Rao (1992). Using this same loss function, of which quadratic loss is a special case, Giles and Giles (1993, 1994) consider the second problem suggested above. They consider the estimation of the scale parameter in a multiple regression model with normal errors after a preliminary test of exact linear restrictions on the coefficient vector, or after a pre-test of variance homogeneity. They find that the risk functions for the pre-test, unrestricted and restricted estimators are robust to mild departures from quadratic loss (at least qualitatively). However, as the degree of asymmetry in the loss function increases, rather different results can emerge. On the basis of this limited information, it seems that the PTE properties may be reasonably robust to departures from quadratic loss which are still symmetric, or only mildly asymmetric. Strong asymmetry in the loss function, however, may lead to results at variance with those in the established literature, and this remains a topic for further investigation.

7.4 Other pre-test problems

As we have seen already, many of the tests that are used in econometrics can be reduced to ones of the validity of exact restrictions on the regression coefficients, or to tests that can be linked to homoskedasticity of the regression errors. Accordingly, the detailed attention that we have paid to the related PTEs effectively covers a range of specific situations, such as testing the 'significance' of an individual regressor, or testing for structural change. Also, there are other closely related pre-test situations that are of interest to economists.

One recent such example is the problem of estimating the regression coefficient vector after a linear restrictions pre-test, but in a situation where there are two sets of linear constraints, one of which contains only valid information but the second of which may contain some invalid information. This problem is studied by Hessenius and Trenkler (undated), who derive necessary and sufficient conditions for the dominance of the PTE in terms of the matrix MSE.[22]

Another example, considered by Griffiths and Judge (1989), involves estimating regression coefficients after the application of Weerahandi's (1987) test of coefficient stability. This test allows for the possibility that the errors may be heteroskedastic across the two subsamples. The component estimators in this case are OLS and the restricted 2SAE. Using Monte Carlo analysis, Griffiths and Judge compare this PTE with the corresponding one based on an asymptotic *F* test[23] and find that although the former PTE is slightly risk-superior to the latter for small degrees of hypothesis error, generally there is no clear advantage in using Weerahandi's 'exact' test, rather than the asymptotic *F* test, in this pre-test environment.

There are other interesting pre-test problems of various sorts which deserve brief mention here. For example, Morey (1984) derives the asymptotic risks of specification PTEs based on Wu–Hausman tests in the context of a linear model which may be mis-specified in the sense that certain of the errors may be correlated with the distur-bances. The two component parts of this PTE for the coefficients are OLS (if the test suggests independence between the errors and the regressors) and instrumental vari-ables (IV) estimation (if the errors and regressors are thought to be correlated). The most interesting feature of Morey's results is that this PTE is strictly dominated by the IV estimator itself. However, to be conservative, and given that the degree of mis-specification will be unknown in practice, Morey recommends against simply using the IV estimator without a pre-test, and instead suggests testing with a much higher significance level than would usually be adopted. In this respect his results accord with those discussed already in the context of autocorrelation pre-testing.

More recently, Özcam et al. (1991) consider an important PTE in the context of the seemingly unrelated regressions (SUR) model. The setting for their analysis is a two-equation SUR model with orthonormal regressors, and the PTE is based on OLS and GLS, depending on whether there is evidence of cross-equation (population) cor-relation between the disturbances. The latter is tested using the corresponding sample correlation coefficient based on the 'restricted' OLS residuals. Although the (squared error) risks of the PTE and its components 'cross' in the usual sense, there are regions of the parameter space over which the PTE's risk is the smallest of the three. As we have seen already, contrary to popular mythology (which is based on the standard 'exact re-strictions' PTE problem) *there are situations in which pre-testing can be advantageous from an MSE viewpoint.*

The pre-test literature has not kept pace fully with certain significant developments in econometrics which are of vital importance to applications in both macroeconomics and financial economics. The modelling of high frequency financial time series now invariably considers the possibility of leptokurtic errors, specifically by specifying some sort of ARCH process for the disturbances. Very little is known about the properties of pre-test strategies in the context of ARCH or GARCH regression errors. The nature of the problem does not allow an analytical treatment, and finite-sample results must be obtained by Monte Carlo simulation.

Engle et al. (1985) consider the following pre-test problem. The model is estimated by OLS and a one-sided version of the Lagrange multiplier test for ARCH(1) errors is applied in its nR^2 form. Depending on the outcome of the test, either the OLS results are retained or the coefficients are re-estimated by maximum likelihood estimation. This PTE is found to be unbiased. Moreover, in terms of finite-sample efficiency, it is found to be little worse than OLS when the errors are free of an ARCH process, much better than OLS when there is an ARCH effect present and almost as good as the maximum likelihood estimator in the latter case. J. A. Giles et al. (1992) consider a related pre-test testing problem. They use Monte Carlo analysis to determine the effects that various pre-tests for ARCH(p) or GARCH(p, q) errors have on the size of a subsequent 't-test' for the significance of a regressor. Their results show that such pre-testing is quite innocuous in samples of a hundred or more observations, but in small samples it may be preferable to use a smaller than usual size for the pre-test.

Empirical macroeconomics has been revolutionized in recent years with the recogni-tion that the use of cointegrated time series has special implications for model formula-tion, estimation and testing. Several tests for the order of integration of time series, and for their possible cointegration, are now routinely used. Pre-test strategies also abound in this context in practice, though their implications are only just beginning to be explored. Again, the asymptotic nature of the tests concerned necessitates the use of Monte Carlo simulation to analyse the finite-sample properties of cointegration PTEs and tests. This remains a fruitful and important area for research, and work under way by the authors[24] considers such issues as the effects that multistage sequential pre-testing for order of integration and the presence of cointegration may have on test sizes and the finite-sample properties of estimators of the parameters of VAR/error correction models after cointegration pre-testing.

8 Conclusions

In this paper we have attempted to provide an overview of preliminary-test problems as they arise in econometrics, and to indicate some of the recent developments in this field. Inevitably, there will be omissions, but hopefully we will have captured the principal thrust of the associated literature while exposing both the historical and recent connections between the different strands of research into pre-testing problems.

A number of specific practical implications that arise from the econometric pre-testing literature have been presented in the paper. However, by way of conclusion it may be appropriate to offer some general comments. First, pre-test estimation and pre-test testing are perhaps the norm rather than the exception in applied econometric analysis, so the issues and results that we have discussed are of direct relevance to economists who engage in empirical work.

Second, once pre-testing takes place the standard 'textbook results' relating to the properties of various estimators and tests generally no longer apply. For instance, estimators which are unbiased under a specified set of assumptions or conditions may be biased if used after one or more preliminary tests relating to the specification of the model. The applied researcher should be aware of this as it may affect the overall strategy that is adopted when specifying, testing and estimating an economic relationship.

Third, and contrary to a commonly encountered viewpoint, this is not to say that pre-testing is necessarily a 'bad' thing. On the contrary, we have given examples of situations in which pre-testing may lead to estimators which have uniformly smaller MSE than can be achieved by applying the estimator without a suitable prior test. The essential point is that the sampling properties (such as bias, efficiency, size and power) of the estimators and tests that economists use in their empirical research are typically altered if pre-testing occurs prior to their application.

Fourth, as with any estimators or tests, the established results are based on various assumptions, including the presumption that the model is 'correctly specified'. If any of these assumptions are violated then typically the established results are affected. One of the recent developments in the pre-testing literature has been an examination of the robustness of established results to the type of assumption violations (such as the omission of regressors, or non-normal errors) that are likely to occur in practice. This makes the literature more directly relevant to practitioners.

Fifth, there are more established results relating to pre-test *estimation* situations than to pre-test *testing* situations. This is an important imbalance, and is one that is being addressed to some degree in current work in the field. Given the nature of the statistical issues involved, it seems likely that these developments will rely more on simulation analysis than on exact distribution theory. In any event, there is an urgent need for more information about the implications of pre-test testing, especially in the context of ARCH–GARCH tests and tests for integration and cointegration with economic time series data.

Sixth, most of the available information concerning the implications of pre-testing in econometrics relates to the application of a single preliminary test. In reality, economists engage in multistage pre-testing in a regression environment. While we have discussed a few results relating to this situation, the available information is very limited. Certainly, multistage pre-testing alters the standard pre-test results, though again it is *not* necessarily the case that things get 'worse' (in some sense) as the degree of pre-testing is increased. However, one general point that does emerge in this context (and in many simple pre-test testing situations) is that it is often advisable to conduct our standard diagnostic tests with nominal significance levels that are far different from those we typically adopt.

Much remains to be done before the full implications of pre-test strategies of the type that economists actually use in their empirical work are properly understood. More information is needed about pre-test testing, multistage pre-testing, the impact of non-normal disturbances and the full sampling distributions of PTEs. However, the recent work in this field has provided us with a good deal of information that is of direct practical benefit to econometricians and applied economists alike.

Notes

This paper was prepared while the authors were receiving support in the form of a University of Canterbury Research Grant 1770901. We are grateful to Kevin Albertson, Offer Lieberman, Kazuhiro Ohtani, Les Oxley, John Small, Alan Wan and a referee for their helpful comments on an earlier draft, and to Alan Wan for supplying us with material for figure 4.
1   For example, see Toyoda and Wallace (1979).
2   For instance, see Toro-Vizcarrondo and Wallace (1968), Wallace and Toro-Vizcarrondo (1969), Goodnight and Wallace (1972), Wallace (1972), Bock et al. (1973), Yancey et al. (1973). See also Judge and Bock (1978) for a summary and a discussion.
3   See, for instance, Brook (1972, 1976), Wallace (1972), Bock et al. (1973), Yancey et al. (1973) and Judge and Bock (1978). Brook (1972, 1976), Bock et al. (1973) and Judge and Bock (1978) also consider the unweighted risk function of the PTE of β itself.
4   These results are discussed, for instance, by Wallace and Asher (1972), Wallace (1977), Judge and Bock (1978), who also further generalize this research, and Judge et al. (1985).
5   $F'_{(m+i, v+j; \lambda)}$ is a non-central F statistic with $m + i$ and $v + j$ degrees of freedom, and non-centrality parameter λ, defined above.
6   Though we do not discuss the Stein-rule family of estimators, it is worth noting that the above analysis has also been considered by, for example, Judge et al. (1983) using Stein-rule estimators as the component estimators. They show that if $k - m \geqslant 3$ then their Stein PTE dominates, under squared error loss, the traditional PTE.
7   See also Gelfand and Dey (1988b).
8   See, for instance, Bancroft (1944) or Toyoda and Wallace (1975).
9   See, for example, Ohtani and Toyoda (1980), Yancey et al. (1984) and Judge and Yancey (1986).
10   For example, Taylor (1977, 1978), Greenberg (1980) and Mandy (1984).
11   See Özcam (1987) for some extensions to this work.

12 Note that James–Stein type estimators exist which have smaller risk than this boundary. See, for instance, Sclove et al. (1972) and Judge and Bock (1978).

13 This is not always the case. For instance, stepwise regression is an obvious counter-example. See, for example, Wallace (1977).

14 Such studies include those of Mandelbröt (1963), Fama (1965), Blattberg and Gonedes (1974), Rainbow and Praetz (1986) and Lau et al. (1990) in respect of returns analyses in the stock, financial and commodity markets.

15 Further discussion of the family of distributions is beyond the scope of this paper. See, for example, Kelker (1970), Chmielewski (1981a) and Muirhead (1982).

16 For example, Box (1952), Thomas (1970), King (1979), Chmielewski (1981a, b), Sutradhar and Ali (1986), Sutradhar (1988), Brandwein and Strawderman (1990).

17 In fact, this result holds for all members of the wider ellibpically symmetric family. See King (1979).

18 That is, the ML and M estimators under a normality assumption.

19 $\nu = \infty$ corresponds to normal errors.

20 Giles (1990) extends these results to the maximum likelihood and the minimum MSE component estimators.

21 See Ohtani (1991c) for related work. He investigates the properties of the inequality restricted estimator when there is a proxy variable in the model, but he does not examine the inequality PTE.

22 See also Pordzik and Trenkler (undated).

23 This is just a scaled Wald statistic.

24 This work is being undertaken with John Small, Matthew Cunneen and Michael Sullivan.

References

Adjibolosoo, B.-S. K. (1989) Measuring the degree of severity of heteroskedasticity and the choice between the OLS estimator and the 2SAE. *Communications in Statistics: Theory and Methods*, A18, 3451–62.

—— (1990a) The degree of severity of heteroskedasticity and the traditional Goldfeld and Quandt pretest estimator. *Communications in Statistics: Simulation and Computation*, B19, 827–36.

—— (1990b) A procedure for improving upon the performance of the traditional heteroskedasticity pretest estimator. *Communications in Statistics: Theory and Methods*, A19, 1899–1912.

Albertson, K. V. (1991) Pre-test estimation in a regression model with a misspecified error covariance matrix. Discussion Paper 9115, Department of Economics, University of Canterbury.

Anderson, T. W. (1971) *An Introduction to Multivariate Statistical Analysis*. New York: Wiley.

Bancroft, T. A. (1944) On biases in estimation due to the use of preliminary tests of significance. *Annals of Mathematical Statistics*, 15, 190–204.

—— and Han, C.-P. (1977) Inference based on conditional specification: a note and a bibliography. *International Statistical Review*, 45, 117–27.

—— and —— (1983) A note on pooling variances. *Journal of the American Statistical Association*, 78, 981–3.

Basmann, R. L. and Hwang, H.-S. (1988) A Monte Carlo study of structural estimator distributions after performance of likelihood ratio pre-tests. Mimeo, SUNY-Binghamton.

Basu, D. (1955) On statistics independent of a complete sufficient statistic. *Sankhya*, 15, 377–80.

Bennett, B. M. (1952) Estimation of means on the basis of preliminary tests of significance. *Annals of the Institute of Statistical Mathematics*, 4, 31–43.

—— (1956) On the use of preliminary tests in certain statistical procedures. *Annals of the Institute of Statistical Mathematics*, 8, 45–52.

Berkson, J. (1942) Tests of significance considered as evidence. *Journal of the American Statistical Association*, 37, 325–35.

Blattberg, R. C. and Gonedes, N. J. (1974) A comparison of the stable and Student distributions as statistical models for stock prices. *Journal of Business*, 47, 244–80.

Bock, M. E., Yancey, T. A. and Judge, G. G. (1973) The statistical consequences of the preliminary test estimators in regression. *Journal of the American Statistical Association*, 68, 109–16.

Box, G. E. P. (1952) Multi-factor designs of first order. *Biometrika*, 39, 49–57.

Brandwein, A. C. and Strawderman, W. E. (1990) Stein estimation: the spherically symmetric case. *Statistical Science*, 5, 356–69.

Brook, R. J. (1972) On the use of minimax regret functions to set significance points in prior tests of estimation. Ph. D. thesis, North Carolina State University.

—— (1976) On the use of a regret function to set significance points in prior tests of estimation. *Journal of the American Statistical Association*, 71, 126–31.

—— and Fletcher, R. H. (1981) Optimal significance levels of prior tests in the presence of multicollinearity. *Communications in Statistics: Theory and Methods*, A10, 1401–13.

Chmielewski, M. A. (1981a) Elliptically symmetric distributions: a review and bibliography. *International Statistical Review*, 49, 67–74.

—— (1981b) Invariant tests for the equality of K scale parameters under spherical symmetry. *Journal of Statistical Planning and Inference*, 5, 341–6.

Chen, E. J. and Saleh, A. K. Md. E. (1991) Estimation of regression parameters when the errors are autocorrelated. Mimeo, Department of Mathematics and Statistics, Carleton University.

Clarke, J. A. (1986) Some implications of estimating a regression scale parameter after a preliminary test of restrictions. M. Sc. thesis, Monash University.

—— (1990) Preliminary-test estimation of the standard error of estimate in linear regression. *Economics Letters*, 34, 21–32.

——, Giles, D. E. A. and Wallace, T. D. (1987a) Estimating the error variance in regression after a preliminary test of restrictions on the coefficients. *Journal of Econometrics*, 34, 293–304.

——, —— and —— (1987b) Preliminary- test estimation of the error variance in linear regression. *Econometric Theory*, 3, 299–304.

Cohen, A. (1965) Estimates of the linear combinations of parameters in the mean vector of a multivariate distribution. *Annals of Mathematical Statistics*, 36, 299–304.

Durbin, J. (1970) Testing for serial correlation in least-squares regression when some of the regressors are lagged dependent variables. *Econometrica*, 38, 410–21.

Engle, R. F., Hendry, D. F. and Trumble, D. (1985) Small-sample properties of ARCH estimators and tests. *Canadian Journal of Economics*, 51, 66–93.

Escobar, L. A. and Skarpness, B. (1986) The bias of the least squares estimator over interval constraints. *Economics Letters*, 20, 331–5.

—— and —— (1987) Mean square error and efficiency of the least squares estimator over interval constraints. *Communications in Statistics: Theory and Methods*, A16, 397–406.

Fama, E. F. (1965) The behaviour of stock market prices. *Journal of Business*, 38, 34–105.

Farebrother, R. W. (1975) Minimax regret significance points for a preliminary test in regression analysis. *Econometrica*, 43, 1005–6.

Folmer, H. (1988) Autocorrelation pre-testing in linear models with AR(1) errors. In T. K. Dijkstra (ed.), *On Model Uncertainty and its Statistical Implications*, Berlin: Springer-Verlag, 39–55.

Fomby, T. B. and Guilkey, D. K. (1978) On choosing the optimal level of significance for the Durbin-Watson test and the Bayesian alternative. *Journal of Econometrics*, 8, 203–13.

Gelfand, A. E. and Dey, D. K. (1988a) Improved estimation of the disturbance variance in a linear regression model. *Journal of Econometrics*, 39, 387–95.

—— and —— (1988b) On the estimation of variance ratio. *Journal of Statistical Planning and Inference*, 19, 121–31.

Giles, D. E. A. (1986) Preliminary-test estimation in mis-specified regressions. *Economics Letters*, 21, 325–8.

—— (1992a) The exact distribution of a simple pre-test estimator. In W. E. Griffiths, M. E. Bock and H. Lütkepohl (eds), *Readings in Econometric Theory and Practice: In Honor of George Judge*, Amsterdam: North-Holland, 57–74.

—— (1992b) Pre-test estimation under absolute error loss. Discussion Paper 9210, Department of Economics, University of Canterbury.

—— and Beattie, M. (1987) Autocorrelation pre-test estimation in models with a lagged dependent variable. In M. L. King and D. E. A. Giles (eds), *Specification Analysis in the Linear Model*, London: Routledge & Kegan Paul, 99–116.

—— and Clarke, J. A. (1989) Preliminary-test estimation of the scale parameter in a mis-specified regression model. *Economics Letters*, 30, 201–5.

—— and Lieberman, O. (1992) Some properties of the Durbin-Watson test after a preliminary *t*-test. *Journal of Statistical Computation and Simulation*, 41, 219–27.

—— and Srivastava, V. K. (1992) The exact distribution of a least squares regression coefficient estimator after a preliminary *t*-test. *Statistics and Probability Letters*, 16, 59–64.

——, Giles, J. A. and Wallace, T. D. (1992a) Pre-test estimation of the regression predictor under a LINEX loss structure. Mimeo, Department of Economics, University of Canterbury.

——, Giles, J. A. and Wong, J. K. (1992b) Properties of a regression pre-test estimator in the presence of GARCH disturbances. Mimeo, Department of Economics, University of Canterbury.

——, Lieberman, O. and Giles, J. A. (1992c) The optimal size of a preliminary test of linear restrictions in a mis-specified regression model. *Journal of the American Statistical Association*, 87, 1153–7.

Giles, J. A. (1990) Preliminary-test estimation of a mis-specified model with spherically symmetric disturbances. Ph. D. thesis, University of Canterbury.

—— (1991a) Pre-testing for linear restrictions in a regression model with spherically symmetric disturbances. *Journal of Econometrics*, 50, 377–98.

—— (1991b) Pre-testing in a mis-specified regression model. *Communications in Statistics: Theory and Methods*, A20, 3221–38.

—— (1992) Estimation of the error variance after a preliminary test of homogeneity in a regression model with spherically symmetric disturbances. *Journal of Econometrics*, 53, 345–61.

—— (1993) Estimation of the scale parameter after a pre-test for homogeneity in a mis-specified regression model. *Communications in Statistics: Theory and Methods*, 22, 1007–29.

—— and Giles, D. E. A. (1993) Preliminary-test estimation of the regression scale parameter when the loss function is asymmetric. *Communications in Statistics: Theory and Methods*, 22, 1709–33.

—— and —— (1994) Risk of a homoskedasticity pre-test estimator of the regression scale under LINEX loss. *Journal of Statistical Planning and Inference*, forthcoming.

—— and Lieberman, O. (1991) The optimal size of a preliminary test for linear restrictions when estimating the regression scale parameter. *Economics Letters*, 37, 25–30.

——, Giles, D. E. A. and Wong, J. K. (1992) The size of a *t*-test after a pre-test for ARCH–GARCH regression errors. Mimeo, Department of Economics, University of Canterbury.

Goodnight, J. and Wallace, T. D. (1972) Operational techniques and tables for making weak MSE tests for restrictions in regression. *Econometrica*, 40, 699–710.

Greenberg, E. (1980) Finite sample moments of a preliminary-test estimator in the case of possible heteroskedasticity. *Econometrica*, 48, 1805–13.

Griffiths, W. E. and Beesley, P. A. A. (1984) The small sample properties of some preliminary test estimators in a linear model with autocorrelated errors. *Journal of Econometrics*, 25, 49–61.

—— and Judge, G. G. (1989) Testing and estimating location vectors under heteroskedasticity. Mimeo, University of New England.

Gurland, J. and McCullough R. S. (1962) Testing equality of means after a preliminary test of equality of variances. *Biometrika*, 49, 403–17.

Han, C.-P., Rao, C. V. and Ravichandran, J. (1988) Inference based on conditional specification: a second bibliography. *Communications in Statistics: Theory and Methods*, A17, 1945–64.

Hasegawa, H. (1989) On some comparisons between Bayesian and sampling theoretic estimators of a normal mean subject to an inequality constraint. *Journal of the Japan Statistical Society*, 19, 167–77.

—— (1991) The MSE of a pre-test estimator of the linear regression model with an interval constraint on coefficients. *Journal of the Japan Statistical Society*, 21, 189–95.

Hessenius, H. and Trenkler, G. (undated) Pre-test estimation in the linear regression model with competing linear constraints. Mimeo, University of Dortmund.

Hirano, K. (1978) A note on the level of significance of the preliminary test in pooling variances. *Journal of the Japan Statistical Society*, 8, 71–5.

Inada, K. (1989) Estimation of variance after preliminary conjecture. *Bulletin of Informatics and Cybernetics*, 23, 183–98.

Jayatissa, W. A. (1977) Tests of equality between sets of coefficients in two linear regressions when disturbance variances are unequal. *Econometrica*, 45, 1291–2.

Judge, G. G. and Bock, M. E. (1978) *The Statistical Implications of Pre-test and Stein Rule Estimators in Econometrics*. New York: North-Holland.

—— and —— (1983) Biased estimation. In Z. Griliches and M. D. Intriligator (eds), *Handbook of Econometrics*, Amsterdam: North-Holland, 599–649.

—— and Takayama, T. (1966) Inequality restrictions in regression analysis. *Journal of the American Statistical Association*, 61, 166–81.

—— and Yancey, T. A. (1981) Sampling properties of an inequality restricted estimator. *Economics Letters*, 7, 327–33.

—— and —— (1986) *Improved Methods of Inference in Econometrics*. Amsterdam: North-Holland.

——, Griffiths, W. E., Hill, R. C. and Lee, T.-C. (1980) *The Theory and Practice of Econometrics*. New York: Wiley.

——, Yancey, T. A. and Bock, M. E. (1983) Pre-test estimation under squared error loss. *Economic Letters*, 11, 347–52.

——, Griffiths, W. E., Hill, R. C., Lütkepohl, H. and Lee, T.-C. (1985) *The Theory and Practice of Econometrics*, 2nd edn. New York: Wiley.

——, Bohrer, R. and Yancey, T. A. (1990) Some statistical implications of multivariate inequality constrained testing. *Communications in Statistics: Theory and Methods*, A19, 413–30.

Kelker, D. (1970) Distribution theory of spherical distributions and a location-scale parameter generalization. *Sankhya*, A32, 419–30.

Kennedy, P. and Simons, D. (1991) Fighting the teflon factor. *Journal of Econometrics*, 48, 15–27.

King, M. L. (1979) Some aspects of statistical inference in the linear regression model. Ph. D. thesis, University of Canterbury.

—— and Giles, D. E. A. (1984) Autocorrelation pre-testing in the linear model: estimation, testing and prediction. *Journal of Econometrics*, 25, 35–48.

Krämer, W. and Sonnberger, H. (1986) *The Linear Regression Model Under Test*. Heidelberg: Physica-Verlag.

Lau, A. H.-L., Lau, H.-S. and Wingender, J. R. (1990) The distribution of stock returns: new evidence against the stable model. *Journal of Business and Economic Statistics*, 8, 217–23.

Leamer, E. E. (1988) Things that bother me. *Economic Record*, 64, 331–5.

Liew, C. K. (1976) Inequality constrained least squares estimation. *Journal of the American Statistical Association*, 71, 746–51.

Lovell, M. C. and Prescott, E. (1970) Multiple regression with inequality constraints: pre-testing bias, hypothesis testing and efficiency. *Journal of the American Statistical Association*, 65, 913–25.

Mandelbröt, B. B. (1963) The variation of certain speculative prices. *Journal of Business*, 36, 394–419.

Mandy, D. M. (1984) The moments of a pre-test estimator under possible heteroskedasticity. *Journal of Econometrics*, 25, 29–33.

Mehta, J. S. (1972) On utilizing information from a second sample in estimating the scale parameter for a family of symmetric distributions. *Journal of the American Statistical Association*, 67, 448–52.

Mittelhammer, R. C. (1984) Restricted least squares, pre-test, OLS and Stein rule estimators: risk comparisons under model misspecification. *Journal of Econometrics*, 25, 151–64.

Mizon, G. E. (1977) Inferential procedures in nonlinear models: an application in a UK cross section study of factor substitution and returns to scale. *Econometrica*, 45, 1221–42.

Morey, M. (1984) the statistical implications of preliminary specification error testing. *Journal of Econometrics*, 25, 63–72.

Muirhead, R. J. (1982) *Aspects of Multivariate Statistical Theory*. New York: Wiley.

Nakamura, A. and Nakamura, M. (1978) On the impact of the test for serial correlation upon the test of significance for the regression coefficient. *Journal of Econometrics*, 7, 199–210.

Ohtani, K. (1983) Preliminary test predictor in the linear regression model including a proxy variable. *Journal of the Japan Statistical Society*, 13, 11–19.

—— (1987a) Some small sample properties of a pre-test estimator of the disturbance variance in a misspecified linear regression. *Journal of the Japan Statistical Society*, 17, 81–9.

—— (1987b) On pooling disturbance variances when the goal is testing restrictions on regression coefficients. *Journal of Econometrics*, 35, 219–31.

—— (1987c) Some sampling properties of the two-stage test in a linear regression with a proxy variable. *Communications in Statistics: Theory and Methods*, A16, 717–29.

—— (1987d) The MSE of the least squares estimator over an interval constraint. *Economics Letters*, 25, 351–4.

—— (1988a) Optimal levels of significance of a pre-test in estimating the disturbance variance after the pre-test for a linear hypothesis on coefficients in a linear regression. *Economics Letters*, 28, 151–6.

—— (1988b) Testing the disturbance variance after a pre-test for a linear hypothesis on coefficients in a linear regression. *Communications in Statistics: Theory and Methods*, A17, 4231–50.

—— (1991a) Some sampling properties of the pre-test estimator for normal variance with the Stein-type estimator. Mimeo, Faculty of Economics, Kobe University.

—— (1991b) Estimation of the variance in a normal population after the one-sided pre-test for the mean. *Communications in Statistics: Theory and Methods*, A20, 219–34.

—— (1991c) Some sampling properties of the inequality constrained least squares estimator in a linear regression model with a proxy variable. Mimeo, Faculty of Economics, Kobe University.

—— and Toyoda T. (1978) Minimax regret critical values for a preliminary test in pooling variance. *Journal of the Japan Statistical Society*, 8, 15–20.

—— and —— (1980) Estimation of regression coefficients after a preliminary test for homoskedasticity. *Journal of Econometrics*, 12, 151–9.

—— and —— (1985) Testing linear hypothesis on regression coefficients after a pre-test for disturbance. *Economics Letters*, 17, 111–14.

—— and —— (1988) Small sample properties of the two-stage test of equality of individual coefficients after a pre-test for homoskedasticity in two linear regressions. *Journal of the Japan Statistical Society*, 18, 23–35.

Özcam, A. (1987) The two stage pre-test estimator and Stein type estimators for the two-sample heteroskedastic linear model. Ph. D. thesis, University of Illinois.

—— and Judge, G. (1991) Some risk results for a two-stage pre-test estimator in the case of possible heteroskedasticity. *Journal of Econometrics*, 48, 355–71.

——, Judge, G., Bera, A. and Yancey, T. (1991) The risk properties of a pre-test estimator for Zellner's seemingly unrelated regression model. Mimeo, Department of Agricultural and Resource Economics, University of California, Berkeley.

Phillips, G. D. A. and McCabe, B. P. (1983) The independence of tests for structural change in regression models. *Economics Letters*, 12, 283–7.

—— and —— (1989) A sequential approach to testing for structural change in econometric models. In W. Krämer (ed.), *Econometrics of Structural Change*, Heidelberg: Physica-Verlag, 87–101.

Pordzik, P. and Trenkler, G. (undated) Pre-test estimation in the linear regression model based on competing restrictions. Mimeo, University of Dortmund.

Rainbow, K. and Praetz, P. D. (1986) The distribution of returns in Sydney wool futures. In B. A. Goss (ed.), *Futures Markets: Their Establishment and Performance*, London: Croom Helm, 191–207.

Rothenberg, T. J. (1984) Hypothesis testing in linear models when the error covariance matrix is nonscalar. *Econometrica*, 45, 1293–8.

Saleh, A. K. Md. E. and Sen, P. K. (1985) On shrinkage M-estimators of location parameters. *Communications in Statistics: Theory and Methods*, A14, 2313–29.

Sawa, T. and Hiromatsu, T. (1973) Minimax regret significance points for a preliminary test in regression analysis. *Econometrica*, 41, 1093–1106.

Sclove, S. L., Morris, C. and Radhakrishnan, R. (1972) Non-optimality of preliminary-test estimators for the multinormal mean. *Annals of Mathematical Statistics*, 43, 1481–90.

Seber, G. A. F. (1964) Linear hypotheses and induced tests. *Biometrika*, 51, 41–8.

Sen, P. K. and Saleh, A. K. Md. E. (1985) On some shrinkage estimators of multivariate location. *Annals of Statistics*, 13, 272–81.

Shukla, N. D. (1979) Estimation of a regression coefficient after two preliminary tests of significance. *Metrika*, 26, 182–93.

Srivastava, S. R. (1976) A preliminary test estimator for the variance of a normal distribution. *Journal of the Indian Statistical Association*, 14, 107–11.

Srivastava, V. K. and Rao, B. B. (1992) Estimation of disturbance variance in linear regression models under asymmetric criterion. *Journal of Quantitative Economics*, 8, 341–52.

Stein, C. (1964) Inadmissibility of the usual estimator for the variance of a normal distribution with unknown mean. *Annals of the Institute of Statistical Mathematics*, 16, 155–60.

Sutradhar, B. C. (1988) Testing hypothesis with t error variable. *Sankhya*, B50, 175–80.

—— and Ali, M. M. (1986) Estimation of the parameters of a regression model with a multivariate t error variable. *Communications in Statistics: Theory and Methods*, A15, 429–50.

Taylor, W. E. (1977) Small sample properties of a class of two stage Aitken estimators. *Econometrica*, 45, 497–508.

—— (1978) The heteroskedastic linear model: exact finite sample results. *Econometrica*, 46, 663–75.

Teichroew, D. (1957) The mixture of normal distributions with different variances. *Annals of Mathematical Statistics*, 28, 510–12.

Thomas, D. H. (1970) Some contributions to radial probability distributions, statistics, and the operational calculi. Ph. D. thesis, Wayne State University.

Thomson, M. (1982) Some results on the statistical properties of an inequality constrained least squares estimator in a linear model with two regressors. *Journal of Econometrics*, 19, 215–31.

—— and Schmidt, P. (1982) A note on the comparison of the mean square error of inequality constrained least squares and other related estimators. *Review of Economics and Statistics*, 64, 174–6.

Toro-Vizcarrondo, C. E. (1968) Multicollinearity and the mean square error criterion in multiple regression: a test and some sequential comparisons. Ph. D. thesis, North Carolina State University.

—— and Wallace, T. D. (1968) A test of the mean square criterion for restrictions in linear regression. *Journal of the American Statistical Association*, 63, 558–72.

Toyoda, T. and Ohtani, K. (1978) Optimal pre-testing procedure in regression. *Keizai Kenkyu*, 29, 39–43.

—— and —— (1986) Testing equality between sets of coefficients after a preliminary test for equality of disturbance variances in two linear regressions. *Journal of Econometrics*, 31, 67–80.

—— and Wallace, T. D. (1975) Estimation of variance after a preliminary test of homogeneity and optimal levels of significance for the pre-test. *Journal of Econometrics*, 3, 395–404.

—— and —— (1976) Optimal critical values for pre-testing in regression. *Econometrica*, 44, 365–75.

—— and —— (1979) Pre-testing on part of the data. *Journal of Econometrics*, 10, 119–23.

Varian, H. R. (1975) A Bayesian approach to real estate assessment. In S. E. Fienberg and A. Zellner (eds.), *Studies in Bayesian Econometrics and Statistics in Honour of Leonard J. Savage*, vol. 1, Amsterdam: North-Holland, 195–208.

Vinod, H. D. and Ullah, A. (1981) *Recent Advances in Regression Methods*. New York: Marcel Dekker.

Wallace, T. D. (1972) Weaker criteria and tests for linear restrictions in regression. *Econometrica*, 40, 689–98.

—— (1977) Pre-test estimation in regression: a survey. *American Journal of Agricultural Economics*, 59, 431–43.

—— and Asher, V. G. (1972) Sequential methods in model construction. *Review of Economics and Statistics*, 54, 172–8.

—— and Toro-Vizcarrondo, C. E. (1969) Tables for the mean square error test for exact linear restrictions in regression. *Journal of the American Statistical Association*, 64, 1649–63.

Wallis, K. F. (1967) Lagged dependent variables and serially correlated errors: a reappraisal of three-pass least squares. *Review of Economics and Statistics*, 49, 555–67.

Wan, A. T. K. (1992) The sampling performance of inequality restricted and pre-test estimators in mis-specified linear regressions. Mimeo, Department of Economics, University of Canterbury.

Weerahandi, S. (1987) Testing regression equality with unequal variances. *Econometrica*, 55, 1211–15.

Wong, J. K. and Giles, J. A. (1991) Optimal critical values of a preliminary test for linear restrictions in a regression model with multivariate Student-t disturbances. Discussion Paper 9114, Department of Economics, University of Canterbury.

Yancey, T. A., Judge, G. G. and Bock, M. E. (1973) Wallace's weak mean square error criterion for testing linear restrictions in regression: a tighter bound. *Econometrica*, 41, 1203–6.

——, —— and Mandy, D. M. (1983) The sampling performance of pre-test estimators of the scale parameter under squared error loss. *Economics Letters*, 12, 181–6.

——, —— and Miyazaki, S. (1984) Some improved estimators in the case of possible heteroskedasticity. *Journal of Econometrics*, 25, 133–50.

——, —— and Bohrer, R. (1989) Sampling performance of some joint one-sided preliminary test estimators under squared error loss. *Econometrica*, 57, 1221–8.

Zellner, A. (1961) Linear regression with inequality constraints on the coefficients. Report 6109, International Centre for Management Science, Rotterdam.

—— (1986) Bayesian estimation and prediction using asymmetric loss functions. *Journal of the American Statistical Association*, 81, 446–51.

5 Sherlock Holmes and the search for truth: a diagnostic tale

Michael McAleer
Department of Economics,
University of Western Australia

1 Introduction

> My name is Sherlock Holmes. It is my business to know what other people don't know.
> (Sherlock Holmes to James Ryder in *The Adventure of the Blue Carbuncle*)

In four novels and fifty-six short stories, Sir Arthur Conan Doyle developed the characters of Mr Sherlock Holmes and his trusted friend and chronicler, Dr John Watson. Conan Doyle had been a practising doctor, which requires a trained eye to diagnose illnesses, often on the basis of superficial symptoms alone. It is therefore not surprising that medical issues seem to arise so frequently in the criminal cases in the adventures of Sherlock Holmes.

> You're like a surgeon who wants every symptom before he can give his diagnosis.
> (J. Neil Gibson to Sherlock Holmes in *The Problem of Thor Bridge*)

The creation of the brilliant sleuth and his partner who, although not possessing genius, stimulated it in his friend was a master-stroke. The Adventures, Memoirs, Return, Last Bow and Case Book of Sherlock Holmes, as well as the four famous novels, are stories of sheer delight, committed to memory by many during their childhood. Econometrics may not have the everlasting charm of Holmesian characters and adventures, or even a famous resident of Baker Street, but there is much in his methodological approach to the solving of criminal cases that is of relevance to applied econometric modelling. Holmesian detection may be interpreted as involving the relationship between data and theory, modelling procedures, deductions and inferences, analysis of biases, testing of theories, specification and respecification of theories, re-evaluation and reformulation of theories, and finally a solution to the problem at hand. With this in mind, can applied econometricians learn anything from the master of detection? A selection of quotes from Conan Doyle (1984) may prove to be instructive.

> I crave for mental exaltation. That is why I have chosen my own particular profession, or rather created it, for I am the only one in the world .... The only unofficial consulting detective ... I am the last and highest court of appeal in 'detection'.
> (Sherlock Holmes to Dr Watson in *The Sign of Four*)

It is my business to know things. That is my trade.
>
> (Sherlock Holmes to Colonel Emsworth in *The Adventure of the Blanched Soldier*)

Well, I have a trade of my own. I suppose I am the only one in the world. I'm a consulting detective . . . .
>
> (Sherlock Holmes to Dr Watson in *A Study in Scarlet*)

No man lives or has ever lived who has brought the same amount of study and of natural talent to the detection of crime which I have done.
>
> (Sherlock Holmes to Dr Watson in *A Study in Scarlet*)

I am a private detective . . . .
(Sherlock Holmes to Lord Mount-James in *The Adventure of the Missing Three-quarter*)

I have been sluggish in mind and wanting in that mixture of imagination and reality which is the basis of my art.
>
> (Sherlock Holmes to Dr Watson in *The Problem of Thor Bridge*)

Sherlock Holmes worked in scenarios that are markedly different from that of the practising econometrician. He was a logician, dealing in the world of the criminal mind. In many situations, human lives were at stake. Herein lies the essential difference between Holmesian methodology – the science of deduction – and applied econometric methodology – the art of data analysis and modelling. Holmes dealt with specific people in specific circumstances. Econometrics frequently deals with aggregated data and average relationships, without necessarily having clear linkages to the underlying behavioural relationships of individuals. Real data are generated by the underlying economic processes, but the data in the adventures of Sherlock Holmes are a product of the life and times of Sir Arthur Conan Doyle.

> You can, for example, never foretell what any one man will do, but you can say with precision what an average number will be up to. Individuals vary, but percentages remain constant. So says the statistician.
>
> (Sherlock Holmes to Dr Watson in *The Sign of Four*)

Are the methodologies used by Holmes and by applied econometricians scientific? It is perhaps unfortunate, or maybe even cause for wry humour, that 'econometrics' contains both 'con' and 'trics', and sounds so much like 'economy tricks' (which is what politicians do). Science is systematic and formulated knowledge, the pursuit of which is enhanced by the testing of existing theories. The inferential strategy used by Holmes combines brilliant powers of observation with an amazing capacity for testing theories and discarding those that are not consistent with the data, regardless of how appealing they might be. Holmes's combination of rigour and imagination can act as a useful role model for applied econometricians and others involved in data analysis.

The selected quotes above might, unfortunately, give Holmes the unwarranted appearance of arrogance. A more accurate description would be a person with no false modesty, as the following quotes make clear.

> To the logician all things should be seen exactly as they are, and to underestimate one's self is as much a departure from truth as to exaggerate one's own powers.
>
> (Sherlock Holmes to Dr Watson in *The Adventure of the Greek Interpreter*)

Such slips are common to all mortals, and the greatest is he who can recognise and repair them. To this modified credit I may, perhaps, make some claim.

(Sherlock Holmes to Dr Watson in *The Disappearance of Lady Frances Carfax*)

The plan of the paper is as follows. Section 2 provides an outline of Holmesian deduction through the various stages of problem solving, theorizing before data, examining the quality of data, the meaning of truth, reconciliation with data, and testing of theories. Section 3 examines some issues of modelling in econometrics, with an emphasis on the historical debate between Keynes and Tinbergen. Diagnostic testing is examined in some detail in section 4, and several of the major tests used in applied econometric modelling are discussed. Tests of functional form are discussed in detail in section 5, concentrating on tests of linear versus log-linear models.

2   Deduction and detection

2.1   Problem solving

That is the problem which we are now about to solve . . . .

(Sherlock Holmes in *The Adventure of the Dancing Men*)

And yet the problem should be capable of ultimate solution.

(Sherlock Holmes to Thorneycroft Huxtable in *The Adventure of the Priory School*)

. . . we shall have reached the solution of the mystery.

(Sherlock Holmes to Thorneycroft Huxtable in *The Adventure of the Priory School*)

. . . I have solved the mystery.

(Sherlock Holmes to Dr Watson in *The Adventure of the Three Students*)

Now, I think that, with a few missing links, my chain is almost complete.

(Sherlock Holmes to Dr Watson in *The Adventure of the Abbey Grange*)

Somewhere in the vaults of the bank of Cox and Co., at Charing Cross, there is a travel-worn and battered tin dispatch-box with my name, John H. Watson, M.D., Late Indian Army, painted upon the lid. It is crammed with papers, nearly all of which are records of cases to illustrate the curious problems which Mr. Sherlock Holmes had at various times to examine. Some, and not the least interesting, were complete failures, and as such will hardly bear narrating, since no final explanation is forthcoming. A problem without a solution may interest the student, but can hardly fail to annoy the casual reader.

(Dr Watson in *The Problem of Thor Bridge*)

Both criminal investigation and econometric analysis involve determining the importance of and the collection of data, and a final explanation of the data after previous explanations (if any) have been rejected against the available evidence. In the context of econometric modelling, the crucial issues involve the data, a set (or sets) of prior beliefs, the development of one or more appropriate explanatory relationships, and testing and evaluation of the resulting model.

As in any social, natural or physical science, econometrics has its limitations. Decision-making under uncertainty must always be so. Economic theories are the products of mathematical analyses and awareness of reality. Although theories can be tested rigorously, it is rarely possible to be certain regarding any inference drawn from data. Holmes had a much easier task in this respect because, after he has solved a mystery, he knows he has the answer – his solution is right or wrong, and he can ascertain which one it is. His methodology is basically one of relying on the facts, of gathering information, of processing observations and of finding a theory that adequately explains the data. He narrows the set of possibilities until only one remains. Like econometricians, Holmes is in search of the truth that generated the data. Confronted with a crime or problem, Holmes assiduously gathers data which are needed for a suitable explanation. Unlike econometrics, however, his searches will frequently yield the truth and the culprit will be apprehended.

As Watson informs, not all of the problems encountered by Holmes resulted in a solution – but this did not make such problems uninteresting. Applied econometricians rarely solve problems, and certainly do not seek conclusive verification of theories. Such a pursuit is in the realm of mathematics, not data analysis in an uncertain world. Holmes is interested in explaining what has occurred, and perhaps even how and why. He achieves his aim by unlocking that precise sequence of events that led to the crime being committed.

In complicated cases, Holmes would occasionally adopt the convenience of a temporary hypothesis before reaching a solution. This has a parallel in applied econometrics, where efficient search strategies can be employed to achieve an adequate model. Holmes did not use statistical analysis to evaluate his theories against the data–only his powers of logic and intuition. But imagination in seeking to discover new evidence and to incorporate it into an overall explanation may also be used to good effect in econometric modelling.

2.2   On theorizing before observing data

I have no data yet. It is a capital mistake to theorise before one has data. Insensibly one begins to twist facts to suit theories, instead of theories to suit facts.
> (Sherlock Holmes to Dr Watson in *A Scandal in Bohemia*)

No data yet.... It is a capital mistake to theorise before you have all the evidence. It biases the judgment.
> (Sherlock Holmes to Dr Watson in *A Study in Scarlet*)

It is a capital mistake to theorise in advance of the facts.
> (Sherlock Holmes to Dr Watson in *The Adventure of the Second Stain*)

I have not all my facts yet.... Still, it is an error to argue in front of your data. You find yourself insensibly twisting them round to fit your theories.
> (Sherlock Holmes to Dr Watson in *The Adventure of Wisteria Lodge*)

We approached the case, you remember, with an absolutely blank mind, which is always an advantage. We had formed no theories. We were simply there to observe and to draw inferences from our observations.
> (Sherlock Holmes to Dr Watson in *The Adventure of the Cardboard Box*)

Facts form the foundations of Holmes's deductive process. His powers of observation permit him to discover, gather and store information. These facts are correct, and are not diluted by the processes used in their collection. Such facts should not, of course, be confused with their interpretation. By contrast, economic data are usually taken as given, and it is frequently both difficult and costly to gather the precise information that econometricians need in order to draw accurate inferences.

Holmes observed the data prior to developing his theories and relied on the data to formulate his theory. By his own admission, he had no prior beliefs as such priors would lead to biased results. Holmesian inference means inferring from the data that sequence of apparently unconnected events that could be organized into a convincing explanation. This is the primary reason for Holmes's reluctance to theorize prior to observing data (he seems to be unsure as to whether he needs *some* or *all* of the data prior to theorizing). Such an approach contrasts markedly with the classical procedure for conducting statistical inference, whereby theorizing precedes examination of the data.

> It is one of those cases where the art of the reasoner should be used rather for the sifting of details than for the acquiring of fresh evidence .... The difficulty is to detach the framework of fact – of absolute undeniable fact – from the embellishments of theorists and reporters.
>
> (Sherlock Holmes to Dr Watson in *The Adventure of Silver Blaze*)

A case similar to Holmesian methodology may be made for using econometric techniques to test economic theories. Textbook theories are based on many, sometimes heroic, assumptions which are often at variance with reality. This is not a problem in itself since assumptions are intended to be *useful*, not realistic. However, the inferences from a theory *are* intended to be realistic, and so a theory should always be tested. Data must be given the last word in deciding on the validity of a theory. In this context, Holmes would undoubtedly be surprised at the gulf which sometimes seems to exist between the economic theorist and the econometrician who tries to test the theory. For example, what is the appropriate relationship between the theory and the methods designed to test it? Are all the data available and are they reliable? Sherlock Holmes did not have insurmountable difficulties in answering these questions as a detective, but he would not have been so successful had he been an econometrician.

2.3   Quality of data

> It is of the highest importance in the art of detection to be able to recognise out of a number of facts which are incidental and which vital.
>
> (Sherlock Holmes to Colonel Hayter in *The Adventure of the Reigate Squire*)

> The principal difficulty in your case ... lay in the fact of there being too much evidence. What was vital was overlaid and hidden by what was irrelevant. Of all the facts which were presented to us, we had to pick just those which we deemed to be essential ....
>
> (Sherlock Holmes to Percy Phelps in *The Adventure of the Naval Treaty*)

> ... let us try to realise what we *do* know so as to make the most of it, and to separate the essential from the accidental.
>
> (Sherlock Holmes to Dr Watson in *The Adventure of the Priory School*)

It is of the highest importance, therefore, not to have useless facts elbowing out the useful ones.

(Sherlock Holmes to Dr Watson in *A Study in Scarlet*)

Having gathered these facts, Watson, I smoked several pipes over them, trying to separate those which were crucial from others which were merely incidental.

(Sherlock Holmes to Dr Watson in *The Adventure of the Crooked Man*)

The process of constructing a model to explain reality uses both the data and the ingenuity of the researcher (or detective). For Holmes, the manipulation of the data was not sanctioned. Facts were to be incorporated into his theory; otherwise, he would alter his theory. A serious problem faced by Holmes was that of a single-occurrence observation, even if other information were associated with its occurrence. Holmes faced limited opportunities to conduct controlled experiments, just as in the case of economics. He did, however, acquire additional data whenever possible, and distinguished between important data and data that could safely be discarded. Irrelevant data were treated as unwanted distractions and were therefore liable to be rejected.

Holmes's quotes may also be relevant for guidance in detecting cause-and-effect relationships. Econometric models attempt to search for suitable relationships between explained and explanatory variables. Holmes attempts to detect factors that could be used to explain how events such as crimes were perpetrated. He also focused his attention on distinguishing between the important and merely coincidental factors. Are the relationships spurious, or are they systematic? Such a question is also of the utmost importance for the applied econometrician.

2.4   Truth

It is an old maxim of mine that when you have excluded the impossible, whatever remains, however improbable, must be the truth.

(Sherlock Holmes to Alexander Holder in *The Adventure of the Beryl Coronet*)

We must fall back upon the old axiom that when all other contingencies fail, whatever remains, however improbable, must be the truth.

(Sherlock Holmes to Dr Watson in *The Adventure of the Bruce-Partington Plans*)

That process... starts upon the supposition that when you have eliminated all which is impossible, then whatever remains, however improbable, must be the truth.

(Sherlock Holmes in *The Adventure of the Blanched Soldier*)

How often have I said to you that when you have eliminated the impossible, whatever remains, *however, improbable*, must be the truth?

(Sherlock Holmes to Dr Watson in *The Sign of Four*)

Eliminate all other factors, and the one which remains must be the truth.

(Sherlock Holmes to Dr Watson in *The Sign of Four*)

In econometrics, 'truth' is a relative term – a benchmark. But, as can be seen from the quotes, Holmes was in no doubt as to the meaning of truth. However, econometricians occasionally seem confused as to the meaning of the term, recalling Peter Pan's confusion between truth and fiction:

> The difference between him and the other boys at such a time was that they knew it was make-believe, while to him make-believe and true were exactly the same thing.
>
> (J.M. Barrie (1986) in *Peter Pan*)

Thus, Peter seemed to equate truth with anything he wanted to believe, whereas the Lost Boys of Neverland were painfully aware of the difference between make-believe and true (such as when they had to make-believe that they had already eaten).

There are many references to 'models' in econometrics, the most well-known dictum perhaps being: 'All models are false, but some are more useful than others'. Models are abstractions from reality and, as such, there are no true models. Thus, Holmes's references to truth as being 'whatever remains' is not appropriate or relevant for applied econometric research since the latter does not rely on deductive reasoning to try to reach an unreachable truth. There are, however, numerous testing procedures available for discovering false models, and these play a vital role in modern applied econometrics. For Holmes, the truth is not an abstraction. Truth exists and it is his mission to uncover it. However, unlike the world of Holmes in which a single event exists or a small number of possibly related events occur, applied econometricians seek to explain an unknown, and frequently unobservable, relation between numerous interdependent factors. Economic systems are far more complicated than the criminal problems and other puzzles Holmes took it upon himself to solve. This complexity is one of the severe limitations facing the econometrician in specifying a model, which is simply a set of assumptions. Assumptions and relationships may also change over time, thereby destroying one of the underlying premises of econometric modelling, namely constancy of the structural relationships. Truth may be constant, but models change.

[A remarkable case called *The Affair of the Mysterious Submarine* was reported in 'Holmes verdict left judge at sea', *The Guardian*, 17 May 1985. Apparently, a dilapidated freighter named the Popi M sank with a full cargo of sugar in calm water off Algeria. The insurers and the owners of Popi M clashed over the legal definition of 'perils of the sea', which may be used to justify insurance claims. The owners claimed that the Popi M had collided with a submarine, a claim which would be justifiable, if true. While admitting that the submarine theory was improbable, Mr Justice Bingham awarded the shipping company compensation on the grounds of Holmes's maxim. Upon appeal, Lord Brandon of Oakbrook overturned the inventive, but unjudicial, reasoning of the High Court judge.]

2.5 Reconciliation with data

> I have devised seven separate explanations, each of which would cover the facts as we know them. But which of these is correct can only be determined by the fresh information... waiting for us.
>
> (Sherlock Holmes to Dr Watson in *The Adventure of the Copper Beeches*)

> Now, my dear Watson, is it beyond the limits of human ingenuity to furnish an explanation which would cover both these big facts?... If the fresh facts which come to our knowledge

all fit themselves into the scheme, then our hypothesis may gradually become a solution.
(Sherlock Holmes to Dr Watson in *The Adventure of Wisteria Lodge*)

It has been a case for intellectual deduction, but when this original intellectual deduction is confirmed point by point by quite a number of independent incidents, then the subjective becomes objective and we can say confidently that we have reached our goal.
(Sherlock Holmes to Robert Ferguson in *The Adventure of the Sussex Vampire*)

What do you think of my theory? . . . When new facts come to our knowledge which cannot be covered by it, it will be time enough to reconsider it.
(Sherlock Holmes to Dr Watson in *The Adventure of the Yellow Face*)

One forms provisional theories and waits for time or fuller knowledge to explode them.
(Sherlock Holmes to Robert Ferguson in *The Adventure of the Sussex Vampire*)

Each fact is suggestive in itself. Together they have a cumulative force . . . . We could not explain the absence of a ticket. This would explain it. Everything fits together.
(Sherlock Holmes to Dr Watson in *The Adventure of the Bruce-Partington Plans*)

I did not foresee the dog, but at least I understand him and he fitted into my reconstruction.
(Sherlock Holmes to Robert Ferguson in *The Adventure of the Sussex Vampire*)

For Holmes the process of arriving at a solution consisted of two distinct stages, namely the assiduous gathering of facts – paying exceptional attention to detail – followed by an intuitive leap into an objective and unifying theory. He was always striving to obtain new evidence. When the facts were at variance with the theory, the theory had to change and not the data.

Circumstantial evidence was not ignored, but was accommodated in a reformulation of the theory.

Circumstantial evidence is a very tricky thing . . . . It may seem to point very straight to one thing, but if you shift your own point of view a little, you may find it pointing in an equally uncompromising manner to something entirely different.
(Sherlock Holmes to Dr Watson in *The Boscombe Valley Mystery*)

Circumstantial evidence is occasionally very convincing . . . .
(Sherlock Holmes to Dr Watson in *The Adventure of the Noble Bachelor*)

The facts should not be confused, as stated previously, with their interpretation. All facts are taken as being correct, but their interpretation may be forced to change. However, Holmes was frequently willing to alter his position to examine the effects on his theory. Such an attitude has its parallel in considerations of statistical robustness.

New theories and hypotheses were constantly being developed by Holmes in a systematic manner, and existing theories were cast aside as they were exploded by 'time or fuller knowledge'. He frequently formulated a theory (or even seven theories) which would be tested against new evidence. The process of developing and appraising existing theories was made abundantly clear. Owing to limited data, at least initially, Holmes typically did not commence with a general theory, but rather with a simple theory which evolved over time. Any theory had to be reconciled with the data and with other competing theories in the search for truth – witness the explanations of the dog and the missing ticket.

2.6 Testing

That is a question which has puzzled many an expert, and why? Because there was no reliable test. Now we have the Sherlock Holmes test, and there will no longer be any difficulty.

(Sherlock Holmes to Dr Watson in *A Study in Scarlet*)

It may well be that several explanations remain, in which case one tries test after test until one or other of them has a convincing amount of support.

(Sherlock Holmes in *The Adventure of the Blanched Soldier*)

... it is as well to test everything.

(Sherlock Holmes to Dr Watson in *The Adventure of the Reigate Squire*)

I have forged and tested every link of my chain ... and I am sure that it is sound.

(Sherlock Holmes to Professor Coram in *The Adventure of the Golden Pince-nez*)

I am inclined to ... test one or two theories which I have formed.

(Sherlock Holmes to Dr Watson in *The Adventure of the Solitary Cyclist*)

That, however, I shall determine by a very simple test....

(Sherlock Holmes to Dr Watson in *The Adventure of the Blue Carbuncle*)

After the data have been filtered through the detective's perceptions and a theory has been constructed, the stage is set for testing. To Holmes, the final theory is the truth, the complete explanation. When all the data have been packaged into a theory, the case is complete and the problem solved, with no doubts as to the veracity of the theory. It is an important component of Holmesian methodology however, to test the various parts, checking for a weak link. The great strength of the master detective's approach is his willingness, indeed his insistence, on abandoning a cherished hypothesis in the light of new and contrary evidence. Given the data, a reliance upon the power of objective reasoning and observation in the search for truth is the true scientific method.

Unlike detection and Holmesian inference in a world of virtual certainty, where false models can nearly always be eliminated decisively by a series of tests, applied econometricians deal with decision-making under uncertainty. However, were all practitioners as willing as Holmes to jettison outmoded models, scientific advancement would be guaranteed, regardless of the methodological stance held by the researcher. It is now accepted by many econometricians as standard practice to employ a wide range of diagnostic tests in the evaluation of empirical models (see, for example, McAleer et al., 1985). Much of the criticism directed at the quality of applied econometric research can be overcome, if not eliminated, by the judicious application of diagnostic testing procedures. As in the case of criminal investigation, a *tested* theory may be shown to have major errors associated with it, in which case it should be a *rejected* theory. But how many economic theories have ever been rejected as being inconsistent with the evidence? Unfortunately, not enough!

The dynamic nature of time series permits a model to be tested as new data constantly become available. Thus, detection of turning points and outliers, the magnitudes of changes in variables, and the manifest failures of predictions from models, all contribute to the testing and evaluation of models. The ability of a model to accommodate new data and to account for the presence of alternative models is, as we have seen, essential to the methodology of Holmes and of the sensible applied econometrician. When a model or theory is not rejected by rigorous testing, it is deemed to be compatible with the data. But if a major fault is detected, there must be a compulsion to consider an alternative.

3   Modelling in econometrics

3.1   Model specification and testing[1]

Econometrics is concerned with the application of statistical or mathematical methods to the analysis of economic data (see, for example, the survey by Pesaran, 1990). Econometric modelling has as its foundation the use of various econometric methods and techniques in evaluating the empirical content of economic relationships. The primary sources of information for use in econometric modelling are economic theory, data, a measurement system, and alternative models for explaining the data. While a notion of 'truth' is deemed essential in many scientific studies, it is unhelpful to apply the scientific methods of the natural and physical sciences uncritically to economics. Econometric modelling is not intended to arrive at the truth, but at an adequate representation of non-experimental economic data.

A model specification is the set of all assumptions which defines the parameter space for purposes of inference. It is therefore an abstraction from reality. Differences in formulating a model specification may arise through (a) different theoretical paradigms; (b) different ways of specifying auxiliary assumptions within a paradigm; or (c) different strategies that may be adopted in the process of model construction. Economic theory often indicates which variables enter into a relationship, but it is frequently not so forthcoming regarding the appropriate functional form or other assumptions which define the parameter space. For these reasons, a specification search is warranted, where by a specification search is meant the set of procedures followed in moving from an initial to a final model specification. It is therefore a research strategy of examining a number of specifications within a modelling cycle of specification, estimation and evaluation. Conflicting views may, of course, arise regarding the justification of the assumptions and the robustness of the inferences to alteration of the assumptions.

Testing procedures, especially the use of diagnostics, are the most common specification search method used in econometrics. Special emphasis has been directed towards developing methods for checking the model specification against the data. There has been debate in the literature as to the appropriate methodology to be adopted for econometric modelling (see, for example, Leamer (1983), McAleer et al. (1985), Pagan (1987) and the readings in Granger (1990)). Although there are dissenters, a consensus seems to have developed among sensible data analysts that diagnostic tests are essential in evaluating econometric models.

As an illustration, consider the linear regression model given by

$$Y_t = \beta_0 + \beta_1 X_t + \beta_2 Z_t + u_t, \qquad u_t \sim D(0, \sigma_u^2) \text{ for all } t = 1, 2, \ldots, T. \tag{1}$$

Defining the information set $I_t = \{Y_{t-1}, Y_{t-2}, \ldots; X_t, X_{t-1}, X_{t-2}, \ldots; Z_t, Z_{t-1}, Z_{t-2}, \ldots\}$, the key assumptions inherent in estimating equation (1) by ordinary least squares (OLS) and in evaluating the adequacy of the model are as follows.

1 Testing for unit roots and cointegration
    (a) Unit root in one variable
    (b) Cointegration
2 Diagnostic testing of the auxiliary assumptions
    (a) Correct functional form: $E(Y_t|I_t) = \beta_0 + \beta_1 X_t + \beta_2 Z_t$ for all $t = 1, 2, \ldots, T$.
    (b) No heteroskedasticity: $E\{[Y_t - E(Y_t|I_t)]^2|I_t\} = \sigma_u^2$ for all $t = 1, 2, \ldots, T$.
    (c) No serial correlation: $E(u_t|I_t) = 0$ for all $t = 1, 2, \ldots T$.
    (d) Explanatory variables are exogenous: $E(u_t X_s) = 0$ and $E(u_t Z_r)$ for all t, s and r.
    (e) Normality of the errors: $u_t \sim N(0, \sigma_u^2)$ for all $t = 1, 2, \ldots T$.
    (f) Structure is constant: $\beta_0, \beta_1, \beta_2$ and σ_u^2 are constant.
    (g) Non-nested models: the model given in equation (1) is adequate in the presence of alternative non-nested models.
    (h) Robustness/lack of sensitivity: the model given in equation (1) is not unduly affected by alterations in the assumptions.

Although the diagnostic tests may suggest alternatives for checking the adequacy of the model, Sherlock Holmes's warning about never losing sight of the alternative is reinforced by examining tables 1 and 2. For any test of the null, there are several possibilities as to the cause of the null hypothesis being rejected, in addition to the specific cause being tested. It is therefore essential to keep the options open. (A specification search has therefore an interesting parallel to the use of medical diagnostics, whereby a symptom may (and frequently does) lead to a misdiagnosis. In situations when the diagnosis is actually correct (i.e. the real cause of the problem is detected), the prescription itself may be inappropriate.)

What can be done about reducing the number of possible causes of rejection? Several of these problems are interrelated, and the tests are, in general, not independent. With regard to the quality of the tests employed in the modelling exercise, is the adequacy of the final specification independent of the procedure by which it was obtained? Unfortunately, it may be taken as being independent only by (foolishly?) ignoring the effects of repeated testing and model respecification on the overall level of significance and on the loss of degrees of freedom.

Thus, some problems associated with the use of diagnostic tests lie in an inability to provide clear answers to the following questions:

1 How many tests should be used?
2 Are the tests independent?
3 What ordering of tests is optimal?
4 Can the tests be used jointly?
5 How many non-nested alternatives should be considered?

6   What are the small sample properties of the tests?
7   Are the tests powerful?
8   Are the tests robust?

Several of these issues will be addressed in the remainder of the paper.

Table 1   Testing for unit roots and cointegration

Test of the null hypothesis		Possibilities for rejecting the null hypothesis
(a) Unit root in one variable	(1)	No unit root
	(2)	Deterministic trend
	(3)	Incorrect transformation of data
	(4)	Incorrect dynamics
	(5)	Structural change
	(6)	Outliers
	(7)	Heteroskedasticity
(b) No cointegration	(1)	Cointegration exists
	(2)	Deterministic trend
	(3)	Incorrect transformation of data
	(4)	Incorrect dynamics
	(5)	Structural change
	(6)	Outliers
	(7)	Omission of variables
	(8)	Heteroskedasticity

Table 2   Diagnostic testing of the auxiliary assumptions

Test of the null hypothesis		Possibilities for rejecting the null hypothesis
(a) Correct functional form	(1)	Incorrect functional form
	(2)	Omitted variables
	(3)	Incorrect transformation of variables
	(4)	Incorrect imposition of restrictions
	(5)	Serial correlation
	(6)	Structural change
	(7)	Predictive failure
	(8)	Outliers
	(9)	Heteroskedasticity
	(10)	Sample selection bias
(b) No heteroskedasticity	(1)	Additive heteroskedasticity
	(2)	Multiplicative heteroskedasticity
	(3)	Omitted variables
	(4)	Incorrect functional form
	(5)	Incorrect transformation of variables
	(6)	Varying coefficients
	(7)	Incorrect dynamics
	(8)	Bilinear models
	(9)	Structural change
	(10)	Predictive failure
	(11)	Outliers

	(12)	Non-normal errors
(c) No serial correlation	(1)	Autoregressive errors
	(2)	Moving average errors
	(3)	Linearly correlated errors
	(4)	Bilinearly correlated errors
	(5)	Nonlinearly correlated errors
	(6)	Omitted variables
	(7)	Incorrect functional forms
	(8)	Incorrect dynamics
	(9)	Incorrect transformation of variables
	(10)	Structural change
(d) Exogeneity	(1)	Endogenous explanatory variables
	(2)	Measurement errors
	(3)	Serial correlation and lagged dependent variables
	(4)	Sample selection bias
(e) Normality	(1)	Skewness
	(2)	Kurtosis
	(3)	Other non-normal distributions
	(4)	Incorrect transformation of variables
	(5)	Structural change
	(6)	Outliers
	(7)	Heteroskedasticity
(f) Parameter constancy	(1)	Structural change
	(2)	Predictive failure
	(3)	Outliers
	(4)	Heteroskedasticity
	(5)	Varying coefficients
(g) Non-nested models	(1)	Incorrect model
	(2)	Incorrect imposition of restrictions
	(3)	Incorrect dynamics
	(4)	Incorrect transformation of variables
(h) Robustness/lack of sensitivity	(1)	Incorrect prior restrictions
	(2)	Influential observations
	(3)	Fragile assumptions
	(4)	Structural change
	(5)	Predictive failure
	(6)	Outliers
	(7)	Choice of sample size
	(8)	Choice of sample period
	(9)	Choice of instruments
	(10)	Inefficient method of estimation

3.2   A historical perspective

Several of the issues highlighted in tables 1 and 2 were argued over half a century ago in a delightfully entertaining, informative and explorative interchange between two prominent figures, Keynes (1939, 1940) and Tinbergen (1940). Many of the arguments are unfocused, but this is not especially surprising since not all of the conceptual apparatus had been invented for a discipline that was at a formative stage. Indeed, even the most rudimentary diagnostic test was not to be developed for several years. Nevertheless, using modern techniques and concepts, it is enlightening to re-examine the debate to focus attention on the differences between a theorist and an applied econometrician. Since some of the issues have been analysed in Hendry (1980) and Pesaran and Smith (1985), only the major points will be raised below.

Although some of Keynes's criticisms of Tinbergen's pioneering econometric methodology remain relevant to this day, they seem to be overly harsh when seen in the context of the contemporary econometrics of 1939–40. Tinbergen's objective is to apply statistical tests to alternative theories of the business cycle. Keynes (1939, p. 559) argues that Tinbergen pays scant attention to the problem of whether the statistical methods here are relevant to applied economics/statistics and, in so doing, raises six major points.

1   The first issue raised by Keynes (1939, p. 559) is perhaps the source of his major disagreement with Tinbergen, namely the appropriate scope and aim of econometrics. He agrees with Tinbergen that testing cannot prove a theory (i.e. a hypothesis regarding the causal relationships between different economic variables) to be correct. This is not controversial because no amount of empirical evidence can prove a theory to be correct. The dispute centres on the possibility of using tests to falsify theories. Keynes notes the stringent requirements that the theory and data must satisfy before concluding that a theory has been refuted. Therefore, Keynes (1939, p. 560) is sceptical regarding the possibility of refutation, and regards the primary role of econometrics as being the estimation of the parameters of the model as determined by economic theorists. For Keynes (1939, p. 560), '[t]he method is one neither of discovery nor of criticism'. On the other hand, Tinbergen finds possibilities for both criticism (or falsification) and discovery.

Keynes argues that estimation and inference seem valid in the context of a correctly specified (or 'true') model, with 'a correct and indubitably complete analysis of the significant factors' (p. 560). There are therefore no omitted variables that are relevant. Tinbergen (1940, p. 141) replies that it is assumed that the explanatory variables are given, the functional form is known and the errors are uncorrelated with the explanatory variables. He also argues that the importance of additional variables may be 'discovered' after observing the data (p. 142).

2   All the significant factors are meant to be measurable. In attempting to clarify the issues, Keynes questions whether omitted variables and/or measurement errors are important. Keynes (p. 561) argues that there are numerous qualitative variables that cannot be measured and implicitly mentions the role of outliers and influential observations.

3   Concern about spurious correlation and specification of variables in levels or in first differences seems to anticipate the literature on unit roots and cointegration. Of course, whether a particular variable should be included in levels or in first differences can be tested formally. Keynes (1939, p. 563, fn 1) parenthetically notes the role of expectations in terms of the rate of profit. Tinbergen (1940, p. 147) responds that attempts have been made to accommodate expectations by examining past behaviour.

4   Keynes questions the use of linear models, as well as extensions to nonlinear models, by Tinbergen and, in particular, the manipulation to 'make it possible to fit any explanation to any facts' (p. 563). Furthermore, he argues that 'to suppose that all economic

forces are of this character... is ridiculous' (p. 564). It is possible that Keynes was arguing for the examination of alternative (non-nested) functional forms. Tinbergen (1940, p. 148) responds that 'curvilinearity is by no means identical with manipulation *at will* of the coefficients', and presents four arguments in favour of examining linear models 'that reduce their degree of ridiculousness' (p. 148).

5   The formulation of lag structures, time trends, integration of time series data, cointegration analysis and manipulation of data seem to be anticipated by Keynes (1939, p. 565). In what would seem to be reasonable, given knowledge at the time, Tinbergen (1940, pp. 151–2) responds that the inclusion of a time trend is a 'catch-all' (p. 151) and that 'trend-differences' may be useful in capturing differences in time series data. Moreover, Tinbergen (1940, p. 150) argues for the use of goodness-of-fit statistics and economic meaning in the specification of the lag structure.

6   What is the relevance of the estimated model to the future, and what is its role in forecasting and as a 'quantitative guide to the future' (Keynes, 1939, p. 566)? Keynes (p. 567) anticipates tests of structural change and of outliers. Tinbergen (1940) seems to be aware of this and argues that not all changes in structure or the presence of outliers will affect the model significantly, and that 'the change in the relations affected may even, perhaps, be estimated' (p. 152). Tinbergen (1940, p. 154) also mentions the importance of choosing between 'competing "explanations" of actual series representing some economic phenomena', perhaps anticipating competing non-nested model specifications.

In his critical appraisal of Tinbergen's econometric methodology and his use of rudimentary statistical techniques, Keynes outlined a research programme, perhaps unconsciously, which subsequently led to the development of numerous econometric techniques that are now widely used in applied econometrics. Keynes characterized Tinbergen thus:

> he is much more interested in getting on with the job than in spending time in deciding whether the job is worth getting on with.
>
> (1939, p. 559)

> No one could be more frank, more painstaking, more free from subjective bias... than Professor Tinbergen. There is no one, therefore, so far as human qualities go, whom it would be safer to trust with black magic.... So let him continue.
>
> (1940, p. 156)

Such assessments were unnecessarily harsh, given the state of knowledge at the time. Criticism of this kind would, of course, be more appropriate for any researcher now ignoring the developments in econometric techniques and methodology over the last half century.

4   Diagnostic testing

A test that is never used has zero power.

The power of a popular test is irrelevant.

4.1   Rationale

As noted in section 3.1, numerous assumptions are made in the process of model construction. The usefulness and reliability of models depend on the assumptions regarding the balance of a linear regression model (namely, investigation of the order of integration of a single variable or vector of variables, as well as examination of the existence of cointegration), the conditional mean (including the choice of functional form, choice of explanatory variables, consideration of lag structure, serial correlation and alternative non-nested models), the properties of the error term (homoskedasticity, no serial correlation, normality and lack of correlation with the explanatory variables), the stability of the parameters over time (involving no structural change, no outliers and no predictive failure) and the robustness to departures from the assumptions.

Serious problems arise when assumption 1(a) is not satisfied, since OLS will not, in general, yield $\sqrt{T}$–consistent estimators. When the variables in equation (1) are not stationary, there may be a cointegrating relation among some or all of the variables which will be stationary, so that assumption 1(b) may be useful to investigate. A serious problem arises when any one of assumptions 2(a) – 2(g) (excluding 2(e)) is not satisfied, since the OLS estimators of the parameters in (1) will be inconsistent or inefficient or the inferences will not be valid. It is well known that when assumption 2(a) is not satisfied OLS (and other estimators) will, in general, yield inconsistent estimators of the parameters in (1) if the incorrect functional form involves omission of relevant explanatory variables. If assumption 2(b) is not satisfied, OLS will yield inefficient estimators, in general. When assumption 2(c) is violated, consistency of OLS depends on whether a lagged dependent variable is present in (1): only exogenous regressors will yield consistent estimators, whereas the presence of a lagged dependent variable will yield inconsistent estimators, in general.

Of course, the consistency of OLS holds when the model given in (1) is *correctly specified*; i.e. serial correlation arises in the true errors and *not* in the residuals. This point is a common cause of confusion, since serial correlation in the residuals may be symptomatic of much more than serial correlation in the errors (see table 2). Thus, it is surprising to read mis-statements such as those in Friedman (1988, p. 230):

> The low values of the Durbin–Watson statistic for the three equations in table 1 led two referees of an earlier version of this paper to question whether the results would remain valid if allowance were made for the indicated strong serial correlation of residuals. Such serial correlation does not bias the estimated coefficients... [sic!]

Friedman (1988, p. 232) seems to recognize that there may be more than one possible reason for rejecting the null hypothesis of no serial correlation by adding the lagged value of the dependent variable as well as using the Cochrane–Orcutt correction for first-order autoregressive errors. However, no discussion is provided of the numerous other alternatives listed in table 2, or why a first-order autoregressive process is chosen over a higher-order autoregressive process or a first- or higher-order moving average process when quarterly data are used.

Fiebig et al. (1992) evaluate the conditions under which OLS will be inefficient relative to the generalized least squares (GLS) estimator when the errors are heteroskedastic and serially correlated. Moreover, they characterize the properties of the OLS estimator in terms of making incorrect inferences because its covariance matrix is no longer given by the conventionally programmed formula. Although these properties are well understood, there are nevertheless several situations in which OLS may be efficient relative to the GLS estimator (which is a best linear unbiased estimator in this case) and/or the covariance matrix is computed correctly. Four cases are given as follows:

1   OLS is efficient and the conventionally programmed standard errors are correct;

2   OLS is efficient and the conventionally programmed standard errors are incorrect;

3   OLS is inefficient and the conventionally programmed standard errors are correct;

4   OLS is inefficient and the conventionally programmed standard errors are incorrect.

While cases 1 and 4 are analysed extensively in the literature, Fiebig et al. (1992) provide several examples of cases 2 and 3 which are drawn from the econometrics literature, and provide necessary and sufficient conditions for models to fall into cases 1, 2 or 3 by establishing a relationship between the design matrix and the error covariance matrix. Using Kruskal's theorem, one of the several equivalent alternative forms of the necessary and sufficient conditions for OLS to be efficient, Fiebig et al. illustrate the theory with several examples, namely: two-step estimators in models with unobserved anticipated and unanticipated variables; seemingly unrelated regression equations; models with a grouped structure; and analysis of partitioned regressions using singular covariance matrices.

4.2   Testing for unit roots and cointegration

Time series analysis will never be the same again since the Dickey–Fuller (DF) and augmented DF (ADF) tests of unit roots, and the concept of cointegration as well as various methods of estimating and testing for cointegration, were developed (see Campbell and Perron (1991) for a valuable survey of the area). The pth-order ADF statistic, denoted ADF(p), is given by the t ratio of the OLS estimate of β in the ADF regression

$$\Delta Y_t = \alpha + \beta Y_{t-1} + \gamma t + \sum_{i=1}^{p} \delta_i \Delta Y_{t-i} + u_t \tag{2}$$

Since the asymptotic distribution of the t ratio is non-standard, the null hypothesis of a unit root is tested using simulated critical values. In table 1 several reasons are given as to why the null hypothesis of a unit root in the variable Y_t might be rejected. Apart from the obvious reason that the null hypothesis is incorrect in that there is no unit root in Y_t and ignoring the small-sample properties of the ADF test statistic, there are several other reasons for rejecting the null hypothesis. The presence or otherwise of a time trend in (2) affects both the calculated and critical values of the ADF (p) statistic, for given p. The value of p is itself affected by the dynamic structure of the variable Y_t with significant differences possible for the autoregressive and moving average cases. Incorrect transformation of the variable Y_t, such as using logarithms rather than levels, can also affect the outcome of the ADF test. Structural change and/or the presence of outliers in the data can bias the results of the ADF test, and the presence of heteroskedasticity will lead to incorrect inferences, in general.

Although several tests of cointegration are available, the Johansen (1988, 1991) procedure seems to be the most widely used. The Johansen procedure tests for the presence of cointegration and, if cointegration exists, estimates the cointegrating vector (or vectors). Johansen's (1991) likelihood ratio test for cointegrating ranks is an extension of the ADF unit root test to the multivariate case, and assumes deterministic cointegration (namely, linear combinations of the variables are stationary). However, stochastic cointegration (namely, linear combinations of the variables are trend stationary) is excluded. Therefore, the use of Johansen's (1991) procedure may lead to biased results in the presence of trend stationarity. As in the case of testing for a unit root in one variable, the null hypothesis of no cointegration may be rejected through the use of incorrect transformation of data, incorrect dynamics in the vector autoregressive (VAR) process, structural change and/or outliers in the VAR process, incorrect omission of non-stationary variables from the one or more cointegrating relationships, and/or heteroskedasticity in the errors of one or more equations of the VAR process. It is therefore essential to check the auxiliary assumptions of the model before determining the possible cause of rejection of the null.

4.3   Testing the auxiliary assumptions

The auxiliary assumptions used in econometric modelling, and tests of their adequacy, are crucial aspects of modern applied econometrics. Reasons for rejecting the various null hypotheses are listed in table 2. A convenient method of testing the assumptions is to use the variable addition approach (see Pagan, 1984). Writing equation (1) in obvious matrix form as $y = X\beta + u$, suppose that the correct specification is $y = X\beta + W\gamma + u$. Therefore a standard F test of the null hypothesis $\gamma = 0$ is a test of the specification given by $y = X\beta + u$. Pagan and Hall (1983, p. 167) argue that it is not necessary to use W to test the original specification $y = X\beta + u$ since the distribution of the test statistic is not affected by replacing W with, say, $\tilde{W}$. However, the power of the test is affected by the choice of $\tilde{W}$, with power being maximized by the choice of correct W. Since the use of any $\tilde{W}$ that is correlated with W will yield a consistent test (i.e. a test that rejects a false null hypothesis with probability one as T approaches infinity), it follows that it would be an incorrect inference to attribute the cause of the rejection of the null to the specific (and arbitrary) use of $\tilde{W}$ in place of W. Moreover, since W is not known in general, the specific cause of a rejection of the null is also not known. Furthermore, when factors such as incorrect functional form, omitted variables, incorrect transformation of variables (such as the use of logarithms or first differences), incorrect imposition of restrictions, serial correlation and dynamic mis-specification, structural change, predictive failure, existence of outliers and sample selection bias yield different matrices $\tilde{W}$ that are correlated with the correct matrix W, which leads to the model $y = X\beta + u$ being incorrect, it is not possible to decipher from the statistical tests which of the various $\tilde{W}$ matrices has highest power, in general.

Tests of correct functional form are increasingly being used in applied research and are an essential tool in the practice of econometric modelling (see section 5 for several variable addition and Lagrange multiplier tests of functional form, specifically, tests of linear versus log-linear regression models). It is straightforward to relate several tests of the null hypothesis of correct functional form to the discussion of the choice of W

and $\tilde{W}$ given above, depending on the specific or general alternative hypothesis that is being entertained. The specific test used is typically developed with W in mind but, in general, it is $\tilde{W}$ that is being used. However, as stated previously, the use of $\tilde{W}$ instead of W does not affect the distribution under the null hypothesis.

4.3.1   Correct functional form

If the variables that should enter into equation (1) are known, any omission from the known set may be tested straightforwardly, that is, the significance of W would be tested by including it in (1). Lack of knowledge of W leads to the use of $\tilde{W}$, with (1) being rejected if $\tilde{W}$ is statistically significant. Several tests of functional form are discussed in detail in section 5. The RESET tests of section 5.3.3 involve adding powers of the fitted values of the dependent variable under the null model $y = X\beta + u$. These added variables constitute the columns of the matrix $\tilde{W}$ in the absence of knowledge of the correct W. Of the many available tests for functional form, variations of the RESET test are the most powerful in general (see, for example, the Monte Carlo results in Godfrey et al., 1988). However, it is also important to be aware of the limitations of the analyses that are involved in numerical simulations. For example, McAleer and Tse (1992) provide Monte Carlo evidence which shows that the rejection frequencies of RESET can be reduced, sometimes dramatically, in the presence of outliers. It is recommended that joint tests for both outliers and incorrect functional form be used in empirical studies, especially in small samples.

Since RESET tests involve the use of fitted values of the dependent variable raised to a known power, the issue of orders of integration of variables needs to be considered. It is not clear how stationary or non-stationary variables are to be treated after being transformed by known transformations which are nonlinear. Granger and Hallman (1991) provide a useful Monte Carlo analysis of some simple nonlinear transformations, but the results are likely to be specific to the experiments conducted. Moreover, the cointegration literature does not seem to have a satisfactory treatment of nonlinearities, being restricted at present to linear relations between non-stationary variables. Thus, if Y_t, X_t and Z_t in (1) are stationary, and if powers of the fitted values of the dependent variable are also stationary, the standard analysis applies. However, if Y_t and at least one of X_t or Z_t are non-stationary, powers of the fitted values of Y_t are also likely to be non-stationary, so that cointegration analysis becomes relevant. Unfortunately, it is not clear how the orders of integration of Y_t, X_t and Z_t affect the orders of integration of the powers of the fitted values of Y_t.

4.3.2   No serial correlation

Numerous variations of tests of serial correlation are available, depending on the specific alternative entertained (that is, depending on the choice of alternative to maximize the power of the test). Specific alternatives that are frequently used are as follows:

$$u_t = \sum_{j=1}^{p} \rho_j u_{t-j} + \varepsilon_t, \qquad \varepsilon_t \sim \text{IID}(0, \sigma_\varepsilon^2) \tag{3}$$

$$u_t = \sum_{j=1}^{q} \theta_i \varepsilon_{t-i} + \varepsilon_t, \qquad \varepsilon_t \sim \text{IID}(0, \sigma_\varepsilon^2) \tag{4}$$

in which (3) is the autoregressive process of order p ($AR(p)$) and (4) is the invertible moving average process of order q ($MA(q)$). The choice of (3) or (4) is predicated by theory or may be determined on an empirical basis. When $p = 1$ in (3) ($q = 1$ in (4)), the most commonly used test of the null hypothesis $\rho_1 = 0$ ($\theta_1 = 0$) is the Durbin–Watson test. More generally, however, replacing the unknown u_{t-j} and ε_{t-i} in (3) and (4) by appropriate estimates, equation (1) may be tested by the addition of the variables $\hat{u}_{t-j}$, namely

$$Y_t = \beta_0 + \beta_1 X_t + \beta_2 Z_t + \sum_{j=1}^{p} \rho_j \hat{u}_{t-j} + \text{error}_t \tag{5}$$

regardless of whether (3) or (4) is the specified alternative (if $p = q$) for the problem under consideration. Breusch (1978) and Godfrey (1978) show that a Lagrange multiplier test constructed for one error process, say $AR(p)$, may be appropriate for $MA(p)$, a result which extends asymptotically to the likelihood ratio and Wald procedures. In the sense that exclusion of the $AR(p)$ or $MA(q)$ error processes is itself a mis-specification of functional form, the null hypothesis of correct functional form may be rejected owing to the presence of serially correlated errors.

It is also possible, if not likely, that the presence of serial correlation in the residuals (rather than the errors) is due to some form of omitted variables, incorrect functional form, incorrect dynamics and/or incorrect transformation of variables. Alternative specifications of u_t that might be considered are bilinear processes such as

$$u_t = \rho_j \varepsilon_{t-j} Y_{t-j} + \varepsilon_t \tag{6}$$

or nonlinear moving average processes such as

$$u_t = \theta_i \varepsilon_t \varepsilon_{t-1} + \varepsilon_t \tag{7}$$

(see Pagan and Hall (1983) for further details). Since error processes such as (6) and (7) lead to non-zero conditional means for u_t, the tests of $\rho_j = 0$ in (6) and $\theta_i = 0$ in (7) may be calculated, respectively, from the following auxiliary regressions:

$$Y_t = \beta_0 + \beta_1 X_t + \beta_2 Z_t + \rho_j \hat{u}_{t-j} Y_{t-j} + \text{error}_t \tag{8}$$

$$Y_t = \beta_0 + \beta_1 X_t + \beta_2 Z_t + \theta_i \hat{u}_t \hat{u}_{t-i} + \text{error}_t. \tag{9}$$

The use of added variables such as $\hat{u}_{t-j}$ in (5), $\hat{u}_{t-j} Y_{t-j}$ in (8) and $\hat{u}_t \hat{u}_{t-1}$ in (9) are examples of choosing alternative matrices $\tilde{W}$ instead of W.

McKenzie et al. (1993) provide numerous economic explanations for specifying error processes as $AR(p)$ or $MA(q)$, including (i) random measurement errors in dynamic models; (ii) the forecasting period exceeding the sampling period in forecasting equations; (iii) solving certain types of rational expectations models; (iv) using a discrete-time approximation to a continuous-time model; (v) using overlapping data on the dependent variable; (vi) estimating an error correction model for a cointegrating relation; and (vii) general formulations of mis-specified relations.

Interesting special cases of regression equation (1) arise when X_t and Z_t involve lagged values of Y_t and u_t follows the MA(q) process. Writing the stationary AR(p) process for Y_t as (10) and rewriting the MA(q) process as (11), namely

$$Y_t = (\phi_1 B + \cdots + \phi_p B^p)Y_t + u_t \qquad \text{or} \qquad \phi(B)Y_t = u_t \qquad (10)$$

$$Y_t = u_t - (\theta_1 B + \cdots + \phi_q B^q)u_t \qquad \text{or} \qquad Y_t = \theta(B)u_t \qquad (11)$$

provides two specifications that are frequently estimated in practice. In (10) and (11), B is the backward shift operator and the roots of $\phi(B) = 0$ and $\theta(B) = 0$ are outside the unit circle. The most common tests of the adequacy of models such as (10) and (11) are the tests of Box and Pierce (1970) and the modifications of the Box–Pierce test statistic provided by Ljung and Box (1978). A serious problem with the use of the Box–Pierce and Ljung–Box tests is that they lack power! Indeed, the extensive Monte Carlo results of McAleer et al. (1988) and Hall and McAleer (1989) show that the powers of both tests are frequently dominated by other computationally convenient tests, so that they would seem to have little in their favour for practical purposes. The use of such tests with low power relies almost entirely on their simplicity and computational convenience, which invites the second observation given at the beginning of section 4.

4.3.3   Exogeneity

The assumption that the explanatory variables are uncorrelated with the equation errors is violated when there are endogenous explanatory variables, measurement errors, serial correlation together with lagged dependent variables, and sample selection bias. When it is unclear whether the explanatory variables in a linear regression equation are correlated with the equation errors, a Durbin (1954)–Wu (1973)–Hausman (1978) test of exogeneity may be used. The original test relied on the difference between an efficient estimator under the null hypothesis of exogeneity and a consistent estimator under the alternative hypothesis of lack of exogeneity. A convenient method of computing the test statistic is to add to the null model $y = X\beta + u$ a matrix of fitted values of the (potentially) endogenous variables from a regression of the columns of X on the columns of M, a matrix of instrumental variables. Since the asymptotic equivalence of the original test statistic and its variable addition counterpart relies on a set of auxiliary assumptions such as lack of serial correlation, no heteroskedasticity and correct functional form, violations of these assumptions will obviously affect the properties of the test statistic.

4.3.4   Parameter constancy

A common assumption in analysing equation (1) is that the regression parameters and the variance of the error term are constant. Such an assumption will be violated when there is structural change, predictive failure, outliers, heteroskedasticity or varying co-efficients. It is possible for the regression parameters to vary (or shift) discretely at given points in time or to vary stochastically over time. Pagan and Hall (1983, p. 173) argue that, since random coefficients lead to heteroskedasticity, it is useful to examine the connection between heteroskedasticity and regression coefficients which vary randomly around a constant mean. In the case of parameters which shift at specified points in time, it is possible to establish the relations between tests of structural change, predictive failure and outliers, as well as a test of a specific type of heteroskedasticity.

McAleer and Tse (1988) show that a test for outliers based on externally studentized residuals is related to a test of predictive failure, and they develop the relationships between tests of outliers, a correlated mean shift and an intercept shift. They also show the independence of a sequential testing procedure for outliers and structural change, which enables the overall size of the joint test for outliers and structural change to be determined exactly. In standard notation, the linear regression model is given by

$$y_t = X_i\beta_i + u_i \qquad (i = 1, 2)$$

in which y_i is $T_i \times 1$, X_i is a $T_i \times k$ matrix of observations on k non-stochastic regressors, β_i is $k \times 1$ and u_i is $T_i \times 1$. The total number of observations available is $T = T_1 + T_2$, where $T_1 > k$ but T_2 is not restricted. It is assumed that $u_i \sim D(0, \sigma_u^2 I_{T_i})$, in which I_{T_i} is the identity matrix of order T_i, so that the errors have constant variances throughout the analysis. It is also assumed that u_1 and u_2 are uncorrelated. The elements of the matrix of regressors are assumed to be uniformly bounded with $T^{-1}(X'X)$ tending to a finite non-singular matrix, where $X' = (X_1' : X_2')$. For purposes of considering a shift in the intercept, the model must contain an intercept term.

The following formulation permits several tests of parametric restrictions, namely

$$\begin{bmatrix} y_1 \\ y_2 \end{bmatrix} = \begin{bmatrix} X_1 & 0 \\ X_2 & I_{T_2} \end{bmatrix} \begin{bmatrix} \beta_1 \\ \delta \end{bmatrix} + \begin{bmatrix} u_1 \\ u_2 \end{bmatrix} \qquad (12)$$

in which δ is $T_2 \times 1$. A test of $\delta = 0$ in (12) is equivalent to testing $\beta_1 - \beta_2$. In (12), the observations are ordered such that the first T_1 are used for estimation and the second T_2 for prediction. When $T_2 > k$, the test of $\delta = 0$ is known as the Chow (1960) test of structural change, or more properly as Chow's first test. However, when T_2 is not restricted, a test of $\delta = 0$ is a test of predictive failure, or Chow's second test. When the mean of the dependent variable is shifted for one or more observations, a related procedure is to test for outliers. If the data have been re-ordered so that the set of observations given by T_2 are possible outliers, a test of $\delta = 0$ is a test of outliers using the mean-shift model. When $T_2 = 1$, a test of $\delta = 0$ is equivalent to a test of outliers based on externally studentized residuals.

When $T_2 > k$, a restricted version of (12) is given by

$$\begin{bmatrix} y_1 \\ y_2 \end{bmatrix} = \begin{bmatrix} X_1 & 0 \\ X_2 & X_2 \end{bmatrix} \begin{bmatrix} \beta_1 \\ \gamma \end{bmatrix} + \begin{bmatrix} u_1 \\ u_2 \end{bmatrix} \qquad (13)$$

in which $\delta = X_2\gamma$ involves $T_2 - k$ restrictions and $\gamma = \beta_2 - \beta_1$. Equation (13) is a reparameterization of

$$\begin{bmatrix} y_1 \\ y_2 \end{bmatrix} = \begin{bmatrix} X_1 & 0 \\ 0 & X_2 \end{bmatrix} \begin{bmatrix} \beta_1 \\ \beta_2 \end{bmatrix} + \begin{bmatrix} u_1 \\ u_2 \end{bmatrix}$$

in which two regression models are estimated separately over two different sample periods. A test of $\gamma = 0$ in (13) is equivalent to a test of $\beta_1 = \beta_2$, namely a test of no structural change. The restriction $\delta = X_2\gamma$ is a correlated mean shift as a function of X_2, rejection of which indicates there are T_2 outliers in the data. Under the assumption of normality of u_1 and u_2, a test of $\delta = X_2\gamma$ is equivalent to the variance ratio test of equality of the error variances against the alternative that the variance of the T_2 observations exceeds that of the T_1 observations. McAleer and Tse (1988, p. 107) note that the algebraic equivalence of the two tests means 'a joint test for outliers and constancy of variances cannot be performed'.

Imposing the $k - 1$ restrictions $X_2\gamma = \alpha i$ on (13), in which i is a $T_2 \times 1$ vector of ones and α is a scalar, leads to

$$\begin{bmatrix} y_1 \\ y_2 \end{bmatrix} = \begin{bmatrix} X_1 & 0 \\ X_2 & i \end{bmatrix} \begin{bmatrix} \beta_1 \\ \alpha \end{bmatrix} + \begin{bmatrix} u_1 \\ u_2 \end{bmatrix} \tag{14}$$

Equation (14) denotes a shift in the intercept. Rejection of $\delta = X_2\gamma = \alpha i$ indicates that there are T_2 outliers present in the data. A test of the single restriction $\alpha = 0$ in (14) leads to the restricted model in which $\beta = \beta_1 = \beta_2$, namely

$$\begin{bmatrix} y_1 \\ y_2 \end{bmatrix} = \begin{bmatrix} X_1 \\ X_2 \end{bmatrix} \beta + \begin{bmatrix} u_1 \\ u_2 \end{bmatrix} \tag{15}$$

for which there is no structural change in the regression parameters and no outliers in the data.

Each of the tests of $\delta = 0$ in (12), $\gamma = 0$ in (13) and $\alpha = 0$ in (14), namely a test of outliers or predictive failure, the analysis of covariance test and a test for an intercept shift, is a computationally straightforward variable addition test. However, the Monte Carlo results of McAleer and Tse (1992) on the robustness of a test of outliers based on the maximum absolute internally studentized residual to functional form mis-specification are worth noting. The assumption of correct functional form is found to be important in accurately detecting outliers. In particular, observations can be incorrectly 'detected' as outliers, sometimes in large proportions, in the presence of functional form mis-specification. Therefore the test of outliers is not robust to mis-specification of the mean of the dependent variable.

In the context of the test procedures discussed above, the Monte Carlo results of Burke et al. (1992) merit attention. Apart from developing modifications of Utt's (1982) 'rainbow' test of general forms of functional form mis-specification, the authors also report the results of Monte Carlo experiments involving the re-ordering of data by leverage values. Application of Chow's first (or analysis of covariance) test, given in (13) above, to the unordered data yields accurate empirical sizes but much lower estimates of power than when the data are re-ordered. Burke et al. (1992, p. 243) argue that, for stationary processes, an absence of re-ordering can lead to inconsistency of the analysis of covariance test in the presence of functional form mis-specification. This may explain the reported low power of Chow's first test against general forms of mis-specification in moderately large samples. The authors also extend the theoretical analysis to cover the effects of using alternative re-ordering schemes not based upon leverage values.

4.3.5   Non-nested models

Tests of functional form mis-specification, serial correlation, exogeneity and parameter constancy seek an appropriate matrix W to maximize the power of the test of the null hypothesis. It is possible, however, that the use of such diagnostic tests will not lead to the rejection of the null because the alternative is not highly correlated with the particular $\hat{W}$ used in the formulation of the test. Non-nested models may arise through the use of an incorrect model, incorrect imposition of restrictions, incorrect dynamic structure or incorrect transformation of variables. Examples of non-nested models are as follows. The use of simple hypotheses, such as testing the simple null $\beta_1 = 0$ in equation (1) against the simple alternative $\beta_1 = 0.5$, leads to a pair of non-nested hypotheses. Competing linear regression models, where the variables in one model cannot be expressed as a linear combination of the variables in the other, provide a common illustration of two non-nested econometric models. The most common method of obtaining non-nested regression models, however, is through the use of non-nested restrictions. An example already encountered is the AR(p) and MA(q) error processes, given in (3) and (4). Although both processes are special cases of the ARMA(p, q), or autoregressive moving average process of order (p, q), they are not special cases of each other through the imposition of restrictions. Both the linear and log-linear regression models, to be examined in detail in section 5, are non-nested, although they are both nested within the more general model of Box and Cox (1964). The linear and Cobb–Douglas production functions are special cases of the constant elasticity of substitution production function, but are themselves non-nested. If the Cobb–Douglas model has multiplicative rather than additive errors, transformation by natural logarithms yields the log-linear regression model. Finally, a different example of non-nested models arises in the case of non-nested probability distributions, such as two- and three-parameter log-normal, gamma and Weibull distributions (for further details, see Bai et al., 1992). Many other examples are listed in McAleer and Pesaran (1986, section 2).

McAleer (1992b) surveys 116 published empirical non-nested papers since Cox (1961, 1962) introduced statistical procedures for testing non-nested (or separate) families of hypotheses. For earlier general surveys, see McAleer and Pesaran (1986) and McAleer (1987). Pesaran (1974) introduced the first procedures for testing a pair of non-nested linear regression models against each other. Numerous techniques have since been developed for testing linear, log-linear, nonlinear and probabilistic discrete choice models against one or more non-nested alternatives. Cox's original ideas have been applied directly to testing a pair of non-nested nonlinear regression models by Pesaran and Deaton (1978), to linear versus log-linear regression models by Aneuryn-Evans and Deaton (1980) and to more than one non-nested alternative by Sawyer (1984). The evidence presented in McAleer (1992b) is that over 90 per cent of published empirical non-nested research uses regression models, namely linear, log-linear, nonlinear and pure time series models, with a substantial majority of these being non-nested linear and log-linear regression models. Moreover, 45 per cent of these published papers examine only paired non-nested models, and 80 per cent of papers with multiple non-nested alternatives use paired tests, namely procedures designed for testing a null model against only a single non-nested alternative.

Given its vintage, the Cox procedure has not been used as frequently as several computationally more straightforward tests. On the basis of Monte Carlo experiments, the small sample type one error properties of the Cox test are not especially good, with the test having a penchant for over-rejecting (sometimes substantially) a true null hypothesis. Although the mean- and variance-adjusted Cox test of Godfrey and Pesaran (1983) has led to improvements in its small sample properties, the adjusted Cox test has seldom been used. For this reason, the brief presentation below concentrates on paired and joint tests of a null linear regression model against paired and multiple alternatives using unadjusted Cox-type tests.

The problem involves $m + 1$ competing non-nested linear regression models which take the form

$$H_0: \; y = X\beta + u_0 \qquad u_0 \sim N(0, \sigma_0^2 I)$$
$$H_i: \; y = Z_i\gamma_i + u_i \qquad u_i \sim N(0, \sigma_0^2 I), \; i = 1, 2, \ldots, m$$

where y is a $T \times 1$ vector of T observations on the dependent variable; $X(Z_i)$ is a $T \times k_0 (T \times k_i)$ matrix of non-stochastic regressors; $\beta(\gamma_i)$ is a $k_0 \times 1$ ($k_i \times 1$) vector of unknown parameters; and u_0 and u_i are $T \times 1$ vectors of disturbance terms. It is assumed that the matrices $T^{-1}X'X$ and $T^{-1}Z_i'Z_i$ converge to well-defined finite positive definite limits; and $T^{-1}X'Z_i$ and $T^{-1}Z_i'Z_j$ ($i \neq j$; $i, j = 1, 2, \ldots, m$) converge to non-zero limits. Relaxation of the conditions for lagged dependent variables is given in White (1982), as well as in the time series literature by McAleer et al. (1988), but relaxation of the conditions to accommodate non-stationary variables would appear to be more difficult. In analysing the asymptotic distributions of some tests, it is also necessary to assume that X, Z_i and Z_j are not orthogonal to each other.

Pesaran (1987) defines the concepts of global and partial non-nested hypotheses based upon the Kullback–Leibler information criterion. Less formally, however, any two linear regression models are assumed to be non-nested in that at least one column of each regressor matrix cannot be expressed as a linear combination of the columns of the others. Since the selection of the null hypothesis is arbitrary, H_0 can be designated as the null and H_i ($i = 1, 2, \ldots, m$) as the m alternative models. A *joint* test is a test of H_0 against the multiple alternatives $H_1, \ldots, H_m$, whereas a *paired* test of H_0 involves only the single alternative H_i (for *any* $i = 1, 2, \ldots, m$).

Dastoor and McAleer (1989) have proposed four possible classifications of tests for competing linear regression models, based on the general auxiliary regression model

$$y = X\delta_0 + Q\delta + u.$$

The augmented matrix $[X : Q]$ is assumed to have full column rank, and the rank of Q, $r(Q)$, equals the number of elements in δ. By an appropriate definition of Q, the following four classes of test statistics may be generated:

(a)   for $m = 1$, a paired (Cox-type) J test of Davidson and MacKinnon (1981), where $Q = Z_1\hat{\gamma}_1, \hat{\gamma}_1 = (Z_1'Z_1)^{-1}Z_1'y$ and $r(Z_1\hat{\gamma}_1)$, and a paired (Cox-type) JA test of Fisher and McAleer (1981), where $Q = Z_1\hat{\gamma}_{10}$, $\hat{\gamma}_{10} = (Z_1'Z_1)^{-1}Z_1'X(X'X)^{-1} X'y$ and $r(Z_1\hat{\gamma}_{10}) = 1$;

(b)   for $m = 1$, a paired F test of Deaton (1982), Dastoor (1983), Gourieroux et al. (1983), Mizon and Richard (1986) (based on encompassing) and McAleer and Pesaran (1986) (based on Roy's (1953) union-intersection principle), where $Q = \overline{Z}_1, \overline{Z}_1$ contains the $k_1 - p$ linearly independent columns of Z_1 that are also linearly independent of the columns of X (i.e. X and Z_1 have p linearly dependent columns) and $r(\overline{Z}_1) = k_1 - p$;

(c)   a joint (Cox-type) J test of Davidson and MacKinnon (1981), where $Q = \hat{G}, \hat{G}$ is the $T \times m$ matrix with ith column $Z_i\hat{\gamma}_i = Z_i(Z_i'Z_i)^{-1}Z_i'y$ $(i = 1, 2, \ldots, m)$ and $r(\hat{G}) = m$, and a joint (Cox-type) JA test of McAleer (1983), where $Q = \hat{H}, \hat{H}$ is the $T \times m$ matrix with ith column $Z_i\hat{\gamma}_{10} = Z_i(Z_i'Z_i)^{-1}Z_i'X(X'X)^{-1}y$ $(i = 1, 2, \ldots, m)$ and $r(\hat{H}) = m$; and

(d)   a joint F test of Dastoor and McAleer (1987) based on any or all of the approaches in (b) above, where $Q = \overline{Z}, \overline{Z}$ contains the k_* linearly independent columns of $Z = [Z_1 : Z_2 : \ldots : Z_m]$ that are also linearly independent of the columns of X, and $r(\overline{Z}) = k_*$.

The paired and joint J tests are asymptotically distributed as χ^2 under H_0 with 1 and m degrees of freedom, respectively. Although the JA test is asymptotically equivalent to the J test under the null and under local alternative hypotheses, when the regressors are non-stochastic the paired and joint JA tests are exactly distributed as $t(T - k_0 - 1)$ and $t(T - k_0 - m)$ under the null, respectively. The paired and joint F tests are exactly distributed as $F(k_1 - p, T - k_0 - k_1 + p)$ and $F(k_*, T - k_0 - k_*)$ under the null, respectively, when the regressors are non-stochastic, and are asymptotically distributed as χ^2 under H_0 with $k_1 - p$ and k_* degrees of freedom, respectively.

Dastoor and McAleer (1989) show that a ranking of the F and Cox-type paired or joint tests of the null hypothesis $\delta = 0$ in the auxiliary regression equation on the basis of asymptotic local power depends on the choice of a local hypothesis. When a local null hypothesis or a local alternative hypothesis for multiple alternatives is used, it is not possible to rank the various tests. However, when a local alternative hypothesis for a single alternative is used, it can be shown that the relative ranking of asymptotic local power is the paired Cox-type test followed by the joint Cox-type test, with the paired and joint F tests equally and least powerful. However, Mizon and Richard (1986) and Dastoor and McAleer (1987) have demonstrated that the paired and joint F tests, respectively, are more widely consistent than their counterpart Cox-type tests. The Monte Carlo results available in the literature suggest that the Cox and J tests have very poor empirical type one error probabilities (or sizes) in finite samples, whereas the F and JA tests have accurate empirical sizes. However, the F and JA tests can have lower finite sample powers than the Cox and J tests when the null is false.

When the linear regression model is given by equation (1) and the two non-nested error processes are given as AR(p) in (3) and MA(q) in (4), King and McAleer (1987) investigated the finite sample performance of the Cox and related tests, as well as point optimal tests. Their Monte Carlo experiments supported previous results in that the Cox test had very poor empirical sizes. McKenzie et al. (1993) developed several tests based on the Cox, F and Cox-type test procedures, and reported Monte Carlo results which conform with previously published results regarding their respective finite sample performance.

4.3.6   Robustness/lack of sensitivity

There are too many diagnostics. One is too many as far as I am concerned.

(Leamer, 1988, p. 332)

The robustness (or lack of sensitivity) of empirical results to changes in the assumptions is an important aspect of applied econometric research. As listed in table 2, inferences may be altered (or even reversed) through the imposition of incorrect prior restrictions, use of influential observations and fragile assumptions, the presence of structural change and predictive failure, incorporation of outliers in the sample, choice of sample period and/or an inefficient method of estimation.

In the context of imposing incorrect prior restrictions regarding the specification of the explanatory variables in a linear regression model, Leamer (1983) attempts to prescribe a solution to such specification uncertainty on the estimated parameters. Leamer's extreme bounds analysis (EBA) partitions the explanatory variables into a set of 'free' variables whose coefficients are not restricted but are always estimated from the regression model and a set of 'doubtful' variables whose coefficients are assigned particular values through linear restrictions. The primary purpose of the analysis is to estimate the effects of one or more 'focus' variables, whose coefficients are given in the form $\beta_{FO} = \Psi'\beta$, which involves a linear combination of the elements of the full parameter vector β. Extreme bounds of β_{FO} refer to the largest and smallest values of the estimated $\hat{\beta}_{FO} = \Psi'\hat{\beta}$, where $\hat{\beta}$ is the restricted least squares estimate of β consistent with the doubtful aspect of the specification, namely the different implications of the linear restrictions. Thus, EBA is intended to analyse the sensitivity (or fragility) of estimates of β_{FO} to alternative model specifications as defined by the restrictions. Since the bounds depend on the prior information, the finding of 'wide' bounds may be interpreted as the existence of fragile inferences, the linear restrictions being incorrect (such as doubtful variables having been inappropriately excluded from the model) or inappropriate linear combinations of the doubtful coefficients having been imposed on the model. In what follows, it is assumed that the other possible reasons for lack of robustness (such as structural change) are not present.

In the linear regression model $y = X\beta + u, u \sim N(0, \sigma_u^2 I)$, subject to the q linear restrictions (or prior information) $R\beta = r$, the matrix R selects those elements of β that are doubtful and r is the vector of prior means. For purposes of the exercise, the focus coefficient is free, $R = (I : 0)$ and $r = 0$ so that the prior mean of $R\beta$ is zero. Extreme bounds are required for $\beta_{FO} = \Psi'\beta$. Let $V = \sigma^2\overline{V}$ represent the covariance matrix of $\tilde{b} = (X'X)^{-1}X'y$, the unrestricted least squares estimate of β. Finally, let D and F denote doubtful and free indices, so that $X\beta$ may be expressed as $X\beta = X_D\beta_D + X_F\beta_F$.

Theorem 3 of Leamer (1981, p. 13) gives the extreme bounds of β_{FO}, when σ^2 is known, as

$$\Psi'\tilde{b} - \frac{1}{2}\Psi'VR'(RVR')^{-1}R\tilde{b} \pm \frac{1}{2}(\Psi'VR'(RVR')^{-1}RV\Psi)^{\frac{1}{2}}(\chi_D^2)^{\frac{1}{2}} \tag{16}$$

in which χ_D^2 is the χ^2 statistic for testing the prior restrictions on the doubtful coefficients. Defining

$$V = \sigma^2\overline{V} = \sigma^2 \begin{bmatrix} \overline{V}_{DD} & \overline{V}_{DF} \\ \overline{V}_{FD} & \overline{V}_{FF} \end{bmatrix} = \sigma^2 \begin{bmatrix} X'_D X_D & X'_D X_F \\ X'_F X_D & X'_F X_F \end{bmatrix}^{-1} \tag{17}$$

it is then straightforward to show that $VR'(RVR')^{-1}R\tilde{b}$ and $VR'(RVR')^{-1}RV$ in equation (16) can be written as

$$\overline{V}R'(R\overline{V}R')^{-1}R\tilde{b} = \begin{bmatrix} \tilde{b}_{\mathrm{D}} \\ \overline{V}_{\mathrm{FD}}\overline{V}_{\mathrm{DD}}^{-1}\tilde{b}_{\mathrm{D}} \end{bmatrix} \tag{18}$$

and

$$\sigma^2\overline{V}R'(R\overline{V}R')^{-1}R\overline{V} = \sigma^2 \begin{bmatrix} \overline{V}_{\mathrm{DD}} & \overline{V}_{\mathrm{DF}} \\ \overline{V}_{\mathrm{FD}} & \overline{V}_{\mathrm{FD}}\overline{V}_{\mathrm{DD}}^{-1}\overline{V}_{\mathrm{DF}} \end{bmatrix}. \tag{19}$$

From the definition of V in equation (17) and standard matrix inversion results, it follows that

$$\overline{V}_{\mathrm{FD}}\overline{V}_{\mathrm{DD}}^{-1}\overline{V}_{\mathrm{DF}} = \overline{V}_{\mathrm{FF}} - (X_\mathrm{F}'X_\mathrm{F})^{-1}. \tag{20}$$

Pre-multiplication of both sides of equations (19) and (20) by Ψ' and $\sigma^2\Psi'$, and post-multiplication by Ψ and $\overline{\Psi}$, respectively, where $\Psi' = (0', \overline{\Psi}')$ and $\overline{\Psi}$ is the sub-vector of Ψ obtained by deleting the zero elements corresponding to the doubtful coefficients, yields

$$\sigma^2\Psi'\overline{V}R'(R\overline{V}R')^{-1}R\overline{V}\Psi = \sigma^2\overline{\Psi}'\overline{V}_{\mathrm{FD}}\overline{V}_{\mathrm{DD}}^{-1}\overline{V}_{\mathrm{DF}}\overline{\Psi}$$
$$= \sigma^2\overline{\Psi}'\overline{V}_{\mathrm{FF}}\overline{\Psi} - \sigma^2\overline{\Psi}'(X_\mathrm{F}'X_\mathrm{F})^{-1}\overline{\Psi}. \tag{21}$$

Since $\sigma^2\overline{V}_{\mathrm{FF}}$ and $\sigma^2(X_\mathrm{F}'X_\mathrm{F})^{-1}$ are, respectively, the covariance matrices of the unrestricted and restricted estimates of the free coefficients, equation (21) may also be written as

$$\Psi'\overline{V}R'(R\overline{V}R')^{-1}R\overline{V}\Psi = \mathrm{var}(\tilde{b}_{\mathrm{FO}})\mathrm{var}(\hat{b}_{\mathrm{FO}}). \tag{22}$$

Turning to equation (18), the vectors Ψ and $\overline{\Psi}$ will select an element of $\overline{V}_{\mathrm{FD}}\overline{V}_{\mathrm{DD}}^{-1}\tilde{b}_{\mathrm{D}}$. A standard partitioned inverse result is that $\overline{V}_{\mathrm{FD}} = -(X_\mathrm{F}'X_\mathrm{F})^{-1}X_\mathrm{F}'X_\mathrm{D}\overline{V}_{\mathrm{DD}}$, so that

$$\overline{V}_{\mathrm{FD}}\overline{V}_{\mathrm{DD}}^{-1}\tilde{b}_{\mathrm{D}} = -(X_\mathrm{F}'X_\mathrm{F})^{-1}X_\mathrm{F}'X_\mathrm{D}\tilde{b}_{\mathrm{D}}. \tag{23}$$

The restricted estimate of β_F is given as

$$\hat{b}_\mathrm{F} = (X_\mathrm{F}'X_\mathrm{F})^{-1}X_\mathrm{F}'y = \tilde{b}_\mathrm{F} + (X_\mathrm{F}'X_\mathrm{F})^{-1}X_\mathrm{F}'X_\mathrm{D}\tilde{b}_{\mathrm{D}}. \tag{24}$$

Using equations (23) and (24) leads to

$$\tilde{b}_\mathrm{F} - \hat{b}_\mathrm{F} = (X_\mathrm{F}'X_\mathrm{F})^{-1}X_\mathrm{F}'X_\mathrm{D}\tilde{b}_{\mathrm{D}} = \overline{V}_{\mathrm{FD}}\overline{V}_{\mathrm{DD}}^{-1}\tilde{b}_{\mathrm{D}}. \tag{25}$$

Substituting equation (25) into (18) and pre-multiplying by Ψ' yields

$$\Psi VR'(RVR')^{-1}R\tilde{b} = \Psi'\overline{V}R'(R\overline{V}R')^{-1}R\tilde{b} = \overline{\Psi}'(\tilde{b}_\mathrm{F} - \hat{b}_\mathrm{F}) = \tilde{b}_{\mathrm{FO}} - \hat{b}_{\mathrm{FO}}. \tag{26}$$

Substitution of equations (22) and (26) into (16) gives

$$\tilde{b}_{\mathrm{FO}} - \frac{1}{2}(\tilde{b}_{\mathrm{FO}} - \hat{b}_{\mathrm{FO}}) \pm \frac{1}{2}[\mathrm{var}(\tilde{b}_{\mathrm{FO}}) - \mathrm{var}(\hat{b}_{\mathrm{FO}})]^{\frac{1}{2}}(\chi_\mathrm{D}^2)^{\frac{1}{2}}$$
$$= \frac{1}{2}(\tilde{b}_{\mathrm{FO}} + \hat{b}_{\mathrm{FO}}) \pm \frac{1}{2}\left\{\left[\mathrm{var}(\tilde{b}_{\mathrm{FO}}) - \mathrm{var}(\hat{b}_{\mathrm{FO}})\right]^{\frac{1}{2}}\chi_\mathrm{D}^2\right\}^{\frac{1}{2}} \tag{27}$$

which are extreme bounds for β_{FO} in the model $y = X\beta + u$. In equation (27), $\frac{1}{2}(\tilde{b}_{FO} + \hat{b}_{FO})$ is the mean of the unrestricted and restricted estimates of β_{FO}, $\text{var}(\tilde{b}_{FO}) - \text{var}(\hat{b}_{FO})$ is the gain in efficiency in imposing the restrictions, and χ_D^2 is the χ^2 statistic for testing the prior restrictions $R\beta - r = 0$ on the doubtful coefficients. Since the extreme bounds are directly related to output from standard regression analysis, it should be clear that EBA provides no information beyond what is already used in applied econometric analysis.

McAleer et al. (1985) present two propositions regarding EBA for cases where the focus variable is doubtful or free. Proposition 1 is concerned with type A fragility (or sampling uncertainty), which is measured as k (a predetermined constant) multiplied by the estimated standard error of the focus coefficient. When the focus variable is doubtful (free), the necessary and sufficient (necessary) condition for type A fragility is that χ_D^2, the χ^2 statistic for the doubtful coefficients to equal their prior means, exceeds k^2. Thus, type A fragility depends on χ_D^2 and the choice of the value of k: for a given k, a larger value of χ_D^2 (indicating that the doubtful coefficients are significant) leads EBA to suggest that inferences are fragile; for a given value of χ_D^2 (which may or may not be significant), a lower value of k would again lead EBA to suggest fragility!

The condition for type B fragility, which arises if there is a change in sign implicit in the bounds for the focus coefficient, is given in proposition 2. When the focus variable is doubtful (free), the necessary and sufficient (necessary) condition for type B fragility to exist is that $\chi_D^2 > \chi_{FO}^2$ where χ_{FO}^2 is the χ^2 statistic for the focus coefficient to equal zero. Thus, type B fragility depends on χ_D^2 and χ_{FO}^2: when the focus coefficient is doubtful, $\chi_D^2 > \chi_{FO}^2$, and so there will always be a sign change for the focus coefficient. In view of such an artificial conclusion regarding fragility, McAleer et al. (1985, p. 296) argue that 'EBA is just an inefficient (and incomplete) way of communicating to readers the fact that the doubtful variables are needed to explain the data...'.

More importantly, however, from the viewpoint of sensible data analysis and econometric modelling, is that several published papers listed in McAleer et al. (1985) which use Leamer's EBA do not provide any other evidence of the usefulness of their estimated models. Although the absence of any diagnostics from virtually all applications of EBA is consistent with Leamer's (1988, p. 332) 'one is too many' predilection for *not* reporting diagnostic tests, it is somewhat worrying in view of the interpretations of fragility given by its exponents. Thus, any inferences regarding fragility which ignore functional form mis-specification and other departures from the standard conditions should be seriously called into question.

In spite of the demonstrated limitations of EBA, it continues to be used uncritically. For example, Levine and Renelt (1992) use a variant of EBA to examine the robustness between long-run growth rates and a selection of economic policy, political and institutional indicators. Treating the focus variable as free throughout their analysis, many existing empirical results are reported as being fragile in that the extreme bounds are statistically significant and of the same sign. However, since the only summary statistic reported is the coefficient of determination, and no diagnostic tests whatsoever are reported, it is hard not to withhold judgement regarding the statistical 'significance' of the extreme bounds or of *any* OLS estimates of the regression parameters. Moreover, the bounds themselves are random variables, and so their standard errors may provide an indication of their reliability. Since the analytical calculation of the standard errors is very difficult, McAleer and Veall (1989) use the bootstrap technique to calculate the standard errors. For the specific empirical example regarding the deterrent effect of capital punishment used in Leamer (1983), McAleer and Veall (1989, p. 106) show 'that the bootstrap estimates of the standard errors of the extreme bounds are sometimes large enough to cast serious doubts on the usefulness of the bounds'.

4.3.7   No heteroskedasticity

When the variance of the error term in equation (1) is not constant, OLS generally yields inefficient estimates and conventionally programmed standard errors which are incorrect. In testing the null hypothesis of homoskedasticity, rejection may be due to one of a number of factors such as the presence of additive or multiplicative heteroskedasticity, omitted variables and/or incorrect functional form, incorrect transformation of variables (such as an inappropriate use of weighted least squares and/or a failure to use the grouping-heteroskedasticity adjustment), the presence of varying coefficients, incorrect dynamics, bilinear models, structural change, predictive failure, outliers and non-normal errors. Several of these factors may be interrelated, such as use of an incorrect conditional mean of the dependent variable or the use of the Box–Cox transformation to adjust for heteroskedastic errors given normality, or to adjust for non-normality given homoskedastic errors.

Insightful analyses of testing for heteroskedasticity via augmenting the conditional variances are given in Pagan and Hall (1983) and Pagan (1984). For example, it is argued in Pagan and Hall (1983, p. 168) that the RESET procedure for detecting functional form mis-specification and White's (1980b) test for heteroskedasticity will lead, in many practical cases, to similar conclusions because mis-specification often leads to significant evidence of heteroskedasticity. White's (1980b) procedure involves regressing the squared OLS residuals from the estimation of the null model on the cross-products of the regressors, and investigating whether or not the R^2 statistic so obtained differs significantly from zero. The suggestion given by White (1980b, p. 825) is that the sample size T multiplied by this R^2 value should be compared with a selected critical value of the χ^2 distribution with degrees of freedom equal to the number of linearly independent non-constant terms in the auxiliary regression. In this form, the test for heteroskedasticity can be thought of as a 'studentized' Lagrange multiplier procedure of the type discussed by Koenker (1981) which does not depend on normality of the errors.

Pagan (1984, p. 115) views departures from heteroskedasticity as augmenting a constant conditional variance with some variable (or variables), say W_t. The alternative hypothesis of heteroskedasticity becomes

$$\sigma_t^2 = \sigma_u^2 + \gamma W_t \tag{28}$$

for $t = 1, 2, \ldots, T$, with the null hypothesis of heteroskedasticity equivalent to $\gamma = 0$. Rewriting equation (28) with OLS estimates $\hat{u}_t^2$ replacing the unknown σ_t^2 yields

$$\hat{u}_t^2 = \sigma_u^2 + \gamma W_t + \text{error}_t \tag{29}$$

where $\text{error}_t = \hat{u}_t^2 - \sigma_t^2$. An asymptotic t test of $\gamma = 0$ (or an asymptotic F test in the case of more than one explanatory variable) is valid for testing homoskedasticity, even in the presence of lagged dependent variables in the regression equation. Since W_t is unknown, in general, replacing W_t in (29) with $\tilde{W}_t$ yields the auxiliary equation used to test the null hypothesis $\gamma = 0$, namely

$$\hat{u}_t^2 = \sigma_u^2 + \gamma \tilde{W}_t + \text{error}_t$$

where $\text{error}_t = \hat{u}_t^2 - \sigma_t^2 + \gamma(W_t - \tilde{W}_t)$.

Different tests are based on different variables $\tilde{W}_t$, or unspecified continuous functions of $\tilde{W}_t$ with first and second derivatives. Pagan (1984, pp. 116–18) provides several examples of the use of different variables $\tilde{W}_t$:

(a) an indicator variable for a structural break at a known point m in the sample (i.e. $\tilde{W}_t = 1$ for $t = 1, \dots, m$ and $\tilde{W}_t = 0$ for $t = m + 1, \dots, T$), which is asymptotically equivalent to the Goldfeld–Quandt test (see Pagan and Hall, 1983);

(b) use of various powers of $\hat{Y}_t$, the OLS fitted values of Y_t under the null hypothesis of homoskedasticity (e.g. the test for heteroskedasticity given in Pesaran and Pesaran's (1991) Microfit 3.0 uses $\tilde{W}_t = \hat{Y}_t^2$);

(c) evolving forms of heteroskedasticity could use a time trend or a time trend multiplied by the regressors in equation (1);

(d) White's (1980b) suggestion of setting $\tilde{W}_t$ to be the cross-products of the regressors (although the Monte Carlo results of Godfrey et al. (1988) suggest that White's test has very low power);

(e) Engle's (1982) autoregressive conditional heteroskedasticity (ARCH), in which the conditional variance is related to the size of past errors (although a multitude of generalizations of ARCH now exists, a simple version would set $\tilde{W}_t$ to $\hat{u}_{t-1}^2$ which is, in effect, a test of an AR(1) process in the squared residuals). For a useful survey of ARCH models, see Bera and Higgins (1993).

An interesting test of heteroskedasticity, which does not fit neatly into the format outlined above, is that of Glejser (1969). The test is based on the auxiliary regression

$$|\hat{u}_t| = \sigma_u^2 + \gamma \tilde{W}_t + \text{error}_t \tag{30}$$

with $\tilde{W}_t$ being chosen as the level, square root, reciprocal or reciprocal square root of one of the explanatory variables in the original equation (1). Although the test of $\gamma = 0$ in (30) does not seem to be affected substantially by the choice of $\tilde{W}_t$, an inability to motivate the use of equation (30) as an augmentation of the conditional variance or conditional standard deviation of u_t in (1) is a drawback of the test procedure.

4.3.8 Normality

Higher-order moments have generally been used to test the validity of normality. Although the null hypothesis of normality can be rejected for reasons such as a variety of non-normal distributions, incorrect transformation of the variables, structural change, outliers and heteroskedasticity, emphasis is generally placed on skewness and kurtosis. Under the null of normality, the third moment of u_t in (1) is zero and the fourth moment is $3\sigma_u^2$. A convenient test of normality against the alternative that the errors have a distribution that is a member of the Pearson family is given in Bera and Jarque (1981).

Their Lagrange multiplier test, LM(N), is asymptotically distributed as $\chi^2(2)$ under the null hypothesis of normality.

The Monte Carlo results of Godfrey et al. (1988) indicate that LM(N) is sensitive to departures from normality in many cases, being powerful against the log-normal alternative for samples as small as $T = 20$. Although power is much lower for alternatives such as a t distribution with five degrees of freedom, in nearly all cases examined the LM(N) test was powerful in detecting highly skewed as well as thick-tailed distributions. However, the Monte Carlo results of Burke et al. (1992) suggest that LM(N) is affected by omitted variables and/or incorrect functional form. For example, the joint presence of non-normality and incorrect functional form can reduce the power of LM(N), so that the sensitivity of the test to the error for which it was designed can be reduced.

5 Testing functional form: linear versus log-linear models

Entia non sunt multiplicanda praeter necessitatem.

(Occam's razor)

5.1 Economic considerations

In practice, ease of interpretation and computation are frequently cited as adequate reasons for choosing a specific functional form for analysing data. Such considerations exemplify Occam's razor which means 'entities are not to be multiplied beyond necessity' or, more loosely translated, 'never use more when fewer will do'. When applied in the context of econometric modelling, this maxim may be seen as an exhortation to avoid using complicated models wherever possible. The interpretation of economic models often focuses on both short- and long-run marginal effects and elasticities. Two functional forms that provide useful information regarding marginal effects are the linear and log-linear regression models: the linear model has constant marginal effects and variable elasticities, while the log-linear model has constant elasticities and variable marginal effects. Although there are models other than these two which have variable elasticities and/or variable marginal effects, linear and log-linear models are useful for economic and statistical reasons. For example, it has been argued that a log-linear model is sensible because it yields a steady state growth path (see Davidson et al., 1978). A log-linear model also imposes non-negative restrictions upon variables and permits a straightforward method of testing whether the dependent variable should be expressed in nominal or real values, whereas a linear model is not amenable for such testing. On the other hand, a linear model is computationally straightforward when there is temporal aggregation of the dependent variable (see Harvey and Pierse, 1984).

The evaluation of functional form is an important aspect of diagnostic testing that seems to have been tackled on a relatively casual basis, and informal practice in these situations has been to present the results for both linear and log-linear models when there is no strong preference for either model. More formally, however, several procedures have been developed for discriminating or choosing between linear and log-linear models, and numerous tests have been devised for examining which of the two is a better approximation to the data generating process. Godfrey et al. (1988) use the following categories for tests of log-linear and linear models:

(a) tests that exploit the fact that one model is tested against a specific non-nested alternative;
(b) tests of both models against the more general model of Box and Cox (1964), using the Lagrange multiplier (LM) principle or methods proposed by Andrews (1971);
(c) diagnostic tests of functional form against an unspecified alternative functional form.

Various tests in (a) and (b) are reviewed in McAleer (1987) and Godfrey et al. (1988). Tests in (c) include the regression specification error test (RESET) of Ramsey (1969, 1974), White's (1980a) functional form test, the differencing test of Plosser et al. (1982) and the Utts (1982) 'rainbow' test for functional form (see Burke et al. (1992) for modifications to the original 'rainbow' test). Kramer et al. (1985) employ some of these tests in evaluating the validity of eleven single-equation empirical models published in the econometric literature. Furthermore, they consider a range of tests that are designed to detect some departures from the classical assumptions of no serial correlation, homoskedasticity and correct functional form. Each of the tests they considered for detecting functional form mis-specification (namely, RESET, the Durbin–Hausman specification test, the differencing test, the LM test of Godfrey and Wickens (1981) and the rainbow test) is designed to test the null hypothesis of correct functional form against an unspecified alternative.

It seems reasonable to suppose that, if there is information regarding the likely nature of mis-specification, then general tests are likely to be less powerful than tests which use this information. It would seem to be primarily for this reason that tests against well-specified alternatives based on the ideas of Cox (1961, 1962) are adopted. An application of such non-nested Cox tests to test linear and log-linear models against each other has been considered by Aneuryn-Evans and Deaton (1980). These authors have presented Monte Carlo evidence suggesting that the Cox test of both linear and log-linear models has acceptable sizes, i.e. acceptable empirical rejection frequencies under the respective null hypotheses. However, Godfrey et al. (1988) provide Monte Carlo evidence suggesting that the Cox test is outperformed in terms of power in finite samples by several computationally straightforward tests.

A different approach to testing linear and log-linear models is to embed both within the general Box–Cox model using an appropriate power transformation and then to test each of them against the more general alternative. The Monte Carlo work of Davidson and MacKinnon (1985) suggests that a specific form of LM test developed by Davidson and MacKinnon (1984) has acceptable size, whereas the version of the LM test developed by Godfrey and Wickens (1981) has size that is unacceptably high. Davidson and MacKinnon (1985, p. 509) also state that the empirical sizes of both tests are too high if the distribution of the errors is thick-tailed rather than normal, but do not report any evidence on the magnitude of the problem. Godfrey et al. (1988) examine the performance of both versions of the LM statistic and show that both are sensitive to non-normal distributions. In fact, the LM test of Davidson and MacKinnon has size that actually *increases* with the sample size, which suggests that it is inadvisable in cases where the error distribution is non-normal, such as gamma or log-normal.

The issue of normality is quite important because, if the linear model is assumed to have normal errors, the log-linear model is not theoretically possible. Moreover, several of the tests rely on the properties of the moments of normal errors for their asymptotic validity (such as the LM tests discussed above). For this reason, Godfrey et al. (1988) examine the effect of non-normality of the errors on the small sample properties of various tests of linear and log-linear models. They also present convenient computational procedures for two tests, namely White's (1980a) functional form test and the rainbow test, and show that they can be regarded as variable addition tests (see Pagan, 1984). These results are useful not only for computational purposes but also because they enable an appreciation of the types of mis-specification that the tests might be most powerful in detecting. White's (1980a) test is re-examined below to relate the procedure to the more familiar RESET test.

5.2   Model specification

Several test procedures will be related to each other below and the similarities and differences between them will be highlighted. The log-linear and linear models to be tested are given by

$$H_0: \log y_t = \beta_0 + \sum_{i=1}^{k} \beta_i \log x_{it} + \varepsilon_{0t}, \qquad \varepsilon_{0t} \sim \text{NID}(0, \sigma_0^2) \tag{31}$$

and

$$H_1: y_t = \beta_0 + \sum_{i=1}^{k} \beta_i x_{it} + \varepsilon_{1t}, \qquad \varepsilon_{1t} \sim \text{NID}(0, \sigma_1^2) \tag{32}$$

in which truncation of ε_{1t} ($t = 1, 2, \ldots, T$) is assumed to be negligible. Other variables, such as seasonal dummies and variables which always enter into the equation linearly, could easily be included in (31) and (32) and would involve only adjustments to degrees of freedom. The cross-product moment matrices of the regressors of H_0 and H_1 are assumed to tend to finite non-singular matrices as the sample size tends to infinity.

For future reference, denote the OLS estimates of the parameters in (31) and (32) as $(\hat{\beta}_0, \hat{\beta}_i, \hat{\sigma}_0^2)$ and $(\tilde{\beta}_0, \tilde{\beta}_i, \tilde{\sigma}_0^2)$, respectively, for $i = 1, 2, \ldots, k$. It follows that

$$\widehat{\log y_t} = \hat{\beta}_0 + \sum_i \hat{\beta}_i \log x_{it} \tag{33}$$

and

$$\tilde{y}_t = \tilde{\beta}_0 + \sum_i \hat{\beta}_i \log x_{it} \tag{34}$$

By $\widehat{\log y_t}$ is meant the fitted value of $\log y_t$ under H_0, whereas $\log \tilde{y}_t$ will be used to denote the logarithm of the fitted value of y_t under H_1.

5.3   Test procedures

Following the scheme adopted by Godfrey et al. (1988), the following three approaches to testing linear and log-linear regression models will be discussed.

(a) Non-nested approach: procedures derived by viewing the log-linear and linear forms as intrinsically non-nested models.

(b) Box–Cox transformation: tests obtained by embedding the two specifications under (31) and (32) in the Box–Cox regression model.

(c) Regression diagnostics: checks for functional form mis-specification when a specific alternative model is not considered.

Several test procedures from (a) and (c) are available in the econometric software package Microfit 3.0 (see Pesaran and Pesaran, 1991), as well as in other packages.

5.3.1 Non-nested approach

Asymptotic tests

The Cox (1961, 1962) test of H_0 and H_1 against each other was derived by Aneuryn-Evans and Deaton (1980). A major difficulty arises in the specification of the error distributions required to obtain the likelihood functions. Since y_t must be strictly positive if the logarithmic transformation is to be applied, the behaviour of ε_{1t} must be restricted to ensure that $y_t > 0$ for all t. The solution adopted by Aneuryn-Evans and Deaton (1980, p. 276) is to assume that the ε_{1t} are independently and identically distributed as symmetrically truncated normal variates (the more plausible assumption of asymmetric truncation is analysed in Bera and McAleer, 1989, p. 216). Such distributional assumptions imply that the calculation of the Cox test of the linear model is quite complicated. The complexity of the computations associated with the direct application of Cox's approach and the fact that standard estimation packages do not permit the evaluation of the test statistics proposed by Aneuryn-Evans and Deaton (1980) have meant that these tests have never been used in practice.

A much simpler approach to testing H_0 and H_1 is given by the extended projection (PE) tests of MacKinnon et al. (1983). These tests are based on the auxiliary linear regressions

$$\log y_t - \widehat{\log y_t} = \beta_0 + \sum_i \beta_i \log x_{it} + \alpha_0 [\tilde{y}_t - \exp(\widehat{\log y_t})] + \varepsilon_t \tag{35}$$

and

$$y_t - \tilde{y}_t = \beta_0 + \sum_i \beta_i x_{it} + \alpha_1 (\widehat{\log y_t} - \log \tilde{y}_t) + \varepsilon_t \tag{36}$$

in which H_0: $\alpha_0 = 0$ is tested against H_{0A}: $\alpha \neq 0$ and H_1: $\alpha_1 = 0$ against H_{1A}: $\alpha_1 \neq 0$. Each of these tests, namely the t-statistics for the OLS estimates of α_0 and α_1 in (35) and (36), respectively, is distributed asymptotically under the null as N(0, 1) or $\chi^2(1)$. Since $\widehat{\log y_t}$ ($\tilde{y}_t$) is a linear combination of the regressors under H_0 (H_1), the tests in (35) and (36) are equivalent to testing $\alpha_0 = 0$ and $\alpha_1 = 0$ in

$$\log y_t = \beta_0 + \sum_i \beta_i \log x_{it} + \alpha_0 [\tilde{y}_t - \exp(\widehat{\log y_t})] + \varepsilon_t \tag{37}$$

and

$$y_t = \beta_0 + \sum_i \beta_i x_{it} + \alpha_1 (\widehat{\log y_t} - \log \tilde{y}_t) + \varepsilon_t \tag{38}$$

In order to examine the effects of using non-directional information regarding the non-nested alternative, a linearization of $\exp(\widehat{\log y_t})$ and $\log \tilde{y}_t$ in (37) and (38), respectively, will be useful. There exists a constant $c\,(>\,0)$ sufficiently large for the following approximations to hold:

$$\log \tilde{y}_t = \log \left(c \frac{\tilde{y}_t}{c} \right) = \log c + \log \left(\frac{\tilde{y}_t}{c} \right)$$

$$\Rightarrow \log \tilde{y}_t = \log c + \log \left(1 + \frac{\tilde{y}_t}{c} - 1 \right) \approx \log c + \frac{\tilde{y}_t}{c} - 1 \tag{39}$$

$$\tilde{y}_t = \exp(\log \tilde{y}_t = \exp \left[c(c^{-1} \log \tilde{y}_t) \right] = \exp(c) \exp(c^{-1} \log \tilde{y}_t)$$

$$\Rightarrow \quad \tilde{y}_t = \exp(c)(1 + c^{-1} \log \tilde{y}_t) = \exp(c) + \left[c^{-1} \exp(c) \right] \log \tilde{y}_t \tag{40}$$

$$\exp(\widehat{\log y_t}) = \exp(c\, c^{-1} \widehat{\log y_t}) \approx \exp(c)(1 + c^{-1} \widehat{\log y_t})$$

$$= \exp(c) + [c^{-1} \exp(c)] \widehat{\log y_t} \tag{41}$$

$$\widehat{\log y_t} = c[\exp(c)]^{-1} \exp(\widehat{\log y_t}) - c \tag{42}$$

The approximations used will not affect the tests under their respective null hypotheses, although power may be altered under the alternative. Substitution of (41) into (37) and (39) into (38) enables the auxiliary regressions to be rewritten as

$$\log y_t = \beta_0 + \sum_i \beta_i \log x_{it} + \alpha_0 \tilde{y}_t + \varepsilon_t \tag{43}$$

and

$$y_t = \beta_0 + \sum_i \beta_i x_{it} + \alpha_1 \widehat{\log y_t} + \varepsilon_t \tag{44}$$

because the remaining terms are subsumed in the intercept and linear combinations with the regressors. The test of H_0: $\alpha_0 = 0$ in (43) and H_1: $\alpha_1 = 0$ in (44), denoted here as J-type tests, are obviously similar to the J test of Davidson and McKinnon (1981) in which the fitted values of the dependent variable from a non-nested alternative model are added to the null. The J-type tests are distributed as N(0, 1) asymptotically under the null.

If the terms $\exp(\widehat{\log y_t})$ and $\log \tilde{y}_t$ in (37) and (38), respectively, have significant roles to play in testing the respective null models, their absence from (43) and (44) should lead to lower power for the J-type tests. A further point to note is that $\tilde{y}_t$ and $\widehat{\log y_t}$ in (43) and (44) will be quite dissimilar in magnitude to the respective dependent variables and associated regressors. It would seem useful, therefore, to alter the magnitudes of the fitted values to reflect more accurately the variations in the dependent variable. Substitution of (40) in (43) and (42) in (44) yields the auxiliary equations

$$\log y_t = \beta_0 + \sum_i \beta_i \log x_{it} + \alpha_0 \log \tilde{y}_t + \varepsilon_t \tag{45}$$

and

$$y_t = \beta_0 + \sum_i \beta_i x_{it} + \alpha_1 \exp(\widehat{\log y_t}) + \varepsilon_t \tag{46}$$

in which the tests of H_0: $\alpha = 0$ and H_1: $\alpha_1 = 0$ are distributed asymptotically as $N(0, 1)$ under their respective null hypotheses.

Exact tests

If the errors of both H_0 and H_1 are assumed NID for all observations, as in (31) and (32), and the regressors are strictly exogenous, then exact tests of H_0 and H_1 can be obtained. Bera and McAleer (1989) derived exact tests by using test variables that depend upon the stochastic observation y_t ($t = 1, 2, \ldots, T$) only through the OLS parameter estimates of the respective null models. This strategy allowed them to appeal to the results of Milliken and Graybill (1970) to derive tests with known null distributions.

The tests suggested by Bera and McAleer (1989) (BM tests) are based on two auxiliary regressions, commencing with

$$\exp(\widehat{\log y_t}) = \beta_0 + \sum_i \beta_i x_{1t} + \eta_{1t} \tag{47}$$

and

$$\log \tilde{y}_t = \beta_0 + \sum_i \beta_i \log x_{1t} + \eta_{0t}. \tag{48}$$

Denoting the OLS residuals from (47) and (48) as $\hat{\eta}_{1t}$ and $\tilde{\eta}_{0t}$, respectively, the tests of H_0 and H_1 are based on the auxiliary regressions

$$\log y_t = \beta_0 + \sum_i \beta_i \log x_{it} + \theta_0 \hat{\eta}_{1t} + \varepsilon_t \tag{49}$$

and

$$y_t = \beta_0 + \sum_i \beta_i x_{it} + \theta_1 \tilde{\eta}_{0t} + \varepsilon_t. \tag{50}$$

The tests in (49) and (50) are denoted BM: the test of H_0: $\theta_0 = 0$ is distributed as $t(T - k - 2)$ under H_0, while the test of H_1: $\theta_1 = 0$, because of possible truncation effects, is approximately distributed as $t(T - k - 2)$ under H_1. Both tests are asymptotically $N(0, 1)$ under the respective null hypotheses in the presence of lagged dependent variables.

5.3.2 The Box–Cox transformation

The PE and BM tests described above represent convenient alternative procedures to the relatively complicated non-nested Cox tests proposed by Aneuryn-Evans and Deaton (1980), but share the same theoretical basis by viewing H_0 and H_1 as non-nested models. As noted in McAleer (1992b), however, there have been few empirical applications of the PE and BM tests in the published literature. A more frequently used method of testing H_0 and H_1 arises when the alternative is not non-nested but is a more general model given by the transformation of Box and Cox (1964), namely

$$H_{BC}: \quad y_t(\lambda) = \beta_0 + \sum_i \beta_i x_{it}(\lambda) + \varepsilon_t, \qquad \varepsilon_t \sim \text{NID}(0, \sigma_\varepsilon^2) \tag{51}$$

in which $z_t(\lambda)$, $z_t = y_t$ or x_{it}, denotes the Box–Cox transformation given by

$$z_t(\lambda) = (z_t^\lambda - 1)/\lambda, \qquad \lambda \neq 0, z_t \geqslant 0$$
$$= \log z_t, \qquad \lambda = 0, z_t > 0$$

The model given in (51) must contain an intercept term (see Schlesselman, 1971). Moreover, the assumption of normality for ε_t in (51), while frequently invoked in practice, is inappropriate since the definition of the Box–Cox transformation implies that $y_t(\lambda)$ in (51) cannot be normally distributed unless $\lambda = 0$. This problem will be ignored for the purposes of describing previous research below. Extensions of the model to account for serial correlation and heteroskedasticity are given in Savin and White (1978) and Zarembka (1974), respectively.

Lagrange multiplier tests

The Box–Cox model in (51) reduces to the log-linear model H_0 when $\lambda = 0$ and to the linear model H_1 when $\lambda = 1$. Strictly speaking, setting $\lambda = 0$ involves a redefinition of the intercept term, but the appropriate parameterization may safely be ignored. Godfrey and Wickens (1981) and Davidson and MacKinnon (1985) develop LM tests for testing H_0 and H_1 against H_{BC}, where the LM tests require only OLS estimation of H_0 and H_1. The corresponding asymptotically equivalent likelihood ratio and Wald tests would require the more complicated estimation of the model H_{BC}, wherein the maximum likelihood estimate of λ has little intrinsic interest.

In order to outline the general form of the LM tests, it will be convenient to denote $\beta' = (\beta_0, \beta_1, \ldots, \beta_k)$ and the $(k + 3)$-dimensional parameter vector $\theta = (\beta', \sigma_\varepsilon^2, \lambda)'$. The log-likelihood function for a typical observation on H_{BC} under the assumption of normally distributed disturbances is given by

$$l_t(\theta) = -\frac{1}{2}\log 2\pi - \frac{1}{2}\log \sigma_\varepsilon^2 + (\lambda - 1)\log y_t - \frac{\left[y_t(\lambda) - \beta_0 - \sum_i \beta_i x_{it}(\lambda)\right]^2}{2\sigma_\varepsilon^2} \qquad (52)$$

for $t = 1, 2, \ldots, T$. The OLS estimates for H_0 and H_1 can then be regarded as elements of constrained maximizers of the function $L_T(\theta) = \sum_{t=1}^{T} l_t(\theta)$, with $\hat{\theta} = (\hat{\beta}', \hat{\sigma}_0^2, 0)'$ maximizing $L_T(\theta)$ subject to $\lambda = 0$, and $\tilde{\theta} = (\tilde{\beta}, \tilde{\sigma}_1^2, 1)'$ being the maximizer when $\lambda = 1$ is imposed. The LM tests of $\lambda = 0$ and $\lambda = 1$ are then checks of significance of $\partial L_T(\hat{\theta})/\partial\lambda$ and $\partial L_T(\hat{\theta})/\partial\lambda$, respectively (see, for example, Breusch and Pagan, 1980).

In general, if θ^* maximizes $L_T(\theta)$ subject to the single restriction $\lambda = c$, with c being some constant, then the LM statistic for testing the validity of this restriction can be written as

$$\mathrm{LM} = \left[\frac{\partial L_T(\theta^*)}{\partial\theta}\right]' \left[B(\theta^*)\right]^{-1} \left[\frac{\partial L_T(\theta^*)}{\partial\theta}\right] \bigg/ T \qquad (53)$$

in which $B(\theta^*)$ has the same probability limit as the average information matrix when $\lambda = c$. The statistic LM will be asymptotically distributed as $\chi^2(1)$ under the null hypothesis $\lambda = c$ for all valid choices of the matrix B. The choice of the B matrix however, may have important consequences for computational costs and finite sample performance in terms of closeness to the χ^2 distribution under the null hypothesis and power under specific alternatives (for further details, see Bera and McKenzie, 1986).

The LM statistics developed by Godfrey and Wickens (1981) and Davidson and MacKinnon (1985) for testing log-linear and linear regression models differ only in their choice of the B matrix, with both pairs of authors avoiding the complications of evaluating the matrix of second partial derivatives $\partial^2 L_T(\theta)/\partial\theta\partial\theta'$. Godfrey and Wickens (1981) employed the usual information matrix equality

$$-E\left[\frac{\partial^2 L_T(\theta)}{\partial\theta\partial\theta'}\right] = E\left[\frac{\partial L_T(\theta)}{\partial\theta}\right]\left[\frac{\partial L_T(\theta)}{\partial\theta}\right]' \tag{54}$$

to derive the expression

$$B(\theta^*) = \sum_t \left[\frac{\partial l_t(\theta^*)}{\partial\theta}\right]\left[\frac{\partial l_t(\theta^*)}{\partial\theta}\right]' \Big/ T$$

which depends only on first-order derivatives. Using the LM test in (53) with the choice of $B(\theta^*)$ given above, Godfrey and Wickens (1981) showed that LM is simply the explained sum of squares for the regression of a vector of ones on the regressor matrix with tth row given by $\partial l_t(\theta^*)/\partial\theta$, for $t = 1, 2, \ldots, T$. This explained sum of squares equals TR^2, that is, the sample size times the uncentred coefficient of determination, or T minus the residual sum of squares, for this auxiliary regression.

The information matrix equality (54) however, is, only applicable when $L_T(\theta)$ is a proper log-likelihood function satisfying the necessary regularity conditions. Since the disturbances of H_{BC} cannot be normally distributed in general, it follows that $l_T(\theta)$ in (52), and hence $L_T(\theta)$, are mis-specified. Consequently, the use of the information matrix equality cannot strictly be justified and the LM test of Godfrey and Wickens (1981) cannot be assumed to be asymptotically valid. The test of $\lambda = 0$ however, would be appropriate under the assumption of normality if the disturbances ε_t of H_{BC} have the truncated normal distribution specified in Poirier (1978). Poirier and Ruud (1979) obtained an LM test of $\lambda = 0$ for this class of truncated Box–Cox regression models and their statistic differs from that of Godfrey and Wickens (1981) only because they evaluate second partial derivatives rather than make use of (54). The derivation is made easier by the fact that the truncation effect in Poirier's specification vanishes under the null hypothesis $\lambda = 0$ so that Poirier's model does not lead to a computationally simple test for the linear variant of H_{BC}.

By making use of properties of normally distributed random variables, Davidson and MacKinnon (1984) derived an alternative expression for a valid form of $B(\theta^*)$. If the underlying model is written as $f_t(y_t, y_{t-1}, \theta) = \varepsilon_t$, where y_t is the dependent variable, y_{t-1} denotes lagged values of $y_t, \varepsilon_t \sim N(0, 1)$ and the Jacobian matrix is lower triangular, then $B(\theta^*)$ may also be expressed as

$$B(\theta^*) = (FF' + JJ')/T$$

where F' and J' have typical elements (t, j) given by $\partial f_t/\partial\theta_j$ and $\partial(\log|\partial f_t/\partial y_t|)/\partial\theta_j$, respectively. This version of the LM statistic may be calculated as the explained sum of squares for an auxiliary regression using $2T$ observations, or as $2T$ minus the residual sum of squares. Strictly speaking, since normality is necessary for the derivation of the LM statistic of Davidson and MacKinnon (1984), their LM procedure is not applicable to the problem of testing H_0 and H_1 against H_{BC} (as used in Davidson and MacKinnon, 1985).

Exact tests
Godfrey and Wickens (1981) also generalize the method of Andrews (1971) for testing restrictions on λ in the Box–Cox model. As before, suppose that $\theta^* = (\beta^{*\prime}, \sigma_\varepsilon^{*2}, c)'$

maximizes $L_T(\theta)$ subject to the constraint $\lambda = c$. The first step of the Andrews procedure for testing $\lambda = c$ is to linearize the transformed variates of H_{BC} around the value specified under the null hypothesis to obtain the approximation

$$y_t(c) = \beta_0 + \sum_i \beta_i x_{it}(c) + (\lambda - c)d_t + \varepsilon_t \tag{55}$$

where

$$d_t = \sum_i \beta_i \frac{\partial x_{it}(c)}{\partial \lambda} - \frac{\partial y_t(c)}{\partial \lambda}. \tag{56}$$

Clearly, the restriction $\lambda = c$ is equivalent to $\lambda - c = 0$, but a direct test of the significance of d_t in (55) cannot be employed because this variable is unobservable; it is worth noting that Andrews (1971) considered a case in which only the dependent variable was transformed, and so did not face the problem of eliminating the coefficients β_i from (56). In order to derive a feasible test variable of the Andrews type, Godfrey and Wickens (1981) suggested that the β_i in (56) be replaced by the corresponding β_i^* and that $\partial y_t(c)/\partial \lambda$ be approximated by a function depending upon the observations $y_1, \ldots, y_T$ only through θ^*. The Andrews-type test involves expanding (51) around $\lambda = 0$ (log-linear) and $\lambda = 1$ (linear) and then evaluating the expansion around estimates obtained under $\lambda = 0$ and $\lambda = 1$, respectively, as in (33) and (34).

A first-order expansion of (51) around $\lambda = 0$ leads, after evaluation under H_0, to the Andrews test of H_0: $\lambda = 0$, namely

$$\log y_t = \beta_0 + \sum_i \beta_i \log x_{it} + \lambda \left[-\frac{1}{2}(\widehat{\log y_t})^2 + \frac{1}{2} \sum_i \hat{\beta}_i (\log x_{it})^2 \right] + \varepsilon_t \tag{57}$$

with the t statistic for $\hat{\lambda}$ in (57) being distributed as $t(T - k - 2)$ under H_0 if the errors of the log-linear model are normally distributed. The null hypothesis H_0: $\lambda = 0$ is tested against a two-sided alternative when no information regarding the alternative is used (see Godfrey and Wickens, 1981, pp. 488, 495, fn 8). The Andrews test of H_1: $\lambda = 0$ involves a first-order expansion of (51) around $\lambda = 1$ and evaluation of the expansion under H_1, namely

$$y_t = \beta_0 + \sum_i \beta_i x_{it} + (1 - \lambda) \left[(\tilde{y}_t \log \tilde{y}_t - \tilde{y}_t + 1) - \sum_i \tilde{\beta}_i(x_{it} \log x_{it} - x_{it} + 1) \right] + \varepsilon_t. \tag{58}$$

The hypothesis H_1: $\lambda = 1$ is tested against a two-sided alternative. As noted in Godfrey and Wickens (1981), an exact test of the null is not available for testing $\lambda = 1$ in (58). However, the t statistic for $\hat{\lambda}$ in (58) is asymptotically distributed as $\chi^2(1)$ under H_1.

An interesting feature of the tests based on the Box–Cox framework is that they can accommodate higher-order expansions of (51) under the null hypothesis. It was conjectured by Andrews (1971, p. 250) and Godfrey and Wickens (1981, p. 492) that such higher-order expansions may lead to increased power in finite samples, the outcome being ambiguous because power decreased with the degrees of freedom for a fixed non-centrality parameter (see Das Gupta and Perlman, 1974). Godfrey et al. (1988) find that power is always lower for the second-order linearization relative to the Andrews tests in (57) and (58). McAleer (1987) discusses alternative methods for imposing restrictions on the signs of λ and $1 - \lambda$ when higher-order expansions of the Box–Cox model are used to test both the log-linear and linear models.

5.3.3   Regression specification error test (RESET)

The variable addition test RESET, developed by Ramsey (1969, 1974) and modified by Ramsey and Schmidt (1976), is calculated by adding powers of the fitted values of the null model. The tests of the log-linear and linear models against a general alternative are based on the auxiliary regressions

$$\log y_t = \beta_0 + \sum_{i=1}^{k} \beta_i \log x_{it} + \sum_{j=2}^{c} \alpha_{0j}(\widehat{\log y_t})^j + \varepsilon_t \tag{59}$$

and

$$y_t = \beta_0 + \sum_{i=1}^{k} \beta_i x_{it} + \sum_{j=2}^{c} \alpha_{1j}(\tilde{y}_t)^j + \varepsilon_t \tag{60}$$

in which $(\widehat{\log y_t})$ and $(\tilde{y}_t)^j$ are the fitted values under H_0 and H_1 respectively, raised to the power j. The test of H_0 given in (59), which will be denoted RESET(c), is the test of H_0: $\alpha_{02} = \alpha_{03} = \ldots = \alpha_{0c} = 0$, and is distributed as $F(c - 1, T - k - c)$ under H_0 if the disturbances are approximately normal. Similarly, the RESET(c) test of H_1 in (60) is the test of H_1: $\alpha_{12} = \alpha_{13} = \ldots = \alpha_{1c} = 0$, which is approximately distributed as $F(c - 1, T - k - c)$ under H_1 if the disturbances are approximately normal. Thursby and Schmidt (1977) have found RESET(4) to work quite well in a comparative study of alternative sets of test variables. Godfrey et al. (1988) find that RESET(3) has accurate size but lower power, in general, than RESET(2). However, it should be remembered that, for a given size of test, using higher exponents of fitted values must be balanced against the potential loss of power through losing degrees of freedom (see Godfrey (1983) for some relevant asymptotic results). Another important point to note is that the RESET auxiliary regressions must be balanced. Thus, if y_t and x_{it} (and $\log y_t$ and $\log x_{it}$) are of a similar order of integration, it is necessary that powers of $\widehat{\log y_t}$ and of $\tilde{y}_t$ also be of similar orders of integration.

McAleer (1987, p. 178) relates RESET-type tests of log-linear and linear models to tests based on the Box–Cox transformation. Consider testing the null hypothesis H_0: $\lambda = 0$ in the auxiliary regression

$$y_t(\lambda) = \beta_0 + \sum_{i} \beta_i \log x_{it} + \varepsilon_t \tag{61}$$

A first-order expansion of $y_t(\lambda)$ around $\lambda = 0$ yields

$$\log y_t = \beta_0 + \sum_{i} \beta_i \log x_{it} + \lambda \left[-\frac{1}{2}(\log y_t)^2 \right] + \varepsilon_t. \tag{62}$$

Evaluation of $(\log y_1)^2$ under H_0 namely $(\widehat{\log y_t})^2$, and substitution in (62) yields RESET(2), namely (59) when $c = 2$. In a similar manner, a second-order linearization of $y_t(\lambda)$ around $\lambda = 0$ in (61) leads to a RESET(3) test of H_0, as in (59) when $c = 3$. Now consider testing the null hypothesis H_1: $\lambda = 1$ in the auxiliary regression

$$y_t(\lambda) = \beta_0 + \sum_i \beta_i x_{it} + \varepsilon_t \qquad (63)$$

for which a first-order linearization is

$$y_t = \beta_0 + \sum_i \beta_i x_{it} + (1 - \lambda)(y_t \log y_t - v_t + 1) + \varepsilon_t. \qquad (64)$$

Under H_1: $\lambda = 1$, substituting $\tilde{y}_t$ for y_t and $\log y_t$ for $\log y_t$ in (64) yields

$$y_t = \beta_0 + \sum_i \beta_i x_{it} + (1 - \lambda)(\tilde{y}_t \log \tilde{y}_t) + \varepsilon_t \qquad (65)$$

since $-\tilde{y}_t + 1$ is perfectly linearly related with the regressors under H_1. Replacing log $\tilde{y}_t$ in (65) with the expression in (39) leads precisely to the RESET(2) test given in (60) when $c = 2$.

5.3.4   White's functional form test

White's (1980a) test for functional form is also worth examining for its connection to RESET. The test procedure is based on the difference between the OLS and weighted least squares (WLS) estimates of the regression parameters. Under the null hypothesis of correct functional form, the OLS and WLS estimators should not be significantly different, whereas if the functional form is not correct the OLS and WLS estimators will tend to different probability limits as T approaches infinity.

The models under H_0 and H_1 can be written in matrix form as

$$y = X\beta + \varepsilon$$

in which y is a $T \times 1$ vector, X is a $T \times (k + 1)$ matrix and ε is a $T \times 1$ vector. White's functional form test statistic, which will be referred to as WFF, can be calculated as a test of significance of

$$q = \hat{\beta}_{WLS} - \hat{\beta}_{OLS}$$

where

$$\hat{\beta}_{WLS} = (X' \Omega^{-1} X)^{-1} X' \Omega^{-1} y$$

$$\hat{\beta}_{OLS} = (X'X)^{-1} X'y$$

and Ω^{-1} is a diagonal matrix whose diagonal elements are given functions (see White (1980a, section 4) for further details). The expression for WFF is given by $q'\{V(q)\}^{-1}q'$, which is distributed asymptotically as $\chi^2(k + 1)$ under the null hypothesis. Several estimates of $V(q)$ are asymptotically valid under H_0. White (1980a, pp. 157–8) provides a relatively complicated estimate of $V(q)$ as well as a simpler form based upon a result given in Hausman (1978), but even the latter is not especially straightforward relative to a variable addition test.

A variable addition interpretation may be provided as follows. Let $\hat{\varepsilon}$ denote the vector of OLS residuals, namely $y = X\hat{\beta}_{\text{OLS}} + \hat{\varepsilon}$, so that

$$\hat{\beta}_{\text{WLS}} - \hat{\beta}_{\text{OLS}} = (X'\Omega^{-1}X)^{-1}X'\Omega^{-1}\hat{\varepsilon}.$$

A test of the significance of q is unaffected by the pre-multiplication of q by a non-singular matrix A since

$$(Aq)'[AV(q)A']^{-1}Aq = q'[V(q)]^{-1}q$$

for all such A. Thus, the WFF test is equivalent to a test of the joint significance of the elements of $X'\Omega^{-1}\hat{\varepsilon}$, which is proportional to the score vector for the quasi-LM test of $\Psi = 0$ in the auxiliary regression (see Breusch and Godfrey, 1986, pp. 51–3)

$$y = X\beta + (\Omega^{-1}X)\Psi + \varepsilon. \tag{66}$$

Accordingly, the original model is simply augmented by the columns of $\Omega^{-1}X$, and a test of $\Psi = 0$ in (66) is distributed as $F(k + 1, T - 2k - 2)$ when Ω is known or is a function of the data only through the fitted value of the dependent variable.

The variable addition form of the WFF test involves generating test variables by scaling the original regressors with the weights employed to derive the WLS estimator and then adding these variables to the initial set of regressors. White (1980a, p. 159, table 2) suggests using weights that are the reciprocals of the squared fitted values under the null hypothesis, so that the typical element of Ω^{-1} is $(\widehat{\log y_t})^{-2}$ for testing H_0 and $(\tilde{y}_t)^{-2}$ for testing H_1. The WFF tests are therefore given by the tests of H_0: $\Psi_{00} = \Psi_{01} = \ldots = \Psi_{0k} = 0$ and H_1: $\Psi_{10} = \Psi_{11} = \ldots \Psi_{1k} = 0$, respectively, in the auxiliary regressions

$$\log y_t = \beta_0 + \sum_{i=1}^{k} \beta_i \log x_{it} + \Psi_{00}(\widehat{\log y_t})^{-2} + \sum_{i=1}^{k} \Psi_{0i}[\log x_{it}(\widehat{\log y_t})^{-2}] + \varepsilon_t \tag{67}$$

and

$$y_t = \beta_0 \sum_{i=1}^{k} \beta_i x_{it} + \Psi_{10}\tilde{y}_t^{-2} + \sum_{i=1}^{k} \Psi_{1i}[x_{it}y(\tilde{y}_t)^{-2}] + \varepsilon_t \tag{68}$$

with the test of H_0 being distributed as $F(k+1, T-2k-2)$ if the disturbances are normally distributed, and the test of H_1 being approximately distributed as $F(k + 1, T - 2k - 2)$. If the typical elements of Ω^{-1} were to be $(\widehat{\log y_t})^2$ for testing H_0 and $\tilde{y}_t^2$ for testing H_1 (67) and (68) would become

$$\log y_t = \beta_0 + \sum_{i=1}^{k} \beta_i \log x_{it} + \Psi_{00}(\widehat{\log y_t})^2 + \sum_{i=1}^{k} \Psi_{0i}[\log x_{it}(\widehat{\log y_t})^2] + \varepsilon_t \tag{69}$$

and

$$y_t = \beta_0 \sum_{i=1}^{k} \beta_i x_{it} + \Psi_{10}\tilde{y}_t^2 + \sum_{i=1}^{k} \Psi_{1i}(x_{it}\tilde{y}_t^2) + \varepsilon_t \tag{70}$$

Setting $\Psi_{0i} = 0$ and $\Psi_{1i} = 0$ for all $i = 1, 2, \ldots, k$ in (69) and (70) leads precisely to RESET(2) tests of H_0 and H_1 respectively, thereby providing an alternative derivation of the RESET procedure.

As in the discussion of RESET, it is necessary that the auxiliary regression models given in (67)–(70) be balanced, otherwise the asymptotic distributions of the OLS estimators will not be standard. However, there is no guarantee that the added variables in the auxiliary regressions will be of the same orders of integration as the original variables.

Notes

This paper is based on part of my inaugural lecture at the University of Western Australia, and was presented as a keynote address to the 9th Biennial Conference on Modelling and Simulation, Gold Coast, Australia, December 1991. It developed from a graduate course in econometric methodology that I taught for several years in the Department of Statistics at the Australian National University. I wish to thank Lisa Busch, Dhammika Dharmapala, Les Godfrey, Mark Gracey, Tony Jakeman, Colin McKenzie, Christine Ong, Les Oxley, Peter Phillips, Colin Roberts and seminar participants at the Bank of Japan, Bond University, Edith Cowan University, Griffith University, Kobe University of Commerce, Kyoto University, Nagasaki University, Osaka University, University of Edinburgh, University of New South Wales and Waseda University for helpful comments and discussions, and to acknowledge the financial support of the Australian Research Council and a Japanese Government Foreign Research Fellowship at Kyoto University.

1   This section is a revised and extended version of McAleer (1992a, pp. 519–23).

References

Andrews, D. F. (1971) A note on the selection of data transformations. *Biometrika*, 58, 249–54.

Aneuryn-Evans, G. and Deaton, A. S. (1980) Testing linear versus logarithmic regression models. *Review of Economic Studies*, 47, 275–91.

Bai, J., Jakeman, A. J. and McAleer, M. (1992) Estimation and discrimination of alternative air pollution models. *Ecological Modelling*, 64, 89–124.

Barrie, J. M. (1986) *Peter Pan*, Harmondsworth: Penguin.

Bera, A. K. and Higgins, M. L. (1993) A survey of ARCH models: properties, estimation and testing. *Journal of Economic Surveys*, 7, 305–66.

—— and Jarque, C. M. (1981) An efficient large sample test for normality of observations and regression residuals. Working Paper in Economics and Econometrics 040, Australian National University.

—— and McAleer, M. (1989) Nested and non-nested procedures for testing linear and log-linear regression models. *Sankhya*, 51, 212–24.

—— and McKenzie, C. R. (1986) Alternative forms and properties of the score test. *Journal of Applied Statistics*, 13, 13–25.

Box, G. E. P. and Cox, D. R. (1964) An analysis of transformations. *Journal of the Royal Statistical Society* B, 26, 211–43.

—— and Pierce, D. A. (1970) Distribution of residual autocorrelations in autoregressive-integrated moving average time series models. *Journal of the American Statistical Association*, 65, 1509–26.

Breusch, T. S. (1978) Testing for autocorrelation in dynamic linear models. *Australian Economic Papers*, 17, 334–55.

—— and Godfrey, L. G. (1986) Data transformation tests. *Economic Journal*, 96, 47–58.

—— and Pagan, A. R. (1980) The Lagrange multiplier test and its applications to model specification in econometrics. *Review of Economic Studies*, 47, 239–53.

Burke, S. P., Godfrey, L. G. and McAleer, M. (1992) Modifications of the rainbow test. In L. G. Godfrey (ed.), *The Implementation and Constructive Use of Mis-specification Tests in Econometrics*, Manchester: Manchester University Press, 233–60.

Campbell, J. Y. and Perron, P. (1991) Pitfalls and opportunities: what macroeconomists should know about unit roots. In O. J. Blanchard and S. Fischer (eds), *NBER Macroeconomics Annual*, vol. 6, Cambridge, MA: MIT Press, 141–201.

Chow, G. C. (1960) Tests of equality between sets of coefficients in two linear regressions. *Econometrica*, 28, 591–605.

Conan Doyle, A. (1984) *The Penguin Complete Sherlock Holmes*. Harmondsworth: Penguin.

Cox, D. R. (1961) Tests of separate families of hypotheses. In *Proceedings of the Fourth Berkeley Symposium on Mathematical Statistics and Probability*, vol. 1, Berkeley, CA: University of California Press, 105–23.

—— (1962) Further results on tests of separate families of hypotheses. *Journal of the Royal Statistical Society B*, 24, 406–24.

Das Gupta, S. and Perlman, M. D. (1974) Power of the noncentral F-test: effect of additional variates on Hotelling's T^2-test. *Journal of the American Statistical Association*, 69, 174–80.

Dastoor, N. K. (1983) Some aspects of testing non-nested hypotheses. *Journal of Econometrics*, 21, 213–28.

—— and McAleer, M. (1987) On the consistency of joint and paired tests for non-nested regression models. *Journal of Quantitative Economics*, 3, 65–84.

—— and —— (1989) Some power comparisons of joint and paired tests for nonnested models under local hypotheses. *Econometric Theory*, 5, 83–94.

Davidson, J. E. H., Hendry, D. F., Srba, F. and Yeo, S. (1978) Econometric modelling of the aggregate time-series relationship between consumers' expenditure and income in the United Kingdom. *Economic Journal*, 88, 661–92.

Davidson, R. and MacKinnon, J. G. (1981) Several tests for model specification in the presence of alternative hypotheses. *Econometrica*, 49, 781–93.

—— and —— (1984) Model specification tests based on artificial linear regressions. *International Economic Review*, 25, 485–502.

—— and —— (1985) Testing linear and loglinear regressions against Box–Cox alternatives. *Canadian Journal of Economics*, 18, 499–517.

Deaton, A. S. (1982) Model selection procedures, or, does the consumption function exist? In G. C. Chow and P. Corsi (eds), *Evaluating the Reliability of Macroeconomic Models*, New York: Wiley, 43–65.

Durbin, J. (1954) Errors in variables. *Review of the International Statistical Institute*, 22, 23–32.

Engle, R. F. (1982) Autoregressive conditional heteroskedasticity with estimates of the variance of United Kingdom inflation. *Econometrica*, 50, 987–1007.

Fiebig, D. G., McAleer, M. and Bartels, R. (1992) Properties of ordinary least squares estimators in regression models with non-spherical disturbances. *Journal of Econometrics*, 54, 321–34.

Fisher, G. R. and McAleer, M. (1981) Alternative procedures and associated tests of significance for non-nested hypotheses. *Journal of Econometrics*, 16, 103–19.

Friedman, M. (1988) Money and the stock market. *Journal of Political Economy*, 96, 221–45.

Glejser, H. (1969) A new test for heteroskedasticity. *Journal of the American Statistical Association*, 64, 316–23.

Godfrey, L. G. (1978) Testing for higher order serial correlation in regression equations when the regressors include lagged dependent variables. *Econometrica*, 46, 1303–10.

—— (1983) Comment on diagnostic tests as residual analysis. *Econometric Reviews*, 2, 229–33.

—— and Pesaran, M. H. (1983) Tests of non-nested regression models: small sample adjustments and Monte Carlo evidence. *Journal of Econometrics*, 21, 133–54.

—— and Wickens, M. R. (1981) Testing linear and log-linear regressions for functional form. *Review of Economic Studies*, 48, 487–96.

——, McAleer, M. and McKenzie, C. R. (1988) Variable addition and Lagrange multiplier tests for linear and logarithmic regression models. *Review of Economics and Statistics*, 70, 492–503.

Gourieroux, C., Monfort, A. and Trognon, A. (1983) Testing nested or non-nested hypotheses. *Journal of Econometrics*, 21, 83–115.

Granger, C. W. J. (ed.) (1990) *Modelling Economic Series: Readings in Econometric Methodology*. Oxford: Oxford University Press.

—— and Hallman, J. (1991) Nonlinear transformations of integrated time series. *Journal of Time Series Analysis*, 12, 207–24.

Hall, A. D. and McAleer, M. (1989) A Monte Carlo study of some tests of model adequacy in time series analysis. *Journal of Business and Economic Statistics*, 7, 95–106.

Harvey, A. C. and Pierse, R. G. (1984) Estimating missing observations in economic time series. *Journal of the American Statistical Association*, 79, 125–31.

Hausman, J. A. (1978) Specification tests in econometrics. *Econometrica*, 46, 1251–71.

Hendry, D. F. (1980) Econometrics – alchemy or science? *Economica*, 47, 387–406.

Johansen, S. (1988) Statistical analysis of cointegrating vectors. *Journal of Economic Dynamics and Control*, 12, 231–54.

—— (1991) Estimation and hypothesis testing of cointegration vectors in Gaussian vector autoregressive models. *Econometrica*, 59, 1551–80.

Keynes, J. M. (1939) Professor Tinbergen's method. *Economic Journal*, 49, 558–68.

—— (1940) Comment. *Economic Journal*, 50, 154–6.

King, M. L. and McAleer, M. (1987) Further results on testing AR(1) against MA(1) disturbances in the linear regression model. *Review of Economic Studies*, 54, 649–63.

Koenker, R. (1981) A note on studentizing a test for heteroskedasticity. *Journal of Econometrics*, 17, 107–12.

Kramer, W., Sonnberger, H., Maurer, J. and Havlik, P. (1985) Diagnostic checking in practice. *Review of Economics and Statistics*, 67, 118–23.

Leamer, E. E. (1981) SEARCH, a linear regression computer package. Unpublished paper, Department of Economics, University of California at Los Angeles.

—— (1983) Let's take the con out of econometrics. *American Economic Review*, 73, 31–43. Reprinted in C. W. J. Granger (ed.), *Modelling Economic Series: Readings in Econometric Methodology*, Oxford: Oxford University Press, 1990, 29–49.

—— (1988) Things that bother me. *Economic Record*, 64, 331–5.

Levine, R. and Renelt, D. (1992) A sensitivity analysis of cross- country growth regressions. *American Economic Review*, 82, 942–63.

Ljung, G. M. and Box, G. E. P. (1978) On a measure of lack of fit in time series models. *Biometrika*, 65, 297–303.

MacKinnon, J. G., White, H. and Davidson, R. (1983) Tests for model specification in the presence of alternative hypotheses: some further results. *Journal of Econometrics*, 21, 53–70.

McAleer, M. (1983) Exact tests of a model against non-nested alternatives. *Biometrika*, 70, 285–8.

—— (1987) Specification tests for separate models: a survey. In M. L. King and D. E. A. Giles (eds), *Specification Analysis in the Linear Model*, London: Routledge & Kegan Paul, 146–96.

—— (1992a) Modelling in econometrics: the deterrent effect of capital punishment. *Mathematics and Computers in Simulation*, 33, 519–32.

—— (1992b) The significance of testing empirical non-nested models. *Journal of Econometrics*, to appear.

—— and Pesaran, M. H. (1986) Statistical inference in non-nested econometric models. *Applied Mathematics and Computation*, 20, 171–211.

—— and Tse, Y. K. (1988) A sequential testing procedure for outliers and structural change. *Econometric Reviews*, 7, 103–11.

—— and —— (1992) The robustness of tests of outliers and functional form. *Journal of Applied Statistics*, 19, 427–36.

—— and Veall, M. R. (1989) How fragile are fragile inferences? A re-evaluation of the deterrent effect of capital punishment. *Review of Economics and Statistics*, 71, 99–106.

——, Pagan, A. R. and Volker, P. A. (1985) What will take the con out of econometrics? *American Economic Review*, 75, 293–307. (Reprinted in C. W. J. Granger (ed.), *Modelling Economic Series: Readings in Econometric Methodology*, Oxford: Oxford University Press, 1990, 50–71.

——, McKenzie, C. R. and Hall, A. D. (1988) Testing separate time series models. *Journal of Time Series Analysis*, 9, 169–89.

McKenzie, C. R., McAleer, M. and Gill, L. (1993) Simple procedures for testing autoregressive versus moving average errors in regression models. Unpublished paper, Faculty of Economics, Osaka University.

Milliken, G. A. and Graybill, F. A. (1970) Extensions of the general linear hypothesis model. *Journal of the American Statistical Association*, 65, 797–807.

Mizon, G. E. and Richard, J.-F. (1986) The encompassing principle and its application to non-nested hypotheses. *Econometrica*, 54, 657–78.

Pagan, A. R. (1984) Model evaluation by variable addition. In D. F.Hendry and K. F.Wallis (eds), *Econometrics and Quantitative Economics*, Oxford: Blackwell, 103–33.

—— (1987) Three econometric methodologies: a critical appraisal. *Journal of Economic Surveys*, 1, 3–24. (Reprinted in C. W. J. Granger (ed.), *Modelling Economic Series: Readings in Econometric Methodology*, Oxford: Oxford University Press, 1990, 97–120.

—— and Hall, A. D. (1983) Diagnostic tests as residual analysis. *Econometric Reviews*, 2, 159–218.

Pesaran, M. H. (1974) On the general problem of model selection. *Review of Economic Studies*, 41, 153–71.

—— (1987) Global and partial non-nested hypotheses and asymptotic local power. *Econometric Theory*, 3, 69–97.

—— (1990) Econometrics. In J. Eatwell, M. Milgate and P. Newman (eds), *The New Palgrave: Econometrics*, London: Macmillan, 1–34.

—— and Deaton, A. S. (1978) Testing non-nested nonlinear regression models. *Econometrica*, 46, 677–94.

—— and Pesaran, B. (1991) *Microfit 3.0: An Interactive Econometric Software Package*. Oxford: Oxford University Press.

—— and Smith, R. (1985) Keynes on econometrics. In T. Lawson and H. Pesaran (eds), *Keynes' Economics: Methodological Issues*, London: Croom Helm, 134–50.

Plosser, C. I., Schwert, G. W. and White, H. (1982) Differencing as a test of specification. *International Economic Review*, 23, 535–52.

Poirier, D. J. (1978) The use of the Box–Cox transformation in limited dependent variable models. *Journal of the American Statistical Association*, 73, 284–7.

—— and Ruud, P. A. (1979) A simple Lagrange multiplier test for lognormal regression. *Economics Letters*, 4, 251–5.

Ramsey, J. B. (1969) Tests for specification errors in classical linear least squares regression analysis. *Journal of the Royal Statistical Society B*, 31, 350–71.

—— (1974) Classical model selection through specification error tests. In P. Zarembka (ed.), *Frontiers in Econometrics*, New York: Academic Press, 13–47.

—— and Schmidt, P. (1976) Some further results on the use of OLS and BLUS residuals in specification error tests. *Journal of the American Statistical Association*, 71, 389–90.

Roy, S. N. (1953) On a heuristic method of test construction and its use in multivariate analysis. *Annals of Mathematical Statistics*, 24, 220–38.

Salkever, D. S. (1976) The use of dummy variables to compute predictions, prediction errors, and confidence intervals. *Journal of Econometrics*, 4, 393–7.

Savin, N. E. and White, K. J. (1978) Estimation and testing for functional form and autocorrelation: a simultaneous approach. *Journal of Econometrics*, 8, 1–12.

Sawyer, K. R. (1984) Multiple hypothesis testing. *Journal of the Royal Statistical Society B*, 46, 419–24.

Schlesselman, J. (1971) Power families: a note on the Box and Cox transformation. *Journal of the Royal Statistical Society B*, 33, 307–11.

Thursby, J. G. and Schmidt, P. (1977) Some properties of tests for specification error in a linear regression model. *Journal of the American Statistical Association*, 72, 635–41.

Tinbergen, J. (1940) On a method of statistical business-cycle research. A reply. *Economic Journal*, 50, 141–54.

Utts, J. M. (1982) The rainbow test for lack of fit in regression. *Communications in Statistics – Theory and Method*, 11, 2801–15.

White, H. (1980a) Using least squares to approximate unknown regression functions. *International Economic Review*, 21, 149–70.

—— (1980b) A heteroskedasticity-consistent covariance matrix estimator and a direct test for heteroskedasticity. *Econometrica*, 48, 817–38.

—— (1982) Regularity conditions for Cox's test of non- nested hypotheses. *Journal of Econometrics*, 19, 301–18.

Wu, D.-M. (1973) Alternative tests of independence between stochastic regressors and disturbances. *Econometrica*, 41, 733–50.

Zarembka, P. (1974) Transformation of variables in econometrics. In P. Zarembka (ed.), *Frontiers in Econometrics*, New York: Academic Press, 81–104.

6 On error correction models: specification, interpretation, estimation

George Alogoskoufis
Birkbeck College, University of London and CEPR
and
Ron Smith
Birkbeck College, University of London

1 Introduction

The notion of an 'error correction model' (ECM) is considered to be a very powerful organizing principle in applied econometrics and has been applied widely, especially since the appearance of the seminal paper by Davidson et al. (1978). It has also prompted a range of statistical developments, most notably the concept of cointegration (Engle and Granger, 1987). In fact, in a recent paper Hylleberg and Mizon (1989) suggest that 'when estimating structural models it is our experience from practical applications that the error correction formulation provides an excellent framework within which it is possible to apply both the data information and the information obtainable from economic theory' (p. 124). Similar views have been expressed by others.

This quotation and others like it raise two sets of questions. The first is related to the fact that the success of the principle has occurred despite the lack of any consensus as to exactly what defines an ECM. The ECM has been interpreted as a method of adjusting a policy instrument to maintain a target variable close to its desired value (Phillips, 1957); a reparameterization of the dynamic linear regression models in terms of differences and levels (some sections of Hendry et al., 1984); a restricted form of a dynamic linear regression model, which imposes long-run proportionality (linear homogeneity) among some regressors (other sections of Hendry et al., 1984); a generalization of the simple 'partial adjustment mechanism' (Hendry and von Ungern Sternberg, 1981); a quasi reduced form derived from special cases of rational expectations models of intertemporal optimization with costs of adjustment (Nickell, 1985); and a particular representation of a vector autoregression appropriate for cointegrated vectors (Engle and Granger, 1987).[1]

The second set of issues raised by the Hylleberg and Mizon quotation is that, contrary to the impression given, most of the applications of the ECM appear to be characterized

140   G. Alogoskoufis and R. Smith

by their relative lack of concern with formal economic theory in general and the modelling of expectations in particular. Using the distinction suggested by Aldrich (1989), the practice of ECM proponents has been to model the time series relationships in the data and then try to interpret the results, rather than to derive relations directly from economic theory, impose the error correction mechanism as an auxiliary adjustment hypothesis, and then estimate the resulting dynamic model. The methodological position of modelling the time series properties of the data and then trying to put interpretations on the resulting model is expounded in various places, one of the early ones being Mizon (1977). This methodological position has been refined in recent years. An influential summing up can be found in Hendry and Wallis (1984).

The present survey has three aims, which are related to the two sets of questions discussed above. The first is to clarify the differences between various specifications of ECMs. We thus provide a brief historical account of their development and evolution, and survey their similarities and differences. Our second aim is to distinguish between different specifications and interpretations of ECMs, and to discuss their economic theoretical status. This enables us to survey the range of controversies that have been provoked. Our third aim is to contribute to the discussion on the specification, estimation and testing of ECMs. We make two points. The first point is that the practice of being cavalier about identification problems and the process of expectations formation, which characterizes some of the most influential proponents of ECMs, can be dangerous as it can lead to very misleading conclusions. The second point, which is seldom recognized, is that ECMs imply tight nonlinear restrictions among the parameters of single dynamic econometric equations. With the exception of special cases these restrictions have so far been ignored in the literature. To illustrate our points we go through an empirical example associated with the early development of the concept, namely the determination of money wages in the United Kingdom. We use annual historical data from 1855 to 1987.

The rest of the paper is organized as follows. In section 2, we examine the evolution of the concept. We go through the approaches of Phillips, Sargan, Hendry and Granger. Section 3 is devoted to theoretical considerations. We briefly survey some of the problems in interpreting long-run parameters and the literature on ECMs as optimal adjustment rules. In section 4 we move to the application of the different concepts, stressing the need for modelling the process of expectations formation and the fact that the predominant specification of ECMs implies a number of nonlinear over-identifying restrictions among the parameters of single dynamic econometric equations. The last section sums up our conclusions.

2   The evolution of the concept

The early development of the ECM is very much a London School of Economics story – Phillips, Sargan and Hendry in particular. Thus, we shall examine the evolution of the concept mainly in terms of their work. Since we are re-reading their work primarily in terms of later developments, rather than in terms of their own contemporary intentions, we are running the risk that the discussion may in places seem anachronistic and we try to point out where our interpretation differs from the concerns of the original authors.

2.1 Phillips

Although there are plausible precursors, Phillips (1954, 1957) introduced the terminology of error correction to economics, in his analysis of feedback control mechanisms for stabilization policy.

Consider a state variable $x(t)$ influenced by a control variable $y(t)$ and exogenous shocks. There is a desired level for $x(t)$, $x^*(t)$, and there is an error associated with it, $e(t) = x^*(t) - x(t)$. What Phillips called 'error correction type stabilization policy' then adjusts the control variable according to proportional, integral and derivative (PID) feedbacks from the errors:

$$y(t) = y^*(t) + f_p e(t) + f_i \int e(t)\, dt + f_d \frac{\partial e(t)}{\partial t}. \tag{1}$$

Phillips's formulation of the control variable was slightly more complicated since he allowed for lags in the policy implementation. In addition he did not provide for the intercept denoted above by y^*. This is the equilibrium level of the control variable, at which $x = x^*$, and is a natural addition to the model (e.g. Turnovsky, 1977, p. 322). The control aspects of the problem with which Phillips was concerned are discussed further in Salmon (1982, 1988).

In discrete time, an equivalent form to (1) is

$$y_t = y_i^* + k_p e_{t-1} + k_i \sum_{i=1}^{\infty} e_{t-i} + k_d \Delta e_t. \tag{2}$$

Applying the first difference operator to (2) gives

$$\Delta y_t = \Delta y_t^* + k_p \Delta e_{t-1} + k_i e_{t-1} + k_d \Delta^2 e_t. \tag{3}$$

This PID equation is the first way of defining the ECM that we might consider. One source of confusion is that subsequent literature, which has started from a model in first differences like (3), has tended to refer to the e_{t-1} term as proportional feedback, whereas in the Phillips formulation it is integral feedback. In addition, later literature has often been specified directly in terms of a target value for y, which may be a function of exogenous variables, dispensing completely with the idea of controlling x around its target.

Although Phillips did not use it explicitly for this purpose, this basic approach can very easily be applied to the concerns of the famous Phillips (1958) article on wage inflation. There he says that the rate of growth of wages depends on the level and change in unemployment and on the rate of inflation. Suppose unemployment is treated as the error (the deviation between actual employment and the target full employment level). Then the wage can be treated as the control variable (of unions say) which feeds back on the error. If we use this interpretation, which is not explicitly given by Phillips himself (see Desai (1984) for a discussion of the derivation of the Phillips curve), then we can write the PID version of his curve in log-linear form as

$$\Delta w_t = \Delta w_t^* + k_p \Delta u_{t-1} + k_i u_{t-1} + k_d \Delta^2 u_t \tag{4}$$

where Δw_t^* is the equilibrium or 'target' wage inflation rate, w is the log of wages and u the unemployment rate.

2.2   Sargan

The next milestone in the evolution of ECMs for econometric purposes is Sargan's (1964) Colston paper. This is primarily a study in econometric methodology dealing with different methods of estimating structural equations with autocorrelated errors. The wage and price equations are used to illustrate the techniques. Sargan estimates an equation of the form

$$\Delta w_t = a_0 + a_1 \Delta p_{t-1} - a_2 u_{t-1} - a_3(w - p)_{t-1} \tag{5}$$

where p is the log of the price level. This is an annual data version of Sargan's equation (15), p. 291, where two additional terms, an incomes policy dummy and a time trend, are being ignored.

Sargan gives two interpretations of this equation. First, he interprets it as the combination of a lagged partial adjustment process, whereby nominal wages adjust to remove part of the gap between actual and 'target' real wages in the previous period, and an equation for target real wages $(w - p)^*$. This interpretation can be written as follows:

$$\Delta w_t = \gamma[(w - p)^*_{t-1} - (w - p)_{t-1}]$$

$$(w - p)^*_t = \omega_t + \theta \Delta p_t - \eta u_t \tag{6a}$$

where γ is the proportion of the gap between past equilibrium and actual real wages that is adjusted in the current period, ω_t represents some exogenous factors (productivity and incomes policies in Sargan's case), η is the semi-elasticity of equilibrium real wages with respect to the unemployment rate and θ is the responsiveness of equilibrium real wages to inflation (*sic*). This formulation is a special case of Phillips's 'error correction', with integral control only, where the error is defined in terms of the deviation of real wages from target. In fact, Phillips's control papers are not referenced, though his (1958) paper is. Gilbert (1989) discusses the influence of Phillips on Sargan's formulation. The Sargan formulation has been widely adopted in subsequent work, and Dawson (1981) extends it to a full PID form.

One strange feature of the interpretation in (6a) is that equilibrium or target real wages depend on price inflation, a clear violation of the homogeneity properties of general equilibrium models. However, this feature can be dispensed with if one assumes that (6a) is an adjustment equation in expected real wages and that inflationary expectations are a function of lagged inflation. Thus (6a) can be modified to

$$\Delta w_t - \Delta p_t^e = \gamma[(w - p)^*_{t-1} - (w - p)_{t-1}]$$
$$(w - p)^*_t = \omega - \eta u_t$$
$$\Delta p_t^e = \pi(1 - \rho) + \rho \Delta p_{t-1}. \tag{6b}$$

The superscript e denotes the expectation of the relevant variable, assumed currently unobserved by wage setters. π and ρ are parameters of an AR(1) expectations process, which under rational expectations could be related to the actual process governing inflation.

Sargan also interprets equation (5) as a Phillips curve, where E is a refined measure of the excess supply of labour.

$$\Delta w_t = \beta_0 + \beta_1 \Delta p_t^e - \beta_2 E_{t-1}$$
$$E_t = u_t + \gamma_2 (w - p)_t \tag{6c}$$

This interpretation suggests that the difference between E and u is positively related to the real wage because of part-time work and temporary labour hoarding.

The point to note at this stage, which is quite crucial for what follows, is that Sargan is quite happy to allow for the same estimates to be given a number of observationally equivalent interpretations. Thus we see that the same econometric equation can be given three quite different theoretical interpretations, with possibly different policy implications, by simply being reparameterized in terms of different unobservables: the target real wage, expected inflation or excess labour supply.

2.3   Hendry

The current popularity of ECMs is largely due to David Hendry, whose work was influenced by both Phillips and Sargan. Gilbert (1986) surveys Hendry's methodological position, which is distributed over many empirical papers. For his contributions on ECMs one of the most influential of these is Davidson et al. (1978). This introduced the ECM form for the aggregate time series relationship between consumers' expenditure and income. Davidson et al. reference Sargan (1964) but not Phillips, and although the estimated relationship is given a 'feedback' interpretation, among many others, the term 'error correction' is not used in the paper. The term is introduced in Hendry (1980), and the links to the PID model are attempted in Hendry and von Ungern Sternberg (1981). Within Hendry's work there are at least two ways that an ECM can be characterized. Both of these appear in Hendry et al. (1984).

For a start, Hendry emphasized the importance of 'general to specific modelling' (Mizon, 1977), and in this context the ECM can be interpreted as a reparameterization of the general 'autoregressive distributed lag' (ADL) or 'dynamic linear regression' (DLR) models.[2]

For example, for two variables y and x, the first-order DLR is

$$y_t = a_0 + b_0 x_t + b_1 x_{t-1} + a_1 y_{t-1} + \varepsilon_t \tag{7}$$

where ε_t is a white noise residual. Equation (7) can be rewritten as

$$\Delta y_t = \alpha_0 + \beta_0 \Delta x_t + \beta_1 x_{t-1} + \alpha_1 y_{t-1} + \varepsilon_t \tag{7a}$$

where $a_0 = \alpha_0, b_0 = \beta_0, \alpha_1 = a_1 - 1, \beta_1 = b_0 + b_1$, or

$$\Delta y_t = \beta_0 \Delta x_t - \lambda(y_{t-1} - \psi_1 x_{t-1} - \psi_0) + \varepsilon_t \tag{7b}$$

where $\lambda = -\alpha_1, \psi_1 = \beta_1/\alpha_1 = (b_0 + b_1)/(1 - a_1), \psi_0 = \alpha_0/\alpha_1$.

This definition of the ECM imposes no restrictions on the DLR, but is in terms of different parameters, which can be given an economic interpretation as impact effects β_0, a scalar adjustment coefficient λ and long-run effects ψ_1. The latter are interpreted as the parameters of an equilibrium relationship about which economic theory is informative. Once again this raises the point that there is a large variety of representations which can be achieved through reparameterizations. They are all observationally equivalent, thus there are no statistical criteria that we can use to choose between them. The questions that arise, then, relate to the parameters of interest from the point of view of economic theory. These questions can only be answered by an explicit theory.

For certain applications, the restriction $\psi_1 = 1$ may be appropriate. For example, for variables in logarithmic form this ensures that the relevant ratios are constant in the long run. This unit restriction is imposed in Davidson et al. through the use of the logarithm of the lagged average propensity to consume. Unit coefficients in logarithmic specifications have a wide range of other applications such as the velocity of money (Hendry, 1980), the wage gap from Cobb–Douglas marginal productivity equations (Bruno and Sachs, 1985) or purchasing power parity (Edison, 1987). They also have applications in levels, such as in the term structure of interest rates. In Hendry's own work the unit coefficient hypothesis seems to have been the most common defining characteristic of the ECM, and this gives us its best known representation, which is an equation of the form

$$\Delta y_t = \alpha + \beta \Delta x_t - \gamma(y_{t-1} - x_{t-1}) + \varepsilon_t. \tag{8}$$

The static long-run solution of this equation (when $y_t = y_{t-1} = y$ and $x_t = x_{t-1} = x$) is

$$y = \frac{\alpha}{\gamma} + x. \tag{9}$$

Davidson et al. interpret $\exp(\alpha/\gamma)$ as an estimate of the long-run average propensity to consume in a consumption function which postulates proportionality between consumers' expenditure and income. This takes the form $Y = KX$.

However, proportionality is a statement about the form of the eventual equilibrium and has little to do with the nature of adjustment processes. Nevertheless, while it seems rather strange to treat a restriction on the character of the equilibrium as the defining characteristic of a model of dynamic adjustment, it is precisely the unit elasticity that makes this popular model operational and more than merely a parameterization of the dynamic linear regression model. We shall return to the question of the restrictions implied by a more general version of these ECMs in section 4 below.

2.4   Granger

The latest twist in the ECM saga has come from Granger and associates. As time series statisticians they noted that most economic series are highly trended with stationary growth rates. This implies that they are integrated of order one, I(1). This means that they become stationary after being differenced once. Then they go on to ask how a stationary variable Δy_t (integrated of order zero) in (7a) could be explained by two non-stationary variables y_{t-1} and x_{t-1}, which are I(1). The two sides of the equation are of different orders of integration, unless the linear combination $y_t - \psi_1 x_t$ is also stationary.

In general, linear combinations of I(1) variables will also be I(1), but if they happen to be I(0), the variables are said to be cointegrated (Engle and Granger, 1987). If they are cointegrated then there exists an error correction representation. Conversely, if there is an error correction representation for the series, they are cointegrated. However, the definition of an error correction representation differs from the earlier ECMs we have used.

Engle and Granger define a vector stochastic process x_t, which is I(1), as having an error correction representation if it can be expressed as

$$A(L)(1 - L)x_t = -\gamma e_{t-1} + \varepsilon_t. \tag{10}$$

L is the backward shift or lag operator, such that $(1-L)x_t = x_t - x_{t-1}$. $A(L)$ is a polynomial in L of the form $\alpha_0 + \alpha_1 L + \alpha_2 L^2 + \cdots$. ε_t is a stationary multivariate disturbance. It is assumed that $A(0) = I$, $A(1)$ has all elements finite and $\gamma \neq 0$. The cointegrating vector is α, where $e_t = \alpha' x_t$ is I(0). There may be more than one such vector. The equilibrium is interpreted as $\alpha' x_t = 0$; thus e_t is interpreted as a measure of the error or deviation from equilibrium.

Engle and Granger (1987) stress the difference from earlier definitions. This definition of an ECM is explicitly multivariate. It does not distinguish between endogenous and exogenous variables, though it may allow some inferences about Granger causality, and current values do not appear on the right-hand side. Homogeneity or unit coefficients are not intrinsic to the definition and the vector α consists of unknown parameters to be estimated. However, these parameters do not necessarily have a theoretical interpretation.

3 Theoretical considerations

At least two conclusions can be drawn from our examination of the evolution of the concept of ECMs in the previous section.

The first is that different authors have different views as to what constitutes an ECM. There seem to be at least three lines, one associated with Phillips, the other associated with Sargan–Hendry, and the last associated with Engle–Granger. Of the three approaches, Phillips and Sargan–Hendry seem to have more common ground, in as much as they seem to be interested in dynamic decision rules of economic agents. For them ECMs seem to be structural representations of dynamic adjustment towards some equilibrium about which economic theory can be informative. Engle, Granger and associates seem to view ECMs not as structural decision rules but as statistical representations only (reduced forms). As a result, their definition of equilibrium is also statistical (variables stay close together).

The second conclusion is that, notwithstanding the differences in emphasis referred to above, all authors seem to envisage a rather limited role for economic theory. In contrast to the Cowles Commission approach which has largely dominated theoretical blueprints of how to specify econometric equations, the ECMs are not directly derived from theory, and therefore the estimated parameters only bear an indirect relation to theoretical parameters of interest. This is clearly borne out by the fact that the leading practitioners are quite happy with alternative interpretations. This is amply illustrated in both Sargan's (1964) paper and Hendry's (1980) contrast of the two methodologies. Practitioners of this alternative approach seem to have to give *ex post* interpretations to their estimated parameters, rather than setting up from the start the relation between their statistical and theoretical parameters of interest. One of the main problems with this approach is that multiple interpretations are given much more emphasis in this methodology than in the Cowles Commission approach. This is clearly illustrated in a well-known problem in this literature, that of solving for long-run parameters.

3.1 'Interpreting' long-run parameters

The derivation of long-run parameters has prompted considerable controversy, which seems to have been bred by the practice of using theory *ex post* as a way to interpret equilibrium relationships. However, the estimated 'long-run coefficients' are likely to be a mixture of adjustment and expectational as well as long-run structural parameters.

To illustrate this suppose the 'long-run' equilibrium in logs is

$$y^* = k + x. \tag{11}$$

Then assume an expectations-augmented ECM short-run relation given by

$$\Delta y_t = \beta(x_t^e - x_{t-1}) + \gamma(y_{t-1}^* - y_{t-1}) \tag{12}$$

where x_t follows a stationary AR(1) process with mean π, and superscript e denotes $E(x_t \mid I_{t-1})$. Equation (12) is of exactly the same form as (8) except that x has been replaced by its expectation. The expectation of x is

$$x_t^e = \pi(1 - \rho) + \rho x_{t-1}. \tag{13}$$

Substituting (13) in (12), in terms of observables the relationship is

$$\Delta y_t = \beta\pi(1 - \rho) + \gamma k + (\beta\rho - \beta + \gamma)x_{t-1} - \gamma y_{t-1} \tag{14}$$

with long-run solution

$$y = \frac{\pi\beta(1 - \rho) + \gamma k}{\gamma} + \left[1 + \frac{\beta(\rho - 1)}{\gamma}\right] x. \tag{15}$$

The long-run coefficient of x will reflect equilibrium, adjustment and expectations parameters. Thus, if one concentrates on (14) only, ignoring the further information given by (13), one would tend to get an estimate of the long-run impact of x on y that is less than unity.[3] This bias will be avoided if one recognizes that since x follows an AR(1) process with mean π, in the long run x ought to be replaced by π. Then (15) reduces to

$$y = k + \pi = k + x. \tag{16}$$

In (16) the calculated long-run elasticity will be the correct one.

The example above, based on expectations, is not the only way in which biases in the calculation of long-run coefficients may arise. This problem can be illustrated by a second type of solution that Davidson et al. (1978) use. This is based on steady state growth effects.

Abstract from expectations in equation (12), and consider the ECM as in equation (8). In a balanced growth path $\Delta y = \Delta x = g$. Then the steady state solution of (8) depends on the growth rates:

$$y = \frac{g(\beta - 1)}{\gamma} + \frac{\alpha}{\gamma} + x. \tag{17}$$

There are many observationally equivalent interpretations that can be given to the 'growth coefficient' $(\beta - 1)/\gamma$. Davidson et al. supposed that the equilibrium depended on the growth rate:

$$y^* = k + x + \psi g. \tag{18a}$$

They then took $(\beta - 1)/\gamma$ as an estimate of ψ, and α/γ as an estimate of k. This was justified by reference to life cycle hypothesis models where the savings ratio is a positive function of the growth rate because of demographic effects. This interpretation was disputed and prompted a considerable controversy (Currie, 1981; Salmon, 1982; Patterson and Ryding, 1984; Kelly, 1985; Nickell, 1985; Pagan, 1985; Osborn, 1986; Taylor, 1987; Hendry and Neale, 1988). We shall return to aspects of this controversy below.

A second interpretation is that the equilibrium is $y = x + k$. Then k is estimated by α/γ, but the adjustment process

$$\Delta y_t = \beta \Delta x_t - \gamma(y_{t-1} - y_{t-1}^*) \tag{18b}$$

is not 'trend neutral' and leads to a steady state bias $y - y^* = g(\beta - 1)/\gamma$ unless $\beta = 1$. The term involving the growth rate is then just a measure of the size of the steady state bias.

A third interpretation uses the same equilibrium condition as the second but an adjustment process

$$\Delta y_t = g + \beta \Delta x_t - \gamma(y_{t-1} - y_{t-1}^*) \tag{18c}$$

where g is a constant, which is the decision-makers' correct estimate of the steady state growth rate. The estimated intercept is $g + \gamma k$ and the extra term just offsets the steady state bias. Thus there is neither steady state bias nor a growth effect in the equilibrium, but α/γ is a biased estimate of k.

Again we have the position that interpretation of the estimated parameters is dependent on theoretical considerations about both the nature of the long-run equilibrium and the adjustment process itself. Parameterizations with quite different theoretical interpretations are observationally equivalent. It may be the case that other evidence can be used to decide between these interpretations (e.g. under the third interpretation we might expect the intercept to shift if the steady state growth shifted) but the estimates themselves cannot inform us about the appropriate interpretation.

What transpires from the above discussion is that there could be multiple interpretations of the estimated equations, even when one starts from the basic premise of an error correction statistical model with long-run homogeneity between y and x.

In view of the above, we shall proceed to assess various ways in which prior theoretical considerations have been used to derive ECMs. We shall concentrate on the strand of the literature associated with the 'LSE approach' as this is the strand that gives relatively more attention to structural relations. Engle, Granger and associates are avowedly only interested in statistical representations (*reduced forms*).

3.2   Error correction models as optimal adjustment rules

Adjustment to equilibrium may come about through *tâtonnement*-type processes as prices and quantities respond to imbalances between demand and supply or as the optimal response of individual agents in an intertemporal context. In the context of ECMs, Hendry and Anderson (1977), Hendry and von Ungern Sternberg (1981), Nickell (1985) and Pagan (1985) provide derivations of ECMs starting from the last case. Common to all the derivations are quadratic loss functions that penalize both deviations from equilibrium and rapid adjustment.

Pagan begins with the problem of an agent who wishes to minimize a myopic quadratic loss function which penalizes both deviations of actual values y_t from target values y_t^* and the deviation of changes in the variable from some normal growth rate α_t. We will treat y_t as being the logarithm of some variable, so Δy_t is a growth rate. In the usual derivation of the partial adjustment model (PAM) α_t is set equal to zero so any growth is penalized. In this case y_t is chosen to minimize

$$\Lambda = \frac{1}{2}(y_t - y_t^*)^2 + \frac{\theta}{2}(\Delta y_t - \alpha_t)^2 \tag{19}$$

where θ is the ratio of the marginal cost of adjustment relative to the marginal cost of being away from equilibrium. The optimal y that minimizes (19) is given by

$$y_t = \phi^{-1}y_t^* + \phi^{-1}\theta y_{t-1} + \phi^{-1}\theta\alpha_t \tag{19a}$$

where $\phi = 1 + \theta$, so $1 - \phi^{-1}\theta = \phi^{-1} = \lambda$. The solution can be written

$$\Delta y_t = \lambda(y_t^* - y_{t-1}) + (1 - \lambda)\alpha_t. \tag{19b}$$

If $\alpha_t = 0$, we get the usual PAM expression

$$\Delta y_t = \lambda(y_t^* - y_{t-1}). \tag{20}$$

Note the similarity of (20) to Sargan's version of the ECM in equation (6a). This version of Sargan's model is none other than the PAM. Equation (20) can also be written as

$$\Delta y_t = \lambda\Delta y_t^* - \lambda(y_{t-1} - y_{t-1}^*). \tag{20a}$$

The standard PAM has the property that the deviation from the long-run equilibrium $(y - y^*)_t$ does not go to zero in steady state when the target grows at a constant rate. Its limit is $g(\lambda - 1)/\lambda$, where in steady state we have assumed that $\Delta y^* = g \neq 0$. Trend neutrality, zero error in steady state, requires that $\alpha_t = \Delta y_t^*$. It is not clear that trend neutrality is necessarily a desirable property. Nickell (1985) argues, using the forward-looking cost of adjustment model discussed below, that with a discount factor less than unity it will not be worth incurring the additional adjustment costs necessary to catch up completely with a growing target. However, this is in the context of a model where any growth is penalized, rather than only growth which differs from some normal level.

Pagan suggests three ways in which trend neutrality can be achieved: through an intercept, which picks up the constant $(1 - \lambda)g$, or by adding, as proxies for α_t, either Δy_{t-1} or Δy_{t-1}^*. Suppose we take Δy_t^* as a proxy for α_t. Then the model becomes

$$\Delta y_t = (1 - \lambda)\Delta y_t^* + \lambda(y_t^* - y_{t-1}) = \Delta y_t^* - \lambda(y_{t-1} - y_{t-1}^*). \tag{21}$$

Equation (21) could also be rewritten as

$$y_t = y_t^* + (1 - \lambda)(y_{t-1} - y_{t-1}^*) \tag{21a}$$

which for $y_t^* = \beta' x_t$ is of exactly the same form as a static model with AR(1) disturbances. Thus this model involves the common factor restrictions (COMFAC) emphasized by Sargan (1964) and Hendry and Mizon (1978). The autoregressive coefficient is equal to $1 - \lambda$. As argued in Hendry et al. (1984), the usual PAM and the AR(1) disturbance models can be seen as special cases of an ECM of the form of (18c).

The question that arises then is whether one could derive the general error correction form from a problem of optimization of quadratic loss function like (19). Hendry and von Ungern Sternberg (1981) justify this form of ECM by augmenting the loss function (19) by a term involving the product of the rate of change of the actual variable and its long-run equilibrium value. Their argument is that if adjustment in the actual variable is in the same direction as the change in the equilibrium, then adjustment will be less costly.

$$\Lambda = \frac{1}{2}(y_t - y_t^*)^2 + \frac{\theta_1}{2}(y_t - y_{t-1})^2 - \theta_2(y_t - y_{t-1})(y_t^* - y_{t-1}^*). \tag{22}$$

Minimizing (22) with respect to y_t and rearranging the first-order condition yields the ECM, as in equation (18c), where

$$\beta = \frac{1 + \theta_2}{1 + \theta_1} \qquad \gamma = \frac{1}{1 + \theta_1}.$$

However, the additional term introduced by Hendry and von Ungern Sternberg (1981) is too *ad hoc* to be satisfactory. In addition, (22), like (19), is myopic and therefore inconsistent with the more plausible theoretical assumption that agents are forward looking.

Nickell (1985) derives the ECM from a forward-looking quadratic costs of adjustment model supplemented by particular forms of stochastic process driving the target. He also examines the Hendry–von Ungern Sternberg type loss function, but we will use the simpler partial adjustment form. Nickell assumes that agents have an infinite horizon and minimize the present value of the one-period losses given by (19).

$$L_t = \sum_{i=t}^{\infty} \delta^i \left[\frac{1}{2}(y_i - y_i^*)^2 + \frac{\theta}{2}\Delta y_i^2 \right] \tag{23}$$

where δ is the discount factor. The Euler equation takes the form

$$\delta y_{t+1} - (1 + \delta + \theta^{-1})y_t + y_{t-1} = -\frac{y_t^*}{\theta} \tag{24a}$$

Solving the Euler equation requires finding the two roots, $\mu_1 < 1 < \mu_2$, which are the solutions of the characteristic equation

$$\delta\mu^2 - (1 + \delta + \theta^{-1})\mu + 1 = 0.$$

Calling the stable root (i.e. the one that is less than unity) μ, the optimal policy is then given by

$$\Delta y_t = (1 - \mu)(\tilde{y}_t - y_{t-1}), \tag{24b}$$

the traditional partial adjustment form but with a forward looking target

$$\tilde{y}_t = (1 - \delta\mu)E\left[\sum_{i=t}^{\infty}(\delta\mu)^i y_{t+i}^*\right] \tag{24c}$$

where the expectation is taken at time t.

To make this operational requires that it be augmented by a model for y_{t+i}^* that will be used to get the rational expectations solution. As Nickell (1985) shows, if y^* follows a random walk with drift g, then (24b) becomes

$$\Delta y_t = \frac{(1 - \mu)\delta\mu g}{1 - \delta\mu} + (1 - \mu)\Delta y_t^* - (1 - \mu)(y_{t-1} - y_{t-1}^*) \tag{25a}$$

which is just partial adjustment with an intercept to track the growing target, written in an error correction form.

Alternatively, assume that the rate of change of y_t^* follows a stationary AR(1) process, which is the same as y_t^* following a second-order autoregression with one unit root. This can be written as

$$\Delta y_t^* = g(1 - \rho) + \rho\Delta y_{t-1}^* + v_t \tag{25b}$$

where g is the steady state growth rate and ρ is the persistence of the growth rate.

With this specification, (24b) becomes

$$\Delta y_t = \frac{\delta\mu(1 - \mu)(1 - \rho)g}{(1 - \delta\mu)(1 - \rho\delta\mu)} + \frac{1 - \mu}{1 - \rho\delta\mu}\Delta y_t^* - (1 - \mu)(y_{t-1} - y_{t-1}^*) \tag{25c}$$

which looks like a standard ECM. Note that if ρ is equal to one, the constant vanishes.

Higher order autoregressive processes for Δy_t^* add further lags in that variable. Nickell comments that, 'Since it is almost a stylised fact that aggregate quantity variables in economics follows a second order autoregression with a root close to unity, we may expect to find the error correction mechanism appearing in many different contexts' (p. 124). Nickell also shows that a random walk with a moving average error also gives rise to an error correction type equation. In each of the cases considered by Nickell the assumed processes for y_t^* can be used to disentangle the adjustment from the expectational parameters (see Alogoskoufis and Nissim (1981) for an early application to the consumption function, and Domowitz and Hakkio (1990) for an international study of money demand). Thus, shifts in the process generating y_t^* ought to be reflected in equations of the form of (25a) and (25b). This suggests tests in the spirit of the Lucas (1976) critique. Thus, one could in principle test whether error correction mechanisms are due to the kind of forward-looking behaviour by checking whether shifts in the process generating y_t^* are reflected in equations of the form of (25b), as is done in Alogoskoufis and Smith (1989) and Hendry (1988).

When Domowitz and Hakkio (1990) implemented this procedure, estimating a generalized version of (25c) that was derived from a cost function of the form of (22), they found that there is no empirical support for the Hendry–von Ungern Sternberg term in the cost function. Without that extra term, the error correction model works well, and the cross equations restrictions cannot be rejected as long as the ECM parameters are allowed to shift with expectational parameters.

4 Specification and estimation of error correction models with an application to wage setting in the United Kingdom

In this section we proceed to discuss in more detail the specification of the alternative ECMs and review alternative methods of estimation. We illustrate the different models and methods and the problems that arise with an example associated with the early evolution of the models, namely wage setting in the United Kingdom. The section is structured as follows. First, we discuss statistical representation of the ECM as a reparameterization of the DLR model or of a vector autoregressive (VAR) model involving cointegrating vectors. The approaches differ in so far as the DLR involves conditioning on current and lagged values whereas the VAR involves conditioning on lagged values only. They both share a common weakness in that the economic interpretation of the estimated parameters is problematic, as neither approach provides a satisfactory solution to the indentification problem. We next consider a structural approach, where economic theory considerations are brought in from the start, and they inform the process of estimation. In this approach there is a clear distinction between behavioural and expectational parameters. Three alternative structural models, corresponding to what we called the Phillips, Sargan and Hendry interpretations in section 2, are estimated. We discuss the relation between the treatment of expectations and the estimation method, and demonstrate the usefulness of nonlinear estimation methods for structural ECMs.

4.1 Statistical representations of error correction models

In the earlier historical review we identified two more 'statistical' versions of the ECM: the Hendry interpretation of the ECM as a reparameterization of a DLR model, and the Granger interpretation of the ECM as a representation for a VAR model involving cointegrating vectors. These approaches are statistical in that the initial objective is to estimate the parameters of a conditional distribution rather than an explicit theoretical model. The approaches differ in whether the distribution is conditional on current and lagged values (the DLR) or only on lagged values (the VAR).

The data used are five series for the UK, 1855–1987. The variables are the logarithms of wages, w, the Feinstein earnings measure; prices, p, the consumers' expenditure deflator; real gross domestic product, y; employment, l, including armed forces; and labour force, n. From these, we can also construct four derived variables: real wages, $w - p$; productivity, $y - l$; the unemployment rate, $n - l$; and the share of wages,

$(w - p) - (y - l)$. There are well-known problems of definition and interpretation with such long runs of data, but here we shall use them primarily to illustrate the specification and estimation of ECMs.

We shall describe the basic time series properties of the data by first estimating a univariate AR model for each variable, i.e. conditioning only on its own past values; then a VAR for all the variables, i.e. conditioning on the full set of past values; and finally the DLR for wages, which conditions on current and lagged variables. We shall also calculate estimates of the long-run or cointegrating vectors.

The univariate time series model has the form

$$\Delta x_t = \alpha_0 + \alpha_1 x_{t-1} + \alpha_2 \Delta x_{t-1} + \alpha_3 t \tag{26}$$

The estimates for the original variables are given in table 1 and for the derived variables in table 2. The F statistic testing against a further lag suggests that second-order autoregressions seem to be adequate to describe these series. Tables 1 and 2 also give a test for serial correlation, the standard error of regression for the univariate AR model, the standard error of regression for the VAR discussed below, and the augmented Dickey–Fuller statistics (ADFs) (Dickey and Fuller, 1981). These ADFs, calculated as the t statistics for α_1, indicate that the variables w, p, y, e and n are all I(1). This is in contrast to Hall (1989) who found, with post-war quarterly data, that w and p were I(2). The hypothesis that p and w were I(2) was tested and rejected. This indicates the sensitivity of the test to sample and the sampling frequency. In addition, the power of the test is low and it is not robust to parameter change (e.g. Perron, 1990). The fragility of inferences about the degree of integration or cointegration should be emphasized. The real wage, $w - p$, and productivity, $y - l$, also appear to be I(1). However, $n - l$ (the unemployment rate) and $(w - p) - (y - l)$ (the share of wages) are I(0). Again for post-war data Hall found u, equivalent to $n - l$, to be I(1). Given these tests, in what follows we shall regard all our series as I(1) except the share and the unemployment rate, which we shall treat as I(0). It is worth noting that since linear combinations of cointegrating vectors are also cointegrating vectors, other combinations such as $w - p - y + n$ would also be cointegrating vectors.

Above we identified the cointegrating vectors from prior theoretical considerations, namely the definition of economically interesting ratios such as the unemployment rate and the labour share. Engle and Granger suggest a two-step procedure for estimating the parameters of a cointegrating vector and the ECM. First run a static regression of y on x to obtain the elements of the cointegrating vector α. The residuals from this regression provide an estimate of the 'error' and can be tested for stationarity. If the errors are I(0), they can be used in a second stage in estimating the short-run error correction mechanism. Table 6 (later) gives the Engle–Granger estimate of the cointegrating regression, obtained by a regression of w on the levels of p, y, l and n, intercept and trend. This had a Durbin–Watson coefficient (DW) of 0.4444 and an ADF of -4.89, again confirming that there exists at least one cointegrating vector. In addition, since the share of wages and unemployment rate seem to be I(0), $w - p - y + l$ was run on $n - l$, intercept and trend. This is given as the restricted Engle–Granger estimates in table 6.

A second-order VAR was then estimated of the same form as (26), but making x the five-element vector, w, p, y, l, n. The derived variables are also regressed on

Table 1   Univariate second-order AR, 1857–1987

$$\Delta x_t = \alpha_0 + \alpha_1 x_{t-1} + \alpha_2 \Delta x_{t-1} + \alpha_3 t$$

	$x = w$	$x = p$	$x = y$	$x = l$	$x = n$
α_0	−0.02	−0.05	0.56*	0.68*	0.28
	(0.02)	(0.04)	(0.25)	(0.26)	(0.15)
$\alpha_1 \times 10^2$	0.08	−0.66	−5.99*	−7.32*	−3.01*
	(0.71)	(0.70)	(2.78)	(2.88)	(1.65)
α_2	0.60*	0.71*	0.26*	0.36*	0.41*
	(0.07)	(0.07)	(0.09)	(0.08)	(0.08)
$\alpha_3 \times 10^3$	0.36	0.35	1.06*	0.39*	0.15
	(0.27)	(0.18)	(0.48)	(0.18)	(0.10)
$\text{AUT}_1(1, 126)$	0.81	2.80	1.12	0.40	0.16
$F (1, 125)$	0.80	2.70	1.22	0.39	0.15
$\text{SER} \times 100$	4.55	3.61	2.98	2.17	0.96
$\text{SER} \times 100 \text{ (VAR)}$	3.81	3.38	2.82	1.94	0.78
ADF_τ	−0.11	−0.93	−2.16	−2.54	−1.82

Asymptotic standard errors are below estimated coefficients. AUT_1 is the F version of the Lagrange multiplier test for first-order residual autocorrelation. F is a test of the exclusion of Δx_{t-2}. ADF is the augmented Dickey–Fuller τ statistic on x_{t-1}.

Table 2   Univariate second-order AR, 1857–1987

$$\Delta x_t = \alpha_0 + \alpha_1 x_{t-1} + \alpha_2 \Delta x_{t-1} + \alpha_3 t$$

	$x = n - l$	$x = w - p$	$x = y - l$	$x = (w - p) - (y - l)$
α_0	0.01	−0.03	0.002	0.85*
	(0.01)	(0.09)	(0.008)	(0.24)
α_1	−0.16*	0.004	−0.007	−0.13*
	(0.05)	(0.01)	(0.02)	(0.04)
α_2	0.22*	0.07	0.02	0.28*
	(0.09)	(0.09)	(0.09)	(0.08)
$\alpha_3 \times 10^3$	0.02	0.11	−0.17	0.20*
	(0.04)	(0.18)	(0.24)	(0.08)
$\text{AUT}_1 (1, 124)$	0.002	0.58	0.02	2.21
$F (1, 125)$	0.0002	0.90	1.52	2.10
$\text{SER} \times 100$	1.88	2.30	2.60	2.84
$\text{SER} \times 100 \text{ (VAR)}$	1.88	2.05	2.39	2.63
ADF_τ	−3.49	0.29	−0.32	−3.55

lagged levels and changes of these five variables. Table 3 gives the residual correlation matrix for the VAR. It is clear that by far the highest contemporaneous correlations are between wages and prices as one might expect. This implies that including current prices in a wage equation or vice versa will produce large, though potentially spurious, improvements in fit.

Table 3

$$\mathrm{VAR}\,\Delta x_t = A_0 + A_1 \Delta x_{t-1} + A_2 x_{t-1}$$

$$x = w, p, y, l, n$$

VAR residual correlation matrix

	w	p	y	l	n
w	1	0.84	0.30	0.38	−0.08
p		1	0.14	0.36	−0.20
y			1	0.55	0.20
l				1	0.28

Granger causality tests

	For x with respect to w	*For w with respect to x*
p	10.3988	1.5018
y	3.9299	1.6789
l	4.1924	0.0783
n	5.5498	1.8983

$F(2, 119)\ 5\% = 3.07$

The existence of cointegrating vectors implies Granger causality between the variables. To pursue this causality tests were conducted by deleting variables in turn from equations of the VAR. The results, also shown in table 3, which focus on the relationship between wages and the other variables, are clear cut. Whereas p, y, l and n are all Granger causal with respect to w, w is not Granger causal with respect to any of these variables. Such Granger non-causaliy of nominal wages with respect to the other variables is a condition required for the strong exogeneity (see Engle et al., 1983) of these other variables with respect to wages. However, as Osborn (1984) points out (p. 94), Granger causality relates to the final equations of an econometric system, and this information is different in nature from the economic causation used in building a structural model.

Table 4 provides estimates for an unrestricted second-order DLR model explaining wages in terms of four other variables. It also gives the long-run solution estimated directly using the 'Bewley' (1979) transform, discussed by Wickens and Breusch (1988). None of the diagnostic statistics for serial correlation, functional form, normality or heteroskedasticity suggest any problem, but the model is clearly over-parameterized, with only half the sixteen estimated parameters being 'significant'. While it would certainly be possible to conduct an *ad hoc* specification search which restricted and reparameterized the DLR to produce a more parsimonious model, we will not follow that route. It is noticeable that, as the residual correlation matrix of the VAR suggested, conditioning on current variables substantially improves the fit, reducing the SER from 3.81 to 1.93. In addition, the long-run coefficients of prices, output and employment are not significantly different from unity.

The Granger–Engle procedure cannot deal with cases, such as this, where there is more than one cointegrating vector. A maximum likelihood procedure for estimation and inference about all the cointegrating vectors is described in Johansen and Juselius (1990). Suppose x_t is a $l \times p$ vector. The VAR can be written

Table 4 Dynamic linear regression, dependent variable w_t

	x_t	x_{t-1}	x_{t-2}
p	0.9638*	−0.9778*	0.1601
	(0.0603)	(0.1510)	(0.1135)
y	0.2743*	−0.5124*	0.3701
	(0.0754)	(0.1113)	(0.0900)
l	−0.1294	0.7455*	−0.5301*
	(0.1234)	(0.1656)	(0.1150)
n	−0.3501	−0.7115	−0.0698
	(0.2511)	(0.3744)	(0.2307)
w		1.0048*	−0.1354
		(0.0846)	(0.0840)

Intercept 1.5902*   Trend$\times 10^3$ 0.4558
(0.7024)   (0.5980)
$R^{-2} = 0.9998$ SER $\times 100 = 1.93$ AUT(1, 114)0.22
FUN(1, 114)1.32   NOR(2)0.6432   HET(1, 129)0.1973

Long-run solution:
$$w = 12.17 + 1.1185p + 1.0105y + 0.6586l - 2.2322n + 0.0035t$$
$$(4.74)(0.677)(0.1784)(0.5491)(0.7488)(0.0047)$$

AUT, FUN, and HET are F-type diagnostics testing respectively against first-order residual autocorrelation, nonlinearity and heteroskedasticity. NOR is the skewness–kurtosis diagnostic of Bera–Jarque, testing against non-normality.
*Absolute t statistic greater than 2.

$$\Delta x_t = \sum \delta_i \Delta x_{t-1} + \pi x_{t-1} + u_t \tag{27}$$

where π is a $p \times p$ matrix. If π is of full rank p, this implies that the vector process x_t is stationary. If the rank of π is zero, i.e. π is the null matrix, then the level terms have no effect and a model in first differences is appropriate. If the rank of π is r between zero and p, then there are $p \times r$ matrices γ and α such that

$$\pi = \gamma\alpha', \tag{28a}$$

i.e. there are r cointegrating vectors

$$e_t = \alpha' x_t, \tag{28b}$$

and (27) can be written in terms of the errors:

$$\Delta x_t = \sum \delta_i \Delta x_{t-i} + \gamma e_{t-1} + u_t \tag{28c}$$

with feedback coefficients or loadings γ.

The estimation method first concentrates the likelihood to remove the effects of the right-hand side differences by regressing Δx_t and x_{t-1} on Δx_{t-i}. These regressions give

Table 5   Johansen–Juselius estimates, from second-order VAR with intercept and trend

λ_i	0.213	0.187	0.119	0.046	0.002
$-T \ln(1 - \lambda_i)$	31.38	27.14	16.60	6.18	0.22
$-T \sum \ln(1 - \lambda_i)$	81.52	50.14	23.00	6.40	0.22
Eigenmatrix					
p	+12.48	−15.00	+14.70	+10.89	+0.39
y	11.01	−22.57	+12.14	−0.79	+7.15
n	−37.22	−28.89	+16.01	+5.96	+21.22
l	+25.68	+16.64	−1.15	−7.05	−13.26
w	−10.25	+16.79	−11.91	−8.03	+1.10

Table 6   Alternative long-run estimates, for wage equation
(coefficients of intercept and trend not reported)

	p	y	l	n	η
Engle–Granger	1.08	0.97	−0.26	−0.95	−0.19
Restricted Engle–Granger	1	1	−0.46	−0.54	0
Johansen 1	1.22	1.07	+2.51	−3.63	−0.12
Johansen 2	0.89	1.34	−0.99	−1.72	−1.71
DLRM	1.12	1.01	+0.66	−2.23	−0.57

$p \times 1$ residual vectors $\boldsymbol{R}_{0t}$, from the $\Delta \boldsymbol{x}_t$ regression, and $\boldsymbol{R}_{1t}$, from the $\boldsymbol{x}_{t-1}$ regression, with covariance matrices

$$S_{ij} = T^{-1} \sum_{t=1}^{T} \boldsymbol{R}_{it} \boldsymbol{R}_{jt}' \qquad i, j = 0, 1; \quad t = 1, \dots, T. \tag{29a}$$

Then the solution to the equation

$$\mid \lambda S_{11} - S_{10} S_{00}^{-1} S_{01} \mid = 0 \tag{29b}$$

gives ranked eigenvalues $\lambda_1, \dots, \lambda_p$ and a matrix of eigenvectors $\boldsymbol{V} = (v_1, \dots, v_p)$. The estimates of α that maximize the likelihood function under the hypothesis $\boldsymbol{\pi} = \gamma \alpha'$ is then the eigenmatrix (v_1, v_r). These have to be normalized to be interpreted. Johansen also provides a test based on λ_i for determining r, the number of cointegrating vectors. These tests use $-T \ln(1 - \lambda_i)$ and $-T \sum \ln(1 - \lambda_i)$, and suggest that there are at least two cointegrating vectors in our data, given by the first two columns of the eigenmatrix.

Table 5 gives the results from the Johansen procedure. These were obtained from the PCFIML module of PC-GIVE, which gives you the Johansen estimates automatically when you estimate a VAR (provided you told it that you were an expert). The first two Johansen cointegrating vectors are given in table 6 renormalized to make the coefficient of wages unity. With post-war data, using the Johansen procedure on $w - p, y, l, u$, and h (the logarithm of weekly hours worked), Hall (1989) identified the cointegrating vector

$$(w - p) = 1.099(y - l) - 0.562u - 0.49h$$

where $u \approx n - l$. This is similar to our first vector except for the effect of hours.

The various procedures give us a number of different estimates of the long-run relationship between w and p, y, l and n. Were target real wages determined by productivity with a unit elasticity (e.g. as the marginal product equation of a Cobb–Douglas), unemployment and trend we would expect a long-run relationship of the form

$$(w - p)^* = (y - l) - \psi u + \delta_0 + \delta_1 t. \tag{30a}$$

Thus in the long-run solutions

$$w = \beta_0 p + \beta_1 y + \beta_2 l + \beta_3 n + \beta_4 t \tag{30b}$$

the restrictions $\beta_0 = 1$, $\beta_1 = 1$, and $1 + \beta_2 + \beta_3 = 0$ should be satisfied. Table 6 summarizes the possible long-run estimates. These are obtained from the Engle–Granger static levels regression; the regression of the share on the unemployment rate and a trend, which satisfies the restrictions above; the first two Johansen cointegrating vectors normalized on wages; and finally the long-run solution from the DLR model. It is clear that, except for the second Johansen vector, β_0 and β_1 are not far from unity, and, except for the second Johansen and the DLR, $\eta = 1 + \beta_2 + \beta_3$ is not too far from zero. However, although economically plausible, these restrictions on the long-run solution would be rejected both for the VAR, $F(3, 119) = 3.45$, and for the DLR, $F(3, 115) = 5.14$. The reason for this seems to be that this measure of the share of wages shifted up to a new level after the Second World War. If a dummy variable which takes the value unity after 1945 is introduced, the restrictions cannot be rejected at the 5 per cent level: for the VAR $F(3, 118) = 1.92$, and for the DLR $F(3, 114) = 2.51$.

Both the DLR and the VAR typically characterize the time series properties of the data by a highly parameterized model. In contrast, more theoretical versions of the ECM tend to imply strong restrictions which leave relatively few parameters to be estimated.

In conclusion, as our example above has shown, the range of statistical techniques utilized has not provided us with anything more than we would have got by taking the economically meaningful linear combinations of the variables and looking at their graphs. In addition, the earlier discussion emphasized that it may be misleading to impute structural interpretations to summaries of the statistical characteristics of the data, such as those provided by the long-run solution of the DLR, the pattern of Granger causality and the cointegrating vectors. The estimated coefficients are likely to be complicated mixtures of equilibrium, adjustment and expectations parameters and disentangling them poses substantial identification problems. This suggests that there are advantages in starting from more structural models.

4.2   Specification of structural error correction models

We next turn to such structural error correction models. The Phillips ECM for wage adjustment is given by equation (4). It postulates that wage inflation is equal to 'equilibrium' or 'target' wage inflation w^* minus three terms related to the lagged unemployment rate, its change and the acceleration of current unemployment. The issue that needs to be resolved before one proceeds to discuss estimation of this version is what determines 'equilibrium' wage inflation.

Different authors take different views about the process of wage determination, and therefore about the underlying model of equilibrium wages. Phillips (1958) seems to think of equilibrium wages as being a function of prices. He seems to view the effect of unemployment as a manifestation of excess supply of labour that will only affect the adjustment process of wages but not the equilibrium level of real wages. We can therefore assume for the Phillips model that equilibrium real wages are independent of the unemployment rate. Then, equilibrium wage inflation is determined by expected price inflation and the rate of change of equilibrium real wages. The following simple model captures this.

$$w_t^* = \omega_t + p_t^e \tag{31}$$

where ω is the exogenous equilibrium real wage and superscript e denotes the expectation of the relevant variable. We have deliberately used the expectation of the price level in order to highlight the role of the modelling of expectations. Clearly, if workers had full information about current variables at the time when wages are set, then one could substitute the actual price level for the expectation. If they did not, then some process of expectations formation has to be assumed.

Applying the first difference operator to (31) and assuming that equilibrium real wages grow at the rate g, we get

$$\Delta w_t^* = g + \Delta p_t^e. \tag{32}$$

Substituting (32) in (4), we get the following expectations-augmented version of the Phillips ECM:

$$\Delta w_t = g + \Delta p_t^e + k_d \Delta^2 u_t + k_p \Delta u_{t-1} + k_i u_{t-1}. \tag{33}$$

We next move on to the Sargan specification. We shall utilize the version referred to in equation (6b). Sargan has a union wage setting model in mind, and for him equilibrium real wages for the union depend on the unemployment rate. Substituting for the 'equilibrium' real wage from the second equation in (6b) into the first, we get

$$\Delta w_t = \Delta p_t^e - \gamma \eta u_{t-1} - \gamma (w - p - \omega)_{t-1}. \tag{34}$$

Finally, the Hendry specification will be based on equation (8), substituting w_t for y_t and w_t^* for x_t. This gives

$$\Delta w_t = \alpha + \beta \Delta w_t^* - \gamma (w - w^*)_{t-1} \tag{35'}$$

Substituting the Sargan version of the equilibrium wage w^* in (35′), we end up with

$$\Delta w_t = (\alpha + \beta g) + \beta \Delta p_t^e - \beta \eta \Delta u_t^e - \gamma (w - p - \omega + \eta u)_{t-1} \tag{35}$$

Equation (35) will form the basis for our models of the 'Hendry' version of ECMs.

4.3   The treatment of expectations

Before one proceeds to estimate the three versions of the ECM (33), (34) and (35), a number of issues have to be resolved.

First and foremost is the treatment of expectations. The approach in the ECM literature has been largely to ignore problems having to do with expectations. In the context of our example, this amounts to replacing actual for expected price inflation in each of the three equations and estimating the equations by a single-equations method. With this treatment of expectations, the alternative ECM equations to be estimated take the form

$$\Delta w_t = g + \Delta p_t + k_d \Delta^2 u_t + k_p \Delta u_{t-1} + k_i u_{t-1} \tag{33a}$$

$$\Delta w_t = \Delta p_t - \gamma \eta u_{t-1} - \gamma (w - p - \omega)_{t-1} \tag{34a}$$

$$\Delta w_t = (\alpha + \beta g) + \beta \Delta p_t - \beta \eta \Delta u_t - \gamma (w - p - \omega + \eta u)_{t-1}. \tag{35a}$$

This practice is widespread in the ECM literature, mainly because of its simplicity. However, it should not be adopted uncritically, especially before one thinks about the identification of the resulting equations.

As an illustration of this point consider a frequent complement to wage equations, which is none other than a price equation. Assume that prices are a markup on unit labour costs, and that productivity follows a random walk. Then, the price equation becomes

$$\Delta p_t = \Delta w_t + v_t \tag{36}$$

where v_t is the innovation to productivity. Any of the three ECM equations (33a), (34a) or (35a) is under-identified in the context of a system with (36). If the wage–price system is viewed as a complete two-equation model the order condition is not satisfied, while if it is viewed as part of a larger macromodel, the order condition may be satisfied but the rank condition will not. Such considerations very seldom seem to find their way into applied research based on ECMs because, despite the focus on weak exogeneity, the choice of theoretical parameters of interest is barely discussed. Yet, poor identification may seriously prejudice one's inferences.

To highlight one simple alternative to this practice of replacing expectations by current variables, consider an alternative assumption. This alternative is based on the hypothesis that wages are set for one year in advance. With this assumption, expectations about current price inflation or the change in the unemployment rate have to be based on information available up to the end of the previous period ($t - 1$). This hypothesis is a version of the Gray (1976) and Fischer (1977) model of wage adjustment. Assume for simplicity that expectations are based on the univariate time series properties of the series in question. Since the price level has been shown to be AR(2) with a unit root, and the unemployment rate has been shown to be AR(2) but stationary (see tables 1 and 2), we shall make the following assumption about the process of expectations formation:

$$\Delta p_t^e = E(\Delta p_t \mid I_{t-1}) = \phi_0 + \phi_1 \Delta p_{t-1} \tag{37}$$

$$\Delta u_t^e = E(\Delta u_t \mid I_{t-1}) = \psi_0 + \psi_1 \Delta u_{t-1} + \psi_2 u_{t-1}. \tag{38}$$

Our focus on univariate forecasting equations for these variables should not be much of a problem. Comparison of standard errors of the AR and VAR models in tables 1 and 2 shows that the SER of the VAR is only marginally smaller than that of the AR for p and u.

Substituting (37) and, where applicable, (38) in the three alternative ECMs (33), (34) and (35), we end up with the following models of wage inflation:

$$\Delta w_t = (g + \phi_0) + \phi_1 \Delta p_{t-1} + k_d \Delta^2 u_t + k_p \Delta u_{t-1} + k_i u_{t-1} \tag{33b}$$

$$\Delta w_t = \phi_0 + \phi_1 \Delta p_{t-1} - \gamma \eta u_{t-1} - \gamma (w - p - \omega)_{t-1} \tag{34b}$$

$$\Delta w_t = \xi + \beta \phi_1 \Delta p_{t-1} - \beta \eta \psi_1 \Delta u_{t-1} + (\beta \psi_2 - \gamma) \eta u_{t-1} - \gamma (w - p - \omega)_{t-1} \tag{35b}$$

where $\xi = \alpha + \beta g + \phi_0 - \beta \eta \phi_0$. These equations are identified even in models with price equations of the form of (36). The timing assumption that wages are set before prices suffices in this case to ensure identification, as current prices are excluded from the wage equations.

The point we want to stress, and which is starkly illustrated by our example, is that the treatment of expectations has important implications for any econometric model, and that ECMs by themselves do not offer an easy escape from the problems that arise. Structural ECMs are at best models of short-run adjustment and, as any other such model, there is a need for auxiliary assumptions about expectations formation. The nature of these assumptions may critically affect the empirical success or failure of the final econometric model.

4.4   Restrictions

The second problem before (33), (34) and (35) are estimated relates to the type of restrictions that they imply for unrestricted dynamic models of the same order. It is often argued that ECMs result in fairly unrestricted and flexible econometric models that are easy to estimate. We shall argue that, if the formal derivations are taken seriously, this is not necessarily the case. We shall briefly deal with the Phillips model and then concentrate on the Sargan and Hendry versions of the ECM.

The Phillips version clearly implies the restriction that both the dependent variable and the variables that affect its equilibrium enter in differenced form. What enters in a fairly unrestricted fashion is the variable that measures the *error*, or *disequilibrium*, which in our example is unemployment.

Let us then concentrate on the Sargan and Hendry versions of ECMs. To see the restrictions that they imply, consider first the general form of Hendry's model:

$$\Delta y_t = \beta \Delta y_t^* - \gamma (y - y^*)_{t-1} + \varepsilon_t \tag{39}$$

where ε is a white noise residual and y^* denotes the equilibrium value of the dependent variable y. Sargan's model is a restricted version of (39), for which $\beta = 0$.

The equilibrium value will in general be specified as

$$y^* = \alpha_0 + \alpha' x \tag{40}$$

where α and x are $k \times 1$ vectors, the x_is being the variables that determine the equilibrium value of y.

Substituting (35) in (34) we get

$$\Delta y_t = \gamma \alpha_0 + \beta \alpha' \Delta x_t - \gamma y_{t-1} + \gamma \alpha' x_{t-1} + \varepsilon_t. \tag{41}$$

Equation (41) is clearly a restricted version of the first-order dynamic linear model

$$\Delta y_t = a_0 + b_0' \Delta x_t + a_1 y_{t-1} + b_1' x_{t-1} + v_t \tag{41a}$$

where $\boldsymbol{b}_0$, $\boldsymbol{b}_1$ are $k \times 1$ vectors and v_t is white noise. The restrictions are given by

$$\frac{b_{0i}}{b_{1i}} = \frac{b_{0j}}{b_{1j}} = \frac{\beta}{\gamma} \qquad \forall i, j = 1, 2, \ldots, k \tag{41b}$$

where b_{0i} and b_{1i} are the ith elements of the b_0 and b_1 vectors respectively.

Clearly there are $k - 1$ restrictions. The reason that such nonlinear restrictions do not appear in the Sargan model of error correction is that this model implies the k restrictions $b_{0i} = 0$, $\forall i = 1, 2, \ldots, k$. What the above suggests is that the Hendry ECM implies one restriction less than the Sargan model, independently of the number of x_is. However, as opposed to the linear restrictions of the Sargan model, these restrictions are nonlinear. This is something that is very seldom recognized, as most applications of ECMs seem to deal with the case of long-run linear homogeneity (e.g. consumption and income, wages and prices) in which these restrictions become linear, as $b_i = b_j$ for all i and j.

In the context of the wage inflation model we have been considering, the equivalent of the unrestricted first-order DLR model is given by

$$\Delta w_t = b_0 + b_1 \Delta p_t^e + b_2 \Delta u_t^e + b_3 (w - \omega)_{t-1} + b_4 p_{t-1} + b_5 u_{t-1}. \tag{42}$$

The theory assumes long-run homogeneity between wages and prices. Thus, it implies the linear restriction $b_3 = -b_4$. This particular linear restriction is not a restriction of the ECM but a restriction emanating from the theory. It is worth emphasizing this, as in many places (e.g. Hendry et al., 1984) it appears as if long-run homogeneity restrictions are something special to the ECM.

The Sargan ECM implies the additional linear restrictions that $b_1 = 1$ and $b_2 = 0$. These are indeed ECM restrictions. The first stems from the assumption that the adjustment takes place in expected real wages, and the second from the assumed nature of the adjustment process. If the assumption was that the adjustment was in nominal wages only, then b_1 would also have been zero. In any case, the Sargan model implies two linear restrictions for the general dynamic model of order one. A third restriction stems from the assumed long-run homogeneity between wages and prices.

The Hendry ECM implies that $b_1/b_2 = b_4/b_5$. This is a nonlinear restriction. Again, the additional linear restriction that $b_4 = 1$ stems from the assumed linear homogeneity between nominal variables.

Having cleared up these issues, we can now move on to estimation.

4.5 Estimation

Before we present estimates of the alternative models, there is a remaining loose end, namely the measurement of the equilibrium real wage ω. To keep matters simple, and given the statistical investigation in section 4.1, we have assumed that this is proportional to average labour productivity. We have also allowed for a shift in the factor of proportionality after the Second World War, by including in all equations a dummy variable that takes the value 0 before 1946 and 1 after. This is intended to capture the rise suggested before in the share of labour in the post-war period.

Ordinary least squares (OLS) estimates of equations (33a), (34a) and (35a) which are based on the assumption of contemporaneous information about prices and unemployment are given in table 7, columns Ia, IIa and IIIa. OLS estimates of the model according

Table 7   OLS estimates of alternative ECMs for wage inflation in the United Kingdom: 1857–1987

	(Ia)	(Ib)	(IIa)	(IIb)	(IIIa)	(IIIb)
Constant	0.012	0.023	0.520	1.735	0.518	1.466
	(0.004)	(0.007)	(0.262)	(0.474)	(0.266)	(0.466)
Δp_t	1.069		1.016		1.016	
	(0.038)		(0.040)		(0.041)	
Δp_{t-1}		0.882		0.751		0.730
		(0.067)		(0.074)		(0.072)
$\Delta^2 u_t$	0.072	−0.914				
	(0.109)	(0.190)				
Δu_{t-1}	−0.263	−1.293				−0.609
	(0.137)	(0.237)				(0.191)
u_{t-1}	0.012	−0.098	−0.050	−0.096	−0.051	0.005
	(0.061)	(0.106)	(0.056)	(0.104)	(0.058)	(0.105)
Δu_t					−0.004	
					(0.108)	
$(w - p - \omega)_{t-1}$			−0.078	−0.263	−0.078	−0.222
			(0.040)	(0.072)	(0.041)	(0.071)
R^2	0.883	0.638	0.886	0.617	0.887	0.646
SER	0.023	0.040	0.022	0.041	0.022	0.040
DW	1.796	1.896	1.872	1.815	1.874	2.045
Lagrange multiplier tests						
AUT (1)	1.295	0.351	0.565	1.687	0.551	0.147
LIN (1)	6.706	0.329	6.182	0.603	6.596	0.473
HET (1)	8.385	4.736	8.749	0.646	8.763	2.280

Dependent variable Δw_t. AUT, LIN and HET are Lagrange multiplier tests for first-order autocorrelation, functional form and heteroskedasticity. They are asymptotically distributed as $\chi^2(1)$. ω has been approximated by the log of average labour productivity and a shift dummy after 1946.

to which wages are set in advance and are therefore based on lagged information are given in columns Ib, IIb and IIIb.

As one would expect, the current information assumption results in a much better fit for all equations. This is hardly surprising, as these estimates are based on a richer conditioning set which includes innovations in prices and unemployment. However, the diagnostics of these equations are worse than for the models that condition on lagged variables only, and the responsiveness of wages to unemployment is very poorly estimated in all cases. The latter problem may be a reflection of under-identification, as in the example we offered above. The restriction of a unitary short-run elasticity between wages and prices cannot be rejected by the relevant t tests in any of the equations. If one were to rely on these estimates, one would have to reject the underlying theory and conclude that the response of wage inflation to unemployment is zero both in the short run and the long run.

Estimation under the assumption that wage setters base their expectation on lagged inflation and unemployment (columns Ib, IIb and IIIb) result in parameters that are more in accord with the underlying theory. The fit of all the equations is worse, but this is a direct consequence of the fact that the conditioning set is smaller, since we are not conditioning on current innovations. The diagnostics show fewer signs of mis-specification, while the point estimates suggest negative short-run elasticities of wage inflation to changes in unemployment. The effect of the level of unemployment on wage inflation is not statistically significant for any of the specifications, whereas the short-run price elasticity is not significantly different from unity for the Mark I specification only. For the Mark II and III specifications it is significantly different from unity at conventional significance levels.

To conclude, from table 7 the assumption that wage setters only use lagged information appears to result in fewer mis-specification problems, and the estimates are consistent with prior theoretical expectations in all versions of ECM. Thus, these results provide an illustration of the importance of decisions about the treatment of expectations, as well as the possible dangers of not tackling the identification problem.

We next concentrate on the more theoretically satisfactory estimates, and address the question of whether the additional (over-identifying) restrictions implied by the Mark II (Sargan) and III (Hendry) version of ECMs are satisfied for wage inflation in the United Kingdom. These additional ECM restrictions are binding in this case because of the rational expectations hypothesis. We shall illustrate these restrictions for the Mark III ECM, which is the more general one.

The Mark III model to be estimated and tested is the following:

$$\Delta w_t = \xi + \beta \phi_1 \Delta p_{t-1} - \beta \eta \psi_1 \Delta u_{t-1} + (\beta \psi_2 - \gamma) \eta u_{t-1} - \gamma(w - p - \omega)_{t-1} + v_{1t} \quad (35b')$$

$$\Delta p_t = \phi_0 + \phi_1 \Delta p_{t-1} + v_{2t} \quad (37')$$

$$\Delta u_t = \psi_0 + \psi_1 \Delta u_{t-1} + \psi_2 u_{t-1} + v_{3t} \quad (38')$$

where the *v*s are (cross-correlated) disturbances. Equations (37′) and (38′) are maintained hypotheses, as we concentrate on the structure of the wage equation. The three-equation model above is a restricted version of a more general three-equation model consisting of (37′), (38′) and an unrestricted wage equation of the form

$$\Delta w_t = a_0 + a_1 \Delta p_{t-1} + a_2 \Delta u_{t-1} + a_3(w - \omega)_{t-1} + a_4 p_{t-1} + a_5 u_{t-1} + \varepsilon_t \quad (35'')$$

The restrictions implied by the system of (35b′), (37′) and (38′) for this unrestricted system are

$$a_3 = -a_4 \quad (43a)$$

$$\frac{a_5}{a_2} = \frac{\psi_2}{\psi_1} + \frac{a_3}{a_1} \frac{\phi_1}{\psi_1} \quad (43b)$$

Equation (43a) is the usual long-run linear homogeneity restriction (in this case between wages and prices), while (43b) is the non-linear ECM restrictions highlighted above in conjunction with the cross-equation rational expectations restrictions. Note that without these additional restrictions the ECM restrictions would not be binding in this case. Apart from the constant, (35b′) has six parameters to be estimated, whereas (35″) has five parameters. Thus, without the cross-equation (rational expectations) restrictions (35b′) is under-identified. It is the combination of the ECM restriction with the rational expectations hypothesis that produces an identified model. In fact the full model is over-identified, as it implies the two restrictions (43a) and (43b).

Table 8   Estimates of structural parameters,
sample 1857–1987

β	1.029	1.000
	(0.047)	
γ	− 0.098	−0.099
	(0.030)	(0.030)
η	−2.306	−2.489
	(1.285)	(1.398)
ϕ_1	0.813	0.816
	(0.050)	(0.050)
ψ_1	0.158	0.155
	(0.077)	(0.076)
ψ_2	−0.112	−0.111
	(0.029)	(0.029)
Likelihood ratio test	2.821	3.243
	$\chi^2(2)$	$\chi^2(3)$

Estimation is by iterative seemingly unrelated regressions. The likelihood ratio test in column 2 tests the restrictions (43a), (43b), while the likelihood ratio test in column 3 tests those two plus the additional restriction that $\beta = 1$.

Table 8 presents the structural estimates of the model. Estimation of the three-equation system is by iterative seemingly unrelated regressions (iterative SURE). The estimates are in accordance with the theoretical priors, and the two restrictions implied by the model cannot be rejected by a likelihood ratio test. The estimate of β is not statistically different from unity (see column 3 where this restriction is imposed) and the long-run responsiveness of real wages to unemployment is correctly signed and statistically significant at 10 per cent. This is to be contrasted with the single-equations estimates in table 7 (column IIIb), where one could not reject the hypothesis of a zero long-run effect of the level of unemployment at this significance level. Furthermore, the nonlinear over-identifying restrictions of this version of the model are not rejected at conventional significance levels.

It is worth noting that η, the structural estimate of the long-run responsiveness of real wages to unemployment, turns out to be of the same order of magnitude as in the Johansen–Juselius cointegrating vectors, and the long-run solution of the unrestricted dynamic linear regression model in table 6, but of a different order of magnitude from the Engle–Granger cointegrating vectors. It is also worth noting that since the estimate of β, the short-run responsiveness of nominal wages to equilibrium nominal wages, is not statistically different from 1, the estimated ECM is observationally equivalent to an expectational model incorporating the common factor restrictions.

To conclude, these results highlight the significance of imposing the nonlinear over-identifying restrictions of Mark III of ECMs, as well as the importance of assumptions about the information set on which the expectations of economic agents are assumed to be based. Inferences about the theoretical parameters of interest may be affected in important ways by decisions concerning these aspects of ECMs.

5   Conclusions

As a particular parameterization of the DLR model or VARs, ECMs are an effective way of characterizing the dynamic multivariate interactions characteristic of economic data. In this use, they are *atheoretical* models in the sense of Cooley and Leroy (1985), and there is no particular problem in substituting one observationally equivalent form of the model for another. One implication of the irrelevance of parameterization is that the only questions that can be asked of the model are those which have the same answer for all observationally equivalent versions of the model. For the purposes of data description, and often forecasting, this is perfectly adequate. For other purposes, this is not true.

In particular, theoretical considerations about forms of adjustment, expectations and equilibrium will determine which is the interesting economic parameterization. In relatively few cases will this correspond to some unrestricted conditional distribution. The choice of parameters of interest is a product of prior theoretical specification. It will reflect considerations such as a belief that they are autonomous or deep, and thus likely to be stable; that they can be interpreted in terms of economic theory, and thus can be compared with prior expectations; and that they are useful, and thus can be used for policy analysis or other purposes.

To quote Frisch's editorial in the first issue of *Econometrica*, 'If we are not to get lost in the overwhelming, bewildering mass of statistical data that are now becoming available, we need the guidance and help of a powerful theoretical framework. Without this no significant interpretation and coordination of our observations will be possible.' We would interpret ECMs as contributing to the powerful theoretical framework, rather than to the bewildering mass of statistical data. As an economic hypothesis about the nature of adjustment, they imply strong and testable restrictions on dynamic models. Although these restrictions have been widely ignored, they can make a significant contribution to the interpretation of the data as our examples illustrate.

Appendix: data set

	PC	Y	N	L	W
1855	−3.2476	10.0368	9.4303	9.3935	4.0775
1856	−3.2404	10.0753	9.4383	9.4067	4.0775
1857	−3.2797	10.0966	9.4462	9.4043	4.0431
1858	−3.3000	10.1032	9.4549	9.3809	4.0254
1859	−3.2816	10.1239	9.4634	9.4375	4.0431
1860	−3.2606	10.1392	9.4712	9.4533	4.0604
1861	−3.2627	10.1886	9.4796	9.4430	4.0604
1862	−3.2359	10.1886	9.4865	9.4263	4.0604
1863	−3.2053	10.1981	9.4940	9.4470	4.0943
1864	−3.1845	10.2135	9.5008	9.4819	4.0943
1865	−3.1773	10.2424	9.5082	9.4902	4.1271
1866	−3.1516	10.2413	9.5149	9.4887	4.1897
1867	−3.1792	10.2549	9.5222	9.4588	4.1897
1868	−3.2123	10.2892	9.5295	9.4611	4.1589

	PC	Y	N	L	W
1869	−3.2090	10.3192	9.5360	9.4765	4.1589
1870	−3.2102	10.3945	9.5432	9.5060	4.1897
1871	−3.1962	10.4569	9.5504	9.5346	4.2341
1872	−3.1506	10.4501	9.5575	9.5482	4.3307
1873	−3.1198	10.4501	9.5645	9.5539	4.4188
1874	−3.1533	10.5085	9.5715	9.5553	4.3944
1875	−3.1722	10.5227	9.5784	9.5568	4.3820
1876	−3.1756	10.5337	9.5853	9.5511	4.3694
1877	−3.1825	10.5422	9.5922	9.5482	4.3567
1878	−3.2052	10.5491	9.5990	9.5360	4.3175
1879	−3.2501	10.5306	9.6058	9.4948	4.2905
1880	−3.2202	10.6043	9.6131	9.5603	4.2905
1881	−3.2316	10.6028	9.6198	9.5847	4.2905
1882	−3.2213	10.6194	9.6297	9.6068	4.3307
1883	−3.2260	10.6620	9.6402	9.6145	4.3307
1884	−3.2532	10.6559	9.6499	9.5666	4.3307
1885	−3.2834	10.6538	9.6601	9.5645	4.3041
1886	−3.2998	10.6648	9.6703	9.5645	4.2905
1887	−3.3052	10.7121	9.6803	9.6024	4.3041
1888	−3.2984	10.7282	9.6903	9.6402	4.3307
1889	−3.2848	10.7479	9.7008	9.6797	4.3944
1890	−3.2823	10.7623	9.7105	9.6897	4.4308
1891	−3.2752	10.7957	9.7208	9.6860	4.4308
1892	−3.2715	10.7807	9.7321	9.6684	4.4308
1893	−3.2790	10.7758	9.7439	9.6671	4.4308
1894	−3.2988	10.8276	9.7550	9.6847	4.4308
1895	−3.3091	10.8573	9.7665	9.7081	4.4308
1896	−3.3125	10.9019	9.7779	9.7451	4.4308
1897	−3.2980	10.9046	9.7892	9.7561	4.4427
1898	−3.2949	10.9589	9.8009	9.7728	4.4773
1899	−3.2878	11.0100	9.8125	9.7926	4.4998
1900	−3.2379	10.9919	9.8239	9.7992	4.5539
1901	−3.2331	11.0310	9.8352	9.8026	4.5433
1902	−3.2331	11.0372	9.8437	9.8042	4.5218
1903	−3.2296	11.0376	9.8527	9.8059	4.5218
1904	−3.2320	11.0437	9.8616	9.8009	4.4998
1905	−3.2280	11.0641	9.8704	9.8201	4.4998
1906	−3.2282	11.0876	9.8792	9.8432	4.5218
1907	−3.2161	11.0907	9.8879	9.8511	4.5747
1908	−3.2116	11.0622	9.8965	9.8168	4.5539
1909	−3.2062	11.0947	9.9055	9.8271	4.5539
1910	−3.1976	11.1279	9.9139	9.8668	4.5539
1911	−3.1962	11.1538	9.9228	9.8929	4.5643
1912	−3.1671	11.1534	9.9311	9.8980	4.5951
1913	−3.1714	11.2048	9.9398	9.9189	4.6052
1914	−3.1740	11.2106	9.9480	9.9159	4.6151
1915	−3.0561	11.2930	9.9566	9.9470	4.7622
1916	−2.8900	11.2895	9.9651	9.9618	4.8903
1917	−2.6651	11.2888	9.9735	9.9688	5.1358
1918	−2.4663	11.2700	9.9818	9.9753	5.3519

	PC	Y	N	L	W
1919	−2.3704	11.1745	9.9906	9.9599	5.4848
1920	−2.2270	11.1065	9.9373	9.9182	5.6276
1921	−2.3167	11.0554	9.9095	9.7930	5.5607
1922	−2.4675	11.0905	9.8926	9.7912	5.3423
1923	−2.5293	11.1246	9.8870	9.8040	5.2627
1924	−2.5366	11.1550	9.8924	9.8188	5.2781
1925	−2.5333	11.2075	9.9108	9.8303	5.2883
1926	−2.5416	11.1655	9.9209	9.8305	5.2627
1927	−2.5655	11.2326	9.9286	9.8593	5.2832
1928	−2.5683	11.2485	9.9398	9.8629	5.2679
1929	−2.5773	11.2722	9.9514	9.8771	5.2730
1930	−2.6052	11.2712	9.9755	9.8582	5.2627
1931	−2.6487	11.2185	9.9950	9.8344	5.2417
1932	−2.6751	11.2155	10.0057	9.8391	5.2204
1933	−2.6968	11.2343	10.0089	9.8593	5.2149
1934	−2.6970	11.2990	10.0121	9.8876	5.2257
1935	−2.6899	11.3371	10.0201	9.9053	5.2417
1936	−2.6826	11.3674	10.0332	9.9364	5.2679
1937	−2.6493	11.4043	10.0493	9.9695	5.2933
1938	−2.6336	11.4326	10.0682	9.9720	5.3327
1939	−2.6061	11.4640	10.0698	10.0114	5.3471
1940	−2.4512	11.5889	10.0766	10.0463	5.5947
1941	−2.3483	11.6427	10.0953	10.0850	5.6836
1942	−2.2793	11.6488	10.1226	10.1182	5.8021
1943	−2.2463	11.6653	10.1290	10.1258	5.8972
1944	−2.2195	11.6183	10.1170	10.1142	5.9135
1945	−2.1916	11.5545	10.0995	10.0953	5.9081
1946	−2.1608	11.5486	10.0618	10.0446	5.9480
1947	−2.0929	11.5272	10.0588	10.0459	6.0210
1948	−2.0324	11.5560	10.0590	10.0460	6.1070
1949	−2.0070	11.5837	10.0588	10.0472	6.1485
1950	−1.9792	11.6320	10.0694	10.0563	6.1944
1951	−1.8890	11.6477	10.0792	10.0685	6.2879
1952	−1.8373	11.6507	10.0827	10.0671	6.3665
1953	−1.8149	11.6918	10.0879	10.0736	6.4249
1954	−1.7964	11.7314	10.1001	10.0883	6.4877
1955	−1.7614	11.7599	10.1098	10.1002	6.5695
1956	−1.7177	11.7778	10.1173	10.1069	6.6477
1957	−1.6844	11.7975	10.1181	10.1051	6.7007
1958	−1.6543	11.8022	10.1135	10.0950	6.7346
1959	−1.6441	11.8403	10.1208	10.1023	6.7616
1960	−1.6330	11.8841	10.1339	10.1195	6.8178
1961	−1.6040	11.9166	10.1431	10.1297	6.8855
1962	−1.5676	11.9292	10.1521	10.1335	6.9197
1963	−1.5505	11.9721	10.1562	10.1350	6.9613
1964	−1.5152	12.0208	10.1629	10.1480	7.0449
1965	−1.4669	12.0453	10.1698	10.1567	7.1229
1966	−1.4277	12.0623	10.1525	10.1384	7.1834
1967	−1.4020	12.0895	10.1471	10.1249	7.2158
1968	−1.3554	12.1290	10.1432	10.1199	7.2975

	PC	Y	N	L	W
1969	−1.3015	12.1454	10.1427	10.1196	7.3742
1970	−1.2445	12.1680	10.1413	10.1167	7.4932
1971	−1.1619	12.1928	10.1348	10.1045	7.6006
1972	−1.0987	12.2140	10.1372	10.1035	7.7215
1973	−1.0196	12.2972	10.1509	10.1273	7.8407
1974	−0.8630	12.2869	10.1893	10.1666	7.9981
1975	−0.6496	12.2716	10.1611	10.1241	8.2317
1976	−0.5040	12.3129	10.1695	10.1183	8.3855
1977	−0.3650	12.3128	10.1739	10.1188	8.4833
1978	−0.2769	12.3535	10.1789	10.1250	8.6180
1979	−0.1501	12.3757	10.1898	10.1399	8.7623
1980	0.0000	12.3480	10.1977	10.1340	8.9268
1981	0.1084	12.3435	10.1938	10.0948	9.0516
1982	0.1918	12.3547	10.1917	10.0760	9.1673
1983	0.2411	12.3936	10.1889	10.0648	9.2551
1984	0.2881	12.4191	10.2078	10.0838	9.3330
1985	0.3385	12.4519	10.2254	10.0992	9.4191
1986	0.3750	12.4861	10.2343	10.1086	9.4927
1987	0.4077	12.5224	10.2333	10.1192	9.5581

All data are in logarithms.

PC, consumer price index; Y, real GDP; N, labour force; L, employment; W, average earnings.

Notes

We would like to acknowledge the comments of two anonymous referees and the editors of this Journal.

1   This list is not exhaustive. Yet another interpretation is provided by Winder and Palm (1989).

2   The former terminology is used in Hendry et al. (1984), while the latter is used by Spanos (1986). In what follows we shall adopt the Spanos terminology.

3   It will only be unbiased if $\rho = 1$. The term bias is used rather loosely here, since the standard estimator of the long-run coefficient does not possess any finite sample moments.

References

Aldrich, J. (1989) Autonomy. *Oxford Economic Papers*, 41, 15–34.

Alogoskoufis, G. S. and Nissim, J. (1981) Consumption income dynamics under rational expectations. *Greek Economic Review*, 3, 128–47.

—— and Smith, R. P. (1989) The Phillips curve and the Lucas critique: some historical evidence. *Birkbeck Discussion Paper in Economics* 89/4, March.

Bewley, R. A. (1979) The direct estimation of the equilibrium response in a linear model. *Economic Letters*, 3, 357–62.

Bruno, M. and Sachs, J. (1985) *Economics of Worldwide Stagflation*. Oxford: Blackwell.

Cooley, T. F. and Leroy, S. L. (1985) Atheoretical macroeconomics. *Journal of Monetary Economics*, 16, 283–308.

Currie, D. A. (1981) Some long run features of dynamic time-series models. *Economic Journal*, 91, 704–15.

Davidson, J. E. H., Hendry, D. F., Srba, F. and Yeo, J. S. (1978) Econometric modelling of the aggregate time series relationship between consumer's expenditure and income in the United Kingdom. *Economic Journal*, 88, 661–92.

Dawson, A. (1981) Sargan's wage equation: a theoretical and empirical reconstruction. *Applied Economics*, 13, 351–63.

Desai, M. (1984) Wages prices and unemployment a quarter of a century after the Phillips curve. In D. F. Hendry and K. Wallis (eds), *Econometrics and Quantitative Economics*, Oxford: Blackwell.

Dickey, D. A. and Fuller, W. A. (1981) The likelihood ratio statistics for autoregressive time series with a unit root. *Econometrica*, 49, 1057–72.

Domowitz, I. and Hakkio, G. S. (1990) Interpreting an error correction model: partial adjustment, forward looking behaviour, and dynamic international money demand. *Journal of Applied Econometrics*, 5, 29–46.

Edison, H. (1987) Purchasing power parity in the long run: a test of the dollar/pound exchange rate (1890–1978), *Journal of Money Credit and Banking*, 19, 376–87.

Engle, R. F., Hendry D. F. and Richard, J. F. (1983) Exogeneity. *Econometrica*, 51, 277–304.

—— and Granger, C. W. J. (1987) Cointegration and error correction: representation, estimation and testing. *Econometrica*, 55, 251–76.

Fischer (1977) Long term contracts, rational expectations and the optimal money supply rule. *Journal of Political Economy*, 85, 191–205.

Gilbert, C. L. (1986) Professor Hendry's econometric methodology. *Oxford Bulletin of Economics and Statistics*, 48, 283–307.

—— (1989) LSE and the British approach to time-series econometrics. *Oxford Economic Papers*, 41, 108–28.

Gray, J. A. (1976) Wage indexation: a macroeconomic approach. *Journal of Monetary Economics*, 2, 221–35.

Hall, S. G. (1989) Maximum likelihood estimation of cointegrating vectors. *Oxford Bulletin of Economics and Statistics*, 51, 213–18.

Hendry, D. F. (1980) Predictive failure and econometric modelling in macro-economics: the transactions demand for money. In P. Ormerod (ed.), *Economic Modelling*, London: Heinemann.

—— (1988) The encompassing implications of feedback versus feedforward mechanisms in econometrics. *Oxford Economic Papers*, 40, 132–49.

—— and Anderson, G. (1977) Testing dynamic specification in small simultaneous systems: an application to a model of Building Society behaviour in the United Kingdom. In M. D. Intriligator (ed.), *Frontiers in Quantitative Economics*, vol. IIIA, Amsterdam: North-Holland.

—— and Mizon, G. (1978) Serial correlation as a convenient simplification, not a nuisance. *Economic Journal*, 88, 549–63.

—— and Neale, A. J. (1988) Interpreting long-run equilibrium solutions in conventional macro models: a comment, *Economic Journal*, 98, 808–17.

—— and von Ungern Sternberg, T. (1981) Liquidity and inflation effects on consumer's expenditure. In A. S. Deaton (ed.), *Essays in the Theory and Measurement of Consumer's Behaviour*, Cambridge: Cambridge University Press.

—— and Wallis, K. (eds) (1984) *Econometrics and Quantitative Economics*. Oxford: Blackwell.

—— , Pagan, A. and Sargan, J. D. (1984) Dynamic specification. In Z. Griliches and M. D. Intriligator (eds), *Handbook of Econometrics*, vol. II, Amsterdam: North-Holland.

Hylleberg, S. and Mizon, G. E. (1989) Cointegration and error correction mechanisms. *Economic Journal (Supplement)*, 99, 113–25.

Johansen, S. and Juselius, K. (1990) Maximum likelihood estimation and inference on cointegration – with applications to the demand for money. *Oxford Bulletin of Economics and Statistics*, 52, 169–210.

Kelly, C. M. (1985) A cautionary note on the interpretation of long-run equilibrium solutions in conventional macro models, *Economic Journal*, 95, 1078–86.

Lucas, R. E. (1976) Econometric policy evaluation: a critique. *Carnegie–Rochester Conference Series on Public Policy*, 2, 19–46.

Mizon, G. E. (1977) Model selection procedures. In M. Artis and R. Nobay (eds), *Studies in Modern Economic Analysis*, Oxford: Blackwell.

Nickell, S. (1985) Error correction, partial adjustment and all that: an expository note. *Oxford Bulletin of Economics and Statistics*, 47, 119–29.

Osborn, D. R. (1984) Causality testing and its implications for dynamic econometric models. *Economic Journal (Supplement)*, 94, 82–96.

—— (1986) A note on error correction mechanisms and steady state error. *Economic Journal*, 96, 208–11.

Pagan, A. (1985) Time series behaviour and dynamic specification. *Oxford Bulletin of Economics and Statistics*, 47, 199–211.

Patterson, K. D. and Ryding, J. (1984) Dynamic time series models with growth effects constrained to zero. *Economic Journal*, 94, 137–43.

Perron, P. (1990) The great crash, the oil price shock and the unit root hypothesis. *Econometrica*, 57, 1361–1401.

Phillips, A. W. (1954) Stabilization policy in a closed economy. *Economic Journal*, 64, 290–323.

—— (1957) Stabilization policy and the time form of lagged responses. *Economic Journal*, 67, 265–77.

—— (1958) The relation between unemployment and the rate of change of money wages 1862–1957. *Economica*, 34, 254–81.

Salmon, M. (1982) Error correction mechanisms. *Economic Journal*, 92, 615–29.

—— (1988) Error correction models, cointegration and the internal model principle. Warwick Economic Research Papers 291.

Sargan, J. D. (1964) Wages and prices in the United Kingdom: a study in econometric methodology. Reprinted in D. F. Hendry and K. Wallis (eds), *Econometrics and Quantitative Economics*, Oxford: Blackwell, 1984.

Spanos, A. (1986) *Statistical Foundations of Econometric Modelling*. Cambridge: Cambridge University Press.

Taylor, M. P. (1987) On long-run solutions to dynamic econometric equations under rational expectations. *Economic Journal*, 97, 215–18.

Turnovsky, S. J. (1977) *Macroeconomic Analysis and Stabilization Policy*. Cambridge: Cambridge University Press.

Wickens, M. R. and Breusch, T. S. (1988) Dynamic specification, the long-run and the estimation of transformed regression models. *Economic Journal (Supplement)*, 98, 189–20.

Winder, C. C. A. and Palm, F. C. (1989) Intertemporal consumer behaviour under structural changes in income. *Econometric Reviews*, 8, 1–88.

7 Econometric modelling using cointegrated time series

Vito Antonio Muscatelli and Stan Hurn
University of Glasgow

1 Introduction

In this paper we provide a survey of some of the developments which have taken place in the area of cointegration in recent years. Given the volume of work which has been produced in this area, any survey is bound to be limited in scope. Our main aim is to focus on some of the practical issues which arise when employing the modelling and testing procedures which have emerged in the literature on cointegration. These issues are likely to be mainly of interest to the applied economist rather than to the specialist in econometric theory.[1]

In order to assist the reader in using some of the modelling and testing procedures surveyed here, at the relevant points in the text we apply some of the procedures to the problem of modelling the demand for money in the United Kingdom. The data used are reproduced in the appendix, and will be used to construct a model for the demand for M1 in the United Kingdom over the sample period 1963.I–1984.IV.[2] We have chosen this particular modelling problem as demand functions for M1 have been estimated with relatively few problems in recent years using the standard 'general-to-specific' modelling procedure (cf. Hendry, 1979; 1985).

We begin, in the next section, by considering some of the basic concepts in modelling with cointegrated variables, taking as our point of departure the Engle–Granger two-stage ordinary least squares (OLS) approach which, because of its inherent simplicity, has received most attention in the recent applied literature. This is then followed in section 3 by an examination of a number of extensions to the basic model. Here we consider issues such as seasonality, multiple cointegration vectors and simultaneity, all of which vividly illustrate that cointegration does not necessarily provide the applied economist with easy short-cuts in time series modelling, in contrast to popular belief. A brief conclusion follows.

2 Modelling with cointegrated variables

2.1 The basic Engle–Granger two-stage procedure

It is useful to begin by defining the concept of cointegration, following Granger (1983) and Engle and Granger (1987). A series is said to be *integrated* of order *d*, or I(*d*) if it requires to be differenced d times to yield a stationary, invertible, non-deterministic autoregressive moving average representation. Suppose that we have a vector x_t containing n variables, all of which are I(d). The series contained in x_t are said to be *cointegrated* if there exists a linear combination $z_t = \alpha' \chi_t$ such that z_t is I($d - b$), where α is known as the cointegrating vector. A particular case of interest to economists, illustrated at length in Engle and Granger (1987), is the following: suppose that the vector χ_t contains two variables y_t and w_t and that they are cointegrated, where $d = b = 1$. In this case, the models for the two variables may be given an error correction mechanism representation:[3]

$$\Delta y_t = A(L)\Delta y_{t-1} + B(L)\Delta w_{t-1} - \gamma_1 z_{t-1} + \varepsilon_{1t}$$
$$\Delta w_t = C(L)\Delta y_{t-1} + D(L)\Delta w_{t-1} - \gamma_2 z_{t-1} + \varepsilon_{2t} \tag{1}$$

where $z_t = y_t - \beta w_t$ and $A(L)$, $B(L)$, $C(L)$ and $D(L)$ are finite-order lag polynomials. In this case the cointegrating vector is $(1, -\beta)$, and it should be noted that all the variables in the two models in (1) are I(0) (i.e. they are stationary).

The existence of cointegration between a set of economic variables provides a statistical foundation for the use of error correction models (ECMs), which have become increasingly popular in the applied literature.[4] The converse of this statement is also true: if an ECM provides an adequate representation of the variables under consideration, then they must be cointegrated. The main reason for the popularity of ECMs is that they provide a way of separating the long-run relationship between the economic variables ($y_t = \beta w_t$) from the short-run responses (the Δy_t, Δw_t terms). From the above discussion it is apparent that in order for the variables to be related in the long run, they must be cointegrated. Therefore, if one can test for cointegration between a vector of economic time series, one is also testing for the presence (or absence) of a long-run equilibrium relationship between them.

A second important reason for the interest shown in cointegration is the so-called superconsistency property of least-squares estimates of the cointegrating vector (i.e. the long-run relationship between the variables concerned). *If the two variables are cointegrated* an OLS regression of y_t on w_t yields a consistent estimate of β (cf. Stock, 1987; Engle and Granger, 1987). Although there is a small-sample bias present in such an estimate, due to the exclusion of the short-run dynamic responses between the two variables, asymptotically these effects are dominated by the long-run relationship between them. Furthermore, as more observations are added, the OLS estimate of the cointegrating vector converges to the true value at a rate $1/T$, where T is the sample size; this rate of convergence is faster than in the case where the variables concerned are stationary, where the rate of convergence is $1/\sqrt{T}$ and hence the estimate is said to be *superconsistent*. Effectively, the presence of cointegration reverses the 'spurious regression' result illustrated by Yule (1926) and, more recently, by Granger and Newbold (1974). However, this requires us to test for the presence of cointegration before accepting the results from such static regressions as valid and, as we shall see below, there are severe difficulties in using statistical tests in order to discriminate between series which are cointegrated and series which are not.

In the light of the superconsistency result, Engle and Granger (1987) have suggested the following two-stage estimation procedure in order to obtain a dynamic model along the lines of equation (1), for a variable y_t in terms of a vector of explanatory variables x_t.

First, one performs a static OLS regression of y_t on x_t in order to obtain the cointegrating vector. Having obtained an estimate of the long-run responses of the model, $\hat{\beta}$, one constructs the estimated ECM term $z_t = y_t - \hat{\beta}x_t$, which is inserted in a dynamic model for Δy_t along the lines of equation (1):

$$\Delta y_t = A(L)\Delta y_{t-1} + B(L)\Delta \chi_t - \gamma(y - \hat{\beta}x)_{t-1} \tag{2}$$

There is one important difference between equation (2) and the ECM representation for the bivariate case in equation (1): in equation (2) we allow for the contemporaneous effect of Δx_t on Δy_t, whilst these contemporaneous feedback effects are excluded in equation (1). This is an issue which we shall return to in section 3.4 as it relates to the concept of exogeneity. For the moment, the reader should assume that (2) represents a valid conditional model, i.e. that the x_t variables are weakly exogenous.

It should be noted that, although the parameter estimates from the static 'first-stage' equation provide consistent estimates of the long-run responses of the model, the same cannot be said of the estimated standard errors of the model. This is because the distribution of the OLS estimator is generally non-normal (see Phillips, 1991). Hence, one cannot utilize these to test, say, the significance of any particular regressor in the long-run equation, or to test whether a particular restriction may be imposed on the long-run responses. It follows that the choice of regressors to enter the 'long-run' relationship has to be made *a priori*, or strictly with reference to the cointegration tests which we shall describe in the next section.

The small-sample bias present in the long-run parameter estimates may vary depending on a number of factors. Banerjee et al. (1986) present some Monte Carlo evidence in this regard. They demonstrate that, in practice, with the standard size of sample available to economists, the bias present may still be large. In bivariate models, this bias is negatively correlated with the R^2 statistic of the static equation, although this conclusion does not carry over to multivariate models. Another important factor is the noise-to-signal ratio, which is the ratio of the standard errors of the disturbance terms in the equations determining the long-run and short-run relationships between the cointegrated variables. Thus, the nature of the data set used may affect the quality of the estimates obtained: whilst a relatively short sample of annual data may yield parameter estimates with small biases, the same may not be true of large samples of high-frequency data (sampled at weekly or daily intervals).[5]

A final point to note is that, *in small samples*, an ECM obtained using the Engle–Granger procedure may not necessarily correspond to the type of model which would be obtained using conventional modelling procedures, such as the 'general-to-specific' methodology.[6] As is well known, the latter begins the search for a dynamic model from a general autoregressive distributed-lag model for y_t:

$$y_t = A(L)y_{t-1} + B(L)x_t + u_t. \tag{3}$$

A model such as (2) is then obtained through a simultaneous process of reduction (eliminating the insignificant lags from (3)) and transformation, in order to arrive at an ECM such as (2). By contrast to the Engle–Granger procedure, in the 'general-to-specific' procedure the modelling of the short-run dynamics and long-run properties of the model are interrelated. This avoids the problem of mis-specification bias present in the estimation of the long-run responses in the first stage of the Engle–Granger procedure, but at the expense of alternative problems. Whilst in the second stage of the Engle–Granger procedure all of the regressors are stationary, the same is not the case in (3), and at various stages of the 'general-to-specific' model selection procedure variables of different orders of integration are used in the same equation. The problem with regressions where the variables employed are not all I(0) is that the asymptotic distributions of the OLS estimators do not generally follow a normal distribution, except in particular cases; in other words, the validity of statistical inference using standard *t* tests may be in doubt. These issues are discussed in detail by Park and Phillips (1988, 1989).[7] In addition, as one simplifies the dynamics of (3) the long-run responses of the model change, because they are not imposed at the outset as is the case in equation (2).

Thus, whilst in large samples we should expect to arrive at the same estimated model whether we are using the two-stage Engle–Granger procedure or alternative model selection procedures, such as 'general-to-specific', in small samples this may not be the case.[8] Furthermore, one cannot say, *a priori*, whether one or other of the methods will be preferable, although one suspects that in small samples the problems of bias in the first stage of the Engle–Granger procedure may be more significant. As pointed out above, although *theoretically*, the variance of an I(1) series dominates that of an I(0) series, and hence we might expect a static OLS regression including only the I(1) regressors to yield estimates with small biases, in *finite samples* the variance of I(0) series often dominates.[9]

To conclude, the application of the Engle–Granger estimation procedure relies on the property of cointegration, which should be established in order to appeal to the consistency properties of the OLS estimator. As cointegration involves verifying that the estimated error correction term (i.e. the residuals from the static OLS regression) are stationary, conventional unit root tests may be employed in order to test for the presence or absence of cointegration. In addition, prior to the estimation of the cointegrating vector, one should verify that all the variables employed in the static regression are indeed of the same order of integration; once again, unit root tests may be used for this purpose.

2.2 Integration and cointegration tests

In order to test for the presence of unit roots, and hence for the degree of integration of individual series, and for cointegration between a number of variables, a number of statistical tests may be used. The most popular are based on the class of tests developed by Dickey and Fuller (1979, 1981). Existing surveys (Diebold and Nerlove, 1988; Pagan and Wickens, 1989; Dolado et al., 1990) already provide an adequate account of the available tests, and we shall restrict ourselves to a simple comparison of the tests which are most commonly used in the applied literature. The basic Dickey–Fuller (DF) statistic to test for the order of integration of the time series x_t is based on the regression

$$x_t = \mu + \alpha x_{t-1} + u_t. \tag{4}$$

It is usually convenient to reparameterize this test regression as follows:

$$\Delta x_t = \mu + (\alpha - 1)x_{t-1} + u_t \tag{5}$$

The t statistic on $\alpha - 1$ in (5) is then used to test the null hypothesis that this coefficient is equal to zero (i.e. that $\alpha = 1$, and there is a unit root in the process for x_t). Unfortunately, the critical values for the t statistic cannot be found from standard statistical tables as the non-stationarity of x_t under the null causes the distribution to be non-standard. Critical values for the various statistics proposed by Dickey and Fuller (including the simple DF test) have been tabulated by Fuller (1976) and Dickey and Fuller (1981). The DF test may be successively applied to differences of the original series in order to discover the value of d, the order of integration.

One problem with (5) is that it does not allow for the possible presence of a deterministic trend in the process for x_t. Thus, in practice it may be more appropriate to model x_t as follows:

$$\Delta x_t = \mu^* + \beta^* t + (\alpha^* - 1)x_{t-1} + u_t \tag{6}$$

One may choose whether equation (5) or equation (6) is more appropriate to test for the order of integration of x_t by checking the t statistic on the β^* parameter[10] (again using the critical values reported by Dickey and Fuller). Indeed, an overall picture of the process generating x_t is given by computing the t statistics for each of the coefficients $\alpha - 1$, μ, β^*, $\alpha^* - 1$ and μ^* in (5) and (6). Dickey and Fuller also suggest a number of F-type statistics to test multiple restrictions on these parameters.

One of the main difficulties with the simple DF tests is that they are based on the assumption that the variable follows a simple first-order autoregression and that the disturbance term is independently and identically distributed (IID). An examination of the residuals from regressions such as (5) and (6) soon demonstrate that this is not so for most economic time series: the problem of 'serial correlation' is endemic.

This problem is usually dealt with by modifying the DF tests. The most popular example is the augmented Dickey–Fuller (ADF) test, in which one takes account of any serial correlation present by entering lagged values of the dependent variable in the regression

$$\Delta x_t = \mu + (\alpha - 1)x_{t-1} + \sum_{i=1}^{n} \gamma_i \Delta x_{t-1} + u_t \tag{7}$$

where n is chosen so as to ensure that the residuals are white noise. The t statistic on $\alpha - 1$ is used instead of the basic DF statistic, but the same critical values are used.

More recently, Phillips and Perron (1988) and Perron (1988) have suggested a non-parametric procedure in order to take account of the serial correlation in the model. Their procedure yields a number of 'modified' DF-type statistics, also known as Z statistics. Full details of these tests are provided in Perron (1988), and the critical values are identical to those used for the traditional DF tests. The full set of modified DF tests available for which critical values are tabulated by Fuller (1976) and Dickey and Fuller (1981) is listed in table 1, together with the null hypothesis for each test. The advantage of these modified Z statistics is that, asymptotically, they eliminate the nuisance parameters which are present in the DF statistics when the errors are not IID. However, the main drawback in computing these Z statistics is that the researcher has to decide *a priori* on the number of residual autocovariances which are to be used in implementing the corrections suggested by Phillips and Perron.

All the unit root tests described above test for the null hypothesis that a series is I(d) against the alternative that it is I($d - 1$). By sequentially differencing the series, one

Table 1

Test statistic	Null hypothesis
Equation (6)	
$Z\{t_\beta\}^*$	$\beta^* = 0$
$Z\{\Phi_2\}$	$\beta^* = 0,\ \mu^* = 0$ and $\alpha^* = 1$
$Z\{\Phi_3\}$	$\beta^* = 0$ and $\alpha^* = 1$
$Z\{\alpha^*\}$	$\alpha^* = 1$
$Z\{t_\alpha^*\}$	$\alpha^* = 1$
Equation (5)	
$Z\{\alpha\}$	$\alpha = 1$
$Z\{t_\alpha\}$	$\alpha = 1$
$Z\{\Phi\}$	$\mu = 0,\ \alpha = 1$
Equation (7)	
ADF	$\alpha = 1$

can of course apply these tests until the series has been reduced to stationarity and the degree of integration has been identified.[11]

Given the definition of cointegration, the above unit root tests can of course be applied to the residuals of the cointegrating regression in the Engle–Granger procedure in order to check whether they are I($d - b$). Thus, when the series in the cointegrating regression are I(1), one can apply the unit root tests to the residuals of the regression in order to check that they are stationary.

The null hypothesis which is tested using the DF and ADF tests (and the corresponding Z tests) is that of no cointegration, with the alternative hypothesis of cointegration. The only problem which arises here is that we cannot use the critical values given in the DF tables which are used in order to test for unit roots for single series. This is because the relevant distribution for the critical values is that under the null hypothesis, which is now different from that which was relevant in testing $\alpha = 1$ in equations (5) and (6). Once again, the appropriate critical values are obtained by simulation methods, and are found to vary considerably with the number of variables in the cointegrating vector. This is because, as we add further regressors to the cointegrating regression, the probability of wrongly rejecting the null hypothesis is increased: a linear combination of a large number of integrated series which are not cointegrated can still look very stationary.

One additional test for cointegration which is also popular, in addition to the DF- and Z-type tests, is the so-called cointegrating regression Durbin–Watson (CRDW) test proposed by Sargan and Bhargava (1983). This is simply the Durbin–Watson test statistic obtained from the residuals of the cointegrating regression, and the series are deemed to be cointegrated if the statistic is significantly greater than zero. Once again, the critical values for this test have to be obtained by Monte Carlo simulation.

The critical values for the DF, ADF and CRDW tests are provided by Engle and Granger (1987) for the simple bivariate case for a sample of 100 observations. Engle and Yoo (1987) provide critical values for samples varying from 50 to 200 observations and for cases with up to five cointegrating regressors. Yoo (1987) tabulates critical values for cases where a deterministic time trend enters the cointegrating regression, although the critical values are similar to those which would have been obtained from

Engle and Yoo (1987) by simply considering the time trend as an additional regressor. As far as the Z tests are concerned, Phillips and Ouliaris (1987) provide critical values for cases where up to five variables are included in the cointegrating regression.

Here we have concentrated mainly on the most popular tests for cointegration, which are based on simple regression analysis. Other procedures have been examined, and these are not analysed fully here for reasons of space. In particular, Phillips and Ouliaris (1988) construct tests for the rank of the cross-spectral matrix. Stock and Watson (1988) examine a 'common trends' approach based on testing for the rank of the cointegrating matrix; a related approach to testing and estimation is developed by Johansen (1988, 1989), and we shall examine the Johansen approach in detail below. Finally, Park and Choi (1988) develop tests based on the *null hypothesis of cointegration*, which are not residual-based like the DF tests.

What about the relative performance of these tests in practice? A number of criteria are relevant here. First, two of the tests, DF and CRDW, are easy to apply. However, this criterion loses a lot of its appeal at a time when computing time is becoming less expensive. Second, one must take into account the assumptions implicit in the construction of the tests. As noted above, the DF-type tests are vulnerable to the criticism that they are only valid when the disturbance term is IID. Although the Z tests were designed to overcome this problem, in practice their application involves an arbitrary truncation of the autocovariances used to correct the DF tests. Overall, one would not advocate the use of the simple DF test in most economic applications, although a ranking between the ADF test and the Z-type tests is more difficult *a priori*. Third, as we have seen, the implementation of the DF and Z-type tests requires assumptions to be made regarding the presence or absence of a constant and/or a deterministic time trend. This has led some observers (cf. Banerjee et al., 1986; Bhargava, 1986) to prefer the CRDW test, which does not rely on any assumptions of this type.

More useful evidence is provided by Monte Carlo studies. Engle and Granger (1987) find that the critical values for both the simple DF test and the CRDW test vary considerably depending on the assumptions made regarding the process generating the data. Molinas (1986) examines the performance of these tests in the presence of moving average errors, and finds that the simple DF and CRDW tests both reject the null hypothesis too often when the process generating the data is an integrated moving average process. Furthermore, the evidence presented in Schwert (1987, 1989) also suggests that when the process is an integrated moving average process, with the moving average parameter close to unity, both the ADF and the Z-type tests reject the null hypothesis of non-stationarity (or non-cointegration) too often,[12] even with very large samples.

In general, it is important to emphasize that the power of all the unit root tests discussed here is quite low, which implies that great care has to be exercised in interpreting the results obtained. The power of all the unit root tests depends critically on the value of the autoregressive parameter α under the alternative hypothesis, but is likely to be very low for values of α less than, but close to, unity. Sargan and Bhargava (1983) note that the CRDW test is more powerful than the DF-type tests, but only when the alternative is a simple stationary *first-order* autoregressive process, which is a very special case.

Overall, the existing Monte Carlo evidence suggests that no test is unambiguously superior to all the others. In the light of this inconclusive evidence and given both the low power of tests for unit roots and that the Engle–Granger procedure relies heavily on these tests at every stage, the results of applying the procedure may be subject to serious doubt. Furthermore, the results obtained may prove to be extremely sensitive to the omission of relevant variables or the inclusion of irrelevant regressors, as we shall see in a later section.

2.3   Order of integration of UK money demand data

The data definitions used in our study of the demand for money are the following: we use the total stock of M1 as the dependent variable (M), and as explanatory variables we use data on total final expenditure on goods and services (TFE) at constant prices as a real income variable (Y), the implicit TFE deflator as a price variable (P) and the treasury bill rate as a measure of the opportunity cost of holding money (R). All the series used are quarterly and seasonally unadjusted, and in what follows all the variables used in regressions will be in logs, except the interest rate.

In order to establish the order of integration of the variables in our data set, we employ both the standard ADF test and some of the Phillips–Perron Z tests described in section 2.2.[13] As we have stated above, all these tests are based on the regression equations (5), (6) and (7) and test both for the presence of a unit root $\alpha = 1$ or $\alpha^* = 1$ and for the absence (or presence) of a deterministic trend $\beta^* = 0$ or a drift term $\mu = 0$. The null hypotheses for all the Z tests reported below are outlined in table 1 above. The values for these test statistics as applied to the series employed (including the real money stock, $M - P$) are reported in table 2.

There are a number of important points to note about these results. To start with, except for Y_t and ΔM_t, the series do not seem to contain a deterministic trend. One interesting aspect of Y_t is that it does not seem to contain a unit root as demonstrated by the $Z\{\alpha\}$ and $Z\{t_\alpha^*\}$ tests in table 2. This seems to confirm the results by Cochrane (1988) for the United States which sees real income as a trend-stationary series. However, if we ignore the presence of a deterministic trend and apply the $Z\{\alpha\}$ and $Z\{t_\alpha^*\}$ tests to TFE, a unit root is detected. This illustrates the difficulties in distinguishing between trend-and difference-stationary series.

In what follows, we shall proceed on the assumption that TFE is difference stationary, so that we can apply the cointegration procedures described in section 2.1. However, one must bear these results in mind in assessing the final model.

A second point to note is that, if we ignore our difficulties with Y_t, all the variables seem to be I(1), except possibly P, which possibly confirms the results in Hall (1986) where prices in the United Kingdom are found to be I(2). Note, however, that as $M - P$ appears to be unambiguously I(1), this may be used as one of the variables in a cointegrating vector, in preference to entering M and P separately.

Finally, we should note that in some cases the Z tests give different results from the ADF test. In particular, whilst the ADF test seems to reject marginally the null hypothesis of a unit root in the interest rate, the Z tests do not reject the hypothesis that $\alpha = 1$. Also, whilst the ADF tests only marginally reject the null hypothesis of non-stationarity for ΔM and $\Delta(M - P)$, this is decisively rejected by the Phillips–Perron tests. This conflict between the results obtained from different unit root tests is difficult to resolve on an *a priori* basis, in the absence of further evidence from Monte Carlo studies. Often when dealing with unit root tests, given their low power, the practice in the applied literature has been to rely on one's theoretical priors when constructing models with cointegrated variables, as we shall see below.

Table 2   Unit root tests

Series	$Z\{t_\beta^*\}$	$Z\{\Phi_2\}$	$Z\{\Phi_3\}$	$Z\{\alpha\}$	$Z\{t_\alpha\}$	$Z\{\Phi_1\}$	ADF
M	2.326	33.01***	7.083**	1.017	2.687	40.78***	1.337
P	2.372	23.94***	3.409	0.367	0.952	29.38***	−0.694
Y	4.712***	8.321***	11.256***	−34.66***	−4.739***	4.658*	−1.058
R	1.512	1.612	3.841	−8.635	−2.286	2.708	−1.953
$M - P$	0.891	0.568	1.548	−6.056	−1.758	1.545	−2.668*
ΔM	3.189**	43.59***	64.78***	−99.89***	−11.38***	52.14***	−2.710*
ΔP	0.452	2.854	3.504	−12.23*	−2.563	3.295	−2.080
ΔY	−0.144	127.6***	133.9***	−94.79***	−16.31***	133.0***	−3.904***
ΔR	−0.575	22.65***	27.56***	−60.45***	−7.387***	27.30***	−4.743***
$\Delta(M - P)$	1.151	24.48***	45.25***	−95.55***	−9.390***	44.09***	−2.814*

*, significance at the 10 per cent level; **, significance at the 5 per cent level; ***, significance at the 1 per cent level.

In the case of Y_t and ΔM_t, the $Z\{\alpha^*\}$ and $Z\{t_\alpha^*\}$ statistics are reported instead of the $Z\{\alpha\}$ and $Z\{t_\alpha\}$ statistics since the null hypothesis of $\beta^* = 0$ is rejected at the 5 per cent level.

In the implementation of the correction suggested by Phillips and Perron (1988), four autocovariances were used.

2.4   Applications of the Engle–Granger two-stage procedure

In the last three to four years, the literature on cointegration employing the Engle–Granger modelling procedure has mushroomed. As a result, it is impossible to provide an adequate survey of all the applied research which has taken place. In this section we merely look at a few representative examples, which illustrate some additional issues involved in applying the procedure.

In section 2.2 we pointed out that the original procedure developed by Engle and Granger (1987) puts great weight on the need for all variables in the static regression to be integrated of the same order and for the second-stage regression to contain only variables which are I(0). This advice is not always heeded in the empirical literature. For example, Hall (1986) uses the Engle–Granger procedure in order to construct a model for real wages in the United Kingdom by proposing the following first-stage static regression:

$$W = \alpha_0 + \alpha_1 P + \alpha_2 R + \alpha_3 U + \alpha_4 H \tag{8}$$

where W is nominal wages, P is prices, R is productivity, H is hours worked (all in logs) and U is the unemployment rate. Unit root tests seem to show that W and P are I(2), whilst all the other variables are I(1), and thus (8) seems inappropriate as a first-stage regression, as the superconsistency properties of the OLS estimator will not hold for α_2, α_3 and α_4. However, as W and P seem to be cointegrated, Hall justifies this procedure on the grounds that W and P cointegrate to yield an I(1) variable, which is then cointegrated with the other variables in the equation. Similarly, the ECM (the second-stage regression) contains variables such as $\Delta W, \Delta H$ and $\Delta^2 U$, which are integrated of different order (respectively I(1), I(0) and I(0)). Once again, this is in conflict with the original aim of the Engle–Granger procedure which was designed in order to produce models in which all the variables are stationary, so that standard statistical inference techniques can be applied.

Hallman (1987) argues that there seems to be a division here between 'UK econometric practice', which worries less about the degree of integration of the regressors employed in adopting model selection procedures such as general-to-specific, and 'standard US practice' in modelling with cointegrated variables (which follows the work of Engle and Granger). The advantage of adhering closely to the Engle–Granger approach in ensuring that only variables integrated of the same order enter the cointegrating regression and that all the variables in the dynamic model are stationary is that at the first stage the estimated parameters of the static regression will be superconsistent, and that at the second stage we can employ standard methods of statistical inference (e.g. standard t tests) in order to select our preferred model.

On the other hand, it is arguable that, given the problems with the testing procedures for integration and cointegration, as long as the chosen set of regressors and regressand cointegrate among themselves so as to produce a stationary residual, we need to worry less about the degree of integration of the individual variables (cf. Dolado et al., 1990). Certainly, this will lead to a non-standard distributional situation, but given that there are severe problems of estimation (small-sample bias) and testing (the low power of the unit root tests), one may well argue that there are few advantages in sticking to the Engle–Granger procedure (cf. Wickens and Breusch, 1988).

Our own view is that there seem to be advantages and disadvantages with both the Engle–Granger procedure and alternative modelling strategies such as 'general-to-specific'. On balance, it would seem to us that to be guided purely by unit root tests in constructing economic relationships is unwise, especially when on a number of occasions 'valid' ECMs (in the sense that the ECM term in the dynamic equation is very significant and correctly signed) seem to be obtainable even when cointegration tests do not formally reject the null hypothesis of no cointegration (see for example Hendry and Ericsson's (1983, 1991) study on the demand for money in the United Kingdom and Jenkinson's (1986) study on employment).

Another point to note is that the omission or inclusion of certain variables from the cointegrating regression can dramatically affect the results obtained from cointegrating regressions. For instance, in modelling the demand for M2 in Italy, Muscatelli and Papi (1990) conclude that a valid cointegration vector which includes money, prices, income and the interest rate can only be found once a proxy for financial innovation in the 1970s and 1980s is included in the cointegrating regression. In modelling the supply of newly industrializing country exports Muscatelli et al. (1990) include a dummy variable to capture the effect of the first oil price shock. Similarly, Drobny and Hall (1989) argue that in order to find a valid cointegration vector for the consumption function in the United Kingdom over the 1966–85 period they have to include a variable to capture the effects of large changes in tax differentials after 1979. In the case of the demand for M1 in the United Kingdom, Hall et al. (1989) found that a financial wealth variable or a measure of stock market turnover has to be included after 1984 to produce a valid set of cointegrating variables. To some extent this result may be due to the rapid growth of the interest-bearing component of M1 in the 1980s, and the inclusion of a measure of the 'own rate of interest' may be useful in finding a cointegrating vector.[14]

This illustrates one of the main problems with the approach proposed by Engle and Granger. Often certain economic variables which one would expect to move together in the long run do not seem to do so unless other variables are included in the relationship.

Thus, for instance, Engle and Granger (1987) find that for the United States wages and prices do not seem to be cointegrated, and the same applies to US money and prices. This is probably due to omitted variables.

As we have already seen, there is an increasing trend for researchers to adopt dummy and proxy variables in order to explain possible structural breaks in the long-run relationship between a number of economic series. Questions have also been raised regarding the nature of some economic time series, which are usually seen as having a stochastic trend (i.e. a unit root). In a univariate context Perron (1987) has questioned whether there is a unit root in gross national product once shift variables are used to proxy the effects of the Great Depression and the oil price shocks. Similarly, Cochrane (1988) has argued, in contrast to the evidence of Nelson and Plosser (1982), that real gross domestic product has fluctuations around a deterministic trend. This matters because the properties of the estimators applied to cointegrated variables critically depend upon the properties of the included regressors. Once again, the prior views of the researcher are likely to dominate the selection or exclusion of particular variables in a model.

The above discussion also raises the following questions. First, to what extent is it justifiable to use the Engle–Granger approach in the presence of deterministic trends in some or all of the data series? Second, is it justifiable to model structural change in the long-run relationship using dummy variables in the cointegrating regression?

The first issue has been addressed by a number of authors.[15] Clearly, if there is both a deterministic and a stochastic trend present in the variable to be modelled, then, in addition to finding a set of variables which are cointegrated with the variable of interest (so as to capture the common stochastic trend), at least one of the regressors should be able to capture the deterministic trend in the variable of interest, to ensure that the residuals are stationary. This highlights the importance of checking (using the tests described in the previous section) whether deterministic trends are present in any of the variables used prior to employing the Engle–Granger procedure, as the distribution of the least-squares estimators may be affected (cf. Stock and Watson, 1988; Sims et al., 1990). Conversely, it makes little sense to use a deterministic time trend as a proxy variable to model a variable which does not contain a deterministic trend component.[16]

Regarding the use of proxies in cointegrating regressions, care obviously needs to be taken that one is not capturing a permanent shift in the long-run relationship under scrutiny. In some instances, dummy variables may be necessary to capture extraordinary events which are unlikely to be repeated (e.g. wars, famines), but by carefully designing a proxy one can *ex post* always fit a 'valid cointegrating vector'.[17] One alternative procedure which has been suggested by Granger (1986) is that of applying time-varying-parameter techniques (e.g. the Kalman filter) to the estimation of the cointegrating regression. Thus one could estimate a constantly evolving long-run relationship, which in the case of relationships such as the demand for money may make a considerable amount of sense: after all, in the presence of a constantly changing financial environment, it is perhaps excessively optimistic to argue that the demand for financial assets will remain invariant over decades. (In contrast, however, Hendry and Ericsson (1991) demonstrate that a model of the demand for money in the United Kingdom over a long historical data period may still be obtained using the Engle–Granger technique, despite the presence of wars and institutional change.)

On the other hand, the problem with varying-parameter techniques is that one may end up confusing long-run trends with what are essentially the short-run dynamics of the model. In our view, unless one is dealing with effects which are likely to alter the long-run behavioural or 'target' relationships under scrutiny for a large part of the sample period,[18] it may be best to restrict the use of dummy variables to the second stage of the Engle–Granger procedure, as they are designed to capture short-run deviations from the long-run 'target' relationships and therefore only belong in the dynamic model. Furthermore, the properties of the least-squares procedure in the presence of a dummy variable have not, to our knowledge, been investigated.

One other area of interest is the application of cointegration techniques to rational expectations models. Although we often interpret ECMs as implying some type of adjustment to past disequilibria, it is well known that an ECM may result from a forward-looking optimization exercise on the part of economic agents (cf. Hendry et al., 1984; Nickell, 1985). Thus, as Campbell and Shiller (1988) point out, finding cointegration (and hence a valid ECM representation) between a number of economic variables need not imply a feedback-only interpretation. This is, of course, only another aspect of the observational equivalence of forward-looking and feedback-only models. The particular example chosen by Campbell and Shiller is the ECM proposed by Marsh and Merton (1987) in order to describe the setting of dividends by firms. The interpretation given by Marsh and Merton is one in which firms adjust dividends so as to reach a desired dividend–price ratio (the 'long-run' relationship). On the other hand, as Campbell and Shiller show, it is perfectly possible to argue that prices react to expectations of *future* dividends and that stock prices also are subject to 'noise'[19] in what they call a 'near-rational expectations model'.

The important point to note here is that cointegration tells us something about long-run equilibrium but nothing about how this equilibrium may be achieved in practice. The Granger representation theorem which demonstrates that cointegrated variables must have an ECM representation does not imply that a feedback interpretation is necessarily correct because of the problem of observational equivalence: an ECM representation may also result from a forward-looking dynamic optimization exercise.[20] If one wishes to discriminate between these two interpretations of the resulting model, the issue becomes one of testing for the superexogeneity of the parameters of interest (i.e. to verify the relevance of Lucas's (1976) critique of econometric policy evaluation). This debate has received a great deal of attention recently, and a number of procedures are analysed and discussed in Hendry (1988), Cuthbertson (1989), Engle and Hendry (1989) and Favero and Hendry (1989).

This discussion also impinges upon the argument that cointegration may be used in order to test for efficient markets. For instance two prices generated by efficient markets cannot be cointegrated as that implies that one variable can be used to forecast the other (cf. Granger, 1986; Granger and Escribano, 1986). Recently, Cerchi and Havenner (1988) have shown that the prices of five different stock prices over the period 1972–9 seemed to be cointegrated, and the resulting model forecasted well out-of-sample. Whilst this seems to contradict the efficient markets hypothesis, the point made by Campbell and Shiller (1988) in the context of the dividend–stock price relationship may be of relevance here. The presence of noise in stock markets may be due to 'fads', in which case we have a 'near-rational expectations' model in which *ex post* there seem to be profitable opportunities but where the observed relationship may be merely a statistical illusion.

One last issue which has been considered in the applied literature is the possibility of nonlinearities, both in the cointegrating (long-run) relationship and in the error correction term. The former type of nonlinearity is considered by Granger (1986), and has not received much attention in the current empirical literature. The latter type of nonlinearity is examined in Escribano (1987) and has been utilized in recent models of the demand for money (cf. Muscatelli and Papi, 1990; Hendry and Ericsson, 1991). The simplest way to implement the idea of a nonlinear adjustment process towards a linear attractor set is to estimate the following model:

$$\Delta y_t = A(L)\Delta y_{t-1} + B(L)\Delta x_t + \sum_{i=1}^{n} \gamma_i Z_{t-1}^i \tag{9}$$

where

$$Z_t = (y - \hat{\beta}x)_t \tag{10}$$

Here the nonlinearity is captured by entering higher powers of the ECM term in the dynamic equation, and the choice of n is open to the researcher, although Hendry and Ericsson (1991) found that using a third-degree polynomial was sufficient to capture the adjustment process. One pitfall of this approach is that even powers of Z_{t-1} must not be found to dominate in the final specification, as they do not suggest a stable error correction adjustment for negative values of Z_{t-1} if the sign of the γ_i parameter (where i is even) is negative.

Having examined some of the existing empirical literature which has attempted to apply the simple Engle–Granger procedure to economic models, we now illustrate some of the more complex issues which have appeared in the recent literature on cointegration. As we shall see, the emergence of these questions casts a shadow of doubt on the appropriateness of the simple Engle–Granger procedure and demonstrates that cointegration is not as convenient a short-cut to dynamic time series modelling as may seem the case at first sight.

3 Some new issues in modelling cointegrated variables

3.1 Seasonality

So far, in discussing the modelling of cointegrated variables we have conveniently ignored the issue of seasonality in the data. However, applied economists often need to construct models with seasonally unadjusted data. The reasons for this are twofold. First, in modelling certain variables which are obviously seasonal in nature, such as the demand for household electricity, consumption or the demand for cash balances, we may actually be interested in modelling the seasonal pattern in the data, for forecasting purposes. Second, as pointed out by Wallis (1974), using seasonally adjusted data can distort the dynamics of the estimated model. It is therefore preferable, whenever possible, to use seasonally unadjusted data in applied work.

The presence of seasonality in data series complicates the estimation and testing procedures which are applied to models with cointegrated variables. The definition of integration must be generalized to include seasonality as follows. The stochastic

Table 3   Cycles implied by the roots of the seasonal difference operator

Root $+1$	Root -1	Root $+i$	Root $-i$
Factor $1-L$	Factor $1+L$	Factor $1-iL$	Factor $1+iL$
$x_{t+1} = x_t$	$x_{t+1} = -x_t$	$x_{t+1} = ix_t$	$x_{t+1} = -ix_t$
	$x_{t+2} = -(x_{t+1}) = x_t$	$x_{t+2} = i(x_{t+1}) = -x_t$	$x_{t+2} = -i(x_{t+1}) = -x_t$
		$x_{t+3} = i(x_{t+2}) = -ix_t$	$x_{t+3} = -i(x_{t+2}) = ix_t$
		$x_{t+4} = i(x_{t+3}) = x_t$	$x_{t+4} = -i(x_{t+3}) = x_t$

process Y is integrated of order (n, s), or $I(n, s)$, if the series is stationary after first-period differencing n times and seasonal differencing s times.[21]

Hasza and Fuller (1982) and Dickey et al. (1984) provide the first attempt at establishing a testing procedure for seasonal unit roots[22] in a univariate series in which the null hypothesis of $I(1,1)$ is tested against the alternatives $I(1,0)$ and $I(0,1)$. Osborn et al. (1988) and Osborn (1990) devise a parameterization of the null hypothesis and Osborn (1990) tabulates the critical values for test statistics based on the following test regression:

$$(1 - L)(1 - L^4)y_t = \alpha_1 Q_{1,t} + \alpha_2 Q_{2,t} + \alpha_3 Q_{3,t} + \alpha_4 Q_{4,t} + B_1(1 - L^4)y_{t-1}$$

$$+ B_2(1 - L)y_{t-4} + \sum_{i=1}^{p} \phi_i(1 - L)(1 - L^4)y_{t-i} + \varepsilon_t \qquad (11)$$

Equation (11) allows the null hypothesis to be tested both by means of separate one-sided t tests on the non-seasonal unit root ($B_1 = 0$ in (11)) and the seasonal root ($B_2 = 0$ in (11)) and also by a joint F test of $B_1 = B_2 = 0$. Notice that (11) contains seasonal dummies Q_{it} to allow for the fact that the statistics might be influenced by the four starting values required for the dependent variable (Perron, 1988).

The drawback of this approach, the resultant tests may be termed OCSB-type tests following Osborn (1990), is that it does not test for all the possible unit roots in a seasonal process. For quarterly data, the seasonal difference operator $1 - L^4$ may be factorized to show all the possible roots in the generating process as follows:

$$1 - L^4 = (1 - L)(1 + L)(1 - iL)(1 + iL) \qquad (12)$$

so that the seasonal process has four possible roots $1, -1, i$ and $-i$. Each of the roots of the seasonal difference operator correspond to different cycles in the time domain. The cycle may be demonstrated by applying the particular factor (corresponding to the root of interest) of the difference operator to any series, say x_t, and observing the number of periods for the original state to be reached. These cycles are shown in table 3.

The root 1 has a single-period cycle; this corresponds, in the frequency domain, to zero frequency and thus captures the long-run behaviour of the series. The root -1 has a two-period cycle which means two cycles per year with quarterly data, whilst the complex roots have a cycle of four periods or one cycle per year in quarterly data. The major problem encountered with the complex roots is that in dealing with quarterly data the effects of the two roots are indistinguishable. Hylleberg et al. (1988) suggest that this problem be dealt with by treating both roots together in an annual cycle.[23]

Tests for seasonal unit roots which consider all the possible roots of the generating process, HEGY-type tests, proceed as follows. Consider the autoregressive process

$$\phi(L)y_t = \varepsilon_t. \tag{13}$$

The process is stationary if all the roots of the polynomial $\phi(L)$ lie outside the unit circle. To test the hypothesis that the roots of $\phi(L)$ lie on the unit circle against the alternative that they lie outside the unit circle Hylleberg et al. (1988) use a polynomial expansion of $\phi(L)$. They show that the polynomial in the lag operator on the left-hand side may be expanded around the roots, 1, -1, i and $-$i to yield terms corresponding to each of the roots and a remainder, η_{1t}, as follows:

$$\psi(L)(1 - L^4) = \pi_1(1 + L + L^2 + L^3)(L) + \pi_2(1 - L + L^2 - L^3)(L)$$
$$+ (\pi_4 + \pi_3 L)(L)(1 - L^2) + \eta_1 \tag{14}$$

The polynomial $\psi(L)$ has a root at 1, -1, i and $-$i if the corresponding terms in π_i are zero.

At this stage it is useful to introduce some simplifying notation. Let the following polynomials in the lag operator be defined.

$$Z_1 = 1 + L + L^2 + L^3. \tag{15a}$$

The filter Z_1 will adjust any series for all roots except that corresponding to the factor $1 - L$ of $1 - L^4$.

$$Z_2 = -(1 - L + L^2 - L^3). \tag{15b}$$

The filter Z_2 will adjust any series for all roots except that corresponding to the factor $1 + L$ of $1 - L^4$.

$$Z_3 = -(1 - L^2). \tag{15c}$$

The filter Z_3 will adjust any series for all roots except those corresponding to the two complex roots in the factor $1 + L^2$ of $1 - L^4$. Rearranging (14), using the filters in (15) above and applying this expansion to (13) yields an estimable equation which allows the null hypothesis of I(0,1) to be tested against the alternatives of I(1,0) and I(0,0):

$$(1 - L^4)y_t = \alpha_1 Q_{1,t} + \alpha_2 Q_{2,t} + \alpha_3 Q_{3,t} + \alpha_4 Q_{4,t} + \delta t + \pi_1 Z_1 y_{t-1}$$
$$+ \pi_2 Z_2 y_{t-1} + \pi_3 Z_3 y_{t-1} + \pi_4 Z_3 y_{t-2} + \sum_{i=1}^{p} \psi_i (1 - L^4)y_{t-i} + \varepsilon_{1t} \tag{16}$$

The null hypothesis of I(0,1), i.e. the presence of non-stationary seasonality, must be accepted unless π_2 *and* either π_3 or π_4 are non-zero. Once again the presence of the seasonal dummies and the linear trend term are also due to the arguments of Perron (1988).

Osborn (1990) outlines a transformation of the HEGY test regression, equation (16), which may be used to test the null hypothesis of I(1,1) against the alternatives of I(2,0) and I(1,0). This would be desirable since many macroeconomic variables are at least

Table 4   OCSB tests

	$B_1 = 0$	$B_2 = 0$	$B_1 = 0$ and $B_2 = 0$
M	0.95	−4.47	4.43
P	4.55	−5.37	5.39
Y	−1.76	−3.62	4.18
R	0.30	−6.29	8.62
$M - P$	0.62	−5.11	5.92
CV 1%	−2.82	−4.35	4.80
CV 5%	−2.11	−3.75	3.79

Null I(1, 1)

I(1,0), making the null hypothesis of the original HEGY test, I(0,1), somewhat limiting. The suggested test equation is[24]

$$(1 - L)(1 - L^4)y_t = \alpha_0 + \alpha_1(Q_{1,t} - Q_{4,t}) + \alpha_2(Q_{2,t} - Q_{4,t}) + \alpha_3(Q_{3,t} - Q_{4,t})$$
$$\pi_1 Z_1 y_{t-1} + \pi_2 Z_2 y_{t-1} + \pi_3 Z_3 y_{t-1} + \pi_4 Z_3 y_{t-2}$$
$$+ \sum_{i=1}^{p} \psi_i (1 - L)(1 - L^4) y_{t-i} + \varepsilon_{2t} \tag{17}$$

The testing procedure is the same as indicated for (16) above and the critical values of the test statistics are given in Osborn (1990).

3.2   Tests of seasonal integration on the UK data set

Having established in section 2.3 that all the series are probably I(1), we then tested for the possible presence of seasonal unit roots. Table 4 reports the OCSB tests and table 5 reports the results of the HEGY tests on non-differenced data. The OCSB test procedure rejects the hypothesis of I(1,1) at the 5 per cent level for all the series and only in the cases of M and Y is rejection at the 1 per cent level not indicated. The rejection of non-stationary seasonality is confirmed by the B_2 statistic for all the series except Y, although in the latter case the joint F test does reject the null of I(1,1) at the 5 per cent level.

Since the OCSB tests reject the hypothesis of I(1,1), in implementing the HEGY framework we use equation (16), which tests I(0,1) against I(1,0), rather than equation (17). The HEGY tests, based on test equation (16), are not as conclusive as the OCSB tests. All the variables show evidence of a unit root at the non-seasonal frequency in terms of the t statistic on π_1. However, we did expect a stronger rejection of seasonal roots in terms of the t statistics on π_2 similar to the conclusive rejection of complex unit roots by the joint F test on π_3 and π_4. Despite these relatively inconclusive results, using the HEGY framework, we believe that the balance of the evidence from both sets of tests confirms the pattern found by Osborn et al. (1988) and Osborn (1990) that seasonal unit roots are found infrequently in tests on UK macroeconomic data.

Table 5   HEGY tests

	$\pi_1 = 0$	$\pi_2 = 0$	$\pi_3 = 0$	$\pi_4 = 0$	$\pi_3 = 0$ *and* $\pi_4 = 0$	$\delta = 0$
M	−1.99	−2.27	−1.39	−3.95	9.36	2.46
P	−2.41	−3.09	−1.30	−5.05	14.50	2.43
Y	−2.03	−1.78	−3.73	−2.38	11.58	1.83
R	−2.81	−2.48	−3.23	−4.82	21.43	2.21
$M - P$	−2.02	−2.44	−1.46	−4.41	11.53	−1.32
CV 1%	−4.15	−3.57	−2.71	−4.05	8.77	{ −2.31 − 3.46 }
CV 5%	−3.52	−2.92	−2.28	−3.44	6.62	

Null I(0,1)

3.3   Seasonal cointegration

The decomposition of the seasonal difference operator into its implied component cycles poses problems for the general form of an ECM. Any series which are all I(0,1) are potentially cointegrated at all the roots of the difference operator $1 - L^4$ and hence at all of the seasonal cycles outlined in table 3.

Definition 1:   Cointegration at the single-period cycle

The vector time series y_t is cointegrated at the single-period cycle (or the long run) corresponding to the root 1 of the factor $1 - L$ of the seasonal process if there exists a cointegrating vector α_1 such that the residuals u_t from

$$\alpha_1' Z_1 y_t = u_t \tag{18}$$

are stationary.

Definition 2:   Cointegration at the two-period cycle

The vector time series y_t is cointegrated at the two-period or biannual cycle corresponding to the root -1 of the factor $1 + L$ of the seasonal process if there exists a cointegrating vector α_2 such that the residuals v_t from

$$\alpha_2' Z_2 y_t = v_t \tag{19}$$

are stationary.

Cointegration at the four-period or annual cycle corresponding to the complex roots of the seasonal polynomial is more difficult to establish as the effects of complex roots are indistinguishable in quarterly data. Yoo (1986) proposes that the cointegration be established on the basis of lags in any vector which purports to reduce the order of integration at the annual cycle. This is termed a *polynomial cointegrating vector*.

Definition 3:   Cointegration at the four-period cycle

The vector time series y_t is cointegrated at the four-period or annual cycle corresponding to the complex roots $+i$ and $-i$ of the factor $1 + L^2$ of the seasonal process if there exists a polynomial cointegrating vector $\alpha_3 + \alpha_4$ such that the residuals w_t from

$$(\alpha'_3 + \alpha'_4 L)Z_3 y_t = w_t \tag{20}$$

are stationary.

There is no guarantee that the series will exhibit cointegration at any of the seasonal cycles or that the cointegrating vectors for the different cycles, should such cointegration exist, will be the same. To construct an ECM which incorporates all the various possible cases of cointegration two criteria must be satisfied. First, the ECM must allow for cointegration at each period of the seasonal cycle. This suggests that an ECM must include a term corresponding to all the possible definitions of cointegration outlined above. Second, all the variables which enter the final error correcting equation should be I(0). For this condition to be satisfied, the terms in the error correction equation should be specified in terms of the pre-filtered data Z_{it} and not in terms of the original vector time series.

The general form of the error correcting mechanism which allows for cointegration at all the frequencies is developed by Hylleberg et al. (1988) and Engle et al. (1990). In its most general form the equation is as follows:

$$\phi(L)(1 - L^4)y_t = \gamma_1 u_{t-1} + \gamma_2 v_{t-1} + (\gamma_3 + \gamma_4 L)w_{t-1} + \varepsilon_t \tag{21}$$

This expression is an error correction representation where both the cointegrating parameters, α_i, and the coefficients on the error correction term, γ_i, may be different at different frequencies and all terms in the equation are stationary.

The estimation of (21) requires estimation of both the α and the γ coefficients. If economic theory suggests values for the cointegrating parameters α_i, then this is easily accomplished. If this is not the case, Hylleberg et al. (1988) and Engle et al. (1990) suggest a generalization of the two-stage procedure proposed by Engle and Granger (1987) which uses the filtered variables Z_{it} in three cointegrating regressions

$$\alpha'_1 Z_1 y_t = u_t \tag{22}$$

$$\alpha'_2 Z_2 y_t = v_t \tag{23}$$

$$(\alpha'_3 + \alpha'_4 L)Z_3 y_t = w_t \tag{24}$$

and allows for the hypothesis of cointegration to be tested at each stage by testing the residuals for stationarity. Then one can proceed to estimate the general ECM in (21).

Writing the model in (21) in terms of the two variables y_t and m_t,

$$\begin{aligned}
(1 - L)(1 - L^4)y_t = &\sum_{i=1}^{m} \beta_i(1 - L)(1 - L^4)y_{t-i} + \sum_{i=1}^{n} \delta_i(1 - L)(1 - L^4)m_{t-i} \\
&+ \gamma_1(Z_1 y_{t-1} - \alpha_{12}Z_1 m_{t-1}) + \gamma_2(Z_2 y_{t-1} - \alpha_{22}Z_2 m_{t-1}) \\
&+ (\gamma_3 + \gamma_4 L)(Z_3 y_{t-1} - \alpha_{32}Z_3 m_{t-1} - \alpha_{41}Z_3 y_{t-2} - \alpha_{42}Z_3 m_{t-2}) \\
&+ \varepsilon_{1t}.
\end{aligned} \tag{25}$$

Two restricted versions of this general model identified by Engle et al. (1990) may have relevance to the practitioner.[25] If there is cointegration at all cycles by the same cointegrating parameter, i.e. if the cointegrating parameters of (25) satisfy the restrictions

$$\alpha_{12} = \alpha_{22} = \alpha_{32} = \alpha$$

$$\alpha_{41} = \alpha_{42} = 0,$$

the ECM collapses to the simple error correction representation (cf. Granger, 1986; Engle and Granger, 1987) expressed in terms of the original variables and not any transforms thereof. Where the model does depart from the original version of the error correcting equation is that, up to a maximum of four lags of the error correcting term, $y_{t-1} - \alpha m_{t-1}$ may enter the equation to capture the four unit roots to be eliminated (Hylleberg et al., 1988). The estimable equation becomes

$$(1 - L^4)y_t = \sum_{i=1}^{m} \beta_i(1 - L^4)y_{t-i} + \sum_{i=1}^{n} \delta_i(1 - L^4)m_{t-i} + \sum_{i=0}^{3} \gamma_i L^i(y_{t-1} - \alpha m_{t-1}) + \varepsilon_{2t} \quad (26)$$

The other useful restricted version of the general model (25) is where there is cointegration at the single-period cycle by seasonally adjusted variables and cointegration at all other cycles by one cointegrating parameter. The restrictions on the αs are

$$\alpha_{12} = \alpha \qquad \alpha_{22} = \alpha_{32} = \alpha_s$$

$$\alpha_{41} = \alpha_{42} = 0$$

and the estimable equation is

$$(1 - L^4)y_t = \sum_{i=1}^{m} \beta_i(1 - L^4)y_{t-i} + \sum_{i=1}^{n} \delta_i(1 - L^4)m_{t-i}$$
$$+ \gamma_1(Z_1 y_{t-1} - \alpha Z_1 m_{t-1})$$
$$+ \sum_{i=0}^{3} \gamma_i L^i[(1 - L)y_{t-1} - \alpha_s(1 - L)m_{t-1}] + \varepsilon_{3t} \quad (27)$$

The common error correcting relation in the differenced variables enters with a maximum lag of 3, so that there are in total three coefficients to estimate on the seasonal error correction term. The model in (27) is similar to those of Birchenhall et al. (1989) and Engle et al. (1989) who consider the merging of short- and long-run forecasts. In the long run, the variable of interest is cointegrated with certain other variables and the normal cointegration analysis is applicable. These studies, however, try to exploit the fact that the variable of interest is a seasonal and may be cointegrated at seasonal cycles with another set of variables, in which case such information should be incorporated in the estimated model. Notice that in both the general version of the ECM and this particular restricted version, seasonal cointegration is used to augment the short-run dynamics of the model. The long-run solution is unchanged from the original simple ECM.

As pointed out above, the use of the general ECM requires separate tests of cointegration at all the cycles of the lag operator. To implement a version of the ECM which includes seasonal error correction terms, the researcher will need

1 to test for cointegration at the single-period cycle by seasonally adjusted variables;
2 to test for cointegration at all seasonal cycles by one cointegrating parameter by the variables adjusted for single-period unit roots;

3 to test for cointegration at the two-period cycle;
4 to test for cointegration at the two complex roots involving the polynomial cointegrating vector.

The tests suggested by Engle et al. (1990) to cover these general cases are reported in table 6. The cointegrating regressions are performed using filtered data which adjust the data for all unit roots except that at the cycle of interest. In all cases the null is that of non-stationarity, or in other words, that the coefficient on the π_i term in the auxiliary regression is zero. The test for cointegration at all seasonal cycles by one cointegrating parameter (case (ii)) is the exception. Since only the root at the single-period cycle is removed, there are potential roots at both the two-period cycle and the annual cycle. As a result, the HEGY framework is used to test for these roots and the appropriate null is I(0,1).

So far there have been very few practical applications of the techniques of seasonal cointegration as the methods are still in the developmental stage. For the United Kingdom the techniques might not be particularly useful because most macroeconomic time series data do not seem to exhibit non-stationary seasonality. However, as noted earlier, Birchenhall et al. (1989) successfully develop a consumption function which attempts to utilize both short- and long-run influences on aggregate consumption. Although they do not rely explicitly on the concept of seasonal cointegration, the idea is similar to that shown in equation (27) above. Engle et al. (1989) develop a model of seasonal cointegration which merges short- and long-run forecasts in the electricity industry. Engle et al. (1990) develop and test a full model of seasonal cointegration for the aggregate consumption function for Japan. Although cointegration at all cycles is rejected, cointegration is shown to exist at the four-period cycles implied by the two complex roots.

3.4 Multiple cointegration vectors

In outlining the Engle–Granger procedure, we have so far assumed that the cointegration vector, which corresponds to the long-run multipliers of the models, is unique. In fact, this need not be the case, except in the simple bivariate case. To illustrate this, we now examine a method for the estimation of cointegration vector(s) in a multivariate framework, proposed by Johansen (1988, 1989).

First consider the following general autoregressive representation for the vector Y, which contains n variables, all of which are I(1):

$$Y_t = c + \sum_{i=1}^{s-1} \phi_i Q_{it} + \sum_{i=1}^{k} \pi_i Y_{t-i} + \varepsilon_t \tag{28}$$

where c is a constant term and the Q_{it} are seasonal dummies to take account of any deterministic seasonality[26] (and s is the seasonal periodicity of the data). The maximum lag of the system, k, is chosen so as to ensure that the residuals are white noise. This VAR system may be rearranged as follows,[27] to yield an ECM representation, along the lines of equation (1):

$$\Delta Y_t = c + \sum_{i=1}^{s-1} \phi_i Q_{it} + \sum_{i=1}^{k-1} \Gamma_i \Delta Y_{t-i} + \Pi Y_{t-k} + \varepsilon_t \tag{29}$$

Table 6   Tests for seasonal cointegration

(i) Test for cointegration at single period by seasonally adjusted variables

$$Z_1 y_t = \kappa + \alpha_{12} Z_1 x_t + u_t$$

Auxiliary regression:

$$(1 - L)u_t = \pi_1 u_{t-1} + \delta_1 Q_{1t} + \delta_2 Q_{2t} + \delta_3 Q_{3t} + \delta_4 Q_{4t} + \delta_5 t + \sum_{i=1}^{4} \phi_i (1 - L)u_{t-i}$$

Test $\pi_1 = 0$. Engle and Granger (1987), Engle and Yoo (1987)

(ii) Test for cointegration at seasonal cycles by common cointegrating parameter

$$(1 - L)y_t = \kappa + \alpha_s (1 - L)x_t + v_t$$

Auxiliary regression:

$$(1 - L^4)v_t = \pi_1 Z_1 v_{t-1} + \pi_2 Z_2 v_{t-1} + \pi_3 Z_3 v_{t-1} + \pi_4 Z_3 v_{t-2}$$
$$+ \delta_1 Q_{1t} + \delta_2 Q_{2t} + \delta_3 Q_{3t} + \delta_4 Q_{4t} + \delta t + \sum_{i=1}^{4} \psi_i (1 - L^4)v_{t-i}$$

Test $\pi_i = 0\ \forall i$. Hylleberg et al. (1988), Osborn et al. (1988), Osborn (1990)

(iii) Test for cointegration at the two-period cycle

$$Z_2 y_t = \kappa + \alpha_{22} Z_2 x_t + v_t$$

Auxiliary regression:

$$(1 + L)v_t = \pi_2(-v_{t-1}) + \delta_1 Q_{1t} + \delta_2 Q_{2t} + \delta_3 Q_{3t} + \delta_4 Q_{4t} + \delta_5 t + \sum_{i=1}^{4} \phi_i (1 - L)v_{t-i}$$

Test $\pi_2 = 0$. Engle and Granger (1987), Engle and Yoo (1987)

(iv) Test for cointegration at the annual cycle: two complex roots

$$Z_3 y_t = \kappa + \alpha_{41} Z_3 y_{t-1} + \alpha_{32} Z_3 x_t + \alpha_{42} Z_3 x_{t-1} + w_t$$

Auxiliary regression:

$$(1 + L^2)w_t = \pi_3(-w_{t-2})\pi_4(-w_{t-1}) + \delta_1 Q_{1t} + \delta_2 Q_{2t} + \delta_3 Q_{3t} + \delta_4 Q_{4t} + \delta_5 t + \sum_{i=1}^{4} (1 + L^2)w_{t-i}$$

Test $\pi_3 = \pi_4 = 0$. Engle et al. (1990)

$$\Gamma_j = -\left(I - \sum_{i=1}^{j} \pi\right) \tag{30a}$$

$$\Pi = -\left(I - \sum_{i=1}^{k} \pi_i\right) \tag{30b}$$

where I is the identity matrix. Notice that, as the ΔY_t and ΔY_{t-1} variables are I(0) and the Y_{t-k} variables are I(1), the system is 'balanced' (in terms of the degree of integration of the left-hand side and the right-hand side variables) only if $\Pi = 0$, in which case the Y variables are not cointegrated as there is no long-run relationship between them, or if the parameters of Π are such that ΠY_{t-k} is also I(0). The latter case applies when the Y variables *are* cointegrated, and in turn implies (see Johansen, 1988) that the rank r of the matrix Π should be less than the number n of variables in the vector Y (i.e. that the matrix Π should not be of full rank). The rank r is also known as the *order of cointegration* (or the cointegration rank) and is equal to the number of distinct cointegration vectors linking the variables in Y. Note that, if $n = 2$ (as in our example in equation (1)), it follows that if the variables are cointegrated there can only be a unique cointegrating vector. This is *not* the case, however, where $n > 2$.

It is useful at this stage to consider the following decomposition of Π:

$$\Pi = \alpha\beta' \tag{31}$$

where β represents the matrix containing the r cointegrating vectors and α represents the matrix of weights with which each cointegrating vector enters each of the ΔY_y equations.

Unfortunately it is not possible to estimate β and α directly using standard estimation methods, but Johansen (1988, 1989) develops a maximum likelihood procedure to estimate these matrices. One additional advantage of Johansen's procedure is that it also suggests likelihood ratio tests which enable us to test for the order of cointegration, r, and for restrictions on individual elements of the cointegration vectors.

The Johansen procedure has received a large amount of attention in the literature. Johansen (1989), Johansen and Juselius (1990), and Juselius (1989) apply the procedure on Danish and Finnish demand for money data. An application of the test procedures to the demand for monetary aggregates in the United Kingdom is provided by Muscatelli (1989a), and Muscatelli and Papi (1990) construct a model of the demand for M2 in Italy. Finally, Hall (1989) demonstrates the use of the Johansen procedure in estimating a real wage equation for the United Kingdom.

It is important to note that the procedure described here is only applicable when one is dealing with a set of I(1) series, but an extension to include I(2) variables is provided by Johansen (1991).

The Johansen procedure may be applied as follows. First one needs to run the following regressions:

$$\Delta Y_t = c + \sum_{i=1}^{s-1} \phi_{0i} Q_{it} + B_{01} \Delta Y_{t-1} + \cdots + B_{0k-1} \Delta Y_{t-k+1} + R_{0t}$$

$$Y_{t-k} = d + \sum_{i=1}^{s-1} \phi_{ki} Q_{it} + B_{k1} \Delta Y_{t-1} + \cdots + B_{kk-1} \Delta Y_{t-k+1} + R_{kt} \tag{32}$$

The fitted residuals $\hat{R}_{0t}$ and $\hat{R}_{kt}$ from (32) are then used in order to construct the following product moment matrices:

$$S_{ij} = \frac{1}{T} \sum_{i=1}^{T} \hat{R}_{it} \hat{R}'_{jt} \qquad (i, j = 0, k) \tag{33}$$

These product moment matrices are then used in order to find the cointegration vectors. This is done by solving the determinant

$$|\lambda S_{kk} - S_{k0} S_{00}^{-1} S_{0k}| = 0 \tag{34}$$

This yields the n estimated eigenvalues $(\hat{\lambda}_1, \ldots, \hat{\lambda}_n)$ and the n estimated eigenvectors $(\hat{v}_1, \ldots, \hat{v}_n)$, which are normalized such that

$$\hat{V}' S_{kk} \hat{V} = I$$

where $\hat{V}$ is the matrix of estimated eigenvectors.

The r cointegrating vectors are given by the r 'most significant' eigenvectors, i.e.

$$\hat{\beta} = (\hat{v}_1, \ldots, \hat{v}_r)$$

and the estimate of α follows immediately from the definition in equation (31).

The problem is that of determining which (and how many) of the eigenvectors in fact represent significant cointegrating relationships. In effect, what we are looking for are those $\hat{\beta}$ vectors which have the largest partial correlation with the stationary variables ΔY_t, conditional on the lags of ΔY_t, and the dummy variables. Thus, we choose those eigenvectors which correspond to the r largest eigenvalues, and in order to find the value of r we can employ the following statistics, suggested by Johansen (1988, 1989):

$$\Lambda_1(q, n) = -T \sum_{i=q+1}^{n} \log(1 - \hat{\lambda}_i) \tag{35}$$

$$\Lambda_2(q, q+1) = -T \log(1 - \hat{\lambda}_{q+1}). \tag{36}$$

The first statistic tests the null hypothesis that $r \leqslant q$ against a general alternative. The second statistic tests the null hypothesis $r = q$ against the alternative $r = q + 1$. The critical values for these tests for r up to 5 are tabulated in Johansen (1988, 1989), and critical values for Λ_1 for values of r up to 10 are computed by Hall et al. (1989).

Thus, the Johansen procedure enables us to test for the order of cointegration and to find the values of the r significant cointegrating vectors. It is important to note that the Johansen procedure may yield quite different estimates for the long-run elasticities of a model compared with the 'static regression' suggested in the Engle–Granger procedure since:

1   the Engle–Granger static regression will not yield consistent estimates of any one of the significant cointegrating vectors if $r > 1$;
2   even if $r = 1$ the two approaches can be expected to yield different results since in the Johansen method the estimate of $\hat{\beta}$ is obtained conditional upon the short-run dynamics of the ΔY_t process as well as on the seasonal dummies;

2   even if $r = 1$ the two approaches can be expected to yield different results since in the Johansen method the estimate of $\hat{\beta}$ is obtained conditional upon the short-run dynamics of the ΔY_t process as well as on the seasonal dummies;

3   the estimates obtained using the Engle–Granger method are based on an arbitrary normalization of the Y variables.[28] The Johansen method uses information from the equations of each of the Y variables in order to obtain the maximum likelihood estimates of $\hat{\beta}$, which are not dependent upon any normalization. As Johansen (1989) demonstrates, the maximum likelihood method and the static regression method will only yield identical results in the special case where $r = 1$ and where the error correction term only enters the equation for the variable of interest. Thus, in the above example, if we partition the vector $Y_t = (y_t\ X_t)$, where y_t is a single variable and X_t contains the remaining $n - 1$ variables, an OLS regression of y_t on the X_t will yield the maximum likelihood estimate of the cointegration vector provided that the restriction $\alpha = (\alpha_1\ 0\ 0\ \dots 0)$ holds.[29]

Having found the significant cointegrating vector(s), we may also test s homogeneous restrictions on all the r vectors of the type[30]

$$R\beta_i = 0 \qquad i = 1, \dots, r$$

where R is $s \times n$, and β_i is $n \times 1$. It is important to note that this is a test where under the null the same s restrictions are imposed on all r cointegrating vectors. More detailed tests relating to individual cointegrating vectors are possible, and we return to discuss these below. The test is carried out by employing the following likelihood ratio test in order to test the null hypothesis that the restriction is valid:

$$\Lambda_3 = T \sum_{i=1}^{r} \frac{1 - \tilde{\lambda}_i}{1 - \hat{\lambda}_i} \tag{37}$$

where r is the order of cointegration established via the Λ_1 and Λ_2 statistics, and $\tilde{\lambda}_i$ and $\hat{\lambda}_i$ represent the estimated characteristic roots from the restricted and unrestricted model respectively. Under the null, this test statistic asymptotically follows a $\chi^2(rs)$ distribution, where s is the number of restrictions imposed on the cointegrating vector(s).

Thus, the Johansen procedure enables us to find maximum likelihood estimates of the long-run relationship(s) which exist between a vector of time series, and also suggests a framework for testing restrictions on the cointegrating vector(s). This is a considerable advantage compared with the Engle–Granger procedure, as it should be recalled that the standard errors from the static regression could not be used for the purposes of conducting statistical tests. The Engle–Granger procedure does not enable us to test for restrictions on the long-run solution of the model, whilst Johansen's suggested procedure does.

The Johansen procedure raises a number of important issues which merit consideration, the first of which is the treatment of the constant in the model. Whether or not the constant should be included in the cointegrating vector(s) depends upon the properties of the individual time series. As Johansen (1989) and Johansen and Juselius (1990) point out, the constant should be included in the cointegrating vector if there is no linear trend in the process generating Y_t. This would imply that in applying the Johansen procedure (equation (32)) the constant term should be excluded as a regressor, and included as a regressand in Y_{t-k}. On the other hand, if the process generating Y_t contains a linear trend, (32) should be estimated as it stands, with c as a regressor. The critical values for the test statistics Λ_1 and Λ_2 vary between these two cases and are tabulated in Johansen (1989) and Johansen and Juselius (1990).

A second general point to be noted is that Johansen's maximum likelihood procedure is not the only one which enables us to test for the order of cointegration. Stock and Watson (1988) propose an alternative approach, known as the 'common trends' approach.[31] A full-information maximum likelihood (FIML) estimator for cointegrated systems is also developed in Phillips (1988, 1991) and Phillips and Hansen (1990). Phillips and Hansen suggest estimators which essentially involve a non-parametric correction of the standard OLS cointegrating regression to take account of bias in finite samples due to two possible sources. The first source of bias has already been mentioned above and is due to the omission of the short-run dynamics in the model. Phillips and Hansen correct for the presence of serial correlation/heterogeneity using a semi-parametric procedure which corresponds to that used in the computation of the Phillips–Perron modified Z tests. The second source of bias is the possible joint dependence of some of the series in the cointegrating vector, i.e. simultaneity bias. Whilst one cannot use conventional IV regression to eliminate this bias in a cointegration framework, Phillips and Hansen employ a semi-parametric correction which exploits the non-stationarity of the series and focuses on the 'long-run' covariance matrix. One advantage of the Phillips–Hansen estimators is that one can obtain asymptotic standard errors for the individual parameters of the cointegrating vector, and they suggest a Wald test in order to test restrictions on the cointegrating vector.[32]

In the light of developments in FIML estimators of cointegrating relationships, recent work by Engle and Yoo (1989) has attempted to refine the simple two-stage procedure. They propose a three-stage procedure which achieves the benefit of FIML with only the addition of a least squares regression starting from the two-step estimates. Consider once again equation (1), the general ECM for two variables. On the assumption that only the first equation has the error correction term,[33] the three-step estimates are obtained by simply regressing the residuals from the ECM on the lagged I(1) variables multiplied by the γ_1 estimate available from the second stage of the original two-stage procedure. The coefficients of this regression are the corrections to the two-stage estimates and the standard errors from this regression are appropriate for inference under the assumption of asymptotic joint normality.[34]

A third point relating to the Johansen procedure is that the estimated cointegrating vectors may be very sensitive to the chosen lag structure for the VAR. One should be careful in choosing a lag length which is just sufficient to overcome serial correlation problems (cf. Hall, 1991), as adding further lags may of course cause large variations in the *point estimates* of the π_i parameters of the VAR, and hence in the elements of Π. Also, the estimated cointegrating vectors are sensitive to other changes in the specification of the model such as the inclusion of other I(0) variables in the VAR, e.g. dummy variables to explain one-off historical aberrations. As the Johansen procedure extracts the estimated cointegrating vectors from a multi-equation system, we should not be surprised to find that the *point estimates* obtained are more sensitive to changes in the specification of the model than single-equation methods such as the Engle–Granger method.

A final question concerns the number of cointegrating vectors found. If we find that $r > 1$, the question remains of how this should be interpreted in economic terms. As we have pointed out in the above discussion, the cointegrating vectors can be interpreted as the long-run equilibrium relationship between a set of variables. If $r > 1$, there is no longer a unique equilibrium towards which the ECM is adjusting. To see this more clearly, let us suppose that the maximum likelihood approach suggests that there are two significant cointegrating vectors β_1 and β_2. Since these are both I(0) by definition, any linear combination of these two will also be I(0):

$$\alpha_1 \beta_1' Y_t + \alpha_2 \beta_2' Y_t \sim \text{I}(0)$$

The ECM in this case must be seen as correcting towards an 'equilibrium subspace', which in this case is two dimensional. Such an apparent indeterminacy in the long-run equilibrium properties of the model is clearly unappealing from the economic point of view. However, this property derives from the fact that a number of variables may be tied together in different ways in the long run in such a multivariate framework. This sometimes causes difficulties in identifying the single long-run relationship of interest from the available data. For example, in recent work on modelling the demand for money (M2) in Italy as a function of prices, incomes and interest rates, both Bagliano and Favero (1990) and Muscatelli (1990) find that there are two distinct cointegrating vectors. Whilst one of these vectors may correspond to the demand for money, the second probably corresponds to a long-run relationship between the two interest rates included in the data set. This suggests that the 'problem' of multiple cointegrating vectors is a symptom of the multivariate framework which is used, and that the addition of further variables *may* help to identify the long-run relationship(s) of interest to the researcher. Basically, the problem is that the procedure is picking all the long-run statistically significant relationships between the variables in Y_t.

How should one therefore deal with a set of variables for which there seems to be more than one statistically significant cointegrating vector? The usual response by applied researchers who are seeking to model a *single* long-run behavioural relationship between the variables included in Y_t when faced with a result that $r > 1$ is to choose to employ only that cointegrating vector which makes 'economic sense'. That is, to choose that vector where the estimated long-run elasticities correspond closely (in both sign and magnitude) to those predicted by economic theory.

Such an *ad hoc* approach seems misplaced once one recognizes that both the Engle–Granger and the Johansen procedure are explicitly multivariate, in the sense that the existence of an error correction formulation for *all* the variables involved is postulated. Indeed, as we have already seen, the main difference between the two approaches is that the Johansen method, unlike the Engle–Granger procedure, explicitly recognizes the multivariate nature of the estimation problem by relying on the maximum likelihood principle. However, neither the Engle–Granger nor the Johansen approaches confront the problem of partitioning of variables into endogenous and (weakly) exogenous, which is central to estimating a single behavioural equation. Therefore, if one arbitrarily selects one of the statistically significant cointegrating vectors in order to move from the Johansen framework to the estimation of a single structural equation, one is implicitly making the assumption that the conditional model which is being isolated is in fact valid. In other words, by doing so one is not discarding any relevant statistical information by focusing on the model for only one of the variables in Y_t.

This is not the case, for example, if one is seeking to model a simultaneous equation model (such as a supply and demand model) where there is more than one long-run behavioural relationship. For example, consider the following simple structural model:

$$y_1 = \alpha_1 y_2 + \alpha_2 x_1$$

$$y_2 = \beta_1 y_1 + \beta_2 x_2. \tag{38}$$

Then, one would expect to find, by applying the Johansen procedure to the vector $Y_1 = (y_1 \ y_2 \ x_1 \ x_2)$, two significant cointegrating vectors ($r = 2$) corresponding to the two behavioural relationships between the variables in Y_t. Unfortunately, the testing procedure suggested by Johansen (1988, 1989) and set out in equation (37) does not enable us to identify the two separate cointegrating vectors, as this would involve the testing of the relevant zero restrictions on x_1 and x_2 implied by the structural model in equation (38). However, the original Johansen (1988, 1989) procedure only permits one to impose and test *the same restriction across all cointegrating vectors simultaneously*. The reason for this is easy to demonstrate. The decomposition of the matrix Π in (31) is essentially arbitrary, as it is apparent that for any non-singular matrix ζ an alternative decomposition can be found which merely rearranges the cointegrating vectors and their respective weights in each equation:

$$\Pi = (\alpha\zeta^{-1})(\zeta\beta). \tag{39}$$

Thus, the Johansen procedure carries with it a fundamental difficulty regarding the identification of separate long-run structural equations, which cannot be easily overcome. This should not come as a surprise given that the approach has its origins in a reduced form representation (equation (29)) and hence it does not provide us with a vehicle which is easily adapted for the analysis of simultaneous structural models.

The problem of identification and estimation of *simultaneous cointegrated models* (SCM) such as that described above has been analysed in some detail by Park (1990). First, let us examine the issue of identification. It turns out that the requirements for the identification of SCMs are similar to those which are applicable to simultaneous equation models in standard econometric analysis. Thus, using the same notation as above, consider a model involving n series Y_t where there are r cointegrating vectors in the $n \times r$ matrix β:

$$\beta'Y_t = \varepsilon_t$$

where the ε_t are I(0) cointegrating errors. As noted above, the matrix β is not uniquely identified, as we can find a non-singular transformation matrix ζ which will yield the same long-run matrix Π. If we wish to identify the separate vectors in β, we require certain restrictions to hold. In particular, in order to identify the cointegrating vector for the ith equation we require the following rank condition to hold, which is both necessary and sufficient:

$$\text{rank}(R_i\beta) = \Gamma$$

where R_i is the $s \times n$ restriction matrix containing the restrictions for the ith equation. This corresponds exactly to the usual rank condition for simultaneous models in econometrics (see for example Judge et al., 1985, ch. 14). Note also that the rank condition reduces to

$$\text{rank}(R_i\beta) = r - 1$$

if we are only considering zero (exclusion) restrictions.

Can one test these restrictions within the Johansen framework? As already noted, the restrictions considered in Johansen (1988, 1989) and tested through the likelihood ratio test in equation (37) are not useful for the identification process.[35] Johansen and Juselius (1990) extend the original Johansen framework to consider the testing of restrictions on the individual r cointegrating vectors[36] using a likelihood ratio test. This therefore permits the applied researcher, having detected r significant cointegrating vectors, to test for appropriate exclusion restrictions on each of the r vectors in order to identify the SCM. However, there are several potential problems here. First, the restricted estimates have to be computed iteratively as pointed out by Johansen and Juselius (1990), which is not a straightforward matter. Admittedly, this is less of a problem as software such as MICROFIT 3.0 allows one to compute such restrictions, but the current version of MICROFIT allows the testing of such restrictions on only one of the cointegrating vectors. Second, Johansen and Juselius (1990) only consider linear homogeneous restrictions on single vectors, whilst in practice when dealing with SCMs one might also be interested in nonlinear restrictions and cross-equation restrictions. Finally, as noted above, the Johansen estimation procedure is sensitive to the specification chosen for the VAR, and hence any tests of identifying restrictions carried out within this framework must be subject to the same qualifications.

An alternative estimation method for the estimation of SCMs is provided by Park (1990), using the concept of *canonical cointegrating regression* (CCR), which involves estimating the cointegrating vectors in an SCM equation by equation.[37] Bagliano et al. (1991a, b) have suggested a procedure to tackle the issue of estimating a simultaneous model with cointegrated variables,[38] which consists of the following steps. First, one begins by setting out an SCM such as (38) above. Second, one employs the Johansen procedure in order to check whether there are, indeed, as many statistically significant cointegrating vectors as the model suggests (in the case of equation (38), one would expect $r = 2$). Thus, one estimates the following reduced form for the model in (38) in order to apply the Johansen procedure:

$$\Delta Y_t = c + \sum_{i=1}^{s-1} \phi_i Q_{it} + \sum_{i=1}^{k-1} \Gamma_i \Delta Y_{t-i} + \Pi Y_{t-k} + \varepsilon_t \tag{40}$$

$$Y_t = (y_1 \ y_2 \ x_1 \ x_2)$$

where s and k are selected as in the case of equation (29). Third, if the second stage is successful, one estimates the single cointegrating vectors by imposing the identifying restrictions and applying the Engle–Granger OLS procedure (in the case of (38) one would estimate the two behavioural equations separately, using OLS), or, alternatively, by employing the Phillips and Hansen (1990) semi-parametric procedure described above, or, as a third alternative, by applying the Johansen procedure to the subsystem containing only the variables present in each cointegrating regression:[39]

$$y_1 = \hat{c}_1 + \hat{\alpha}_1 y_2 + \hat{\alpha}_2 x_1 + \hat{u}_{1t}$$
$$y_2 = \hat{c}_2 + \hat{\beta}_1 y_2 + \hat{\beta}_2 x_2 + \hat{u}_{2t}$$
$$\hat{Z}_t^1 = (y_1 - \hat{c}_1 - \hat{\alpha}_1 y_2 - \hat{\alpha}_2 x_1) \tag{41}$$
$$\hat{Z}_t^2 = (y_2 - \hat{c}_2 - \hat{\beta}_1 y_2 - \hat{\beta}_2 x_2).$$

Fourth, one can impose the two error-correction terms obtained from the third step as restrictions on the unrestricted reduced form (40):

$$\Delta Y_t = c^* + \sum_{i=1}^{s-1} \phi_i^* Q_{it} + \sum_{i=1}^{k-1} \Gamma_i^* \Delta Y_{t-i} + \Pi^* \hat{Z}_{t-k} + \eta_t \tag{42}$$
$$\hat{Z}_{t-k} = (\hat{Z}_{t-k}^1 \; \hat{Z}_{t-k}^2).$$

The validity of the restrictions imposed on the reduced form (i.e. $\Pi^* = \Pi$) may be tested by applying a likelihood ratio test to assess the transition from (40) to (42). Fifth, if this restriction on the long-run properties of the model is accepted, one can move from the reduced form given by (42) to a structural representation,[40] by imposing and testing the appropriate over-identifying restrictions (see Hendry et al., 1988).

One issue which should be confronted when estimating SCMs is whether the structural interpretation sought is appropriate. The five-step procedure suggested by Bagliano, Favero and Muscatelli tests the appropriateness of the identifying restrictions at the fourth stage, when we move from the unrestricted to the restricted VAR. If each individual cointegrating vector has been estimated using the Engle–Granger procedure, then one cannot, of course, use *t*-tests to evaluate the significance of single variables in each cointegrating vector. However, one could assess the significance of the variables included in the cointegrating vectors through the application of the third step of the Engle–Yoo (1989) procedure to each equation in the SCM. Finally, if one uses the Phillips–Hansen (1990) procedure to estimate the single cointegrating vectors,[41] then one can compute asymptotic standard errors for each estimated parameter of the cointegrating vector.

Of course, tests of cointegration may provide useful insights into whether individual cointegrating equations in an SCM have been correctly identified.[42] In so far as a subset of the series in the Y_t vector are not cointegrated, this would indicate that the exclusion (identifying) restrictions are inappropriate; i.e. if in equation (38) y_1, y_2 and x_1 do not form a valid cointegrating vector, this might indicate that the zero restriction on x_2 is not valid.

For examples of estimated SCMs see Muscatelli (1990) and Muscatelli et al. (1992) who model the demand and supply for exports, Bagliano et al. (1991a, b) who construct a model of money demand and interest-rate-setting behaviour for Italy, Chow (1991) who constructs a multiplier-accelerator model, and Clements and Mizon (1991) who examine UK wage-price behaviour.

The discussion in this section illustrates how, in recent years, the literature on estimating cointegrated systems has moved away from the original method proposed by Engle and Granger (1987) to include issues such as the specification of the short-run dynamics of the model and the estimation of multi-equation models.

Table 7   Johansen procedure-eigenvalue statistics

H_0: order of cointegration	$\Lambda_1(q,n)$	$\Lambda_2(q,q+1)$
$q = 0$	44.22***	28.79***
$q = 1$	15.43	9.84
$q = 2$	5.59	5.59

***, the null hypothesis has been rejected at the 1 per cent significance level.
The critical values reported in table III of Johansen (1989) were used.
The sample period was 1963.I–1984.IV.

3.5   The Johansen procedure and the demand for money in the United Kingdom

In the case of our demand for money model in the United Kingdom, we are not obviously concerned with the issue of how to handle a simultaneous model, as previous research (cf. Hendry 1979, 1985) has suggested that a valid conditional model may be constructed for the demand for M1 in the United Kingdom.

As the data have been shown not to exhibit non-stationary seasonality, we can ignore the problems caused by seasonal integration and apply the standard Johansen procedure on $M - P$, Y and R. The values obtained for the Λ_1 and Λ_2 statistics, which enable us to determine the order of cointegration of the system, are shown in table 7. In implementing the Johansen procedure, we included the constant in the cointegrating vectors, as except for TFE there did not seem to be a time trend in the process generating the series. We also included three seasonal dummies, and following Johansen (1988, 1989), we used centred dummy variables.[43] Interestingly, the estimated eigenvalue statistics are *sensitive to the specification of the seasonal dummy variables*, and hence the inclusion of standard as opposed to centred seasonal dummies will lead to different results. This once again highlights the sensitivity of the Johansen procedure to the specification of the VAR.

Four lags of the $\Delta(M - P)$, ΔY and ΔR variables were included in order to capture the short-run dynamics of the model, and the first eight residual correlations for each equation (up to three decimal places) are reported in table 8. As can be readily seen, the correlograms are quite flat, except for the interest rate equation and for a peak in the real money stock equation in the second period. The residual autocorrelations for these equations did not decrease markedly when further lags were added (cf. Hall (1991) for some of the issues involved in choosing the appropriate lag length in the application of the Johansen procedure).

The results from table 7 indicate that whilst the null hypothesis of no cointegrating vectors can be decisively rejected in favour of the alternative that $r = 1$, the null that $r = 1$ cannot be rejected. This suggests that a single cointegrating vector is present, which may be interpreted as our long-run demand for M1 relationship. Looking at the estimated long-run elasticities in table 8, we see that the real income elasticity is close to unity. Given that previous studies (Hendry, 1979; 1985) have also found a unit income elasticity, we decided to test a unit restriction, and the Λ_3 likelihood ratio

Table 8   Johansen procedure – estimated long-run elasticities

Sample period: 1963.I–1984.IV

Estimated cointegrating vector:
$M - P = 0.709 + 1.069Y - 15.843R$

Estimated restricted cointegrating vector:
$M - P - Y = 1.3625 - 15.071R$

Residual autocorrelations:
$\Delta(M - P)$ equation: { 0.013 0.573, −0.061, 0.092, −0.001, −0.002, −0.002, −0.002 }
ΔY equation: { 0.049, −0.045, −0.058, −0.311, 0.000, 0.000, 0.000, 0.000 }
ΔR equation: { −0.389, −0.301, 0.348, −0.152, 0.000, 0.000, 0.000, 0.000 }

statistic suggested by Johansen was found to be 0.001, which is clearly insignificant at the 5 per cent level as it is approximately distributed as a $\chi^2(1)$ statistic under the null. Thus, the restriction was imposed, and the resulting long-run elasticities are also reported in table 8.

As a single cointegrating vector has been found, we decided to check whether a static regression, as suggested by the Engle–Granger procedure, would yield the same results. The following two static regressions were estimated over the sample period 1963.I–1984.IV:

$$M - P = 11.111 - 0.043Y - 1.956R \tag{43}$$
$$R^2 = 0.550 \qquad \text{CRDW} = 0.363$$

$$M - P - Y = -0.082 - 5.620R \tag{44}$$
$$R^2 = 0.692 \qquad \text{CRDW} = 0.264$$

As can be readily observed, these results do not correspond at all with those obtained from the Johansen procedure, and in fact the values obtained for the income elasticity have the wrong sign! In addition, whilst the CRDW statistic in equation (43) marginally rejects the null of no cointegration, the same cannot be said of equation (44). This illustrates the dangers, which were stressed in section 2, of relying on a procedure which may suffer from a large degree of small-sample bias in omitting the short-run dynamics. Even with a reasonably large sample, the bias may still be very significant. On the basis of these results, the simple Engle–Granger procedure seems to be entirely inappropriate for this particular data set.[44]

As a check on whether serial correlation/heterogeneity bias was at the root of these results, we computed the Phillips–Hansen modified OLS estimator. The following estimated equation was obtained:

$$(M - P)_t = 10.40 + 0.025Y_t - 2.43R_t$$
$$(1.07) \quad (0.10) \quad (0.47)$$
$$R^2 = 0.534 \qquad Z(t_{\hat{\alpha}}) = -3.24 \tag{43'}$$

where numbers in parentheses represent asymptotic standard errors. These results do not differ markedly from the OLS estimates in equation (43), and thus the difference from the Johansen estimates do not seem to be due to mis-specification bias. Note, however, that if one drops the constant term from (43′) the income variable becomes significant and has a unit coefficient:

$$(M - P)_t = 1.00Y_t - 6.67R_t$$
$$\quad\quad\quad (0.07) \quad (0.77)$$

(43″)

Here the Wald test suggested by Phillips and Hansen (1990) cannot reject the null of a unit income elasticity. The point estimates in (43″) are closer to those obtained using the Johansen procedure, and this once again highlights the sensitivity of the estimates to the specification of the cointegrating vector, including the constant, seasonal dummies, and other deterministic variables.

We now construct a dynamic model for the demand for M1, having constructed an ECM term Z_{t-1} with the (restricted) cointegrating vector obtained from the Johansen procedure. We began by estimating the following general model over the period 1963.I–1982.IV, leaving aside eight periods to assess the model's *ex ante* forecast performance:

$$\Delta(M - P)_t = c + \sum_{i=1}^{3} \phi_i Q_{it} + \alpha(L)\Delta(M - P)_{t-1} + \beta(L)\Delta X_t + \gamma Z_{t-1} + u_t$$
$$X_t = (P_t \ Y_t \ R_t).$$

(45)

Note that we have included ΔP terms as well as terms in $\Delta(M - P)$ on the right-hand side of the equation in order to allow for a non-instantaneous adjustment of nominal money balances to changes in the price level. Note also that current values of the explanatory variables ΔX_t have been entered in (45) as we are assuming that the explanatory variables are weakly exogenous. Initially four lags were included for each regressor (except Z_{t-1}, the dummies and the constant term). By successively eliminating insignificant regressors and imposing data-acceptable restrictions on the regression parameters, we obtained the following model:

$$\Delta(M - P)_t = 0.016 \quad + 0.420\Delta(M - P)_{t-2} - 1.268\Delta P_t + 0.522\Delta_2 P_{t-1}$$
$$\quad\quad (0.008) \quad (0.074) \quad\quad\quad\quad (0.251) \quad\quad (0.159)$$
$$\quad\quad + 0.210\Delta Y_{t-1} - 0.273\Delta_2 T_{t-3} - 0.710\Delta R_t - 0.014 Z_{t-1}$$
$$\quad\quad\quad (0.114) \quad\quad\quad (0.080) \quad\quad\quad (0.134) \quad\quad (0.007)$$
$$\quad\quad + \text{'seasonal dummies'}$$

(46)

$R^2 = 0.817 \quad\quad \tilde{\sigma} = 1.54 \text{ per cent} \quad\quad DW = 2.05$
$\xi_1(8) = 3.87 \quad\quad \eta_1(8, 64) = 3.33^* \quad\quad \eta_2(5, 59) = 0.46$
$ARCH(4, 56) = 0.17 \quad\quad \eta_6(17, 46) = 1.038 \quad\quad RESET(1) = 0.062$
Sample period: 1964.II–1982.IV

where η_2 tests for fifth-order serial correlation in the residuals, η_1 is the Chow test over the forecast period (1983.I–1984.IV), ξ_1 is an asymptotically valid test for parameter constancy, ARCH is a test for fourth-order ARCH, RESET is a first-order RESET test and η_6 is White's test for heteroscedasticity due to squares of the regressors. All the standard errors reported in brackets are heteroscedastic-consistent standard errors.[45]

Almost all the diagnostics are satisfactory, except for the Chow test over the forecast period, which seems to provide evidence of a structural break. To some extent this may be due to the fact that, as we pointed out in section 1, there was a large increase in interest-bearing M1 after 1982, and this may well have affected the constancy of the model. On the other hand, as shown by Muscatelli (1989b) a constant model may be found over the period to 1984.IV using the general-to-specific method. Muscatelli (1989b) reports the following results, using the same data set as that employed here:[46]

$$\Delta M_t = \begin{matrix} 0.744 \\ (0.582) \end{matrix} - \begin{matrix} 0.177\Delta M_{t-3} \\ (0.105) \end{matrix} - \begin{matrix} 0.406(\Delta P_{t-1} - \Delta P_{t-4}) \\ (0.119) \end{matrix}$$

$$- \begin{matrix} 0.610R_t \\ (0.106) \end{matrix} + \begin{matrix} 0.267Y_t \\ (0.078) \end{matrix} - \begin{matrix} 0.164Y_{t-3} \\ (0.076) \end{matrix} - \begin{matrix} 0.172(M-P)_{t-1} \\ (0.032) \end{matrix}$$

$$+ \text{ 'seasonal dummies'} \tag{47}$$

$R^2 = 0.783 \qquad \hat{\sigma} = 1.50 \text{ per cent} \qquad \text{DW} = 2.38$

$\xi_1(8) = 1.52 \qquad \eta_1(8, 64) = 1.28 \qquad \eta_2(5, 59) = 1.65$

$\text{ARCH}(4, 56) = 0.58 \qquad \eta_6(17, 46) = 1.72 \qquad \text{RESET}(1) = 1.37$

Sample period: 1964.II–1982.IV.

This demonstrates the point already made in our discussion in section 2: different model selection procedures need not lead to models with identical properties in finite samples. Whether equation (47) is a 'better' model of the demand for M1 because it passes all diagnostic tests is a matter for dispute, as it has been *designed* to do so, whilst it is less easy to design a model such as (46) to fit the data perfectly as the long-run properties of the model are imposed at the outset. On the other hand, the long-run properties imposed on the model in equation (46) may not correspond as closely to reality, as they have been estimated using a procedure which is only valid in large samples. Of course one way of attempting to discriminate between the models in equations (46) and (47) is to use non-nested tests.[47] These are not reported in full here for reasons of space, but they were generally inconclusive, with equation (47) marginally favoured in terms of the encompassing F test (see Godfrey and Pesaran, 1983; McAleer and Pesaran, 1986) and in terms of the Akaike and Schwarz information criteria.

However, ultimately the choice of model selection procedure is likely to depend on the particular modelling context, and Monte Carlo evidence may be able to shed more light on the properties of different procedures, particularly in cases where, as in equation (47), variables integrated of different orders enter the same regression.

4 Conclusion

To conclude, the main message of this paper is that recent developments in cointegration have come a long way from the simple modelling prescription offered by Engle and Granger (1987) in their suggested two-stage procedure. It is often the case that, faced with conflicting statistical evidence from unit root tests with low power, the researcher has little option but to impose his prior views upon the model. This illustrates the difficulties involved in relying on unit root tests as pre-tests in building econometric models. Further issues such as seasonality, simultaneity, multiple cointegrating vectors and non-linearities all contribute to make the construction of dynamic time series models with cointegrated variables a hazardous pursuit. Contrary to popular belief, the concept of 'cointegration' does not offer any easy short-cuts in the construction and estimation of dynamic time series models in economics.

Appendix: Tutorial data set

	M	R	Y	P
1963: I	8.88810	0.03510	10.67800	−1.63500
1963: II	8.91560	0.03690	10.74600	−1.61890
1963: III	8.93050	0.03720	10.75200	−1.62050
1963: IV	8.98460	0.03720	10.78900	−1.60280
1964: I	8.95840	0.03980	10.75600	−1.60450
1964: II	8.96930	0.04360	10.80000	−1.58430
1964: III	8.99110	0.04620	10.80200	−1.58130
1964: IV	9.01420	0.05470	10.83800	−1.56770
1965: I	8.98720	0.06510	10.77900	−1.55570
1965: II	9.00050	0.06120	10.81800	−1.54380
1965: III	9.01160	0.05560	10.83200	−1.54080
1965: IV	9.05060	0.05450	10.85100	−1.52720
1966: I	9.03940	0.05560	10.81400	−1.51900
1966: II	9.03360	0.05650	10.83800	−1.50370
1966: III	9.04380	0.06580	10.84900	−1.49640
1966: IV	9.04910	0.06620	10.86000	−1.48450
1967: I	9.03880	0.06000	10.84100	−1.48420
1967: II	9.05500	0.05300	10.87400	−1.47690
1967: III	9.09750	0.05440	10.88100	−1.47260
1967: IV	9.13260	0.06570	10.90000	−1.46610
1968: I	9.10290	0.07400	10.89000	−1.44590
1968: II	9.12040	0.07140	10.90100	−1.42850
1968: III	9.13510	0.06950	10.92900	−1.41410
1968: IV	9.17330	0.06660	10.96100	−1.40440
1969: I	9.11820	0.07180	10.89100	−1.38980
1969: II	9.09920	0.07830	10.93200	−1.38250
1969: III	9.11570	0.07820	10.94300	−1.36970
1969: IV	9.17440	0.07710	10.97900	−1.35730
1970: I	9.13710	0.07540	10.90500	−1.33680
1970: II	9.17800	0.06890	10.96200	−1.31680
1970: III	9.19810	0.06830	10.97100	−1.29390
1970: IV	9.26430	0.06820	11.01700	−1.27910
1971: I	9.26930	0.06740	10.93800	−1.25850
1971: II	9.28360	0.05670	10.99000	−1.23450
1971: III	9.32210	0.05390	11.01000	−1.21320
1971: IV	9.36790	0.04520	11.04400	−1.19920

	M	R	Y	P
1972: I	9.37420	0.04360	10.98000	−1.18530
1972: II	9.41850	0.04590	11.02500	−1.17070
1972: III	9.43560	0.05970	11.02000	−1.14390
1972: IV	9.49510	0.07150	11.10000	−1.12820
1973: I	9.46810	0.08130	11.09300	−1.10440
1973: II	9.53470	0.07540	11.10200	−1.09130
1973: III	9.51190	0.10250	11.11700	−1.04930
1973: IV	9.54450	0.11620	11.14100	−1.00480
1974: I	9.50170	0.11990	11.06800	−0.95787
1974: II	9.53250	0.11360	11.10300	−0.89963
1974: III	9.55840	0.11180	11.12500	−0.85112
1974: IV	9.64580	0.10960	11.13900	−0.80250
1975: I	9.64380	0.10010	11.06600	−0.73806
1975: II	9.67420	0.09380	11.07400	−0.68020
1975: III	9.72750	0.10170	11.08800	−0.63297
1975: IV	9.76890	0.11120	11.12400	−0.59904
1976: I	9.78700	0.09040	11.09200	−0.56265
1976: II	9.81410	0.10190	11.10500	−0.52675
1976: III	9.86410	0.11260	11.13400	−0.49414
1976: IV	9.87650	0.13990	11.17200	−0.45642
1977: I	9.88150	0.11200	11.11200	−0.41982
1977: II	9.92380	0.07720	11.12200	−0.38322
1977: III	10.00100	0.06550	11.14000	−0.36159
1977: IV	10.07100	0.05440	11.17700	−0.35041
1978: I	10.09700	0.05970	11.14300	−0.32276
1978: II	10.11700	0.09490	11.16500	−0.29942
1978: III	10.16800	0.09380	11.18200	−0.27619
1978: IV	10.22300	0.11910	11.20300	−0.25279
1979: I	10.22200	0.11780	11.15900	−0.22607
1979: II	10.23600	0.13790	11.21500	−0.18980
1979: III	10.27400	0.13820	11.22100	−0.13856
1979: IV	10.30400	0.16490	11.24200	−0.10048
1980: I	10.27400	0.16970	11.19900	−0.05655
1980: II	10.29300	0.16320	11.17100	−0.01134
1980: III	10.29400	0.14860	11.18700	0.02109
1980: IV	10.34300	0.13580	11.18800	0.04439
1981: I	10.35600	0.11870	11.14400	0.06282
1981: II	10.39000	0.12240	11.14400	0.09367
1981: III	10.40700	0.15720	11.19100	0.11541
1981: IV	10.50600	0.15390	11.20600	0.13245
1982: I	10.50100	0.12920	11.17500	0.14663
1982: II	10.52600	0.12660	11.17200	0.17030
1982: III	10.55100	0.10120	11.19300	0.18290
1982: IV	10.61300	0.09960	11.22000	0.19315
1983: I	10.63900	0.10490	11.20900	0.21273
1983: II	10.66400	0.09510	11.19500	0.22420

	M	*R*	*Y*	*P*
1983: III	10.67500	0.09170	11.24400	0.23412
1983: IV	10.71900	0.09040	11.26800	0.24285
1984: I	10.75400	0.08560	11.24100	0.25738
1984: II	10.79800	0.09060	11.23300	0.27467
1984: III	10.82700	0.10240	11.26800	0.28672
1984: IV	10.86200	0.09330	11.31700	0.29773

Notes

We are grateful to three anonymous referees, Les Oxley and Colin Roberts and numerous other readers for extremely useful comments on earlier versions of this paper. The usual disclaimer applies.

1 Those readers who wish to study in detail some of the more theoretical aspects of integration and cointegration are already well served by a number of excellent surveys (see Granger, 1986; Engle, 1987; Hylleberg and Mizon, 1989a; Pagan and Wickens, 1989; Dolado et al., 1990).

2 This sample was chosen on pragmatic grounds. In the late 1980s the increasing presence of interest-bearing current accounts tends to cause a major structural break in the demand for M1 in the United Kingdom.

3 Strictly speaking, the models in (1) should be modified to include a moving average term where a finite autoregressive representation for $(y_t w_t)$ is not possible (see Granger, 1986; Hylleberg and Mizon, 1989a).

4 See for instance Davidson et al. (1978), Hendry and Mizon (1978), Hendry and Ericsson (1983).

5 For an example of cointegrating vectors estimated on small annual samples in the context of LDC/NIC exports, see Muscatelli et al. (1990).

6 See also the survey by Pagan (1987) and Harvey (1989).

7 See also Pagan and Wickens (1989).

8 For a comparison of the two techniques, when they are applied to the same data set, see Cuthbertson and Barlow (1989).

9 See Pagan and Wickens (1989) for a vivid illustration of this point. The Monte Carlo experiments of Banerjee et al. (1986) in fact detect precisely this problem.

10 Dolado and Jenkinson (1987) and Dolado et al. (1990) suggest an alternative sequential testing procedure, which is based on the results reported by West (1988) and Durlauf and Phillips (1988). These authors show that, in models where there is no time trend and a drift term is present (or vice versa), the t statistics of the model will have limiting normal distributions and it is no longer necessary to refer to the DF tables. This point is illustrated in detail in Dolado et al. (1990) and in Pagan and Wickens (1989). For our purposes, suffice it to say that this result is an *asymptotic* one, and that Hylleberg and Mizon (1989b) have shown, using simulation methods, that it only holds in certain circumstances. Thus, it is not clear whether one should rely on this result in practice.

11 See Dickey and Pantula (1987) for an alternative sequential testing procedure to test for up to d unit roots in a series.

12 Of the two types of test, the ADF test seems less prone to this difficulty, although it still suffers from serious problems, even with large samples.

13 The following packages were employed in obtaining the estimates in this paper. The estimates of the basic unit root tests and the Johansen procedure were computed using routines written by the authors for the RATS package, version 2.1. The results for the

Johansen procedure were confirmed using MICROFIT 3.0. The results for the modified unit root Z tests were confirmed using Peter Burridge's ROOTINE software, which was also used to compute the Phillips-Hansen (1990) modified OLS estimator. The seasonal cointegration tests were computed using routines written by the authors for TSP, and the regression estimates were computed using alternatively PC-GIVE, version 6.0, and MICROFIT 3.0. In order to facilitate the reproduction of the results obtained in this paper using the tutorial data set, we can supply any interested reader with the appropriate MICROFIT data files and list files for our estimated models in equations (46) and (47) on receipt of a formatted 3.5 inch diskette and a stamped self-addressed envelope.

14 As in the US study by Baba et al. (1988), this measure may need to be adjusted for 'learning behaviour', as economic agents gradually become aware of the availability of interest-bearing accounts.

15 Hylleberg and Mizon (1989a) provide a useful survey of this problem.

16 See for instance Vaciago and Verga (1989), Muscatelli and Papi (1990).

17 The model by Muscatelli and Papi (1990) may be subject to this criticism.

18 For example, the 'Great Crash' and 'Productivity Slowdown' highlighted by Perron (1987).

19 This may be due to so-called 'fads' in stock prices. For an analysis of the effects of noise traders on financial markets, see Campbell and Kyle (1986) Poterba and Summers (1987) and Miller et al. (1989).

20 For a discussion of the issues relating to the rational expectations approach to modelling the consumption function, see Campbell (1987), Campbell and Shiller (1987), MacDonald and Speight (1989) and Favero (1991).

21 Note that our definition of seasonal integration, which is used throughout and applies to quarterly data, is based on the Box and Jenkins (1976) approach to time series analysis. On this definition the following adjustment is required for an SI(1,1) variable to achieve stationarity:

$$SI(1, 1) = (1 - L)(1 - L^4).$$

The definition favoured by Hylleberg et al. (1988) and Engle et al. (1989) relates to the seasonal adjustment polynomial

$$S(L) = (1 + L + L^2 + L^3)$$

and defines the adjustment required for an SI(1,1) variable to achieve stationarity as

$$SI(1, 1) = (1 - L)S(L).$$

22 All the examples in this section refer to the case of seasonally unadjusted quarterly data. The models may be generalized to samples with other frequencies.

23 In other words the models implied by

$$x_{t+1} = iX_t$$

and

$$x_{t+1} = -iX_t$$

are not valid when dealing with '*real*' data. Where the model is valid,

$$x_{t+2} = -X_t$$

and both roots predict the same value for the variable of interest.

24   It was pointed out by an anonymous referee that the application of the difference operator $1 - L$ to equation (16) in the text to yield (17) means that the error term in (17) becomes $\varepsilon_{2t} = (1 - L)\varepsilon_{lt}$.

This is a non-invertible moving average process and as a result some doubt may be expressed as to the validity of this particular testing procedure.

25   Engle et al. (1990) point out that if cointegration exists at the four-period cycle in terms of a polynomial vector in $y_t, y_{t-1}, m_t, m_{t-1}$ then a valid cointegrating relationship may also be established between y_t, m_t, m_{t-1} only. There is therefore some ambiguity as to the importance of y_{t-1} in this vector, a problem which has not yet been resolved satisfactorily in the theoretical literature.

26   In what follows we shall ignore the possible presence of stochastic seasonality, as the Johansen (1988, 1989) procedure does not take this possibility into account. Clearly modifications to the procedure would be required in order to deal with cointegration at seasonal frequencies of the type described in sections 3.1–3.3.

27   See Johansen (1988, 1989), Wickens and Breusch (1988) and Hylleberg and Mizon (1989a).

28   In the bivariate case with two variables x and y, the Engle–Granger method will yield different estimates of the long-run multiplier if y is regressed on x and if x is regressed on y. As we know from basic econometrics, this discrepancy depends upon the value of the R^2 statistic.

29   In other words the x_t are at least weakly exogenous with respect to y_t in the sense of Engle et al. (1983).

30   The notation employed here corresponds to that in Pesaran and Pesaran (1991). Note that in Johansen (1989) and Johansen and Juselius (1990) the following notation is used. They define an orthogonal $n \times (n - s)$ matrix A such that $R'A = 0$. The restrictions are then expressed as $A\phi_i = \beta_i, i = 1,\ldots,l$, where the ϕ_i are unknown.

31   See also Phillips and Ouliaris (1988).

32   One of the Phillips–Hansen corrected estimators, the fully modified OLS estimator (and the relevant Wald test procedure) is computable using Peter Burridge's ROOTINE software.

33   As before, this requires us to assume that w_t is weakly exogenous.

34   See Engle and Yoo (1989) for a description of the three- stage procedure for the slightly more difficult case when w_t is not weakly exogenous with respect to y_t.

35   These restrictions applied across *all* cointegrating vectors $R\beta = 0$ are labelled *cointegrating identities* by Park (1990) as they play a similar role to identities in simultaneous equation econometric models in that they do not help in the identification process.

36   This is hypothesis H_6 in Johansen and Juselius (1990).

37   Although Park (1990) also considers systems methods of estimation.

38   An analysis of multivariate systems with cointegrated variables is also provided by Davidson and Hall (1991) and Chow (1991).

39   Although it should be apparent that the Johansen procedure applied to the subsystems may not necessarily yield unique cointegrating vectors.

40   For a discussion of the relationship between closed system VARs such as those discussed by Johansen (1988, 1989) and Johansen and Juselius and conditional systems where some of the variables are treated as (strongly) exogenous, see Davidson and Hall (1991) and Clements and Mizon (1991). Essentially this step involves testing the ability of a structural representation to encompass the closed VAR (see Hendry and Mizon, 1992).

41   See Muscatelli et al. (1992).

42   In this context the tests for cointegration by *variable addition*, (see for example Park, 1988) might be particularly useful in identifying the individual equations in an SCM.

43   The standard seasonal dummies $Q_1 - Q_4$ can be centred by modifying them as follows: $Q_{1C} = Q_1 - 0.25, Q_{2C} = Q_2 - 0.25, Q_{3C} = Q_3 - 0.25, Q_{4C} = Q_4 - 0.25$ following Johansen

(1989). Of course, one problem with this is that in obtaining our estimates for tables 7 and 8 we have only included three dummies $Q_{1c} - Q_{3C}$, as the model contains an intercept term; however, we have retained these centred dummy variables as this seems to be the procedure adopted by Johansen (1989). The $Q_{1C} - Q_{3C}$ dummy variables are included in the data set available from the authors.

44 The results do not change markedly by including seasonal dummies in the regression.

45 For further details of the diagnostic tests reported, see *inter alia* Hendry (1986). These tests are carried out in order to check the data congruency of the model.

46 Note that (47) has ΔM as the dependent variable instead of $\Delta(M - P)$. However, following Hendry (1979) (47) may be reparameterized in terms of $\Delta M_t - \Delta P_{t-1}$.

47 This was suggested by an anonymous referee, as in this case the two modelling procedures yield two non-nested alternatives. The tests were computed using MICROFIT 3.0, and can be carried out by re-expressing either equation (46) in terms of nominal balances, or equation (47) in terms of real balances and adding ΔP_t as a regressor.

References

Baba, Y., Hendry, D. F. and Starr, R. M. (1988) U.S. money demand 1960–1984. *Discussion Paper*, Nuffield College, Oxford.

Bagliano, F. C. and Favero, C. A. (1990) Money demand instability, rational expectations and policy regimes: the case of Italy 1964–1986. *Paper presented at the EEA Congress*, Augsburg, September 1989.

——, —— and Muscatelli, V. A. (1991a) Cointegration and simultaneous models: an application to the demand for money in Italy. *University of Glasgow Discussion Paper* 9108.

——, —— and —— (1991b) Cointegrazione, simultaneita' ed errata specificazione: un applicazione alla domanda di moneta in Italia. In Banca d'Italia, *Ricerche Applicate e Modelli per la Politica Economica*, vol. 1, Rome: Banca d'Italia, 91–122.

Banerjee, A., Dolado, J. J., Hendry, D. F. and Smith, G. W. (1986) Exploring equilibrium relationships in econometrics through static models: some Monte Carlo evidence *Oxford Bulletin of Economics and Statistics*, 48, 253–77.

Bhargava A. (1986) On the theory of testing for unit roots in observed time series. *Review of Economic Studies*, 53, 369–84.

Birchenhall, C. R., Bladen-Hovell, R., Chui, A. P. L., Osborn, D. R. and Smith, J. P. (1989) A seasonal model of consumption. *Economic Journal*, 99, 837–43.

Box, G. E. P. and Jenkins, G. M. (1976) *Time Series Analysis: Forecasting and Control*, revised edn. San Francisco, CA: Holden-Day.

Campbell, J. Y. (1987) Does saving anticipate declining labor income? An alternative test of the permanent income hypothesis. *Econometrica*, 55, 1249–73.

—— and Kyle, A. S. (1986) Smart money, noise trading and stock price behaviour. *Mimeo*, Princeton University.

—— and Shiller, R. J. (1987) Cointegration and tests of present value models. *Journal of Political Economy*, 95, 1062–88.

—— and —— (1988) Interpreting cointegrated models. *Journal of Economic Dynamics and Control*, 12, 505–22.

Cerchi, M. and Havenner, A. (1988) Cointegration and stock prices: the London Walk on Wall Street revisited. *Journal of Economic Dynamics and Control*, 12, 332–46.

Chow, G. C. (1991) The multiplier–accelerator model in the light of cointegration. Princeton Research Memorandum 357.

Clements, M. P. and Mizon, G. E. (1991) Empirical analysis of macroeconomic time series: VAR and structural models. *European Economic Review*.

Cochrane, L. J. W. (1988) How big is the random walk in GNP. *Journal of Political Economy*, 96, 893–920.

Cuthbertson, K. (1989) The econometric implications of feedforward versus feedback mechanisms: a reply to Hendry. *Mimeo*, University of Newcastle.

—— and Barlow, D. (1989) The determination of liquid asset holdings of the U.K. personal sector. *Mimeo*, University of Newcastle.

Davidson, J. E. H. and Hall, S. G. (1991) Cointegration in recursive systems. *Economic Journal (Supplement)*, 101, 239–51.

——, Hendry, D. F., Srba, F. and Yeo, S. (1978) Econometric modelling of the aggregate time-series relationship between consumer's expenditure and income in the United Kingdom. *Economic Journal*, 88, 661–92.

Dickey, D. A. and Fuller, W. A. (1979) Distribution of the estimators for autoregressive time series with a unit root. *Journal of the American Statistical Association*, 84, 427–31.

—— and —— (1981) Likelihood ratio statistics for autoregressive time series with a unit root. *Econometrica*, 50, 1057–72.

—— and Pantula, S. (1987) Determining the order of differencing in autoregressive processes. *Journal of Business and Economic Statistics*, 15, 455–61.

——, Hasza, H. P. and Fuller, W. A. (1984) Testing for unit roots in seasonal time series. *Journal of the American Statistical Association*, 79, 355–67.

Diebold, F. X. and Nerlove, M. (1988) Unit roots in economic time series: a selective survey. In T. B. Fomby and G. F. Rhodes (eds), *Advances in Econometrics: Cointegration, Spurious Regressions and Unit Roots*, Greenwich, CT: JAI Press.

Dolado, J. J. and Jenkinson, T. (1987) Cointegration: a survey of recent developments. *Applied Economics Discussion Paper*, Institute of Economics and Statistics, Oxford.

—— —— and Sosvilla-Rivero, S. (1990) Cointegration and unit roots. *Journal of Economic Surveys*, 4, 249–73.

Drobny, A. and Hall, S. G. (1989) An investigation of the long-run properties of aggregate non-durable consumers' expenditure in the U.K. *Economic Journal*, 99, 454–60.

Durlauf, S. N. and Phillips, P. C. B. (1988) Trends versus random walks in time series analysis. *Econometrica*, 56, 1333–54.

Engle, R. F. (1987) On the theory of cointegrated economic time series. Paper presented at ESEM 87, Copenhagen.

—— and Granger, C. W. J. (1987) Cointegration and error-correction: representation, estimation and testing. *Econometrica*, 55, 251–76.

—— and Hendry, D. F. (1989) Testing superexogeneity and invariance. *Mimeo*, University of Oxford.

—— and Yoo B. S. (1987) Forecasting and testing in cointegrated systems. *Journal of Econometrics*, 35, 143–59.

—— and —— (1989) Cointegrated economic time series: a survey with new results. *Discussion Paper*, University of California at San Diego.

——, Hendry, D. F. and Richard, J.-F. (1983) Exogeneity. *Econometrica*, 51, 277–304.

——, Granger, C. W. J. and Hallman, J. (1989) Combining short-and long-run forecasts: an application of seasonal co-integration to monthly electricity sales forecasting. *Journal of Econometrics*, 39, 45–62.

——, —— and Hylleberg, S. (1990) Seasonal cointegration: the Japanese consumption function 1970: 1–1985:4. *Discussion Paper*, University of California at San Diego.

Escribano A. (1987) Error-correction systems: non-linear adjustments to linear long-run relationships. *CORE Discussion Paper* 8730.

Favero, C. A. (1991) Error correction specifications for the U.K. consumers' expenditure and the Lucas critique. *Mimeo*, Queen Mary College, London.

—— and Hendry, D. F. (1989) Testing the Lucas critique: a review. Paper presented at the Australasian Meeting of the Econometric Society.

Fuller, W. A. (1976) *Introduction to Statistical Time Series*. New York: Wiley.

Godfrey, L. G. and Pesaran, M. H. (1983) Tests on non-nested regression models: small sample adjustments and Monte Carlo evidence. *Journal of Econometrics*, 21, 133–54.

Granger, C. W. J. (1983) Cointegrated variables and error-correcting models. *Discussion Paper*, University of California at San Diego.

—— (1986) Developments in the study of cointegrated economic variables. *Oxford Bulletin of Economics and Statistics*, 48, 213–28.

—— and Escribano, A. (1986) Limitation on the long-run relationship between prices from an efficient market. *Discussion Paper*, University of California at San Diego.

—— and Newbold, P. (1974) Spurious regressions in econometrics. *Journal of Econometrics*, 2, 111–20.

Hall, S. G. (1986) An application of the Engle–Granger two step estimation procedure to United Kingdom aggregate wage data. *Oxford Bulletin of Economics and Statistics*, 48, 229–40.

—— (1989) Maximum likelihood estimation of cointegration vectors: an example of the Johansen procedure. *Oxford Bulletin of Economics and Statistics*, 51, 213–18.

—— (1991) The effect of varying length VAR models on the maximum likelihood estimates of cointegrating vectors. *Scottish Journal of Political Economy*, 38, 317–23.

——, Henry, S. G. B. and Wilcox, J. (1989) The long-run determination of the U.K. monetary aggregates. In S. G. B. Henry and K. D. Patterson (eds), *Economic Modelling at the Bank of England*, London: Chapman and Hall.

Hallman, J. (1987) Cointegrated systems and error correction. *Discussion Paper*, University of California at San Diego.

Harvey, A. C. (1989) *The Economic Analysis of Time Series*, 2nd ed. Deddington: Philip Allan.

Hasza, D. P. and Fuller, W. A. (1982) Testing for nonstationary parameter specifications in seasonal time series models. *Annals of Statistics*, 10, 1209–16.

Hendry, D. F. (1979) Predictive failure and econometric modelling in macroeconomics: the transactions demand for money. In P. Ormerod (ed.), *Modelling the Economy*, Oxford: Heinemann Educational.

—— (1985) Monetary economic myth and econometric reality. *Oxford Review of Economic Policy*, 1, 72–84.

—— (1986) Empirical modelling in dynamic econometrics. *Applied Economics Discussion Paper*, Institute of Economics and Statistics, Oxford.

—— (1988) The encompassing implications of feedback versus feedforward mechanisms in econometrics. *Oxford Economic Papers*, 40, 132–49.

—— and Ericsson, N. R. (1983) Assertion without empirical basis: an econometric appraisal of Friedman and Schwartz. Panel Paper 22, Bank of England Panel of Academic Consultants.

—— and —— (1991) An econometric analysis of the U.K. money demand in 'Monetary Trends and the United Kingdom by Milton Friedman and Anna J. Schwartz'. *American Economic Review*, 81, 8–38.

—— and Mizon, G. E. (1978) Serial correlation as a convenient simplification, not a nuisance: a comment on a study of the demand for money by the Bank of England. *Economic Journal*, 88, 549–63.

—— and —— (1992) Evaluating dynamic econometric modelling by encompassing the VAR. In P. C. B. Phillips (ed), *Models, Methods and Applications of Econometrics, Essays in Honour of Rex Bergstrom*, Oxford: Blackwell.

——, Pagan, A. R. and Sargan, J. D. (1984) Dynamic specification. In Z. Griliches and M. D. Intriligator, (eds), *Handbook of Econometrics*, vol. 2, Amsterdam: Elsevier.

——, Neale, A. and Srba, F. (1988) Econometric analysis of small linear systems using PC-FIML. *Journal of Econometrics*, 38, 203–26.

Hylleberg, S. and Mizon, G.E. (1989a) Cointegration and error-correction mechanisms. *Economic Journal (Supplement)*, 99, 113–25.

—— and —— (1989b) A note on the distribution of the least squares estimator of a random walk with drift. *Economic Letters*, 29, 225–30.

——, Engle, R. F., Granger, C. W. J. and Yoo, B. S. (1988) Seasonal integration and cointegration. *Discussion Paper*, University of California at San Diego.

Jenkinson, T. J. (1986) Testing neo-classical theories of labour demand: an application of cointegration techniques. *Oxford Bulletin of Economics and Statistics*, 48, 241–52.

Johansen, S. (1988) Statistical analysis of cointegration vectors. *Journal of Economic Dynamics and Control*, 12, 231–54.

—— (1989) Likelihood based inference on cointegration: theory and applications. *Mimeo*, Institute of Mathematical Statistics, University of Copenhagen.

—— (1991) A statistical analysis of cointegration for I(2) variables. *Preprint* 1991, n.2, *Institute of Mathematical Statistics, Copenhagen*.

—— and Juselius, K. (1990) Maximum likelihood estimation and inference on cointegration with applications to the demand for money. *Oxford Bulletin of Economics and Statistics*, 52, 169–209.

Judge, G. G., Griffiths, W. E., Hill, R. E., Lutkepohl, H. and Lee, T.-S. (1985) *The Theory and Practice of Econometrics*, 2nd edn. New York: Wiley.

Juselius, K. (1989) Stationary disequilibrium error processes in the Danish money market: an application of ML cointegration. Mimeo, University of Copenhagen.

Lucas, R. E. (1976) Econometric policy evaluation: a critique. In K. Brunner and A. H. Meltzer (eds), *The Phillips Curve and Labor Markets*, Amsterdam: North-Holland.

MacDonald, R. and Speight, A. C. H. (1989) Consumption, saving and rational expectations: some further evidence for the U.K. *Economic Journal*, 99, 83–91.

Marsh, T. A. and Merton, R. C. (1987) Dividend behaviour for the aggregate stock market. *Journal of Business*, 60, 1–40.

McAleer, M. and Pesaran, M. H. (1986) Statistical inference in non-nested econometric models. *Applied Mathematics and Computation*, 20, 271–311.

Miller, M. H., Weller, P. and Williamson, J. W. (1989) The stability properties of target zones. In R. C. Bryant, D. A. Currie, J. A. Frenkel, P. R. Masson and R. Portes (eds), *Macroeconomic Policies in an Interdependent World*, Washington, DC: International Monetary Fund.

Molinas, C. (1986) A note on spurious regressions with integrated moving average errors. *Oxford Bulletin of Economics and Statistics*, 48, 252–62.

Muscatelli, V. A. (1989a) Cointegration and the long-run properties of the demand for money in the U.K. *Discussion Paper*, University of Glasgow.

—— (1989b) A comparison of the 'rational expectations' and 'general-to-specific' approaches to modelling the demand for M1. *Oxford Bulletin of Economics and Statistics*, 51, 353–73.

—— (1990) Exogeneity, cointegration and the demand for money in Italy. *Discussion Paper*, University of Glasgow.

—— and Papi, L. (1990) Cointegration, financial innovation and modelling the demand for money in Italy. *The Manchester School*, 58, 242–59.

——, Srinivasan, T. G. and Vines, D. A. (1990) The empirical modelling of NIE exports: an evaluation of different approaches. *Discussion Paper*, University of Glasgow.

—— and —— (1992) Demand and supply factors in the determination of NIE exports: a simultaneous error-correction model for Hong Kong. *Economic Journal*, 102, 1467–7.

Nelson, C. R. and Plosser, C. I. (1982) Trends and random walks in macroeconomic time series: some evidence and implications. *Journal of Monetary Economics*, 10, 139–62.

Nickell, S. J. (1985) Error correction, partial adjustment and all that: an expository note. *Oxford Bulletin of Economics and Statistics*, 47, 119–30.

Osborn, D. R. (1990) A survey of seasonality in U.K. macroeconomic variables. *Discussion Paper*, University of Manchester.

——, Chui, A. P. L., Smith, J. P. and Birchenhall, C. R. (1988) Seasonality and the order of integration for consumption. *Oxford Bulletin of Economics and Statistics*, 50, 361–77.

Pagan, A. R. (1987) Three econometric methodologies: a critical appraisal. *Journal of Economic Surveys*, 1, 3–24.

—— and Wickens, M. S. (1989) A survey of some recent econometric methods. *Economic Journal*, 99, 962–1025.

Park, J. Y. (1988) Testing for unit roots and cointegration by variable addition. *CAE Working Paper* n. 88–30, *Cornell University*.

—— (1990) Maximum likelihood estimation of simultaneous cointegrated models. *Memo* 1990–18, *Institute of Economics, University of Aarhus*.

—— and Choi, B. (1988) A new approach to testing for a unit root. *CAE Working Paper* n. 88–23, *Cornell University*.

—— and Phillips, P. C. B. (1988) Statistical inference in regressions with integrated processes: Part 1. *Econometric Theory*, 4, 408–67.

—— and —— (1989) Statistical inference in regressions with integrated processes: Part 2. *Econometric Theory*, 5, 468–97.

Perron, P. (1987) The Great Crash, the oil price shock and unit root hypothesis. *Mimeo*, University of Montreal.

—— (1988) Trends and random walks in macroeconomic time series. *Journal of Economic Dynamics and Control*, 12, 333–46.

Pesaran, M. H. and Pesaran, B. (1991) *Microfit 3.0*. Oxford: Oxford University Press.

Phillips, P. C. B. (1988) Spectral regression for cointegrated time series. *Cowles Foundation Discussion Paper* 872, Yale University.

—— (1991) Optimal inference in cointegrated systems. *Econometrica*, 59, 283–306.

—— and Hansen, B. E. (1990) Statistical inference in instrumental variables regression with I(1) processes. *Review of Economic Studies*, 57, 99–125.

—— and Ouliaris, S. (1987) Asymptotic properties of residual based tests for cointegration, *Discussion Paper* 847, Yale University.

—— and —— (1988) Testing for cointegration using principle component methods. *Journal of Economic Dynamics and Control*, 12, 205–30.

—— and Perron, P. (1988) Testing for unit roots in time series regressions. *Biometrika*, 75, 335–46.

Poterba, J. M. and Summers, L. H. (1987) Mean reversion in stock prices: evidence and implications, *Mimeo*, Massachusetts Institute of Technology.

Sargan, J. D. and Bhargava, A. (1983) Testing residuals from least squares regression for being generated by the Gaussian random walk. *Econometrica*, 51, 153–74.

Schwert, G. W. (1987) Effects of model misspecification on tests for unit roots in macroeconomic data. *Journal of Monetary Economics*, 20, 73–103.

—— (1989) Tests for unit roots: a Monte Carlo investigation. *Journal of Business and Economic Statistics*, 7, 147–59.

Sims, C. A., Stock, J. H. and Watson, M. W. (1990) Inference in linear time series models with some unit roots. *Econometrica*, 58, 113–44.

Stock, J. (1987) Asymptotic properties of least squares estimators cointegrating vectors. *Econometrica*, 55, 1035–56.

—— and Watson, M. W. (1988) Testing for common trends. *Journal of the American Statistical Association*, 83, 1097–1107.

Vaciago, G. and Verga, G. (1989) Nuovi strumenti finanziari e stabilita' della domanda di moneta. *Note Economiche*, 18, 1–23.

Wallis, K. F. (1974) Seasonal adjustment and relations between variables. *Journal of the American Statistical Association*, 69, 18–31.

West, K. (1988) Asymptotic normality when regressors have a unit root. *Econometrica*, 56, 1397–1417.

Wickens, M. R. and Breusch, T. S. (1988) Dynamic specification, the long-run and the estimation of transformed regression models. *Economic Journal (Supplement)*, 98, 189–205.

Yoo, B. S. (1986) Multi-cointegrated time series and generalised error-correction models. *Discussion Paper*, University of California at San Diego.

—— (1987) Cointegrated time series: structure forecasting and testing. *Ph.D. Dissertation*, University of California at San Diego.

Yule, G. U. (1926) Why do we sometimes get nonsense-correlations between time series? A study in sampling and the nature of time series. *Journal of the Royal Statistical Society*, 89, 1–64.

8 On ARCH models: properties, estimation and testing

Anil K. Bera
University of Illinois at Urbana-Champaign
and
Matthew L. Higgins
University of Wisconsin-Milwaukee

1 Introduction

The history of autoregressive conditional heteroskedasticity (ARCH) models is indeed a very short one, for they were introduced by Robert Engle only a decade ago. Within this brief period, however, the ARCH literature has grown in a spectacular fashion. The numerous applications of ARCH models defies observed trends in scientific advancements. Usually, applications lag theoretical developments, but Engle's original ARCH model and its various generalizations have been applied to numerous economic and financial data series of many countries, while it has seen relatively fewer theoretical advancements.

The concept of ARCH might be only a decade old, but its roots go far into the past, possibly as far as Bachelier (1900), who was the first to conduct a rigorous study of the behaviour of speculative prices. There was then a period of long silence. Mandelbrot (1963a, b, 1967) revived the interest in the time series properties of asset prices with his theory that 'random variables with an infinite population variance are indispensable for a workable description of price changes' (cf. 1963b, p. 421). His observations, such as that unconditional distributions have thick tails, variances change over time and large (small) changes tend to be followed by large (small) changes of either sign, are 'stylized facts' for many economic and financial variables. Figures 1, 2 and 3 present three typical data series on price changes. These are, respectively, the weekly rate of return on the US dollar–British pound exchange rate, changes in the three-month treasury bill rate and the growth rate of the New York Stock Exchange (NYSE) monthly composite index. The first noticeable thing is that for all three series the means appear to be constant, while the variances change over time. In particular, for the treasury bill rate, there is a dramatic increase in the variance in the late 1970s and early 1980s. Sample statistics from these series overwhelmingly support Mandelbrot's other stylized facts.

Prior to the introduction of ARCH, researchers were very much aware of changes in variance, but used only informal procedures to take account of this. For example, Mandelbrot (1963a) used recursive estimates of the variance over time and Klien (1977) took five-period moving variance estimates about a ten-period moving sample mean.

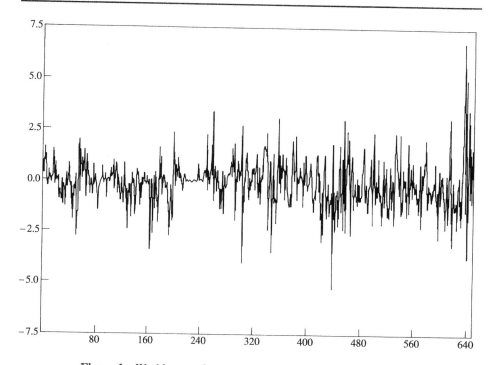

Figure 1   Weekly rate of return on the dollar–pound exchange rate.

Engle's (1982) ARCH model was the first formal model which seemed to capture the stylized facts mentioned above.

The ARCH model is useful not only because it captures some stylized facts, but also because it has applications to numerous and diverse areas. For example, it has been used in asset pricing to test the intertemporal capital asset pricing model, the consumption-based capital asset pricing model and the arbitrage pricing theory, to develop volatility tests for market efficiency and to estimate the time-varying systematic risk in the context of the market model. It has been used to measure the term structure of interest rates; to develop optimal dynamic hedging strategies; to examine how information flows across countries, markets and assets; to price options; and to model risk premia. In macroeconomics, it has been successfully used to construct debt portfolios of developing countries, to measure inflationary uncertainty, to examine the relationship between exchange rate uncertainty and trade, to study the effects of central bank interventions, and to characterize the relationship between the macroeconomy and the stock market.

The literature on ARCH is so vast that it is almost impossible to provide a comprehensive review. There are already a few survey papers on this topic. In particular, we would refer readers to Engle and Bollerslev (1986) and Bollerslev et al. (1992). The latter paper noted several hundred papers that apply the ARCH methodology to various financial markets. Some recent references to the very rapidly growing bibliography include Bekaert (1992), Bollerslev and Hodrick (1992), Duffee (1992), Koedijk et al. (1992) and Ng and Pirrong (1992), just to name a few. The purpose of this review paper is rather modest. Our aim is to provide an informal account of recent theoretical

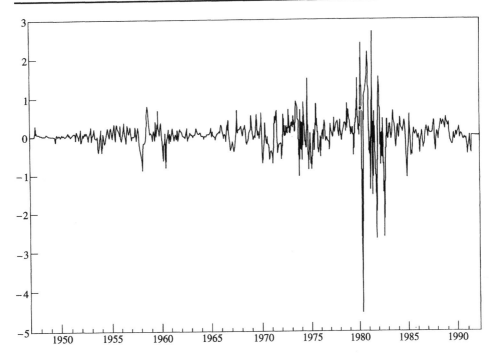

Figure 2 First difference of the three-month treasury bill rate.

advances and their impact on applied work. It should be mentioned that our use of the term 'ARCH' does not refer to Engle's original model. By ARCH, we mean the phenomenon of conditional heteroskedasticity in general and all models to capture this phenomenon.

The plan of the paper is as follows. The basic ARCH models are described in the next section. As these models capture various stylized facts, they can be given different interpretations, and these are discussed in section 3. It has been found that the basic ARCH models are unable to capture all observed phenomena, such as the leverage effect, excess kurtosis and the high degree of nonlinearity. Generalizations of the basic ARCH models to capture these phenomena are the subject matter of section 4. Forecasting with ARCH models is treated in section 5. The following sections, 6 and 7, review further generalizations, such as multivariate ARCH and ARCH-in-mean (ARCH-M) models. In sections 8 and 9, we discuss estimation and testing of ARCH models. The last section concludes the paper with a few remarks. At the end of the paper, we include a complete glossary of the acronyms for the ARCH models which we describe in the survey.

2 Autoregressive conditional heteroskedasticity

In this section, we introduce the original ARCH model of Engle (1982). We begin by defining the ARCH process, and heuristically describe its properties. We emphasize the properties of the ARCH model which make it appealing for modelling the volatility of

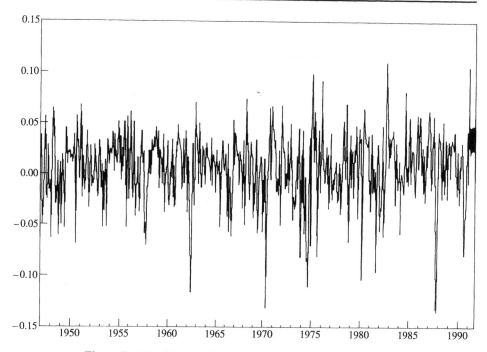

Figure 3   Monthly rate of return on the NYSE composite index.

economic time series. Subsequently, we introduce the generalized ARCH (GARCH) model of Bollerslev (1986), which provides a parsimonious parameterization for the conditional variance. The properties of the ARCH process are then formally characterized by describing its unconditional moments. We also discuss how aggregating an ARCH process over time affects the moments of the process.

2.1   Definition of the process

An ARCH process can be defined in a variety of contexts. We will define it in terms of the distribution of the errors of a dynamic linear regression model. The dependent variable y_t is assumed to be generated by

$$y_t = x_t'\xi + \varepsilon_t \qquad t = 1, \ldots, T \tag{1}$$

where x_t is a $k \times 1$ vector of exogenous variables, which may include lagged values of the dependent variable, and ξ is a $k \times 1$ vector of regression parameters. The ARCH model characterizes the distribution of the stochastic error ε_t conditional on the realized values of the set of variables $\Psi_{t-1} = \{y_{t-1}, x_{t-1}, y_{t-2}, x_{t-2}, \ldots\}$. Specifically, Engle's (1982) original ARCH model assumes

$$\varepsilon_t \mid \Psi_{t-1} \sim \mathrm{N}(0, h_t) \tag{2}$$

where

$$h_t = \alpha_0 + \alpha_1 \varepsilon_{t-1}^2 + \cdots + \alpha_q \varepsilon_{t-q}^2 \tag{3}$$

with $\alpha_0 > 0$ and $\alpha_i \geqslant 0, i = 1, \ldots, q$, to ensure that the conditional variance is positive. Note that since $\varepsilon_{t-i} = y_{t-i} - x'_{t-i}\xi, i = 1, \ldots q, h_t$ is clearly a function of the elements of Ψ_{t-1}.

The distinguishing feature of the model (2) and (3) is not simply that the conditional variance h_t is a function of the conditioning set Ψ_{t-1}, but rather the particular functional form that is specified. Episodes of volatility are generally characterized as the clustering of large shocks to the dependent variable. The conditional variance function (3) is formulated to mimic this phenomenon. In the regression model, a large shock is represented by a large deviation of y_t from its conditional mean $x'_t\xi$, or equivalently, a large positive or negative value of ε_t. In the ARCH regression model, the variance of the current error ε_t, conditional on the realized values of the lagged errors $\varepsilon_{t-i}, i = 1, \ldots, q$, is an increasing function of the magnitude of the lagged errors, irrespective of their signs. Hence, large errors of either sign *tend* to be followed by a large error of either sign. And similarly, small errors of either sign *tend* to be followed by a small error of either sign. The order of the lag q determines the length of time for which a shock persists in conditioning the variance of subsequent errors. The larger the value of q, the longer the episodes of volatility will tend to be.

A linear function of lagged squared errors, of course, is not the only conditional variance function that will produce clustering of large deviations. Any monotonically increasing function of the absolute values of the lagged errors will lead to such clustering. However, since variance is expected squared deviation, a linear combination of lagged squared errors is a natural measure of the recent trend in variance to translate to the current conditional variance h_t. Alternative formulations of the conditional variance function have been found to be useful and these formulations will be discussed in depth in section 4.1.

To illustrate the characteristic appearance of ARCH data, we generate artificial samples from (2). An explicit generating equation for an ARCH process is

$$\varepsilon_t = \eta_t \sqrt{h_t}, \tag{4}$$

where $\eta_t \sim$ IID N(0,1) and h_t is given by (3). Since h_t is a function of the elements of Ψ_{t-1}, and therefore is fixed when conditioning on Ψ_{t-1}, it is clear that ε_t as given in (4) will be conditionally normal with $E(\varepsilon_t \mid \Psi_{t-1}) = \sqrt{h_t}E(\eta_t \mid \Psi_{t-1}) = 0$ and $\text{var}(\varepsilon_t \mid \Psi_{t-1}) = h_t, \text{var}(\eta_t \mid \Psi_{t-1}) = h_t$. Hence, the process specified by (4) is identical to the ARCH process (2). The generating equation (4) reveals that ARCH rescales an underlying Gaussian innovation process η_t by multiplying it by the conditional standard deviation which is a function of the information set Ψ_{t-1}. First, for comparison when ARCH is not present in the data, in figure 4 we present a plot of 500 realizations of $\varepsilon_t = \eta_t$, setting $h_t = 1$ by imposing $\alpha_0 = 1$ and $\alpha_i = 0$ for $i = 1, \ldots, q$. The displayed data are simply Gaussian white noise, the process usually assumed for the errors in a linear model. Then, using the same η_t shown in figure 4, figures 5 and 6 are plots of $\varepsilon_t = \eta_t \sqrt{h_t}$ for which the h_t are respectively

$$h_t = 0.1 + 0.9\varepsilon_{t-1}^2 \tag{5}$$

and

$$h_t = 0.1 + 0.36\varepsilon_{t-1}^2 + 0.27\varepsilon_{t-2}^2 + 0.18\varepsilon_{t-3}^2 + 0.09\varepsilon_{t-4}^2. \tag{6}$$

To make the scale of the data comparable in all three figures, the parameter values in (5) and (6) were chosen to make the unconditional variances of the ARCH processes

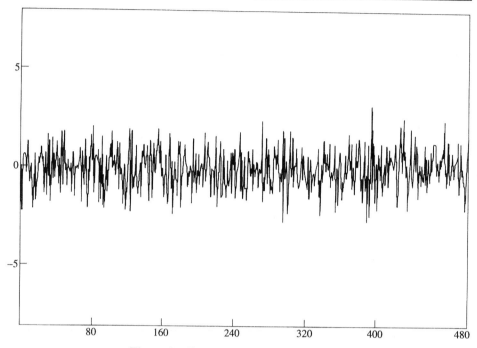

Figure 4   Simulated Gaussian white noise.

equal to unity. After section 2.3, it will be clear why the conditional variance functions (5) and (6) imply that the unconditional variances of the processes are unity. We do not notice any clustering of the observations in figure 4. Figures 5 and 6, however, have close resemblance to our earlier figures 1, 2 and 3. In particular, the closeness of figures 2 and 6 is quite striking. Comparing figures 5 and 6, we also note that, as expected, the episodes of volatility are longer for ARCH(4).

2.2   Generalized autoregressive conditional heteroskedasticity

In the first empirical applications of ARCH to the relationship between the level and the volatility of inflation, Engle (1982, 1983) found that a large lag q was required in the conditional variance function. This would necessitate estimating a large number of parameters subject to inequality restrictions. To reduce the computational burden, Engle (1982, 1983) parameterized the conditional variance as

$$h_t = \alpha_0 + \alpha_1 \sum_{i=1}^{q} w_i \varepsilon_{t-i}^2$$

where the weights

$$w_i = \frac{(q+1) - i}{\frac{1}{2}q(q+1)}$$

decline linearly and are constructed so that $\sum_{i=1}^{q} w_i = 1$. With this parameterization, a large lag can be specified and yet only two parameters are required to be estimated in

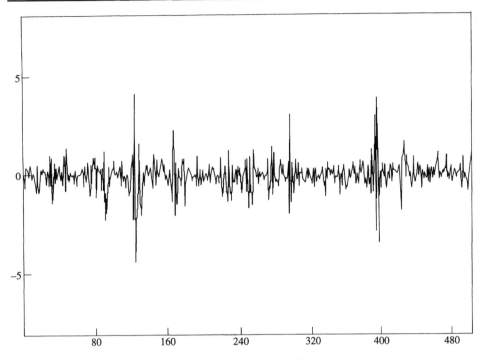

Figure 5   Simulated ARCH(1) data.

the conditional variance function. Although linearly declining weights are plausible, the formulation does put undue restrictions on the dynamics of the ARCH process.

Bollerslev (1986) proposed an extension of the conditional variance function (3), which he termed generalized ARCH (GARCH), that has proved to be very useful in empirical work. The GARCH model was also independently proposed by Taylor (1986), who used a different acronym. They suggested that the conditional variance be specified as

$$h_t = \alpha_0 + \alpha_1 \varepsilon_{t-1}^2 + \cdots + \alpha_q \varepsilon_{t-q}^2 + \beta_1 h_{t-1} + \cdots + \beta_p h_{t-p} \tag{7}$$

where the inequality restrictions

$$\begin{aligned}
\alpha_0 &> 0 \\
\alpha_i &\geqslant 0 \quad \text{for } i = 1, \ldots, q \\
\beta_i &\geqslant 0 \quad \text{for } i = 1, \ldots, p
\end{aligned} \tag{8}$$

are imposed to ensure that the conditional variance is strictly positive. A GARCH process with orders p and q is denoted as GARCH(p, q). The motivation of the GARCH process can be seen by expressing (7) as

$$h_t = \alpha_0 + \alpha(B)\varepsilon_t^2 + \beta(B)h_t$$

where $\alpha(B) = \alpha_1 B + \cdots + \alpha_q B^q$ and $\beta(B) = \beta_1 B + \cdots + \beta_p B^p$ are polynomials in the backshift operator B. If the roots of $1 - \beta(Z)$ lie outside the unit circle, we can rewrite (7) as

$$h_t = \frac{\alpha_0}{1 - \beta(1)} + \frac{\alpha(B)}{1 - \beta(B)} \varepsilon_t^2$$

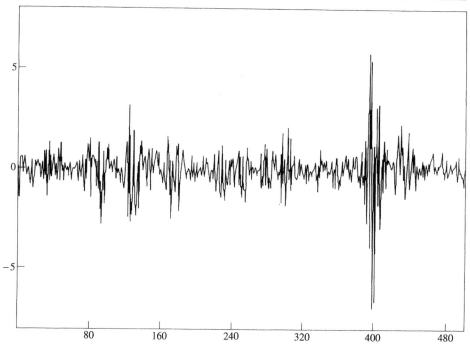

Figure 6   Simulated ARCH(4) data.

$$= \alpha_0^* + \sum_{i=1}^{\infty} \delta_i \varepsilon_{t-i}^2 \tag{9}$$

where $\alpha_0^* = \alpha_0/[1 - \beta(1)]$ and the coefficient δ_i is the coefficient of B^i in the expansion of $\alpha(B)[1 - \beta(B)]^{-1}$. Hence, expression (9) reveals that a GARCH(p, q) process is an infinite order ARCH process with a rational lag structure imposed on the coefficients. The generalization of ARCH to GARCH is similar to the generalization of an MA process to an ARMA process. The intention is that GARCH can parsimoniously represent a high-order ARCH process.

Although the restrictions (8) are sufficient to ensure that the conditional variance of a GARCH(p, q) process is strictly positive, Nelson and Cao (1992) demonstrated that weaker sufficient conditions can be found (see also Drost and Nijman, 1992). They pointed out that from the *inverted* representation of h_t in (9)

$$\alpha_0^* > 0 \text{ and } \delta_i \geqslant 0 \qquad i = 1, \ldots, \infty \tag{10}$$

are sufficient to ensure that the conditional variance is strictly positive. Expressing α_0^* and the δ_i in terms of the original parameters of the GARCH model, Nelson and Cao showed that (10) does not require that all the inequalities in (8) hold. For example, in a GARCH(1, 2) process, $\alpha_0 > 0, \alpha_1 \geqslant 0, \beta_1 \geqslant 0$ and $\beta_1\alpha_1 + \alpha_2 \geqslant 0$ are sufficient to guarantee that $h_t > 0$. Therefore, in the GARCH(1, 2) model, α_2 may be negative. They presented general results for GARCH(1, q) and GARCH(2, q), but suggested that a derivation for GARCH processes with $p \geqslant 3$ is difficult. Nelson and Cao cited several empirical studies, such as French et al. (1987), Baillie and Bollerslev (1989), and Engle et al. (1990a), which report negative coefficients and yet satisfy the conditions for a positive conditional variance based on (10). They concluded that the inequality restrictions (8) should not be imposed in estimation, as violation of these inequalities does not necessarily imply that the conditional variance function is mis-specified.

2.3 Unconditional moments of the ARCH model

Above, we described verbally the properties of ARCH and illustrated the visual appearance of ARCH with computer-generated data. The unconditional moments of the ARCH process formally characterize these properties. Engle (1982) gave expressions for many of the moments, and stated necessary and sufficient conditions for the existence of the moments for the original linear ARCH process (3). Milhoj (1985) provided additional moments. Subsequently, Bollerslev (1986) extended these results to the GARCH process.

The derivation of the unconditional moments of the ARCH process is possible through extensive use of the following important probability result:

Law of iterated expectations Let Ω_1 and Ω_2 be two sets of random variables such that $\Omega_1 \subseteq \Omega_2$. Let y be a scalar random variable. Then $E(y \mid \Omega_1) = E[E(y \mid \Omega_2) \mid \Omega_1]$.

In the context of this paper, Ω_1 and Ω_2 are information sets available at different periods in time. A special case of the law is frequently employed to find the moments of the ARCH process. If $\Omega_1 = \emptyset$ is the empty set, then $E(y) = E[E(y \mid \Omega_2)]$. This expression is useful because it relates an unconditional moment to a conditional moment. Since the ARCH model is specified in terms of its conditional moments, it provides a method for deriving unconditional moments.

Using the law of iterated expectations, we can easily derive the fundamental properties of an ARCH process. First, consider the unconditional mean of a GARCH(p, q) error ε_t with conditional variance (7). Applying the law of iterated expectations, $E(\varepsilon_t) = E[E(\varepsilon_t \mid \Psi_{t-1})]$. However, because the GARCH model specifies that $E(\varepsilon_t \mid \Psi_{t-1}) = 0$ for all realizations of Ψ_{t-1}, it immediately follows that $E(\varepsilon_t) = 0$. Thus, the GARCH process has mean zero.

Next, consider the unconditional variance of the GARCH(p, q) process. Although the variance of ε_t can be evaluated in general, for simple illustration we consider the GARCH(1, 1) process. Using (7), with $p = q = 1$, and the law of iterated expectations

$$
\begin{aligned}
E(\varepsilon_t^2) &= E[E(\varepsilon_t^2 \mid \Psi_{t-1})] \\
&= E(h_t) \\
&= \alpha_0 + \alpha_1 E(\varepsilon_{t-1}^2) + \beta_1 E(h_{t-1}) \\
&= \alpha_0 + (\alpha_1 + \beta_1) E(\varepsilon_{t-1}^2)
\end{aligned}
$$

which is a linear difference equation for the sequence of variances. Assuming the process began infinitely far in the past with a finite initial variance, the sequence of variances converges to the constant

$$
\sigma_\varepsilon^2 = E(\varepsilon_t^2) = \frac{\alpha_0}{1 - \alpha_1 - \beta_1}
$$

if $\alpha_1 + \beta_1 < 1$. For the general GARCH(p, q) process, Bollerslev (1986) gave the necessary and sufficient condition

$$\alpha(1) + \beta(1) = \sum_{i=1}^{q} \alpha_i + \sum_{i=1}^{p} \beta_i < 1 \tag{11}$$

for the existence of the variance. When this condition is satisfied, the variance is

$$\sigma_\varepsilon^2 = E(\varepsilon_t^2) = \frac{\alpha_0}{1 - \alpha(1) - \beta(1)}.$$

Although the variance of ε_t conditional on Ψ_{t-1} changes with the elements of the information set, unconditionally the ARCH process is *homoskedastic*. Considering figures 5 and 6 again, the visual appearance of the generated data conveys the impression that the unconditional variance changes with time. This false perception results from the clustering of large deviations. A major contribution of the ARCH literature is the finding that apparent changes in the volatility of economic time series may be predictable and result from a specific type of nonlinear dependence rather than exogenous structural change in the variance.

The nature of the unconditional density of an ARCH process can be analysed by the higher order moments. As ε_t is conditionally normal, for all odd integers m, $E(\varepsilon_t^m \mid \Psi_{t-1}) = 0$. The skewness coefficient is immediately seen to be zero. Since ε_t is continuous, this implies that the unconditional distribution is symmetric. Higher moments indicate further properties of the ARCH process. An expression for the fourth moment of a general GARCH(p, q) process is not available, but Engle (1982) gave it for the ARCH(1) process and Bollerslev (1986) generalized it to the GARCH(1, 1) case. Engle's result for the ARCH(1) case requires $3\alpha_1^2 < 1$ for the fourth moment to exist. Simple algebra then reveals that the kurtosis is

$$\frac{E(\varepsilon_t^4)}{\sigma_\varepsilon^4} = 3 \left(\frac{1 - \alpha_1^2}{1 - 3\alpha_1^2} \right)$$

which is clearly greater than 3, the kurtosis coefficient of the normal distribution. Therefore, the ARCH(1) process has tails heavier than the normal distribution. This property makes the ARCH process attractive because the distributions of asset returns frequently display tails heavier than the normal distribution. Although no known closed form for the unconditional density function of an ARCH process exists, Nelson (1990b) demonstrated that under suitable conditions, as the time interval goes to zero, a GARCH(1, 1) process approaches a continuous time process whose stationary unconditional distribution is a Student's t. Nelson's result indicates why heavy-tailed distributions are so prevalent with high frequency financial data.

That the parameterization of the ARCH process does not *a priori* impose the existence of unconditional moments is an important characteristic of the model. It has long been suggested, at least as early as Mandelbrot (1963b), that the distribution of asset returns are such that the variance may not exist. In empirical applications of GARCH, estimated parameters frequently do not satisfy (11). The fact that the ARCH model admits an infinite variance is desirable because such behaviour may be a characteristic of the data generating process that should be reflected in the estimated model. Also, fortunately, as will be noted in section 8, even for GARCH models with infinite variances, standard results on consistency and asymptotic normality might still be valid.

Above we considered the univariate distribution of a single ε_t. The moments of the joint distribution of the ε_t also reveal important properties of the ARCH process. For $k \geqslant 1$, the autocovariances of the GARCH(p, q) process are

$$
\begin{aligned}
E(\varepsilon_t \varepsilon_{t-k}) &= E[E(\varepsilon_t \varepsilon_{t-k} \mid \Psi_{t-1})] \\
&= E[\varepsilon_{t-k} E(\varepsilon_t \mid \Psi_{t-1})] \\
&= 0.
\end{aligned}
$$

Since the GARCH process is serially uncorrelated, with constant mean zero, the process is weakly stationary if the variance exists, i.e. if (11) holds. A remarkable property of a GARCH process, first demonstrated by Nelson (1990a) for GARCH(1, 1), is that it may be strongly stationary without being weakly stationary. Bougerol and Picard (1992) extended Nelson's result to the GARCH(p, q) process and stated necessary and sufficient conditions for strong stationarity. These conditions are very technical and will not be described here. That the GARCH process may be strongly stationary without being weakly stationary stems from the fact that weak stationarity requires that the mean, variance and autocovariances be *finite* and time invariant. Strong stationarity requires that the distribution function of any finite set of ε_t is invariant under time translation. Finite moments are not required for strong stationarity. The results of Nelson (1990a) and Bougerol and Picard (1992) show that the unconditional variance may be infinite and yet the GARCH process may still be strongly stationary.

The lack of serial correlation is an important characteristic of the ARCH process which makes it suitable for modelling financial time series. The efficient market hypothesis asserts that past rates of return cannot be used to improve the prediction of future rates of return. In (1), suppose the y_t is the rate of return on an asset and that $\xi = 0$ so that there is no regression component in the model. Then y_t is identical to ε_t and becomes a pure GARCH process. The optimal prediction of the return y_t is the expectation of the return conditional on any available information. But because the GARCH model specifies $E(y_t \mid \Psi_{t-1}) = E(y_t) = 0$, the past observations on y_t contained in Ψ_{t-1} do not alter the optimal prediction of the rate of return. Therefore, the presence of ARCH does not represent a violation of market efficiency.

Of course, the lack of serial correlation does not imply that the ε_t are independent. Above, we suggested that the qualitative appearance of data generated from an ARCH process arises from the particular type of dependence. Bollerslev (1986) gave a representation for the GARCH(p, q) process which reveals the nature of the dependence. Letting $v_t = \varepsilon_t^2 - h_t$, the squared error can be written as

$$
\begin{aligned}
\varepsilon_t^2 &= h_t + v_t \\
&= \alpha_0 + \sum_{i=1}^{m} (\alpha_i + \beta_i) \varepsilon_{t-i}^2 - \sum_{i=1}^{p} \beta_i (\varepsilon_{t-1}^2 - h_{t-i}) + v_t \\
&= \alpha_0 + \sum_{i=1}^{m} (\alpha_i + \beta_i) \varepsilon_{t-i}^2 - \sum_{i=1}^{p} \beta_i v_{t-i} + v_t
\end{aligned}
\tag{12}
$$

where $m = \max(p, q)$, $\alpha_i = 0$ for $i > q$ and $\beta_i = 0$ for $i > p$. Because $E(v_t \mid \Psi_{t-1}) = 0$, the law of iterated expectations reveals that v_t has mean zero and is serially uncorrelated. Therefore, from (12) we see that ε_t^2 has an ARMA(m, p) representation. The autocorrelation and partial autocorrelation functions of the squared process ε_t^2 will have the familiar patterns of those from an autoregressive moving average process. Bollerslev (1988) has suggested that these autocorrelation functions of ε_t^2 may be used to identify the orders p and q of the GARCH process. In practice, the identification of the order of a GARCH(p, q) has not posed much of a problem, at least in comparison with the earlier modelling experience with ARMA(p, q) processes. In applied work, it has been frequently demonstrated that the GARCH(1, 1) process is able to represent the majority of financial time series. A data set which requires a model of order greater than GARCH(1, 2) or GARCH(2, 1) is very rare.

2.4   Illustrative example with the weekly dollar–pound exchange rate

The ARCH model has been widely applied to the study of the dynamics of the rate of return on holding foreign currencies (see Bollerslev et al. (1992, pp. 37–46) for a survey of applications). In this section, we illustrate the properties of conditionally heteroskedastic data by estimating ARCH and GARCH models for the weekly rate of return in the US–British currency exchange market. The data are the weekly spot exchange rate from January 1973 to June 1985. There are 651 observations. Let s_t denote the spot price of the British pound in terms of the US dollar. We then analyse the continuously compounded percentage rate of return, $r_t = 100 \log(s_t/s_{t-1})$, from holding the British pound for one week. These data are plotted in figure 1.

We begin by identifying and estimating an AR process for the mean of r_t. The autocorrelation and partial autocorrelation functions of r_t suggest that the data can be represented by an AR(3) process. The estimated model is given by

$$r_t = -0.07 + 0.27 r_{t-1} - 0.08 r_{t-2} + 0.10 r_{t-3} \qquad l(\hat{\theta}) = -971.70$$
$$\quad\;\; (0.04) \;\; (0.04) \qquad\;\; (0.04) \qquad\;\; (0.04)$$

where the standard errors are shown in parentheses and $l(\hat{\theta})$ is the value of the maximized log likelihood function assuming that the data are normally distributed. Box–Pierce statistics computed from the residuals indicate that the AR(3) process adequately accounts for the serial correlation in the data. The higher order moments of the residuals, however, reveal that nonlinearity is present in the data and that the unconditional distribution is non-normal. In table 1, we present the skewness and kurtosis coefficients of the residuals, and the autocorrelations of the squared residuals. If the errors of the AR process are independent, the autocorrelations of the squared residuals should be approximately zero. From table 1, the autocorrelations at lags 1, 2, 3, 4 and 7 exceed twice their asymptotic standard errors, suggesting the presence of nonlinear dependence in the data. The skewness coefficient conveys some evidence of asymmetry in the unconditional distribution. The kurtosis coefficient is significantly greater than 3, which indicates that the unconditional distribution of the data has much heavier tails than a normal distribution.

As emphasized in section 2.3, nonlinear dependence and a heavy-tailed unconditional distribution are characteristic of conditionally heteroskedastic data. We maintain the

AR(3) specification for the conditional mean of r_t, but now specify the error as an ARCH(q) process. The autocorrelations of the squares of the AR residuals suggest dependence through order 7. Therefore, we initially estimated an ARCH(7) model, but found α_7 to be insignificant. We re-specified the errors as ARCH(6) and estimated the model by the maximum likelihood method to obtain

$$r_t = -0.06 + 0.27r_{t-1} + 0.03r_{t-2} + 0.07r_{t-3} \qquad l(\hat{\theta}) = -919.72$$
$$\quad\;\; (0.03)\;\; (0.05) \qquad (0.05) \qquad (0.04)$$
$$h_t = 0.42 + 0.23\varepsilon^2_{t-1} + 0.21\varepsilon^2_{t-2} + 0.05\varepsilon^2_{t-3}$$
$$\quad\; (0.06)\;\; (0.06) \qquad (0.06) \qquad (0.04)$$
$$\quad\; + 0.05\varepsilon^2_{t-4} + 0.07\varepsilon^2_{t-5} + 0.12\varepsilon^2_{t-6}$$
$$\quad\; (0.04) \qquad (0.04) \qquad (0.05)$$

The ARCH parameters α_1, α_2 and α_6 are highly significant. The ARCH model also produces a significant increase in the value of the log likelihood. A likelihood ratio test easily rejects the null of an AR(3) process with independent Gaussian errors against the alternative of an AR(3) process with conditionally normal ARCH(6) errors. Notice that the coefficient of r_{t-2} loses its significance. Frequently, after ARCH is accounted for, the initial specification of the mean must be re-evaluated.

The ARCH(6) model can apparently explain the nonlinear dependence in the residuals. In table 1, we present the autocorrelations of the squared standardized residuals $\hat{\eta}^2_t = \hat{\varepsilon}^2_t / h_t$. None of the first eight autocorrelations are significant at any reasonable significance level. The skewness coefficient of the standardized residuals is different in sign from the AR residuals and larger in magnitude, but still not excessively big. The sample kurtosis coefficient of the standardized residuals is smaller than the coefficient for the AR residuals, but is still significantly greater than 3. This suggests that the unconditional distribution of the conditionally normal ARCH process is not sufficiently heavy tailed to account for the excess kurtosis in the data. The rejection of the conditional normality assumption is frequently encountered in applications of the ARCH model. As will be discussed in section 4.2, there are ways to take account of this excess kurtosis.

In section 2.2, we demonstrated how the GARCH model can provide a parsimonious parameterization of a high-order ARCH process. To illustrate this, we estimate an AR(3) model for r_t with the conditional variance of the errors specified as GARCH(1, 1). Maintaining the conditional normality assumption, the estimated model is

$$r_t = -0.05 + 0.27r_{t-1} - 0.003r_{t-2} + 0.08r_{t-3} \qquad l(\hat{\theta}) = -920.02$$
$$\quad\;\; (0.04)\;\; (0.05) \qquad (0.05) \qquad (0.04)$$
$$h_t = 0.09 + 0.17\varepsilon^2_{t-1} + 0.77h_{t-1}.$$
$$\quad\; (0.03)\;\; (0.04) \qquad (0.05)$$

The estimates of the AR parameters are similar to the estimates for ARCH(6) errors, with only the coefficient of r_{t-2} changing sign and becoming even less significant. The autocorrelations of the squares of the GARCH(1, 1) standardized residuals, shown in table 1, are insignificant and similar in magnitude to those for the ARCH(6) standardized residuals. This indicates that the GARCH(1, 1), which requires estimation of only three conditional variance parameters, can account for the nonlinear dependence as well as the

Table 1 Summary statistics for the standardized residuals from AR, ARCH and GARCH models for the rate of return on the weekly US–British exchange rate

	Autocorrelations of squared residuals								Skewness	Kurtosis
	1	2	3	4	5	6	7	8		
AR(3)	0.16	0.14	0.22	0.15	0.06	0.05	0.11	0.00	0.22	6.78
AR(3)+ARCH(6)	0.01	−0.02	−0.01	0.01	−0.04	−0.02	−0.02	0.02	−0.45	6.40
AR(3)+GARCH(1,1)	0.02	0.00	−0.02	0.00	−0.05	0.01	−0.03	−0.02	−0.41	6.21

The asymptotic standard error of the autocorrelations of the squared standardized residuals is $1/\sqrt{T} = 0.04$.
The asymptotic standard errors of the skewness and kurtosis coefficients are respectively 0.096 and 0.192.

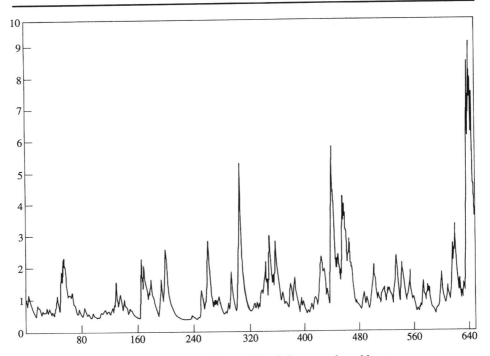

Figure 7   Conditional variance of the dollar–pound weekly return.

ARCH(6) model, which requires estimation of seven conditional variance parameters. The skewness and kurtosis coefficients of the standardized GARCH(1, 1) residuals, also given in Table 1, are almost identical to the coefficients for the standardized ARCH(6) residuals. The value of the maximized ARCH(6) log likelihood is marginally greater than the value of the GARCH(1, 1) log likelihood. But any model selection criteria, such as AIC or BIC, which penalizes a model for additional parameters, would select the GARCH(1, 1) specification over the ARCH(6) specification. Finally, in figure 7 we present a plot of the estimates of the conditional variances, h_t, from the GARCH(1, 1) model. The conditional variances show considerable variation over time. Comparing the plot of the weekly returns in figure 1 with the plot of the conditional variances in figure 7, it is clear that a clustering of large deviations, of either sign, in the returns is associated with a rise in the conditional variance.

2.5   Temporal aggregation of ARCH processes

One of the important issues in time series modelling is temporal aggregation. It is well known that a high frequency (e.g. fitted to daily data) ARMA process aggregates to a low frequency (fitted to, say, weekly data) ARMA process. A natural question is whether ARCH models also possess this property. Drost and Nijman (1992) considered this issue in detail and we follow their analysis. Let us consider the ARCH model (2) and (3) with $q = 1$, i.e.

$$\varepsilon_t \mid \Psi_{t-1} \sim N(0, h_t) \tag{13}$$

where

$$h_t = E(\varepsilon_t^2 \mid \Psi_{t-1}) = \alpha_0 + \alpha_1 \varepsilon_{t-1}^2 \qquad t = 1, 2, \ldots, T. \tag{14}$$

Suppose we want to find the corresponding model for ε_t when $t = 2, 4, \ldots, T$. The information set will consist of only $\{y_{t-2}, x_{t-2}, y_{t-4}, x_{t-4}, \ldots\}$ and we will denote it by $\Psi_{t-(2)}$. Drost and Nijman showed that

$$E(\varepsilon_t \mid \Psi_{t-(2)}) = 0$$
$$E(\varepsilon_t^2 \mid \Psi_{t-(2)}) = \alpha_0(1 + \alpha_1) + \alpha_1^2 \varepsilon_{t-2}^2 \qquad t = 2, 4, \ldots, T$$
$$= h_{t(2)}, \text{ say}.$$

In general, if we consider $t = m, 2m, \ldots, T$, then

$$E(\varepsilon_t \mid \Psi_{t-(m)}) = 0$$
$$E(\varepsilon_t^2 \mid \Psi_{t-(m)}) = \alpha_0 \frac{1 - \alpha_1^m}{1 - \alpha_1} + \alpha_1^m \varepsilon_{t-m}^2.$$

Therefore, in terms of the first two moments, an ARCH process is closed under temporal aggregation and we have an algebraic relationship between the parameters corresponding to high and low frequency data. It is interesting to note that, as $m \to \infty$, $E(\varepsilon_t^2 \mid \Psi_{t-(m)}) \to \alpha_0/(1 - \alpha_1)$, so that in the limit the aggregate process behaves like a conditional homoskedastic model as pointed out by Diebold (1988). If we consider the reverse operation of going from a low frequency model to a higher one, in the limit the process will have an integrated ARCH structure as noted by Nelson (1990b).

Now let us consider the distributional part of the specification (13), which can be stated as

$$\varepsilon_t / \sqrt{h_t} \mid \Psi_{t-1} \sim \text{IID N}(0, 1) \qquad t = 1, 2, \ldots, T. \tag{15}$$

We need to check the conditional distribution of $\varepsilon_t^* = \varepsilon_t / \sqrt{h_{t(2)}}, t = 2, 4, \ldots, T$. Drost and Nijman (1992) showed that

$$E(\varepsilon_t^{*4} \mid \Psi_{t-(2)}) = 3 + 6 \left(\frac{\alpha_0}{h_{t(2)}} - 1 \right)^2.$$

Therefore, the conditional moments of ε_t^* depend on the information set and hence the conditional distribution of ε_t^* does not have the IID structure (15). Also the distribution is no longer normal. Therefore, from a distributional point of view, an ARCH process is not closed under aggregation.

For practical purposes, if we specify an ARCH model only in terms of moments, it is possible to estimate the low frequency parameters from the estimation of a high frequency model and vice versa. Drost and Nijman (1992) demonstrated this using the empirical results of Baillie and Bollerslev (1989), who fitted a GARCH(1, 1) model to several exchange rates. For the Swiss franc, the estimates of α_1 and β_1 from the daily data were 0.073 and 0.907. Using the relationship between the parameters of high and low frequency data, Drost and Nijman showed that the implied weekly estimates are 0.112 and 0.792. Baillie and Bollerslev's estimates using the actual weekly data were 0.121 and 0.781. Except for the Japanese yen, Drost and Nijman found that direct estimates were very close to the implied weekly estimates.

3 Interpretations of ARCH

Apart from their simplicity, the main reason for the success of ARCH models is that they take account of the many observed features of the data, such as thick tails of the distribution, clustering of large and small observations, nonlinearity and changes in our ability to forecast future values. Therefore, it is not surprising that these models can be interpreted in a number of ways, and we discuss some of these interpretations in this section.

3.1 Random coefficient interpretation

In the last section, we noted that ARCH takes account of the clustering of large and small errors and the fatness of the tail part of the distribution (excess kurtosis) as observed in many financial data series. One of the major considerations for introducing ARCH by Engle (1982, p. 989) was that econometricians' ability to predict the future varies from one period to another. Predictions are usually done by using a conditional mean model. Uncertainty about the conditional mean can be expressed by a random coefficient formulation. Consider a random coefficient AR(1) process

$$y_t = \phi_t y_{t-1} + \varepsilon_t$$

where $\phi_t \sim (\phi, \alpha_1)$ and $c_t \sim (0, \alpha_0)$ are independent. Then $E(y_t \mid \Psi_{t-1}) = \phi y_{t-1}$ as with the fixed AR(1) process; however, now $\text{var}(y_t \mid \Psi_{t-1}) = \alpha_0 + \alpha_1 y_{t-1}^2$, which has the same form as (3). To obtain a general ARCH(q) model in our regression context from a random coefficient framework, we need to start with the following set-up:

$$y_t = x_t'\xi + \varepsilon_t \tag{16}$$

$$\varepsilon_t = \sum_{i=1}^{q} \phi_{it}\varepsilon_{t-i} + u_t$$

$$= \sum_{i=1}^{q} (\phi_i + \eta_{it})\varepsilon_{t-1} + u_t \tag{17}$$

where $\eta_t = (\eta_{1t}, \ldots, \eta_{qt})' \sim (0, A_{q\times q})$ and $u_t \sim (0, \sigma_u^2)$ are independent. It immediately follows that

$$E(\varepsilon_t \mid \Psi_{t-1}) = \phi'\underline{\varepsilon}_{t-1},$$

where $\phi = (\phi_1, \ldots, \phi_q)'$, and $\underline{\varepsilon}_{t-1} = (\varepsilon_{t-1}, \ldots, \varepsilon_{t-q})'$, and that

$$\text{var}(\varepsilon_t \mid \Psi_{t-1}) = \underline{\varepsilon}_{t-1}' A \underline{\varepsilon}_{t-1} + \sigma_u^2. \tag{18}$$

If $A = ((\alpha_{ij}))$ is a diagonal matrix with $A = \text{diag}(\alpha_1, \ldots, \alpha_q)$ and $\sigma_u^2 = \alpha_0$, then

$$\text{var}(\varepsilon_t \mid \Psi_{t-1}) = \alpha_0 + \sum_{i=1}^{q} \alpha_i \varepsilon_{t-i}^2$$

as we have in (3). A non-diagonal A specifies an ARCH process with additional cross-product terms between the past errors. The intuition behind the inclusion of the cross-product terms is that they take account of the effect of the interaction between the lagged residuals on the conditional variance. White's (1980) test for heteroskedasticity has a similar feature which includes the cross-products of the regressors as the test variables while the operational form of the Breusch and Pagan (1979) test does not. The model (18) was discussed in detail by Bera et al. (1992) who called it the augmented ARCH (AARCH) model (see also Tsay, 1987). If we add linear terms of ε_{t-1} in (18), we obtain the quadratic ARCH (QARCH) model of Sentana (1991). Bera et al. (1990) extended the framework (16) and (17) to give the GARCH(p, q) model a random coefficient interpretation. It is immediately seen that, unlike ARCH, AARCH is not symmetric in the sense that the conditional variance depends on the sign of the individual lagged ε_ts.

In their empirical analysis of exchange rate data, Cheung and Pauly (1990) found that many of the off-diagonal elements of A were significantly different from zero and concluded that a random coefficient formulation provided a richer formulation of time-varying volatility than did the standard ARCH characterization. Bera et al. (1990) also noted similar results when they reconsidered Engle's (1983) model for measuring the variability of US inflation. They found that the estimate of the coefficient of the AARCH term $\varepsilon_{t-4}\varepsilon_{t-7}$ was -0.195 with a t statistic of 4.89. Their resulting specification of an AR-AARCH model passed the specification tests and diagnostic checks they performed, while Engle's original ARCH model had some unexplained serial correlation and conditional heteroskedasticity. An empirical application in Sentana (1991) with a century of daily US stock returns provided support for his QARCH model. Coefficients of all the cross-product terms were highly significant.

Bera and Lee (1993) established the connection between random coefficients and ARCH in a somewhat indirect way. They applied White's (1982) information matrix test to a linear regression model with autocorrelated errors. The information matrix test had six distinct components, and a special case of one component, which corresponded to the autocorrelation parameter ϕ, was found to be identical to Engle's (1982) Lagrange multiplier test for ARCH. Given Chesher's (1984) interpretation of the information matrix test as a test for parameter variation, it can be said that as far as the test is concerned the presence of ARCH is 'equivalent' to random variation in the autocorrelation coefficient. In our above analysis, we noted that both ARCH and the random coefficient model lead to the same first two conditional moments. Under the additional assumption of conditional normality, all the moments, and hence the two processes themselves, will be identical.

One byproduct of the random coefficient representation of the ARCH model is that standard results from the time series literature can be used to derive the necessary and sufficient conditions for stationarity. Andel (1976), Nicholls and Quinn (1982) and Ray (1983) stated simple conditions for second-order stationarity of the AR process with random coefficients. In section 2.3, we noted that the stationarity condition for an ARCH(q) process in the absence of autocorrelation is $\sum_{i=1}^q \alpha_i < 1$. As demonstrated in Bera et al. (1990), the presence of autocorrelation leads to a different stationarity condition. For example, the stationarity condition for an ARCH(q) process in the presence of first-order serial correlation is

$$\frac{1}{1-\phi_1^2} \sum_{i=1}^q \alpha_i < 1.$$

In the absence of autocorrelation, $\sum_{i=1}^{q} \alpha_i < 1$ is sufficient for weak stationarity. This clearly demonstrates that the presence of autocorrelation can make a stationary ARCH process non-stationary.

3.2   A conditional mixture model interpretation

Following the work of Clark (1973) and Tauchen and Pitts (1983), Gallant et al. (1991) provided an interesting rationale for the presence of conditional heteroskedasticity and heterogeneity in the higher order moments of asset prices. Let us write the observed price change y_t as

$$y_t = \mu_t + \sum_{i=1}^{I_t} \zeta_i \tag{19}$$

where $\zeta_i \sim \text{IID N}(0, \tau^2)$. Here μ_t can be viewed as the forecastable component, the ζ_i are the incremental changes and I_t is the number of times new information comes to the market in period t. I_t is a serially dependent unobservable random variable and is independent of $\{\zeta_i\}$. Because of the randomness of I_t, y_t is not normally distributed; it is in fact a mixture of normal distributions. Here we can view y_t as a subordinated stochastic process, where $y_t - \mu_t$ is subordinate to ζ_i and I_t is the directing process. Equation (19) can be written as

$$y_t - \mu_t + \tau I_t^{1/2} \nu_t \tag{19a}$$

with $\nu_t \sim \text{N}(0, 1)$. Then, conditional on the information set Ψ_{t-1} and I_t, we have the conditional heteroskedastic normal distribution

$$y_t \mid \Psi_{t-1}, I_t \sim \text{N}(\mu_t, \tau^2 I_t). \tag{20}$$

Since I_t is not observable, in practice we can work only with the conditional distribution $y_t \mid \Psi_{t-1}$. From the general result that if a random variable is conditionally (on I_t) normal, unconditionally it must be non-normal, a realistic distribution for $y_t \mid \Psi_{t-1}$ would be conditional heteroskedastic and non-normal.

Framework (20) is very general, and a variety of interesting cases can be derived from this. When I_t is a constant c, we have

$$y_t \mid \Psi_{t-1} \sim \text{N}(\mu_t, c\tau^2)$$

which is our standard homoskedastic model. If our information set Ψ_{t-1} also includes I_t, then

$$y_t \mid \Psi_{t-1} \sim \text{N}(\mu_t, \tau^2 I_t).$$

This is a conditional heteroskedastic-normal model. However, the assumption about the knowledge of I_t is not realistic. For the general case (20) the first four moments are

$$E[(y_t - \mu_t) \mid \Psi_{t-1}] = 0$$
$$E[(y_t - \mu_t)^2 \mid \Psi_{t-1}] = \tau^2 E(I_t \mid \Psi_{t-1})$$
$$E[(y_t - \mu_t)^3 \mid \Psi_{t-1}] = 0$$
$$E[(y_t - \mu_t)^4 \mid \Psi_{t-1}] = \tau^4 3 E(I_t^2 \mid \Psi_{t-1}).$$

Hence, the conditional kurtosis

$$\frac{E[(y_t - \mu_t)^4 \mid \Psi_{t-1}]}{E[(y_t - \mu_t)^2 \mid \Psi_{t-1}]^2} = \frac{3E(I_t^2 \mid \Psi_{t-1})}{E(I_t \mid \Psi_{t-1})^2} \tag{21}$$

exceeds 3. Therefore, it is not surprising that in many empirical studies the normal ARCH model could not capture most of the excess kurtosis in the data, while a conditional t or some non-normal ARCH models worked somewhat better (see, for example, Engle and Bollerslev, 1986; Bollerslev, 1987; Baillie and Bollerslev, 1989; Gallant and Tauchen, 1989; Hsieh, 1989; Gallant et al., 1991; Lee and Tse, 1991). Conditional t or other non-normal distributions do not of course solve all the problems, since the quantity in (21) is not necessarily time invariant. The conditional t distribution, for example, although it allows kurtosis to exceed 3, assumes constant conditional kurtosis. Note that the kurtosis in (21) will be time invariant if I_t and Ψ_{t-1} are independent. To take account of the time-varying higher moments, Hansen (1992) generalized the conditional t model by expressing the corresponding shape parameter (the degrees of freedom) as a function of the information set. We will discuss this model in section 4.2.

Bera and Zuo (1991) suggested a specification test for ARCH models which examines the constancy of the kurtosis of the standardized residuals of the estimated ARCH model. They call it a test for heterokurtosis. The test is derived using the information matrix test principle and hence is a test for heterogeneity of the ARCH parameters. As we discussed earlier, conditional heteroskedasticity can be viewed as a randomness of the AR parameters. Conditional heterokurtosis is related to the heterogeneity of the ARCH parameters. Mizrach (1990) used a generalization of the ARCH model which allowed for time-varying coefficients in the conditional variance equation, and found the model to perform better than the standard GARCH model in an exchange rate application.

At this point a question could be raised: why in many empirical applications do ARCH models work remarkably well? To explain this, we again follow Gallant et al. (1991). As noted before, the conditional variance is

$$E[(y_t - \mu_t)^2 \mid \Psi_{t-1}] = \tau^2 E(I_t \mid \Psi_{t-1}).$$

Denoting $y_t - \mu_t = \tau I_t^{1/2} \nu_t$ as the error ε_t, we have

$$\begin{aligned} \mathrm{cov}(\varepsilon_t^2, \varepsilon_{t-j}^2) &= \tau^4 \mathrm{cov}(I_t \nu_t^2, I_{t-j} \nu_{t-j}^2) \\ &= \tau^4 \mathrm{cov}(I_t, I_{t-j}). \end{aligned}$$

If the I_t are serially dependent, which seems plausible *a priori*, that will introduce correlation in the squared errors. The ARCH methodology tries to capture this correlation.

Using US daily stock return data, Lamoureux and Lastrapes (1990a) provided empirical evidence in support of the hypothesis that ARCH is a manifestation of the time dependence in the rate of information arrival to the market. They assumed that I_t in (19) is serially correlated and expressed it as

$$I_t = \gamma_0 + \gamma(B)I_{t-1} + u_t \tag{22}$$

where γ_0 is a constant, $\gamma(B)$ is a lag polynomial and u_t is white noise. Defining $\Omega_t = E[(y_t - \mu_t)^2 \mid I_t] = \tau^2 I_t$ and using (22) we have

$$\Omega_t = \tau^2 \gamma_0 + \gamma(B)\Omega_{t-1} + \tau^2 u_t$$

which has a similar structure to that of a GARCH model. Since I_t is not observable, Lamoureux and Lastrapes used daily trading volume, V_t, as a proxy for the daily information that flows into the market. When V_t was included as an extra variable in the GARCH(1,1) model (7), its coefficient was highly significant for all of the twenty stocks they considered. Also, inclusion of V_t in h_t made the ARCH effects (coefficients α_1 and β_1) become negligible for most of the stocks. To summarize, this empirical work supports the view that ARCH in daily stock returns is an outcome of the time dependence in the news that flows into the market.

To evaluate the role of news in the determination of volatility in the foreign exchange markets, Engle et al. (1990a) provided a test of two hypotheses – heat waves and meteor showers. The heat wave hypothesis states that the major sources of disturbances come from *within* a market, while the meteor shower hypothesis states that disturbances come from spillovers *between* markets. They used the intra-daily yen–dollar exchange rate in the Tokyo, European, New York and Pacific markets. To test the two hypotheses, they included the squared innovations from the other markets in the specification of each h_t. Coefficients of all of these variables were found to be highly significant, thus lending support to the meteor shower hypothesis. In fact, they found that the foreign news was more important than the past domestic news. In particular, Japanese news had the greatest impact on the volatility of all markets except the Tokyo market.

3.3 Nonlinear model interpretation

It is clear that one of the essential features of the ARCH model is $\text{cov}(\varepsilon_t^2, \varepsilon_{t-j}^2) \neq 0$, although $\text{cov}(\varepsilon_t, \varepsilon_{t-j}) = 0$ for $j \neq 0$. In other words, ARCH postulates a nonlinear relationship between ε_t and its past values. There are many nonlinear time series models such as the bilinear, threshold autoregressive, exponential autoregressive and nonlinear moving average models that can also exhibit this property (see Tong, 1990). For simplicity, we concentrate on the bilinear model and its relation to the ARCH model. A time series $\{\varepsilon_t\}$ is said to follow a bilinear model if it satisfies (see Granger and Andersen, 1978; Tong, 1990)

$$\varepsilon_t = \sum_{i=1}^{p} \phi_i \varepsilon_{t-i} + \sum_{j=1}^{r}\sum_{k=1}^{s} b_{jk}\varepsilon_{t-j}u_{t-k} + u_t \tag{23}$$

where u_t is a sequence of IID $(0, \sigma_u^2)$ variables. The first two conditional moments for this process are

$$E(\varepsilon_t \mid \Psi_{t-1}) = \sum_{i=1}^{p} \phi_i \varepsilon_{t-i} + \sum_{j=1}^{r}\sum_{k=1}^{s} b_{jk}\varepsilon_{t-j}u_{t-k}$$

$$\text{var}(\varepsilon_t \mid \Psi_{t-1}) = \sigma_u^2.$$

These conditional moments contrast with those of an ARCH process in which the conditional mean is, in general, a constant but the conditional variance is time varying. Their unconditional moments, however, might be similar. For example, the bilinear model

$$\varepsilon_t = b_{21}\varepsilon_{t-2}u_{t-1} + u_t$$

has $E(\varepsilon_t) = 0$ and $\text{cov}(\varepsilon_t^2, \varepsilon_{t-2}^2) = b_{21}^2\sigma_u^2$. As this process is autocorrelated in squares, it will exhibit temporal clustering of large and small deviations like an ARCH process. In fact, a bilinear model is quite similar to an ARCH model in that it can also be represented as a varying coefficient model. Equation (23) can be written as

$$
\begin{aligned}
\varepsilon_t &= \sum_{j=1}^{m}[\phi_j + A_j(t)]\varepsilon_{t-j} + u_t \\
&= \sum_{j=1}^{m}\phi_{jt}\varepsilon_{t-j} + u_t, \text{ say,}
\end{aligned}
\tag{24}
$$

where $m = \max(p, r)$ and $A_j(t) = \sum_{k=1}^{s}b_{jk}u_{t-k}$ with $\phi_i = 0, i \geqslant p+1, b_{jk} = 0, j \geqslant r+1$ (see Tong, 1990, p. 114). The basic difference between (17) and (24) is that in the former the coefficients are purely random, whereas in (24) the varying coefficient part $A_j(t)$ has a structure which is a linear function of the lagged innovations u_t.

There is yet another way of looking at the similarities and differences between ARCH and bilinear models. Although both models take account of nonlinear dependence, ARCH represents the dependence in a multiplicative fashion,

$$
\begin{aligned}
\varepsilon_t &= u_t f_1(\varepsilon_{t-1}, \varepsilon_{t-2}, \dots; u_{t-1}, u_{t-2}, \dots) \\
&= u_t f_{1t}, \text{ say,}
\end{aligned}
\tag{25}
$$

while a bilinear model postulates an additive structure

$$
\begin{aligned}
\varepsilon_t &= f_2(\varepsilon_{t-1}, \varepsilon_{t-2}, \dots; u_{t-1}, u_{t-2}, \dots) + u_t \\
&= f_{2t} + u_t, \text{ say,}
\end{aligned}
\tag{26}
$$

where $f_1(\cdot)$ and $f_2(\cdot)$ are some well-defined nonlinear functions. Hsieh (1989) exploited these differences to discriminate between the two types of nonlinearities. Higgins and Bera (1991) suggested a Cox non-nested procedure to test these two models against each other.

From a practical point of view, these models have different implications. Using a bilinear model we can improve the point forecast over standard ARMA modelling, but cannot assess the accuracy of the forecast interval. On the other hand, the ARCH specification makes it possible to forecast the conditional variance without any additional gain in point forecastability. It is quite possible that the data may be represented by a joint ARCH–bilinear model such as the one suggested by Weiss (1986a). Higgins and Bera (1989, 1991) developed simple procedures for detecting the joint presence of ARCH and bilinearity.

The empirical results on this topic are somewhat mixed. Hsieh (1989) finds that the ARCH model is able to account for the nonlinearities in the daily German mark,

Canadian dollar and Swiss franc, but not in the British pound nor the Japanese yen. The ARCH standardized residuals exhibited substantial nonlinearity for the latter two currencies and, for the British pound, more non-normality (excess kurtosis) than the raw data. Diebold and Nason (1990) addressed the issue of whether conditional heteroskedasticity actually exists in exchange rate data or whether it is just a reflection of mis-specification in the conditional mean of the model. They tackled the problem by estimating the conditional mean through a nonparametric regression and testing the residuals for the presence of ARCH. ARCH was found in the nonparametric residuals, implying that conditional heteroskedasticity was not due to mis-specification of the mean. Higgins and Bera (1991) applied the Cox test to six weekly exchange rates. For the Canadian dollar the GARCH model was not rejected, and for the British pound the bilinear was not rejected. For the other currencies, the French franc, the German mark, the Japanese yen and the Swiss franc, both of the models were found to be inadequate.

Lastly, we should mention an inherent problem in using a nonlinear conditional mean specification to model financial data. For a nonlinear conditional mean model to explain the sort of volatility observed in practice, the variation in the conditional first moment would have to be enormous, implying huge unexploited profit opportunities for the traders. Possibly, for this reason, models which are nonlinear in the mean have not become as popular in analysing financial data. The ARCH models do not have this drawback because changes in volatility are represented by changes in the conditional variance, linking volatility to a natural measure of risk.

3.4 Other interpretation

Continuing with the question of why ARCH is so prevalent in empirical studies, there are a number of other interesting explanations, such as Mizrach's (1990) learning model and Stock's (1988) time deformation hypothesis. Mizrach (1990) developed a model of asset pricing and learning in which ARCH disturbances evolve out of the decision problem of economic agents. He showed that errors made by the agents during the learning process are highly persistent, and that the current errors are dependent on all past errors. This leads the conditional variance to have an ARCH-like structure with a long lag.

Stock (1988) established the link between time deformation and ARCH models. Any economic variable, in general, evolves on an 'operational' time scale, while in practice it is measured on a 'calendar' time scale. And this inappropriate use of a calender time scale may lead to volatility clustering since, relative to the calendar time, the variable may evolve more quickly or slowly (see Diebold, 1986a). Stock (1988) showed that a time deformation model of a random variable ε_t can be approximated by

$$\varepsilon_t = \rho_t \varepsilon_{t-1} + \nu_t \qquad \nu_t \mid \Psi_{t-1} \sim \mathrm{N}(0, h_t)$$

where $h_t = \alpha_0 + \alpha_1 \varepsilon_{t-1}^2$. Stock also established that, when a relatively long segment of operational time has elapsed during a unit of calendar time, ρ_t is small and h_t is large, i.e. the time-varying autoregressive parameter is inversely related to the conditional variance.

A number of researchers investigated the empirical relationship between autocorrelation and volatility (see for example Kim, 1989; Oedegaard, 1991; Sentana and

Wadhwani, 1991; LeBaron, 1992). Oedegaard found that the first-order autocorrelation of the Standard and Poor (S&P) 500 daily index decreased over time, which he attributed to the introduction of new financial markets such as options and futures on the index. However, when ARCH was explicitly introduced into the model, the evidence of time-varying autocorrelation became very weak. The other papers detected the simultaneous presence of autocorrelation and ARCH, and found them to be inversely related. LeBaron (1992) used the following model:

$$y_t = a + f(h_t)y_{t-1} + \varepsilon_t$$

$$\varepsilon_t \mid \Psi_{t-1} \sim N(0, h_t)$$

$$f(h_t) = b_0 + b_1 \exp(-h_t/b_2) \tag{27}$$

where h_t was specified as a GARCH$(1,1)$ model. The function $f(\cdot)$ took account of the changing autocorrelation parameter. For estimation, LeBaron set b_2 to the sample variances of the various series he considered. Since

$$\frac{df(h_t)}{dh_t} = -\frac{b_1}{b_2} \exp\left(-\frac{h_t}{b_2}\right)$$

the coefficient b_1 measures the influence of volatility on autocorrelation. For the S&P 500 composite daily index from January 1928 to May 1990, the estimate of b_1 was 0.36 with a t value of 11.70. When the sample was divided into three subsamples, the estimate of b_1 did not change very much. For other data series, he used the weekly return for the S&P 500 index, the Center for Research and Securities Prices (CRSP) value-weighted index, the Dow index and IBM returns. The general result was that lower correlations were connected with periods of high volatility. As possible explanations, LeBaron mentioned non-trading and the accumulation of news. Some stocks do not trade close to the end of the day and information arriving during that period is reflected on the next day's trading. This induces serial correlation. At the same time, non-trading results in overall lower trade volume, which has a strong positive relationship with volatility. When new information reaches the market very slowly, for traders the optimal action is to do nothing until enough information is accumulated. This leads to low trade volume and high correlation. Finding the exact causes of serial correlation and its relationship with volatility is still an open empirical problem. The relationship noted in (27) requires further investigation and some other models need to be examined.

4   Extensions of the model

In the original exposition of the ARCH model, it was natural for Engle (1982) to assume that the conditional variance function was linear in the squared errors and that the conditional distribution was normal. He acknowledged, however, that the linearity and conditional normality assumptions may not be appropriate in particular applications. Subsequent empirical work has borne this out. In this section, we survey alternative formulations of the conditional variance function and conditional distribution which have proved useful in applied research.

4.1   Nonlinear conditional variance

One of the first difficulties encountered with the linear ARCH model was that the estimated α_1 coefficients were frequently found to be negative. To avoid this problem Geweke (1986) and Milhoj (1987a) suggested the log ARCH model (see also Pantula, 1986)

$$\log(h_t) = \alpha_0 + \alpha_1 \log(\varepsilon_{t-i}^2) + \cdots + \alpha_q \log(\varepsilon_{t-q}^2). \tag{28}$$

Taking the exponential of both sides of (28), $h_t = e^{(\cdot)}$ is strictly positive, and therefore no inequality restrictions are required for the α_1s to ensure that the conditional variance is strictly positive. To determine whether the linear model (3) or the logarithmic model (28) provided a better fit to actual data, Higgins and Bera (1992) proposed a nonlinear ARCH (NARCH) model, which still requires non-negativity restrictions but includes linear ARCH as a special case and log ARCH as a limiting case. They specified the conditional variance as

$$h_t = [\phi_0(\sigma^2)^\delta + \phi_1(\varepsilon_{t-1}^2)^\delta + \cdots + \phi_q(\varepsilon_{t-q}^2)^\delta]^{1/\delta} \tag{29}$$

where $\sigma^2 > 0, \phi_i \geqslant 0, \delta > 0$ and the ϕ_i are such that $\sum_{i=0}^q \phi_i = 1$. The motivation of the NARCH model can be seen by rearranging (29) to give

$$\frac{h_t^\delta - 1}{\delta} = \phi_0 \frac{(\sigma^2)^\delta - 1}{\delta} + \phi_1 \frac{(\varepsilon_{t-1}^2)^\delta - 1}{\delta} + \cdots + \phi_q \frac{(\varepsilon_{t-q}^2)^\delta - 1}{\delta}, \tag{30}$$

from which it is evident that the NARCH model is a Box–Cox power transformation of both sides of the linear ARCH model. It is apparent that, when $\delta = 1$, (30) is equivalent to the linear ARCH model and that, as $\delta \to 0$, (30) approaches the log ARCH model (28). Higgins and Bera (1992) estimated (29) with weekly exchange rates and found that δ was typically significantly less than one and much closer to zero, indicating that the data favoured the logarithmic rather than the linear ARCH model. Extensions of the above functional forms to the GARCH process are straightforward.

A possible limitation of the functional forms described above is that the conditional variance function h_t is symmetric in the lagged ε_ts. Nelson (1991) suggested that a symmetric conditional variance function may be inappropriate for modelling the volatility of returns on stocks because it cannot represent a phenomenon known as the 'leverage effect', which is the negative correlation between volatility and past returns. In a symmetric ARCH model, h_t is not affected by the sign of ε_{t-i}, and therefore h_t is uncorrelated with past errors. To rectify this, Nelson began by defining $\varepsilon_t = \eta_t \sqrt{h_t}$, where η_t is independent and identically distributed with $E(\eta_t) = 0$ and $\text{var}(\eta_t) = 1$. He suggested that in the general ARCH formulation

$$h_t = h(\eta_{t-1} \ldots, \eta_{t-q}, h_{t-1}, \ldots, h_{t-p}) \tag{31}$$

h_t can be viewed as a stochastic process in which η_t serves as the forcing variable for both the conditional variance and the error. He then chose $h(\cdot)$ in (31) to produce the desired dependence. To avoid non-negativity restrictions on parameters, Nelson maintained the logarithmic specification (28) and proposed

$$\log(h_t) = \alpha_0 + \sum_{i=1}^q \alpha_i g(\eta_{t-i}) + \sum_{i=1}^p \beta_i \log(h_{t-i}) \tag{32}$$

where

$$g(\eta_t) = \theta_{\eta_t} + \gamma(\mid \eta_t \mid -E \mid \eta_t \mid). \tag{33}$$

The conditional variance (32), with (33), is known as exponential GARCH (EGARCH). It is easy to see that the sequence $g(\eta_t)$ is independent with mean zero and constant, if finite, variance. Therefore, (32) represents a linear ARMA model for $\log(h_t)$ with innovation $g(\eta_t)$. The properties of the EGARCH model are determined by the careful construction of the function (33). These properties are as follows.

1   The innovation to the conditional variance is piecewise linear in η_t, with slopes $\alpha_i(\theta + \gamma)$ when η_t is positive and $\alpha_i(\theta - \gamma)$ when η_t is negative. This produces the asymmetry in the conditional variance.
2   The first term in (33) allows for correlation between the error and future conditional variances. For example, suppose that $\gamma = 0$ and that $\theta < 0$. Then a negative η_t will cause the error to be negative and the current innovation to the variance process to be positive.
3   The second term in (33) produces the ARCH effect. Suppose that $\theta = 0$ and $\gamma > 0$. Whenever the absolute magnitude of η_t exceeds its expected value, the innovation $g(\eta_t)$ is positive. Therefore, large shocks increase the conditional variance.

Nelson (1991) fitted the EGARCH model to the excess daily return on the CRSP value-weighted stock market index from July 1962 to December 1987. The estimate of θ was -0.118 and had a standard error of 0.008, confirming a highly significant negative correlation between the excess return and subsequent volatility. For other applications of the EGARCH model see, for example, Pagan and Schwert (1990) and Taylor (1990).

Building on the success of the EGARCH model to represent asymmetric responses in the conditional variance to positive and negative errors, a series of papers have proposed other ARCH models which allow a very general shape in the conditional variance function. Although these models are parametric, and estimated by maximum likelihood, they are nonparametric in spirit because the shape of the conditional variance function is largely determined by the data themselves. Glosten et al. (1991) and Zakoian (1990) independently suggested a conditional standard deviation of the form

$$\sqrt{h_t} = \alpha_0 + \sum_{i=1}^{q} \alpha_i^+ \varepsilon_{t-i}^+ - \sum_{i=1}^{q} \alpha_i^- \varepsilon_{t-i}^-, \tag{34}$$

where $\varepsilon_t^+ = \max[\varepsilon_t, 0]$ and $\varepsilon_t^- = \min\{\varepsilon_t, 0\}$ (see also Rabemananjara and Zakoian, 1993). The parameters are constrained by $\alpha_0 > 0, \alpha_i^+ \geqslant 0$ and $\alpha_i^- \geqslant 0$ for $i = 1, \dots, q$, to ensure that the conditional standard deviation is positive. Zakoian referred to this formulation as a threshold ARCH (TARCH) model because the coefficient of ε_{t-i} changes when ε_{t-i} crosses the *threshold* of zero. When $\varepsilon_{t-i} > 0$ the conditional standard deviation is linear in ε_{t-i} with slope α_i^+, and when $\varepsilon_{t-i} < 0$ the conditional standard deviation is linear in ε_{t-i} with slope $-\alpha_i^-$. This allows for asymmetry in the conditional variance in the fashion of EGARCH.

Gourieroux and Monfort (1992) proposed that a step function over the support of the conditioning error vector $\varepsilon_{-t-1} = (\varepsilon_{t-1}, \dots, \varepsilon_{t-q}')'$ can approximate a highly non-linear conditional variance function. Let $A_1, \dots, A_m$ be a partition of the support of ε_t. Gourieroux and Monfort consider a conditional variance of the form

$$h_t = \alpha_0 + \sum_{i=1}^{m}\sum_{j=1}^{q}\alpha_{ij}1_{Ai}(\varepsilon_{t-j}) \tag{35}$$

where $1_A(\varepsilon_t)$ is the indicator function of the set A, which takes the value one when $\varepsilon_t \in A$ and zero otherwise. They describe (35) as a qualitative TARCH (QTARCH) model because the conditional variance is determined by the region in R^q in which ε_{-t-1} lies, rather than by the continuous values of the elements of ε_{-t-1}.

Engle and Ng (1991) provided a summary of asymmetric ARCH models and introduced several new models of their own. They concentrated on the GARCH(1, 1) process and the functional relationship $h_t = h(\varepsilon_{t-1})$, which they term the 'news impact curve'. They proposed the parametric models

$$h_t = \alpha_0 + \alpha_1(\varepsilon_{t-1} + \gamma)^2 + \beta h_{t-1} \tag{36}$$

$$h_t = \alpha_0 + \alpha_1(\varepsilon_{t-1}/h_{t-1}^{1/2} + \gamma)^2 + \beta h_{t-1} \tag{37}$$

$$h_t = \alpha_0 + \alpha_1(\varepsilon_{t-1} + \gamma h_{t-1}^{1/2})^2 + \beta h_{t-1}. \tag{38}$$

In the standard GARCH(1, 1) model, while holding h_{t-1} constant, h_t is a parabola in ε_{t-1} that takes its minimum at $\varepsilon_{t-1} = 0$. In the conditional variance function (36), the introduction of the parameter γ shifts the parabola horizontally so that the minimum occurs at $\varepsilon_{t-1} = -\gamma$. This produces asymmetry because if, for example, $\gamma < 0$, then $h_t = h(-\varepsilon_{t-1})$ exceeds $h_t = h(\varepsilon_{t-1})$ for $\varepsilon_{t-1} > 0$. The model (37) is similar to (36) except that the conditional variance is quadratic in the standardized error $\varepsilon_{t-1}/h_{t-1}^{1/2}$. In (38) the minimum of h_t occurs at $-\gamma h_{t-1}^{1/2}$, which varies with the information set. Engle and Ng (1991) also proposed a very flexible functional form, which is similar to the QTARCH model but is piecewise linear over the support of ε_{t-1} rather than a step function as in (35). They characterized this model as 'partially nonparametric' (PNP). They partitioned the support of ε_{t-1} into intervals, where the boundaries of the intervals are $\{\tau_{m-},\ldots,\tau_{-1},0,\tau_1,\ldots,\tau_{m+}\}$, m^- is the number of intervals below zero and m^+ is the number of intervals above zero. Engle and Ng then specified

$$h_t = \alpha + \sum_{i=0}^{m^+}\theta_i P_{it}(\varepsilon_{t-1} - \tau_i) + \sum_{i=0}^{m^-}\delta_i N_{it}(\varepsilon_{t-1} - \tau_{-i})\beta h_{t-1} \tag{39}$$

where the variables P_{it} and N_{it} are defined as

$$P_{it} = \begin{cases} 1 & \text{if } \varepsilon_{t-1} > \tau_i \\ 0 & \text{otherwise} \end{cases} \quad \text{and} \quad N_{it} = \begin{cases} 1 & \text{if } \varepsilon_{t-1} < \tau_{-i} \\ 0 & \text{otherwise.} \end{cases}$$

From (39), h_t will be linear with a different slope over each interval. For example, if ε_{t-1} is positive and lies in the interval (τ_i, τ_{i+1}), then the slope coefficient is $\theta_1 + \cdots + \theta_i$. Engle and Ng chose the τ_i to be multiples of the unconditional standard deviation of the series.

Engle and Ng (1991) also conducted an experiment to compare the ability of asymmetric ARCH models to represent the conditional variance of stock returns. Using daily observations on the Japanese TOPIX stock index from January 1980 to September 1987, Engle and Ng fitted GARCH(1, 1) versions of the EGARCH and TARCH models, and the models given by (36), (37) and (38). All of the fitted models confirmed the presence of the leverage effect. But using a series of diagnostic tests, which we describe in section 9, Engle and Ng concluded that the simple parametric models (36), (37) and (38) significantly underestimated the volatility produced by large negative errors. The EGARCH and TARCH models, however, adequately represented this 'negative size' effect. Engle and Ng also estimated the PNP model and used the fitted conditional variance function as a baseline by which to compare the other asymmetric ARCH models. Relative to the prediction of the PNP model, the three models given in (36), (37) and (38) again underpredicted volatility for large negative ε_{t-1} and overpredicted volatility for large positive ε_{t-1}. The fitted conditional variance functions of the EGARCH and TARCH models were very close to the PNP's, but the EGARCH model significantly over-stated volatility for extremely large negative ε_{t-1}. Although based on only one data set, Engle and Ng's results indicate that for a parsimonious and highly parametric model EGARCH can represent an asymmetric conditional variance remarkably well. Whether any inadequacies in the EGARCH functional form for representing the volatility of stock returns justifies the additional computational effort of estimating a more flexible model like the TARCH, QTARCH or PNP models may largely depend on the peculiarities of the individual data set and the ultimate purpose of the empirical analysis.

In the context of estimating risk premia, Pagan and Hong (1991) suggested that no parametric functional form is sufficiently general to represent the diverse types of data which display conditional heteroskedasticity. With data from French et al. (1987) and Engle et al. (1987), Pagan and Hong (1991) used a nonparametric kernel estimator of the conditional variance and demonstrated that the nonparametric estimators give different conclusions about the effect of the risk premium on asset returns than do the standard parametric ARCH models. In section 8, we will briefly discuss the nonparametric approach suggested by Pagan and Hong (1991). Undoubtedly, as research on ARCH phenomena continues, new empirical regularities of conditional heteroskedasticity will be discovered and new functional forms will be put forward to model these regularities.

4.2   Non-normal conditional distribution

As described in section 2.3, an attractive feature of the ARCH process is that even though the conditional distribution of the error is normal the unconditional distribution is non-normal with tails thicker than the normal distribution. In spite of this property, early empirical work with ARCH models for daily exchange rates indicated that the implied unconditional distributions of estimated ARCH models were not sufficiently leptokurtic to represent the distribution of returns. In the linear regression model with conditionally normal ARCH errors, suppose that $\hat{\varepsilon}_t$ and $\hat{h}_t$ are estimates of the error and conditional variance. Then the standardized residuals $\hat{\varepsilon}_t/\hat{h}_t^{1/2}$ should be approximately N(0, 1). Hsieh (1988, 1989), McCurdy and Morgan (1988) and Milhøj (1987b), however, demonstrated for a variety of currencies that the sample kurtosis coefficient of the standardized residuals often exceeded 3.

The frequent inability of the conditionally normal ARCH model to pass this simple diagnostic test has led to the use of conditional distributions more general than the normal distribution. Let $\eta_t = \varepsilon_t/h_t^{1/2} = (y_t - x_t', \xi)/h_t^{1/2}$ be the standardized error. In this approach, the conditional distribution of η_t is specified as

$$\eta_t \mid \Psi_{t-1} \sim f(\eta, \theta) \tag{40}$$

where θ is a low-dimension parameter vector whose value determines the shape of the conditional distribution of η_t. In the conditionally normal ARCH model, θ is absent and $f(\eta)$ is simply the N(0, 1) density. Bollerslev (1987) was the first to adopt this approach and specified $f(\eta, \theta)$ as a conditional t distribution, where θ, a scalar, is the degrees of freedom of the distribution. The conditional t distribution allows for heavier tails than the normal distribution and, as the degrees of freedom go to infinity, includes the normal distribution as a limiting case. Bollerslev suggested that a test for conditional normality could be conducted by testing that the reciprocal of the degrees of freedom equals zero. Using the daily rate of return in the spot market for the German mark and the British pound from March 1980 to January 1985, Bollerslev estimated GARCH(1, 1) models with conditional t distributions and rejected the hypothesis of conditional normality. The sample kurtosis coefficients of the standardized residuals were very close to the kurtosis coefficients of the t distribution evaluated at the estimated parameters. With the German mark, for example, the sample kurtosis coefficient of the standardized residuals $\hat{\varepsilon}_t/\hat{h}_t^{1/2}$ was 4.63, while the implied kurtosis of the fitted t distribution was 4.45, suggesting that the conditional t distribution adequately accounted for the excess kurtosis in the unconditional distribution. Bollerslev presented similar results for the daily rate of return on five S&P stock indexes. Engle and Bollerslev (1986), Baillie and Bollerslev (1989) and Hsieh (1989) also found that employing a conditional t distribution helped account for the excess kurtosis in daily exchange rates. Spanos (1991) demonstrated that if the observed data are assumed to have an uncorrelated multivariate t distribution, the conditional distribution of the error also has a t distribution, with an ARCH structure for the variance.

Other specifications of the conditional distribution of the ARCH process have been suggested. Nelson (1991) employed a generalized error distribution (GED) with his EGARCH model. The GED encompasses distributions with tails both thicker and thinner than the normal, and includes the normal as a special case. For a stock price index, Nelson found evidence of non-normality in the conditional distribution, but concluded that tails of the estimated GED were not sufficiently thick to account for a large number of outliers in the data. Lee and Tse (1991) suggested that the conditional distribution may not only be leptokurtotic but also asymmetric. They argued that for rates of return which cannot be negative, such as nominal interest rates, the conditional distribution should be skewed to the right. They used a distribution based on the first three terms of the Gram–Charlier series that allows for both thick tails and skewness. Using interest rates from the Singapore Asian dollar market, Lee and Tse estimated their model but failed to find any evidence of skewness.

As with parametric specifications of the conditional variance function, no single parametric specification of the conditional density (40) appears to be suitable for all conditionally heteroskedastic data. Applications in which none of the above conditional distributions appear to be appropriate are often encountered. For example, Hsieh (1989) found that a GARCH(1, 1) model with either a conditional t or a conditional GED distribution could not adequately represent daily returns on the British pound nor the

Japanese yen. Hansen (1992) recently suggested an approach to allow more flexibility in the conditional distribution within a parametric framework. While conventional ARCH models allow the mean and variance to be time varying, Hansen argues that other properties of the conditional distribution, such as skewness and kurtosis, should also be time varying and a function of the current information set. More formally, Hansen proposed that the conditional distribution (40) should be generalized to

$$\eta_t \mid \Psi_{t-1} \sim f(\eta, \theta_t) \tag{41}$$

where the parameters θ_t, which determine the shape of the conditional density, are themselves a function of the elements of the information set Ψ_{t-1}. Hansen refers to (41) as an autoregressive conditional density (ARCD) model.

To illustrate the use of an ARCD model, Hansen estimated a GARCH model with a conditional t distribution and time- varying degrees of freedom for the monthly excess holding yield on short-term US treasury securities. To allow the tail thickness of the conditional distribution to be determined by the information set, the degrees of freedom were parameterized as logistic transformation of a quadratic function of the lagged error and the difference between the one-month yield and the instantaneous yield. A likelihood ratio test rejected a conditional t distribution with constant degrees of freedom in favour of the ARCD model. A time plot of the estimated degrees of freedom revealed that the degrees of freedom varied considerably over time, with a mean of about 5 but frequently reaching 30 and 2.1, the upper and lower bounds imposed by the logistic transformation.

5　Forecasting with ARCH models

A very important use of ARCH models is the evaluation of the accuracy of forecasts. In standard time series methodology which uses conditionally homoskedastic ARMA processes, the variance of the forecast error does not depend on the current information set. If the series being forecasted displays ARCH, the current information set can indicate the accuracy by which the series can be forecasted. Below, we demonstrate how this is possible. Engle and Kraft (1983) were the first to consider the effect of ARCH on forecasting. Baillie and Bollerslev (1992) extended many of their results. The discussion below draws heavily from these two papers.

5.1　Measurement of forecast uncertainty

We illustrate the effects of ARCH on the measurement of forecast uncertainty in the context of predicting a univariate linear time series. Consider the ARMA(k, l) process

$$\phi(B)y_t = \theta(B)\varepsilon_t \tag{42}$$

where $\phi(B) = 1 - \phi_1 B - \cdots - \phi_k B^k$, $\theta(B) = 1 + \theta_1 B + \cdots + \theta_1 B^l$, B is the backshift operator and ε_t is a GARCH(p, q) process. We consider forecasting the value of the process s periods from an origin t, which is given by

$$y_{t+s} = \sum_{i=1}^{k} \phi_i y_{t+s-i} + \sum_{i=1}^{l} \theta_i \varepsilon_{t+s-i} + \varepsilon_{t+s}.$$

The optimal predictor is the mean of y_{t+s} conditional on the available information up to period t, Ψ_t. Because $E(\varepsilon_{t+s} \mid \Psi_t) = 0$, the optimal predictor is

$$E(y_{t+s} \mid \Psi_t) = \sum_{i=1}^{k} \phi_i E(y_{t+s-i} \mid \Psi_t) + \sum_{i=1}^{l} \theta_i E(\varepsilon_{t+s-i} \mid \Psi_t) \tag{43}$$

where

(a) $E(y_{t+s-i} \mid \Psi_t)$, for $i < s$, is given recursively by (43);
(b) $E(y_{t+s-i} \mid \Psi_t) = y_{t+s-i}$, for $i \geqslant s$;
(c) $E(\varepsilon_{t+s-i} \mid \Psi_t) = 0$, for $i < s$;
(d) $E(\varepsilon_{t+s-i} \mid \Psi_t) = \varepsilon_{t+s-i}$, for $i \geqslant s$.

Expression (43) is the standard recursive relation for the optimal point forecast of the conventional ARMA process, which can be found for example in Box and Jenkins (1976, p. 129). Therefore, the presence of ARCH does not affect the way in which the point forecast is constructed. This is because ARCH introduces dependence in high-order moments and only affects the uncertainty in the point forecast.

To consider the effect of ARCH on the uncertainty of the point forecast, we require an expression for the forecast error. Assuming the roots of $\phi(B) = 1 - \phi_1 B - \cdots - \phi_k B^k$ lie outside the unit circle, the ARMA process (42) can be inverted to give

$$y_{t+s} = \sum_{i=0}^{\infty} \gamma_i \varepsilon_{t+s-i} \tag{44}$$

where γ_i is the coefficient of B^i in the expansion of $\phi(B)^{-1}\theta(B)$. Using the moving average representation, the optimal predictor is

$$E(y_{t+s} \mid \Psi_t) = \sum_{i=s}^{\infty} \gamma_i \varepsilon_{t+s-i} \tag{45}$$

Let $e_{t,s}$ be the forecast error from origin t with forecast horizon s. Subtracting (45) from (44), the forecast error

$$e_{t,s} = y_{t+s} - E(y_{t+s} \mid \Psi_t) = \sum_{i=0}^{s-1} \gamma_i \varepsilon_{t+s-i} \tag{46}$$

is seen to be a linear combination of the innovations from $t + 1$ to the horizon $t + s$. The uncertainty in a forecast can be measured by the variance of the forecast error conditional on the information Ψ_t used to construct the forecast. Using (46), the variance of the forecast error is

$$\mathrm{var}(e_{t,s} \mid \Psi_t) = \sum_{i=0}^{s-1} \gamma_i^2 E(\varepsilon_{t+s-i}^2 \mid \Psi_t). \tag{47}$$

Expression (47) reveals how ARCH affects the conditional variance of the forecast error. When ARCH is present, $E(\varepsilon_{t+s-i} \mid \Psi_t)$ will depend on the elements of Ψ_t and will, in general, be time varying. In contrast, for a conditionally homoskedastic model in which $E(\varepsilon_{t+s-i} \mid \Psi_t) = \sigma_\varepsilon^2$, the variance of the forecast error reduces to

$$\text{var}(e_{t,s} \mid \Psi_t) = \sigma_\varepsilon^2 \sum_{i=0}^{s-1} \gamma_i^2.$$

In this case, the variance of the forecast error does not depend upon the elements of the information set Ψ_t, but only on the length s of the forecast horizon.

To make (47) operational, for constructing prediction intervals for example, it is necessary to evaluate the expectations $E(\varepsilon_{t+s-i}^2 \mid \Psi_t)$. This can be done by using the ARMA(m, p) representation of the square of a GARCH(p, q) process (see equation (12)):

$$\varepsilon_{t+s}^2 = \infty_0 + \sum_{i=1}^{m}(\alpha_i + \beta_i)\varepsilon_{t+s-i}^2 - \sum_{i=1}^{p} \beta_i \nu_{t+s-i} + \nu_{t+s}.$$

The conditional expectations are then seen to be

$$E(\varepsilon_{t+s}^2 \mid \Psi_t) = \alpha_0 + \sum_{i=1}^{m}(\alpha_i + \beta_i)E(\varepsilon_{t+s-i}^2 \mid \Psi_t) - \sum_{i=1}^{p} \beta_i E(\nu_{t+s-i} \mid \Psi_t) \qquad (48)$$

where

(a) $E(\varepsilon_{t+s-i}^2 \mid \Psi_t)$, for $i < s$, is given recursively by (48);
(b) $E(\varepsilon_{t+s-i}^2 \mid \Psi_t) = \varepsilon_{t+s-i}^2$, for $i \geqslant s$;
(c) $E(\nu_{t+s-i} \mid \Psi_t) = 0$, for $i < s$;
(d) $E(\nu_{t+s-i} \mid \Psi_t) = \nu_{t+s-i}$, for $i \geqslant s$.

The expression for $E(\varepsilon_{t+s}^2 \mid \Psi_t)$ in (48) is completely analogous to the optimal predictor $E(y_{t+s} \mid \Psi_t)$ in (43).

As an example of constructing estimates of the variance of the forecast, consider the stationary AR(1) process

$$y_t = \phi_1 y_{t-1} + \varepsilon_t \qquad | \phi_1 | < 1$$

where ε_t is a GARCH(1, 1) process. The optimal point forecasts follow the recursion

$$E(y_{t+s} \mid \Psi_t) = \phi_1 E(y_{t+s-1} \mid \Psi_{t-1})$$

where the first-period forecast is $E(y_{t+1} \mid \Psi_t) = \phi_1 y_t$. Inverting the AR(1) process, the coefficients in (45) are seen to be $\gamma_i = \phi_1^i$. Therefore, from (47), the variance of the forecast error is

$$\text{var}(e_{t,s} \mid \Psi_t) = \sum_{i=0}^{s-1} \phi_1^{2i} E(\varepsilon_{t+s-i}^2 \mid \Psi_t) \qquad s \geqslant 1$$

where the expectations can be computed recursively by

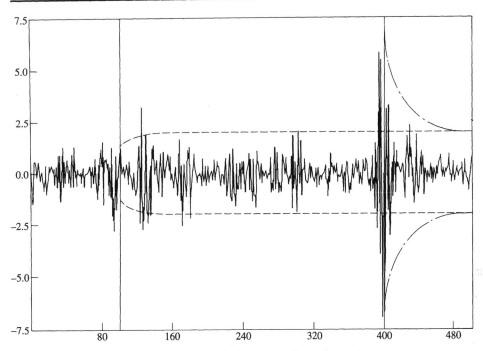

Figure 8 Two standard error prediction intervals.

$$E(\varepsilon_{t+s}^2 \mid \Psi_t) = \alpha_0 + (\alpha_1 + \beta_1)E(\varepsilon_{t+s-1}^2 \mid \Psi_t) \qquad s > 1$$

with the initial expectation $E(\varepsilon_{t+1}^2 \mid \Psi_t) = \alpha_0 + \alpha_1\varepsilon_t^2 + \beta_1 h_t$.

To further demonstrate the effect of ARCH on the construction of forecast intervals, in figure 8 we present prediction intervals for the generated ARCH(4) data that were displayed in figure 6. Since the process has a constant conditional mean of zero, the optimal point forecast of the series is simply zero. The prediction intervals are then $\pm 2E(\varepsilon_{t+s}^2 \mid \Psi_t)^{1/2}$, where $E(\varepsilon_{t+s}^2 \mid \Psi_t)$ is given in (48). The information sets Ψ_{100} and Ψ_{400} on which the intervals are based were chosen because $t = 100$ was a tranquil period for the series and $t = 400$ was a volatile period. Notice that for Ψ_{100} the prediction intervals increase monotonically, indicating that uncertainty increases with the forecast horizon, while for Ψ_{400} the intervals decrease, indicating that certainty in the point forecast increases with the forecast horizon. Although at first sight it may seem peculiar that the accuracy of a forecast can increase as we forecast further into the future, this phenomenon is very plausible in the context of ARCH models. If the forecast is constructed in a highly volatile period, an ARCH model will convey that volatility is likely to persist for several periods. But as the forecast horizon increases, the volatility is likely to return to its typical level, and therefore the expected accuracy of the point forecast actually increases as we forecast further ahead. Also notice that, for both information sets, the intervals converge to $\pm 2\sigma_\varepsilon$, where σ_ε is the unconditional standard deviation of the process. In an important class of ARCH models, the conditional variances of the forecast errors may not converge to the unconditional variance of the process. We characterize this class of models in the next section.

5.2   Persistence in variance

When ARCH is present, current information is useful for assessing the accuracy by which a process can be forecast. It is interesting to consider how the available information Ψ_t affects the forecast uncertainty as the forecast horizon s increases. For $s > p$, the conditional variance (48) of the innovation to the forecast error reduces to

$$E(\varepsilon_{t+s}^2 \mid \Psi_t) = \alpha_0 + \sum_{i=1}^{m} (\alpha_i + \beta_i) E(\varepsilon_{t+s-i}^2 \mid \Psi_t) \tag{49}$$

which is a linear difference equation for the sequence $\{E(\varepsilon_{t+s}^2 \mid \Psi_t)\}_{s=p+1}^{\infty}$. If the roots of $1 - (\alpha_1 + \beta_1)Z - \cdots - (\alpha_m + \beta_m)Z^m = 1 - \alpha(Z) - \beta(Z)$ lie outside the unit circle, the solution sequence of (49) converges to

$$\sum_{s \to \infty} E(\varepsilon_{t+s}^2 \mid \Psi_{t-1}) = \frac{\alpha_0}{1 - \alpha_1 - \cdots - \alpha_q - \beta_1 - \cdots - \beta_p}$$

which is the unconditional variance of the innovation. In this case, as the forecast horizon becomes very large, the conditioning set provides no information about the variance of ε_{t+s}. If, however, the roots of $1 - \alpha(z) - \beta(z)$ lie on or inside the unit circle, this will not be the case. For example, consider a GARCH(1, 1) process with $1 - \alpha(Z) - \beta(Z)$ having a unit root, implying $\alpha_1 + \beta_1 = 1$. Then (49) reduces to

$$E(\varepsilon_{t+s}^2 \mid \Psi_t) = \alpha_0 + E(\varepsilon_{t+s-1}^2 \mid \Psi_t).$$

which has the solution

$$E(\varepsilon_{t+s}^2 \mid \Psi_t) = s\alpha_0 + E(\varepsilon_t^2 \mid \Psi_t).$$

Therefore, when $\alpha_1 + \beta_1 = 1$, the conditional variance grows linearly with the forecast horizon and the dependence on the information set persists through $E(\varepsilon_t^2 \mid \Psi_t)$.

Engle and Bollerslev (1986) were the first to consider GARCH processes with $\alpha(1) + \beta(1) = 1$ as a distinct class of models, which they termed integrated GARCH (IGARCH). They pointed out the similarity between IGARCH processes and processes that are integrated in the mean. For a process that is integrated in the mean, i.e. one that must be differenced to induce stationarity, a shock in the current period affects the level of the series into the indefinite future. In an IGARCH process, a current shock persists indefinitely in conditioning the future variances. The IGARCH model is important because a remarkable empirical regularity, repeatedly observed in applied work, is that the estimated coefficients of a GARCH conditional variance sum close to unity. For example, Baillie and Bollerslev (1989) estimated GARCH(1, 1) models for six US exchange rates and found $\hat{\alpha}_1 + \hat{\beta}_1$ ranging between 0.94 and 0.99 for the six series. Bollerslev and Engle (1989) considered multivariate IGARCH processes and defined a concept of cointegration in variance which they termed *co-persistence*. A set of univariate IGARCH processes are co-persistent if there exists a linear combination of the processes which is *not* integrated in variance. Nelson (1990a) has cautioned that drawing an analogy with processes that are integrated in the mean, however, may be somewhat misleading. As described in section 2.3, Nelson (1990a) demonstrated that although IGARCH models are not weakly stationary, because they have infinite variances, they can be strongly stationary. Processes that are integrated in the mean are not stationary in any sense.

The consistent finding of very large persistence in variance in financial time series is perplexing because currently no theory predicts that this should be the case. Lamoureux and Lastrapes (1990b) argued that large persistence may actually represent mis-specification of the variance and result from structural change in the unconditional variance of the process, as represented by changes in α_0 in (7). A discrete change in the unconditional variance of a process produces clustering of large and small deviations which may show up as persistence in a fitted ARCH model. To illustrate this possibility, Lamoureux and Lastrapes used seventeen years of daily returns on the stocks of thirty randomly selected companies and estimated GARCH$(1, 1)$ models holding α_0 constant and allowing α_0 to change discretely over subperiods of the sample. For the restricted model, in which α_0 is constant, the average estimate of $\alpha_1 + \beta_1$ for the thirty companies was 0.978, while for the unrestricted model, in which α_0 is allowed to change, the average estimate fell to 0.817. Lamoureux and Lastrapes also present Monte Carlo evidence which demonstrated that the maximum likelihood estimator of $\alpha_1 + \beta_1$ has a large positive bias when changes in the unconditional variance are ignored.

6 Multivariate ARCH models

As economic variables are interrelated, generalization of univariate models to the multivariate and simultaneous set-up is quite natural – this is more so for ARCH models. Apart from possible gains in efficiency in parameter estimation, estimation of a number of financial 'coefficients' such as the systematic risk (beta coefficient) and the hedge ratio requires sample values of covariances between relevant variables. The motivation for multivariate ARCH also stems from the fact that many economic variables react to the same information and hence have non-zero covariances conditional on the information set. For simplicity, we concentrate on two variables, and using our earlier notation as in (19a) let

$$
\begin{aligned}
y_{1t} &= \mu_{1t} + \tau_1 I_t^{1/2} \nu_{1t} \\
y_{2t} &= \mu_{2t} + \tau_2 I_t^{1/2} \nu_{2t}
\end{aligned}
\tag{50}
$$

where y_{1t} and y_{2t} are two time series driven by the same directing process I_t and

$$
\begin{pmatrix} \nu_{1t} \\ \nu_{2t} \end{pmatrix} \sim \mathrm{N}\left[\begin{pmatrix} 0 \\ 0 \end{pmatrix}, \begin{pmatrix} 1 & c_{12} \\ c_{12} & 1 \end{pmatrix} \right].
$$

Then we have

$$
\begin{pmatrix} y_{1t} \\ y_{2t} \end{pmatrix} \mid \Psi_{t-1}, I_t \sim \mathrm{N}\left[\begin{pmatrix} \mu_{1t} \\ \mu_{2t} \end{pmatrix}, I_t \begin{pmatrix} \tau_1^2 & c_{12}\tau_1\tau_2 \\ c_{12}\tau_1\tau_2 & \tau_2^2 \end{pmatrix} \right].
\tag{51}
$$

This is the bivariate counterpart of (20) and provides a rationale behind higher-dimensional ARCH processes. As discussed in section 3.2, several special cases can be derived from (51).

Let us now consider an $N \times 1$ vector time series $y_t = (y_{1t}, \ldots, y_{Nt})'$. We can express a general form of the multivariate GARCH model as

$$y_t \mid \Psi_{t-1} \sim \mathrm{N}(\mu_t, H_t)$$

where μ_t is an $N \times 1$ vector and H_t is an $N \times N$ matrix. Of course, the conditional distribution could be something other than normal. As in the univariate case, one main problem is the specification of H_t. In fact, we will soon realize that the problem is more serious here. Even if we confine ourselves to linear specifications for multivariate ARCH, there are many choices.

To express H_t in a vector form, we use the 'vech' notation which stacks the lower triangular elements of a symmetric matrix in a column. A somewhat general form of H_t can be written as

$$\mathrm{vech}(H_t) = \mathrm{vech}(\Sigma) + \sum_{i=1}^{q} A_i \mathrm{vech}(\varepsilon_{t-i}\varepsilon'_{t-i}) + \sum_{i=1}^{p} B_i \mathrm{vech}(H_{t-i}) \qquad (52)$$

where $\varepsilon_t = (\varepsilon_{1t}, \ldots, \varepsilon_{Nt})'$, Σ is an $N \times N$ positive definite matrix and A_i and B_i are $N(N+1)/2 \times N(N+1)/2$ matrices. This is a direct generalization of our earlier univariate GARCH(p,q) model given in equation (7). Representation (52) is called the 'vech representation' of a multivariate ARCH model. For $N = 2$ and $p = q = 1$, (52) takes the form

$$\mathrm{vech}(H_t) = \begin{bmatrix} h_{11,t} \\ h_{12,t} \\ h_{22,t} \end{bmatrix} = \begin{bmatrix} \sigma_{11} \\ \sigma_{12} \\ \sigma_{22} \end{bmatrix} + \begin{bmatrix} a_{11} & a_{12} & a_{13} \\ a_{21} & a_{22} & a_{23} \\ a_{31} & a_{32} & a_{33} \end{bmatrix} \begin{bmatrix} \varepsilon^2_{1,t-1} \\ \varepsilon_{1,t-1}\varepsilon_{2,t-1} \\ \varepsilon^2_{2,t-1} \end{bmatrix}$$
$$+ \begin{bmatrix} b_{11} & b_{12} & b_{13} \\ b_{21} & b_{22} & b_{23} \\ b_{31} & b_{32} & b_{33} \end{bmatrix} \begin{bmatrix} h_{11,t-1} \\ h_{12,t-1} \\ h_{22,t-1} \end{bmatrix}. \qquad (53)$$

The two main problems concerning the specification of H_t are that it should be positive definite for all possible realizations and some exclusion restrictions should be imposed so that the number of parameters to be estimated is not very large. Formulation (52) will be difficult to estimate, for it has $[N(N+1)/2]\{1 + [N(N+1)/2](p+q)\}$ parameters, which for the special bivariate case (53) amounts to twenty-one parameters–still too large.

Engle et al. (1986) published the first paper on multivariate ARCH models. They considered a bivariate ARCH model which was (53) without the lagged h_t components. For that model, they showed that necessary conditions for H_t to be positive definite are

$$\sigma_{11} > 0, \sigma_{22} > 0, \sigma_{11}\sigma_{22} - \sigma^2_{12} > 0$$

$$a_{11} \geqslant 0, a_{13} \geqslant 0, a_{31} \geqslant 0, a_{33} \geqslant 0$$

$$a_{11}a_{33} - a^2_{22} \geqslant 0 \qquad (54)$$

$$a_{11}a_{13} - \tfrac{1}{4}a^2_{12} \geqslant 0, a_{11}a_{31} - a^2_{21} \geqslant 0$$

$$a_{31}a_{33} - \tfrac{1}{4}a^2_{32} \geqslant 0, a_{13}a_{33} - a^2_{23} \geqslant 0$$

Note that in (52) and (53), each $h_{ij,t}$ depends on lagged squared residuals and past variances of all the variables in the system. One simple assumption that could be made to reduce the number of parameters is to specify that a conditional variance depends only on its own lagged squared residuals and lagged values. The assumption amounts to taking A_i and B_i to be diagonal matrices. In that case, conditions in (54) reduce to

$$\sigma_{11} > 0, \sigma_{22} > 0, \sigma_{11}\sigma_{22} - \sigma_{12}^2 > 0$$
$$a_{11} \geqslant 0, a_{33} \geqslant 0, a_{11}a_{33} - a_{22}^2 \geqslant 0. \tag{55}$$

From (52), the 'diagonal representation' for $p = q = 1$ can be expressed as

$$h_{ij,t} = \sigma_{ij} + a_{ij}\varepsilon_{i,t-1}\varepsilon_{j,t-1} + b_{ij}h_{ij,t-1} \qquad i,j = 1, 2, \ldots, N. \tag{56}$$

This form was used by Bollerslev et al. (1988) for their analysis of returns on bills, bonds and stocks, and by Baillie and Myers (1991) and Bera et al. (1991) for hedge ratio estimation in commodity markets.

The diagonal representation appears to be too restrictive, and at the same time positive definiteness of the resulting H_t, in general, is not easy to check and also difficult to impose at the estimation stage (see (55)). Baba Engle, Kraft and Kroner (1990) suggested the following parameterization, known as the 'BEKK representation', which is almost guaranteed to be positive definite:

$$H_t = \Sigma + \sum_{i=1}^{q} A_i^{*\prime}\varepsilon_{t-i}\varepsilon_{t-i}^\prime A_i^* + \sum_{i=1}^{p} B_i^{*\prime}H_{t-i}B_i^* \tag{57}$$

where A_i^* and B_i^* are $N \times N$ matrices. If Σ is positive definite, then so is H_t. For $N = 2$ and $p = q = 1$, (57) will have only eleven parameters compared with the twenty-one parameters of the vech representation (53), as (57) now takes the form

$$\begin{bmatrix} h_{11,t} & h_{12,t} \\ h_{12,t} & h_{22,t} \end{bmatrix} = \begin{bmatrix} \sigma_{11} & \sigma_{12} \\ \sigma_{21} & \sigma_{22} \end{bmatrix} + \begin{bmatrix} a_{11}^* & a_{12}^* \\ a_{21}^* & a_{22}^* \end{bmatrix}^\prime \begin{bmatrix} \varepsilon_{1,t-1}^2 & \varepsilon_{1,t-1}\varepsilon_{2,t-1} \\ \varepsilon_{1,t-1}\varepsilon_{2,t-1} & \varepsilon_{2,t-1}^2 \end{bmatrix}$$
$$\times \begin{bmatrix} a_{11}^* & a_{12}^* \\ a_{21}^* & a_{22}^* \end{bmatrix} + \begin{bmatrix} b_{11}^* & b_{12}^* \\ b_{21}^* & b_{22}^* \end{bmatrix}^\prime \begin{bmatrix} h_{11,t-1} & h_{12,t-1} \\ h_{12,t-1} & h_{22,t-1} \end{bmatrix} \begin{bmatrix} b_{11}^* & b_{12}^* \\ b_{21}^* & b_{22}^* \end{bmatrix} \tag{58}$$

By taking the vech of (57), it can be shown that under certain nonlinear restrictions on A_i^*, B_i^*, A_i and B_i, (52) and (57) are equivalent (see Baba et al., 1990). The relationship is easily seen by comparing the special cases (53) and (58).

Bollerslev (1990) introduced an attractive way to simplify H_t. He assumed that the conditional correlation matrix of $\varepsilon_t = (\varepsilon_{1t}, \ldots, \varepsilon_{Nt})^\prime$ is constant and expressed H_t as

$$H_t = \mathrm{diag}(\sqrt{h_{11,t}}, \ldots, \sqrt{h_{NN,t}})R\,\mathrm{diag}(\sqrt{h_{11,t}}, \ldots, \sqrt{h_{NN,t}}) \tag{59}$$

where R is the time-invariant correlation matrix. When $N = 2$, this representation takes the form

$$H_t = \begin{bmatrix} \sqrt{h_{11,t}} & 0 \\ 0 & \sqrt{h_{22,t}} \end{bmatrix} \begin{bmatrix} 1 & \rho \\ \rho & 1 \end{bmatrix} \begin{bmatrix} \sqrt{h_{11,t}} & 0 \\ 0 & \sqrt{h_{22,t}} \end{bmatrix} \tag{60}$$

where $|\rho| < 1$ is the correlation coefficient between ε_{1t} and ε_{2t}, and the individual variances $h_{11,t}$ and $h_{22,t}$ are assumed to be standard univariate ARCH(p, q) processes, for example

$$h_{11,t} = \sigma_{11} + \sum_{i=1}^{q} \alpha_{1i}\varepsilon_{1,t-i}^2 + \sum_{i=1}^{p} \beta_{1i}h_{11,t-i}. \tag{61}$$

For positive definiteness of H_t in this constant correlation representation, we need $\sigma_{11} > 0, \alpha_{ij} \geqslant 0, \beta_{ik} \geqslant 0, i = 1,\ldots,N, j = 1,\ldots,q, k = 1,\ldots,p$. Many of the recent applications of bivariate ARCH use this representation (see, for example, Baillie and Bollerslev, 1990; Bollerslev, 1990; Baillie and Myers, 1991; Bera et al., 1990; Kroner and Claessens, 1991; Kroner and Sultan, 1991). However, it is quite obvious that constant correlation is a strong assumption. Bera and Roh (1991) suggested a test for the constant correlation hypothesis and found that the null hypothesis is rejected for many financial data series.

None of the above forms takes account of the motivation behind multivariate ARCH discussed earlier. Diebold and Nerlove (1989) were the first to exploit the theory that only a few factors influence all the variables $(y_1,\ldots,y_N)$ and their conditional variances. They suggest a one-factor multivariate ARCH model represented as

$$y_t = \lambda F_t + \eta_t \tag{62}$$

where $\eta_t = (\eta_{1t},\ldots,\eta_{Nt}), \eta_{it} \sim (0, \sigma_{ii}), i = 1,\ldots,N$ and the unobservable factor F_t is conditionally distributed as $F_t \mid \Psi_{t-1} \sim N(0, h_t)$. Then

$$\text{var}(y_t \mid \Psi_{t-1}) = h_t\lambda\lambda' + \text{diag}(\sigma_{11},\ldots,\sigma_{NN}) \tag{63}$$

and we can specify a univariate GARCH process for h_t. The effect of the common factor F_t on y_i is measured by λ_i ($i = 1,\ldots,N$). Their application of this model to seven weekly exchange rate series gave superior results compared with seven separate univariate ARCH models.

Harvey et al. (1992) presented a more general unobserved component model that includes (62) as a special case and allows for richer dynamics in the mean of y_t. They consider the model

$$y_t = Z_t\alpha_t + \Lambda\eta_t + \eta_t^*$$

in which α_t is an $m \times 1$ state vector that evolves according to the transition equation

$$\alpha_t = T_t\alpha_{t-1} + \Gamma\varepsilon_t + \varepsilon_t^*$$

where T_t and Z_t are observable matrices and the $m \times 1$ vector ε_t^* and the $N \times 1$ vector η_t^* are conditionally homoskedastic. Conditional heteroskedasticity is introduced through the scalar processes ε_t and η_t, which are assumed to follow univariate ARCH processes. The state space formulation provides a convenient representation for estimation and prediction by means of a Kalman filter. Higgins and Majin (1992) applied a univariate version of this model to measure the time-varying volatility of both the latent *ex ante* real interest rate and the market's forecast errors of inflation from the observable *ex post* real interest rate.

To discuss Engle's (1987) multivariate ARCH model with a k-factor structure, we start with a slight generalization of the BEKK representation (57), namely

$$H_t = \Sigma + \sum_{j=1}^{k} \left[\sum_{i=1}^{q} A_{ij}^{*\prime} \varepsilon_{t-i} \varepsilon_{t-i}' A_{ij}^* + \sum_{i=1}^{p} B_{ij}^{*\prime} H_{t-i} B_{ij}^* \right] \qquad (64)$$

where A_{ij}^* and B_{ij}^* are $N \times N$ matrices and $k \ll N$. Engle obtained a very parsimonious structure for H_t by restricting the rank of A_{ij}^* and B_{ij}^* to one (see also Lin, 1992). More specifically, he assumed that these matrices have the same left and right eigenvectors g_j and f_j, i.e.

$$A_{ij}^* = \alpha_{ij} f_j g_j' \qquad \text{and} \qquad B_{ij}^* = \beta_{ij} f_j g_j'$$

with

$$f_j g_j' = \begin{cases} 0 & \text{for } j \neq l \\ 1 & \text{for } j = 1 \end{cases}$$

where f_j and g_i are $N \times 1$ vectors, $j, l = 1, 2, \ldots, N$. Using these expressions for A_{ij}^* and B_{ij}^* in (64) we have the k-factor GARCH(p, q) model

$$H_t = \Sigma + \sum_{j=1}^{k} g_j g_j' \left[\sum_{i=1}^{q} \alpha_{ij}^2 f_j' \varepsilon_{t-i} \varepsilon_{t-i}' f_j + \sum_{i=1}^{p} \beta_{ij}^2 f_j' H_{t-i} f_j \right]. \qquad (65)$$

In the Diebold and Nerlove model the factor is an unobserved latent variable, while in the k-factor GARCH model the jth factor, F_{jt}, is a linear combination of the residuals, namely $F_{jt} = f_j' \varepsilon_t$. Therefore,

$$\text{var}(F_{jt} \mid \Psi_{t-1}) = f_j' H_t f_j = h_{jt}^* \text{ (say).} \qquad (66)$$

Substituting (65) into (66), we have

$$h_{jt}^* = f_j' \Sigma f_j + \sum_{i=1}^{q} \alpha_{ij}^2 F_{j,t-i}^2 + \sum_{i=1}^{p} \beta_{ij}^2 h_{j,t-i}^*.$$

Therefore, each h_{jt}^* has a GARCH(p, q) structure, $j = 1, \ldots, k$. This enables us to express (65) as

$$H_t = \Sigma + \sum_{j=1}^{k} g_j g_j' [h_{jt}^* - f_j' \Sigma f_j]$$

$$= \Sigma^* + \sum_{j=1}^{k} g_j g_j' h_{jt}^* \qquad (67)$$

where

$$\Sigma^* = \Sigma - \sum_{j=1}^{k} g_j g_j' f_j' \Sigma f_j.$$

Expression (67) demonstrates that the conditional variance of ε_t is regulated completely by the conditional variance of the k factors. Also, for $k = 1$, we can see the similarities between (63) and (67). Engle (1987), Kroner (1988), Lin (1992) and Engle et al. (1990) discussed other interesting properties of the k-factor GARCH model. Two notable applications of this model are that of Engle et al. (1990b) to explain the excess return for treasury bills and that of Ng et al. (1992) to study the behaviour of stock returns.

Lin (1992) examined the finite-sample properties of various estimators, such as maximum likelihood and two-stage estimators, for the factor GARCH(1, 1) model through simulation. Estimators were found to be, in general, unbiased. And, as predicted by asymptotic theory, the maximum likelihood estimators were most efficient. The major problems in estimation are devising methods for finding the number of factors and the factor weights.

7   ARCH-M models

It is reasonable to expect that the mean and variance of a return move in the same direction. Denoting the mean by μ_t, we can express this idea as

$$\mu_t = \xi_0 + \delta g(h_t)$$

where $g(h_t)$ is a monotonic function of the conditional variance h_t, with $g(\alpha_0) = 0$. In finance models, $\delta g(h_t)$ represents the risk premium, i.e. the increase in the expected rate of return due to an increase in the variance of the return. Existence of risk premia in foreign exchange markets and the term structure of interest rates have been studied extensively. Most of the earlier studies concentrated on detecting a *constant* risk premium. ARCH in the mean (ARCH-M) models, first proposed by Engle et al. (1987), provide a new approach by which we can test for and estimate a *time-varying* risk premium. In the regression set-up, an ARCH-M model is specified as

$$y_t = x_t'\xi + \delta g(h_t) + \varepsilon_t \tag{68}$$

where

$$\varepsilon_t \mid \Psi_{t-1} \sim N(0, h_t)$$

and h_t is an ARCH or GARCH process. The presence of h_t in the conditional mean is the distinctive feature of this model.

To examine the properties of the ARCH-M model, we consider a simple version of (68), namely

$$y_t = \delta h_t + \varepsilon_t$$

where $\varepsilon_t \mid \Psi_{t-1} \sim N(0, h_t)$ and $h_t = \alpha_0 + \alpha_1 \varepsilon_{t-1}^2$. We can then write

$$y_t = \delta \alpha_0 + \delta \alpha_1 \varepsilon_{t-1}^2 + \varepsilon_t$$

where ε_t follows an ARCH(1) process. From this expression, and using $E(\varepsilon_{t-1}^2) = \alpha_0/(1 - \alpha_1)$, it immediately follows that

$$E(y_t) = \delta_{\alpha 0} \left(1 + \frac{\alpha_0}{1 - \alpha_1} \right)$$

which can be viewed in finance models as the unconditional expected return for holding a risky asset. Similarly,

$$\text{var}(y_t) = \frac{\alpha_0}{1 - \alpha_1} + \frac{(\delta\alpha_1)^2 2\alpha_0^2}{(1 - \alpha_1)^2(1 - 3\alpha_1^2)}.$$

In the absence of a risk premium $\text{var}(y_t) = \alpha_0/(1 - \alpha_1)$. Therefore, the second component of $\text{var}(y_t)$ is due to the presence of a risk premium which makes y_t more dispersed. Finally, the ARCH-M effect makes y_t serially correlated, since (see Hong, 1991)

$$\rho_1 = \text{corr}(y_t, y_{t-1}) = \frac{2\alpha_1^3\delta^2\alpha_0}{2\alpha_1^2\delta^2\alpha_0 + (1 - \alpha_1)(1 - 3\alpha_1^2)}$$

$$\rho_k = \text{corr}(y_t, y_{t-k}) = \alpha_1^{k-1}\rho_1 \qquad k = 2, 3, \ldots.$$

From the expressions for ρ_1 and ρ_2, it is easily seen that the admissible region for (ρ_1, ρ_2) will be very restrictive. Bollerslev (1988) obtained similar results for the GARCH process. ARCH-M models introduce some interesting problems in terms of estimation and testing which will be discussed in the following sections.

In most applications, $g(h_t) = \sqrt{h_t}$ has been used (see, for example, Domowitz and Hakkio, 1985; Bollerslev et al. 1988), although Engle et al. (1987) found that $g(h_t) = \log(h_t)$ worked better in their estimation of the time-varying risk premia in the term structure. Pagan and Hong (1991) commented that the use of $\log(h_t)$ is problematic since, for $h_t < 1$, $g(h_t)$ will be negative, and also when $h_t \to 0$, the effect on y_t will be infinite.

8 Estimation

The most commonly used estimation procedure for ARCH models has been the maximum likelihood approach. The log likelihood function of the standard ARCH regression model

$$y_t \mid \Psi_{t-1} \sim \text{N}(x_t'\xi, h_t)$$

is given by

$$l(\theta) = \frac{1}{T}\sum_{t=1}^{\tau} l_t(\theta)$$

where

$$l_t(\theta) = \text{constant} - \frac{1}{2}\log(h_t) - \frac{\varepsilon_t^2}{2h_t^2} \tag{69}$$

and $\theta = (\xi', \gamma')'$. Here ξ and γ denote the conditional mean and conditional variance parameters respectively. One attractive feature of this normal likelihood function is that the information matrix is block diagonal between the parameters ξ and γ. To see this, note that the (i, j)th element of the off-diagonal block of the information matrix can be written as

$$\frac{1}{T}\sum_{t=1}^{T} E\left[\frac{\partial^2 l_t}{\partial\xi_i\partial\gamma_j}\right] = \frac{1}{T}\sum_{t=1}^{T} E\left[\frac{1}{2h_T^2}\frac{\partial h_t}{\partial\xi_i}\frac{\partial h_t}{\partial\gamma_j}\right]. \tag{70}$$

If h_t is a symmetric function of the lagged errors in the sense of Engle (1982), then the last expression in square brackets is anti-symmetric and therefore has expectation zero. The ARCH, GARCH, log ARCH and NARCH models given in (3), (7), (28) and (29) respectively are all symmetric according to the definition of Engle (1982).

The advantage of having this block diagonality is that, under the likelihood framework, estimation and testing for the mean and variance parameters can be carried out separately (see Engle, 1982, p. 996; Bollerslev, 1986, p. 317; Higgins and Bera, 1992, p. 996). Most of the applied work on ARCH models use the Berndt, Hall, Hall and Hausman (1974) algorithm (BHHH) to maximize $l(\theta)$. Starting from estimates of the rth iteration, the $(r + 1)$th step of the BHHH algorithm can be written as

$$\xi^{(r+1)} = \xi^{(r)} + \left[\sum_{t=1}^{T} \left(\frac{\partial l_t}{\partial \xi} \right) \left(\frac{\partial l_t}{\partial \xi} \right)' \right]^{-1} \sum_{t=1}^{T} \frac{\partial l_t}{\partial \xi}$$

and

$$\gamma^{(r+1)} = \gamma(r) + \left[\sum_{t=1}^{T} \left(\frac{\partial l_t}{\partial \gamma} \right) \left(\frac{\partial l_t}{\partial \gamma} \right)' \right]^{-1} \sum_{t=1}^{T} \frac{\partial l_t}{\partial \gamma}$$

where the derivates are evaluated at $\xi^{(r)}$ and $\gamma^{(r)}$. The block diagonality of the information matrix no longer holds for the ARCH-M model in (68) and the asymmetric models like AARCH in (18) and EGARCH in (32). For these models, the BHHH algorithm needs to be carried out jointly for both the conditional mean and the variance parameters.

For most applications it is very difficult to justify the conditional normality assumption in (69). Therefore, the log likelihood function $l(\theta)$ may be mis-specified. However, we can still obtain estimates of ξ and γ by maximizing $l(\theta)$ and such estimators are called quasi maximum likelihood estimators (QMLEs). Weiss (1986a) was the first to study the asymptotic properties of the QMLE of ARCH models. His important finding was that, as long as the first two conditional moments are correctly specified, ξ and γ will be consistently estimated even if the conditional normality assumption is violated. To state the asymptotic distribution of the QMLE $\hat{\theta} = (\hat{\xi}, \hat{\gamma}')$ let us denote

$$A = -\frac{1}{T} E \left[\frac{\partial^2 l(\theta_0)}{\partial \theta \, \partial \theta'} \right] \qquad \text{and} \qquad B = \frac{1}{T} E \left[\left(\frac{\partial l(\theta_0)}{\partial \theta} \right) \left(\frac{\partial l(\theta_0)}{\partial \theta} \right)' \right] \qquad (71)$$

where θ_0 is the true value of the parameter. Then under certain regularity conditions

$$\sqrt{T}(\hat{\theta} - \theta_0) \xrightarrow{L} N(0, A^{-1} B A^{-1})$$

and consistent estimators of A and B are given by

$$\hat{A} = -\frac{1}{T} \sum_{t=1}^{T} \frac{\partial^2 l_t(\hat{\theta})}{\partial \theta \, \partial \theta'} \qquad \text{and} \qquad \hat{B} = \frac{1}{T} \sum_{t=1}^{T} \left(\frac{\partial l_t(\hat{\theta})}{\partial \theta} \right) \left(\frac{\partial l_t(\hat{\theta})}{\partial \theta} \right)'.$$

Robust inference about θ can be achieved using this result. If the normality assumption is correct, $A = B$ and valid inference can be drawn using either $\hat{A}^{-1}$ or $\hat{B}^{-1}$ as the covariance matrix estimator. Bollerslev and Wooldridge (1992) generalized the univariate

ARCH results of Weiss (1986a) to the multivariate GARCH case under a different set of regularity conditions. Although the specification of a univariate ARCH model in Weiss (1986a) was very general, he assumed a finite fourth moment of the error term. As an example, for the ARCH(2) model this condition requires (see Bollerslev, 1986)

$$3\alpha_1^2 + 3\alpha_2^2 - 3\alpha_2^3 + 3\alpha_1^2\alpha_2 + \alpha_2 < 1$$

which might be difficult to justify in practice. For higher order ARCH and GARCH models, the condition will restrict models to a small part of the parameter space. Bollerslev and Wooldridge (1992) did not assume finiteness of the fourth moment, but instead they required $l_t(\theta)$ and its derivatives to satisfy a uniform weak law of large numbers which is not easy to verify. Lumsdaine (1991a) established the consistency and asymptotic normality of the QMLE of the GARCH(1, 1) and IGARCH(1, 1) models under a different set of assumptions. Her basic conditions are

$$E\left(\frac{\partial h_t}{\partial \theta} h_t^{-1}\right) < \infty \qquad \text{and} \qquad E\left[\left(\frac{\partial h_t}{\partial \theta}\right)\left(\frac{\partial h_t}{\partial \theta}\right)' h_t^{-2}\right] < \infty$$

and these are easy to verify. For simplicity, consider an ARCH(1) model

$$h_t = \alpha_0 + \alpha_1 \varepsilon_{t-1}^2.$$

Then

$$E\left[\left(\frac{\partial h_t}{\partial \alpha_1}\right)^2\right] = E(\varepsilon_{t-1}^4)$$

might not exist, and yet

$$E\left[\left(\frac{\partial h_t}{\partial \alpha_1}\right)^2 h_t^{-2}\right] = E\left(\frac{\varepsilon_{t-1}^4}{\alpha_0^2 + \alpha_1^2\varepsilon_{t-1}^4 + 2\alpha_0\alpha_1\varepsilon_{t-1}^2}\right)$$

may exist because here both the numerator and the denominator grow at the same rate. In terms of the standardized variable $\varepsilon_t^* = \varepsilon_t/\sqrt{h_t}$, Lumsdaine's assumptions are that ε_t^* is independent and identically distributed and drawn from a symmetric and unimodal density with thirty-two finite moments. Lee and Hansen (1991) obtained similar results under the somewhat weaker condition that ε_t^* is stationary and ergodic with a bounded fourth conditional moment. Lumsdaine (1991a) and Lee and Hansen (1991) showed that the QMLE for the IGARCH(1, 1) model has the same asymptotic distribution as that of the GARCH(1, 1) model. This result is important because it establishes that the difficulties of the unit root model are not encountered with IGARCH.

S.-W. Lee (1991) extended all these asymptotic distribution results to the GARCH (1, 1)-M and IGARCH(1, 1)-M models. As discussed in Lee, these models pose additional difficulties because, unlike the GARCH model, the conditional variance of a GARCH-M model is a *nonlinear* difference equation. To see this, note from (68) that for a GARCH(1, 1)-M model

$$h_t = \alpha_0 + \alpha_1 \varepsilon_{t-1}^2 + \beta_1 h_{t-1}$$
$$= \alpha_0 + \alpha_1 [y_{t-1} - x_t'\xi - \delta g(h_{t-1})]^2 + \beta_1 h_{t-1}.$$

To avoid the difficulties associated with nonlinear difference equations, Lee (1991) used the fact that at the true parameter value h_t is a linear difference equation.

Engle and González-Rivera (1991) pointed out that although the QMLE is consistent and asymptotically normal, it can be inefficient. They demonstrated that the loss of efficiency due to mis-specification could be severe when the true distribution is asymmetric and a normal quasi likelihood function is used. They suggested a semiparametric approach in which one maximizes the log likelihood function $l(\theta) = (1/T)\Sigma_t l_t(\theta)$, where the non-constant part of $l_t(\theta)$ in (69) is replaced by

$$-\frac{1}{2}\log(h_t) + \log[g(\varepsilon_t/h_{1/2}^t)].\tag{72}$$

Engle and González-Rivera (1991) used a nonparametric method to estimate the function $g(\cdot)$. To do this, they started with an initial estimator of θ, obtained $\hat{\varepsilon}_t/\hat{h}_t^{1/2}$, used these values to estimate $g(\cdot)$ and then maximized $l(\theta)$ to get a revised estimate of θ. The procedure was repeated until it converged. Their Monte Carlo results indicated that there is substantial gain in efficiency from using the semiparametric method over QMLE.

Another attractive way to estimate ARCH models without assuming normality is to apply the generalized method of moments (GMM) approach as advocated by Rich et al. (1991) (see also Sabau, 1987, 1988). For simplicity, consider an ARCH(1) model and define the following two errors:

$$\varepsilon_t = y_t - x_t'\xi$$
$$\nu_t = \varepsilon_t^2 - \alpha_0 - \alpha_1\varepsilon_{t-1}^2$$
$$= (y_t - x_t'\xi)^2 - \alpha_0 - \alpha_1(y_{t-1} - x_{t-1}'\xi)^2.$$

Then the GMM estimator is obtained from the following two moment conditions:

$$E(\varepsilon_t \mid Z_t) = 0 \qquad \text{and} \qquad e(\nu_t \mid Z_t) = 0$$

where z_t is a set of predetermined variables. The asymptotic distribution of the GMM estimator follows directly from the general formula is Hansen (1982). Weiss (1986a) and Pantula (1988) studied the asymptotic properties of least-squares estimators which also do not require a normality assumption. They proved the consistency and asymptotic normality of such estimators. However, as can be expected, least-squares estimators are less efficient than GMM estimators and maximum likelihood estimators with a correct likelihood function. It would be interesting to compare the finite-sample properties of all these estimators.

We previously mentioned the importance of correct specification of the conditional variance function h_t. All the forms of h_t we discussed in section 4 are fully parametric. Pagan and Hong (1991) argued that the existing parametric forms are not very convincing owing to the lack of optimizing theory in their formulation. They advocated nonparametric estimation of h_t, as originally suggested by Pagan and Ullah (1988). They even recommended estimating both the conditional mean, m_t, and the conditional variance, h_t, nonparametrically since mis-specification in the conditional mean might exaggerate the variation in h_t. Many nonparametric techniques are available in the statistics literature. For their empirical application, Pagan and Hong (1991) used the kernel method and the Fourier series approximation of Gallant (1982). These procedures estimate the first two conditional moments by relating them to the past values of y_t. If r lags of y_t are chosen, then m_t and h_t can be estimated by using the formulae

$$\hat{m}_t = \sum_{\substack{i=1 \\ i \neq t}}^{T} \omega_{it} y_i \qquad \text{and} \qquad \hat{h}_t = \sum_{\substack{i=1 \\ i \neq t}}^{T} \omega_{it} y_i^2 - \hat{m}_t^2$$

where ω_{it} are the kernel weights. For the Gaussian kernel

$$\omega_{it} = \frac{\kappa_{it}}{\sum_{\substack{i=1 \\ i \neq t}}^{T} \kappa_{it}}$$

where $\kappa_{it} = \exp[-\frac{1}{2} \sum_{s=1}^{s} h_s^{-2}(y_{i-s} - y_{s-t})^2]$, h_s being the bandwidth (for details see Pagan and Hong, 1991, p. 60). The empirical applications of Pagan and Hong (1991) showed the advantages of the nonparametric approach. They plotted the nonparametric $\hat{h}_t$ against y_{t-1} and found a high degree of nonlinearity which would be difficult to capture by simple parametric models. Also, Cox non-nested tests for parametric versus nonparametric models rejected the Engle et al. (1987) specification of the ARCH-M model for excess holding yields on treasury bills. The nonparametric method does require much larger data sets. Fortunately, we do have large data sets for economic and financial variables where ARCH models are generally applied. Of course, results from nonparametric analysis are not as easily interpreted in terms of response coefficients as those obtained from a parametric method. However, at the very least, nonparametric methods can point out deficiencies in the existing parametric models and offer some guidance for modification.

Not much is known about the finite-sample distribution of the different estimators discussed above. Engle et al. (1985), Bollerslev and Wooldridge (1992) and Lumsdaine (1991b) reported some Monte Carlo results on the QMLE. For the GARCH(1, 1) model, Bollerslev and Wooldridge (1992) found the QMLE of α_1 to be biased upward, the QMLE of β_1 to be biased downward and the overall estimate of $\alpha_1 + \beta_1$ to be slightly biased downward. This was consistent with the ARCH(1) results of Engle et al. (1985). Lumsdaine (1991b) reported that in small samples QMLEs are not normally distributed and rather skewed. For example, she found $\hat{\beta}_1$ to be skewed to the right. This is similar to the downward bias observed by Bollerslev and Wooldridge (1992). Lumsdaine (1991b) also observed some pile-up for the estimator of β_1. Surprisingly, the pile-up was at the zero boundary. In most applications β_1 seems to take values above 0.5 and so this may not be taken as a small-sample effect.

Geweke (1988a, b, 1989) argued that a Bayesian approach rather than the classical one might be more suitable for estimating ARCH models due to two distinct features of these models. First, as we noted earlier, some inequality restrictions must be imposed on the parameters to ensure positivity of h. In the classical estimation framework, these restrictions are somewhat impractical to impose. However, under the Bayesian paradigm, diffuse priors can incorporate these inequalities. Second, most of the time the main interest is not in the individual parameters but in h_t, which is a function of the parameters. Exact posterior distributions and means of

h_t can be obtained quite easily using Monte Carlo integration with importance sampling. The recent introduction of Gibbs sampling to the Bayesian econometrics literature might make the task even easier. Geweke's successful application to inflation and stock price data demonstrated the viability of the Bayesian approach for estimating ARCH models. Unfortunately, this approach has not been pursued by other researchers.

9   Testing

The introduction of ARCH to econometrics has led to many interesting testing problems. The basic test for the ARCH model is testing for the presence of ARCH, i.e. a test for the null hypothesis H_0: $\alpha_q = \alpha_2 = \cdots = \alpha_1 = 0$ in (3). Engle (1982) derived the Lagrange multiplier (LM) statistic for testing H_0 which is computed as TR^2, where T is the number of observations and R^2 is the coefficient of multiple determination from the regression of $\hat{\varepsilon}_t^2$ on a constant and $\hat{\varepsilon}_{t-1}^2, \ldots, \hat{\varepsilon}_{t-q}^2$ the $\hat{\varepsilon}_t$ being the OLS residuals from model (1). Under H_0, the LM statistic asymptotically follows a χ_q^2 distribution. The structure of the test is the same as that of the Breusch and Pagan (1979) and Godfrey (1978) 'static' heteroskedasticity test in the regression model. As noted in Bera and Lee (1993), this test is also a special case of the information matrix test applied to the regression model (1) with an AR(q) error structure and can be viewed as a test for randomness of the AR parameters $\phi_1, \ldots, \phi_q$.

A convenient way of looking at a general test for ARCH is to give it a moment test interpretation, the moment condition being

$$E\left(\frac{\varepsilon_t^2}{\alpha_0} - 1 \Big| z_t\right) = 0 \tag{73}$$

where z_t is some vector of variables. For Engle's test, $z_t = (1, \varepsilon_{t-1}^2, \varepsilon_{t-2}^2, \ldots, \varepsilon_{t-q}^2)$. If the alternative model is GARCH, as given in (7), then z_t would be specified as $z_t = (1, \varepsilon_{t-1}^2, \varepsilon_{t-2}^2, \ldots, \varepsilon_{t-q}^2, h_{t-1}, \ldots, h_{t-p})$. When estimated under H_0, z_t becomes $z_t = (1, \hat{\varepsilon}_{t-1}^2, \hat{\varepsilon}_{t-2}^2, \ldots, \hat{\varepsilon}_{t-q}^2, \alpha_0, \ldots, \hat{\alpha}_0)$. Therefore, the last p elements of $\hat{z}_t$ are redundant and a test for no conditional heteroskedasticity against an ARCH(q) or a GARCH(p, q) will be identical (see Bollerslev, 1986; J. H. Lee, 1991). For the AARCH model (18), $z_t = (1, \varepsilon_{t-1}^2, \varepsilon_{t-2}^2, \ldots, \varepsilon_{t-q}^2, \varepsilon_{t-1}\varepsilon_{t-2}, \ldots, \varepsilon_{t-1}\varepsilon_{t-q})$ and the test is carried out by running a regression of $\hat{\varepsilon}_t^2$ on a constant and the squares and cross-products of $\hat{\varepsilon}_{t-i}, i = 1, 2, \ldots, q$ (see Bera and Lee, 1993; Bera et al., 1992).

A complication arises when H_0 is tested against an ARCH-M model given in (68). The conditioning set z_t is the same as in the ARCH case, namely $z_t = (1, \varepsilon_{t-1}^2, \varepsilon_{t-2}^2, \ldots, \varepsilon_{t-q}^2)$. However, we note that, when the null hypothesis of no ARCH is imposed on the model, the nuisance parameter δ is not identified. This renders the information matrix singular under H_0, and thereby invalidates the standard distribution of the LM test. However, note that for a given value of δ, say δ^*, the LM statistic is perfectly well behaved and has the form (see Domowitz and Hakkio, 1985)

$$\text{LM}(\delta^*) = \frac{1}{2 + \delta^{*2}} \gamma' Z \left[Z'Z - \frac{\delta^{*2}}{2 + \delta^*} Z'X(X'X)^{-1}X'Z \right]^{-1} Z'\gamma \tag{74}$$

where γ is a $T \times 1$ vector with tth element $\gamma_t = (\hat{\varepsilon}_t^2 \mid \hat{\alpha}_0 - 1) + (\delta^* \hat{\varepsilon}_t \mid \hat{\alpha}_0)$. The second component of this LM test is due to the non-block diagonality of the information matrix between the conditional mean and variance parameters. It is clear that when $\delta^* = 0, LM(\delta^*)$ reduces to Engle's test for ARCH. Any arbitrary choice of δ will lead to a suboptimal test.

The same problem is faced for the NARCH model (29). When $\alpha_1 = \alpha_2 = \cdots = \alpha_q = 0$ in (29), the parameter δ becomes unidentified. For a fixed value of δ, again say δ^*, the LM statistic $S(\delta^*)$ can be computed as TR^2, where the R^2 is obtained by a regression of $\hat{\varepsilon}_t^2$ on an intercept and

$$\frac{(\hat{\varepsilon}_{t-i}^2)^{\delta*} - 1}{\delta^*} \qquad i = 1, 2, \ldots, q.$$

Therefore, in our conditional moment test framework

$$z_t = \left[1, \frac{(\varepsilon_{t-1}^2)^{\delta*} - 1}{\delta^*}, \ldots, \frac{(\varepsilon_{t-q}^2)^{\delta*} - 1}{\delta^*} \right]$$

which is the Box–Cox transformation of the lagged squared residuals. It is obvious that, when $\delta^* = 1$, z_t reduces to the conditioning set of Engle's test. To overcome the non-identification of δ, Bera and Higgins (1992) followed the procedure of Davies (1977, 1987) and suggested basing the test on a critical region of the form

$$\left\{ S = \sup_{\delta^*} S(\delta^*) > \omega \right\} \tag{75}$$

where ω is a suitably chosen constant. However, unlike $S(\delta^*)$, S does not have an asymptotic χ_q^2 distribution under the null hypothesis. It is clear that if χ_q^2 critical values are used, the type-I error probability of the test will be too high. Davies (1987) provided an approximation to the p value of the test as

$$\Pr[\chi_q^2 > S] + V \frac{\exp(-S/2)S^{(p-1)/2}}{2^{p/2}(p/2)^{1/2}} \tag{76}$$

where V measures the variation in $\sqrt{S(\delta)}$ over values of δ corresponding to different alternative hypotheses. This V can be estimated by

$$V = \sum_{j=1}^{R} \mid \sqrt{S(\delta_j)} - \sqrt{S(\delta_{j-1})} \mid$$

where δ_0 and δ_R are the lower and upper bounds for δ, and $\delta_1, \delta_2, \ldots, \delta_{R-1}$ are the turning points of $\sqrt{S(\delta)}$. The second component in (76) can be viewed as the correction factor to the standard χ^2 p value due to the scanning across a range of values of δ. Monte Carlo results and an empirical illustration presented by Bera and Higgins (1992) suggest that the above procedure is more powerful than the standard LM test for ARCH when the true process has $\delta \neq 1$. Bera and Ra (1991) applied the same technique to the ARCH-M model and obtained similar results. Hansen (1991) developed a simulation approach which approximates the asymptotic null distribution of statistics which have the structure of S. Andrews and Ploberger (1992) also considered the general problem of testing when a nuisance parameter exists only under the alternative hypothesis and derived asymptotically optimal tests in terms of weighted average power in the class of all tests with a given significance level. Andrews (1993) used the latter approach for testing the presence of conditional heteroskedasticity with GARCH(1, 1) as the alternative model.

One drawback of using the LM test principle in testing H_0: $\alpha_1 = \alpha_2 = \cdots = \alpha_q = 0$ is that it does not take account of the one-sided nature of the alternative hypothesis, i.e. that the α_i cannot take negative values. We can expect some loss of power due to this omission, although the two-sided LM test will have the correct size asymptotically. Demos and Sentana (1991) and Lee and King (1991) suggested some one-sided versions of the LM test. Demos and Sentana's version of the one-sided LM test can be obtained as the sum of the squared t ratios associated with the positive coefficients of the OLS regression of $\hat{\varepsilon}_t^2$ on 1, $\hat{\varepsilon}_{t-1}^2, \ldots, \hat{\varepsilon}_{t-q}^2$, while Lee and King's version is based on the sum of the scores $\partial l(\theta)/\partial \alpha_i, i = 1, \ldots, q$. Lee and King (1991) carried out a Monte Carlo study of the finite-sample power properties of the two-sided and their one-sided LM statistics, and found that the one-sided version of the test has better power.

In the moment condition (73), the term $\varepsilon_t^2/\alpha_0 - 1$ is essentially a result of the normality assumption. If we consider a general log-density function of the form (72), then $\varepsilon_t^2/\alpha_0 - 1$ could be replaced by $\phi(\varepsilon_t/\sqrt{\alpha_0})\varepsilon_t/\sqrt{\alpha_0} - 1$, where $\phi = -g'/g$ is the score function. For the normal distribution $\phi(\varepsilon_t/\alpha_0) = \varepsilon_t/\alpha_0$. As in Engle and González-Rivera (1991), the score function can be estimated nonparametrically. As a general test for ARCH under non-normality, we can think of running a regression of $\phi_t \varepsilon_t$ on z_t. In our discussion above of the TR^2 type test statistics, we noted various tests by changing the independent variable set z_t with the same dependent variable $\hat{\varepsilon}_t^2$. Now we can think of different dependent variables corresponding to various non-normal distributions. For example, if we assume a double exponential distribution, we need to run the regression of $|\hat{\varepsilon}_t|$ on z_t. This is known as the Glejser (1969) test for heteroskedasticity. In the context of testing static heteroskedasticity and autocorrelation in the regression model, Bera and Ng (1991) successfully used such nonparametric tests and these could easily be adapted to ARCH models (also see Pagan and Pak, 1993).

Any general test for nonlinear dependence may also detect conditional heteroskedasticity. The BDS test of Brock, Dechert and Scheinkman (1987) is frequently used in empirical work with ARCH models (see for example Hsieh, 1989; Gallant et al. 1991; and Higgins and Bera, 1992). The BDS test measures nonlinearity by the proportion of 'm-histories', $y_t^m = \{y_t, y_{t+1}, \ldots, y_{t+m-1}\}$, which lie within a specified distance of one another. Hsieh (1989) and Brock et al. (1991) demonstrated by Monte Carlo experiments that the BDS test has good power against ARCH alternatives.

All of the above tests are only for detection of the possible presence of conditional heteroskedasticity and do not provide any information regarding the form of the conditional variance function h_t. As we mentioned earlier, correct specification of h_t is very important. The accuracy of forecast intervals depends on selecting an h_t which correctly relates the future variances to the current information set. Also Pagan and Sabau (1987a) showed that an incorrect functional form for h_t can result in inconsistent maximum likelihood estimates of the conditional mean parameters. This is more likely to happen when h_t is asymmetric or for the ARCH-M models. Most of the empirical papers indirectly test for the correct specification of h_t and other accompanying assumptions by studying the properties of the standardized residuals $\hat{\varepsilon}_t^* = \hat{\varepsilon}_t / \hat{h}_t^{1/2}$. The basis of considering ε_t^* is that under our set-up

$$\varepsilon_t^* = \frac{\varepsilon_t}{h_t^{1/2}} \mid \Psi_{t-1} \sim N(0, 1).$$

Therefore, if the model is correctly specified, $\hat{\varepsilon}_t^*$ should behave as white noise. The various diagnostic checks that are commonly used include testing the normality of $\hat{\varepsilon}_t^*$ and considering the sample autocorrelations of $\hat{\varepsilon}_t^*$. These diagnostics are helpful in detecting certain mis-specifications, but we cannot expect them to be very powerful tests.

Using the Newey (1985) and Tauchen (1985) principle of moment tests, Pagan and Sabau (1987b) suggested a consistency test for ARCH models. The test is based on the moment condition $E[h_t(\varepsilon_t^2 - h_t)] = 0$. Therefore, the test could be carried out by regressing $\hat{\varepsilon}_t^2 - \hat{h}_t$ on a constant and $\hat{h}_t$, and testing whether the coefficient of $\hat{h}_t$ is zero. However, if $\hat{h}_t$ is symmetric and the model is not of the ARCH-M type, then mis-specification of $\hat{h}_t$ will not lead to inconsistency and consequently the test will not have any power.

In most ARCH models, mis-specification may not lead to inconsistency, but it might make likelihood-based inference invalid. In that case, mis-specification can be tested through the information matrix equality, i.e. by testing $A = B$ which are defined in equation (71). Bera and Zuo (1991) suggested such a test. One component of the information matrix test can be calculated by running a regression of $\hat{\varepsilon}_t^{*4} - 6\hat{\varepsilon}_t^{*2} + 3$ on the cross-products of $\hat{\varepsilon}_{t-i}^{*2}$, where $\hat{\varepsilon}_t^* = \hat{\varepsilon}_t / \hat{h}_t^{1/2}$ is as above. This is essentially a test for heterokurtosis, and it can also be viewed as a test for randomness of the parameters in the specified h_t.

Another simple test for an estimated ARCH model like (3) is derived in Higgins and Bera (1992). The relevant null hypothesis for this is $H_0 : \delta = 1$ in the NARCH model (29). The LM statistic for testing H_0 can be calculated by running a regression of $\hat{\varepsilon}_t^2$ on z_t, where

$$z_t = (1, \hat{\varepsilon}_{t-1}^2, \ldots, \hat{\varepsilon}_{t-q}^2, \pi_t - \hat{h}_t \log(\hat{h}_t))$$

with

$$\pi_t = \sum_{i=1}^{q} \hat{\alpha}_i \hat{\varepsilon}_{t-i}^2 \log(\hat{\varepsilon}_{t-i}^2).$$

The test can be viewed as a diagnostic check of the adequacy of the ARCH model (3) after it has been estimated. Starting from a different alternative model, Hall (1990) derived a simple LM test for an estimated ARCH model. The alternative distribution for his heteroskedastic normal model is that the distribution is a member of the family with semiparametric probability density functions considered by Gallant and Tauchen (1989). His test is based on the possible correlations of $\hat{\varepsilon}_t / \hat{h}_t$ and $\hat{\varepsilon}_t^2 / \hat{h}_t^2$ with the information set. Simulation results reported in his paper indicate that the LM test which uses all the information under the null hypothesis has good finite-sample properties in moderate to large samples.

Engle and Ng (1991) proposed a battery of tests designed to detect mis-specification of a maintained conditional variance function. Let S_t^- be a dummy variable that takes the value 1 when ε_{t-1} is negative and zero otherwise. Similarly, let S_t^+ be a dummy variable that takes the value 1 when ε_{t-1} is positive and zero otherwise. Engle and Ng suggested standardizing the residual with the null h_t, regressing $\hat{\varepsilon}_t^{*2}$ on an intercept, $S_t^-, S_t^- \hat{\varepsilon}_{t-1}$ and $S_t^+ \hat{\varepsilon}_{t-1}$, and testing that the coefficients on the three constructed regressors are zero using an F or TR^2 statistic. The first regressor, S_t^-, represents the *sign bias* test which is intended to detect an asymmetric influence by the lagged negative and positive errors on the conditional variance which may not be incorporated in the conditional variance function specified under the null hypothesis. The second regressor, $S_t^- \hat{\varepsilon}_{t-1}$, should be significant if the impact of large negative errors versus small negative errors on the conditional variance is different from the impact implied by the null h_t. This component of the regression is called the *negative size bias* test. The third regressor, $S_t^+ \hat{\varepsilon}_{t-1}$, represents the *positive size bias* test and should detect different impacts of large positive errors versus small positive errors on the conditional variance. Engle and Ng point out that the components of the test can be conducted individually if a particular form of mis-specification is suspected.

The introduction of conditional heteroskedasticity in econometrics also leads to another interesting problem. Diebold (1986b) demonstrated that the presence of ARCH invalidates the standard asymptotic distribution theory of the sample autocorrelations, and hence of the Box–Pierce and Box–Ljung test statistics for serial correlation. For simplicity, consider the test for $\phi_1 = 0$ in

$$y_t = x_t \xi + \varepsilon_t$$

$$\varepsilon_t = \psi_1 \varepsilon_{t-1} + u_t$$

(77)

where $u_t \sim (0, \sigma_u^2)$ and $\mathrm{var}(\varepsilon_t \mid \Psi_{t-1}) = \alpha_0 + \alpha_1 \varepsilon_{t-1}^2$. As we noted, having ARCH of the above form is equivalent to ϕ_1 being random or u_t being heteroskedastic. Then the problem is equivalent to testing for the significance of a regression coefficient under heteroskedasticity. We know that the use of White's (1980) consistent estimator for the variance–covariance matrix provides asymptotically valid inference in the presence of an unknown form of heteroskedasticity. Therefore, a robust way to test $\phi_1 = 0$ is to run a regression of the OLS residuals $\hat{\varepsilon}_t$ on x_t and $\hat{\varepsilon}_{t-1}$ and test the significance of the coefficient of $\hat{\varepsilon}_{t-1}$ using White's standard error. Wooldridge (1990) suggested exactly this procedure for testing autocorrelation in the presence of ARCH (see also Davidson and MacKinnon, 1985; Bollerslev and Wooldridge, 1992; MacKinnon, 1992). Note that the standard LM approach for testing first-order autocorrelation is to regress $\hat{\varepsilon}_t$ on x_t and $\hat{\varepsilon}_{t-1}$ and use a TR^2 statistic. The robust procedure involves two regressions:

1   run $\hat{\varepsilon}_{t-1}$ on x_t and save the residuals as $\tilde{\varepsilon}_{t-1}$;
2   compute TR^2 from running 1 on $\hat{\varepsilon}_t \tilde{\varepsilon}_{t-1}$.

The statistic TR^2 asymptotically follows a χ_1^2 distribution under the null hypothesis of no serial correlation. Steps 1 and 2 are equivalent to using White's consistent variance-covariance matrix estimator as mentioned above. Monte Carlo results reported in Bollerslev and Wooldridge (1992) indicate that the size of the robust version of the LM test is much closer to the nominal size than the size of the standard LM test. Bera et al. (1992) derived LM tests for autocorrelation which take account of specific forms of ARCH disturbances. Of course, the validity of such tests depends on the correct specification of the ARCH process. In practice, the tests could be very useful by specifying different forms of conditional heteroskedasticity and then testing for serial correlation. Being fully parametric, this test could be expected to have higher power when h_t is specified correctly.

10 Epilogue

Research on modelling conditional first moments started many decades ago, and that field is still very active. The problems currently being investigated, just to name a few, are structural change, different kinds of nonlinearities, cointegration and finite-sample properties of estimators and test statistics. It is safe to say that most of the problems encountered in modelling the first moment also transmits to ARCH, i.e. conditional second moment modelling. In this survey paper, we have provided a brief account of these problems. For years to come, researchers will be occupied with topics like structural change in ARCH, co-persistence, asymptotic and finite-sample statistical inference for ARCH, and procedures robust in the presence of ARCH. We have also noted that ARCH models have their own unique problems which are not present in modelling the conditional mean. Gradually, we will also see more rigorous economic foundations for ARCH models than those currently available. Therefore, the frontiers of ARCH will keep on moving further, though possibly not at the spectacular rate we observed in its first decade of existence. The success of ARCH might even tempt researchers to model higher order moments – the third and fourth – in a systematic way. From that we might learn more about the behaviour of speculative prices, and economic variables in general, a tradition started by Louis Bachelier almost a century ago.

Notes

We are grateful to three anonymous referees and editor Les Oxley for many helpful suggestions and detailed comments on the earlier version of the paper. Thanks are also due to Ken Kroner for his comments. However, we retain the responsibility for any remaining errors. Financial support from the Research Board of the University of Illinois is gratefully acknowledged.

Glossary

AARCH	augmented autoregressive conditional heteroskedasticity
ARCD	autoregressive conditional density
ARCH	autoregressive conditional heteroskedasticity
ARCH-M	autoregressive conditional heteroskedasticity in the mean
EGARCH	exponential autoregressive conditional heteroskedasticity
GARCH	generalized autoregressive conditional heteroskedasticity
IGARCH	integrated generalized autoregressive conditional heteroskedasticity
NARCH	nonlinear autoregressive conditional heteroskedasticity
PNP ARCH	partially nonparametric autoregressive conditional heteroskedasticity
QARCH	quadratic autoregressive conditional heteroskedasticity
QTARCH	qualitative threshold autoregressive conditional heteroskedasticity
TARCH	threshold autoregressive conditional heteroskedasticity

References

Andel, J. (1976) Autoregressive series with random parameters. *Mathematische Operations forschung und Statistik, Series Statistics*, 7, 736–41.

Andrews, D. W. K. (1993) An introduction to econometric applications of empirical process theory for dependent random variables. *Econometric Reviews*, forthcoming.

—— and Ploberger, W. (1992) Optimal tests when a nuisance parameter is present only under the alternative. *Cowles Foundation Discussion Paper* 1015.

Baba, Y., Engle, R. F., Kraft, D. F. and Kroner, K. F. (1990) Multivariate simultaneous generalized ARCH. Mimeo, Department of Economics, University of California at San Diego.

Bachelier, L. (1900) Théorie de la spéculation. *Annales de l'Ecole Normale Supérieure*, 17, 21–86.

Baillie, R. T. and Bollerslev, T. (1989) The message in daily exchange rates: a conditional variance tale. *Journal of Business and Economic Statistics*, 7, 297–305.

—— and —— (1990) A multivariate generalized ARCH approach to modeling risk premia in forward foreign exchange rate markets. *Journal of International Money and Finance*, 16, 109–24.

—— and —— (1992) Prediction in dynamic models with time-dependent conditional variances. *Journal of Econometrics*, 52, 91–113.

—— and Myers, R. J. (1991) Bivariate GARCH estimation of optimal commodity futures hedge. *Journal of Applied Econometrics*, 16, 109–24.

Bekaert, G. (1992) The time-variation of expected returns and volatility in foreign exchange markets. Mimeo, Northwestern University.

Bera, A. K. and Higgins, M. L. (1992) A test for conditional heteroskedasticity in time series models. *Journal of Time Series Analysis*, 13, 501–19.

—— and Lee, S. (1993) Information matrix test, parameter heterogeneity and ARCH: a synthesis. *Review of Economic Studies*, 60, 229–40.

—— and Ng, P. T. (1991) Robust tests for heteroskedasticity and autocorrelation using score functions. Mimeo, Department of Economics, University of Illinois at Urbana-Champaign.

—— and Ra, S-S. (1991) A test for conditional heteroskedasticity in the ARCH-M model. Mimeo, Department of Economics, University of Illinois at Urbana-Champaign.

—— and Roh, J.-S. (1991) A moment test of the constancy of the correlation coefficient in the bivariate GARCH model. Mimeo, Department of Economics, University of Illinois at Urbana-Champaign.

—— and Zuo, X. (1991) Specification test for a linear regression model with ARCH process. Mimeo, Department of Economics, University of Illinois at Urbana-Champaign.

——, Higgins, M. L. and Lee, S. (1990) On the formulation of a general structure for conditional heteroskedasticity. Mimeo, Department of Economics, University of Illinois at Urbana-Champaign.

——, Garcia, P. and Roh, J.-S. (1991) Estimation of time-varying hedge ratios for agricultural commodities: BGARCH and random coefficient approaches. Mimeo, Department of Economics, University of Illinois at Urbana-Champaign.

——, —— and —— (1992) Interaction between autocorrelation and conditional heteroskedasticity: a random coefficient approach. *Journal of Business and Economic Statistics*, 10, 133–42.

Berndt, E. K., Hall, B. H., Hall, R. E. and Hausman, J. (1974) Estimation and inference in nonlinear structural models. *Annals of Economic and Social Measurement*, 4, 653–65.

Bollerslev, T. (1986) A generalized autoregressive conditional heteroskedasticity. *Journal of Econometrics*, 31, 307–27.

—— (1987) A conditionally heteroskedastic time series model for speculative prices and rates of return. *Review of Economics and Statistics*, 69, 542–7.

—— (1988) On the correlation structure of the generalized autoregressive conditional heteroskedastic process. *Journal of Time Series Analysis*, 9, 121–31.

—— (1990) Modelling the coherence in short-run nominal exchange rates: a multivariate generalized ARCH approach. *Review of Economics and Statistics*, 72, 498–505.

—— and Engle, R. F. (1989) Common persistence in conditional variances. *Econometrica*, 61, 167–86.

—— and Hodrick, R. J. (1992) Financial market efficiency tests. *Kellogg Graduate School of Management Working Paper* 132.

—— and Wooldridge, J. M. (1992) Quasi-maximum likelihood estimation and inference in dynamic models with time-varying covariances. *Econometric Reviews*, 11, 143–79.

——, Engle, R. F. and Wooldridge, J. M. (1988) A capital asset pricing model with time-varying covariances. *Journal of Political Economy*, 96, 116–31.

——, Chou, R. Y. and Kroner, K. F. (1992) ARCH modelling in finance: a review of the theory and empirical evidence. *Journal of Econometrics*, 52, 5–59.

Bougerol, P. and Picard, N. (1992) Stationarity of GARCH processes and of some nonnegative time series. *Journal of Econometrics*, 52, 115–27.

Box, G. and Jenkins, G. (1976) *Time Series Analysis, Forecasting and Control*, revised ed. San Francisco, CA: Holden-Day.

Breusch, T. S. and Pagan, A. R. (1979) A simple test for heteroskedasticity and random coefficient variation. *Econometrica*, 47, 239–53.

Brock, W., Dechert, W. D. and Scheinkman, J. (1987) A test for independence based on the correlation dimension. Mimeo, University of Wisconsin-Madison.

——, Hsieh, D. A. and LeBaron, B. (1991) *Nonlinear Dynamics, Chaos and Instability*. Cambridge, MA: MIT Press.

Chesher, A. D. (1984) Testing for neglected heterogeneity. *Econometrica*, 52, 865–71.

Cheung, Y-W. and Pauly, P. (1990) Random coefficient modelling of conditionally heteroskedastic processes: short run exchange rate dynamics. Paper presented at the International Conference on ARCH Models, June 1990, Paris.

Clark, P. K. (1973) A subordinated stochastic process model with finite variance for speculative prices. *Econometrica*, 41, 135–56.

Davidson, R. and MacKinnon, J. G. (1985) Heteroskedasticity-robust tests in regression directions. *Annales de l'INSEE*, 59/60, 183–218.

Davies, R. B. (1977) Hypothesis testing when a nuisance parameter is present only under the alternative. *Biometrika*, 64, 247–54.

—— (1987) Hypothesis testing when a nuisance parameter is present only under the alternative. *Biometrika*, 74, 33–43.

Demos, A. and Sentana, E. (1991) Testing for GARCH effects: a one-sided approach. Mimeo, Financial Market Group, London School of Economics.

Diebold, F. X. (1986a) Modelling the persistence of conditional variances: a comment. *Econometric Reviews*, 5, 51–6.

—— (1986b) Testing for serial correlation in the presence of heteroskedasticity. *Proceedings of the American Statistical Association, Business and Economic Statistics Section*, 323–8.

—— (1988) *Empirical Modeling of Exchange Rate Dynamics*. New York: Springer.

—— and Nason, J. A. (1990) Nonparametric exchange rate prediction. *Journal of International Economics*, 28, 315–32.

—— and Nerlove, M. (1989) The dynamics of exchange rate volatility: a multivariate latent factor ARCH model. *Journal of Applied Econometrics*, 4, 1–21.

Domowitz, I. and Hakkio, C. S. (1985) Conditional variance and the risk premium in the foreign exchange market. *Journal of International Economics*, 19, 47–66.

Drost, F. C. and Nijman, T. E. (1992) Temporal aggregation of GARCH processes. *Econometrica*, forthcoming.

Duffee, G. R. (1992) Reexamining the relationship between stock returns and stock return volatility. *Federal Reserve Board Finance and Economics Discussion Series* 191.

Engle, R. F. (1982) Autoregressive conditional heteroskedasticity with estimates of the variance of U.K. inflation. *Econometrica*, 50, 987–1008.

—— (1983) Estimates of the variance of U.S. inflation based upon the ARCH model. *Journal of Money, Credit, and Banking*, 15, 286–301.

—— (1987) Multivariate ARCH with factor structures – cointegration in variance. *Discussion Paper* 87–27, University of California at San Diego.

—— and Bollerslev, T. (1986) Modelling the persistence of conditional variances. *Econometric Reviews*, 5, 1–87.

—— and González-Rivera, G. (1991) Semiparametric ARCH models. *Journal of Business and Economic Statistics*, 9, 345–59.

—— and Kraft, D. (1983) Multiperiod forecast error variances of inflation estimated from ARCH models. In A. Zellner (ed.), *Applied Time Series Analysis of Economic Data*, Washington, DC: Bureau of the Census.

—— and Ng, V. K. (1991) Measuring and testing the impact of news on volatility. Mimeo, Department of Economics, University of California at San Diego.

——, Hendry, D. and Trumble, D. (1985) Small-sample properties of ARCH estimates and tests. *Canadian Journal of Economics*, 18, 66–93.

——, Granger, C. W. J. and Kraft, D. (1986) Combining competing forecasts of inflation using a bivariate ARCH model. *Journal of Economic Dynamics and Control*, 8, 151–65.

——, Lilien, D. M. and Robins, R. P. (1987) Estimating time varying risk premia in the term structure: the ARCH-M model. *Econometrica*, 55, 391–407.

——, Ito, T. and Lin W-L. (1990a) Meteor showers or heat waves? Heteroskedastic intra-daily volatility in the foreign exchange market. *Econometrica*, 58, 525–42.

——, Ng, V. and Rothschild, M. (1990b) Asset pricing with a FACTOR-ARCH covariance structure: empirical estimates for treasury bills. *Journal of Econometrics*, 45, 213–37.

French, K. R., Schwert, G. W. and Stambaugh, R. F. (1987) Expected stock returns and volatility. *Journal of Financial Economics*, 19, 3–30.

Gallant, A. R. (1982) Unbiased determination of production technologies. *Journal of Econometrics*, 20, 285–323.

—— and Tauchen, G. (1989) Seminonparametric estimation of conditionally constrained heterogeneous processes: asset pricing applications. *Econometrica*, 57, 1091–1129.

——, Hsieh, D. A. and Tauchen, G. (1991) On fitting a recalcitrant series: the pound/dollar exchange rate, 1974–1983. In W. A. Barnett, J. Powell and G. Tauchen (eds), *Nonparametric and Semiparametric Methods in Econometrics and Statistics*, Cambridge: Cambridge University Press.

Geweke, J. (1986) Modelling the persistence of conditional variances: comment. *Econometric Reviews*, 5, 57–61.

—— (1988a) Comments on Poirier: operational Bayesian methods in econometrics. *Journal of Economic Perspectives*, 2, 159–66.

—— (1988b) Exact inference in models with autoregressive conditional heteroskedasticity. In E. Berndt, H. White and W. Barnett (eds), *Dynamic Econometric Modeling*, Cambridge: Cambridge University Press.

—— (1989) Exact predictive densities in linear models with ARCH disturbances. *Journal of Econometrics*, 44, 307–25.

Glejser, H. (1969) A new test for heteroskedasticity. *Journal of the American Statistical Association*, 64, 316–23.

Glosten, L. R., Jagannathan, R. and Runkle, D. (1991) Relationship between the expected value and the volatility of the nominal excess return on stocks. Mimeo, Northwestern University.

Godfrey, L. G. (1978) Testing for multiplicative heteroskedasticity. *Journal of Econometrics*, 8, 227–36.

Gourieroux, C. and Monfort, A. (1992) Qualitative threshold ARCH models. *Journal of Econometrics*, 52, 159–99.

Granger, C. W. J. and Andersen, A. P. (1978) *An Introduction to Bilinear Time Series Models.* Göttingen: Vandenhoeck and Ruprecht.

——, Robins, R. P. and Engle, R. F. (1984) Wholesale and retail prices: bivariate time series modeling with forecastable error variances. In D. A. Belsley and E. Kuh (eds), *Model Reliability*, Cambridge, MA: MIT Press.

Hall, A. (1990) Lagrange multiplier tests for normality against semiparametric alternatives. *Journal of Business and Economic Statistics*, 8, 417–26.

Hansen, B. E. (1991) Inference when a nuisance parameter is not identified under the null hypothesis. *Rochester Center for Economic Research Working Paper* 296.

—— (1992) Autoregressive conditional density estimation, *Rochester Center for Economic Research Working Paper* 332.

Hansen, L. P. (1982) Large sample properties of the method of moment estimators. *Econometrica*, 50, 1029–54.

Harvey, A., Ruiz, E. and Sentana, E. (1992) Unobserved component time series models with ARCH disturbances. *Journal of Econometrics*, 52, 129–57.

Higgins, M. L. and Bera, A. K. (1989) A joint test for ARCH and bilinearity in the regression model. *Econometric Reviews*, 7, 171–81.

—— and —— (1991) ARCH and bilinearity as competing models for nonlinear dependence. Mimeo, Department of Economics, University of Wisconsin-Milwaukee.

—— and —— (1992) A class of nonlinear ARCH models. *International Economic Review*, 33, 137–58.

—— and Majin, S. (1992) Measuring the volatility of the *ex ante* real interest rate: a structural ARCH approach. Mimeo, University of Wisconsin-Milwaukee.

Hong, P. Y. (1991) The autocorrelation structure for the GARCH-M process. *Economic Letters*, 37, 129–32.

Hsieh, D. A. (1988) The statistical properties of daily foreign exchange rates: 1974–1983. *Journal of International Economics*, 24, 129–45.

—— (1989) Testing for nonlinear dependence in daily foreign exchange rate changes. *Journal of Business*, 62, 339–68.

Kim, C. M. (1989) Volatility effect on time series behavior of exchange rate changes. Working Paper, Korea Institute for International Economic Policy.

Klien, B. (1977) The demand for quality-adjusted cash balances: price uncertainty in the U.S. demand for money function. *Journal of Political Economy*, 85, 692–715.

Koedijk, K. G., Stork, P. A. and De Vries, C. G. (1992) Conditional heteroskedasticity, realignments and the European monetary system. Mimeo, Katholieke Universiteit Leuven.

Kroner, K. F. (1988) Estimating and testing for factor ARCH. Mimeo, University of Arizona.

—— and Claessens, S. (1991) Optimal currency composition of external debt: applications to Indonesia and Turkey. *Journal of International Money and Finance*, 10, 131–48.

—— and Sultan, J. (1991) Exchange rate volatility and time varying hedge ratios. In S. G. Rhee and R. P. Change (eds), *Pacific-Basin Capital Markets Research*, vol. II, Amsterdam: North-Holland.

Lamoureux, G. C. and Lastrapes, W. D. (1990a) Heteroskedasticity in stock return data: volume versus GARCH effects. *Journal of Finance*, 45, 221–9.

—— and —— (1990b) Persistence in variance, structural change, and the GARCH model. *Journal of Business and Economic Statistics*, 8, 225–34.

LeBaron, B. (1992) Some relations between volatility and serial correlations in stock market returns. *Journal of Business*, 65, 199–219.

Lee, J. H. (1991) A Lagrange multiplier test for GARCH models. *Economic Letters*, 37, 265–71.

—— and M. L. King (1991) A locally most mean powerful based score test for ARCH and GARCH regression disturbances. *Journal of Business and Economic Statistics*, 11, 17–27.

Lee, S.-W. (1991) Asymptotic properties of the maximum likelihood estimator of the GARCH-M and IGARCH-M models. Mimeo, Department of Economics, University of Rochester.

—— and Hansen, B. E. (1991) Asymptotic properties of the maximum likelihood estimator and test of the stability of parameters of the GARCH and IGARCH models. Mimeo, Department of Economics, University of Rochester.

Lee, T. K. Y. and Tse, Y. K. (1991) Term structure of interest rates in the Singapore Asian dollar market. *Journal of Applied Econometrics*, 6, 143–52.

Lin, W.-L. (1992) Alternative estimators for factor GARCH models – a Monte Carlo comparison. *Journal of Applied Econometrics*, 7, 259–79.

Lumsdaine, R. L. (1991a) Asymptotic properties of the quasi-maximum likelihood estimator in GARCH(1, 1) and IGARCH(1, 1) models. Mimeo, Department of Economics, Princeton University.

—— (1991b) Finite sample properties of the maximum likelihood estimator in GARCH(1, 1) and IGARCH(1, 1) models: a Monte Carlo investigation. Mimeo, Department of Economics, Princeton University.

MacKinnon, J. G. (1992) Model specification tests and artificial regression. *Journal of Economic Literature*, 30, 102–46.

Mandelbrot, B. (1963a) The variation of certain speculative prices. *Journal of Business*, 36, 394–419.

—— (1963b) New methods in statistical economics. *Journal of Political Economy*, 71, 421–40.

—— (1967) The variation of some other speculative prices. *Journal of Business*, 40, 393–413.

McCurdy, T. H. and Morgan, I. (1988) Testing the martingale hypothesis in Deutsche mark futures with models specifying the form of the heteroskedasticity. *Journal of Applied Econometrics*, 3, 187–202.

McLeod, A. I. and Li, W. K. (1983) Diagnostic checking ARMA time series models using squared-residual autocorrelations. *Journal of Time Series Analysis*, 4, 269–73.

Milhøj, A. (1985) The moment structure of ARCH processes. *Scandinavian Journal of Statistics*, 12, 281–92.

—— (1987a) A multiplicative parameterization of ARCH models. *Research Report* 101, Institute of Statistics, University of Copenhagen.

—— (1987b) A conditional variance model for daily observations of an exchange rate. *Journal of Business and Economic Statistics*, 5, 99–103.

Mizrach, B. (1990) Learning and conditional heteroskedasticity in asset returns. Mimeo, Department of Finance, The Wharton School, University of Pennsylvania.

Nelson, D. B. (1990a) Stationarity and persistence in the GARCH(1, 1) model. *Econometric Theory*, 6, 318–34.

—— (1990b) ARCH models as diffusion approximations. *Journal of Econometrics*, 45, 7–38.

—— (1991) Conditional heteroskedasticity in asset returns: a new approach. *Econometrica*, 59, 347–70.

—— and Cao, C. Q. (1992) Inequality constraints in the univariate GARCH model. *Journal of Business and Economic Statistics*, 10, 229–35.

Newey, W. (1985) Maximum likelihood specification testing and conditional moment tests. *Econometrica*, 53, 1047–70.

Ng, V. K. and Pirrong, S. C. (1992) Disequilibrium adjustment, volatility, and price discovery in spot and futures markets. Mimeo, University of Michigan.

——, Engle, R. F. and Rothschild, M. (1992) A multi-dynamic-factor model for stock returns. *Journal of Econometrics*, 52, 245–66.

Nicholls, D. F. and Quinn, B. G. (1982) *Random Coefficient Autoregressive Models: An Intro-duction*. New York: Springer.

Oedegaard, B. A. (1991) Empirical tests of changes in autocorrelation of stock index returns. Mimeo, Graduate School of Industrial Administration, Carnegie Mellon University.

Pagan, A. R. and Hong, Y. S. (1991) Nonparametric estimation and the risk premium. In W. A. Barnett, J. Powell and G. Tauchen (eds), *Nonparametric and Semiparametric Methods in Econometrics and Statistics*, Cambridge: Cambridge University Press.

—— and Pak, Y. (1991) Tests for heteroskedasticity. In G. S. Maddala, C. R. Rao and H. D. Vinod (eds), *Handbook of Statistics*, vol. 11, Amsterdam: North-Holland.

—— and Sabau, H. (1987a) On the inconsistency of the MLE in certain heteroskedastic regression models. Mimeo, Department of Economics, University of Rochester.

—— and —— (1987b) Consistency tests for heteroskedastic and risk models. Mimeo, Department of Economics, University of Rochester.

—— and Schwert, G. W. (1990) Alternative models for conditional stock volatility. *Journal of Econometrics*, 45, 267–90.

—— and Ullah, A. (1988) The econometric analysis of models with risk terms. *Journal of Applied Econometrics*, 3, 87–105.

Pantula, S. G. (1986) Modelling the persistence of conditional variances: comment. *Econometric Reviews*, 5, 79–97.

—— (1988) Estimation of autoregressive models with ARCH errors. *Sankhyā: The Indian Journal of Statistics, Series B*, 50, 119–38.

Rabemananjara, R. and Zakoian, J. M. (1993) Threshold ARCH models and asymmetries in volatility. *Journal of Applied Econometrics*, 8, 31–49.

Ray, D. (1983) On the autoregressive model with random coefficients. *Calcutta Statistical Association Bulletin*, 32, 135–42.

Rich, R. W., Raymond, J. and Butler, J. S. (1991) Generalized instrumental variables estimation of autoregressive conditional heteroskedastic models. *Economics Letters*, 35, 179–85.

Sabau, H. C. L. (1987) The structure of GMM and ML estimators in conditionally heteroskedastic models. Working Paper 153, Faculty of Economics, Australian National University.

—— (1988) Some theoretical aspects of econometric inference with heteroskedastic models. Ph.D. dissertation, Australian National University.

Sentana, E. (1991) Quadratic ARCH models: a potential re-interpretation of ARCH models. Mimeo, Department of Economics and Financial Markets Group, London School of Economics.

—— and Wadhwani, S. (1991) Feedback traders and stock returns autocorrelations: evidence from a century of daily data. *Review of Economic Studies*, 58, 547–63.

Spanos, A. (1991) A parametric approach to dynamic heteroskedasticity: the Student's *t* and related models. Mimeo, Department of Economics, Virginia Polytechnic Institute and State University.

Stock, J. H. (1988) Estimating continuous-time processes subject to time deformation. *Journal of the American Statistical Association*, 83, 77–85.

Tauchen, G. (1985) Diagnostic testing and evaluation of maximum likelihood models. *Journal of Econometrics*, 30, 415–43.

—— and Pitts, M. (1983) The price variability–volume relationship on speculative markets. *Econometrica*, 51, 485–505.

Taylor, S. J. (1986) *Modelling Financial Time Series*. Chichester: Wiley.

—— (1990) Modelling stochastic volatility. Mimeo, Department of Accounting and Finance, University of Lancaster.

Tong, H. (1990) *Non-linear Time Series, A Dynamical System Approach.* Oxford: Clarendon Press.

Tsay, R. S. (1987) Conditional heteroskedastic time series models. *Journal of the American Statistical Association*, 82, 590–604.

Weiss, A. A. (1986a) Asymptotic theory for ARCH models: estimation and testing. *Econometric Theory*, 2, 107–31.

—— (1986b) ARCH and bilinear time series models: comparison and combination. *Journal of Business and Economic Statistics*, 4, 59–70.

White, H. (1980) A heteroskedastic-consistent covariance matrix and a direct test for heteroskedasticity. *Econometrica*, 48, 421–48.

—— (1982) Maximum likelihood estimation of misspecified models. *Econometrica*, 50, 1–25.

Wooldridge, J. M. (1990) A unified approach to robust regression-based specification tests. *Econometric Theory*, 6, 17–43.

Zakoian, J.-M. (1990) Threshold heteroskedastic model. Mimeo, INSEE, Paris.

9 Nonlinear time series models in economics

Terence C. Mills
University of Hull

1 Introduction

The last decade or so has witnessed a surge of interest in the examination of nonlinear phenomena in economics. Although the roots of nonlinear economic dynamics lie in the trade cycle models of Kaldor (1940), Hicks (1950) and Goodwin (1951), new models of nonlinear dynamics are now being developed in many areas: for an impressive list of references, see the excellent recent survey by Baumol and Benhabib (1989).

A major reason for this explosion of interest is that the presence of nonlinearities, particularly those characterized by 'chaos', has been shown to have important implications for the properties of many theoretical economic models. Grandmont (1985), for example, develops a deterministic macroeconomic model which leads to substantially more activist policy conclusions than do typical rational expectations models, while Day and Shafer (1985) show that both cyclic and chaotic dynamic behaviour can easily arise in the standard fixed price Keynesian model with a nonlinear investment schedule. Baumol and Benhabib (1989) provide references that show that both cyclic and chaotic dynamics can arise in a number of competitive models of intertemporal general equilibrium, these being of interest since they demonstrate that prices and output can oscillate even under standard competitive assumptions such as market clearing, perfect information and perfect foresight.

The presence of undetected nonlinearities can also make forecasting extremely difficult, since the two basic forecasting devices – extrapolation and the estimation of a structural forecasting model – both become questionable when, for example, time paths of economic variables may exhibit vastly fluctuating patterns of oscillation, which alter without warning, and when small changes in parameter values of an underlying model (which can, after all, only be estimated from limited data sets) may alter the qualitative character of the forecast beyond recognition. These effects are both features of chaotic dynamics and a detailed discussion of the implications such phenomena have for forecasting is to be found in Baumol and Quandt (1985).

Many dynamic economic models can be characterized by a difference equation in a single variable (as, for example, the Samuelson model of the accelerator–multiplier cycle). It is also the case that any theorem about nonlinear behaviour in n-dimensional simultaneous first-order systems (another popular characterization of dynamic economic models) must also apply to a single nth-order difference equation. Since difference equations also lie at the heart of extrapolative methods of forecasting, we will focus attention on nonlinear extensions to the general class of model that such equations belong to, the auto regressive integrated moving average (ARIMA) process, which has been extensively analysed and popularized by Box and Jenkins (1976).

Our point of departure, therefore, will be the standard ARIMA model for a single, non-seasonal, time series $\{x_t\}$:

$$\phi(B)\nabla^d x_t = \theta_0 + \theta(B)a_t \tag{1}$$

where B is the lag operator whose defining property is $B^j x_t = x_{t-j}$ and $\nabla = 1 - B$ is the difference operator. The appearance of $\nabla^d x_t$ in (1) implies that x_t has been differenced d times: x_t thus has d *unit roots* and, equivalently, is said to be integrated of order d, denoted I(d) (see Engle and Granger, 1987).

This definition of integration is strictly correct only if the polynomials $\phi(B) = 1 - \phi_1 B - \cdots - \phi_p B^p$ and $\theta(B) = 1 - \theta_1 B - \cdots - \theta_q B^q$ have no unit roots themselves. More precisely, we must assume that $\phi(B) = 0$ and $\theta(B) = 0$ have roots which lie outside the unit circle, so that both polynomials are invertible: $\nabla^d x_t$ is then stationary and invertible, being generated by an ARMA(p, q) process. The integrated series x_t is generated by an ARIMA(p, d, q) process.

The error, or innovation, $\{a_t\}$ is typically assumed to be a sequence of independent, zero mean random variables, with constant variance σ_a^2, drawn from a fixed distribution, usually the normal (or Gaussian), i.e. $\{a_t\}$ is assumed to be white noise.

Although the introductory discussion of nonlinearity has emphasized the concept of 'chaotic dynamics', i.e. a dynamic mechanism that is very simple and deterministic yet yields a time path so complicated that it will pass most standard tests of randomness, the model (1) can be extended in many 'nonlinear' ways, if this term is defined in a flexible enough manner. We shall concentrate on four types of modifications, which we will argue have important implications for the way in which economists typically investigate the stochastic behaviour of observed time series.

Section 2 considers using transformations of x_t rather then x_t itself. All economists are familiar with the logarithmic transformation and most are acquainted with the class of power transformations introduced by Box and Cox (1964), of which the logarithmic is but a special case. They may be less familiar with the implications that the use of power transformations have for constructing forecasts of x_t and with methods of jointly estimating the transformation parameter along with the other parameters of the model. Also discussed in this section are other transformations that may be relevant to certain types of time series.

Section 3 considers relaxing the usual restriction that the order of integration d is a non-negative integer value, typically 0, 1 or, sometimes, 2. This leads to the class of *fractionally differenced* or, to borrow terminology from the hydrology literature, *long-memory* models. Such models have interesting implications for long-run forecasting and for the debate about how persistent shocks are to economic time series (see Diebold and Rudebusch, 1989).

The assumption that the innovation sequence $\{a_t\}$ is independently and identically distributed (IID) with constant variance can be relaxed in a number of ways. Of particular interest here is the case when we allow the sequence to be uncorrelated, rather than independent. While it is still true that, if we restrict attention to models that are just *linear* functions of past innovations, then these past values will contain no information with which to forecast the current innovation, they may well contain useful information if we allow *nonlinear* functions of past innovations; for a general discussion of this point, containing many examples, see Granger (1983).

While there are a wide variety of nonlinear models that have been developed in the time series literature to capture various departures from the standard assumption of constant variance IID innovations, many have found little application in economics. In section 4 we consider those nonlinear models that are, at least potentially, useful for modelling economic series, the majority of which have been explicitly designed to capture nonlinear economic phenomena rather than being taken from other scientific disciplines, such as engineering, geology and oceanography. One important class that do, however, have their origins in the natural sciences are the chaos models discussed above and the application of this concept to economics is discussed here, although, as surveys of chaos in economic models already exist (e.g. Baumol and Benhabib, 1989; Scheinkman, 1990), this discussion will necessarily be brief.

An important aspect of nonlinear modelling is detecting whether time series do, in fact, contain important nonlinearities and hence the development of testing procedures is paramount. It is important to emphasize that examining plots of the data will typically be of little use: many time series generated by nonlinear, possibly chaotic, processes are usually indistinguishable from random series. Such departures from linearity will therefore not be established by simple 'eyeballing' of the data, or even by using standard statistical tests of randomness. A number of the tests that have been proposed are discussed in section 5, where the evidence to date on the prevalence of nonlinearity in economic series is also surveyed. Section 6 completes the survey by providing a perspective on some of the current issues in nonlinear time series modelling in economics.

2   Transforming time series

2.1   Power transformations

The logarithmic transformation is frequently used in the modelling of economic time series. In regression models this is usually because such a transformation provides slope coefficients that can be interpreted as (constant) elasticities, but in univariate time series models it is used either because the first differences of the logarithms approximate the percentage change of the series, or because the level of the series appears to be related to its variability, specifically if it is proportional to the standard deviation. In the latter case, taking logarithms will help to induce more homoskedastic and normally distributed residuals.

If the level of the series is proportional to its *variance*, however, taking logarithms will 'over-transform' the series and the appropriate transformation is the square root. The well-known Box and Cox (1964) class of power transformations provides a general family to which the logarithmic and square root both belong. For a time series x_t, these transformations are given by

$$y_t = x_t^{(\lambda)} = \begin{cases} (x_t^\lambda - 1)/\lambda & \lambda \neq 0 \\ \ln x_t & \lambda = 0. \end{cases} \tag{2}$$

A model for y_t can then be developed from which forecasts may be generated. It is typically the case, however, that forecasts of the originally observed series x_t are required. An obvious way of calculating such forecasts is to apply the inverse of the power transformation (2) to the forecasts of y_t, i.e.

$$x_t = \begin{cases} (\lambda y_t + 1)^{1/\lambda} & \lambda \neq 0 \\ \exp(y_t) & \lambda = 0. \end{cases} \tag{3}$$

This 'naive' retransformation to obtain the forecast of x_t however, will, provide a minimum mean *absolute* error (MMAE) forecast, since it will equal the *median* of the conditional probability density function of x_t (see Pankratz and Dudley, 1987). This forecast is well known to be optimal for an *absolute* forecast error loss function, but typically in economics we assume the loss function to be *quadratic*, in which case a minimum mean *squared* error forecast (MMSE) will be optimal. This is given by the *mean* of the conditional probability density function of x_t. Thus, if a quadratic loss function is assumed, so that MMSE forecasts are optimal, two questions naturally arise: by how much do MMAE forecasts of x_t deviate from MMSE forecasts, and how can MMSE forecasts be found?

Granger and Newbold (1976) present general theoretical results for various transformations, but give results for only the two cases considered above, the logarithmic ($\lambda = 0$) and the square root ($\lambda = 0.5$). They show that when $\lambda = 0$ the MMSE h-step-ahead forecast made at origin n is given by

$$\hat{x}_{n+h} = \exp\left(\hat{y}_{n+h} + \frac{1}{2}\sigma_h^2\right)$$

where σ_h^2 is the h-step-ahead forecast error variance associated with $\hat{y}_{n+h}$. The relative bias from using the MMAE forecast

$$\tilde{x}_{n+h} = \exp(\hat{y}_{n+h})$$

is therefore

$$B = (\tilde{x}_{n+h} - \hat{x}_{n+h})/\hat{x}_{n+h} = \exp\left(-\frac{1}{2}\sigma_h^2\right) - 1.$$

When $\lambda = 0.5$, Granger and Newbold show that

$$\hat{x}_{n+h} = \hat{y}_{n+h}^2 + \sigma_h^2$$
$$\tilde{x}_{n+h} = \hat{y}_{n+h}^2$$

and so

$$B = -\frac{\sigma_h^2/\hat{y}_{n+h}^2}{1 + (\sigma_h^2/\hat{y}_{n+h}^2)}.$$

These theoretical results suggest that using the naive retransformation may give forecasts of x_t that deviate substantially from MMSE forecasts. In an empirical study, however, Nelson and Granger (1979) found using $\tilde{x}_{n+h}$ rather than $\hat{x}_{n+h}$ to be only moderately worthwhile, giving better forecasts in about 60 per cent of the cases when some twenty-one macroeconomic series were forecast over various horizons, with a similar performance being found in simulation experiments.

While a number of important qualifications to, and alternative interpretations of, Nelson and Granger's results were offered by Poirier (1980), the forecasting issue has recently been reinvestigated by Pankratz and Dudley (1987). In general, the relationship between $\hat{x}_{n+h}$ and $\tilde{x}_{n+h}$ is given by

$$\hat{x}_{n+h} = G\tilde{x}_{n+h}$$

where G is an integral with no closed form solution for a general value of λ. Pankratz and Dudley evaluate G numerically, providing values of the per cent bias

$$100B = \frac{100(1 - G)}{G}$$

for various combinations of λ and $r = \sigma_h/(\hat{y}_{n+h} + \lambda^{-1})$, the ratio of the forecast standard deviation of $\hat{y}_{n+h}$ to the sum of the forecast and the inverse of the power transformation. For many combinations ($|\lambda| > 0.1$, $|r| < 0.1$), only a small bias is found, often in the region of ± 1 per cent (Pankratz and Dudley show that we must have $|r| \leqslant 0.25$ for the transformation to produce a normal density for y_t having negligible truncation: this is related to one of Poirier's criticisms of the Nelson and Granger (1979) study). For $|\lambda| < 0.1$ and $|r| > 0.1$, however, the bias can be enormous; for example, the bias associated with $\lambda = 0.1$ and $r = 0.25$ is -86 per cent, while even for $|r| = 0.1$ the bias is -34 per cent!

These theoretical findings go a long way towards explaining the modest improvement in forecast accuracy reported by Nelson and Granger when a non-biasing procedure was used with the Box–Cox transformation. In twelve of their twenty-one series they found $\lambda > 0.6$, and Pankratz and Dudley provide evidence to suggest that the associated values of $|r|$ were rather small: exactly the conditions under which little bias is found. Furthermore, the greatest bias is found for values of λ close to zero, the value that is probably the most popular choice of econometricians.

2.2 Estimation issues

The discussion so far has avoided aspects of estimation. If we simply wish to choose a value of the transformation parameter λ independently of the other parameters of the ARIMA model to be fitted to $x_t^{(\lambda)}$, then there a number of methods available. Robust techniques based on exploratory methods of data analysis are discussed in Mills (1990, ch. 4), while more formal estimation techniques may be based on the maximum likelihood (ML) technique of Box and Cox (1964).

Unfortunately, as Granger and Newbold (1976) show theoretically and Nelson and Granger (1979) show by way of an empirical example, the identified ARIMA model tends to change as λ changes. Joint ML estimation of all parameters, with some alternatives, is discussed in Granger and Newbold (1977, ch. 9.2) and Nelson and Granger (1979), along with some of the potential drawbacks found using such methods. A major problem of using ML techniques is that the residuals from the ARIMA model fitted to $x_t^{(\lambda_0)}$, where λ_0 is the ML estimate of λ, are often still significantly non-normal; Nelson and Granger conclude that using power transformation takes the residuals nearer to normality but rarely does it actually achieve normality. An extension of the analysis to seasonal time series is provided by Ansley et al. (1977).

2.3   Other transformations

The class of power transformations (2) strictly are defined only for $x_t > 0$. As the majority of economic time series are naturally positive this does not often constitute a binding constraint, but even if negative values do occur, or at least have non-zero probability of occurring, a constant μ can always be added to ensure that $\Pr[(x_t + \mu) < 0]$ is negligible.

A more important data constraint is when a variable is bounded both from above and below. For a variable known to lie between 0 and 1, Wallis (1987) suggests using the logistic transformation

$$g(x_t) = \ln\left(\frac{x_t}{1 - x_t}\right)$$

and shows that this has a number of advantages over, for example, the logarithmic. In particular, an attractive feature of the logistic transformation is its symmetry. An example of a series bounded as $0 \leqslant x_t \leqslant 1$ is the unemployment rate, and hence $1 - x_t$ is its complement, the employment rate. Since

$$\ln\left(\frac{x_t}{1 - x_t}\right) = -\ln\left[\frac{1 - x_t}{1 - (1 - x_t)}\right]$$

the autocorrelation functions (ACFs) for the logistic transformations of x_t and $1 - x_t$ are identical and it is therefore of no consequence whether one chooses to work with the unemployment or the employment rate, which is certainly not true for the logarithmic transformation.

Other transformations have occasionally been used in the modelling of economic time series. Granger and Hughes (1971), for example, found that the transformation

$$g(x_t) = x_t \bigg/ \frac{1}{2m + 1} \sum_{j = -m}^{m} x_{t-j}$$

was useful when both the mean and variance trend together.

2.4   Asymmetric time series

As argued above, one of the principal reasons for employing a transformation is to turn a skewed marginal distribution into a more normal distribution. Wecker (1981) argues, however, that observed skewness in a time series might result from the series being generated by an *asymmetric* model, *i.e.* one in which x_t responds in a different fashion to the innovation a_t depending on whether the innovation is positive or negative. This may be illustrated by the asymmetric first-order moving average (MA(1)) process defined as

$$x_t = a_t - \theta^+ a_{t-1}^+ - \theta^- a_{t-1}^-$$

where

$$a_t^+ = \max(a_t, 0)$$

and

$$a_t^+ = \min(a_t, 0)$$

are positive and negative innovations respectively. Wecker shows that, unlike the symmetric MA(1) process where the mean of x_t is zero, the mean of the asymmetric MA(1) process is

$$\mu \frac{\theta^- - \theta^+}{\sqrt{2\pi}}$$

if we assume, for simplicity, that $a_t \sim N(0, 1)$. The asymmetric series x_t has variance

$$E(x_t - \mu)^2 = \sigma^2 = 1 + \frac{(\theta^+)^2 + (\theta^-)^2}{2} - \mu^2$$

and lag one autocovariance

$$E(x_t - \mu)(x_{t-1} - \mu) = \gamma_1 = -\frac{\theta^+ + \theta^-}{2}$$

with $\gamma_k = 0$ for $k \geqslant 2$. The symmetric MA(1) process is obtained when $\theta^+ = \theta^- = \theta$, in which case the familiar results $\mu = 0$, $\sigma^2 = 1 + \theta^2$ and $\gamma_1 = -\theta$ are obtained. Moreover, if $\theta^- = -\theta^-$, $\gamma_1 = 0$ and the asymmetric process becomes indistinguishable from white noise with mean $(-2\theta^+)/\sqrt{2\pi}$. Using this mean to make forecasts will result in a forecast error variance of

$$1 - \frac{\pi - 2}{\pi}(\theta^+)^2$$

rather than the true innovation variance of unity. For $-\theta^- = \theta^+ = -0.9$ this represents an increase in forecast error variance of about 30 per cent over what would be possible if the forecasts were made using the true asymmetric model.

Note that the sample ACF will give no clue as to whether the series is being generated by an asymmetric or a symmetric process, and any observed skewness in the marginal distribution of x_t may well prompt the application of a power transformation. Wecker suggests that, unknown to analysts, asymmetric time series may abound, but are analysed as either white noise processes, if $\theta^- \approx -\theta^+$, or as symmetric processes of power transformed series.

Wecker provides details of ML estimation and of a test for symmetry, and investigates the asymmetric MA(1) model on a variety of industrial price change series. Some of these series are quoted prices and, it is argued, should thus be asymmetric, while others, being transactions prices, should be symmetric. Wecker confirms these predictions, and also finds that for all asymmetric series the estimate of θ^- is large and positive, while that for θ^+ is small and non-positive, thus providing support for the view that when market conditions change, quoted prices are not revised immediately, this delay operating more strongly against reductions in price quotations than against increases.

3   Fractional integration and long-memory models

3.1   ARFIMA models

Much of the analysis of economic time series considers the case when the order of differencing, d, is either 0 or 1. If the latter, x_t is I(1) and its ACF declines linearly. If the former, x_t is stationary (I(0)) and its ACF will exhibit an exponential decay: observations separated by a long time span may therefore be assumed to be independent, or at least nearly so. The implications of economic time series being I(1), i.e. having a unit root, have been the subject of much analysis: Christiano and Eichenbaum (1990), for example, discuss the implications of output having a unit root for both the permanent income hypothesis and real business cycle models; the presence of a unit root is an implication of many models of efficient markets, and integration of individual series is a necessary pre-condition for a group of series to be cointegrated (Engle and Granger, 1987).

However, many empirically observed time series, although satisfying the assumption of stationarity (perhaps after some differencing transformation), exhibit a dependence between distant observations that, although small, is by no means negligible. Such series are particularly found in hydrology, where this 'persistence' is known as the Hurst phenomenon (see, for example, Mandelbrot and Wallis, 1969; Hosking, 1984), but many economic time series also exhibit similar characteristics of extremely long persistence. This may be characterized as a tendency for large values to be followed by large values of the same sign in such a way that the series seem to go through a succession of 'cycles', including long cycles whose length is comparable with the total sample size.

This viewpoint has been persuasively argued by Mandelbrot (1969, 1972) in extending his work on non-Gaussian (marginal) distributions in economics (Mandelbrot, 1963) to an exploration of the structure of serial dependence in economic time series. While Mandelbrot considered processes that were of the form of discrete-time fractional Gaussian noise, attention has recently focused on an extension of the ARIMA class (1) to model long-term persistence.

We have so far considered only integer values of d in (1). If d is non-integer, however, x_t is said to be *fractionally integrated*, and the model (1) for such values of d is referred to as ARFIMA (AR fractionally IMA) by Diebold and Rudebusch (1989). This notion of fractional integration (or, equivalently, fractional differencing) seems to have been proposed independently by Hosking (1981) and Granger and Joyeux (1980). To make the concept operational, we may use the binomial series expansion

$$\nabla^d = (1 - B)^d = \sum_{k=0}^{\infty} \begin{bmatrix} d \\ k \end{bmatrix} (-B)^k$$

$$= 1 - dB - \frac{d(1-d)}{2!}B^2 - \frac{d(1-d)(2-d)}{3!}B^3 - \cdots \qquad (4)$$

How does the ARFIMA model incorporate 'long-memory' behaviour? For $0 < d < \frac{1}{2}$, it can be shown that the ACF of such a model declines *hyperbolically* to zero, i.e. at a much slower rate than the exponential decay of a standard ARMA ($d = 0$) process. For $d \geqslant \frac{1}{2}$, the variance of x_t is infinite, and hence the process is non-stationary. Examples of how autocorrelations vary with d are provided in, for example, Hosking (1981) and Diebold and Rudebusch (1989). Typically, autocorrelations from fractionally integrated processes remain noticeably positive at very high lags, long after the autocorrelations from $I(0)$ processes have declined to (almost) zero.

Hosking (1982) has proposed a simple fractionally differenced model which combines both long memory and seasonality:

$$(1 - 2\phi B + B^2)^d x_t = a_t \qquad |d| < \frac{1}{2}, |\phi| < 1.$$

Despite having only two parameters, this model can describe a wide range of seasonal behaviour. Its ACF is characteristic of a damped sine wave in which correlations eventually die away to zero, unlike the non-stationary seasonal process $(1 - B^s)x_t = a_t$, but the rate of decay is less rapid than for the stationary process $(1 - \phi B^s)x_t = a_t$. Setting $\phi = 0.866$ corresponds to a seasonal period of $s = 12$, negative values of ϕ correspond to short periodicities and values near 1 yield ACFs reminiscent of the sample ACFs of ARIMA(0,1,0) or nearly non-stationary AR(1) processes.

The intuition behind the concept of long memory and the limitation of the integer-d restriction emerge more clearly in the frequency domain. $\{x_t\}$ will display long memory if its spectral density, $f_x(\vartheta)$, increases without limit as the frequency ϑ tends to zero:

$$\lim_{\vartheta \to 0} f_x(\vartheta) = \infty.$$

If $\{x_t\}$ is ARFIMA then $f_x(\vartheta)$ behaves like ϑ^{-2d} as $\vartheta \to 0$, so that d parameterizes its low frequency behaviour. When $d = 1$, $f_x(\vartheta)$ thus behaves like ϑ^{-2} as $\vartheta \to 0$, whereas when the integer-d restriction is relaxed a much richer range of spectral behaviour near the origin becomes possible. Indeed, the 'typical spectral shape' of economic time series (Granger, 1966), which exhibits montonically declining power as frequency increases (except at seasonals), is well captured by an $I(d)$ process with $0 < d < 1$. Moreover, although the levels of many series have spectra that appear to be infinite at the origin, and so might seem to warrant first differencing, after such differencing they often have no power at the origin. This suggests that first differencing takes out 'too much' and that using a fractional d is thus a more appropriate form of 'detrending'.

3.2   Estimation of ARFIMA models

Since it is the parameter d that enables long-term persistence to be modelled, the value chosen for it is obviously crucial in any empirical application. Typically, this value will be unknown and must therefore be estimated. A number of methods have been proposed, but there is yet to become a large enough body of experimental evidence to suggest which are the clearly superior techniques, although this will surely become available before long.

Some early suggestions are summarized in Mills (1990, ch. 11.7), and Pagan and Wickens (1989) discuss briefly ML estimation of d and tests to determine whether $d = 1$ or $d \neq 1$. The approach that seems the most successful, however, is that proposed by Geweke and Porter-Hudak (1983). By writing

$$(1 - B)^d x_t = (1 - B)(1 - B)^{d-1} x_t = (1 - B)^{\bar{d}} z_t,$$

where $z_t = (1 - B)x_t$ and $\bar{d} = d - 1$, the ARFIMA model can be written (ignoring the constant θ_0 for convenience) as

$$(1 - B)^{\bar{d}} z_t = \phi^{-1}(B)\theta(B)a_t = u_t.$$

The spectral density of z_t is given by

$$f_z(\vartheta) = |1 - \exp(-i\vartheta)|^{-2\bar{d}} f_u(\vartheta) = [4\sin^2(\vartheta/2)]^{-\bar{d}} f_u(\vartheta)$$

where $f_u(\vartheta)$ is the spectral density of the stationary process u_t. It then follows that

$$\ln\{f_z(\vartheta)\} = \ln\{f_u(\vartheta)\} - \bar{d}\ln\{4\sin^2(\vartheta/2)\}$$

and, given the sample $\{z_t, t = 1, \ldots, T\}$, this leads Geweke and Porter-Hudak to propose estimating d by regressing the periodogram $I_t(\vartheta_j)$ at frequencies $\vartheta_j = 2\pi j/T$, where $0 < k_1 \leqslant j \leqslant K \leqslant T$, against a constant and $\ln[4\sin^2(\vartheta_j/2)]$. As pointed out by Pagan and Wickens (1989), Kunsch (1986) shows that frequencies around the origin need to be excluded to get a consistent estimator, and shows how k_1 should vary with T. K should also expand with sample size and setting $K = T^{0.5}$ has been found to work well.

Having obtained an estimate of $\tilde{d}$, and hence d, x_t can be transformed by the long-memory filter (4), truncated at each point to the available sample. The transformed series is then modelled as an ARMA process. Further details of this procedure and discussion of its properties may be found in Geweke and Porter-Hudak (1983) and Diebold and Rudebusch (1989).

3.3   Applications of fractional integration

The potential macroeconomic relevance of ARFIMA models is demonstrated by Granger (1980) in the context of aggregation. Granger shows that if the components of an aggregate series follow AR(1) processes, and if the parameters of these processes are beta-distributed in the cross-section, then aggregation yields a fractionally integrated macroeconomic series. Haubrich and Lo (1989) exploit this result in a real business cycle model with beta-distributed intrasectoral input–output coefficients to obtain fractionally integrated aggregate output.

The presence of fractional integration in observed output is investigated by Diebold and Rudebusch (1989), specifically within the context of examining the persistence of macroeconomic fluctuations. They find that the long-run response of various US output series to innovations depends crucially on the estimate of d: in general the estimates are in the range $0.5 < d < 0.9$. Although long-memory behaviour is clearly found, the measures of persistence are rather less than those obtained when a 'unit root', $d = 1$, is assumed: the fifty-quarter impulse response of output to a shock is roughly 0.7, compared with values of around 1.5 for $d = 1$. A major drawback with all calculations of this type is that the confidence interval associated with any univariate persistence estimate is likely to be quite wide: the confidence that can be placed in *any* estimate of the long-run response of an economic variable to an unexpected shock is low because there are so few independent observations on long-run behaviour available in the data (see also Christiano and Eichenbaum (1990) who arrive at this conclusion from a rather different analysis).

Granger and Joyeux (1980) and Geweke and Porter-Hudak (1983) concentrate on using ARFIMA models for forecasting. The latter investigation was particularly interesting. They considered three-monthly US food indices, and found that the sample ACFs of the first differences exhibited the slow decay typical of long-memory models, the first fifty sample autocorrelations all being positive in each case, most being significantly different from zero. Estimates of d ranged from 0.42 to 0.70 and out-of-sample forecasts from both the simple fractionally differenced model $\nabla^{1+d}x_t = a_t$ and for the more sophisticated model where the errors follow an ARMA process tended to be more accurate, for long forecast horizons, than those from conventional ARMA models. While more evidence is obviously needed, fractional differencing and the associated ARFIMA class of processes may be a useful addition to the set of models that can produce decent long-run forecasts.

4   Nonlinear extensions of ARMA models

4.1   The bilinear model

If x_t is I(0), possibly after some prior differencing transformations, then the ARMA model

$$\phi(B)x_t = \theta_0 + \theta(B)a_t \tag{5}$$

is a finite-sample approximation to the *Wold decomposition*

$$x_t = \mu + a_t + \psi_1 a_{t-1} + \psi_2 a_{t-2} + \cdots \tag{6}$$

where $\mu = E(x_t)$. For this decomposition to exist, the $\{a_t\}$ must be a sequence of *uncorrelated* random variables. It is usually the case that we make the stronger assumption that the $\{a_t\}$ are *independent* although, if the distribution from which the sequence is drawn is assumed to be normal, the two assumptions are identical. The *bilinear* model extends (5) to

$$\phi(B)x_t = \theta_0 + \theta(B)a_t + \sum_{i=1}^{m}\sum_{j=1}^{k} \delta_{ij}x_{t-i}a_{t-j}. \tag{7}$$

The second term on the right-hand side of (7) is a bilinear form in a_{t-j} and x_{t-i}, and this accounts for the nonlinear character of the model: if all the δ_{ij} are zero, (7) reduces to the linear ARMA model (6). Bilinear models have the property that, although they involve only a finite number of parameters, they can approximate with arbitrary accuracy any 'reasonable' nonlinear relationship (Priestley, 1980).

Little analysis has been carried out on the general bilinear form (7), but Granger and Andersen (1978) have analysed the properties of several simple bilinear forms, characterized as

$$x_t = a_t + \delta x_{t-i}a_{t-j}.$$

Maravall (1983) considers an alternative form of bilinearity in which x_t is given by the Wold decomposition (6) but where the *uncorrelated* sequence $\{a_t\}$ is bilinear in a_t and the white noise sequence $\{\varepsilon_t\}$:

$$a_t = \varepsilon_t + \sum_{i=1}^{m}\sum_{j=1}^{k} \delta_{ij}\varepsilon_{t-i}a_{t-j}.$$

Although the bilinear model is a natural extension of the ARMA process, few economic applications have appeared. Subba Rao and Gabr (1980) and Poskitt and Tremayne

(1986) have used economic time series essentially to illustrate the methodology of identifying, estimating and forecasting from bilinear models. Maravall's (1983) application is more detailed in that he uses a bilinear specification to model and forecast a Spanish currency series. His conclusion is that bilinear models are particularly appropriate for series with sequences of outliers, during which periods a different 'regime' seems to apply. When the 'normal' regime operates, the bilinear part of the model is mostly dormant; it only becomes operative when atypical behaviour sets in, and then it acts so as to smooth outliers.

Other models are, of course, available for modelling such 'bursts' of volatility, the most popular and widely used being the autoregressive conditional heteroskedastic (ARCH) process. As Weiss (1986) demonstrates, there are, in fact, very close links between the bilinear and ARCH models and it may be difficult to distinguish between them in empirical applications. ARCH models are not considered here as they are the subject of another survey paper.

4.2   State-dependent models

Using the concept of 'Volterra expansions', Priestley (1980) shows that a general relationship between x_t and a_t can be represented as

$$x_t = F(x_{t-1}, \ldots, x_{t-p}, a_{t-1}, \ldots, a_{t-q}) + a_t. \tag{8}$$

If F is assumed analytic, the right-hand side of (8) can be expanded in a Taylor's series expansion about an arbitrary but fixed time point, allowing the relationship to be written as the state-dependent model (SDM) of order (p, q):

$$x_t - \sum_{i=1}^{p} \phi_i(\boldsymbol{x}_{t-1})x_{t-i} = \mu(\boldsymbol{x}_{t-1}) + a_t - \sum_{i=1}^{q} \theta_i(\boldsymbol{x}_{t-1})a_{t-i} \tag{9}$$

where $\boldsymbol{x}_t$ denotes the state vector

$$\boldsymbol{x}_t = (a_{t-q+1}, \ldots, a_t, x_{t-p+1}, \ldots x_t).$$

As Priestley (1980, p. 54) remarks, this model 'has a natural and appealing interpretation as a locally linear ARMA model in which the evolution of the process at time $(t-1)$ is governed by a set of AR coefficients $\{\phi_i\}$, a set of MA coefficients $\{\theta_i\}$, and a local mean μ, all of which depend on the "state" of the process at time $(t-1)$'.

Indeed, if μ, $\{\phi_i\}$ and $\{\theta_i\}$ are all taken as constants, i.e. as independent of $\boldsymbol{x}_{t-1}$, (9) reduces to the usual ARMA(p, q) model. Moreover, if only μ and $\{\phi_i\}$ are taken as constants but we set

$$\theta_i(\boldsymbol{x}_{t-i}) = \theta_i - \sum_{j=1}^{p} \delta_{ij}x_{t-j} \qquad i = 1, \ldots, q$$

then the SDM reduces to the bilinear model (7), with the $\theta_i(\boldsymbol{x}_{t-i})$ being linear functions of $(x_{t-1}, \ldots x_{t-p})$.

The SDM class of nonlinear models can also be shown to include the *threshold AR* model (Tong and Lim, 1980), the *exponential AR* model (Haggan and Ozaki, 1981) and various other nonlinear specifications that have been developed over recent years. Although Haggan et al. (1984) provide an extensive study of the application of SDMs to a wide variety of nonlinear time series, no economic data are used and it must remain to be seen whether such models are found to be useful for the modelling of economic time series.

4.3 Other nonlinear time series models in economics

Perhaps the reason why few of the SDM class of nonlinear models have found applications in economics is that they were not developed with economic time series specifically in mind. Economic time series have features that often are not found in other types of series and thus require models to be developed specifically to account for these features.

Two types of economic time series that appear to have such special features are macroeconomic aggregates and financial data, and we shall particularly concentrate on these areas in discussing a number of nonlinear models that are appearing in the literature.

4.3.1 Business cycle asymmetries

There has been considerable interest in recent years in the question of whether the correlation properties of macroeconomic series differ across various phases of the 'business cycle'; in particular, much attention has been focused on the apparent asymmetry of the cycle, with long, gradual expansion being followed by short, steep contraction. One way of potentially modelling this form of cyclical behaviour is through the asymmetric model discussed in section 2.4, where different parameters are associated with positive and negative innovations. An alternative approach is through a *nonlinear moving average* model such as that considered by Robinson (1978):

$$x_t = a_t + \theta_1 a_{t-1} + \theta_2 a_{t-1} a_{t-2} \tag{10}$$

where positive and negative innovations have differential effects on x_t through the interaction term $a_{t-1} a_{t-2}$. For example, the model will generate different forecasts for upswings and downswings; the realizations $\{a_t, a_{t-1}, a_{t-2}\}$ and $\{-a_t, -a_{t-1}, -a_{t-2}\}$ would yield, respectively,

$$\hat{x}_{t,1}^{\mathrm{u}} = \theta_1 a_1 + \theta_2 a_t a_{t-1}$$

and

$$\hat{x}_{t,1}^{\mathrm{d}} = -\theta_1 a_t + \theta_2 a_t a_{t-1}$$

where $\hat{x}_{t,1}^u$ and $\hat{x}_{t,1}^d$ are forecasts that relate to upswings and downswings respectively. If θ_1 is positive and θ_2 is negative, then the model in (10) would yield the sharp drops and gradual increases in $\{x_t\}$ that are a feature of business cycle asymmetry.

Unfortunately, both types of model are quite cumbersome to estimate and the nonlinear moving average model does not have easily tractable properties, such as invertibility. Neftci (1984, 1986) argues in favour of using *linear* models whose innovations have asymmetric densities, preferring to model the asymmetry property of business cycles as a finite state Markov process in which the states depend on whether the zero mean, stationary series $\{x_t\}$ is rising or falling, i.e.

$$s_t = \begin{cases} 1 & \text{if } \nabla x_t > 0 \\ 0 & \text{if } \nabla x_t \leqslant 0. \end{cases}$$

Hamilton (1989) generalizes this approach to consider the following model. Suppose initially that $\{x_t\}$ is given by

$$x_t = s_t + a_t \tag{11}$$

where the transition between states is governed by a first-order Markov process:

$$\Pr(s_t = 1 | s_{t-1} = 1) = p$$
$$\Pr(s_t = 0 | s_{t-1} = 1) = 1 - p$$
$$\Pr(s_t = 0 | s_{t-1} = 0) = q$$
$$\Pr(s_t = 1 | s_{t-1} = 0) = 1 - q.$$

The stochastic process for s_t is thus strictly stationary and, in fact, has the following AR(1) representation:

$$s_t = (1 - q) + \lambda s_{t-1} v_i \tag{12}$$

where

$$\lambda = -1 + p + q,$$

Conditional on $s_{t-1} = 1$, the innovation v_t has the distribution

$$v_t = 1 - p \qquad\qquad \text{with probability } p$$
$$v_t = -p \qquad\qquad \text{with probability } 1 - p$$

while, conditional on $s_{t-1} = 0$, it has the distribution

$$v_t = -(1 - q) \qquad\qquad \text{with probability } q$$
$$v_t = q \qquad\qquad \text{with probability } 1 - q.$$

Although v_t is uncorrelated with lagged values of s_t,

$$E(v_t | s_{t-j} = 1) = E(v_t | s_{t-j} = 0) = 0 \qquad \text{for } j = 1, 2, \ldots,$$

it is not independent of such lagged values since, for example,

$$E(v_t^2 | s_{t-1} = 1) = p(1 - p)$$
$$E(v_t^2 | s_{t-1} = 0) = q(1 - q).$$

Substituting (12) into (11) yields

$$x_t - \lambda x_{t-1} = (1 - q) + v_t + a_t - \lambda a_{t-1}$$

or

$$x_t - \lambda x_{t-1} = (1 - q) + u_t - \theta u_{t-1} \tag{13}$$

where $|\theta| < 1$, along with σ_u^2, satisfies

$$(1 + \theta^2)\sigma_u^2 = (1 + \lambda^2)\sigma_u^2 + \sigma_v^2$$
$$-\theta\sigma_u^2 = -\lambda\sigma_a^2$$

in which

$$\sigma_v^2 = E(v_t^2) = p(1 - p)\pi + q(1 - q)(1 - \pi),$$

π being the limiting unconditional probability $\Pr(s_t = 1)$. As for v_t, the innovation u_t is uncorrelated with u_{t-j} for $j > 0$, but is not independent. Thus, while the ARMA(1, 1) model (13) could be used to forecast x_{t+h} as a linear function of $x_t, x_{t-1}, \ldots$, these forecasts are not optimal; nonlinear forecasts that exploit the serial dependence of the white noise series u_t will be superior. Hamilton (1989, p. 362) shows that these are given by

$$\hat{x}_{t,h} = \pi + \lambda^h \left[\Pr(s_t = 1 \mid x_t, x_{t-1}, \ldots) - \pi \right]$$

where $\Pr(s_t = 1 \mid x_t, x_{t-1}, \ldots)$ is a nonlinear function of $x_t, x_{t-1}, \ldots$.

Non-stationary series and serially correlated noise are easily analysed in this set-up. Suppose, following Hamilton (1989, p. 366), that we now have

$$\tilde{x}_t = n_t + \tilde{z}_t$$

where $\tilde{x}_t$ is I(1), the trend component n_t is given by

$$n_t = \alpha_0 + \alpha_1 s_t + n_{t-1}$$

and $\tilde{z}_t$ follows an ARIMA(r, 1, 0) process

$$\nabla\tilde{z}_t = \phi_1 \nabla\tilde{z}_{t-1} + \cdots + \phi_r \nabla\tilde{z}_{t-r} + a_t.$$

With $x_t = \nabla\tilde{x}_t$ and $z_t = \nabla\tilde{z}_t$, we then have

$$x_t = \alpha_0 + \alpha_1 s_t + z_t$$

$$z_t = \phi_1 z_{t-1} + \cdots + \phi_r z_{t-r} + a_t.$$

Hamilton estimates this model, using ML methods, on logarithms of post-war US output. The estimates of α_0 and α_1 are -0.36 and 1.52 respectively, implying that in state $s_t = 0$ there is a negative growth rate of -0.4 per cent per quarter, while in state $s_t = 1$ there is positive growth of $\alpha_0 + \alpha_1 = 1.2$ per cent. Since the autoregressive coefficients ϕ_1 and ϕ_2 (r was set at 4) were close to zero, Hamilton infers that the first- and second-order serial correlation properties of logarithmic changes of output seem to be better captured by shifts in states than by an ARIMA process, as has been commonly used: see, for example, Diebold and Rudebusch (1989).

Hamilton also shows that, conditional on being in state 0, the expected duration of a 'recession' is $(1 - q)^{-1}$, estimated as 4.1 quarters, while the expected duration of an 'expansion' is $(1 - p)^{-1}$, estimated to be 10.5 quarters, thus confirming the asymmetric nature of business cycles. These are fairly close to the historical average durations of recessions and expansions according to the conventional National Bureau of Economic Research datings.

Hamilton further shows that this Markov model provides better forecasts than linear ARIMA models and that it also allows for heteroscedastic errors, the presence of which are indeed found in the output series. Finally, the model implies that a move from, for example, expansion to recession is associated with a 3 per cent decrease in the present value of future output and a 3 per cent drop in the long-run forecast level of output.

4.3.2   Time deformation models

Stock (1987, 1988) examines the question of business cycle asymmetry in a somewhat different way by emphasizing the distinction between 'economic' or 'operational' time and 'calendar' or 'observational' time, leading to the class of *time deformation* models. These relate the continuous latent process $\xi(s)$, evolving in economic time s, to the observable process x_t, evolving in calendar time t. When observed at discrete points in calendar time, x_t and $\xi(s)$ are related by

$$x_t = \xi[g(t)] \qquad t = 1, 2, \ldots, T.$$

Specification of the time deformation model consists of two parts: the choice of $g(t)$ and the specification of the latent process $\xi(s)$. Stock assumes the latter to be generated by a stable, continuous (economic) time, rth-order, linear stochastic differential equation. The time transformation $g(t)$ takes the form

$$\nabla g(t) = \frac{\exp(c'z_{t-1})}{T^{-1}\sum_{t=2}^{T}\exp(c'z_{t-1})} \tag{14}$$

where z_{t-1} is an m-dimensional vector of variables observed at time $t-1$ and c is an m-dimensional vector of unknown parameters. Note that if $c = 0$, $\nabla g(t) = 1$ and there is no time deformation.

When $r = 1$ the model for $\xi(s)$ can be written as

$$d\xi(s) = A\xi(s)ds + d\zeta(s)$$

where $\zeta(s)$ is a continuous-time white noise process with variance σ_ζ^2. For $s > s'$, this has the solution, conditional on $\xi(s')$,

$$\xi(s) = \exp[A(s - s')]\xi(s') + \int_{s'}^{s} \exp[A(s - v)]d\zeta(v).$$

If we let $s = g(t)$ and $s' = g(t - 1)$, the observable process x_t has the discrete-time representation

$$x_t = \exp\{A[\nabla g(t)]\}x_{t-1} + v_t \qquad v_t \sim N(0, \sigma_t^2)$$

where

$$\sigma_t^2 \sigma_\zeta^2 \frac{1 - \exp[2A\nabla g(t)]}{2A}$$

and where the normal distribution for v_t is conditional on $\nabla g(t)$. Thus the shift in time scale induces nonlinearities in the discrete calendar-time representation both through the autoregressive coefficient and through the limits of integration of the error term. In particular, the process has a time-varying conditional mean and is heteroskedastic. Stock (1988) provides some specific examples of the types of models produced for various choices of the time transformation $g(t)$ given by (14): both ARCH models and switching regressions can be obtained.

Using this time deformation model, Stock (1987, 1988) presents results, estimated using a Kalman filter algorithm, to suggest that there is evidence that post-war US output evolves on a time scale other than calendar time. The models imply that output exhibits stochastic cyclical behaviour in operational time rather than in observational time, but that the periodicity of the cycle is much shorter than the periods typically associated with business cycles.

In Stock (1989), time deformation models are used to investigate hysteresis in both US and UK post-war unemployment. The results indicate substantial, and statistically significant, nonlinearities in the unemployment process, indicating a nonlinear relationship between the operational and observational time scales of unemployment. Stock interprets the results as suggesting that if unemployment has been stable then its dependence on previous levels is increased, whereas if it has been rising in the recent past then its dependence is reduced, with the error associated with forecasts of future unemployment being consequently increased. The results thus resemble descriptions of hysteresis in unemployment as being the result of shifts between multiple equilibria.

4.3.3 Nonlinear dynamics and chaos

The methods discussed above all have in common the aim of modelling *stochastic* nonlinearities in macroeconomic time series. This would seem a natural approach to take by econometricians used to dealing with stochastic time series processes, but recently a literature has begun to develop that considers the question of whether such series could be generated by nonlinear *deterministic* laws of motion. This has been prompted by findings in the natural sciences of completely deterministic processes that generate behaviour which looks random under standard statistical tests: processes that are termed 'deterministic chaos'. A simple example is provided by Brock (1986), where a formal development of deterministic chaos models is provided. Consider the difference equation

$$x_t = f(x_{t-1}) \qquad x_0 \in [0, 1]$$

where

$$f(x) = \begin{cases} x/a & x \in [0, a] \\ (1-x)/(1-a) & x \in [a, 1], \ 0 < a < 1. \end{cases}$$

Most trajectories of this difference equation generate the same ACFs as an AR(1) process for x_t with parameter $\phi = 2a - 1$. Hence, for $a = \frac{1}{2}$, the trajectory will be indistinguishable from white noise, although it has been generated by a purely deterministic nonlinear process.

Are such models useful in economics? The results of Boldrin and Montrucchio (1986), for example, suggest that they might be, for they show that one can generate a policy function in a nonlinear deterministic model that, from the linear point of view, is exactly as if it were generated from a log-linear stochastic growth model. Baumol and Benhabib (1989) provide further illustrations of models leading to chaotic behaviour in such diverse areas as the relationship between profits and advertising, the linkage between productivity growth and R & D expenditures, and growth models in which the propensity to save out of wages is lower than out of profits. Moreover, as mentioned in section 1, there have been numerous other important contributions of chaos models to economic theory: further references are, for example, Stutzer (1980), Day (1983) and Deneckere and Pelican (1986). In all these models, highly nonlinear deterministic recursions embodying chaotic dynamics generate time series which appear to be stochastic, often failing to be rejected as random using standard statistical tests.

4.3.4   Conditional variance models for financial time series

Other than the ARCH class of models, there have been numerous conditional variance models proposed over recent years. Hsu (1977, 1979) considers a simple model in which the variance alters at a single, but unknown, point in time, estimating this change-point by ML techniques; Bayesian analyses of this model are provided by Hsu (1982) and Menzefricke (1981), and robust estimation is discussed by Davis (1979). Ali and Giacotto (1982) extend the model to contain more than one jump in variance while Tyssedal and Tjostheim (1982) allow the variance to depend on time in a continuous fashion.

Clark (1973) develops a model in which the conditional variance is a deterministic function of an exogenous variable, while Tauchen and Pitts (1983) extend this to a stochastic setting, with Taylor (1986) providing further extensions.

The typical area of application of these conditional variance models is that of financial markets, where daily time series of considerable length are available. Such models are felt to be needed because the early work of Mandelbrot (1963) and Fama (1965) found that conventional statistical analysis of daily price changes in financial markets was inadequate in that normal distributions do not satisfactorily model the observed data; conditional variance models do not force the distribution of x_t to be normal.

Financial time series have characteristics peculiar to themselves, and published research into their properties is diffuse and often relatively inaccessible. It is fortunate, then, that Taylor (1986) provides both a survey and a modern presentation of the modelling of such series.

5   Tests for nonlinearity

As the last section, in particular, has demonstrated, a wide variety of nonlinear models have been proposed for modelling economic time series. Not surprisingly, a number of tests for nonlinearity have also been proposed, but since the form of nonlinearity is often difficult to specify *a priori*, many tests are 'diagnostic' in nature, i.e. a clear alternative to the null hypothesis of linearity is not specified, and this, of course, leads to difficulties in discriminating between the possible causes of 'nonlinear mis-specification'.

Of the early proposals, Subba Rao and Gabr (1980) suggest a frequency domain test, while McLeod and Li (1983) show that the autocorrelations and associated portmanteau statistics of the squared residuals from a fitted ARMA model can be used to test for non-linear dependence, such tests being particularly suited when the alternative hypothesis is of the ARCH type.

Keenan (1985) and Tsay (1986) provide a regression type test that appears to have good power against the nonlinear moving average and bilinear alternatives, but possibly has low power against ARCH models. This uses the Volterra expansion of x_t used by Priestley (1980) to obtain (8), which allows x_t to be written in the very general form

$$x_t = \mu + \sum_{i=-\infty}^{\infty} \psi_i a_{t-i} + \sum_{i,j=-\infty}^{\infty} \psi_{ij} a_{t-i} a_{t-j} + \sum_{i,j,k=-\infty}^{\infty} \psi_{ijk} a_{t-i} a_{t-j} a_{t-k} + \cdots \quad (15)$$

Obviously, x_t will be nonlinear if any of the higher order coefficients $\{\psi_{ij}\}, \{\psi_{ijk}\}, \ldots,$ are nonzero; if not, we obtain the usual linear Wold decomposition (6). This test of nonlinearity is, then, essentially a test of no multiplicative terms in (15) and is based on a sequence of regressions using x_t and its cross-products. Tests based on the estimated bispectrum have also been developed: see, for example, Ashley et al. (1986) and Brockett et al. (1988), although these too appear to have low power against ARCH alternatives.

Since bilinearity and ARCH have similar properties, and may often be mistaken for each other, a number of tests of these extensions of the ARMA model have been proposed recently. Weiss (1986) shows that a Lagrange multiplier test of bilinearity in (7) is the familiar TR^2 statistic calculated from the regression of $\hat{a}_t$ on a constant, $x_{t-1}, \ldots, x_{t-p}$, and $x_{t-i}\hat{a}_{t-j}, i = 1, \ldots, m, j = 1, \ldots, k$, the $\hat{a}_t$ being obtained from fitting the linear ARMA model under the null hypothesis.

However, if the test is conducted in the assumed presence of ARCH, it cannot be represented as a TR^2 statistic from an auxiliary regression. This has led Higgins and Bera (1989) to propose a joint test for ARCH and bilinearity which, using the additive property of Lagrange multiplier tests, is calculated as the sum of the test statistics for each component, both of which can be computed from auxiliary regressions.

A further test that is creating considerable interest is the BDS statistic, based on the concept of the *correlation integral*: see, for example, Brock (1986), Brock and Sayers (1988), Brock and Dechert (1988), Hsieh (1989) and Scheinkman (1990). For an observed series $\{x_t: t = 1, \ldots, T\}$, the correlation integral $C_N(l, T)$ is defined as

$$C_N(l, T) = \frac{2}{T_N(T_N - 1)} \sum_{t < s} I_l(x_t^N, x_s^N)$$

where

$$x_t^N = (x_t, x_{t+1}, \ldots, x_{t+N-1})$$

and

$$x_s^N = (x_s, x_{s+1}, \ldots, x_{t+N-1})$$

are called '*N*-histories', $I_l(x_t^N, x_s^N)$ is an indicator function that equals unity if $\|x_t^N - x_s^N\| < l$ and zero otherwise, $\| \cdot \|$ being the sup-norm, and $T_N = T - N + 1$.

The correlation integral is an estimate of the probability that any two *N*-histories, x_t^N and x_s^N, are within l of each other. From it we may define the *correlation dimension* of $\{x_t\}$ as

$$v = \lim_{l \to 0} \frac{\log C_N(l, T)}{\log l}$$

if the limit exists.

Physicists use the correlation dimension to distinguish between chaotic deterministic systems and stochastic systems, the intuition being that if the data are generated by a chaotic system then the dimension v should be 'small'. Unfortunately, there is no proper statistical theory to underpin this intuition: indeed, the estimated correlation dimension may be substantially biased even in samples of 2000. An alternative strategy uses the result that if the x_ts are IID then

$$C_N(l, T) \to C_1(l, T)^N \qquad \text{as } T \to \infty$$

and

$$w_N(l, T) = \frac{\sqrt{T}[C_N(l, T) - C_1(l, T)^N]}{\sigma_n(l, T)}$$

has a standard normal limiting distribution, where the expression for the variance $\sigma_n^2(l, T)$ may be found in, for example, Hsieh (1989, p. 343). Thus the BDS statistic $w_N(l, T)$ tests the null hypothesis that a series is IID, it is a diagnostic test since a rejection of this null is consistent with some type of dependence in the data, which could result from a linear stochastic system, a nonlinear stochastic system or a nonlinear deterministic system. Additional diagnostic tests are therefore needed to determine the source of the rejection, but simulation experiments do suggest that the BDS test has power against simple linear deterministic systems as well as nonlinear stochastic processes.

It should be emphasized, however, that all these tests are designed to distinguish between linear and nonlinear *stochastic* dynamics: they are not, as yet, capable of distinguishing nonlinear stochastic dynamics from deterministic chaotic dynamics, although the rejection of linearity may, of course, motivate the investigation of chaotic models.

Given that the presence of important nonlinear dynamics may, for example, make standard linear rational expectations models quite misleading, what evidence has so far accumulated concerning the presence of nonlinear dynamics? Apart from the applications of the specific nonlinear models discussed earlier, there have been numerous recent studies providing general tests of nonlinearity in economic time series.

The evidence for macroeconomic series is rather mixed. There appears, from the results presented in Brock and Sayers (1988) and Scheinkman and LeBaron (1989a), to be little evidence of nonlinear dynamics in output. For industrial production and employment series, however, there do seem to be important nonlinearities, as judged from the results of a variety of tests reported by Brock and Sayers (1988), Scheinkman and LeBaron (1989a) and Ashley and Patterson (1989). Similar nonlinearities have also been found in Divisia monetary aggregates (Barnett and Chen, 1988).

It is in financial time series that evidence of nonlinear dynamics abounds. Ashley and Patterson (1986, 1989), Scheinkman and LeBaron (1989b), Hinich and Patterson (1985, 1989) and De Gooijer (1989) all present evidence that stock returns contain important nonlinearities, even though they use different tests on data collected over different sampling periods and intervals. Both Brockett et al. (1988) and Hsieh (1989) find similar nonlinear dependence in daily exchange rates.

6   Conclusions

In this paper we have surveyed a variety of classes of nonlinear models that have been used to model economic time series. Rather than provide a mere summary of these models in this concluding section we shall attempt to emphasize certain relationships between them, the implications they have for economic modelling, and the areas in which we feel nonlinear models to be potentially at their most useful.

In section 2, the popular class of instantaneous power transformations and the less familiar asymmetric time series model were both found to be useful for turning a skewed marginal distribution into a more normal distribution. While power transformations, particularly the logarithmic, have been employed almost by default by economists, the analysis of Wecker (1981) shows that the presence of asymmetric time series may, in fact, be much more prevalent than might first be thought and their use for modelling price series should seriously be considered. In any event, obtaining unbiased forecasts from power transformed series has been shown to require very careful analysis, a fact that has not been appreciated sufficiently by many applied economists.

The notion of fractional integration developed in section 3 generalizes the concept of integrated series and leads to a class of models that incorporate long-memory behaviour. The potential relevance of fractionally integrated time series has been demonstrated in three areas: aggregation, long-horizon forecasting and for examining the persistence of macroeconomic fluctuations, where the results of Diebold and Rudebusch (1989) suggest that the response of output to innovations may depend crucially on the value of d that is chosen.

Related to this point is the recent analysis of Sowell (1990a), who shows that the presence of fractionally integrated errors can have extremely serious effects on conventional unit root tests. These findings are particularly important when related to the work of Christiano and Eichenbaum (1990), who highlight the severe inferential problems inherent in distinguishing between series containing unit roots and those that are trend stationary. We thus feel that an important research area is that of determining the extent of fractional integration in economic time series, along with the development of appropriate methods of estimation and inference: on this point, see Sowell (1990b).

Various nonlinear extensions of ARMA models were considered in section 4. The general class of state-dependent models would appear to have only limited application to the modelling of economic time series and, indeed, only superficial examples have yet been provided. Of greater potential are the bilinear class, although even here there is some doubt as to whether they are a viable alternative to the more popular ARCH class of models, to which they are closely linked and from which they may be difficult to distinguish in empirical applications.

The well-documented observation that business cycles are asymmetric, having long, gradual expansions followed by short, steep contractions, has provided a rich field for nonlinear modelling. The asymmetric models discussed above, however, have not been used: attention has focused rather on discrete-state Markov processes, where the mean growth rate of a non-stationary series may be subject to occasional, discrete shifts, and on time deformation models, which emphasize the distinction between economic and calendar time. Although empirical applications of these two approaches are limited so far, it is our view that they nevertheless yield important insights into the nature of business cycle fluctuations not offered by conventional linear time series modelling, and that further research into their development and application is of paramount importance in this fundamental area of macroeconomic analysis.

Models of deterministic chaos have begun to intrigue economic theorists and thus it is natural for methods of detecting its presence to have begun to be developed. At the present time, however, these testing procedures are at too early a stage of development for us to be convinced that economic series are indeed characterized by deterministic chaos: the results so far reported reveal the presence of nonlinearities in many series, particularly financial, but do not find evidence of low-dimensional deterministic chaos. We suspect that nonlinearities in economic time series will be predominantly of the stochastic variety, and thus feel that the tests of nonlinearity discussed in section 5 should be available to, and be used by, any economic modeller.

We thus conclude by restating our view that economic time series often contain important nonlinearities that can take many forms; there are a number of tests available to detect such nonlinearities and many types of processes to model them. The models and tests surveyed in this paper offer a rich extension to the time series techniques available to researchers and should become essential tools in the kit of any modeller of economic time series.

Acknowledgements

I would like to thank Les Oxley and two anonymous referees for helpful comments on earlier drafts. The usual disclaimer applies, of course.

References

Ali, M. M. and Giacotto, C. (1982) The identical distribution hypothesis for stock market prices – location and scale shift alternatives. *Journal of the American Statistical Association*, 77, 19–28.

Ansley, C. F., Spivey, W. A. and Wrobleski, W. J. (1977) A class of transformations for Box–Jenkins seasonal models. *Applied Statistics*, 26, 173–8.

Ashley, R. A. and Patterson, D. M. (1986) A nonparametric, distribution-free test for serial dependence in stock returns. *Journal of Financial and Quantitative Analysis*, 21, 221–7.

—— and —— (1989) Linear versus nonlinear macroeconomies: a statistical test. *International Economic Review*, 30, 685–704.

——, —— and Hinich, M. J. (1986) A diagnostic test for nonlinear serial dependence in time series fitting errors. *Journal of Time Series Analysis*, 7, 165–78.

Barnett, W. A. and Chen, P. (1988) The aggregation-theoretic monetary aggregates are chaotic and have strange attractors: an econometric application of mathematical chaos. In W. A. Barnett, E. R. Berndt and H. White (eds), *Dynamic Econometric Modelling*, Cambridge: Cambridge University Press, 199–246.

Baumol, W. J. and Benhabib, J. (1989) Chaos: significance, mechanism, and economic applications. *Journal of Economic Perspectives*, 3 (1), 77–105.

—— and Quandt, R. E. (1985) Chaos models and their implications for forecasting. *Eastern Economic Journal*, 11, 3–15.

Boldrin, M. and Montrucchio, L. (1986) On the indeterminacy of capital accumulation paths. *Journal of Economic Theory*, 40, 26–39.

Box, G. E. P. and Cox, D. R. (1964) An analysis of transformations. *Journal of the Royal Statistical Society, Series B*, 26, 211–43.

—— and Jenkins, G. M. (1976) *Time Series Analysis: Forecasting and Control*, revised edn. San Francisco, CA: Holden-Day.

Brock, W. A. (1986) Distinguishing random and deterministic systems: abridged version. *Journal of Economic Theory*, 40, 168–95.

—— and Dechert, W. D. (1988) Theorems on distinguishing deterministic from random systems. In W. A. Barnett, E. R. Berndt and H. White (eds), *Dynamic Econometric Modelling*, Cambridge: Cambridge University Press, 247–68.

—— and Sayers, C. L. (1988) Is the business cycle characterized by deterministic chaos? *Journal of Monetary Economics*, 22, 71–90.

Brockett, P. L., Hinich, M. J. and Patterson, D. M. (1988) Bispectral based tests for the detection of Gaussianity and linearity in time series. *Journal of the American Statistical Association*, 83, 657–64.

Christiano, L. J. and Eichenbaum, M. (1990) Unit roots in real GNP: do we know, and do we care? *Carnegie-Rochester Conference Series on Public Policy*, 32, 7–62.

Clark, P. K. (1973) A subordinated stochastic process model with finite variance for speculative prices. *Econometrica*, 41, 135–55.

Davis, W. W. (1979) Robust methods for detection of shifts of the innovation variance of a time series. *Technometrics*, 21, 313–20.

Day, R. (1983) The emergence of chaos from classical economic growth. *Quarterly Journal of Economics*, 98, 201–13.

—— and Shafer, W. (1985) Keynesian chaos. *Journal of Macroeconomics*, 7, 277–95.

De Gooijer, J. G. (1989) Testing non-linearities in world stock market prices. *Economics Letters*, 31, 31–5.

Deneckere, R. and Pelikan, S. (1986) Competitive chaos. *Journal of Economic Theory*, 40, 13–25.

Diebold, F. X. and Rudebusch, G. D. (1989) Long memory and persistence in aggregate output. *Journal of Monetary Economics*, 24, 189–209.

Engle, R. F. and Granger, C. W. J. (1987) Co-integration and error correction: representation, estimation and testing. *Econometrica*, 55, 251–76.

Fama, E. F. (1965) The behaviour of stock market prices. *Journal of Business*, 38, 34–105.

Geweke, J. and Porter-Hudak, S. (1983) The estimation and application of long memory time series models. *Journal of Time Series Analysis*, 4, 221–38.

Goodwin, R. M. (1951) The nonlinear accelerator and the persistence of business cycles. *Econometrica*, 19, 1–17.

Grandmont, J. M. (1985) On endogenous competitive business cycles. *Econometrica*, 53, 995–1045.

Granger, C. W. J. (1966) The typical spectral shape of an economic variable. *Econometrica*, 34, 150–61.

—— (1980) Long memory relationships and the aggregation of dynamic models. *Journal of Econometrics*, 14, 227–38.

—— (1983) Forecasting white noise. In A. Zellner (ed.), *Applied Time Series Analysis of Economic Data*, Washington, DC: US Department of Commerce, Bureau of the Census, 308–14.

—— and Andersen, A. P. (1978) *An Introduction to Bilinear Time Series Models*. Göttingen: Vandenhoeck and Ruprecht.

—— and Hughes, A. D. (1971) A new look at some old data: the Beveridge wheat price series. *Journal of the Royal Statistical Society, Series A*, 134, 413–28.

—— and Joyeux, R. (1980) An introduction to long memory time series models and fractional differencing. *Journal of Time Series Analysis*, 1, 15–29.

—— and Newbold, P. (1976) Forecasting transformed series. *Journal of the Royal Statistical Society, Series B*, 38, 189–203.

—— and —— (1977) *Forecasting Economic Time Series*. New York: Academic Press.

Haggan, V. and Ozaki, T. (1981) Modelling non-linear vibrations using an amplitude-dependent autoregressive time series model. *Biometrika*, 68, 189–96.

——, Heravi, S. M. and Priestley, M. B. (1984) A study of the application of state-dependent models in non-linear time series analysis. *Journal of Time Series Analysis*, 5, 69–102.

Hamilton, J. D. (1989) A new approach to the economic analysis of nonstationary time series and the business cycle. *Econometrica*, 57, 357–84.

Haubrich, J. G. and Lo, A. W. (1989) The sources and nature of long term memory in the business cycle. Rodney White Center Working Paper 5–89, Wharton School, University of Pennsylvania.

Hicks, J. (1950) *A Contribution to the Theory of the Trade Cycle*. Oxford: Clarendon Press.

Higgins, M. L. and Bera, A. K. (1989) A joint test for ARCH and bilinearity in the regression model. *Econometric Reviews*, 7, 171–81.

Hinich, M. J. and Patterson, D. M. (1985) Evidence of nonlinearity in daily stock returns. *Journal of Business and Economic Statistics*, 3, 69–77.

—— and —— (1989) Evidence of nonlinearity in the trade-by-trade stock market return generating process. In W. A. Barnett, J. Geweke and K. Shell (eds), *Economic Complexity: Chaos, Sunspots, Bubbles, and Nonlinearity*, Cambridge: Cambridge University Press, 383–409.

Hosking, J. R. M. (1981) Fractional differencing. *Biometrika*, 68, 165–76.

—— (1982) Some models of persistence in time series. In O. D. Anderson (ed.), *Time Series Analysis: Theory and Practice 1*, Amsterdam: North-Holland, 641–54.

—— (1984) Modelling persistence in hydrological time series using fractional differencing. *Water Resources Research*, 20, 1898–1908.

Hsieh, D. A. (1989) Testing for nonlinear dependence in daily foreign exchange rates. *Journal of Business*, 62, 339–68.

Hsu, D. A. (1977) Tests for variance shift at an unknown time point. *Applied Statistics*, 26, 279–84.

—— (1979) Detecting shifts of parameter in gamma sequences with applications to stock price and air traffic flow analysis. *Journal of the American Statistical Association*, 74, 31–40.

—— (1982) A Bayesian robust detection of shift in the risk structure of stock market returns. *Journal of the American Statistical Association*, 77, 29–39.

Kaldor, N. (1940) A model of the trade cycle. *Economic Journal*, 50, 78–92.

Keenan, D. M. (1985) A Tukey nonadditivity-type test for time series nonlinearity. *Biometrika*, 72, 39–44.

Kunsch, H. (1986) Discrimination between monotonic trends and long-range dependence. *Journal of Applied Probability*, 23, 1025–30.

Mandelbrot, B. B. (1963) New methods in statistical economics. *Journal of Political Economy*, 71, 421–40.

—— (1969) Long-run linearity, locally Gaussian process, *H*-spectra, and infinite variances. *International Economic Review*, 10, 82–111.

—— (1972) Statistical methodology for nonperiodic cycles: from the covariance to R/S analysis. *Annals of Economic and Social Measurement*, 1/3, 259–90.

—— and Wallis, J. R. (1969) Some long-run properties of geophysical records. *Water Resources Research*, 5, 321–40.

Maravall, A. (1983) An application of nonlinear time series forecasting. *Journal of Business and Economic Statistics*, 3, 350–5.

McLeod, A. J. and Li, W. K. (1983) Diagnostic checking ARMA time series models using squared-residual correlations. *Journal of Time Series Analysis*, 4, 269–73.

Menzefricke, U. (1981) A Bayesian analysis of a change in the precision of a sequence of independent random normal variables at an unknown time point. *Applied Statistics*, 30, 141–6.

Mills, T. C. (1990) *Time Series Techniques for Economists*, Cambridge: Cambridge University Press.

Neftci, S. N. (1984) Are economic time series asymmetric over the business cycle? *Journal of Political Economy*, 92, 307–28.

—— (1986) Is there a cyclical time unit? *Carnegie- Rochester Conference Series on Public Policy*, 24, 11–48.

Nelson, H. R. and Granger, C. W. J. (1979) Experience with using the Box–Cox transformation when forecasting economic time series. *Journal of Econometrics*, 10, 57–69.

Pagan, A. R. and Wickens, M. R. (1989) A survey of some recent econometric methods. *Economic Journal*, 99, 962–1025.

Pankratz, A. and Dudley, U. (1987) Forecasts of power-transformed series. *Journal of Forecasting*, 6, 239–48.

Poirier, D. J. (1980) Experience with using the Box–Cox transformation when forecasting economic time series: a comment. *Journal of Econometrics*, 14, 277–80.

Poskitt, D. S. and Tremayne, A. R. (1986) The selection and use of linear and bilinear time series models. *International Journal of Forecasting*, 2, 101–14.

Priestley, M. B. (1980) State-dependent models: a general approach to nonlinear time series analysis. *Journal of Time Series Analysis*, 1, 47–71.

Robinson, P. M. (1978) Estimation of a nonlinear moving average process. *Journal of Stochastic Processes*, 3, 135–56.

Scheinkman, J. A. (1990) Nonlinearities in economic dynamics. *Economic Journal (Supplement)*, 100, 33–48.

—— and LeBaron, B. (1989a) Nonlinear dynamics and GNP data. In W. A. Barnett, J. Geweke and K. Shell (eds), *Economic Complexity: Chaos, Sunspots, Bubbles, and Nonlinearity*, Cambridge: Cambridge University Press, 213–27.

—— and —— (1989b) Nonlinear dynamics and stock returns. *Journal of Business*, 62, 311–37.

Sowell, F. (1990a) The fractional unit root distribution. *Econometrica*, 58, 495–505.

—— (1990b) Maximum likelihood estimation of fractionally integrated time series models. *Econometrica*, forthcoming.

Stock, J. H. (1987) Measuring business cycle time. *Journal of Political Economy*, 95, 1240–61.

—— (1988) Estimating continuous time processes subject to time deformation: an application to postwar GNP. *Journal of the American Statistical Association*, 83, 77–85.

—— (1989) Hysteresis and the evolution of postwar U.S. and U.K. unemployment. In W. A. Barnett, J. Geweke and K. Shell (eds), *Economic Complexity: Chaos, Sunspots, Bubbles, and Nonlinearity*, Cambridge: Cambridge University Press, 361–82.

Stutzer, M. (1980) Chaotic dynamics and bifurcations in a macro model. *Journal of Economic Dynamics and Control*, 2, 353–76.

Subba Rao, T. and Gabr, M. M. (1980) A test for linearity of stationary time series. *Journal of Time Series Analysis*, 1, 145–58.

Tauchen, G. E. and Pitts, M. (1983) The price variability–volume relationship on speculative markets. *Econometrica*, 51, 485–505.

Taylor, S. J. (1986) *Modelling Financial Time Series*, New York: Wiley.

Tong, H. and Lim, K. S. (1980) Threshold autoregression, limit cycles, and cyclical data. *Journal of the Royal Statistical Society, Series B*, 42, 245–92.

Tsay, R. S. (1986) Nonlinearity tests for time series. *Biometrika*, 73, 461–6.

Tyssedal, J. S. and Tjostheim, D. (1982) Autoregressive processes with a time dependent variance. *Journal of Time Series Analysis*, 3, 209–17.

Wallis, K. F. (1987) Time series analysis of bounded variables. *Journal of Time Series Analysis*, 8, 115–23.

Wecker, W. E. (1981) Asymmetric time series. *Journal of the American Statistical Association*, 76, 16–21.

Weiss, A. A. (1986) ARCH and bilinear time series models: comparison and combination. *Journal of Business and Economic Statistics*, 4, 59–70.

10 Testing the rational expectations hypothesis in macroeconometric models with unobserved variables

Les Oxley
University of Edinburgh
and
University of Western Australia

and

Michael McAleer
University of Western Australia
and
Kyoto University

1 Introduction

Expectations play an important role in many areas of economics, such as in macroeconomic dynamics and microeconomic intertemporal optimization. The 1970s and 1980s saw the development of a number of models where unexpected events, 'surprises' or 'news' began to play a prominent role in the analysis of economic behaviour (see, for example, Sargent and Wallace, 1975). Developments in economic theory led to empirical applications. Economic models were formulated, estimated and tested in which the independent variables in one equation were either predicted/fitted values or the levels or squares of residuals generated from another equation.

Such models with 'generated regressors' (GRs) gradually began to permeate major areas of economics. The effect of 'news' in efficient markets was considered by Frenkel (1981) and this was followed by many empirical applications, including models of exchange rate determination by, for example, MacDonald (1983a, b, 1985). Models of the consumption function with a specific role for 'surprise' income include those of Hall (1978), Bean (1986) and Muellbauer (1983). Furthermore, the conversion of survey-based expectations from qualitative response data to a quantitative series typically produces GRs (see, for example, Pesaran, 1984, 1987; Smith and McAleer, 1992a). However, the most influential body of literature, derived from the work of Barro (1977), relates to the effects of 'unanticipated' monetary growth. This important and widely cited article initiated an industry of empirical applications, some of which will be discussed in section 4. In particular, those papers which report only uncorrected ordinary least squares (OLS) results will be highlighted and reference will be made therein to the problems of inefficiency and inconsistency of the standard errors, to be discussed in section 3. Other models, such as those attempting to test the 'buffer-stock' notion, also involve some concept of 'unanticipated money' (see, for example, Carr and Darby, 1981; MacKinnon and Milbourne, 1984; Carr et al., 1985; Cuthbertson and Taylor, 1987, 1989).

Although clearly important, expectational and surprise variables are typically not directly observable. At the theoretical level, such a characteristic is of little practical significance since conclusions can be derived on the basis of the assumed generic properties of the expectation formation mechanism, e.g. convergence in an adaptive expectations regime or orthogonality in rational expectations (RE). However, if such conclusions are to be tested, the lack of observability of variables assumes far greater importance. In the absence of direct measurement of expectations, typically from surveys, some form of indirect measurement is clearly required.

Backward-looking mechanisms, such as adaptive or autoregressive expectations, derived as a weighted average of past observations of the variable, were generally superseded in the 1970s and 1980s by the 'model-consistent' forward-looking hypothesis of RE. The RE hypothesis gained increasing support, in part, because of its conditional nature, namely a measure of expectations that was derived as being consistent with a particular underlying structural model.

The main purpose of this survey is to review critically the econometric issues which arise in models with unobserved variables. It will be assumed throughout that such variables are stationary and not cointegrated. Further, the issue of the observational equivalence of rational and non-rational models will not be addressed. For an excellent discussion see Pesaran (1987). Since the seminal work of Pagan (1984, 1986), a number of theoretical developments have occurred, in relation both to estimation, e.g. Hoffman (1987) and McAleer and Smith (1990), and to inferences in hypothesis testing, e.g. Gauger (1989). Both estimation and inference are assuming greater importance in applied economics as the prevalence of models which are estimated using GRs, either implicitly or explicitly, increases substantially. With the widespread adoption of RE and a continuing popularity for New Classical macroeconomic (NCM) ideas, the statistical properties of GR models, particularly their strengths and weaknesses, need to be clearly understood.

The most prolific area of empirical applications utilizing GRs relates to variants of the Barro (1977) model. Barro formulates tests of the NCM monetary neutrality proposition which, by necessity, require some measure of monetary surprises. This issue produced a massive and continuing research programme, stemming from Barro (1977) through to McAleer and McKenzie (1991a). This emphasis will be reflected by using variants of the Barro approach to illustrate important empirical issues relating to estimating RE models in general and GR models in particular. However, GR problems permeate many areas of economics and the issues highlighted here have considerably more importance than simply tests of monetary neutrality.

In section 2 we consider how GRs arise as a consequence of the *economic modelling process*. Emphasis here will fall upon NCM models of monetary neutrality and four testable neutrality propositions will be developed. Section 3 discusses the estimation of models with GRs and some emphasis is placed on the efficiency of (uncorrected) two-step estimation (2SE) under various conditions. The properties of efficient estimation are also discussed and the role of separate tests of neutrality and rationality is highlighted. Section 4 discusses a number of empirical results relating to GR models in general, and to tests of the NCM monetary neutrality hypothesis in particular, and highlights the problems associated with drawing valid inferences in such models. Concluding remarks are given in section 5.

2   Generated regressors

In this section, various conditions under which GRs may arise as a consequence of the *economic modelling* of a particular problem are illustrated. Four examples are considered: qualitative response models; exchange rate models with a specific role for 'news'; 'surprise' consumption functions; and New Classical 'surprise supply functions' of the Sargent and Wallace (1975) type which underpin the empirical models of Barro (1977).

GRs arise in a number of ways and the manner in which they enter the equation(s) of interest affects both identification and estimation. Pagan (1984) identifies three different theoretical situations where GRs are produced: (i) *predictor GRs*, where the regressors are constructed as predictions from another equation; (ii) *residual GRs (levels)*, where the regressors are obtained as the residuals from another regression; (iii) *residual GRs (variance)*, where the variance rather than the level of the 'surprise' is of interest. Clearly, combinations of such cases exist: e.g. predictor and residual GRs are included in the NCM models of the natural rate–rational expectations (NR–RE) hypothesis, which will be discussed below. Less common are examples of residual GRs (variance), but these include the models of Makin (1982), Mullineaux (1980) and Levi and Makin (1980), which test for the effects of inflation uncertainty on real economic activity.

2.1   Qualitative response models

Testing of expectations formation hypotheses may be based either on directly observed expectations data or on indirect expectations data. Few empirical studies have been based on direct observations whereas many have relied on indirectly observed (i.e. *generated*) expectations series. Tests of the rational expectations hypothesis (REH) are typically indirect tests, being based on model-consistent expectations. As the name suggests, model-consistent expectations equate individual subjective expectations to the objective expectations of a model and are therefore not invariant to the model specification used. Indirect tests also require several restrictive assumptions, such as knowledge of the information set, homogeneity of information across individuals and knowledge of the 'true' structural model and its parameter values.

Pesaran (1987, p. 207) argues that:

> Only when direct observations on expectations are available is it possible to satisfactorily compare and contrast alternative models of expectations formation.

But what precisely is meant by 'direct observations'? In practice, 'direct' survey response expectations data are typically of a qualitative nature, whereas what are required are quantitative series. Two methods are available for converting qualitative response data into a quantitative expectations series, namely the probability approach and the regression model approach.

2.1.1   The probability method

The probability method was developed by Theil (1952) and is discussed in detail by Pesaran (1987). It is assumed that there is some indifference interval (a_{it}, b_{it}) around zero within which individuals report the expected change in a variable as being zero, but report the variable as having changed outside the indifference interval. A number of key assumptions are made, namely: (i) each agent (firm) has its own subjective probability distribution, which is identical and independent, defined over its own future percentage change in some variable x_t conditional on its own information set; (ii) the subjective probability distribution across agents (firms) in many different industries can be aggregated to form a probability distribution $h(x_{t+1}|\Omega_t)$, where x_{t+1} is the weighted sum of each firm's percentage change in some variable and Ω_t is the union of individual information sets; (iii) the indifference interval is assumed to be constant across both individuals and time, so that $(a_{it}, b_{it}) = (a, b)$ for all i and t (for further details, see Pesaran, 1987).

It follows from the assumptions that

$$\Pr(x_{t+1} \leqslant a | \Omega_t) = H_t(a) = {}_tF^e_{t+1} \tag{1}$$

$$\Pr(x_{t+1} \geqslant b | \Omega_t) = 1 - H_t(b) = {}_tR^e_{t+1} \tag{2}$$

where H_t is the cumulative density function of X_t and ${}_tF^e_{t+1}$ (${}_tR^e_{t+1}$) is the percentage of firms expecting a fall (rise) in x_{t+1}. Equations (1) and (2) can be solved to yield estimates of ${}_tx^e_{t+1}$ and ${}_t\sigma^e_{t+1} = \{E[(x_{t+1} - {}_tx^e_{t+1})^2 | \Omega_t]\}^{1/2}$. The choice of functional form for H_t is a matter of convenience, with the standard normal, the logistic and the scaled-t distributions being commonly used (see Smith and McAleer (1992a) for an extensive empirical example comparing these and other methods).

The uniform distribution provides an interesting example of a GR which is, in effect, the same algebraic solution as a special case of Pesaran's (1984, 1987) nonlinear regression model (namely, Pesaran's reinterpretation of Anderson's (1952) approach as a linear regression model). Assume that x_t is a random drawing from a uniform distribution over the range $({}_tx^e_{t+1} - q, {}_tx^e_{t+1} + q)$. Equations (1) and (2) can be written as

$$_tF^e_{t+1} = \frac{-{}_tx^e_{t+1} + q - a}{2q} \tag{3}$$

$$_tR^e_{t+1} = \frac{{}_tx^e_{t+1} + q - b}{2q} \tag{4}$$

Solving (3) and (4) for ${}_tx^e_{t+1}$ yields

$$_tx^e_{t+1} = \alpha/{}_tR^e_{t+1} - \beta/{}_tF^e_{t+1} \tag{5}$$

where $\alpha = 2q(q - a)/(2q - a - b)$ and $\beta = 2q(q - b)/(2q - a - b)$. Relating x_t to the percentage change of firms reporting a fall (F_t) or rise (R_t) in period t leads to the equation

$$x_t = \alpha R_t - \beta F_t + \xi_t. \tag{6}$$

OLS estimates of α and β from (6) may be substituted in (5) to yield forecasts given by

$$_t\hat{x}^e_{t+1} = \hat{\alpha}\,{}_tR^e_{t+1} - \hat{\beta}\,{}_tF^e_{t+1}. \tag{7}$$

As Pesaran (1987, p. 226) observes, such a substitution assumes that the aggregate distribution and the indifference intervals are the same between realizations and expectations. Use of the OLS estimates $\hat{\alpha}$ and $\hat{\beta}$ to obtain $_t\hat{x}^e_{t+1}$ leads to a GR in the orthogonality test.

2.1.2 The regression method

Pesaran (1984, 1987) developed the regression method as an alternative to the probability method by making quantitative expectations a function of a regression model instead of a specific probability distribution. If x_t is composed of a weighted combination of firms responding that it increased (denoted x^+_{it}) and decreased (denoted x^-_{it}), then

$$x_t = \sum_{i=1}^{r} w^+_{it} x^+_{it} + \sum_{i=1}^{f} w^-_{it} x^-_{it} \tag{8}$$

where w^+_{it} (w^-_{it}) is the weight on a particular firm reporting a rise (fall) during t. Following Pesaran (1987), who argues for an asymmetric relationship between rises and falls, assume that all firms reporting an increase or decrease behave according to

$$x^+_{it} = \alpha + \gamma x_t + \varepsilon^+_{it} \qquad (\alpha \geqslant 0, 0 \leqslant \gamma \leqslant 1) \tag{9}$$

$$x^-_{it} = -\beta + \varepsilon^-_{it} \qquad (\beta \geqslant 0) \tag{9'}$$

where ε^+_{it} and ε^-_{it} are independent white noise processes. Substituting from (9) and (9') into (8) yields

$$x_t = \frac{\alpha R_t - \beta F_t}{1 - \gamma R_t} + \xi_t \tag{10}$$

$$\xi_t = \left(\sum_{i=1}^{r} w^+_{it} \varepsilon^+_{it} + \sum_{i=1}^{f} w^-_{it} \varepsilon^-_{it} \right) \Big/ (1 - \gamma R_t) \tag{11}$$

in which ξ_t is heteroskedastic through R_t (if the weights vary over time) and may be serially correlated through the weights or through R_t. Using consistent estimates $\hat{\alpha}, \hat{\beta}$ and $\hat{\gamma}$ from (10), together with the expectations variables, the expectations series are obtained through

$$_t\hat{x}^e_{t+1} = \frac{\hat{\alpha}_t R^e_{t+1} - \hat{\beta}_t F^e_{t+1}}{1 - \hat{\gamma}_t e_{t+1}}. \tag{12}$$

Setting $\gamma = 0$ yields Pesaran's reinterpretation of Anderson's (1952) approach as a linear regression model based on a symmetric relationship between rises and falls. Noting that (10) and (12) collapse to (6) and (7), respectively, upon setting $\gamma = 0$, but with a different interpretation of the parameters, it is clear that the expectations series based on the regression method also lead to a GR in conducting the orthogonality test of the REH.

Thus, when direct measures of expectations are available only qualitatively, a specific model (or conversion procedure) is required to convert the qualitative responses into a quantitative expectations series for empirical analysis. It would seem to be arguable, therefore, that direct observations lead to direct tests of the REH because such tests are not independent of the particular conversion procedure used. A more appropriate conclusion would be that direct observations can provide further empirical evidence for testing the REH. However, since a rejection of the REH could be due to an inappropriate conversion procedure (i.e. an incorrect choice of probability distribution or regression model), tests of possible functional form mis-specification are necessary for sensible empirical analysis.

2.2   Market efficiency and the exchange rate

Applying the theory of RE formation and market efficiency to the foreign exchange rate market produces the familiar result that the forward exchange rate should be an unbiased predictor of the corresponding future spot rate. For example, in a one-period-ahead model, the model is given by

$$s_t = f_{t-1} + \psi_t \tag{13}$$

where s_t is the logarithm of the spot exchange rate at time t, f_{t-1} is the logarithm of the forward rate set in period $t - 1$ corresponding to the expected spot rate at t, and ψ_t is a zero mean and independent disturbance term.

Orthogonality tests can be invoked to test for efficiency and RE as a joint hypothesis (see, for example, Frenkel, 1980; MacDonald, 1983a, b, 1985; MacDonald and Ta, 1987). However, an extension of the implications of (13) relates to the effect of 'news'.

Equation (13) implies that the forward rate provides an unbiased forecast of the future spot rate, but the *actual* spot rate may differ from the prediction owing to the effect of 'news'. This leads to an extension of (13) as follows:

$$s_t - f_{t-1} = \alpha + \beta(Z_t - Z_t^e) + \psi_t \tag{14}$$

where Z_t is a vector of variables used to forecast the exchange rate (such as monetary growth rates) and Z_t^e denotes their expectation based upon information at time $t - 1$; β is a vector of parameters, α is a scalar parameter and ψ_t is a zero mean and independent disturbance term. As such 'news' entering the system is measured from an auxiliary equation by estimating Z_t^e in $Z_t - Z_t^e$, it thereby leads to a case of *residual GRs (levels)*.

2.3   Surprise consumption functions

The view that current income changes will have little effect on current consumption behaviour, an implication of Friedman's (1957) life cycle model of consumption, was formalized and tested by Hall (1978). In particular, assuming constant real interest rates and no transitory elements in consumption, the life cycle hypothesis would imply

$$c_t = (1 + \gamma)c_{t-1} + \varepsilon_t \tag{15}$$

where c_t is real consumption, γ is a scalar parameter and ε_t is the revision in life cycle income determined in $t - 1$ for period t onwards, i.e. 'surprise' life cycle income. Assuming RE, each agent would have a model of life cycle income and any innovations would have the properties of non-systematic surprises, namely they would have zero mean and be independently distributed. As such, equation (15) may be viewed as a 'surprise consumption function', commonly referred to as Hall's consumption function.

Muellbauer (1983) shows that if ε_t is assumed to be proportional to the surprise in human capital, where human capital is defined as the discounted present value of expected labour and transfer income, and expected human capital is approximated by a linear combination of past y and c, such as

$$y_t = \beta_0 + \beta_1 y_{t-1} + \beta_2 y_{t-2} + \beta_3 c_{t-1} + u_t \tag{16}$$

then ε_t will be proportional to u_t. In particular, if $\varepsilon_t = \rho u_t$ with ρ a scalar parameter, then (15) can be written as

$$c_t = (1 + \gamma)c_{t-1} + \rho(y_t - \beta_0 - \beta_1 y_{t-1} - \beta_2 y_{t-2} - \beta_3 c_{t-1}) + \varepsilon_t, \tag{17}$$

thereby yielding a *residual GRs (levels)* model where a test of $\rho = \gamma = 0$ would be a test of Hall's consumption function.

Davidson and Hendry (1981) generalize Hall's (1978) approach to test explicitly for the effect of current and past income, i.e. a test of $\alpha_4 = 1$ and $\alpha_0 = \alpha_1 = \alpha_2 = \alpha_3 = 0$ in

$$c_t = \alpha_0 + \alpha_1 y_t + \alpha_2 y_{t-1} + \alpha_3 y_{t-2} + \alpha_4 c_{t-1} + \eta_t, \tag{18}$$

but they also replace y_t with its expected value y_t^e formulated in period $t - 1$. This case is an example of a *predictor GR*.

2.4   NCM models of the NR–RE hypothesis

2.4.1   An NCM model

The NCM challenge to the short-run potency of systematic monetary policy is derived from three crucial assumptions:

1   full instantaneous price flexibility in all markets;
2   a concentration on aggregate supply rather than demand, modelled according to the Sargent and Wallace (1975) 'surprise supply' function; and
3   adoption of Muth-rational versions of expectation formation.

A simple statement of NCM claims is that real variables, such as output or employment, deviate from their long-run or NR levels only in response to unanticipated, or 'surprise', monetary policy. Note the concentration on monetary policy, the issue of fiscal policy being far less contentious (see, for example, Buiter, 1980). A somewhat fuller discussion of various forms of surprise supply function, mainly associated with the work of Lucas, is presented in section 2.4.2.

To examine the theoretical underpinnings of the model and the role of 'surprises', consider the following.

1   A Sargent and Wallace surprise supply function:

$$y_t^s = \bar{y}_t + \lambda(p_t - p_t^e) + \zeta_t \qquad \lambda > 0 \tag{19}$$

where y_t^s is the logarithm of aggregate supply, $\bar{y}_t$ is the logarithm of the NR level of output, p_t is the logarithm of the price level, p_t^e denotes the expectation of p_t formed at $t - 1$, ζ_t is a zero mean and independent disturbance term, and λ is a scalar.

2 An aggregate demand function:

$$y_t^d + p_t = v_t + m_t \tag{20}$$

where y_t^d is the logarithm of aggregate demand, m_t the logarithm of the money supply and v_t the logarithm of the velocity of circulation.

3 Full instantaneous market clearing:

$$y_t^d = y_t^s = y_t. \tag{21}$$

4 A policy reaction function:

$$m_t = Z_t \gamma + \eta_t \tag{22}$$

where Z_t is a vector of variables used to explain the monetary growth process, γ is a vector of parameters and η_t is a zero mean and independent disturbance term.

Often the policy reaction function is modelled as a simple feedback rule:

$$m_t = m_{t-1} + g + \eta_t \tag{22'}$$

where g is a constant. Clearly, more sophisticated mechanisms can be constructed (see, for example, Pesaran, 1987).

It is important to note that m_t is assumed exogenous with respect to y_t and p_t. Furthermore, v_t in (20) is often assumed to be a constant, although this is not crucial to the analysis. However, it must be exogenous with respect to both y_t and p_t. Assuming that $E(\eta_t) = 0$ yields $m_t^e = Z_t \gamma$ in (22), in which case $E(m_t^e - m_t) = 0$.

Following from the above, the NCM model based upon a Sargent and Wallace surprise supply function produces a pseudo-reduced form equation where output deviates from its NR level only in response to *unanticipated* changes in the quantity of money:

$$\tilde{y}_t = \beta(m_t - m_t^e) + \zeta_t \qquad \beta > 0 \tag{23}$$

where $\tilde{y}_t = y_t - \bar{y}_t$ and ζ_t is a zero mean and independent disturbance term. The above yields a *residual GRs (levels)* model.

The NCM models examined in sections 3 and 4 below typically constitute a mixture of predictor and residual GRs and comprise a policy reaction function given by equation (22) and an output equation represented by

$$\tilde{y}_t = \sum_{i=0}^{N} \beta_i(m_{t-i} - m_{t-i}^e) + \sum_{i=0}^{P} \delta_i m_{t-i}^e + \zeta_t \tag{24}$$

where the terms on the right-hand side relate to unanticipated and anticipated (or expected) monetary growth respectively. Methods of measuring or estimating values for such monetary variables will be discussed in section 3.

2.4.2   Alternative surprise supply functions

The Sargent and Wallace (1975) aggregate surprise supply function produces real effects because of misperceptions about systematic versus non-systematic monetary growth rates. Economic agents face a 'signal extraction' problem. Such signal extraction problems permeate NCM models, and arise for a number of different reasons.

There are instances where the term *Lucas surprise supply function* is attached to the NCM policy-ineffectiveness propositions. However, care must be exercised in such instances as Lucas has three discernible versions of aggregate supply response models, namely the Lucas islands, Lucas and Rapping and Lucas 'serial correlation in output' approaches. The three variants of aggregate supply will be discussed below.

The Lucas (1972) islands model
Lucas (1972) produces a theoretical rationale for the aggregate supply model of Sargent and Wallace (1975) based upon informational asymmetries between workers and firms in local markets, the so-called islands model. Both workers and firms are assumed to have full information on local wages and prices, but lack information on the general price level. Firms respond to local market price surprises, supplying more today if the local price exceeds the normal or expected price, which is typically assumed to be the average of prices in all comparable markets. This relation is captured in the equation

$$y_{Lt} - y_{Lt}^* = \alpha(p_{Lt} - p_{Lt}^e) + \zeta_{Lt} \tag{25}$$

where y_{Lt} denotes output in the local market at time t, p_{Lt} the local price and p_{Lt}^e the expected price in *all markets* based upon only the local information set at time $t - 1$ and ζ_{Lt} is a zero mean and independent disturbance term. The variable y_{Lt}^* denotes the normal level of local output, implying that firms adjust their outputs relative to normal in response to perceived changes in relative prices. In the situation considered here, 'normal' is not necessarily associated with the concept of an NR level of output. When observing a change in p_{Lt}, firms have to decide whether such a change is a consequence of simply a change in all prices or a change in relative prices.

An important corollary of the Lucas (1972) model relates to the variability of the local versus aggregate price level (or their rates of change). Any increase in the general price level engineered, for example, by monetary policy will initially increase local output. However, if repeated, increases in the general price level will tend to increase its variability without having local output effects. Therefore, output effects engineered by monetary shocks will tend to be smaller the higher is the variability of the general price level. The islands hypothesis was tested by Lucas (1973), Makin (1982), Mullineaux (1980) and Kormendi and Mequire (1991), and generally involves some form of residual GRs (variance) approach.

The Lucas and Rapping (1969) intertemporal substitution supply function
Although the original Lucas and Rapping (1969) model considers the determination of labour supply, their intertemporal substitution in production approach has been widely used as a microeconomic rationale for a surprise supply function. As will be seen, however, monetary neutrality is not a generic property of this particular theoretical underpinning.

If producers perceive that prices at t are higher than those expected at $t + 1$, it may (depending on the firm's rate of discount on future profits) be more profitable to sell at t, thereby producing more at t and less at $t + 1$. Such expectations will clearly have real effects even when fully perceived by all agents. The Lucas and Rapping intertemporal supply function will take the form

$$y_t - y_t^\dagger = \alpha(p_t - p_{t+1}^e) + r_t + \zeta_t \tag{26}$$

where $y_t - y_t^\dagger$ denotes the deviation of actual output at t from its expected profit maximizing level $y_t^\dagger$, caused by the incentive to shift production intertemporally, r_t is the discount factor, p_{t+1}^e denotes the expectation of prices in $t + 1$ based upon information available in period t, and ζ_t is a zero mean and independent disturbance term.

An important assumption in this approach is whether price increases will be temporary or permanent. There will be no large switch to production at t if permanent, although temporary increases will create large real effects. However, like the islands model, extracting temporary from permanent effects may take time, with real effects being produced in the interim.

This formulation of a surprise supply function has not attracted much attention from applied economists, perhaps partly because of the theoretical possibility of non-neutrality of systematic monetary policy. An exception to the general rule is the work of Thoma (1989).

The Lucas (1973, 1975) serial correlation in output approach

One implication of the Sargent and Wallace aggregate supply function under RE is that deviations in output from the NR will be serially independent. Casual empiricism, however, highlights considerable serial correlation in output (see Pesaran's (1982) reference to an LSW (Lucas, Sargent and Wallace) model, and Pesaran's (1987) Lucas surprise supply function). Pesaran (1982) argues that, with serial correlation in output, the implications above can only hold if the NR varies *pro-cyclically*, thereby contradicting the standard practice of NCM wherein the NR is approximated by an exponential trend. Lucas's (1973) response to such contradictions is to formulate the model as

$$\tilde{y}_t = \sum_{i=1}^N \mu_i y_{t-i} + \gamma(p_t - p_t^e) + \varepsilon_t \tag{27}$$

where $\tilde{y}_t = y_t - \tilde{y}_t$ is the deviation of output from the NR, p_t and p_t^e are actual and expected prices based on information at time $t - 1$, μ_i and γ are constant parameters, and ε_t is a zero mean and independent disturbance term.

Lucas (1975) refers to information confusion and serial correlation in the capital stock in an attempt to rationalize (27). Sargent (1979) refers to the existence of adjustment costs involved in hiring and firing labour. The problem with (27), as Pesaran (1982) highlights, is that tests of the NCM hypothesis are no longer a trivial matter. The essence of Pesaran's critique relates to the interpretation of causality tests when past actions of the authorities to stabilize output have been effective. In particular, perfect stabilization, namely keeping actual output at its NR, would support the NCM hypothesis, or at least be unable to reject it.

2.4.3 Some testable implications of the NCM–RE model

When considering tests of the NCM claims regarding monetary neutrality and the effects of GRs on such hypotheses, it is important to isolate the nature of the various propositions under review. As will become apparent, the NCM–RE neutrality hypothesis is typically a joint hypothesis, and is one which may be rejected for a number of reasons. The statistical outcome based on a model which includes GRs, however, may be symptomatic of the estimation procedure used as well as the model specification. Both of these issues will be highlighted in section 3 below.

PROPOSITION P1 – WEAK NEUTRALITY (or 'structural' neutrality, as in Attfield et al. (1991, p. 159)): *For any generally accepted, but not necessarily rational, expectation formation mechanism, real variables will only be affected by monetary policy if such policy is unanticipated.*

This proposition, in one sense, constitutes the null hypothesis against which others are to be compared, particularly RE (table 1). It may not be a particularly interesting economic proposition in its own right, but in models which exhibit observational equivalence, or where RE are assumed but not tested, it may be the strongest conclusion not rejected by the data.

Clearly, the term 'generally accepted' is very wide-ranging, at least in principle. However, some model of expectation formation must be stipulated explicitly if the notion of anticipated policy is to have meaning. Models such as adaptive, extrapolative or autoregressive expectations formation are clearly permissible. The basic characteristic of P1 is that expectations are not constrained to be rational, highlighting the important implication that neutrality can arise in non-rational models.

Empirical applications which maintain the hypothesis of RE when testing for neutrality should fall, strictly speaking, within the province of P1, and not P2 or P3 as stated below. Such contributions include Barro (1977) and Bellante et al. (1982), where neutrality is not rejected for the USA. Darrat (1985a) and Makin (1982), however, reject neutrality for Canada and the USA, respectively, while maintaining the assumption of RE. As will be seen in section 4 and as illustrated by table 5, explicit tests of RE and neutrality may not lead to rejection of such maintained hypotheses, particularly for the USA (see, for example, Leiderman, 1980).

PROPOSITION P2 – SEMI-STRONG NEUTRALITY (or the 'weak neutrality theorem', as in Begg (1982, p. 143)): P1 together with *Muth rationality replacing the 'generally accepted' expectations mechanism.*

This appears to be the basic NCM monetary neutrality proposition. However, in practice the actual proposition formulated is somewhat stronger and is presented as P3 below.

PROPOSITION P3 – STRONG NEUTRALITY (or the 'strong neutrality theorem', as in Begg (1982, p. 143)): P2 together with '*systematic monetary policy cannot affect the NR level of output*'.

The assumption that systematic monetary policy cannot affect the NR level of output is a maintained hypothesis in most NCM models, including the original work of Barro

Table 1   Hypothesis testing framework for propositions P1–P4

Proposition	Anticipated money	Unanticipated money	Auxiliary assumption, RE
ACCEPT null hypothesis (P1–P4)[a]			
P1	Not significant	*And* significant	Not required
P2	Not significant	*And* significant	*And* required
P3	Not significant	*And* significant	*And* required
P4	Not significant	*And* not significant	No assumption regarding rationality
REJECT null hypothesis (P1–P4)[b]			
P1	Significant	*Or* not significant	Not required
P2	Significant	*Or* not significant	*Or* required
P3	Significant	*Or* not significant	*Or* required
P4	Significant	*Or* significant	No assumption regarding rationality

[a] Monetary neutrality may still be supported with the rejection of RE (refer to P1).
[b] P4 is *rejected* if any of P1–P3 *is not rejected or* if any of P1–P3 *is rejected* due to the significance of anticipated money.

(1977) and subsequent applications (see, for example, Attfield et al., 1981b; Cuthbertson and Taylor, 1986; Gochoco, 1986; Hoffman and Schlagenhauf, 1982). It is typically the case that the assumption is not tested empirically, although an implication of the results of Pesaran (1982) and McAleer and McKenzie (1991a) in testing NCM models against Keynesian models is that systematic policy does affect the NR of unemployment. Keynesian or activist models have theoretical underpinnings which clearly reject P3. Note, however, that in this case P3 constitutes a joint hypothesis testing approach, involving RE and *two* independent forms of neutrality.

PROPOSITION P4 – STRICT NEUTRALITY: *Monetary variables, whether anticipated or unanticipated, have no effects on real variables.*

As with P1, P4 might be viewed simply within a classical hypothesis testing framework (see table 1). However, P4 has economic validity if we consider it as a testable implication of the real business cycle approach to macroeconomics (see, for example, Kydland and Prescott, 1982). For completeness, RE and non-RE versions should perhaps be presented, but this seems unnecessarily cumbersome. In particular, except for the Philippines, El Salvador and Argentina in Attfield and Duck (1983) and Mexico (non-traded goods) in Montiel (1987), the empirical papers to be discussed below all implicitly reject P4.

2.4.5 Rejection of the propositions

As presented, propositions P1–P4 are not a simple set of transitive hypotheses, although clearly P1, P2 and P3 are. One of the major complications which arises in hypothesis testing is the joint nature of the hypotheses. Table 1 presents the hypothesis testing framework, and the propositions are discussed in detail below.

Proposition 1 will be rejected if:

1 both anticipated and unanticipated policy affects real variables;
2 anticipated policy affects real variables but unanticipated policy does not;
3 proposition P4 is not rejected.

Notice that the auxiliary hypothesis of RE is not required in testing P1, so that its rejection does not lead to rejection of the maintained hypothesis.

As detailed below in section 4, P1 is rejected for a number of countries based upon either 1 or 2 above, and is rejected for Argentina, El Salvador and the Philippines in Attfield and Duck (1983), and for Mexico in Montiel (1987), based upon 3.

Proposition P2 will be rejected as for P1, but also if testable RE restrictions are rejected.

Proposition P3 will be rejected as for P2, but also if systematic monetary policy affects the NR level of real variables.

Such a hypothesis is not, however, explicitly tested, partly because the NR is often (implicitly) approximated by a simple time trend, so that P2 and P3 become synonymous in empirical applications. However, as noted above, support for Keynesian models against NCM models in Pesaran (1982) and McAleer and McKenzie (1991a) could be construed as a rejection of P3, in addition to the significant effects of anticipated monetary growth which both papers identify.

Proposition P4 will be rejected if any of P1–P3 is not rejected or if any of P1–P3 is rejected due to the significance of anticipated money.

This rejection strategy demonstrates why propositions P1–P4 are not nested. In particular, P4 can be rejected for two separate reasons.

3 Measures of unobserved variables–unanticipated money growth

In section 2, models which give rise to GRs were discussed and the economic importance of 'unanticipated', 'surprise' or 'news' terms was stressed. The first major obstacle faced when seeking to test the importance of such variables is their general lack of observability. In this section we classify various methods used to measure such variables concentrating, *by way of example*, on measures of unanticipated money growth. The strengths and weaknesses of each approach are highlighted and examples of various types of models used are provided. First, four basic *methods* of determining unanticipated monetary variables are defined. The approach is easily generalized to other measures of 'news', 'surprise' or 'unexpected' variables.

Method A: Consistent methods using two-step estimation
This is the most common approach involving OLS estimation and includes, as a separate category, recursive and rolling estimation. Consistency in this instance refers to the inefficiently estimated parameters and not to their (typically) inconsistent standard errors.

Method B: Efficient methods
Method B uses models of expectations formation within an estimation framework to produce efficient estimates. This method necessarily involves the imposition of non-linear cross-equation restrictions and has the advantage in an NCM testing framework of allowing separate tests of neutrality and rationality, a feature which is unavailable under method A.

Method C: Correct two-step estimation methods
Method C is an improvement on method A in that it produces correct inferences by a correction to the conventionally programmed OLS standard errors. However, the approach lacks the flexibility of method B in that rationality remains a maintained hypothesis which is not empirically tested. To date this important method has not been widely adopted by researchers, no doubt because it involves recomputation of correct OLS standard errors. Important exceptions to this general rule are Cuthbertson and Taylor (1986) and McAleer and McKenzie (1991a). Monte Carlo evidence presented in Hoffman and Schlagenhauf (1991) suggests that, in large samples, method C performs as well as method B in detecting failure of neutrality.

Method G: Generalized Least Squares methods
Method G corrects the non-spherical error structure produced by the introduction of GRs as part of the estimation procedure. Rather than correcting the structural errors *after* estimation, the correction is incorporated through generalized least squares (GLS) estimation.

3.1   Model categorization and classification

Within these four basic methods are classified two important *categories* of models:

1   *full sample period* estimation;
2   *recursive projections*, namely repeated estimation and production of one-step-ahead forecast errors.

These two categories have important methodological implications for the role of RE models in expectations formation.
   Within these two categories we can identify four different *classifications:*

(a)   *structural models*;
(b)   *time series models*, ranging from simple autoregressive (AR) to autoregressive integrated moving average (ARIMA) models;

(c) *survey-based measures* of anticipated variables, for example the Livingston data of Carlson (1977);

(d) *inferred approach*, which uses a maintained model to infer expectations of variables.

Therefore, there are, in principle, four *methods*, two *categories* and four *classifications* of models to measure specifically unanticipated monetary variables. However, the approach clearly generalizes to other examples. In practice, not all of these combinations are used. As an example, Barro (1977) is a method A1(a) approach while Attfield et al. (1981a) is an A1(a)–(b) and B1(a)–(b).

In order to consider the *methods, categories* and *classifications* in more detail, consider the following developments.

3.2   The methods in more detail

To aid discussion of the methods of estimation to be discussed, consider equations (22) and (24) which are presented as equations (28) and (29) below:

$$m_t = Z_t\gamma + \eta_t \tag{28}$$

$$\tilde{y}_t = \sum_{i=0}^{N} \beta_i(m_{t-i} - m_{t-i}^e) + \sum_{i=0}^{P} \delta_i m_{t-i}^e + \zeta_t \tag{29}$$

where m_t is the logarithm of the money supply; Z_t is a vector of variables used to explain the monetary growth process; y_t is the logarithm of output; $\bar{y}_t$ the NR level of output, with $\tilde{y}_t = y_t - \bar{y}_t$; m_{t-i}^e is the expectation of m for period $t - i$ based upon information known at period $t - i$; γ, β and δ are constant parameters; and η_t and ζ_t are zero mean and independent disturbance terms.

3.2.1   Method A: Two-step estimation

A feature common to all categories within this group is that anticipations of policy parameters are estimated in isolation from the rest of the system. From a model of expectations formation like (28), unanticipated policy is approximated either by a simple OLS residual or by a one-step-ahead forecast error. After measures of anticipated money, m_t^e, and unanticipated money, η_t, have been established, they are treated as non-stochastic inputs into the second stage of the process, namely the estimation of a relationship such as (29).

Method A1(a)–(d): Two-step estimation
As described above, some form of policy reaction function (28) is estimated for the period of interest, with OLS residuals used as proxies for unanticipated policy. In Barro (1977), (28) is formulated as

$$DM_t = a_0 + a_1DM_{t-1} + a_2DM_{t-2} + a_3FEDV_t + a_4UN_{t-1} + u_t \tag{30}$$

where DM is the annual average money growth rate of M1, FEDV is a measure of real federal government expenditure relative to trend, and UN is a measure of the annual average unemployment rate in the working population. The a_i ($i = 1, \ldots, 4$) are parameters to be estimated and u_t is assumed to be a zero mean and serially uncorrelated disturbance which represents unanticipated money growth. In Barro (1977), equation (30) was estimated for the period 1941–73 to produce a series of OLS residuals to be used as GRs in the following structural equation:

$$\text{UN}_t = b_0 + b_1\text{DMR}_t + b_2\text{DMR}_{t-1} + b_3\text{DMR}_{t-2} + b_4\text{MIL}_t + b_5\text{MINW}_t + v_t. \tag{31}$$

Equation (31) was estimated by OLS for the period 1946–73. Models such as (31) will be discussed later, and the variables are defined as follows: MIL is a measure of military conscription, MINW is a minimum wage variable, and v_t is a zero mean and independent disturbance term. All other variables are as above.

Equation (31) is a structural equation classification, i.e. A1(a), which is the most popular approach to be found in the literature. Examples include the seminal work of Barro (1977, 1978, 1981), Barro and Rush (1980), Bellante et al. (1982), Darrat (1985a, b), Gordon (1982), Leiderman (1980), Montiel (1987), Pesaran (1982, 1988), Rush (1985), Rush and Waldo (1988) and Sheehey (1984).

As an extension of 2SE, McAleer and McKenzie (1991a) produce multivariate 2SE (M2SE) results. They estimate a three-equation system comprising a univariate structural equation of unemployment together with a bivariate expectations system.

Examples of the A1(b) classification are much less common. The most notable is the work of Makin (1982), where he uses an ARIMA model of the form

$$(1 - \phi_1 L)m_t = (1 - \Delta_1 L^4 - \Delta_2 L^8 - \Delta_3 L^{12})(1 - \phi_2 L^2) + \delta_t \tag{32}$$

where m_t relates to money growth, L is the lag operator, ϕ_1 is an autoregressive coefficient, ϕ_2 a moving average coefficient, Δ_i ($i = 1, 2, 3$) is a seasonal moving average coefficient, and δ_t is a random disturbance term. Equation (32) is used to model US money growth for 1953–75 using both bi-annual and quarterly data. Makin (1982) also uses Carlson's (1977) Livingston inflation expectations survey data, thereby entering classifications A1(b) and A1(c). One problem with equation (32) is that it implies non-stationarity. Examples of the A1(d) classification include Amihud (1982), which is based upon a measure of the public's prediction of inflation as inferred from market nominal interest rates.

The *main strength* of the A1 method is its ease of implementation. Equations such as (30) are estimated only once, typically by OLS, thereby producing time series approximations of the unanticipated money variable. However, there are several weaknesses, some of which are common to all method A approaches while others are restricted to A1.

A serious weakness might appear to be full-sample estimation since the econometrician uses unavailable future information in the formulation of current expectations and shocks. An obvious defence is of the 'as if' variety. Investigators are attempting to 'discover' the data generation process (DGP) and, *conditional on the estimated model being stable*, no injustice to the spirit of RE is made by the A1 approach. This conditioning is crucial. Estimated policy reaction functions which exhibit stability clearly offer some credence to the argument. However, studies which omit any tests of stability, or treat them in a cursory manner, should be treated with extreme caution. Therefore, *stability tests of policy reaction functions should be considered a necessary part of the testing methodology.* A further methodological weakness suffered by A1(b) methods is that, in using only time series of, typically, money growth, they omit information which might be useful in explaining the variable of interest. This is not within the spirit of RE.

Apart from these specific weaknesses, A1 methods suffer from a number of generic shortcomings. The first is the GR problem which will be discussed later under method C. As McAleer and McKenzie (1991a) show, *the GR problem can lead to biases in a number of diagnostic test statistics.* In particular, variable addition tests of the Ramsey (1969, 1974) RESET variety, and Godfrey (1978) and Breusch and Godfrey (1981) tests of serial correlation, may require corrections to the asymptotic standard errors to provide valid inferences. Both sets of tests are biased towards rejection of the null and hence require correction.

Further, variable addition non-nested tests, such as the J test of Davidson and Mac-Kinnon (1981) and the JA test of Fisher and McAleer (1981), will also be biased towards rejection of the null hypothesis. The variance-adjusted Cox- and Wald-type tests of Godfrey and Pesaran (1983), based upon the ratios of sums of estimated error variances, would also seem to yield biased test statistics. In addition, the original Cox test will be incorrectly computed, but the direction of bias is unclear. Second, whatever is omitted from z_t in (28) is incorporated into the OLS residuals, so that the problem of mis-specification of (28) is important. The degree of importance depends on the nature of the test statistics being constructed; see, for example, Hoffman and Schlagenhauf (1984) and McAleer and Smith (1990) for Monte Carlo simulation results based upon mis-specified functions. This potential mis-specification problem also permeates methods B, C and G, so that no extra weight should be attached to it as a criticism of method A1 alone.

Finally, methods A, C and G have the weakness, in an NCM–RE testing framework, that they do not allow the formulation of separate tests of the rationality of expectations formation and the neutrality of policy. Therefore, the hypothesis of RE is *always maintained.*

Method A2(a)–(d): Recursive estimation

Adhering to the nature of RE, this approach uses only information known at the time expectations are formulated. Unanticipated policy is approximated by one-step-ahead forecast errors. To produce a time series of unanticipated money growth of length n requires n regressions updated period by period with additional Z_t data.

The main strength of the approach is methodological. Only data available at the time expectations are formed are actually used in the modelling process. Furthermore, in principle, stability tests of the reaction function need not be a prerequisite to their being used in the second stage. However, evidence of varying parameters not only causes econometric inference problems but also suggests some form of adaptive or learning behaviour in expectations formation, which is a controversial issue in its own right. Such evidence has particular significance given that methods A, C and G treat RE as a maintained hypothesis.

The main weaknesses of the approach, apart from those generic to method A (for further details, see McAleer and McKenzie, 1992) are its operational inconvenience and data constraints. To produce a time series of $t = 1, 2, \ldots, T$ proxies requires T

updated regressions. Evidence of varying parameters may simply be a consequence of a lack of available data used in representing early values of the variable of interest.

The A2 approach has been used by several authors, including Beladi and Samanta (1988) (A2(a) and A2(c)), Sheehan (1985) (A2(a)) and Sheffrin (1979) (A2(b)). The use of the Kalman filter as a means of updating will also be included in this category. Few examples besides Cuthbertson and Taylor (1986) are available.

3.2.2   Method B: Efficient methods

One of the main attractions of RE over alternative models of expectations formation is that expectations formed 'rationally' are *internally consistent*. By this is meant that RE are the outcome inferred by a macroeconomic model constructed to satisfy certain characteristics, such as long-run neutrality, market clearing and market efficiency. The crucial feature of RE is that expectations are produced as part of estimation. Method A simply assumes that models like (28) exhibit RE and can be used 'as if' (28) and (29) are the correctly specified economic system. Method B approaches, however, check for internal consistency by comparing the expectations produced without imposing correct specification.

The estimators produced by method B are also efficient compared with those produced by method A, conditional on the model being correct. *However, it is not clear whether uncorrected standard errors are greater than, less than or equal to the efficient estimates*, since the uncorrected standard errors are *understated* (see Murphy and Topel (1985) and McAleer and McKenzie (1991a) for empirical demonstrations of this problem). In a sense, method B uses all available information at all stages of estimation, whereas the second stage of 2SE uses only a summary measure of anticipated and unanticipated money, namely the first-step predictions or residuals. Method B uses all available information by the imposition of the RE *cross-equation restrictions*.

Consider a two-equation version of the generic system:

$$m_t = Z_t \gamma + \eta_t \tag{33}$$

$$\tilde{y}_t = \sum_{i=0}^{N} \beta_i (m_{t-i} - m_{t-i}^{e}) + \sum_{i=0}^{P} \delta_i m_{t-i}^{e} + \zeta_t \tag{34}$$

where the variables are as defined in section 3.2. Further, for identification purposes, η and ζ are assumed to have zero contemporaneous covariance, i.e. $E(\eta_t \zeta_t) = \sigma_{\eta\zeta} = 0$ (see Pesaran, 1987, p.171).

Measures of both anticipated money, m_t^{e}, and unanticipated money, $m_t - m_t^{e}$, are internally consistent using method B. Thus, invoking RE, (34) may be rewritten as

$$\tilde{y}_t = \sum_{i=0}^{N} \beta_i (m_{t-i} - Z_{t-i}\gamma) + \sum_{i=0}^{P} \delta_i Z_{t-i}\gamma + \zeta_t \tag{35}$$

or as

$$\tilde{y}_t = \sum_{i=0}^{N} \beta_i' (m_{t-i} - Z_{t-i}\gamma) + \sum_{i=0}^{P} \delta_i m_{t-i} + \zeta_t \tag{36}$$

where $\beta_i' = \beta_i - \delta_i$. Unanticipated money is now approximated by $m_{t-i} - Z_{t-i}\gamma$ and anticipated money by $Z_{t-i}\gamma$. Estimation of the model involves joint estimation of equations (33) and (35) (or 36) as a system using, for example, full-information maximum likelihood (FIML). This approach is efficient since estimation imposes cross-equation restrictions, i.e. the estimated value of γ in equation (33) must equal the estimated value of γ in (35) or (36) if the model is to incorporate Muth rationality.

Apart from efficiency the main advantage of method B over the A, C and G alternatives is the ability to test, in an NCM–RE testing framework, the implied RE and neutrality as separate hypotheses. Moreover, systems estimation does not suffer from the GR problem.

The main disadvantages of the method, apart from those generic to category 1, are computational. Estimation of (33) and (35) (or 36) as a system necessarily involves some form of nonlinear estimation.

Attfield et al. (1981b) demonstrate two equivalent methods of estimating systems like (33) and (35). Imposing neutrality, consider the two-equation system

$$m_t = Z_t\gamma + \eta_t$$

$$\tilde{y}_t = \sum_{i=0}^{N} \beta_i(m_{t-i} - Z_{t-i}\gamma) + \varepsilon_t \tag{37}$$

where all variables are as defined in section 3.2 and η_t and ε_t are uncorrelated, zero mean, independent disturbance terms. Estimation of (37) by OLS produces consistent but inefficient estimates. However, either of the following procedures produces efficient estimates.

I. *Constrain the off-diagonal elements of the covariance matrix of errors of the system to zero*, i.e.

$$E \begin{bmatrix} \eta_t \\ \varepsilon_t \end{bmatrix} [\, \eta_t \quad \varepsilon_t \,] = \begin{bmatrix} \sigma_{\eta\eta} & 0 \\ 0 & \sigma_{\varepsilon\varepsilon} \end{bmatrix}.$$

This nonlinear seemingly unrelated regression estimation (SURE)-type constraint is required to ensure that the system residuals are contemporaneously uncorrelated, a necessary condition for identifying β_0. The imposition of such covariance restrictions on the equation errors is computationally straightforward.

As an alternative to imposing covariance restrictions, equivalent residual properties can be produced indirectly as follows.

II. *Estimate the system with implicit covariance restrictions*, i.e.

$$m_t = Z_t\gamma + \eta_t$$

$$\tilde{y}_t = \sum_{i=0}^{N} \beta_i(m_{t-i} - Z_{t-i}\gamma) + \varepsilon_t. \tag{38}$$

System (38) can be estimated by nonlinear least squares (NLLS) without invoking constraints on the residuals across equations.

Technique II is computationally simpler than I, but it does not produce a direct estimate of β_0 or its standard error. Unlike technique I, an estimate of β_0 is extracted from the covariance matrix of errors from the reduced form. In particular,

$$E \begin{bmatrix} \eta_t \\ \varepsilon_t \end{bmatrix} [\eta_t \quad \varepsilon_t] = \begin{bmatrix} \sigma_{\eta\eta} & \beta_0 \sigma_{\eta\eta} \\ \beta_0 \sigma_{\eta\eta} & \beta_0^2 \sigma_{\eta\eta} + \sigma_{\varepsilon\varepsilon} \end{bmatrix}.$$

Estimation by either technique I or II, however, involves the minimization of the same criterion and therefore produces equivalent estimates (see Attfield et al. (1981b, pp. 340–1) for an explicit demonstration). Each technique, however, has operational strengths and weaknesses.

Estimation by technique II is relatively straightforward, except for extracting the standard errors for the estimate β_0. To quote from Attfield et al. (1981, p. 374), this involves:

> applying to the variance–covariance matrix, the Jacobian transformation between β_0 and the elements $\sigma_{\eta\eta}, \beta_0 \sigma_{\eta\eta}$ and $\beta_0^2 \sigma_{\eta\eta} + \sigma_{\varepsilon\varepsilon}$. (our notation)

Estimation by technique I, however, produces direct estimates of β_0 and its standard error, but only after estimation involving covariance restrictions on the errors of the system.

Examples of applications of method B include Attfield et al. (1981a, b) (B1(a)), Barro (1981) (B1(b)), Hoffman and Schlagenhauf (1982) (B1(a)), Leiderman (1980) (B1(a)), and Mishkin (1982, 1983) (B1(a)).

3.2.3   Method C: Corrected two-step estimation

The two-step methods discussed in section 3.2.1 treat the proxies for unanticipated and anticipated policy as fixed regressors in the second step of estimating an equation like (29) or (31). Such proxies are the result of previous estimation and therefore are referred to as GRs.

Pagan (1984) discusses the general issue of GRs, of which the policy ineffectiveness models comprise a special case, and shows that the errors in a two-step procedure are non-spherical. Full discussion and demonstration of the phenomenon is presented in section 3.3 below.

As noted in section 3.2.1, the uncorrected 2SE method, although consistent, produces inefficient estimates. However, as Mishkin (1982) suggests, the important issue may not be efficiency but the potentially invalid inferences based on both t and F tests. The conventionally programmed OLS estimates of the covariance matrix of the β_1 and δ_1 parameters tends to understate the true covariance matrix. Pagan's (1984) theorem 8, however, provides some solace:

> The estimated (OLS) standard errors in Barro-type procedures are no greater than the true standard errors.

Therefore, non-rejection of neutrality based upon uncorrected 2SE standard errors cannot be reversed by using the corrected standard errors. However, although uncorrected standard errors will be less than or equal to the correct standard errors, the same outcome cannot be guaranteed when comparing efficiently estimated standard errors. The correct standard errors will be greater than or equal to the efficiently estimated standard errors, but a simple relationship between the efficient and uncorrected standard errors does not exist (see Murphy and Topel, 1985; McAleer and McKenzie, 1991a).

The clear advantage of corrected 2SE is the validity of inferences. However, being a variant of method A, it suffers from the same generic problems, including its inability to test rationality and neutrality separately in an NCM testing framework. Given such strengths, including power of the test (see Hoffman and Schlagenhauf, 1984), it seems to have attracted little attention in empirical studies. A notable exception includes Cuthbertson and Taylor (1986), who produce models classified as C1(a), (b), C2(a) and both B1(a) and B1(b).

3.2.4   Method G–Hoffman (1987)

In this method, rather than simply correcting the covariance matrix *after* OLS estimation, Hoffman (1987) incorporates the non-spherical error structure through GLS estimation.

Method G produces two major improvements over method A: (i) the use of an appropriate covariance matrix for use in hypothesis testing; and (ii) the incorporation of the non-spherical disturbance term in estimation. The degree of gain in efficiency over uncorrected 2SE depends upon two factors discussed in footnote 4 in Gauger (1989, p. 388):

> The greater the noise in the auxiliary equation, or the difference between δ_i and β_i parameters, the greater the deficiency between the error covariance matrix implied in standard 2SOLS [two-step OLS] and the correct covariance matrix.

Such factors were considered in a series of empirical replications reported in table 1 of Gauger (1989) where, as expected, noisy 'auxiliary' equations led to the largest number of inferential reversals when either corrected 2SE or GLS estimation was used.

3.3   Formulation of tests of the neutrality propositions

In this section tests of the neutrality propositions are discussed in detail, with the formulation of separate tests of neutrality and rationality being highlighted.

Two types of test are used to evaluate the various neutrality propositions as follows.

Type 1 is based upon tests of linear coefficients, with the test statistics following either the *t* or *F* distribution. Such tests are associated with the 2SE procedure which always maintains the RE hypothesis.

Type 2 is based upon tests of systems, with the test statistic following the χ^2 distribution. At least two variants of this type of test exist, with both requiring efficient estimation of the underlying system, namely method B. The first variant is a joint test of neutrality and rationality, while the second considers the two hypotheses separately.

3.3.1   Type 1 tests

Maintaining the RE hypothesis, type 1 tests consider the significance of the estimated β_i and δ_i in, for example, (35) using individual or joint tests of significance. Equivalently, goodness-of-fit tests can be constructed to compare models which exclude either anticipated or unanticipated money variables from a general specification such as (35).

The main advantage of type 1 tests is the ease of implementation using standard output from OLS estimation. However, OLS (or 2SE) induces the GR problem, so that appropriate corrections may be required if the standard errors are to be consistent (see section 3.5 below).

3.3.2   Type 2 tests

These tests permit two variants, namely *joint* tests of the rationality and neutrality hypothesis and *separate* tests of rationality (maintaining neutrality) and neutrality (maintaining rationality). Such tests require the use of method B estimation.

Consider once again the system

$$m_t = Z_t\gamma + \eta_t$$

$$\tilde{y}_t = \sum_{i=0}^{N} \beta_i(m_{t-i} - Z_{t-i}\gamma^*) + \sum_{i=0}^{P} \delta_i Z_{t-i}\gamma^* + \varepsilon_t \qquad (39)$$

where η and ε are assumed to be uncorrelated. Notice that γ^* is not constrained to equal γ. Imposing neutrality and rationality jointly on the system (39) would impose restrictions such that

$$m_t = Z_t\gamma + \eta_t$$

$$\tilde{y}_t = \sum_{i=0}^{N} \beta_i(m_{t-i} - Z_{t-i}\gamma) + \varepsilon_t. \qquad (40)$$

Rationality is imposed by requiring $\gamma^* = \gamma$, while neutrality is imposed upon setting $\delta_i = 0$ $(i = 0, 1, \ldots, N)$. Tests of the joint type therefore involve comparison of the two systems (39) and (40).

Alternatively, separate tests can either assume that expectations are formed rationally and allow the data to determine neutrality or can assume neutrality and test for rationality. In the former case, the restrictions imposed on (39) would imply

$$m_t = Z_t\gamma + \eta_t$$

$$\tilde{y}_t = \sum_{i=0}^{N} \beta_i(m_{t-i} - Z_{t-i}\gamma) + \sum_{i=0}^{P} \delta_i Z_{t-i}\gamma + \varepsilon_t. \qquad (41)$$

Tests of this form would involve comparing system (41) with (39). A test of rationality with neutrality maintained constrains the system (39) to

$$m_t = Z_t\gamma + \eta_t$$

$$\tilde{y}_t = \sum_{i=0}^{N} \beta_i(m_{t-i} - Z_{t-i}\gamma^*) + \varepsilon_t. \qquad (42)$$

This separate test would involve comparing system (42) with (39).

The main problem with the joint test is that it may be rejected for three reasons, namely non-rationality, non-neutrality, or both. If the null is rejected, it will not be clear which is the precise cause of the rejection. The main advantage of the separate test is precisely the weakness of its joint counterpart.

3.3.3 Formulation of likelihood ratio tests

Both the joint and separate forms of the type 2 test require the comparison of the constrained and unconstrained systems, which typically involves the use of likelihood ratio tests. Mishkin (1982) considers two operational versions as follows.

$$L^* = -2\log\left(\frac{L^c}{L^u}\right)^a \sim \chi^2(q) \tag{43}$$

where L^c is the maximized likelihood value of the constrained system, L^u is the maximized likelihood value of the unconstrained system and q is the number of constraints imposed. However, when imposing covariance restrictions on systems errors to identify β_0, some econometric software packages do not print out maximized log-likelihood values. In this case, we can redefine (43) as

$$L^* = n\log\left(\frac{\det\hat{\Omega}^c}{\det\hat{\Omega}^u}\right)^a \sim \chi^2(q) \tag{44}$$

where $\det\hat{\Omega}$ is the determinant of the matrix given by

$$\hat{\Omega} = \begin{bmatrix} \dfrac{SSR_1}{N} & 0 \\ 0 & \dfrac{SSR_2}{N} \end{bmatrix}$$

with SSR_1 the sum of the squared residuals (SSR) from the first equation of the system and SSR_2 the SSR from the second equation of the system; N is the number of observations, c indicates the constrained system and u the unconstrained system. Systems of higher dimension involve exactly the same procedures. The SSR values and the matrix $\hat{\Omega}$ are those produced from imposing the covariance restrictions.

Mishkin (1982), however, highlights possible small-sample problems with the two L^* versions due to the potentially large differences in the degrees of freedom in the constrained and unconstrained systems. For this reason, he produces an alternative to L^*, namely:

$$L^{**} = 2n\log\left(\frac{SSR^c}{SSR^u}\right)^a \sim \chi^2(q). \tag{45}$$

In small samples, $L^{**} < L^*$, thereby implying a greater probability of non-rejection of the null. The severity of the difficulties with L^* depends upon the differences in degrees of freedom between the two systems. Mishkin (1982, fn 9) suggests that differences may be small in practice.

3.3.4 An example

Consider the system produced by Siegloff and Groenewold (1987), who investigated the neutrality and rationality hypotheses using seasonally adjusted Australian data for 1962(2)–1985(5). Their unconstrained system comprises

$$M_t = t\gamma_1 + \gamma_2 M_{t-1} + \gamma_3 r_{t-1} + \gamma_4 r_{t-2} + \eta_t$$

$$
\begin{aligned}
U_t = {}& \alpha_0 + \alpha_1 t + \beta_0 M_t + \beta_1 M_{t-1} + \beta_2 M_{t-2} + \beta_3 M_{t-3} + \beta_4 M_{t-4} \\
& + (\delta_0 - \beta_0)(\gamma_1^* + \gamma_2^* M_{t-1} + \gamma_3^* r_{t-1} + \gamma_4^* r_{t-2}) \\
& + (\delta_1 - \beta_1)(\gamma_1^* + \gamma_2^* M_{t-2} + \gamma_3^* r_{t-2} + \gamma_4^* r_{t-3}) \\
& + (\delta_2 - \beta_2)(\gamma_1^* + \gamma_2^* M_{t-3} + \gamma_3^* r_{t-3} + \gamma_4^* r_{t-4}) \\
& + (\delta_3 - \beta_3)(\gamma_1^* + \gamma_2^* M_{t-4} + \gamma_3^* r_{t-4} + \gamma_4^* r_{t-5}) \\
& + (\delta_4 - \beta_4)(\gamma_1^* + \gamma_2^* M_{t-5} + \gamma_3^* r_{t-5} + \gamma_4^* r_{t-6}) + w_t
\end{aligned}
\tag{46}
$$

where r is the nominal rate of interest (represented by the two-year government bond rate), M is money growth (various definitions), U is the unemployment rate, η_t and w_t are zero mean and independent disturbance terms which are assumed to be mutually uncorrelated, and the $\alpha, \beta, \delta, \gamma$ and γ_i^* are parameters to be estimated.

System (46) is the unconstrained system with neither rationality nor neutrality imposed. To test the data consistency of a joint hypothesis would involve the formulation of a likelihood ratio test based upon a comparison of (46) with a system subject to the following constraints:

$$\gamma_i^* = \gamma_i \ (i = 1, 2, 3, 4) \qquad \text{and} \qquad \delta_i = 0 \ (i = 1, 2, 3, 4).$$

Tests of such joint constraints were decisively rejected by the data. Tests of rationality, with neutrality maintained, involve the constraints $\delta_i = 0$ $(i = 1, 2, 3, 4)$. Using Australian data, the necessary cross-equation restrictions were not supported by the data. Finally, tests of neutrality, with rationality maintained, involve the constraints $\gamma_i^* = \gamma_i$ $(i = 1, 2, 3, 4)$, which were rejected. Both these separate test results were found to be robust to systems comprising shorter lags and alternative measures of money growth.

3.3.5   Other tests of neutrality

Cecchetti (1986, p. 409) derived a test of neutrality which is 'valid when the information set used to form expectations is incorrectly specified and the effect of anticipated policy on deviations of output from the natural rate, varies over time'. The various tests of neutrality discussed above depend upon two crucial assumptions:

1   that the differences between the 'true' and measured expectations (i.e. the measurement errors) are identically zero;
2   that the parameters are time invariant.

Cecchetti's test procedure is invariant to 1 or 2.
Consider the following simplified model:

$$y_t = \tilde{y}_t + \sum_{i=0}^{N} \beta_i m_{t-i} + w_t \tag{47}$$

where $y_t, \tilde{y}_t$ and β_i are as previously defined, w_t is a zero mean and independent disturbance term, and m is the expectation error defined as

$$E(\Delta M_t | \Gamma_{t-1}) = \Delta M_t - m_t \tag{48}$$

in which E is the expectations operator and Γ_{t-1} is the information set at $t-1$ used in forming expectations of the money stock at time t. If anticipated money is neutral, then

$$E[(y_t - \bar{y}_t)|\Gamma_{t-1}] = 0 \tag{49}$$

such that output deviations must be orthogonal to the lagged information set or a subset thereof.

The test of neutrality involves a regression of lagged values of the chosen information set, Z say, on deviations in output from their NR levels, and a subsequent test of orthogonality. Using both vector autoregressive (VAR) and instrumental variable (IV) methods with Z, and Haugh (1976) type tests of orthogonality, Cecchetti (1986, p. 422) is able to conclude that: 'there is no credible evidence for policy neutrality [in the USA]. This rejection must lead one to question the basis of NCM models.'

3.3.6   The AUDI approach to neutrality testing

In an attempt to explain real output variability, Frydman and Rappoport (1987) introduce the acronym 'AUDI' to refer to the hypothesis that the 'anticipated–unanticipated distinction is irrelevant'. The importance of AUDI, if supported, is twofold: (i) many of the econometric problems such as GRs, consistent versus efficient estimation, separate tests of RE and neutrality, disappear; (ii) NCM propositions P2 and P3 become irrelevant.

Consider the standard two-equation system

$$m_t = Z_t\gamma + \eta_t \tag{50}$$

$$\tilde{y}_t = \sum_{i=0}^{N} \beta_i(m_{t-i} - Z_{t-i}\gamma) + \sum_{i=0}^{P} \delta_i Z_{t-i}\gamma + \varepsilon_t.$$

The AUDI hypothesis is given by $\delta_i = \beta_i$ ($i = 0, 1, 2, \ldots, N$). If valid, output can be rewritten as

$$\tilde{y}_t = \sum_{i=0}^{N} \delta_i m_{t-i} + \varepsilon_t. \tag{51}$$

A test of monetary neutrality in (51) then becomes $\delta_i = 0$ ($i = 1, 2, \ldots, N$). If AUDI is supported (i.e. if $\delta_i = \beta_i$), mismeasurement of expectations will not affect the efficiency of estimators or the validity of inferences under the null hypothesis.

Frydman and Rappoport (1987) conclude, using US data, that: 'Our results demonstrate the stylized fact that raw money growth affects real output, in the short run, irrespective of whether it is anticipated or not'. This conclusion is supported by Pesaran (1982, 1988) using UK data. Other tests of the AUDI hypothesis include Kormendi and Meguire (1991).

3.4   When is two-step estimation efficient?

Sections 3.2.1–3.2.4 briefly outlined four methods of estimating models which include GRs. Problems inherent in method A estimation, uncorrected 2SE, were outlined and some solutions were discussed, including correct 2SE (method C) and estimation by GLS (method G).

Assuming that the expectations equation is correctly specified, McKenzie and McAleer (1992a) provide conditions under which 2SE will be as efficient as using maximum likelihood. Efficiency in this context relates either to single-equation efficiency or the efficiency of a subset of parameters. The conditions under which 2SE is efficient depend crucially upon the form of the model that is estimated.

3.4.1   Current anticipated and other variables

Consider the model given by

$$y = z^*\delta + X\beta + e \tag{52}$$

$$z = z^* + \eta = W\alpha + \eta. \tag{53}$$

Equations (52) and (53) correspond to model 2 in Pagan (1984) where y and z are $T \times 1$ vectors of endogenous variables; z^* is a $T \times 1$ vector comprising the conditional expectation of z; e and η are $T \times 1$ vectors of zero mean random disturbances with variances σ_e^2 and σ_η^2 respectively; X is a $T \times k$ matrix of exogenous or predetermined variables; W is a $T \times q$ matrix of predetermined variables; δ is an unknown scalar parameter; and α and β are unknown parameters of dimensions $k \times 1$ and $q \times 1$ respectively.

Assuming zero contemporaneous covariance between equation errors, $\sigma_{e\eta} = 0$, the first stage of 2SE involves regressing z on W to obtain the OLS fitted values $\hat{z}$. The second stage replaces z^* in (52) with $\hat{z}$ such that (52) becomes

$$y = \hat{z}\delta + X\beta + u \tag{54}$$

where $u = e + (z^* - \hat{z})\delta = e - \delta P_w \eta$, $P_w = W(W'W)^{-1}W'$ and $\hat{z} = W\hat{\alpha} = P_w z$. Assuming W to be non-stochastic and $\delta \neq 0$, the non-spherical nature of u is given by

$$V = E(uu') = \sigma_e^2 I + \delta^2 \sigma_\eta^2 P_w. \tag{55}$$

Equation (55) illustrates why conventionally programmed OLS estimation of V based upon $\sigma_e^2 I$ will under-estimate the true value of V. Under such conditions, *2SE estimates of α and β are generally not single equation efficient* unless

(a) X is orthogonal to W;
(b) X appears in W;
(c) $\beta = 0$; or
(d) $\delta = 0$.

Relaxation of the assumption that $\sigma_{e\eta} = 0$ to allow $\sigma_{e\eta} \neq 0$ yields the additional condition

(e) $\delta \sigma_\eta^2 - 2\sigma_{e\eta} = 0$.

3.4.2   Current anticipated, unanticipated and other variables

In an extension of Pagan's (1984) model 4, McAleer and McKenzie (1991b) consider

$$y = z^*\delta + (z - z^*)\gamma + X\beta + e \tag{56}$$

$$z = z^* + \eta = W\alpha + \eta. \tag{57}$$

Maintaining the assumption $\sigma_{e\eta} = 0$, which is now required for the identification of γ, *2SE of δ, γ and β is not generally single equation efficient unless*

(a) X is orthogonal to W;
(b) X appears in W;
(c) $\beta = 0$; or
(d) $\gamma = \delta$.

However, McAleer and McKenzie (1991b) prove that *2SE of γ is always asymptotically efficient when taken as a subset of equation (56).*

3.4.3 Current and lagged anticipated and unanticipated variables

Model 5 of Pagan (1984) adds lagged values of both anticipated and unanticipated variables to model 4 as follows:

$$y = z^*\delta_1 + z^*_{-1}\delta_2 + \eta\gamma_1 + \eta_{-1}\gamma_2 + e \tag{58}$$

$$z = z^* + \eta = W\alpha + \eta \tag{59}$$

$$z^*_{-1} = W_{-1}\alpha. \tag{60}$$

Assuming $\sigma_{e\eta} = 0$ for purposes of identifying γ_1, McAleer and McKenzie (1991b) establish the following results.

1 If $\delta_1 \neq 0, \delta_2 \neq 0$ and W does not contain z_{-1}: *2SE is not single equation efficient for $\delta_1, \delta_2, \gamma_1$ or γ_2; however, 2SE of γ_1 and γ_2 is asymptotically efficient when taken as a subset of equation (58).*
2 If $\delta_1 \neq 0, \delta_2 \neq 0$ and W contains z_{-1}: *2SE is not single equation efficient for $\delta_1, \delta_2, \gamma_1$ or γ_2; however, 2SE of γ_1 is asymptotically efficient when taken as a subset of equation (58).*
3 If $\delta_1 = \delta_2 = 0$ and W does not contain z_{-1}: *2SE will be asymptotically single equation efficient.*
4 If $\delta_1 = \delta_2 = 0$ and W contains z_{-1}: *2SE of γ_1 and γ_2 is not single equation efficient; however, γ_1 is asymptotically efficient when taken as a subset of equation (58).* The addition of other regressors to the structural equation will also produce inefficient estimators. Even when $\delta_1 = \delta_2 = 0$, 2SE is asymptotically single equation efficient and only if X is asymptotically orthogonal to both W and W_{-1}.

3.4.4 Mis-specification of the expectations equation

So far we have considered various efficiency results based upon a correctly specified model, in particular the expectations equation. McKenzie and McAleer (1992b) consider several extensions of Pagan (1986) with reference to the effects of both under-specified and over-specified expectations equations. Under-specification generally leads to the 2SE and the estimator of the error variance being inconsistent. When the errors of the structural and expectation equations are uncorrelated, it is shown that 2SE based on an over-specified expectation equation will generally lead to a loss of efficiency compared with 2SE based on a correctly specified expectation equation. Barro's model is used to provide an illustration of these results, together with some results when the estimator is based on an under-specified expectation equation. Some apparent counter-intuitive results are derived by comparison with standard results on mis-specification analysis. The problem of obtaining consistent parameter estimates based on 2SE is also considered in a model with future expectations when the expectation equation is under-specified.

Under-specification

Proposition 3.2 in Pagan (1986) considers the consistency of 2SE of the parameters in (56) in the presence of an under-specified expectations equation. Assuming $\gamma = 0$ and $X \subset W$, McKenzie and McAleer (1992b) consider the efficiency of a consistent two-step estimator based on an under-specified expectations equation relative to its correctly specified alternative.

Consider a model where current anticipated, unanticipated and other variables enter as in (56) and (57) above. Represent under-specification by a conformable partitioning of W and α into $[W_1 : W_2]$ and $\alpha' = (\alpha'_1 : \alpha'_2)$, *where $\alpha_2 \neq 0$ in the true model.* Denoting $\alpha_1^* = (W_1'W_1)^{-1}W_1'z$, then α_1^* will in general be an inconsistent estimator of α_1. Setting $\gamma = 0$ as in Pagan (1986) and replacing $W\hat{\alpha}_1$, a consistent estimator based upon OLS applied to (57), by $W_1\alpha_1^*$ yields

$$y = (W_1\alpha_1^*)\delta + X\beta + u_1 \tag{61}$$

$$y = K^*\psi + u_1. \tag{62}$$

It is demonstrated that:

1   if $\gamma \neq 0$, *OLS applied to (62) will in general be inconsistent;*
2   if $\gamma = 0$, with non-stochastic W_1, W_2 and $X \subset W_1$, then *OLS applied to (62) will produce a consistent estimate of ϕ even if $\sigma_{e\eta} \neq 0$.*

Over-specification

In this case, over-specification is represented by $\alpha_2 = 0$ *in the true model.* McKenzie and McAleer (1992b) demonstrate the following.

1   With $\sigma_{e\eta} = 0$ and $\gamma \neq 0$, *2SE based on the correctly specified equation is never less efficient than 2SE based on the over-specified expectations equation.* Furthermore, when $X \subset W_1$ or $\delta - \gamma = 0$, *both estimators are equally efficient.* This result appears to be robust to the inclusion of lagged anticipated and unanticipated variables.
2   If $\gamma = 0, \sigma_{e\eta} \neq 0, X \notin W_1$ and $\delta - \gamma \neq 0$, *2SE based on an over-specified expectations equation may be more efficient than one based on the correctly specified equation. In this case, the result is ambiguous. If $X \subset W_1$ or $\delta = 0$, both 2SEs are equally efficient.*

3.4.5   Tests of the REH and measurement errors

The unbiasedness and orthogonality tests which are frequently used to test the REH are based upon the equation given by

$$x_t = \alpha + \beta_{t-1}x_t^e + M_t\phi + v_t \qquad v_t \sim D(0, \sigma_v^2) \ \forall t. \tag{63}$$

In equation (63), x_t is the variable of interest for period t, $_{t-1}x_t^e$ is the expectation of this variable at time t formed at $t-1$, M_t is a vector of variables known at time t and is regarded as relevant in determining expectations (and expectations errors) and $t = 2, 3, \ldots, T$. The unbiasedness test sets $\phi = 0$ in (63) and is a test of the joint null hypothesis that $\alpha = 0$ and $\beta = 1$. Since (63) can be rewritten as

$$x_t - {}_{t-1}x_t^e = \alpha + (\beta - 1)_{t-1}x_t^e + M_t\phi + v_t$$

setting $\phi = 0$ and testing $\alpha = \beta - 1 = 0$ is, in effect, examining the orthogonality of the forecast error with respect to the current mean forecast.

A serious problem with the unbiasedness test of $\alpha = \beta - 1 = 0$ in

$$x_t = \alpha + \beta_{t-1}x_t^e + v_t \qquad v_t \sim D(0, \sigma_v^2) \ \forall t \tag{64}$$

is that the series $_{t-1}x_t^e$ are generated by another equation. The presence of such a GR implies that the conventionally programmed OLS standard errors are biased downward (see section 3.3.1). McAleer and Smith (1990) provide extensive Monte Carlo evidence of the degree of under-estimation of the conventionally programmed OLS standard errors for various simple linear models in small samples, and show that the problem can be very serious.

The nature of the problem considered here is quite different from that analysed by Pagan (1984) (and section 3.2.3) and is considered in detail by McAleer and McKenzie (1991c). Taking equation (64) as the structural equation, the expectations equations are given by

$$x_t = W_t\gamma + \xi_t \qquad \xi_t \sim D(0, \sigma_\xi^2) \ \forall t$$
$$_{t-1}x_t^e = Z_t\gamma$$

which can be written in matrix notation as

$$x = W\gamma + \xi \tag{65}$$
$$_{-1}x^e = Z\gamma. \tag{66}$$

The variables in W and Z are obtained from survey data. Many surveys seek to ascertain firms' perceived industrial performance in the quarter prior to the survey and their expected performance in the forthcoming quarter. Each firm is required to answer the question from its own perspective, and to specify the direction of change of a range of variables such as prices, output, employment and stocks. Thus, W would include information such as the fractions of firms reporting, say, a price rise and a price fall, with the remainder in the 'stay-the-same' category; Z would include information on the fractions of firms expecting a price rise and a price fall.

An estimate of $_{-1}x^e$ may be obtained by applying OLS to equation (65) to obtain $\hat\gamma = (W'W)^{-1}W'x$ and then substituting $\hat\gamma$ into equation (66) to yield

$$_{-1}\hat{x}_t^e = Z\hat\gamma = Z(W'W)^{-1}W'x.$$

The structural equation to be estimated may be rewritten as

$$x = \alpha + \beta_{-1}\hat{x}^e + v + \beta(_{-1}x^e - _{-1}\hat{x}^e)$$

or

$$x = \alpha + \beta_{-1}\hat{x}^e + u \tag{67}$$

in which

$$u = v + \beta(_{-1}x^e - _{-1}\hat{x}^e) = v + \beta(Z\gamma - Z\hat{\gamma})$$

or

$$u = v - \beta Z(W'W)^{-1}W'\xi. \tag{68}$$

Consequently, the covariance matrix of u is given by

$$V = \sigma_v^2 I - \beta\sigma_{v\xi}[Z(W'W)^{-1}W' + W(W'W)^{-1}Z'] + \beta^2\sigma_\xi^2 Z(W'W)^{-1}Z'$$

where $\sigma_v^2 = E(v_t^2)$, $\sigma_{v\xi} = E(v_t\xi_t)$, $\sigma_\xi^2 = E(\xi_t^2)$, and v_t and ξ_t are assumed to be homoskedastic and serially uncorrelated. In contrast to Pagan's (1984) well-known result discussed above, where the conventionally programmed OLS standard errors are no greater than the correct OLS standard errors, the structure of V above raises the possibility that this inequality no longer holds.

Estimating equation (67) using the correct OLS method yields standard errors given by

$$\mathrm{var}(\hat{\delta}_{\mathrm{OLS}}) = (X^{*'}X^*)^{-1}X^{*'}VX^*(X^*X^*)^{-1}$$

where $\hat{\delta}_{\mathrm{OLS}} = (X^{*'}X^*)^{-1}X^{*'}x$, $\delta = (\alpha, \beta)'$, $X^* = (\iota, _{-1}\hat{x}^e)$ and ι is a column of unit elements. An additional problem with equations (64) and (67) is that the expectations series are likely to be measured with error as aggregate (or 'average') expectations are unlikely to appear in an individual's information set. Therefore, a test of unbiasedness based on equation (67) should not be interpreted as a test of the REH. Indeed, as Pesaran (1987, p. 210) notes, measurement errors are likely to be present even when they are directly observed, although individuals are more likely to report correctly the expected direction of future changes than a point estimate of its future value.

Accommodating the measurement error problem alone requires that (67) be estimated by the use of instrumental variables (IV), whereas combining measurement error with a GR requires the use of correct IV. The correct IV standard error estimates are calculated from

$$\mathrm{var}(\hat{\delta}_{IV}) = (X^{*'}P_s X^*)^{-1}X^{*'}P_s VP_s X^*(X^{*'}P_s X^*)^{-1}$$

where $\hat{\delta}_{IV} = (X^{*'}P_s X^*)^{-1}X^{*'}P_s x$, $P_s = S(S'S)^{-1}S'$ and S is the matrix of instruments used in estimating equation (67).

The orthogonality test sets $\alpha = 0$ and $\beta = 1$ in equation (63) and tests $\phi = 0$, namely

$$x_t - _{t-1}x_t^e = M_t\phi + v_t \qquad v_t \sim \mathrm{D}(0, \sigma_v^2) \ \forall t. \tag{69}$$

Unlike the unbiasedness test which examines the orthogonality of the forecast error with respect to the current mean forecast, the orthogonality test examines whether the forecast error is orthogonal to information known at time *t*. In equation (69), the null hypothesis is $\phi = 0$ so that the null is rejected if the informational variables are significant. The conventionally programmed OLS standard errors are again inconsistent. Using equations (65) and (66) to generate $_{-1}\hat{x}^e$, equation (69) may be rewritten in matrix notation as

$$x - {}_{-1}\hat{x}^e = M\phi + v + ({}_{-1}x^e - {}_{-1}\hat{x}^e) = M\phi + u$$

where *u* is given by the expression in equation (68) with $\beta = 1$. For purposes of calculating the correct OLS standard errors of $\hat{\phi} = (M'M)^{-1}M'(x - {}_{-1}\hat{x}^e)$, the covariance matrix of *u* is given by

$$V = \sigma_v^2 I - \sigma_{v\xi}[Z(W'W)^{-1}W' + W(W'W)^{-1}Z'] + \sigma_\xi^2 Z(W'W)^{-1}Z'$$

which is simply the covariance matrix for the unbiasedness test subject to the restriction $\beta = 1$. Since the information known at time *t* is assumed to be measured without error, there is no need for IV or correct IV standard errors in calculating the orthogonality test statistics.

It is interesting to note that imposing unbiasedness in (64) enables an alternative estimate of $_{t-1}x_t^e$ to be obtained from

$$x_t = {}_{t-1}x_t^e + v_t = Z_t\gamma + v_t \qquad v_t \sim \text{D}(0, \sigma_v^2) \ \forall t$$

or, in matrix form,

$$x = {}_{-1}x^e + v = Z\gamma + v. \tag{70}$$

Applying OLS to (57) gives

$$\tilde{\gamma} = (Z'Z)^{-1}Z'x$$

and an estimate of $_{-1}x^e$ is obtained as

$${}_{-1}\tilde{x}^e = Z\tilde{\gamma} = Z(Z'Z)^{-1}Z'x = P_z x$$

where $P_z = Z(Z'Z)^{-1}Z'$. Substitution of $Z\tilde{\gamma}$ for $_{-1}x^e$ in (69) yields

$$x - {}_{-1}\tilde{x}^e = M\phi + v + ({}_{-1}X^e - {}_{-1}\tilde{x}^e) = M\phi + u$$

where $u = v + ({}_{-1}x^e - {}_{-1}\tilde{x}^e) = v + (Z\gamma - Z\tilde{\gamma})$. Under H_0: $\phi = 0$,

$$u = v + Z\gamma - P_z x = v + Z\gamma - P_z(Z\gamma + v) = (I - P_z)v$$

so that $\text{var}(u) = \sigma_v^2(I - P_z) \leqslant \sigma_v^2 I$. Thus, contrary to the standard well-known result, the conventionally programmed OLS standard errors will in this case be no less than the correct OLS standard errors.

3.4.6 Newey–West Covariance Matrix Estimates

When GRs are present, it is clearly advisable to calculate correct OLS standard errors or to use alternative estimation methods such as FIML or IV to yield consistent standard error estimates. However, these procedures can be computationally cumbersome to implement. Newey and West (1987) (NW) provide a method for calculating a positive semi-definite covariance matrix that is consistent in the presence of unknown forms of heteroskedasticity and autocorrelation. Smith and McAleer (1992b) examine whether the NW covariance matrix can approximate the known non-spherical nature of the disturbance covariance matrix in equations containing GRs, and thereby provide a simple and convenient method for obtaining consistent standard error estimates for these models.

The NW covariance matrix is calculated as

$$\hat{S}_T = \hat{\Omega}_0 + \sum_{j-1}^{m} \omega(j,m)[\hat{\Omega}_j + \hat{\Omega}_j'] \qquad \omega(j,m) = 1 - \frac{j}{m+1}$$

where

$$\hat{\Omega}_j = \sum_{t=j+1}^{T} e_t P_t' P_{t-k} e_{t-k},$$

e_t are the residuals from an equation such as (43) and P_t is the vector of explanatory variables from the same equation. For each model, NW standard errors are calculated using different lag lengths m.

Smith and McAleer (1992b) find a tendency for the NW procedure to over-reject a true null hypothesis, which contrasts with the correct OLS and FIML result reported in Hoffman and Schlagenhauf (1984) and McAleer and Smith (1990). In particular, the empirical type-I error probabilities of the NW procedure tend to be closer to the large probabilities obtained by the (incorrect) 2SE procedure. It is also found that the rejection frequencies become larger as further lags are included in the calculation of the NW covariance matrix. These findings are supported by two illustrative empirical applications, namely the Barro (1977) money growth/unemployment model and the orthogonality tests of quantitative expectations derived from qualitative responses in Smith and McAleer (1992a).

4   Empirical generated regressor models

4.1   Overview

The seminal paper by Pagan (1984) seems to have marked the beginning of serious discussion of the major econometric issues raised by GR models. However, the warnings issued seem to have been ignored by many researchers. Table 2 presents the frequency of post-1986 published papers where uncorrected (OLS) 2SE results are reported. The starting year of 1986 has been chosen to allow a reasonable time, namely two years, for Pagan's (1984) paper to be widely disseminated. *Since 1986, fifty-one papers have been published reporting uncorrected (OLS) 2SE results.* A glance at table 2 reveals that *the problem seems to be worsening,* since more rather than fewer published papers include uncorrected 2SE results. Specifically, the period 1986–8 produced eighteen cases compared with thirty-three for the period 1989–91. Table 3 disaggregates the

Table 2 Published papers reporting
uncorrected (OLS) 2SE

Year	Frequency
1986	4
1987	10
1988	4
1989	9
1990	13
1991	11
1986–8	18
1989–91	33
Total	51

Table 3 Classification by topic of empirical papers
reporting uncorrected (OLS) 2SE results, post-1986

Topic	Frequency
Monetary neutrality	19
Demand for money	5
Labour/employment	2
International trade	2
Other macroeconomic	14
Other	9
Total	51

figures by type of application. A large number of cases relate to tests of money neutrality, an issue which is discussed at length below, with the second most frequent case being models of money demand. Macroeconomic issues account, in general, for thirty-eight of the fifty-one cases identified, although this list does not pretend to be exhaustive.

It could be argued that, given the results presented in section 3, in some instances the inferences drawn in these papers might be unaffected by the inclusion of GRs. While this might be true *in some cases*, it is generally not acknowledged by the authors and requires careful scrutiny of the specific formulation of the model. Furthermore, certain new results presented in section 3 complicate any such fortuitous defence of the publication of uncorrected 2SE results. By way of example, this issue will be illustrated by a careful discussion of empirical tests of the NCM monetary neutrality question raised in section 3.

4.2 Empirical tests of the NCM monetary neutrality hypothesis

In section 2.4 the NCM model of monetary neutrality based upon the notion of a 'surprise supply' function and 'unanticipated monetary growth' was outlined and the role of GRs was highlighted. Section 3 involved a discussion of various measures of unanticipated money growth and proposed a method of categorization and classification

Table 4   Classification of empirical tests of monetary neutrality

Method of estimation	Pre-1986	Post-1986	Total
Uncorrected (OLS) 2SE	20	18	38
Efficient/corrected[a]	11	10	21
Unclear	–	1	1
Total	31	29	60

[a]May additionally report uncorrected (OLS) 2SE.

to aid understanding of the model and interpretation of the empirical results. Furthermore, the issue of stability tests of the expectation equation (policy reaction function) was stressed.

In this section these and other issues will be used to scrutinize sixty papers which test the monetary neutrality hypothesis. Table 4 presents a breakdown of the papers by type of estimation. The paper by Atesoglu and Dutkowsky (1990) has been classified as using efficient estimation techniques for the purposes of tables 4 and 6, although it merits an entry in tables 2 and 3. The justification for its inclusion in tables 2 and 3 is that inferences are drawn on the basis of invalid F tests derived via uncorrected 2SE methods.

Table 5 presents a breakdown of the papers by author (column 1), data period and country of study (column 2) and type of estimation method (column 3). Column 4 identifies whether the expectation equation was tested for stability, the type of test (if applicable) and the result, namely stable (s) or not stable (ns). Column 5 identifies the diagnostics actually reported. (Table 6 analyses the entries in columns 4 and 5 in greater detail.) The significance of current/lagged/joint unanticipated money growth is reported in column 6, and the results of tests of neutrality (column 7) and rationality (column 8) are classified by type of test. Further details on interpretation are given in the key. However, it is useful to consider the format of columns 6–8 in detail at this point, prior to the detailed discussion which follows.

Column 6 identifies whether *current* and *lagged* values of the unanticipated money growth variables are individually or *jointly* significant. A question mark denotes that, because of the GR problem discussed in section 3, the reported result is uncertain. Further, all current-valued variable results are also robust. Column 7 considers the results of neutrality tests by outcome and type, where the types are defined in section 3. A question mark in this column also indicates uncertain results due to the GR problem, but now a 'yes' result is robust. Rationality tests can be implemented only when estimation involves the imposition of cross-equation restrictions. Column 8 presents type 1 and type 2 joint (j) and separate (s) test results. An entry n.a. in column 8 denotes that tests of rationality are 'not applicable' for this type of estimation method as rationality is *always* a maintained hypothesis.

Given the statistical implications of the GR problem, *what can validly be inferred from the sixty cited papers testing the NCM neutrality propositions based upon uncorrected and corrected 2SE, GLS, and efficient estimation method results?*

Table 5 Empirical tests of monetary neutrality

1 Author(s)	2 Data	3 Estimation method(s)	4 Stability tests of expectations equation	5 Diagnostics actually reported	6 Significant: current/ lagged/joint, unanticipated	7 Neutrality/ type	8 Rationality/ type
Ahmed (1987)	Canada, annual data, 1961–74	A1(a)	No tests	DW	No*/–/No* (*general tendencies)	No tests	n.a.
Alogoskoufis and Pissarides (1983)	UK, annual data, 1950–80	A1(a) B1(a)	Chow 1, (s)	h	Yes/Yes/–	No tests	Yes/j
Amihud (1982)	USA, annual data, 1954–78	A1(d)	No tests	DW	Yes/–/–	Yes/1	n.a.
Askari (1986)	Canada, quarterly seasonally adjusted data, 1967(?) – 1981(?)	A1(a)	Chow 1, (s)	None	No/No/–	No?/1	n.a.
Atesoglu and Dutkowsky (1990)	USA, quarterly seasonally adjusted data, 1956.II–1985.I	B1(a)	Chow 1, (s)	DW	Yes/No/–	No/s	Yes/s
Attfield et al. (1981a)	UK, quarterly seasonally adjusted data, 1963.I–1978.IV	A1(a) B1(a)	Chow 1, (s)	DW	Yes/Yes/–	Yes/1 and 2j	Yes/j
Attfield et al. (1981b)	UK, annual data, 1946 – 77	A1(a) B1(a)	Chow 1, (s)	DW, h, Q	Yes/Yes/–	Yes/1 and 2j	Yes/j
Attfield and Duck (1983)	UK, USA, Canada, Netherlands, Denmark, Australia, Colombia, Philippines, El Salvador, Argentina, Guatemala, annual data, 1951–78	B1(a)	Chow 1, (s)	None?	No/Yes*/– (*except Philippines, El Salvador and Argentina)	Yes/2j	Yes/j
Attfield and Duck (1986)	UK, annual data, 1946–83	B1(a)	?, (ns)	DW, Q	–/–/–	Neutrality inferred	Yes/?
Barro (1977)	USA, annual data, 1941–73	A1(a)	No tests	DW	Yes/Yes?/Yes?	Yes/1	n.a.
Barro (1978)	USA, annual data, 1941–76	A1(a) B1(a)?	No tests	DW	Yes/Yes?/Yes?	Yes/1	?

(Table 5 cont.)

1 Author(s)	2 Data	3 Estimation method(s)	4 Stability tests of expectations equation	5 Diagnostics actually reported	6 Significant: current/ lagged/joint, unanticipated	7 Neutrality/ type	8 Rationality/ type
Barro (1981)	USA, annual data, 1941–78	A1(a) B1(a)	Chow 1, (⎯)	DW	Yes/Yes/–	Ambiguous	Ambiguous
Barro and Rush (1980)	USA, annual data, 1941–77, and quarterly seasonally adjusted data, 1941.I–1978.I	A1(a) B1(a)	Utilize Barro (1981)	DW	Yes/Yes/–	Ambiguous	Ambiguous
Bean (1984)	UK, quarterly seasonally adjusted data, 1963.I–1982.I	A1(a)	Chow 1, (ns)	DW	–/–/No	No?/1 (M1) Yes/1 (£M3)	n.a.
Beladi and Samanta (1988)	UK, annual data, 1952–83	A1(a) A2(a), A2(b)	Chow 1, (⎯)	DW	Yes/Yes?/No	No?/1	n.a.
Bellante et al. (1982)	UK, annual data, 1952–83	A1(a) A2(a), A2(b)	Chow 1, (⎯)	DW, h	No/Yes?/–	Yes/1	n.a.
Bryant (1991)	Australia, Canada, Japan, Switzerland and Sweden, annual data, 1950–86	A1(a)	No tests	None	No/No/–	Yes/1	n.a.
Canarella and Pollard (1989)	Argentina, Bolivia, Brazil, Chile, Colombia, Ecuador, El Salvador, Guatemala, Honduras, Mexico, Nicaragua, Panama, Paraguay, Peru, Uruguay, Venezuela, annual data, 1950–83	A1(b)	No tests	DW, Q, h	No/Yes?/Yes? (general tendencies)	Neutrality imposed	n.a.
Cecchetti (1986)	USA, quarterly data, 1957.I–1984.III	See text	No tests	Q, h	–/–/–	Ambiguous/ See text	See text
Chan (1988)	USA, quarterly data, 1952.II–1986.II, 1920.I–1960.IV and monthly data, 1964(8)–1979(9)	B1(a)	LR, (ns)	None	Yes/Yes/No	Ambiguous	No tests

Study	Data	Model	Test	Method	Results		
Choudhary and Parai (1991)	Argentina, Bolivia, Brazil, Chile, Colombia, Costa Rica, Guatemala, Mexico, Nicaragua, Paraguay, Peru, Uraguay, Venezuela, annual data, 1952–87	A1(a)	Chow 1, (s) (all countries)	DW, Q,F*	No/Yes?/Yes? (general tendencies)	No?/1	n.a.
Chrystal and Chatterji (1987)	USA, annual data, 1948–82	A1(a)	No tests	DW	Yes/Yes?/Yes? (general tendencies)	No?/1	n.a.
Cuthbertson and Taylor (1986)	UK, quarterly seasonally adjusted data, 1964.II–1981.IV	C1(a), C1(b) C2(a) B1(a) B2(a)	No tests	h, Q*	Yes/–/–	No/2s	No/s
Dadkhah and Valbuena (1985)	Germany, France, Italy, Spain, annual data, 1950–83	A1(a)	No tests	DW	No/No*/– (*except Italy)	Ambiguous/1	n.a.
Darrat (1985a)	Italy, quarterly data, 1960.1–1982.IV	A1(a)	Chow 1, (s)	DW, Q	Yes/Yes?/Yes?	No?/1	n.a.
Darrat (1985b)	Canada, quarterly data, 1960.1–1982.IV	A1(a)	Chow 1 and (s) Farley and Hinich (1970),	DW, Q	No/Yes?/Yes?	Yes/1	n.a.
Darrat (1987)	Denmark, annual data, 1953–83	A1(a)	Chow 1, (s)	DW, G, LM(H)	No/No/No	No?/1	n.a.
Driscoll et al. (1983)	UK, annual data, 1946–79	B1(a)	CUSUM and CUSUMSQ, (s)	DW, h	–/–/–	No/2s	No/s
Dutkowsky (1987)	USA, annual data, 1949–84	A1(a)	CUSUM, (s)	DW, h	Yes/Yes?/–	No tests	n.a.
Dutkowsky and Atesoglu (1986)	USA, annual data, 1941–83	A1(a)	Chow 1, (s)	DW, CUSUM, CUSUMSQ	Yes/Yes?/–	Ambiguous/1	n.a.
Frydman and Rappoport (1987)	USA, quarterly seasonally adjusted data, 1948.III–1976.IV	A1(a)	Chow 1, (s)	None	AUDI, see text	See text	n.a.
Gauger (1988)	USA, quarterly seasonally adjusted data, 1955.I–1986.II	A1(a) G1(a)	Chow 1, (ms)	None	Yes/Yes/Yes	No/1	No tests

(Table 5 cont.)

1 Author(s)	2 Data	3 Estimation method(s)	4 Stability tests of expectations equation	5 Diagnostics actually reported	6 Significant: current/ lagged/joint/ unanticipated	7 Neutrality/ type	8 Rationality/ type
Glick and Hutchinson (1990)	USA, quarterly seasonally adjusted data, 1960.IV–1985.IV	A1(a)	No tests	Q	No/Yes?/Yes?	No?/1	n.a.
Gochoco (1986)	Japan, monthly seasonally adjusted and unadjusted data, 1973(1)–1985(6)	B1(a)	Chow 1 (s)	None	Yes/Yes/–	No/1 and 2s	Yes/s
Gordon (1982)	USA, quarterly data, 1892.IV–1980.IV	A1(a)	Chow 1, ns	h, DW	No/Yes?/–	Ambiguous/1	n.a.
Grossman (1979)	USA, quarterly data, 1947.I–1975.III	A1(a) A2(a), A2(b)	No tests	DW	Yes/Yes?/Yes?	Model not identified	n.a.
Helliwell (1986)	Canada, annual data, 1954–82 USA, annual data, 1960–82	A1(a)	No tests	DW, Chow 1	Yes/Yes/– No/–/–	No?/1 No?/1	n.a.
Hoffman and Schlagenhauf (1982)	Canada, Italy, Germany, Japan, UK, USA, quarterly data, 1960.I–1980.IV	A1(a) B1(a)	?, (s)	DW, Q*	Yes/Yes/–	No*/2s (*except Canada)	Yes*/s (*except Germany, Japan and UK)
Kormendi and Meguire (1991)	46 countries, annual data, 'post-war' –1987	A1(b)	No tests	No conventional tests	–/–/	Neutrality imposed	n.a.
Leiderman (1980)	USA, annual data, 1946–73	B1(a)	No tests	None	Yes/Yes/–	Yes/2s	Yes/s
Leiderman (1983)	USA, annual data, 1948–76, and quarterly data 1974.III–1977.IV	A1(a)	No tests	DW	Yes/Yes/–	Yes/1	n.a.
Makin (1982)	USA, bi-annual and quarterly, 1953.I–1975.IV	A1(a), A1(b), A1(c) A2(a)	No tests	DW	No/No/–	No?/1	n.a.
McAleer and McKenzie (1991a)	USA, annual data, 1941–85	A1(a) (B1)a	No tests	RESET(2) LM(SC), LM(H), LM(N)	Yes/Yes/Yes	Yes/2s	Yes/j

Study	Data	Model	Tests	Tests			
Mishkin (1982)	USA, quarterly seasonally adjusted, 1954.I–1976 (?)	A1 (a) B1(a)	Chow 1, (s)	DW	Yes/Yes/–	Yes/1 and 2s	No/s
Mishkin (1983)	USA, quarterly seasonally adjusted, 1954.I–1976 (?)	A1(a) B1(a)	Chow 1, (ns)	DW	Yes/No/–	No/2s (generally)	No/s (generally)
Mohabbat and Al-Saji (1991)	Iraq, quarterly data, 1961.I–1977.II	A1(a)	Chow 1, (s)	DW	No/No/–	No?/1	n.a.
Montiel (1987)	Mexico, annual data, 1953–75	A1(a)	No tests	DW, Q	Yes/–/–	Ambiguous/1	n.a.
Mullineaux (1980)	USA, bi-annual? data, 1952–75	A1(a), A1(c)	No tests	DW	No/Yes?/Yes?	No tests	n.a.
Pesaran (1982)	USA, annual data, 1941–73	A1(a)	No tests	DW	Yes/Yes?/–	No?/1	n.a.
Pesaran (1988)	USA, annual data, 1948–76	A1(a)	No tests	DW, h, LM(SC), LM(H), LM(N), RESET(1)	Yes/Yes?/–	No?/1	n.a.
Rush (1985)	USA, annual data, 1880–1913	A1(a)	No tests	DW	No/No/No	Yes/1	n.a.
Rush (1986)	USA, annual data, 1917–83	A1(a) B1(a)	Chow 1, s	DW	Yes/Yes/–	Yes/1 and 2j	Yes/j
Rush and Waldo (1988)	USA, annual data, 1941–85	A1(a)	No tests	DW	–/–/–	No tests	n.a.
Sheehan (1985)	USA, quarterly data, 1954.I–1981.IV	A1(a), A2(a)	No tests	DW	Yes/Yes?/Yes?	Ambiguous/1	n.a.
Sheehey (1984)	Uruguay, Brazil, Chile, Argentina, Bolivia, Colombia, Peru, Paraguay, Mexico, Equador, Costa Rica, Honduras, Nicaragua, Venezuela, El Salvador, Guatemala, annual data 1948–72	A1(a)	No tests	DW	No/–/– (general tendencies)	Yes/1 (generally)	n.a.
Sheffrin (1979)	USA, quarterly seasonally adjusted data, 1952.IV–1975.III	A2(b)	No tests	DW	Yes/Yes?/–	No tests	n.a.
Siegloff and Groenewold (1987)	Australia, quarterly seasonally adjusted data, 1962.II–1985.III	B1(a)	No tests	LM(SC)	–/–/–	No/s	No/s

(Table 5 cont.)

1 Author(s)	2 Data	3 Estimation method(s)	4 Stability tests of expectations equations	5 Diagnostics actually reported	6 Significant: current/ lagged/joint, unanticipated	7 Neutrality/ type	8 Rationality/ type
Small (1979)	USA, annual data, 1941–73	A1(a)	No tests	DW	No/Yes?/–	No tests	n.a.
Thoma (1989)	UK, USA, Germany, Canada, quarterly seasonally adjusted data, 1964.I–1983.IV	B1(b)	No tests	DW, Q, Q*	Yes/Yes/–	No*/2s (*except Canada)	Yes/s
Wogin (1980)	Canada, annual data, 1927–72	A1(a)	Chow 1 (s)	DW	Yes/Yes?/Yes?	Yes/1	n.a.

Estimation method(s): For definitions, see section 3.

Chow 1 refers to Chow's (1960) first test for structural change.

CUSUM and CUSUMSQ refer to Brown et al.'s (1975) test for structural change.

DW refers to the Durbin–Watson (1950, 1951) statistic.

h refers to Durbin's (1970) statistic.

Q refers to the Box–Pierce (1970) portmanteau statistic.

Q* refers to the Ljung–Box (1978) portmanteau statistic.

G is the Geary (1970) non-parametric test for serial correlation.

LM(SC), LM(N) and LM(H) refer, respectively, to Lagrange multiplier tests for serial correlation, normality and heteroskedasticity.

RESET(2) refers to Ramsey's (1969, 1974) test for functional form mis-specification based upon the squares of the fitted values.

F refers to a non-nested F test.

s denotes that a stable relationship was identified; ns denotes an unstable relationship based upon the particular test of structural stability.

AUDI refers to the acronym 'anticipated–unanticipated distinction is irrelevant', used by Fry-Iman and Rappoport (1987).

Interpretation of column 6

The three entries separated by a slash (/) relate, respectively, to a significant coefficient on the *current valued unanticipated 'surprise' variable*; a significant coefficient on the *lagged unanticipated variable*; *jointly significant coefficients on current and lagged unanticipated variables*.

A question mark (?) in column 6 denotes that the true inference is uncertain because of the underestimation of the true standard errors due to the GR problem.

A question mark (?) anywhere else but in column 6 denotes that the information is unclear from the paper. A dash (–) denotes that the relevant value was not reported.

Interpretation of column 7

A 'yes' entry denotes that the null hypothesis of monetary neutrality was not rejected. This result is robust to the underestimation of the true standard errors due to the GR problem. A 'no' entry denotes rejection of the null hypothesis. This result is not robust to the GR problem and uncorrected 2SE results are therefore unresolved and represented by a question mark (?). The entry following the slash (/) denotes the type of test used to derive the outcome, either type 1 or 2 with the latter either joint (j) or separate (s).

Interpretation of column 8

A 'yes' entry denotes that the null hypothesis of rationality of expectation formation implied by the satisfaction of necessary cross-equation restrictions is not rejected by the data. A 'no' entry denotes rejection of the null. Rationality tests can only be undertaken in efficiently estimated models, and hence any GR uncertainty does not apply. The entry following the slash (/) denotes the type of type 2 test undertaken, either separate (s) or joint (j). An entry n.a. denotes that rationality tests are not applicable in this case because of the type of estimation method.

Table 6   Empirical tests of monetary neutrality

Method of estimation	No stability test(s) of expectations equation	No diagnostic test(s) reported	Only DW reported	No stability test(s) on the expectations equation and (at best) only DW reported	Total
All cases	30[a]	8	27	19	60[a]
Uncorrected (OLS) 2SE	24	3	20	18	38
Efficient, corrected	5	5	7	1	21

[a] Due to the uncertainty of the estimation method, the Cecchetti (1986) paper has not been assigned a specific method of estimation although it is included in the 'All cases' entry.

4.2.1   Tests of the monetary neutrality hypothesis–uncorrected 2SE results, pre-1986

Table 5 presents results from twenty papers published pre-1986. Of these twenty, fourteen (70 per cent) present no stability tests of the expectation equation; fifteen (75 per cent) present only the Durbin–Watson (DW) statistic as a diagnostic test; and fourteen report no stability test on the expectation equation *and* (at best) *only* the DW statistic. On the basis of these results, we should have little confidence in the validity of many of the empirical results presented.

What can be validly inferred in these twenty cases? First, being estimated by OLS, the REH is always maintained. Hence, column 8 is not relevant. However, columns 6 and 7 allow discussion of the empirical validity of the NCM monetary neutrality hypothesis.

The inferences relating to the statistical *insignificance* of current and lagged surprises are unaffected by the inclusion of GRs in Dadkhah and Valbuena (1985) and Makin (1982), and current surprises remain insignificant in Darrat (1985b) and Gordon (1982). The results from Bean (1984) and Rush (1985) on the joint insignificance of current and lagged surprises are also robust to the GR problem. With the exception of Amihud (1982) and Sheehey (1984), who report only the significance of current surprises, the results from the remaining fourteen papers on the *significance* of surprise variables *are* affected by the GR problem. In particular, the reported *significance* of lagged surprises is now uncertain. However, of the nineteen papers which report the significance of current monetary surprises, ten report significant effects and nine insignificant.

4.2.2   Tests of the monetary neutrality hypothesis– uncorrected 2SE results, post-1986

Table 5 presents results on the eighteen post-1986 published papers which test the monetary neutrality hypothesis. Of the eighteen cases noted, ten do not test the stability of the expectations equation, three report no diagnostic tests whatsoever for any of the estimated equations, and five report only the DW statistic. Furthermore, four cases report no tests of stability of the expectations equation and (at best) only the DW statistic. This is of considerable concern given the recent nature of such papers. Such characteristics give little confidence overall in the adequacy of the models. However, columns 5 and 6 are especially revealing with regard to the problems of interpretation arising from the use of GRs.

The inferences derived by Askari (1986), Bryant (1991), Helliwell (1986) and Mohabbat and Al-Saji (1991) regarding the statistical *insignificance* of current and lagged 'surprises' are unaffected by the inclusion of GRs, as are the majority of inferences derived by Ahmed (1987). However, much of the emphasis in Ahmed (1987) revolves around results which imply support for the NCM neutrality propositions which, given the presence of GRs, must be regarded as unresolved. Montiel's (1987) results are also unaffected since attention is restricted solely to the effects of current surprises, which are found to have a significant positive effect.

Although the results of Askari (1986) and Bryant (1991) on the significance of 'surprise' effects are robust, both use non-nested tests, in particular the J test of Davidson and MacKinnon (1981). As noted in section 3.2.1 and in McAleer and McKenzie (1991a), uncorrected 2SE will yield biased test statistics, in this case towards rejection of the (NCM) null. Bryant (1991) reports a rejection of the NCM model against a Keynesian alternative, with no rejection of the Keynesian model against the NCM alternative, in four of the five countries considered. Similar results are found in Askari (1986). On the basis of the theoretical evidence and the dramatic empirical reversals reported in McAleer and McKenzie (1991a), considerable caution should be exercised in interpreting such results.

In all other cases some reservation must be held regarding the inferences drawn in respect of the significance of the 'surprise' effects, at least those denoted by a question mark. All eight of the reported unambiguous results regarding the significance of lagged 'surprises' are contaminated by the effects of the inclusion of GRs. Four of the seven joint tests of current and lagged surprises are similarly contaminated. In these cases the actual significance of unanticipated money growth and partial support for the NCM neutrality hypothesis is unclear.

Tests results are robust under the null hypothesis of neutrality; however, a rejection becomes questionable because of the GR problem. For this reason, the non-neutrality inferred by Askari (1986), Beladi and Samanta (1988), Chrystal and Chatterji (1987), Glick and Hutchinson (1990), Helliwell (1986), Mohabbat and Al-Saji (1991) and Pesaran (1988) is unresolved. Furthermore, Pesaran (1988) reports the RESET and Breusch and Godfrey (1981) serial correlation tests, both of which may be biased when uncorrected 2SE is used in the construction of the test statistic (see McAleer and McKenzie, 1991a).

4.2.3 Tests of the monetary neutrality hypothesis–efficient estimation results, all cases

Conditional on the model being correctly specified, efficiently estimated models produce valid inferences. However, such conditioning is crucial. Of the twenty-one cases of efficient estimation considered, five present no tests of the stability of the expectation equation, five report no diagnostic checks, and seven report only DW. However, only in one case is no stability test of the expectations equation and (at best) only the DW reported. Again, little overall confidence can be expressed in the general adequacy of the reported models, although some clear exceptions emerge. One extra feature of efficient estimation is that it affords the opportunity to test rationality and neutrality separately.

Of the twenty-one papers, seventeen report *significant* positive effects of *current* monetary surprises, with only one (Attfield and Duck, 1983) reporting insignificant values, the remaining reporting no value. This is in sharp contrast to the results noted above. In fifteen cases, mainly drawn from the seventeen above, *lagged* surprises are also significant, with Attfield and Duck (1983) reporting significant lagged effects. Atesoglu and Dutkowsky (1990) and Mishkin (1983) also present a reversal, with insignificant lagged surprises but significant current surprises. In only three cases is the joint significance of monetary surprises tested, being insignificant in Chan (1988) and significant in McAleer and McKenzie (1991a). Owing to the uncertainties in the method of estimation, the results of Barro (1978) and Cecchetti (1986) have been omitted from the analysis. *Overall, there seems to be strong evidence in favour of monetary surprises exerting significant positive effects on real variables.* However, the significance of anticipated money growth requires careful consideration before firm empirical support can be found for NCM monetary neutrality.

Column 7 reports the results of both type 1 and type 2 joint and separate tests of monetary neutrality. An equal number, eight, find in favour of an against the null hypothesis of monetary neutrality!

Tests of rationality are reported in column 8. Of the Seventeen unambiguous results, twelve do not reject the cross-equation constraints imposed by the REH, the exceptions being Cuthbertson and Taylor (1986), Driscoll et al. (1983), Mishkin (1982, 1983) and Siegloff and Groenewold (1987).

4.2.4   Tests of the monetary neutrality hypothesis–corrected 2SE and GLS estimation, all cases

The only instances of corrected 2SE and method G (GLS estimation) reported relate to Cuthbertson and Taylor (1986) and Gauger (1988), although McAleer and McKenzie (1991a) report comparisons of the effects of correcting 2SE results. Cuthbertson and Taylor's (1986) results have been reviewed earlier, with Gauger (1988) finding current, lagged and joint 'surprises' significant and anticipated money non-neutral. Rationality is a maintained hypothesis under GLS estimation.

4.2.5   Any general tendencies?

Given the plethora of papers discussed, it is not surprising that few general conclusions emerge. One issue of concern is the general lack of confidence which can be held in the empirical specification of many of the reported models. Specification tests and tests of the stability of the expectations equation are often not reported, so that two possible routes can be followed to establish the balance of empirical support for the NCM neutrality propositions. First, general tendencies can be established. On balance, it appears that *both* unanticipated and anticipated monetary growth exert significant effects on real variables, with support for the former being generally stronger than for the latter. Tests of rationality are somewhat more clearly in favour of the REH.

Alternatively, individual cases can be identified where more confidence can be placed in the validity of the results. On this basis, six possible candidates emerge, namely Attfield et al. (1981a, b), Hoffman and Schlagenhauf (1982), Mishkin (1982, 1983) and McAleer and McKenzie (1991a). All suffer from minor criticisms either in the paucity of diagnostic test results or in the failure to adequately (or unambiguously) check the stability of the expectations equation. However, considerable confidence overall can be placed in the inferences. On such a basis, rationality is not rejected, with the exception of Mishkin (1982, 1983); neutrality is accepted, with the exception of Mishkin (1983) and Hoffman and Schlagenhauf (1982); and current, lagged and jointly significant 'surprises' are identified for all cases, except lagged 'surprises' in Mishkin (1983). It therefore appears that *no general tendencies emerge*.

5   Concluding remarks

The 1980s and 1990s saw a growth in the number of empirical applications where models with GRs were estimated. Economic reasons for such models were discussed in section 2. Some of the econometric issues associated with the inclusion of GRs were highlighted in Pagan's (1984) seminal contribution. It appears, however, that the warnings issued therein have in many cases been ignored. The late 1980s produced a growing number of published empirical applications where uncorrected 2SE results were presented, with no (apparent) warnings as regards their interpretation.

The main purpose of this paper has been to review and update the econometric issues raised by models with GRs. Such issues were discussed in section 3, where both established and new results were highlighted. It was stressed that, although 2SE would not generally be single equation efficient, under certain circumstances a subset of coefficients may be efficiently estimated and valid inferences may be drawn. In particular, the coefficient attached to current 'surprises' would be efficiently estimated in models where the expectations equation is correctly specified (formal proofs are given in McAleer and McKenzie, 1991b).

The effects of mis-specification of the expectations equation were considered, together with some consequences of measurement errors. Some interesting and counter-intuitive cases were identified, thereby reinforcing the notion that the inclusion of GRs in a model can lead to considerable problems of interpretation. In particular, care must be exercised in the interpretation of (possibly) biased 'standard' test statistics, such as t and F, and several variable addition and non-nested tests, such as Ramsey's (1969, 1974) RESET test, Breusch and Godfrey's (1981) test of serial correlation, Davidson and MacKinnon's (1981) J test and Fisher and McAleer's (1981) JA test. The theoretical problems of 2SE were highlighted and several solutions were offered, including the use of corrected 2SE and efficient estimation methods. The strengths and weaknesses of all methods of estimation in the relevant models was examined.

In addition to the theoretical issues discussed, the literature on tests of the NCM monetary neutrality hypothesis was examined. Overall, sixty papers were considered and the type of estimation method was identified in each case. The validity of inferences presented was analysed and the uncertainties emerging as a consequence of the use of uncorrected 2SE results and the GR problem were identified. The results derived from efficient estimation methods were also considered, allowing discussion of separate tests of neutrality and rationality. General conclusions on the empirical validity of the NCM neutrality propositions seem difficult to establish and two attempts to give such a view were presented.

It is clear that models which include GRs will continue to be popular and will be subjected to empirical testing. It is also clear that the ease of 2SE will continue to attract many practitioners. However, the possible dangers of using uncorrected 2SE should now be well understood, as should the benefits of using alternative estimation procedures. Uncorrected 2SE should be used with considerable caution. Ideally, corrected 2SE or efficient methods would replace such methods. In many instances, such as separate tests of rationality and neutrality, efficient estimation methods are required.

Note

The authors wish to thank David Hendry, Soren Johansen, Keith McLaren, Hashem Pesaran, Jeremy Smith, seminar participants at the Australian National University, Bank of Japan, Fukuoka University, Hiroshima University, Keio University, Kobe University, Monash University, Otaru University of Commerce, Tokyo Center for Economic Research, University of Canterbury, University of Strathclyde, University of Tokyo, University of Tsukuba, University of Waikato, University of Western Australia, Yokohama National University and especially Colin McKenzie, for helpful comments and discussions. The second author wishes to acknowledge the financial support of the Australian Research Council and a Japanese Government Foreign Research Fellowship at Kyoto University.

References

Ahmed, S. (1987) Wage stickiness and the non-neutrality of money: a cross-industry analysis. *Journal of Monetary Economics*, 20, 25–50.

Alogoskoufis, G. and Pissarides, C. A. (1983) A test of price sluggishness in the simple rational expectations model: UK 1950–80. *Economic Journal*, 93, 616–28.

Amihud, Y. (1982) Unanticipated inflation and economic activity. *Economics Letters*, 9, 327–35.

Anderson, O. (1952), The business test of the IFO-Institute for Economic Research, Munich, and its theoretical model. *Revue de l'Institut International de Statistique*, 20, 1–17.

Askari, M. (1986) A non-nested test of the new classical neutrality proposition for Canada. *Applied Economics*, 18, 1349–57.

Atesoglu, H. S. and Dutkowsky, D. H. (1990) Interest volatility and the macro rational expectations hypothesis. *Journal of Macroeconomics*, 12, 97–109.

Attfield, C. L. F. and Duck, N. (1983) The influence of unanticipated money growth on real output: some cross country estimates. *Journal of Money, Credit and Banking*, 15, 442–54.

—— and —— (1986) Distinguishing between rational expectations and 'Keynesian' models of the business cycle in the presence of a structural break in the money growth process. *Economics Letters*, 21, 133–5.

——, Demery, D. and Duck, N. (1981a) Unanticipated monetary growth, output, and the price level: UK 1946–77. *European Economic Review*, 16, 367–85.

——, —— and —— (1981b) A quarterly model of unanticipated monetary growth, output and the price level in the UK 1963–78. *Journal of Monetary Economics*, 8, 331–50.

——, —— and —— (1991) *Rational Expectations in Macroeconomics: An Introduction to Theory and Evidence*, 2nd edn. Oxford: Blackwell.

Barro, R. J. (1977) Unanticipated money growth and unemployment in the United States. *American Economic Review*, 67, 101–15.

—— (1978) Unanticipated money, output and the price level in the United States. *Journal of Political Economy*, 86, 549–80.

——(1981) Unanticipated money growth and economic activity in the United States. In R. J. Barro (ed.), *Money, Expectations and Economic Policy*, New York: Academic Press, ch. 5.

——and Rush, M. (1980) Unanticipated money and economic activity. In S. Fischer (ed.), *Rational Expectations and Economic Policy*, Chicago, IL: NBER and University of Chicago Press, ch. 2.

Bean, C. R. (1984) A little bit more evidence on the natural rate hypothesis for the UK. *European Economic Review*, 25, 279–92.

——(1986) The estimation of 'surprise' models and the 'surprise' consumption function. *Review of Economic Studies*, 53, 497–516.

Begg, D. K. H. (1982) *The Rational Expectations Revolution in Macroeconomics: Theories and Evidence*. Oxford: Philip Allan.

Beladi, H. and Samanta, S. (1988) Unanticipated monetary policy and real output – some evidence from the UK economy. *Applied Economics*, 20, 721–9.

Bellante, D., Morrell, S. and Zardkoohi, A. (1982) Unanticipated money growth in the UK: 1946–77. *Southern Economic Journal*, 49, 62–76.

Box, G. E. P. and Pierce, D. A. (1970) Distribution of residual autocorrelations in autoregressive-integrated-moving average time series models. *Journal of the American Statistical Association*, 65, 1509–26.

Breusch, T. S. and Godfrey, L. G. (1981) A review of recent work on testing for autocorrelation in dynamic simultaneous models. In D. Currie, R. Nobay and D. Peel (eds), *Macroeconomic Analysis: Essays in Macroeconomics and Econometrics*, London: Croom Helm.

Brown, R. L., Durbin, J. and Evans, J. M. (1975) Techniques for testing the constancy of regression relations over time (with discussion). *Journal of the Royal Statistical Society B*, 37, 149–92.

Bryant, W. D. A. (1991) Non-nested tests of the new classical versus Keynesian models: further evidence. *Applied Economics*, 23, 385–90.

Buiter, W. H. (1980) The macroeconomics of Dr. Pangloss: a critical survey of the new classical macroeconomics. *Economic Journal*, 90, 34–50.

Canarella, G. and Pollard, S. K. (1989) Unanticipated monetary growth, output, and the price level in Latin America: an empirical investigation. *Journal of Development Economics*, 30, 345–58.

Carlson, J. A. (1977) A study of price forecasts. *Annals of Economic and Social Measurement*, 6, 27–56.

Carr, J. and Darby, M. (1981) The role of money supply shocks in the short-run demand for money. *Journal of Monetary Economics*, 8, 183–200.

——, —— and Thornton, D. L. (1985) Monetary anticipations and the demand for money: reply. *Journal of Monetary Economics*, 16, 251–7.

Cecchetti, S. G. (1986) Testing short-run neutrality. *Journal of Monetary Economics*, 17, 409–23.

Chan, L. K. C. (1988) Unanticipated monetary policy and real economic activity, some cross-regime evidence. *Journal of Monetary Economics*, 22, 439–59.

Choudhary, M. A. S. and Parai, A. K. (1991) Anticipated monetary policy and real output: evidence from Latin American countries. *Applied Economics*, 23, 579–86.

Chow, G. C. (1960) Tests of equality between sets of coefficients in two linear regressions. *Econometrica*, 28, 591–605.

Chrystal, K. A. and Chatterji, M. (1987) Money and disaggregate supply in the United States, 1950–1982. *European Economic Review*, 31, 1211–28.

Cuthbertson, K. and Taylor, M. P. (1986) Monetary anticipations and the demand for money in the UK: testing the rationality of buffer-stock money. *Journal of Applied Econometrics*, 1, 355–65.

—— and —— (1987) Monetary anticipations and the demand for money: some evidence for the United Kingdom. *Weltwirtschaftliches Archiv*, 123, 509–20.

—— and ——(1989) Anticipated and unanticipated variables in the demand for M1 in the United Kingdom. *The Manchester School of Economic and Social Research*, 57, 319–39.

Dadkhah, K. M. and Valbuena, S. (1985) Non-nested tests of the new classical versus Keynesian models: evidence from European countries. *Applied Economics*, 17, 1083–98.

Darrat, A. F. (1985a) Anticipated money and real output in Italy: some tests of the rational expectations approach. *Journal of Post-Keynesian Economics*, 8, 81–90.

——(1985b) Unanticipated inflation and real output: the Canadian experience. *Canadian Journal of Economics*, 18, 146–55.

—— (1987) The policy ineffectiveness proposition: some further tests. *Economics Letters*, 25, 117–22.

Davidson, J. E. and Hendry, D. (1981) Interpreting econometric evidence: consumers' expenditure in the UK. *European Economic Review*, 16, 177–92.

Davidson, R. and MacKinnon, J. G. (1981) Several tests for model specification in the presence of alternative hypotheses. *Econometrica*, 49, 781–93.

Driscoll, M. J., Ford, J. L. and Mullineux, A. (1983) The gains and losses to predicting nominal income by disaggregating via the new classical aggregate supply and rational expectations hypothesis. *Empirical Economics*, 8, 42–62.

Durbin, J. (1970) Testing for serial correlation in least-squares regressions when some of the regressors are lagged dependent variables. *Econometrica*, 38, 410–21.

——and Watson, G. S. (1950) Testing for serial correlation in least squares regression I. *Biometrika*, 37, 409–28.

—— and ——(1951) Testing for serial correlation in least squares regression II. *Biometrika*, 38, 159–78.

Dutkowsky, D. H. (1987) Unanticipated money growth, interest rate volatility and unemployment in the United States. *Review of Economics and Statistics*, 69, 144–8.

——and Atesoglu, H. (1986) Unanticipated money growth and unemployment: post sample forecasts. *Southern Economic Journal*, 53, 413–21.

Farley, J. and Hinich, M. J. (1970) A test for a shifting slope coefficient in a linear model. *Journal of the American Statistical Association*, 65, 1320–9.

Fisher, G. R. and McAleer, M. (1981) Alternative procedures and associated tests of significance for non-nested hypotheses. *Journal of Econometrics*, 16, 103–19.

Frenkel, J. A. (1980) Exchange rates, prices and money, lessons from the 1920s. *American Economic Association, Papers and Proceedings*, 70, 235–42.

——(1981) Flexible exchange rates, prices and the role of 'news': lessons from the 1970s. *Journal of Political Economy*, 87, 665–705.

Friedman, M. (1957) *A Theory of the Consumption Function*. Princeton, NJ: Princeton University Press.

Frydman, R. and Rappoport, P. (1987) Is the distinction between anticipated and unanticipated money growth relevant in explaining aggregate output? *American Economic Review*, 77, 693–703.

Gauger, J. (1988) Disaggregate level evidence on monetary neutrality. *Review of Economics and Statistics*, 70, 676–80.

——(1989) The generated regression correction: impacts upon inferences in hypothesis testing. *Journal of Macroeconomics*, 11, 383–95.

Geary, R. C. (1970) Relative efficiency of count of sign change for assessing residual auto-regression in least-squares regression. *Biometrika*, 57, 123–7.

Glick, R. and Hutchinson, M. (1990) New results in support of the fiscal policy ineffectiveness proposition. *Journal of Money, Credit and Banking*, 22, 288–304.

Gochoco, M. S. (1986) Tests of monetary neutrality and rationality hypotheses: the case of Japan 1973–85. *Journal of Money, Credit and Banking*, 18, 458–66.

Godfrey, L. G. (1978) Testing against general autoregressive and moving average error models when the regressors include lagged dependent variables. *Econometrica*, 41, 1293–302.

—— and Pesaran, M. H. (1983) Tests of non-nested regression models: small sample adjustments and Monte Carlo evidence. *Journal of Econometrics*, 21, 133–54.

Gordon, R. J. (1982) Price inertia and policy ineffectiveness in the US: 1890–1980. *Journal of Political Economy*, 90, 1087–117.

Grossman, J. (1979) Nominal demand policy and short-run fluctuations in unemployment and prices in the US. *Journal of Political Economy*, 87, 1063–85.

Hall, R. E. (1978) Stochastic implications of the life-cycle, permanent income hypothesis: theory and evidence. *Journal of Political Economy*, 86, 971–87.

Haugh, L. D. (1976) Checking the independence of stationary time series: a univariate residual cross-correlation approach. *Journal of the American Statistical Association*, 71, 378–85.

Helliwell, J. F. (1986) Supply-side macroeconomics. *Canadian Journal of Economics*, 19, 597–625.

Hoffman, D. L. (1987) Two-step generalized least squares estimators in multi-equation generated regressor models. *Review of Economics and Statistics*, 69, 336–46.

—— and Schlagenhauf, D. E. (1982) An econometric investigation of the monetary neutrality and rationality propositions from an international perspective. *Review of Economics and Statistics*, 64, 562–71.

—— and —— (1984) Tests of rationality, neutrality and market efficiency: a Monte Carlo analysis of alternative test statistics. *Journal of Monetary Economics*, 10, 339–63.

Kormendi, R. C. and Meguire, P. (1991) Cross-country tests of the Lucas proposition revisited. *Journal of Business and Economic Statistics*, 9, 152–9.

Kydland, F. and Prescott, E. (1982) Time to build and aggregate fluctuations. *Econometrica*, 50, 1345–70.

Leiderman, L. (1980) Macroeconomic testing of the rational expectations and structural neutrality hypothesis for the US. *Journal of Monetary Economics*, 6, 69–82.

—— (1983) The response of real wages to unanticipated money growth. *Journal of Monetary Economics*, 11, 73–88.

Levi, M. D. and Makin, J. (1980) Inflation uncertainty and the Phillips curve: some empirical evidence. *American Economic Review*, 70, 1022–7.

Ljung, G. M. and Box, G. E. P. (1978) On a measure of lack of fit in time series models. *Biometrika*, 65, 297–303.

Lucas, R. E. (1972) Expectations and the neutrality of money. *Journal of Economic Theory*, 4, 103–24.

—— (1973) Some international evidence on output–inflation tradeoffs. *American Economic Review*, 68, 326–34.

—— (1975) An equilibrium model of the business cycle. *Journal of Political Economy*, 83, 1113–44.

—— and Rapping, L. (1969) Real wages, employment and inflation. *Journal of Political Economy*, 77, 721–54.

MacDonald, R. (1983a) Tests of efficiency and the impact of 'news' in three foreign exchange markets: the experience of the 1920s. *Bulletin of Economic Research*, 35, 123–44.

—— (1983b) Some tests of the rational expectations hypothesis in the foreign exchange market. *Scottish Journal of Political Economy*, 30, 235–50.

—— (1985) 'News' and the 1920s experience with floating exchange rates. *Economics Letters*, 17, 379–83.

—— and Ta, G. (1987) The Singapore dollar: tests of the efficient markets hypothesis and the role of 'news'. *Applied Economics*, 19, 569–79.

MacKinnon, J. G. and Milbourne, R. D. (1984) Monetary anticipations and the demand for money. *Journal of Monetary Economics*, 13, 263–74.

Makin, J. (1982) Anticipated money, inflation uncertainty and real economic activity. *Review of Economics and Statistics*, 64, 126–34.

McAleer, M. and McKenzie, C. R. (1991a) Keynesian and new classical models of unemployment revisited. *Economic Journal*, 101, 359–81.

—— and —— (1991b) When are two step estimators efficient? *Econometric Reviews*, 10, 235–52.

—— and —— (1991c) Cointegration and direct tests of the rational expectations hypothesis paper presented at the Australasian Meetings of the Econometric Society, Sydney, July 1991.

—— and —— (1992) Recursive estimation and generated regressors. *Economics Letters*, 39, 1–5.

—— and Smith, J. (1990) A Monte Carlo comparison of OLS, IV, FIML and bootstrap standard errors for linear models with generated regressors. Working Paper in Economics and Econometrics 207, Australian National University.

McKenzie, C. R. and McAleer, M. (1992a) On efficient estimation and correct inference in models with generated regressors: a general approach. Unpublished paper, Department of Economics, University of Western Australia.

—— and —— (1992b) On the effects of misspecification errors in models with generated regressors. Unpublished paper, Department of Economics, University of Western Australia.

Mishkin, F. (1982) Does anticipated monetary policy matter? An econometric investigation. *Journal of Political Economy*, 90, 22–51.

—— (1983) *A Rational Expectations Approach to Macroeconometrics: Testing Policy Ineffectiveness and Efficient Markets Models.* Chicago, IL: NBER and University of Chicago Press.

Mohabbat, K. A. and Al-Saji, A. K. (1991) The effect on output of anticipated and unanticipated money growth: the case of an oil- producing country. *Applied Economics*, 23, 1493–7.

Montiel, P. J. (1987) Output and unanticipated money in the dependent economy model. *International Monetary Fund Staff Papers*, 34, 228–59.

Muellbauer, J. (1983) Surprises in the consumption function. *Economic Journal (Supplement)*, 93, 34–50.

Mullineaux, D. J. (1980) Unemployment, industrial production and inflation uncertainty in the US. *Review of Economics and Statistics*, 62, 163–9.

Murphy, K. M. and Topel, R. H. (1985) Estimation and inference in two step econometric models. *Journal of Business and Economic Statistics*, 3, 370–9.

Newey, W. K. and West, K. D. (1987) A simple, positive semi- definite, heteroskedasticity and autocorrelation consistent covariance matrix. *Econometrica*, 55, 703–8.

Pagan, A. R. (1984) Econometric issues in the analysis of regressions with generated regressors. *International Economic Review*, 25, 221–47.

—— (1986) Two stage and related estimators and their applications. *Review of Economic Studies*, 53, 517–38.

Pesaran, M. H. (1982) A critique of the proposed tests of the natural rate-rational expectations hypothesis. *Economic Journal*, 92, 529–54.

—— (1984) Expectations formations and macro-econometric modelling. In P. Malgrange and P. A. Muet (eds), *Contemporary Macroeconomic Modelling*, Oxford: Basil Blackwell.

—— (1987) *The Limits to Rational Expectations.* Oxford: Basil Blackwell.

—— (1988) On the policy ineffectiveness proposition and a Keynesian alternative: a rejoinder. *Economic Journal*, 98, 504–8.

Ramsey, J. B. (1969) Tests of specification errors in classical linear least squares regression analysis. *Journal of the Royal Statistical Society B*, 31, 350–71.

—— (1974) Classical model selection through specification error tests. In P. Zarembka (ed.), *Frontiers in Econometrics*, New York: Academic Press.

Rush, M. (1985) Unexpected monetary disturbances during the gold standard era. *Journal of Monetary Economics*, 15, 309–21.

—— (1986) Unexpected money and employment: 1920–83. *Journal of Money, Credit and Banking*, 18, 259–74.

—— and Waldo, D. (1988) On the policy ineffectiveness proposition and a Keynesian alternative. *Economic Journal*, 98, 498–503.

Sargent, T. J. (1979) *Macroeconomic Theory*. New York: Academic Press.

—— and Wallace, N. (1975) Rational expectations, the optimal monetary instrument and the optimal money supply rule. *Journal of Political Economy*, 83, 241–54.

Sheehan, R. G. (1985) Money, anticipated changes and policy ineffectiveness. *American Economic Review*, 75, 524–9.

Sheehey, E. J. (1984) Money and output in Latin America: some tests of a rational expectations approach. *Journal of Development Economics*, 14, 203–18.

Sheffrin, S. (1979) Unanticipated money growth and output fluctuations. *Economic Inquiry*, 17, 1–13.

Siegloff, E. S. and Groenewold, N. (1987) Policy ineffectiveness: tests with Australian data. *Australian Economic Papers*, 26, 179–87.

Small, D. H. (1979) Unanticipated money growth and unemployment in the US: comment. *American Economic Review*, 69, 996–1009.

Smith, J. and McAleer, M. (1992a) Alternative procedures for converting qualitative response data to quantitative expectations: an application to Australian manufacturing. Unpublished paper, Department of Economics, University of Western Australia.

—— and —— (1992b) Newey–West covariance matrix estimates for models with generated regressors. Unpublished paper, Department of Economics, University of Western Australia.

Theil, H. (1952) On the time shape of economic macro variables and the Munich business test. *Revue de l'Institut International de Statistique*, 20, 105–20.

Thoma, M. A. (1989) Do prices lead money? A re-examination of the neutrality hypothesis. *Economic Inquiry*, 27, 197–217.

Wogin, G. (1980) Unemployment and monetary policy under rational expectations. *Journal of Monetary Economics*, 6, 59–68.

11 Nonparametric and semi-parametric methods for economic research

Miguel A. Delgado
Universidad Carlos III
and
Peter M. Robinson
London School of Economics

1 Introduction

Econometrics is concerned with drawing statistical inferences from economic data. Statistical inferences must be based on a probability model for the data. The probability model may describe the joint distribution of the data, or it may only describe the conditional distribution of one set of observables given values of another set, or some aspect of this conditional distribution such as the conditional expectation (regression function).

In econometrics the probability model has most usually been parametric, i.e. a given function involving a finite number of unknown parameters. In particular, a linear parametric function is often assumed. If the number of parameters is small relative to the number of observations, precise estimation of the parameters is possible, and consequently, reliable statistical inferences. Because many economic data sets are usually small, e.g. annual post-war macroeconomic time series, a parametric approach is sometimes essential. However, it is important that the parametric model be accurately chosen. Consistent parameter estimation generally requires an exactly correct choice of parametric model. Of course, this is never possible in practice. But economic theory may be insufficient to provide much confidence in any given parametric model as even a good approximation. Given a candidate set of explanatory variables, a purely arbitrary functional form for a regression function is often used in much applied research, usually a form which is linear in the parameters owing to its desirable computational implications.

A nonparametric model makes no precise assumptions about functional form. Instead, the data are allowed to 'speak for themselves'. A nonparametric model provides a more robust approach to statistical inference because it is more likely to approximately capture the true underlying structure. With a very large amount of data, good estimates of a nonparametric model can be obtained. A nonparametric approach is especially useful at an exploratory level, to provide a rough indication of which variables are relevant to the analysis of a particular problem, or of the functional form of a regression model, or of the distributional form of a disturbance random variable. Nowadays many large economic data sets are available, such as cross-sectional survey data consisting of thousands of observations, or intra-daily financial time series recorded at fine intervals of time, and these provide scope for reasonably precise estimation of a number of nonparametric models.

Semiparametric models provide a compromise between parametric and nonparametric models. A semiparametric probability model has two components, a parametric and a nonparametric one. Interest usually focuses on the estimation of the parametric component, the generality afforded by the nonparametric component providing a more robust environment for this than a pure parametric model. Because parameters, such as regression coefficients, may have a ready economic interpretation, there is some advantage over the nonparametric approach in retaining some element of finite parameterization. Semiparametric estimation is likely to require more data than parametric estimation. On the other hand it is likely to require fewer data than nonparametric estimation; indeed a satisfactorily precise nonparametric analysis involving a large number of explanatory variables would probably require an astronomically large sample, larger than any likely to be available in economic problems, and larger than any that we might have the resources to process.

This paper attempts to survey useful developments in nonparametric and semiparametric estimation. The literature is vast and rapidly growing, and so a comprehensive bibliography, let alone a full account of this literature, would be out of the question. In section 2 we discuss estimation of the probability density function. While of some direct interest in itself in economic research, our discussion of this topic also introduces themes relevant to nonparametric regression analysis, which is discussed in section 3, and both nonparametric density and regression estimates feature in semiparametric estimation, which is discussed in section 4. The paper places some stress on one important topic on which much of the progress has been recent, namely data-driven choice of smoothing numbers. We also refer to some economic applications of the various methods. Published empirical applications to economic data are not widespread, but the paper is written with the expectation that as the methodology becomes more widely known and better understood it will find greater use by applied economists.

2 Density estimation

Probability density estimates are useful in exploratory data analysis of econometric data sets. A number of statistical procedures use density and derivative-of-density estimates; e.g. discriminant and cluster analysis; the estimation of probabilities, hazard rates, conditional densities and score functions; simulation; testing for unimodality and independence etc. Our discussion of this topic will also involve themes useful in sections 3 and 4 below.

The density estimation problem consists of estimating the functional form of the density from data. That is, the density $f(\cdot)$ of an r-valued random vector X is estimated by $\hat{f}_n(\cdot)$ from data $\{X_1, X_2, \ldots, X_n\}$. Unless otherwise stated the X_i are assumed to be independent in what follows.

One approach to density estimation is *parametric*. Assuming that f belongs to a parametric family of densities, the parameters can be estimated, e.g. by maximum likelihood, from the observed data set. Economic models usually do not justify a precise parameterization but they may provide information on certain features of the density shape, e.g. skewness, kurtosis, multimodality, monotonicity etc. For instance, it is known, from casual observation, that income distributions are skewed to the right like the log-normal and gamma distributions and a vast number of mixture distributions.

Nonparametric estimation provides a way of avoiding the imposition of a rigid functional form on the density *a priori*. Hildenbrand and Hildenbrand (1980) compared nonparametric estimates of the income distribution with maximum likelihood based on the log-normal and gamma densities. They found that nonparametric density estimates are indeed skewed to the right but that their shape is very different from those of the log-normal and gamma. The literature on nonparametric density estimation is immense. Some books on the topic are Tapia and Thompson (1978), Hand (1982), Prakasa Rao (1983), Devroye and Györfi (1985), Silverman (1986) and Devroye (1987); some survey papers are Rosenblatt (1971), Wegman (1982), Tarter and Kronmal (1976), Fryer (1977), Leonard (1978), Bean and Tsokos (1980) and Izenman (1991); and an extensive (but inevitably out-of-date) bibliography is in Wertz and Schneider (1979). We next present some density estimation techniques used in nonparametric estimation and then we discuss some applications in economics.

2.1   Some techniques

The traditionally most popular method is the histogram. In order to construct a histogram, the data set $\{X_1, X_2, \ldots, X_n\}$ is divided into a number n of partitions $A_{n1}, A_{n2}, \ldots, A_{nm}$ and $f(x)$ is estimated by

$$\hat{f}(x) = n^{-1} \sum_{j=1}^{n} \sum_{i=1}^{m} \frac{1(X_j \in A_{ni})1(x \in A_{ni})}{\lambda(A_{ni})} \tag{1}$$

where $1(\cdot)$ is the indicator function and $\lambda(A)$ is the Lebesgue measure of the partition A, i.e. the length of the interval when $r = 1$, the area when $r = 2$, the volume when $r = 3$ or the hypervolume when $r > 3$. When n is large, (1) is a good approximation to

$$\sum_{i=1}^{m} \frac{\Pr(X \in A_{ni} \quad \text{and} \quad x \in A_{ni})}{\lambda(A_{ni})} \tag{2}$$

which, in turn, is expected to approximate $f(x)$ well when the partitions are fine. The size of the partitions has to be chosen by the practitioner. In particular, in the cubic histogram each partition A_{nj} is of the type $\Pi_{i=1}^{r}[a_i k_i h, a_i(k_i + 1)h]$, where a_i are positive constants, k_i are integers and h is a positive parameter. Then $\lambda(A_{nj}) = h^r \Pi_{i=1}^{r} a_i$. The parameter h, called the *binwidth*, controls the hypervolume of the partition and thus the smoothness of the histogram. As h decreases, the number of peaks in the histogram tends to increase. A small h produces estimates with smaller bias but greater variance than estimates based on large h. This tradeoff between degree of smoothing, bias and variance is shared by all nonparametric curve estimates.

It is clear that the choice of smoothing will affect the shape of the histogram. The histogram competes with more sophisticated nonparametric density estimates because it is easy to compute and is available in many econometric packages. However, some undesirable properties of the histogram are not shared by other nonparametric estimates. The choice of the origin may greatly affect the shape of the histogram (Silverman 1986, ch. 1) provides several examples). The choice of the coordinate directions in multiple dimensions (i.e. the a_i) also affects the histogram estimates. Contours are difficult to draw in one dimension. The discontinuity of the histogram prevents estimation of derivatives; these are useful for their own sake and as intermediate tools in various statistical procedures. Finally, the asymptotic rate of convergence of the histogram to the true density, according to different measures, can be better for alternative density estimates (see section 2.2 below).

The *frequency polygon* smooths out the block-line shape of the histogram by connecting the middle points of each class in the histogram. Another possibility consists of using the histogram method with different 'bins' centred about the point to be estimated. Rosenblatt (1956) proposed the *naive* estimate, for $r = 1$,

$$\hat{f}(x) = \frac{\hat{F}(x+h) - \hat{F}(x-h)}{2h} \tag{3}$$

where $F(x) = n^{-1}\Sigma_j 1(X_j \leqslant x)$ is the empirical distribution function. The density estimate in (3) is proportional to the relative frequency of the data in an interval of length h and centred about x. The length of the interval has the same role as the bin-width number and is called a *bandwidth*. Since $F(x)$ is an unbiased estimate of $F(x)$ with good statistical properties, the population distribution function, (3) is expected to be a good estimate of $f(x) = dF(x)/d(x)$ as $h \to 0$.

When $r > 1$, the naive estimator is defined as

$$\hat{f}(x) = n^{-1} \sum_{i=1}^{n} \frac{1[X_i \in S(x,h)]}{\lambda[S(x,h)]} \tag{4}$$

where $S(x,h)$ is the sphere in $\mathbb{R}^r$-centred at x with radius h and $\lambda(\cdot)$ denotes Lebesgue's measure. The numerator in (4) is an unbiased estimator of $\Pr[X \in S(x,h)]$, and by Lebesgue's theorem

$$\lim_{h \downarrow 0} \frac{\Pr[X \in S(x,h)]}{\lambda[S(x,h)]} = f(x). \tag{5}$$

Then, it is expected that the estimate in (4) will approximate the true density $f(x)$ well for large sample sizes and h small. Note that

$$\hat{f}(x) = (nh^r)^{-1} \sum_{i} \frac{1(\|x - X_i\|h^{-1} \leqslant 1)}{\lambda[S(0,1)]}$$

$$= (nh^r)^{-1} \sum_{i} K[(x - X_i)h^{-1}] \tag{6}$$

where $\| \cdot \|$ is the Euclidean norm and $K(t) = 1(\|t\| \leqslant 1)/\lambda[S(0,1)]$ is the rectangular density on the r-dimensional sphere. Rosenblatt (1956) also suggested smoothing the estimate (4) by replacing the rectangular window in (6), which is a uniform density, by a general function $K\colon \mathbb{R}^r \to \mathbb{R}$ such that $\int_{\mathbb{R}^r} K(u)du = 1$, called a kernel. When $K(\cdot)$ is a density, the resulting density estimate is also a density. In such a case, (6) can be seen as a mixture of densities where each component has the same weight n^{-1}. Popular kernels are:

Gaussian $K(t) = (2\pi)^{-r/2} \exp(-t't/2)$

Epanechnikov $K(t) = \lambda[S(0,1)]^{-1}(r+2)\dfrac{1 - t't}{2/1(t't < 1)}$

where t is an r-dimensional vector and the prime indicates transposition.

The derivatives of the density are estimated by the derivatives of the density estimate assuming a suitable smooth kernel is used (the Gaussian produces derivative estimates of any order; the uniform, none). That is, if $f^{(s)}(x)$ is the sth derivative of f at scalar x, it is estimated by

$$\hat{f}^{(s)}(x) = n^{-1} \sum_{i=1}^{n} K^{(s)} \frac{h^{-1}(x - X_i)}{h^{r+s}}$$

where $K^{(s)}$ is the sth derivative of the kernel.

Instead of using a scalar bandwidth, one can use a matrix of bandwidths when $r > 1$, in order to take into account the correlation between the components in the vector X, i.e.

$$\hat{f}(x) = n^{-1} \sum_{i=1}^{n} K \frac{H^{-1}(x - X_i)}{\det(H)} \tag{7}$$

where H is a positive definite matrix. Then (6) is a particular case of (7) with $H = \text{diag}(h, \ldots, h)$. Sometimes, it may be convenient to scale the observations by the sample covariance matrix $\hat{\Sigma}$ as suggested by Fukunaga (1972), i.e. use $H - h\hat{\Sigma}$ in (7). Robinson (1983) pointed out that with diagonal bandwidths in a time series context 'the estimated distribution would suggest a "whiter" X_i than is the case, unless X_i is truly white noise'. Kernel density estimates are straightforward to program, but they do entail heavy computation, especially when n is large, the density is to be computed at many points x and estimates for several choices of bandwidth are to be found. However, $\hat{f}(\cdot)$ has a convolution form and may thus be computed by using the Fast Fourier Transform algorithm. Silverman (1982) developed this idea for $r = 1$. To estimate the density at a point x, this method requires only the order of $n \log n$ computations, instead of an order of n^2 operations using the naive approach, and not all the computations have to be redone when a new bandwidth is used.

The histograms and kernel estimates discussed above are not locally sensitive to such peculiarities in the data as sparsity in the tails of the density. If the smoothing parameter (binwidth or bandwidth) is too small, values in the tails of the data will provoke bumps or modes in the resulting density estimates. If the smoothing parameter is made too large, in order to avoid such effects, the resulting estimate will be oversmoothed and all the modes may be ironed even in the central part of the density. Several methods implement a local adaptive smoothing where the smoothing parameter is allowed to vary with the data.

An alternative to the histogram estimate (1) is the *variable partition histogram* suggested by Anderson (1965) and Van Ryzin (1973). When $r = 1$, the partitions depend on the order statistics $X_{(1)}, \ldots, X_{(n)}$. An integer $m \in [2, n]$ is chosen to be the number of bins in the histogram. Then set $k = [n/m]([\cdot]$ indicates nearest integer) and define partitions $A_{1n} = [X_{(1)}, X_{(k)}], A_{2n} = [X_{(k)}, X_{(2k)}], \ldots, A_{mn} = [X_{((m-1)k)}, X_{(n)}]$. Each partition is of different width and contains about k data points. The density is estimated by (1) using the new partitions. The generalization to multidimensions has been studied by Gessaman (1970).

The basic idea of variable histogram estimates can be also applied to kernels. Fix and Hodges (1951) and Loftsgarden and Quesenberry (1965) noted that (5) can be approximated in another way, by making the radius of the sphere depend on the sparsity of the data around x, i.e.

$$\hat{f}(x) = n^{-1} \sum_{i=1}^{n} \frac{1[X_i \in S(x, R_k)]}{\lambda[S(x, R_k)]} \tag{8}$$

where R_k is the minimal value for which $\Sigma_{i=1}^{n} 1[X_i \in S(x, R_k)] = k$. That is, the smoothing parameter is the Euclidean distance between x and its kth nearest neighbour in the data set. This is called a *nearest neighbour* estimate. Like the naive estimate, the estimate in (8) is expected to perform well for large sample sizes when $R_k \to 0$ (i.e. $k \to \infty$). Friedman et al. (1975) proposed an efficient algorithm for locating nearest neighbours. The algorithm has been implemented by Delgado (1990b). Note that (8) can be written as

$$\hat{f}(x) = \frac{k}{(n\lambda)[S(0, 1)]R_k^r}.$$

The estimated density is not a density itself since $\int_{\mathbb{R}^r} \hat{f}(x)dx = \infty$. Mack and Rosenblatt (1979) proposed to make (8) smoother by using a general kernel, i.e.

$$\hat{f}(x) = n^{-1} \sum_{i=1}^{n} K \frac{R_k^{-1}(x - X_i)}{R_k^r}. \tag{9}$$

Then (8) is a particular case of (9) where K is the uniform density on the unit sphere and is known as *uniform nearest neighbour* estimate. The estimate (9) is the locally adaptive smooth counterpart of (6), where a different h depending on x is used at each point. The nearest neighbour estimate provides fatter but smoother tails than the kernel.

The *variable kernel* estimate proposed by Breiman et al. (1977) adapts the amount of smoothing to the local density of the data, avoiding the problem of density estimates with infinite mass under the tails presented by the nearest neighbours. The variable kernel estimate is defined as

$$\hat{f}(x) = n^{-1} \sum_{i=1}^{n} \frac{K(hd_{i,k})^{-1}(x - X_i)}{(d_{i,k}H)^r} \tag{10}$$

where $d_{i,k}$ is the Euclidean distance from X_i to its kth nearest neighbour. Note that the same smoothing is used for each x. Breiman et al. (1977) proposed a two-step procedure for estimating the window width. In a first step, a pilot estimate $\hat{f}(x)$ is computed using kernels or nearest neighbours such that $\hat{f}(X_i) > 0$ for all i. In a second step, *local bandwidth factors* $\lambda_i = [\hat{f}(X_i)/g]^{-\alpha}$ are defined, where $g = \exp[n^{-1} \sum_i \log \hat{f}(X_i)]$ and $a \in [0, 1]$ is a sensitivity parameter. The density is estimated by

$$\hat{f}(x) = n^{-1} \sum_{i=1}^{n} \frac{K(h\lambda_i)^{-1}(x - X_i)}{(\lambda_i h)^r}.$$

This is known as an *adaptive kernel* estimate. Note that a bandwidth has to be chosen for the pilot estimate as well as the sensitivity parameter α. Breiman et al. (1977) recommended using a nearest neighbour estimate as the pilot estimate with a very large value of k and setting $\alpha = 1/r$. Abramson (1982) found that the method is quite insensitive to the pilot estimate and that $\alpha = 1/2$ is a good choice.

Other methods not discussed here are *orthogonal series* (e.g. Fourier series, Laguerre series, Legendre series and Hermite series) and *maximum likelihood* (e.g. convolution sieves and penalized maximum likelihood). These methods are discussed by Prakasa Rao (1983), Devroye and Györfi (1985) and Silverman (1986).

Whittle (1958) found that many nonparametric density estimates can be expressed in terms of a *delta sequence* $\{\delta_m(x, y), m > 0\}$ which satisfies the condition

$$\int \delta_m(x, y)\phi(y)\,\mathrm{d}y \to \phi(x) \text{ as } m \to \infty$$

for every infinitely differential function ϕ with compact support. Then, many density estimators can be written in the form

$$\hat{f}(x) = n^{-1} \sum_{i=1}^{n} \delta_m(x, X_i).$$

For instance, for the kernel estimate $\delta_m(x, y) = m^r K[m(x - y)]$.

2.2   Asymptotic properties and automatic choice of the smoothing number

Rosenblatt (1956) noted that all the estimates of the density function satisfying relatively mild regularity conditions are biased. Then, he evaluated the asymptotic mean square error (MSE) of kernel estimates.

The naive estimator in (3) is asymptotically unbiased when $h = h_n$ is a function of the sample size n and

$$h \to 0 \quad \text{as} \quad n \to \infty. \tag{11}$$

The empirical distribution function $n\hat{F}(x)$ is distributed as a binomial with parameters n and $F(x)$. Therefore

$$E[\hat{f}(x)] = \frac{F(x + h) - F(x - h)}{2h \to f(x)} \quad \text{under (11).}$$

Rosenblatt (1956) noted that, assuming the first three derivatives of $f(\cdot)$ exist,

$$F(x + h) - F(x - h) = 2hf(x) + f^{(2)}(x)h^3/3 + \mathrm{O}(h^4).$$

Since

$$\mathrm{MSE} = E\left\{[\hat{f}(x) - f(x)]^2\right\} = \frac{f(x)}{2h} + \frac{f^{(2)}(x)^2 h^4}{36} + \mathrm{O}[(nh)^{-1} + h^4]$$

then squared mean consistency is provided by (11) and

$$nh \to \infty \quad \text{as} \quad n \to \infty. \tag{12}$$

Rosenblatt (1956) also proposed general kernel estimates and gave an expression for the asymptotic MSE. The asymptotic properties of the kernel estimate were studied in detail by Parzen (1962). Cacoullos (1966) studied the asymptotic properties of kernel estimates for multivariate densities in (5). We discuss results for the general kernel estimate (7) following Robinson (1983).

Bochner's theorem (Bochner, 1955) is used for proving many asymptotic results in kernel estimation. The generalization of this theorem to a general kernel with a matrix of bandwidths H is as follows.

BOCHNER'S THEOREM Let $q : \mathbb{R}^r \to \mathbb{R}$ be a Borel function such that

(i) $q(\cdot)$ is continuous at x,

(ii) $\int_{\mathbb{R}^r} | q(u) | \, du < \infty$,

(iii) $\int_{\mathbb{R}^r} K(u) \, du = \chi < \infty$,

(iv) $\int_{\mathbb{R}^r} | K(u) | \, du < \infty$,

(v) $\lim_{\|u\| \to \infty} \|u\| \, | K(u) | = 0$,

(vi) $\lim_{n \to \infty} \|H\|^r \det(H)^{-1} < \infty$,

(vii) $\lim_{n \to \infty} H = 0$.

Then

$$\hat{q}(x) = \det(H)^{-1} \int K[H^{-1}(x - u)] q(u) \, du \to q(x) \int K(u) \, d(u) \text{ as } n \to \infty.$$

The conditions of this theorem are very mild. Note that condition (vi) holds when H is a diagonal matrix with equal components.

Then asymptotic unbiasedness follows under the conditions in the theorem, taking $q(u) = f(u)$ and $\chi = 1$, since

$$\hat{q}(x) = E[\hat{f}(x)] = \det(H)^{-1} \int K[H^{-1}(x - u)] f(u) du \to f(x) \text{ as } n \to \infty.$$

Consistency follows assuming also that

(viii) $\int_{\mathbb{R}^r} K(u)^2 du = \alpha < \infty$,

(ix) $n \det(H) \to \infty$.

Note that under independence

$$\text{var}[(\hat{f}(x)] = [n \det(H)]^{-1} \hat{q}(x) + n^{-1} \left\{ E[\hat{f}(x)] \right\}^2$$

where

$$\hat{q}(x) = [\det(H)]^{-1} \int K[H^{-1}(x - u)]^2 f(u) du \to f(x)\alpha \text{ as } n \to \infty.$$

When the density function is smooth, the bias rate of convergence can be improved by using higher order kernels proposed by Bartlett (1963). For simplicity consider the case

$r = 1$. We say that a kernel K is of class 0 if it belongs to the class of symmetric kernels about zero which integrate to 1. A *class s kernel* is a class 0 kernel for which

(a) $\int |t|^s |K(t)| \, dt < \infty$

(b) $\int t^l K(t) \, dt = 0 \qquad l = 1, \ldots, s - 1$

$\qquad\qquad\qquad\qquad\qquad\qquad\qquad\qquad\qquad\qquad\qquad\qquad$ (13)

In view of the symmetry of the kernels, (b) automatically holds for all even values of $l < s$. Most class 0 kernels are class 2 kernels. The order of a class 0 kernel is the largest integer such that $K(\cdot)$ obeys (13). Then if

(x) $f(\cdot)$ is s times boundedly differentiable,

(xi) $K(\cdot)$ is of order s,

(xii) $\sup_u (1 + |u|^2) |K(u)| < \infty$,

$E[\hat{f}(x) - f(x)] = O(h^s)$. Robinson (1988a) provided formulae for constructing higher order kernels of any degree. This bias reduction technique is crucial in many semiparametric procedures. The density estimate can be negative for kernels of order $s > 2$. This undesirable feature is not so important in semiparametric estimation where nonparametric estimates are only used as an intermediate tool. Applying a Taylor expansion, we obtain an expression for the mean integrated squared error (MISE):

$$\text{MISE} = (s!)^{-2} \beta_s^2 h^{2s} \int f^{(s)}(x)^2 dx + n^{-1} h^{-1} \alpha + o[(nh)^{-1} + h^{2s}] \qquad (14)$$

where $\beta_s = \int t^s K(t) \, dt$. The MISE is a measure of the discrepancy between the estimated and the true density. Then the MISE depends on the bandwidth, the kernel, and the smoothness of the density through the term $\int f^{(s)}(x)^2 dx$, known as the *difficulty factor*. From (14), the bandwidth number which minimizes the asymptotic expansion of the MISE is

$$h_{\text{opt}} \approx \left(\frac{\alpha(s!)^2}{2s \beta_s^2 \int f^{(s)}(x)^2 dx} \right)^{1/(2s+1)} n^{-1/(2s+1)}. \qquad (15)$$

Substituting this expression in (14) we obtain the optimal rate of convergence in L_2:

$$\inf_h \text{MISE} = O(n^{-2s/(2s+1)}).$$

Devroye and Györfi (1985) obtained the optimal rate of convergence of the mean integrated absolute error (MIAE):

$$\text{MIAE} = E \left[\int_{-\infty}^{\infty} |\hat{f}(x) - f(x)| \, dx \right].$$

This is a more robust measure for comparing densities than the MISE. The optimal rate of convergence of the MIAE is $O(n^{-2/(2s+1)})$.

Using calculus of variations, Epanechnikov (1969) proved that the kernel which minimizes α, subject to $K(\cdot)$, a bounded and even density and $\beta_2 = 1$, is the Epanechnikov kernel. The choice of kernel is not crucial. Values of α for different kernels are close. For instance, the ratio of the αs corresponding to the Epanechnikov and Gaussian kernels is 1.051. The choice of the bandwidth number is more important.

Optimal bandwidths can be 'estimated' from the data using (15). Assuming $f(\cdot)$ belongs to a particular parametric family of densities (e.g. the Gaussian), the parameters of the density are estimated (e.g. by maximum likelihood or by a robust procedure) under the assumed parametric model and then β_s and α are computed by numerical integration. This parametric method has been proposed by Deheuvels (1977) and Deheuvels and Hominal (1980). Suppose we use the Epanechnikov kernel and we assume that $f(x) = f(x, \theta)$ where $\theta = (\mu, \sigma, \gamma)$ is a vector of parameters, μ is the location parameter, σ is the scale parameter and γ is a vector of shape parameters. Then

$$h_{\text{opt}} \approx D_2(\theta)^{1/5} n^{-1/5} \qquad D_2(\theta) = 15 \left[\int f^{(2)}(x)^2 \, \mathrm{d}x \right]^{-1}. \qquad (16)$$

It is not necessary to mention location and scale parameters since

$$D_2(\mu, \sigma, \gamma)^{1/5} = \sigma D_2(0, 1, \gamma)^{1/5}.$$

Let $\hat{\sigma}$ be a robust estimate of σ (e.g. the least absolute deviation (LAD) estimate or any other robust estimate of the scale). Then the optimal bandwidths are estimated by

$$\hat{h}_{\text{opt}} \approx \hat{\sigma} D_2(0, 1, \hat{\gamma})^{1/5}$$

where $\hat{\gamma}$ is an estimate of γ computed by any method. Some densities do not have shape parameters (e.g. unimodal densities) and therefore it is only necessary to compute the scale parameter from the data. For instance with the normal density and using the Epanechnikov kernel

$$\hat{h}_{\text{opt}} \approx 2.345 \hat{\sigma} n^{-1/5}.$$

In practice one may report graphs of the density estimates, computing the optimal bandwidth based on different parametric densities.

Woodroofe (1970) proposed to avoid parameterizing the density in (15) and (16) by estimating it from a preliminary bandwidth, i.e.

$$\hat{h}_{\text{opt}} = D_2(\hat{f}, h_0)^{1/5} n^{-1/5} \qquad D_2(\hat{f}, h_0) = 15 \left[\int \hat{f}^{(2)}(x)^2 \mathrm{d}x \right]^{-1}.$$

$\hat{f}(x)$ is computed from a given bandwidth h_0. This method is also not completely automatic since h_0 has to be determined by the practitioner. An alternative, suggested by Scott et al. (1977), is to use an iterative procedure, estimating $\hat{h}_{\text{opt}}$ as the solution to

$$\hat{h}_{\text{opt}} = D_2(\hat{f}, \hat{h}_{\text{opt}})^{1/5}.$$

These methods exclude a large number of densities for which $\int f^{(2)}(x)^2 \mathrm{d}x$ is not defined or is infinite.

An alternative is to treat h as a parameter which is estimated by optimizing some criterion function. For instance Duin (1976) and Habbema et al. (1978) proposed choosing h to maximize the cross-validated likelihood

$$L(h) = \Pi_{i=1}^{n} \hat{f}_{(-i)}(X_i)$$

where

$$\hat{f}_{(-i)}(x) = (n-1)^{-1} \sum_{\substack{j=1 \\ j \neq i}} K \frac{h^{-1}(x - X_j)}{h^r}.$$

The cross-validation (i.e. the exclusion of the own observation) is due to the fact that $\Pi_{i=1}^{n} \hat{f}(X_i)$ is always maximized for $h = 0$. Chow et al. (1983) proved the consistency of this cross-validated estimate assuming that $f(\cdot)$ has compact support, but Schuster and Gregory (1981) have found that consistency may not be possible when the density does not have a compact support. However, we can always make a suitable transformation of X such that the corresponding density is defined on a compact. Once the density of the transformation has been estimated we can obtain the density estimate of X. Simulation studies (see for example Scott and Factor, 1981) have shown that the maximum likelihood cross-validation is very sensitive to outliers and to the form of K.

Hall (1983a, b), Rudemo (1982) and Bowman (1985) suggested using the cross-validated estimated MSE as a criterion function. Then the criterion function is

$$M(h) = \int \hat{f}(x)^2 dx - 2n^{-1} \sum_{i=1}^{n} \hat{f}_{(-i)}(X_i).$$

Stone (1984) found that the h minimizing this function is the best, in the sense of minimizing the MISE.

A central limit theorem for $\hat{f}(x)$ is useful in practice for constructing confidence intervals. For simplicity, consider the case $r = 1$ and a kernel of order 2. Under conditions mentioned above

$$\text{cov}[(nh)^{1/2}\hat{f}(x), (nh)^{1/2}\hat{f}(y)] \to 0 \text{ as } n \to \infty$$

and for $[x_1, \ldots, x_s]$ fixed

$$(nh)^{1/2}\left\{ \hat{f}(x_1) - E[\hat{f}(x_1)], \ldots, \hat{f}(x_s) - E[\hat{f}(x_s)] \right\} \xrightarrow{d} N(0, V\alpha)$$

where $V = \text{diag}[f(x_1), \ldots, f(x_s)]$.

Since
$$(nh)^{1/2}E[\hat{f}(x) - f(x)] = O[(nh^5)^{1/2}]$$

the asymptotic distribution of $(nh)^{1/2}[\hat{f}(x) - f(x)]$ is not centred at zero. Assuming that

$$nh^5 \to \gamma < \infty \text{ as } n \to \infty,$$

then for $[x_1, \ldots, x_s]$ fixed points

$$(nh)^{1/2}[\hat{f}(x_1) - f(x_1), \ldots, \hat{f}(x_s) - f(x_s)] \xrightarrow{d} N(\gamma^{1/2}\beta_2 B/2, V\alpha)$$

where $B = [f^{(2)}(x_1), \ldots, f^{(2)}(x_s)]'$. The bias disappears when $\gamma = 0$. Note that when $\gamma = 0$ the bandwidth is not optimal. This result can be used for constructing confidence intervals, since V is consistently estimated by

$$\hat{V} = \text{diag}[\hat{f}(x_1), \ldots, \hat{f}(x_s)].$$

Interestingly, the density is estimated more imprecisely on regions where the mass is concentrated.

The asymptotic variance is the same for general kernels (7), but the normalizing factor is $[n \det(H)]^{1/2}$. Asymptotic results are not affected under weak dependence. In particular, the asymptotic variance of $\hat{f}(x)$ is unaffected when X_i are strong mixing (Robinson, 1983).

Optimal rates of convergence of density estimates have been established by Stone (1980).

Uniform consistency for kernel estimates has been established by Bertrand-Retali (1978). Devroye and Györfi (1985) have proved that (11) and (12) are necessary and sufficient conditions for $\int |\hat{f}(x) - f(x)| \, dx$ to converge to zero with probability one, for any $f(\cdot)$, assuming only that the kernel is a non-negative function which integrates to unity.

The consistency of the histogram was established by Rèvèsz (1972). Freedman and Diaconis (1981a) have studied the uniform convergence properties. The histogram has L_2 optimal rate of convergence $n^{-2/3}$ (Scott, 1979) and the optimal L_1 rate is $n^{-1/3}$ (Devroye and Györfi, 1985). The histogram can be adjusted to enjoy a faster rate of convergence $n^{-4/5}$ in L_2 by smoothing out the block-line shape of the histogram. It has been done using the average shifted histogram (Scott, 1985a) and the *frequency polygon* (Scott, 1985b).

The consistency of nearest neighbour estimates has been established by Loftsgaarden and Quesenberry (1965) and Moore and Yackel (1977) assuming that

$$k/n \to 0 \text{ and } k \to \infty \text{ as } n \to \infty.$$

L_2 properties have been studied by Rosenblatt (1979) and Mack and Rosenblatt (1979). Devroye and Györfi (1985) noted that it is impossible to study the L_1 properties of nearest neighbour estimates because of their infinite integral. Devroye and Györfi (1985) gave L_1 results for the variable histogram. Similar results for the L_2 case can be found in Prakasa Rao (1983), Lecoutre (1986) and Kogure (1987). The optimal MISE, is of the same order as that of the classical histogram. Devroye and Györfi (1985) gave conditions for L_1 consistency of the variable kernel estimate for all f and Devroye and Penrod (1986) proved strong uniform consistency.

Nonparametric kernel density estimates for weakly dependent processes have been studied, for example, by Roussas (1969), Rosenblatt (1971), Robinson (1983), Yakowitz (1985), Roussas (1988), Tran (1989), Hart and Vieu (1990) and Silveira (1990) and Robinson (1987d) and Hall and Hart (1989a, b) considered strongly dependent processes. The asymptotic properties of the histogram under weak serial dependence have been studied by Györfi (1987) and Tran (1989).

2.3 Applications

Density estimates are recommended as a first step in *exploratory data analysis*. Density estimates of residuals from parametric regression may be useful as a preliminary specification tool. Robinson (1987b) considered density estimates of innovations in time series models, based on estimated residuals.

Fix and Hodges (1951) were the first to propose using nonparametric density estimates in application to *discriminatory data analysis*. In discrimination, density estimates $\hat{f}_A(\cdot)$ and $\hat{f}_B(\cdot)$ are computed from samples from two different populations A and B. Then a particular observation $\mathfrak{F}$ is assigned to the population A if $\hat{f}_A(\mathfrak{F}) > \hat{f}_B(\mathfrak{F})$. This method has been applied in medicine in order to perform diagnosis on a disease. The variables are random vectors containing dummies, which indicate the performance of diagnostic tests, and certain individual characteristics of the patient. One envisages applications of these methods to investigate the success of employment training programmes or other social experiments.

In *cluster analysis* the problem is to divide the data set into clusters or classes. Roughly speaking, the problem now is to find from how many and which populations the observations are coming. Several cluster and discrimination methods, using nonparametric density estimation, were reviewed by Prakasa Rao (1983) and Silverman (1986).

Devroye and Györfi (1985) proposed several algorithms for *simulation* from the estimated density and any standard uniform random number generator. They discussed inversion, rejection and order statistics methods for densities estimated from kernels or the histogram. They showed that quite large sample sizes are required for generating observations indistinguishable from observations generated from the true density. These simulation methods are useful in constructing bootstrap estimates. The classical bootstrap performs random sampling with replacement from the empirical distribution of the data. A *smooth bootstrap* consists of generating observations from the estimated density.

Another application is in *testing unimodality*. Silverman (1981, 1983) used the idea that, as the amount of smoothing increases, the number of modes or bumps in the estimated density tends to decrease. Thus Silverman proposed finding a critical bandwidth h_{crit} such that the nonparametric density estimate is unimodal for any $h \geqslant h_{crit}$. If the true density is unimodal one expects a small h_{crit} and for multimodal densities a large h_{crit}. The h_{crit} is found by a grid search. This idea forms the basis of creating statistics based on h_{crit}. Silverman (1983) proved that, as $n \to \infty$, $h_{crit} \to 0$ when the density is unimodal but h_{crit} is bounded away from zero otherwise. The h_{crit} is assessed against a standard family of unimodal densities. Silverman also suggested avoiding use of a parametric family by using the smoothed bootstrap. A large number of samples, with the original sample size, are generated from the estimated density $\hat{f}_{crit}$ computed with h_{crit}. For each replicated sample, new densities are estimated using h_{crit}. Then the proportion of replications producing multimodal densities is the *p*-value. Craig (1991) has compared these methods with the *dip* tests of Hartigan and Hartigan (1985) in the context of a test for unimodality of fixed costs of labour adjustment. The dip statistic is the maximum difference between the empirical distribution function and the unimodal distribution function that minimizes the maximum difference. The dip test is asymptotically larger for the uniform distribution than for any distribution in a larger class of distributions.

Tests of independence can also be performed using nonparametric density estimates. Traditionally tests for serial dependence are based on the sample serial correlation or serial rank-based correlation procedures (e.g. Spearman's test). These tests may not be suitable in the analysis of stock market prices, where the dependence may be non-linear (e.g. autoregressive conditionally heteroskedastic or bilinear processes). Such subtle alternatives to the independence hypothesis may be detected using nonparametric density estimates. The null hypothesis for testing independence between continuous random variables X and Y can be expressed as H_0: $f(x,y) = f(x)f(y)$ for all x and y. Robinson (1991c) proposed using the Kullback and Leibler distance, i.e.

$$I = \int\int f(x,y)\left\{\log f(x,y) - \log[f(x)f(y)]\right\} \, \mathrm{d}x \, \mathrm{d}y.$$

This is approximated using kernel estimates of the joint and marginal densities. For example, in order to test serial independence in time series, i.e. independence of X_i and X_{i+1}, a possible statistic is

$$\hat{I}_n = n^{-1} \sum_i c_i \left\{\log[\hat{f}(X_i, X_{i+1})] - 2\log[(\hat{f}(X_i)]\right\}$$

for a sequence of weights c_i. Robinson (1991c) showed consistency of the test based on $\hat{I}_n$ against strong mixing alternatives and, for suitable c_i, asymptotic normality under the null. He applied the resulting test in testing independence of exchange rates for different currencies using daily, weekly and monthly data. Chan and Tran (1992) proposed using the L_1 distance rather than the Kullback–Leibler distance and used histogram instead of kernel estimates. Their test resembles tests based on contingency tables. They showed that the test is consistent when the series is absolutely regular. However, they did not obtain the asymptotic distribution of the statistic under the null and therefore the implementation of their test relies on the estimation of critical values using permutations of the original series. Neither Robinson (1991c) nor Chan and Tran (1992) considered data-dependent bandwidths or binwidths in their theory.

Cumulative distribution functions can be estimated using kernel estimates. In particular the cumulative distribution $F(x)$ is estimated by $\hat{F}(x) = n^{-1}\sum_i \mathcal{K}(x - X_i)$, where $\mathcal{K}(\cdot)$ is the cumulative distribution of the kernel (see Prakasa Rao, 1983). One may prefer to use the empirical cumulative distribution $\hat{F}(x) = n^{-1}\sum_i 1(X_i \leqslant x)$, which is unbiased, avoids the choice of a smoothing parameter, and is computationally very convenient. However, the empirical cumulative distribution may be unsuitable for estimating probabilities under the tails of the density where data are scarce. In such cases a smooth estimator may be preferred. Other functionals, like $f^{(s)}(x)$, $\int f^{(s)}(x)\mathrm{d}x$ or $\int f(x)^2\mathrm{d}x$ or, can be estimated by substituting for the true density the estimated density inside the integrals.

The hazard rate $H(x) = f(x)/[1 - F(x)]$ can be estimated by $\hat{H}(x) = \hat{f}(x)/[1 - \hat{F}(x)]$. Relevant surveys are by Singpurewalla and Wong (1983) and Hassani et al. (1986).

The conditional density $f(y|X = x) = f(y,x)/f(x)$ is estimated by $\hat{f}_{Y|X}(y) = \hat{f}(y,x)/\hat{f}(x)$ (Nadaraya, 1964; Watson, 1964; Rosenblatt, 1969).

Other important applications of density estimates are the computation of regression functions, which will be covered in the next section, and semiparametric estimates, which will be covered in section 4.

3 Nonparametric regression

Econometric models describe the relationship between economic variables. This relationship is often represented by means of conditional moments. In particular, given an

$r \times 1$ vector of explanatory variables X, a $q \times 1$ vector of response variables Y and a known function g: $\mathbb{R}^q \to \mathbb{R}$, one is interested in estimating

$$m(x) = E[g(Y) \mid X = x] \tag{17}$$

The function $m(\cdot)$ is called a *regression curve*.

Regression curves can be estimated by parametric methods. That is, $m(x)$ is assumed to follow a particular parametric form (e.g. $m(x) = x'\beta$, where β is a vector of unknown parameters) and then the parameters are estimated using some loss function. Economic models usually provide information on some features of the regression curve. For instance, it is known that, for normal goods, the regression curve of expenditure with respect to income has positive first derivatives and negative second derivatives. However, many competing functional forms can be in agreement with economic theory principles.

Nonparametric regression estimates do not impose a rigid functional form on the regression function. Given a data set $\{(Y_i, X_i), i = 1, \ldots, n\}$, the nonparametric estimate of $m(x)$ is a weighted average of $g(Y_i)$, where the heavier weights are given to the observations with X_i closest to x; i.e. $m(x)$ is estimated by

$$\hat{m}(x) = \sum_i g(Y_i) W_{ni}(x) \tag{18}$$

where $\{W_{ni}(x), i = 1, \ldots, n\}$ is a sequence of weights which sum up to unity. The idea is that $g(Y_i)$s with X_is close to x possess more information on $m(x)$ than observations far away from x. Therefore, $W_{ni}(x)$ will be small when X_i is far away from x. When $W_{ni}(x) = n^{-1}$ all i, (18) is a consistent estimate of $E[g(Y)]$ but an inconsistent estimate of $m(x)$.

Nonparametric regression may be used in explanatory data analysis. Hildenbrand and Hildenbrand (1980), Härdle and Jerison (1988), Härdle (1990) and Bierens and Pott-Buter (1991) have obtained nonparametric estimates of Engle curves for different goods. Nonparametric predictors from time series have also been used to investigate the forecastability of rates of return of gold by Prescott and Stengos (1988) and Härdle and Vieu (1989) and of exchange rates by Diebold and Nason (1990). Nonparametric estimates constructed from parametric residuals may be useful in model specification, e.g. to check structure in the residuals or the presence of heteroskedasticity. Estimates of derivatives of the regression function are computed in the same way as density derivatives. In particular, the sth derivative of $m(x)$, $m^{(s)}(x)$, is estimated by

$$\hat{m}^{(s)}(x) = \sum_i g(Y_i) W_{ni}^{(s)}(x) \tag{19}$$

where $W_{ni}^{(s)}(x) = \partial W_{ni}(x)/\partial x$, when the weight function is s-times differentiable. From (19), one can obtain estimates of elasticities and other functionals. Nonparametric regression has also been used in many semiparametric problems. Recent surveys on nonparametric regression are Collomb (1981, 1985) and a book on the topic is given by Härdle (1990).

We next present some specific nonparametric regression techniques, then we discuss automatic choices of the smoothing parameter, and finally we discuss some applications.

3.1   Some techniques

Nonparametric density estimates can be represented as a sum of weights, i.e.

$$\hat{f}(x) = \sum_i w(x, X_i).$$

Noting that

$$m(x) = \int g(y) f[g(y) \mid X = x] \, dy = \int g(y) f[g(y), x] \, dy / f(x)$$
$$= P_{g(y)}(x) / f(x),$$

the problem is to find an estimate of $P_{g(y)}(x)$. When $g(Y) = 1$, it follows that $P_1(x) = f(x)$ and is estimated by $\hat{f}(x)$. Then it seems sensible to estimate $P_{g(y)}(x)$ by

$$\hat{P}_{g(y)}(x) = \sum_i g(Y_i) w(x, X_i). \tag{20}$$

It is possible to construct weights

$$W_{ni}(x) = \frac{w(x, X_i)}{\sum_i w(x, X_i)}. \tag{21}$$

So, the histogram produces partition estimates with weights

$$W_{ni}(x) = 1(X_i \in A_{nj}) \left[\sum_{i=1}^n 1(X_i \in A_{nj}) \right]^{-1}. \tag{22}$$

when $x \in A_{nj}$. The partition estimate is just the arithmetic average of the Y_is with corresponding X_is in the same bin as x. These types of weights were proposed by McMurtry and Fu (1966), Hill (1969) and Jarvis (1970) among others. Since $\sum_{i=1}^n 1(X \in A_{nj})$ can be equal to zero for some partitions, it has been suggested that (22) might be replaced by $W_{ni}(x) = n^{-1}$ when $\sum_{i=1}^n 1(X_i \in A_{nj}) = 0$ for $x \in A_{nj}$ (see Györfi, 1991). *Variable partition estimates* are constructed in the same way but using the variable histogram. The *kernel estimates* use weights

$$W_{ni}(x) = \frac{K[(x - X_i)/h]}{\sum_i K[(x - X_i)/h]} \tag{23}$$

with $W_{ni}(x) = 0$ in the case $0/0$. These weights were proposed by Nadaraya (1964) and Watson (1964). More general weights using kernels like those employed in (7) are

$$W_{ni}(x) = \frac{K[H^{-1}(x - X_i)]}{\sum_i K[H^{-1}(x - X_i)]}. \tag{24}$$

These weights were introduced by Robinson (1983).

The *nearest neighbour estimates* use weights

$$W_{ni}(x) = \frac{K[(x - X_i)/R_k]}{\sum_i K[(x - X_i)/R_k]}. \tag{25}$$

When $K(\cdot)$ is the uniform kernel we have weights

$$W_{ni}(x) = 1(X_i \text{ is one of the } k \text{ nearest neighbours of } x)/k \tag{26}$$

where $1(A)$ is the indicator function of the event A. These weights were introduced by Royall (1966), Cover (1968) and Cover and Hart (1967), and weights (25) were introduced by Collomb (1980).

Stone (1977) and Devroye (1978) introduced a general class of nearest neighbour weights. Since the individual coordinates are usually measured in dissimilar units, Stone proposed transforming them to the unit metric before applying the Euclidean metric. The scales used have to satisfy certain conditions. These conditions are met by the sample standard deviation, provided that X admits a nondegenerate distribution and has finite second moments. Then the random (pseudo) metric corresponding to the scales $\{s_{nj}, j = 1, \ldots, r\}$ is defined by

$$\rho_n(u, v) = \left[\sum_{i=1}^{r} s_{ni}^{-1}(u_i - v_i)^2 \right]^{1/2}$$

where $u = (u_1, \ldots, u_r)$ and $v = (v_1, \ldots, v_r)$. Let c_{ni} be such that

$$c_{1n} \geqslant \ldots \geqslant c_{nn} \geqslant 0, c_{ni} = 0 \text{ for } 1 > n \text{ and } \sum_{i=1}^{n} c_{ni} = 1.$$

For $1 \leqslant i \leqslant n$,

$$W_{ni}(x) = \frac{c_{nv_i}(x) + \ldots + c_{nv_i}(x) + \lambda_i(x) - 1}{\lambda_i(x)}, \tag{27}$$

$$\nu_i(x) = (1 + \#[l : l \neq i, \rho_n(X_l, x) < \rho_n(X_i, x)])$$

and

$$\lambda_i(x) = (1 + \#[l : l \neq i, \rho_n(X_l, x) = \rho_n(X_i, x)])$$

This tie-breaking rule is computationally expensive. Devroye (1978) suggested breaking the ties by comparing indices, i.e. when X_i and X_j are equally close to x, according to the defined metric, X_i is said to be closer to x if $i < j$. Then, the weights are just $W_{ni}(x) = c_{n\nu_i}$. Stone (1977) required the weights (27) to satisfy, for asymptotic theory,

(i) $c_{nl} \rightarrow 0$

$$\tag{28}$$

(ii) $\displaystyle\sum_{i \geqslant n\alpha} c_{ni} \rightarrow 0$ for all $\alpha > 0$ as $n \rightarrow \infty$.

Devroye (1978) required (28)(i) and that there exists a sequence of numbers $k = k_n$ such that, in asymptotic theory,

$$k \to \infty, k/n \to 0 \text{ and } \sum_{i=k+1}^{n} c_{ni} \to 0 \text{ as } n \to \infty. \tag{29}$$

Devroye (1982) proved that (28) and (29) are equivalent. These properties are satisfied by the following weights:

Uniform $c_{ni} = k^{-1}$ when $i \leqslant k$ and $c_{ni} = 0$ otherwise, with $k \to \infty$ and $k/n \to 0$ as $n \to \infty$,

Triangular $c_{ni} = 2(k - i + 1)/(k + k^2)$ when $i \leqslant k$ and $c_{ni} = 0$ otherwise, with $k \to \infty$ and $k/n \to 0$ as $n \to \infty$,

Exponential $c_{ni} = h(1 + h)^{-1}[1 - (1 - h)^{-n}]^{-1}$, with $h \to 0$ and $nh \to \infty$.

In order to check that these weights satisfy (29), Devroye (1978) recommended taking $k \approx (n/h)^{1/2}$ in (29).

Since $m(x) = P_{g(y)}(x)/f(x)$, one can exploit any available information on $f(x)$, e.g. when $f(x)$ is known (which is highly unlikely in practice) $m(x)$ can be estimated by $\hat{m}(x) = \hat{P}_{g(y)}(x)/f(x)$ (Johnston, 1982).

In the fixed design model, where the explanatory variables are non-random and possibly equispaced on the interval [0, 1], Priestley and Chao (1972) proposed weights (with $r = 1$)

$$W_{ni}(x) = (X_i - X_{i-1})h^{-1}K[(x - X_i)/h].$$

Gasser and Müller (1979) defined weights for the fixed design model

$$W_{ni}(x) = h^{-1} \int_{S_{i-1}}^{S_i} K\left(\frac{x - u}{h}\right) du \tag{30}$$

where $X_{i-1} \leqslant S_{i-1} \leqslant X_i$ is chosen between the ordered Xs. Cheng and Lin (1981) considered the case $S_i = X_i$.

Yang (1981) and Stute (1984) considered a type of nearest neighbour estimate with weights

$$W_{ni}(x) = n^{-1}h^{-1}K\left[\frac{\hat{F}(x) - \hat{F}(X_i)}{h}\right] \tag{31}$$

where $\hat{F}(\cdot)$ is the empirical cumulative distribution. These weights are of the form (23) where we use the fact that $\sum_i n^{-1}h^{-1}K\left\{[\hat{F}(x) - \hat{F}(X_i)]/h\right\} \to 1$, under the usual conditions on h.

Nonparametric regression in a time series context has been studied by Watson (1964), Roussas (1969), Bosq (1980), Robinson (1983), Doukhan and Ghindès (1980, 1983), Collomb (1984), Yakowitz (1985, 1987) and Bierens (1990) among others.

Note that the weights in (18) can be interpreted as minimizing a square loss function, i.e.

$$\hat{m}(x) = \operatorname*{argmin}_{\mu} \sum_{j}[g(Y_j) - \mu]^2 W_{nj}(x).$$

Then $\hat{m}(x)$ is highly sensitive to the effect of just one isolated observation Y_i, particularly if the corresponding X_i is close to x. The idea of robust estimation of a location parameter has been adapted to this context. In particular, the influence of outlying observations is reduced by substituting for the quadratic loss function a convex function $\rho(\cdot)$ with bounded derivative $\phi(\cdot)$. That is, the robust conditional location functional $r(x)$ defined by the equation

$$E\{\phi[g(Y) - r(x)] \mid X = x\} = 0$$

is estimated by the solution to

$$\sum_j \phi[g(Y_j) - r(x)]W_{ni}(x) = 0. \tag{32}$$

This estimator was proposed by Tsybakov (1982), Robinson (1984) and Härdle (1984) using kernels. Härdle and Tsybakov (1990) extended it to simultaneous robust estimation of conditional location and scale using kernels, and Boente and Fraiman (1989, 1990) to location-invariant robust estimates, estimating the conditional scale *a priori*, using kernel and nearest neighbour estimates.

Conditional quartiles can be estimated from the estimated cumulative conditional distribution $F(\mathcal{G} \mid X = x)$:

$$\hat{F}(\mathcal{G} \mid X = x) = \sum_j 1[g(Y_j) \leqslant \mathcal{G}]W_{nj}(x). \tag{33}$$

Then the αth conditional quartile ζ_α is estimated by $\hat{\zeta}_\alpha$ such that

$$\hat{F}(\hat{\zeta}_\alpha \mid X = x) = \alpha, \tag{34}$$

These quartile estimates were defined by Stone (1977) using general consistent weights. He also proposed L estimates computed by functions of conditional quartile estimates.

Stone (1977) also defined *local linear weights* as follows. Let us define $Z_i' = (1, X_i')$; then $\hat{\beta} = [\sum_i Z_i Z_i' W_{ni}(x)]^{-1} \sum_i Z_i g(Y_i) W_{ni}(x)$ minimizes the function

$$\sum_j [g(Y_j) - \beta'Z_j]^2 W_{nj}(x).$$

The weights $V_{ni}(x) = x'[\sum_i Z_i Z_i' W_{ni}(x)]^{-1} \sum_i Z_i W_{ni}(x)$ are called local linear weights. These weights may be inconsistent and Stone proposed a transformation of $V_{ni}(x)$ which produces consistent weights. Cleveland (1979), Cleveland and Devlin (1988) and Cleveland et al. (1988) proposed local linear polynomial weights which are robustified by means of an iterative procedure.

3.2   Asymptotic properties and automatic choice of the smoothing number

The general kernel estimate using weights (24) can be expressed as

$$\hat{m}(x) = \hat{P}_{g(y)}(x)/\hat{f}(x)$$

where

$$\hat{P}_{g(y)}(x) = [n \det(H)]^{-1} \sum_j g(Y_j) K[H^{-1}(x - X_j)] \tag{35}$$

estimates

$$\hat{P}_{g(y)}(x) = m(x)f(x).$$

The asymptotic unbiasedness of $\hat{P}_{g(y)}(x)$ follows from Bochner's theorem, taking $q(u) = \hat{P}_{g(y)}(u)$, with $f(\cdot)$ and $m(\cdot)$ continuous at x and $E \mid m(X) \mid < \infty$. Then

$$\begin{aligned}
\hat{q}(u) = E[\hat{P}_{g(y)}(x)] &= \det(H)^{-1} E\left\{ g(Y)K[H^{-1}(x - X)]\right\} \\
&= \det(H)^{-1} E\left\{ m(X)K[H^{-1}(x - X)]\right\} \\
&= \det(H)^{-1} \int P_{g(y)}(U)K[H^{-1}(x - u)]\, du \\
&\to P_{g(y)}(x) \text{ as } n \to \infty.
\end{aligned}$$

The asymptotic bias of $\hat{P}_{g(y)}(x)$ can be reduced, when $P_{g(y)}(x)$ admits enough derivatives, by using higher order kernels, as in density estimation. In particular, using kernels of order two and assuming also that the first two derivatives of $P_{g(y)}(x)$ exist and are bounded and (xii), when $r = 1$,

$$E[\hat{P}_{g(y)}(x) - P_{g(y)}(x)] \approx 2^{-1}h^2\beta_2 \frac{\partial^2 P_{g(y)}(x)}{\partial x^2}.$$

Mean square consistency follows assuming also (vii)–(ix) and that $s^2(x) = E[g(Y)^2 \mid X = x]$ is continuous at x, since assuming independence

$$\mathrm{var}[\hat{P}_{g(y)}(x)] = [n\det(H)]^{-1}\hat{Q}(x) + n^{-1}E[\hat{P}_{g(y)}(x)]$$

where

$$\hat{Q}(x) = [\det(H)]^{-1} \int s(u)^2 f(u)K[H^{-1}(x - u)]\, du \to s(x)^2 f(x)\alpha \text{ as } n \to \infty.$$

Therefore, $\hat{m}(x)$ is also consistent, applying Slutsky's theorem. Strictly, the moments of kernel estimates may only exist under restrictive conditions in view of the random denominator $\hat{f}(x)$.

The sequence of weights $\{W_{ni}(x), i \geqslant 1\}$ is said to be *universally L_s consistent*, for $s \geqslant 1$ fixed, if

$$E\left[\int \mid \hat{m}(x) - m(x) \mid^s f(x)\, dx\right] \to 0 \text{ as } n \to \infty$$

for all possible distributions of (Y, X) such that $E \mid g(Y) \mid^s < \infty$.

Stone (1977) gave necessary and sufficient conditions for the universal consistency of weights and he applied his result to prove the universal consistency of nearest neighbour weights. Devroye and Wagner (1980) and Spiegelman and Sacks (1980) proved the L_s universal consistency of kernel weights and Györfi (1991) the universal consistency of partition estimates. An important feature of many of these results is that, despite the motivation given for kernel estimates, X need not have a density, so that discrete-valued regressors are permitted.

Schuster (1972) established for $r = 1$, under conditions stated above and

$$nh^3 \to \infty, nh^5 \to 0 \quad \text{as} \quad n \to \infty,$$

for $\{x_1, \ldots, x_s\}$ distinct fixed points,

$$(nh)^{1/2}[\hat{m}(x_1) - m(x_1), \ldots, \hat{m}(x_s) - m(x_s)] \xrightarrow{d} N(0, \alpha W)$$

where $W = \text{diag}[\sigma^2(x_1)/f(x_1), \ldots, \sigma^2(x_s)/f(x_s)]$ and $\sigma^2(x) = \text{var}(Y|X = x)$. The conditional variance is consistently estimated by

$$\hat{\sigma}^2(x) = \sum_i Y_i^2 W_{ni}(x) - \left[\sum_i Y_i W_{ni}(x)\right]^2.$$

Hence,

$$\hat{W} = \text{diag}[\hat{\sigma}^2(x_1)/\hat{f}(x_1), \ldots, \hat{\sigma}^2(x_s)/\hat{f}(x_s)]$$

is a consistent estimate of W that can be used for constructing consistent confidence intervals. Robinson (1983) proved that, for $r > 1$ and using weights (24), the asymptotic variance is the same but the normalizing factor is $[n \det(H)]^{1/2}$. He also proved that the asymptotic variance is unaffected under weak dependence where the regressors are lagged values of the dependent variable and assuming that the series is strong mixing.

The plug-in method is more difficult to implement than in density estimation. The MSE of $\hat{m}(x)$ may not exist because it is a ratio between random variables. The following linearization is often applied:

$$\hat{m}(x) - m(x) \approx \frac{\hat{P}_{g(y)}(x) - m(x)\hat{f}(x)}{f(x)}.$$

Then, the MSE of $\hat{m}(x)$ is approximated by

$$E[\hat{P}_{g(y)}(x) - m(x)\hat{f}(x)]^2/f(x)^2 \approx (nh)^{-1}\sigma^2(x)\alpha f(x)^{-1}$$
$$+ h^4 \left[\frac{\beta_2\{m^{(2)}(x) + 2m^{(1)}(x)[\partial \log f(x)/\partial x]\}}{2}\right]^2$$

where $m^{(i)}(x) = \partial^i m(x)/\partial x^i$. The 'optimal bandwidth' which minimizes the above expression is proportional to $n^{-1/5}$ and depends on the unknowns $\sigma^2(x), f(x), f^{(1)}(x)$, $m^{(1)}(x), m^{(2)}(x)$. All these unknowns must be estimated when implementing the plug-in procedure.

Alternatively, other measures of accuracy can be employed. The mean integrated weighted squared error (MIWSE) is defined as

$$E\left\{\int [m(x) - \hat{m}(x)]^2 f(x)V(x)\,dx\right\} \tag{36}$$

where $V(\cdot)$ is a weighting function. Stone (1982) provided the lower and optimal rate of convergence in this sense, under certain smoothness conditions on $m(\cdot)$ and $f(\cdot)$.

The MIWSE can be estimated from the data by the averaged weighted squared error (AWSE)

$$\text{AWSE} = n^{-1} \sum_j \{g(Y_j) - \hat{m}(X_j)\}^2 V(X_j).$$

The bandwidth minimizing this function will be too small since $\hat{m}(X_j) \to g(Y_j)$ as $h \to 0$, for fixed n. Clark (1975) proposed the leave-one-out cross-validation function

$$\text{CV}(h) = \sum_j [g(Y_j) - \hat{m}_{(j)}(X_j)]^2 V(X_j) \qquad (37)$$

where $\hat{m}_{(j)}(x) = \Sigma_{i \neq j} g(Y_i) W_{ni}(x)$ and $W_{ni}(x)$ are kernel weights.

An alternative to the leave-one-out cross-validation function is to use some penalizing function. In this case h is chosen to be $\hat{h} = \text{argmin}_h Q(h)$, where

$$Q(h) = \sum_j [g(Y_j) - \hat{m}(X_j)]^2 \Psi(n^{-1}h^{-1}) V(X_j),$$

where $\Psi(\cdot)$ is the penalizing function which corrects for too small h. Examples of penalizing functions are:

$\Psi(n^{-1}h^{-1}) = [1 - n^{-1}h^{-1}K(0)]^{-2}$ Craven and Wahba (1979); Li (1985)

$\Psi(n^{-1}h^{-1}) = \exp[2n^{-1}h^{-1}K(0)]$ Akaike (1970)

$\Psi(n^{-1}h^{-1}) = [1 + n^{-1}h^{-1}K(0)]/[1 - n^{-1}h^{-1}K(0)]$ Akaike (1974)

$\Psi(n^{-1}h^{-1}) = [1 - 2n^{-1}h^{-1}K(0)]^{-1}$ Rice (1984)

Härdle and Marron (1985a, b) have proved that, under certain regularity conditions, all these data-driven bandwidths are asymptotically optimal with respect to different accuracy measures. Consistent cross-validated smoothing parameters in the nearest neighbour case have been obtained by Li (1984). Li (1987) proved the asymptotic optimality of several cross-validation criteria where the smoothing parameter takes discrete values, with application to nearest neighbours estimation. Andrews (1991a) has generalized his result to models with heteroskedastic disturbances.

3.3 Applications

Nonparametric regression estimates can be employed to check the goodness of particular parameterizations of conditional expectations and the usefulness of candidate explanatory variables without specifying functional form. Plots of parametric and nonparametric fitting are useful in this respect.

Bierens and Pott-Buter (1991) demonstrated the usefulness of nonparametric regression analysis for functional specification of household Engle curves. Household demand functions and equivalence scales are estimated from econometric models where the demand function is specified in advance, directly or indirectly, via the specification of the utility function or cost function. The functional form of the model is chosen on the basis of tractability rather than on the basis of prior knowledge of the true functional form. The probability of choosing the correct model is small due to the many functional forms theoretically admissible. Mis-specification of functional form leads to inconsistent parameter estimates and the equivalence scales will also be inconsistently estimated. Bierens and Pott-Buter (1990) noted that the life cycle consumption hypothesis leads to demand systems that relate specific demand to net income, prices and household composition, plus a heteroskedastic error term. The demand functions involved are conditional expectations functions. The functional form of the Engle curve is estimated by nonparametric kernel regression using the 1980 Budget Survey for the

Netherlands. Two Engle curves are estimated for expenditure on food, clothing and footwear, and for other expenditures. The regressors are net income and number of children in the age group 0–15 and in the age group 16 or over. They plotted the Engle curves of expenditure versus net income for the different household categories. Then, parametric models were chosen in accordance with the nonparametric regression results. The final specifications of the Engle curves are linear, depending on income and the number of children in the two age groups.

Stone (1977) proposed estimates of conditional variances, covariances and correlation functions. In particular the conditional variance of Y given the vector of regressors X, $\sigma^2(x) = \text{var}(Y \mid X = x)$, is estimated by

$$\hat{\sigma}^2(x) = \sum_i Y_i^2 W_{ni}(x) - \left[\sum_i Y_i W_{ni}(x) \right]^2. \tag{38}$$

Rose (1978) proposed other conditional variance estimates in the linear regression model when it is known that $E(Y \mid X = x) = x'\beta$, where β is a vector of unknown parameters. A possible estimate of $\sigma^2(x)$ is

$$\hat{\sigma}^2(x) = \sum_j (Y_i - X_i'\hat{\beta})^2 W_{ni}(x) \tag{39}$$

where $\hat{\beta}$ is some preliminary estimate of β, e.g. the least squares estimate.

Elasticity and other economic functional estimates can be computed from the estimates of the derivatives of the regression curve.

Another important application is in prediction of time series. The regression function in this case is an autoregressive process of unknown functional form, i.e. let $Z_i' = (X_{i-1}, X_{i-2}, \ldots, X_{i-p})$ and

$$m(\mathcal{F}) = E(X \mid Z = \mathcal{F}).$$

In efficient asset markets, it is widely agreed that high frequency asset returns are linearly unpredictable, conditionally heteroskedastic and conditionally leptokurtic. Empirical and theoretical results are consistent with the conjecture that nonlinearities may be present in asset returns' conditional means. However, the out-of-sample forecasting of linear models has not been improved on by any nonlinear model. Diebold and Nason (1990) provide several explanations for this fact: nonlinearities may be present in even-ordered conditional moments, nonlinearities such as outliers may be present, and it is difficult to find the correct parametric model. They estimated the conditional expectation of ten major dollar spot rates using the nonparametric local weighted regression proposed by Cleveland (1979) and Cleveland and Devlin (1988). They found that nonparametric regression does not improve the out-of-sample prediction of a simple random walk. These results are consistent with those of Prescott and Stengos (1988) who were unable to improve forecasts of gold prices in the Canadian market using kernel regression.

Nonparametric estimates of conditional variances in a time series context are useful for estimating the stock return volatility in asset markets. Pagan and Schwert (1990) compared the nonparametric conditional stock volatility estimates with parametric estimates such as the autoregressive conditionally heteroskedastic (ARCH) model, generalized ARCH (GARCH), exponential GARCH and Markov's switching regime.

An important application consists of testing the difference between regression curves. Suppose that we have data $\{(X_i, Y_i, Z_i), 1 \leqslant i \leqslant n\}$ from the random variable (X, Y, Z). We want to test the hypothesis H_0: $m_y = m_z$ where $m_y(x) = E(Y \mid X = x)$ and $m_z(x) = E(Z \mid X = x)$. King (1989) proposed the statistic

$$\hat{\tau}_n = n^{-1} \sum_i [\hat{m}_y(X_i) - \hat{m}_z(X_i)]^2 \tag{40}$$

where $\hat{m}_y(\cdot)$ and $\hat{m}_z(\cdot)$ are kernel estimates which employ the same bandwidth. He obtained the small-sample distribution of such a statistic on the assumption that the error terms in each regression are normally distributed and the asymptotic distribution of $\hat{\tau}_n$, after suitable normalization, when the bandwidth tends to zero as $n \to \infty$. Härdle and Marron (1990) obtained a similar test where the difference between the two regressions is parameterized. Hall and Hart (1990) proposed a statistic

$$\hat{S}_n = \left[\sum_{j=0}^{n-1} \left(\sum_{i=j+1}^{j+m} D_i \right)^2 \right] \left[n \sum_{j=0}^{n-1} \frac{(D_{i-1} - D_i)^2}{2} \right]^{-1}$$

where m is the integer part of nh for fixed h, $D_i = Y_i - Z_i$ for $1 \leqslant i \leqslant n$, and $D_i = D_{i-n}$ for $n + 1 \leqslant i \leqslant n + m$. They proved, keeping h fixed, that $\hat{S}_n$ provides an asymptotically powerful test, and the asymptotic distribution of $\hat{S}_n$, under the null, is a Wiener process. They proposed to determine the critical values by bootstrap, which are more accurate than the critical values obtained by the asymptotic approximation. Hall and Hart (1990) generalized this test to the testing of several nonparametric functions and regression curves which depend on different regressors.

Many other applications of nonparametric regression are found in semiparametric problems which are discussed in the next section.

4   Estimation of semiparametric models

Many if not most econometric models are semiparametric. A parametric structure explaining some basic economic phenomena (e.g. utility or cost functions) is usually known and one is interested in the estimation of these parameters and in making inferences on the assumed structure from the data. However, many features of the data generating process are of unknown form. The full functional form of the distribution cannot usually be justified from economic theory and is unlikely to be of specific economic interest. In the recent econometric literature, estimation of a number of semiparametric models requires nonparametric estimation of certain functionals in the first step. In these models, it is explicitly recognized that certain features of the underlying distribution of the data are unknown while others follow a known parametric model. The goal is to obtain estimates for the parametric part that are asymptotically equivalent to those obtained when the nonparametric part of the model is perfectly known.

In nonparametric estimation, 'nature' only provides a data set $\{Z_i, i \geqslant 1\}$, and different features of the underlying data generating process are estimated from these data. In semiparametric estimation, 'nature' also provides some parametric relationship between variables. For instance,

$$E(Y \mid X = x) = x'\beta \tag{41}$$

$$E(Y \mid X = x, Z = \mathcal{F}) = x'\beta + \mu(\mathcal{F}) \text{ with } \mu \text{ unknown} \tag{42}$$

$$\text{median}(Y \mid X = x, W = w) = x'\beta. \tag{43}$$

In (41) and (43), the parameters of interest β can be consistently estimated by parametric methods, e.g. least squares or robust estimation. The problem in this case is to choose the most appropriate objective function. Semiparametric estimates improve the efficiency of simple consistent parametric estimates by incorporating estimates of some unknown nonparametric function in the objective function. Consistent estimates are sometimes impossible to obtain by parametric methods (e.g. in (42)) but they can be obtained by semiparametric estimation.

Thus, in a semiparametric problem one combines a known function of the parameter of interest (e.g. $x'\beta$) with a nonparametric shape function G, such as the density of the disturbances, regression functions, conditional quantiles etc. A semiparametric estimate is adaptive if it is asymptotically as efficient as the infeasible estimate which employs a correct finite parameterization of G. (In what follows, when referring to 'efficiency' we shall always mean 'asymptotic efficiency'.) The property of adaptation refers to the existence of such an estimate. Unfortunately, adaptation is not always possible.

Stein (1956) proved that a necessary condition for adaptation is that for every finite parameterization G_η of G, where η is a finite-dimensional vector, the limiting covariance matrix of the infeasible estimate of β and the nuisance parameters vector η is block diagonal. It implies that knowledge of η cannot improve estimation of β. Bickel (1982) gave a condition for a less general class of Gs having the heuristic interpretation that the efficient estimate based on a given G is still root-n-consistent when G is mis-specified. Manski (1984) gave a necessary condition for adaptation of a subset of parameters in β and Schick (1986) gave a condition that is necessary in models more general than Bickel's.

Begun et al. (1983) showed how to obtain lower bounds for the asymptotic covariance matrix of estimates of β when adaptation is not possible. These bounds, called semiparametric efficiency bounds, have been calculated for certain econometric models (see Chamberlain, 1986, 1990; Cosslett, 1987; Newey, 1990b).

In order to conserve space and to achieve a more unified presentation we focus on methods which employ the smoothed nonparametric density or regression estimates introduced in sections 2 and 3. Thus we omit such important semiparametric methods as least absolute deviations estimates of censored regression (where nonparametric estimation occurs only in computing standard errors) and maximum score estimates of discrete choice models (which are asymptotically non-normal and are not root-n-consistent). Some of these methods were included in the survey by Robinson (1988b). Not a great deal of work has been done on the choice of data-dependent bandwidth in semiparametric problems, though of course the rules described in sections 2 and 3 can be applied.

In the rest of this section we present different semiparametric estimates. Surveys of the semiparametric literature are Robinson (1988b), Newey (1990b) and Härdle (1990). Most semiparametric work, including the bulk of the work referred to below, has employed the kernel or nearest neighbour nonparametric estimates discussed above. Another semiparametric method which is proving popular in a variety of semiparametric problems is series estimation (see for example Andrews, 1991b; Newey, 1991).

4.1 Full adaptive estimation

Bickel (1982) considered the linear regression model (41). Under regularity conditions, the Cramer–Rao efficiency bound is achieved by the one-step score estimate

$$\bar{\beta} = \tilde{\beta} - \left[\sum_i X_i X_i' f^{(1)}(U_i)^2 f(U_i)^{-2} \right]^{-1} \sum_i X_i f^{(1)}(U_i) f(U_i)^{-1}$$

where $\tilde{\beta}$ is a preliminary root-n-consistent estimate and $U_i = Y_i - \beta' X_i$. However, the density of the disturbances U_i is nonparametric and the disturbances themselves are unobserved. Stone (1975), for the case $X = 1$ and β scalar, and Bickel (1982), for the general regression case, suggested an estimate of approximately the form

$$\hat{\beta} = \tilde{\beta} - \left[\sum_i X_i X_i' \hat{f}^{(1)}(\tilde{U}_i)^2 \hat{f}(\tilde{U}_i)^{-2} \right]^{-1} \sum_i X_i \hat{f}^{(1)}(\tilde{U}_i) \hat{f}(\tilde{U}_i)^{-1} \tag{44}$$

where $\tilde{U}_i = Y_i - \tilde{\beta}' X_i$ and $\hat{f}(\tilde{U}_i)$ and $\hat{f}^{(1)}(\tilde{U}_i)$ are kernel estimates of $f(\cdot)$ and $f^{(1)}(\cdot)$ Bickel proved that $\hat{\beta}$ is as efficient as the infeasible $\bar{\beta}$, assuming that the U_i are independently and identically distributed, symmetric and independent of X_i. Symmetry is not necessary for adaptive estimation of the slope coefficient. Bickel required splitting of the sample into two parts. The residuals $\tilde{U}_i$ are computed from one part of the sample and the density and its derivatives are estimated from the other. Schick (1986) employed a less drastic form of sample splitting. Manski (1984) extended Bickel's results to nonlinear regression, avoiding independence between disturbances and regressors. A Monte Carlo study of bandwidth choice is reported in Hsieh and Manski (1987). Kreiss (1987) extended these results to adaptive estimation of the coefficients of an autoregressive moving average (ARMA) model. He did not require the sample splitting of Bickel. Steigerwald (1990) considered an extension to regression models with ARMA errors.

Engle and González-Rivera (1991) have applied this method to the estimation of ARCH models with conditional density of unknown form. They assumed a linear functional form for the conditional expectation and the conditional variance of stock returns. Then, using ordinary least squares, they estimated the parameters of the conditional mean and variance in order to estimate the standardized residuals. The density function of the standardized residuals is estimated by a kernel estimate. Then the log-likelihood function based on the estimated density is maximized with respect to the parameters of the conditional mean and variance. The information matrix is not block diagonal, and the resulting semiparametric estimate is not proved to be adaptive. However, they reported encouraging Monte Carlo results.

There are other semiparametric estimates, based on nonparametric estimates of the score function, that achieve certain efficiency bounds. Newey and Powell (1987a, b) used nonparametric score estimates to achieve semiparametric efficiency bounds within a certain class of distributions for censored regression models under symmetry and conditional quantile restrictions. Lee (1990) has used also estimates of the score function in sample selection models. His semiparametric estimate achieves the Chamberlain (1986) bound in the binary selection model.

4.2   Asymptotically efficient estimation in the presence of heteroskedasticity of unknown form

Consider model (41) with $\mathrm{var}(Y \mid X = x) = \sigma^2(x)$ of unknown form. The infeasible weighted least squares estimate

$$\bar{\beta} = \left[\sum_i \frac{X_i X_i'}{\sigma^2(X_i)} \right]^{-1} \sum_i \frac{X_i Y_i}{\sigma^2(X_i)}$$

is Gauss–Markov efficient under suitable regularity conditions. Rose (1978) suggested estimating $\sigma^2(X_i)$ by (38) or (39) and then estimating the coefficients by

$$\hat{\beta} = \left[\sum_i \frac{X_i X_i'}{\hat{\sigma}^2(X_i)} \right]^{-1} \sum_i \frac{X_i Y_i}{\hat{\sigma}^2(X_i)} \tag{45}$$

This estimate has been proved to be as efficient as $\bar{\beta}$ by Carroll (1982) using (38) with kernel weights for the single regression model, assuming that $\sigma^2(\cdot)$ is a smooth function and the regressor admits a density with compact support and is bounded away from zero. Robinson (1987a) relaxed Carroll's assumptions to moment conditions in the general multiple regression model using (38) with nearest neighbour weights. He did not require continuity of $\sigma^2(\cdot)$, and indeed allowed X to have a discrete or mixed distribution, not only a continuous one. Lee (1990c) presented Monte Carlo results using a data driven bandwidth. Delgado (1992) has extended Robinson's results to the multiple equations nonlinear regression model and Delgado (1989) has proved adaptation in the nonlinear regression model using (39).

A natural application of this method is to count regression models. When Y is a count variable taking values $0, 1, 2, \ldots$, the conditional variance is typically a function of the conditional mean. The usual estimation approach in econometrics is maximum likelihood (ML). Under regularity conditions, the ML estimate is asymptotically efficient if the conditional distribution of Y given X is correctly specified (e.g. a Poisson, a geometric or a negative binomial). Furthermore, when the conditional distribution is incorrectly specified, the pseudo ML (PML) estimate may be consistent but asymptotically inefficient (e.g. the Poisson ML). The usefulness of the Poisson model is limited by the fact that the variance is equal to the conditional mean, which is rarely obviously true using microeconomic data. Other likelihood functions, like the geometric or negative binomial, may yield inconsistent pseudo ML (PML) estimates under misspecification. In this sort of model, it is typically assumed that $E(Y \mid X = x) = g(x, \beta_0)$, where β_0 are unknown parameters and $g(x, \beta)$ is always positive for any value of β, e.g. $g(x, \beta) = \exp(x'\beta)$. The semiparametric weighted nonlinear least squares estimate

$$\hat{\beta} = \underset{\beta}{\mathrm{argmin}} \sum_i \frac{[Y_i - g(x, \beta)]^2}{\hat{\sigma}^2(X_i)}$$

is asymptotically equally efficient to the Poisson ML estimate when the likelihood is correctly specified, but it is more efficient than the Poisson PML estimate when the conditional distribution is not Poisson. The semiparametric estimate is, in general, more inefficient than other ML estimates when the likelihood is correctly specified. But it is consistent more generally than PML estimates under mis-specification.

Delgado and Kniesner (1990) considered the problem of modelling worker absenteeism on London buses. In their application, Y is the number of absence spells of up to 7 days in 1985. X is a vector consisting of the numbers of absences in 1984 and 1983 and variables including pay grades, non-wage characteristics of employment, worker's personal and economic characteristics, the employer's technological and economic traits, and the legal and economic environment. There were $n = 5101$ observations, a promising number for semiparametric estimation because sufficiently good nonparametric conditional variance estimates are likely to be obtainable. It was assumed that $g(x, \beta) = \exp(x'\beta)$, which is common in regression models of counts. They computed semiparametric estimates as well as ordinary least squares and ML (based on various models). It was found that the semiparametric and negative binomial ML results were similar.

Müller and Stadtmüller (1987) obtained efficient estimates in the fixed design model with unknown heteroskedasticity, using weights (38). Harvey and Robinson (1988) considered a non-stationary time series regression model with trending regressors and stationary autoregressive disturbances which were multiplied by an unknown time-varying factor. They obtained efficient estimates of the regression parameters using a Cochrane–Orcutt algorithm where the residuals are standardized by a nonparametric estimate of the heteroskedasticity based on partition weights. Robinson (1986) also used weights (36) to obtain estimates of time-varying parameters and heteroskedastic variances which are a function of time.

Robinson (1987b) has proposed applying semiparametric methods to the estimation of models with ARCH effects, where the conditional variance is of unknown form. The conditional variances and their derivatives are estimated by nonparametric regression. Then, estimates of the parameters of the conditional mean are obtained by substituting the nonparametric estimates in the normal equations of the Gaussian log-likelihood. Applications of this method may be found in Whistler (1989) and Lee (1990b).

The estimate defined in (45) can be arbitrarily influenced by outlying observations. Delgado (1990a) proposed using the estimates defined in (38) and (45) with nearest neighbour weights to correct for heteroskedasticity in the linear regression model using robust estimates. This estimate is implicitly defined as the solution to

$$\sum_i \Psi \left(\frac{Y_i - X_i'\hat{\beta}}{\hat{\sigma}(X_i), X_i} \right) \frac{X_i}{\hat{\sigma}(X_i)} = 0 \tag{46}$$

where $\Psi(\cdot)$ is a bounded function and $\hat{\sigma}(X_i) = [\hat{\sigma}^2(X_i)]^{1/2}$. Delgado proved, under regularity conditions, that this estimate is asymptotically as efficient as the infeasible estimator which employs the true $\sigma(X_i)$ in (46).

4.3   Optimal semiparametric instrumental variable estimators

Consider a nonlinear simultaneous equations model expressed by the conditional moment restriction

$$E[U(\beta_0, Y, X) \mid X] = 0 \tag{47}$$

where $U(\cdot)$ is a $q \times 1$ vector of known functions, β is an unknown $p \times 1$ vector of parameters, X is an $r \times 1$ random variable and Y is an $s \times 1$ random variable. It is also assumed that

$$\mathrm{var}[U(\beta_0, Y, X) \mid X = x] = \Omega$$

where Ω is positive definite and independent of x. Let H_i be a matrix of instruments such that

$$H_i = R(X_i, \beta_0)\Omega^{-1}$$

where

$$R(X_i, \beta) = E\left[\frac{\partial U(\beta, Y, X)}{\partial \beta}\bigg| X = X_i\right].$$

When U is nonlinear in Y, in general at least some elements of $R(X_i, \beta)$ are of unknown functional form, because (47) produces insufficient information. Amemiya (1977) defined the optimal nonlinear three-stage least squares (NL3SLS) estimate as

$$\bar{\beta} = \underset{\beta}{\mathrm{argmin}} \sum_i U_i(\beta)'H_i'\left(\sum_i H_i \Omega H_i'\right)^{-1}\sum_i H_i U_i(\beta).$$

Arbitrary instruments uncorrelated with U_i will generally produce root-n-consistent but asymptotically inefficient estimates. Let $\bar{\beta}$ be some preliminary root-n-consistent estimate of β. When the (α, τ)th component of $R(\beta, X_i)$, $r_{\alpha\tau}(\beta, X_i)$, is of unknown functional form, it is estimated by

$$\hat{r}_{\alpha\tau}(X_i) = \sum_j c_{\alpha\tau}(Y_j, X_j, \tilde{\beta})W_{nj}(X_i)$$

where $c_{\alpha\tau}(Y_j, X_j, \beta)$ is the (α, τ)th component of the matrix $\partial U(\beta, Y_i, X_i)/\partial\beta$. The variance matrix Ω is estimated by its sample analogue.

$$\hat{\Omega} = n^{-1}\sum_j U_j(\tilde{\beta})U_j(\tilde{\beta})'.$$

Then the optimal instruments H_i are estimated by $\hat{H}_i = \hat{R}_i\hat{\Omega}^{-1}$, where $\hat{R}_i$ has (α, τ)th component $\hat{r}_{\alpha\tau}(X_i)$, and β is estimated by

$$\bar{\beta} = \underset{\beta}{\mathrm{argmin}} \sum_i U_i(\beta)'\hat{H}_i'\left(\sum_i \hat{H}_i\hat{\Omega}\hat{H}_i'\right)^{-1}\sum_i \hat{H}_i U_i(\beta).$$

This feasible NL3SLS estimate has been proposed by Newey (1990a). Newey (1990a) has proved, under conditions similar to Robinson (1987a), that the corresponding one-step estimate is asymptotically efficient.

If certain independence assumptions are added to (47), Robinson (1991a) has shown that estimates as efficient as Newey's can be obtained by estimating $R(\beta, X_i)$ by resampling techniques. In particular, if

$$c_{\alpha\tau}(Y_i, X_i, \beta) = t_{\alpha\tau}[\xi(\beta), h(\beta_0, Y_i, X_i), X_i]$$

where $t_{\alpha\tau}(\cdot), \xi(\cdot)$ and $h(\cdot)$ are known functions, $V_i = h(\beta_0, Y_i, X_i)$ is independent of X_i. Then,

$$\hat{r}_{\alpha\tau}(X_i) = T^{-1} \sum_{j \in \mathfrak{J}} t_{\alpha\tau}[\xi(\tilde{\beta}), h(\tilde{\beta}, Y_j, X_j,), X_i]$$

where $\mathfrak{J}$ is a subset of size T of the integers $\{1, 2, \ldots, n\}$. Robinson (1991a) proved that the resulting NL3SLS estimate of β is as efficient as the infeasible estimate, under regularity conditions which allow for lagged independent variables or serially correlated disturbances, but requires independence between V and X, often tantamount to independence between U and X, strengthening the conditional moment restriction (47). An advantage is that the estimate avoids the choice of a smoothing parameter. The number of elements in $\mathfrak{J}$ has to increase with n but at an arbitrarily slow rate, where this rate may affect a Berry–Esseen-type bound (i.e. the rate of convergence to the limiting distribution).

Application of these methods is interesting in transformed regression models, where PML generally yields inconsistent estimates. Consider for instance the transformed model.

$$U(\beta, Y_i, X_i) = \frac{\text{arcsinh}(\lambda Y_i)}{\lambda} - \alpha - \theta' X_i$$

where Y is a scalar and $\beta = (\lambda, \alpha, \theta')'$ is the vector of parameters. Then

$$R(X_i, \beta) - (r(X_i), -1, -X_i)$$

where

$$r(X_i) = E\left[\frac{\partial U(\beta_0, Y, X)}{\partial \lambda} \bigg| X = X_i\right]$$

$$= E\left\{\tanh\left[\lambda_0\left(\alpha_0 + \beta_0' X + \frac{\tilde{U}}{\lambda_0^2}\right)\right] - \frac{\alpha_0 + \beta' X}{\lambda_0} \bigg| X = X_i\right\}.$$

Root-n-consistent estimates of θ are obtained using arbitrary instruments, uncorrelated with U. The resulting estimates $\tilde{\theta} = (\tilde{\alpha}, \tilde{\lambda}, \tilde{\beta}')'$ are inefficient. However, efficient estimates are obtained by applying Newey's method, estimating $r(X_i)$ by

$$\hat{r}(X_i) = \sum_j \left\{\tanh\left[\tilde{\lambda}\left(\tilde{\alpha} + \tilde{\beta}' X_j + \frac{\tilde{U}_j}{\tilde{\lambda}^2}\right)\right] - \frac{\tilde{\alpha} + \tilde{\beta}' X_j}{\tilde{\lambda}}\right\} W_{nj}(X_i).$$

Assuming X is independent of U, we can apply Robinson's method. The estimate of $r(X_i)$ is given by

$$\hat{r}(X_i) = T^{-1} \sum_{j \in \mathfrak{J}} \left\{\tanh\left[\tilde{\lambda}\left(\tilde{\alpha} + \tilde{\beta}' X_j + \frac{\tilde{U}_j}{\tilde{\lambda}^2}\right)\right] - \frac{\tilde{\alpha} + \tilde{\beta}' X_j}{\tilde{\lambda}}\right\}.$$

Note that $V_i = U_i$ in this case.

These methods have been extended and applied to the estimation of price elasticities of demand for car attributes and fuel efficiency by Lee (1990a).

4.4   Semiparametric partially linear models

Semiparametric estimates of model (42) have been considered by Spiegelman (1976), Green et al. (1985), Engle et al. (1986), Rice (1986), Heckman (1986), Robinson (1988a), Speckman (1988), Carroll and Härdle (1989) and others.

Note that

$$E(Y \mid Z = \mathfrak{F}) = E(X \mid Z = \mathfrak{F})' \beta + \gamma(\mathfrak{F}).$$

Then, with serially uncorrelated and homoskedastic errors, an efficient estimate of the slope coefficients is obtained by regressing $Y_i - E(Y \mid Z = Z_i)$ on $X_i - E(X \mid Z = Z_i)$, assuming X and Z are not functionally related. A feasible version can be constructed by estimating the conditional expectations by nonparametric methods. In particular, Robinson (1988a) proposed estimating β by

$$\hat{\beta} = \left\{ \sum_i X_i^* X_i^{*\prime} \hat{I}_i \right\}^{-1} \sum_i X_i^* Y_i^* \hat{I}_i$$

where $X_i^* = X_i - \hat{m}_X(Z_i)$ and $Y_i^* = Y_i - \hat{m}_Y(Z_i)$, $m_X(Z_i)$ and $\hat{m}_Y(Z_i)$ are higher order kernel estimates of $E(X \mid Z = Z_i)$ and $E(Y \mid Z = Z_i)$, respectively, and $\hat{I}_i = 1[\hat{f}(Z_i) > b]$ where $\hat{f}(Z_i)$ is the corresponding density estimate of Z evaluated at Z_i and b is a small trimming number. Under regularity conditions $\hat{\beta}$ is root-n-consistent and asymptotically normal. Chamberlain (1990) has shown that it achieves a semiparametric efficiency bound. Higher order kernels are used in order to make the bias of $\hat{\beta}$ (see Speckman, 1988) converge at the appropriate rate. Lee (1990c) has provided Monte Carlo results using data-driven bandwidths.

Lee (1989) has applied this approach to the estimation of the 'surprise' consumption function. The model can be expressed as follows:

$$Y_i = \beta'[X_i - E_i(X_i)] - \gamma' E_i(X_i) + U_i$$

where Y_i is consumption and X_i is a vector observable, $E_i(X_i)$ is an unobservable vector of agents' expectations of X_i, and U_i is a scalar unobservable. The vector $X_i - E_i(X_i)$ consists of 'surprises' or 'news'. It is assumed that agents have rational expectations, i.e.

$$E_i(X_i) = E(X_i \mid \mathfrak{J}_i),$$

where $\mathfrak{J}_i$ is the information set at time i. Further, it is assumed that $\mathfrak{J}_i$ can be summarized by a vector of observables Z_i, so that

$$E(X_i \mid \mathfrak{J}_i) = E(X_i \mid Z_i).$$

It is supposed that $h(\mathfrak{F}) = E(X \mid Z = \mathcal{F})$ is nonparametric; we know the information set governing agents' expectations but we do not know by which mechanism these are formed. The consumption function can be described as semiparametric. We can rewrite the model as

$$Y_i = \beta' X_i + (\gamma - \beta)' h(Z_i) + U_i$$
$$= \beta' X_i + \phi(Z_i) + U_i,$$

where $\phi(Z_i) = (\gamma - \beta)'h(Z_i)$ is of unknown functional form. This is a partially linear regression model. Robinson (1989) considered an alternative but related class of statistics which provides tests of certain hypotheses (such as $\beta = 0$) under fairly general serially dependent, stationary, observations on X_i, Z_i and Y_i. Lee (1989) used US quarterly data and considered the model

$$\Delta C_i = \gamma_i + \gamma_2 E_i(r_i) + \gamma_3 E_i(I_i) + \beta_1[r_i - E_i(r_i)] + \beta_2[I_i - E_i(I_i)] + U_i$$

where C_i is consumption, $\Delta C_i = C_i - C_{i-1}, I_i$ is income and r_i is the interest rate. Lee suggested that the information set $\mathfrak{J}_i$ might initially comprise a large number of variables, such as three lags of C, I, nominal interest rates, averaged hours worked per capita, government expenditures, inflation and stock prices. Because $n = 133$ only, nonparametric estimates of $E_i(r_i)$ and $E_i(I_i)$ when Z_i is a 21-dimensional vector will be hopelessly imprecise, and though the effect on estimates of β_1 and β_2 is likely to be less serious it is clearly desirable to seek a Z_i which contains much of the information in the twenty-one variables but is of much smaller dimension. This is an extremely difficult and delicate task, especially as the possibly nonlinear character of $h(\cdot)$ makes a linear components procedure possibly inadequate. Lee employed a principal components procedure based on certain nonlinear functions, as well as linear ones, and found it possible to choose a two-dimensional Z_i. Among his conclusions, the semiparametric tests tended to find semiparametric coefficients insignificant, and the estimates of the surprise coefficients tended to differ between parametric and semiparametric methods. The semiparametric estimates were found to be sensitive to the choice of bandwidth number, but not excessively so.

Stock (1989) uses this semiparametric estimate for nonparametric policy analysis. He considers model (42) where observations are drawn from different cells. The variables Z include policy variables that can be modified by the policy maker, and X are dummy variables indicating the cell-specific effects. The dependent variables measure the success of the policy. Then the objective of this research is to estimate the benefit of a particular policy by the average

$$B_n = n^{-1} \sum_j [E(Y \mid X = X_j, Z = Z_j) - E(Y \mid X = X_j, Z = Z_j^*)]$$

$$= n^{-1} \sum_j [\gamma(Z_j) - \gamma(Z_j^*)]$$

where Z_i and Z_i^* are the values of Z before and after the policy intervention. Stock (1989) proposed to estimate B_n by

$$\hat{B}_n = n^{-1} \sum_j [W_{nj}(Z_i) - W_{nj}(Z_i^*)](Y_j - \hat{\beta}'X_j)$$

and obtained the asymptotic distribution of $\hat{B}_n$ under regularity conditions and after suitable normalization. Stock (1991) applied this procedure to the estimation of the mean hazardous waste clean-up benefits. In his application, equation (42) is interpreted as a hedonic price equation, where Y is the price of a house and Z are waste related and waste not related housing characteristics. The housing waste related characteristics are proxy variables indicating the risk of the waste site. These variables are a function of the distance from the house to the waste site, the area of the waste site, and whether or not the waste site is hazardous. The not waste related characteristics are the size of the lot, living area in the house, a measure of the neighbour status, the age of the house, and the distance from the house to the centre of the town weighted by the town population. The data consist of 324 single family homes in eleven western and northwestern Boston suburbs. The dependent variable is the sale price of the house between April 1978 and March 1981 deflated to 1980 prices according to the annual National Association of Realtors. Stock (1991) compared ordinary least squares results, assuming $\gamma(\cdot)$ is linear, and the semiparametric methods. He found that the range of semiparametric benefit estimates was comparable with the range of estimates using least squares. However, both semiparametric and parametric methods resulted in imprecise estimates of the benefit of cleaning up the hazardous waste site.

The approach of Engle et al. (1986) and Heckman (1986) is based on spline estimates. Powell (1989) and Newey et al. (1990) considered (42) where $Z_i = W_i'\delta, W_i$ are observable variables and δ is an unknown vector of parameters with application to censored regression models. In this model δ can be estimated root-n-consistently and then a similar approach to that discussed above is employed. Ahn and Powell (1990) considered Z_i to be an unobservable regression function which can be estimated nonparametrically.

Semiparametric estimates such us those described in sections 4.1 to 4.4 are included in a general class considered by Andrews (1990). He also explicitly considered hypothesis testing rules in semiparametric models, estimates which avoid sample splitting, and allowance for serial dependence and mild heterogeneity.

4.5   Semiparametric estimation based on averaged nonparametric estimates and their derivatives

Powell et al. (1989) proposed an estimate of

$$\delta = E[f(X)m^{(1)}(X)]$$

where $m^{(1)}(x)$ are the first derivatives of the unknown regression function $m(x) = E(Y \mid X = x)$ and $f(\cdot)$ is the density of X. It is interesting in a number of econometric applications to limited dependent variable models where we have an index model of the form

$$E(Y \mid X = x) = m(x'\beta_0)$$

where β_0 is an $r \times 1$ vector of unknown parameters. In this case $\delta = c\beta_0$, where c is an unknown constant. Powell et al. noted that, under mild regularity conditions, integration by parts produces

$$\delta = -2E[Yf^{(1)}(X)].$$

Thus, $f^{(1)}(\cdot)$ can be estimated by kernels and δ by

$$\hat{\delta}_n = -2n^{-1} \sum_i Y_i \hat{f}_{(i)}^{(1)}(X_i)$$

$$= \left(\frac{n}{2}\right)^{-1} \sum_{i=1}^{n-1} \sum_{j=i+1}^{n} p_{ij}$$

where $p_{ij} = -h^{-r-1}K^{(1)}[(X_i - X_j)/h](Y_i - Y_j)$, $K^{(1)}$ is the vector of first derivatives of the kernel function and $\hat{f}^{(1)}(\cdot)$ is the derivative of $\hat{f}_i(\cdot)$ defined in (16). Applying asymptotic theory for U statistics, they proved that

$$n^{1/2}\text{var}[r(X,Y)]^{-1/2}[\hat{\delta}_n - E(\hat{\delta}_n)]/2 \xrightarrow{d} N(0, I_r)$$

where

$$r(x,y) = f(x)m^{(1)}(x) - [y - m(x)]f^{(1)}(x).$$

A kernel estimate of $r(X_i, Y_i)$ is

$$\hat{r}(X_i, Y_i) = (n-1)^{-1}\sum_{\substack{j \neq 1 \\ j \neq i}}^{n} p_{ij}.$$

Since $E[r(X,Y)] = \delta$, a consistent estimate of $\text{var}[r(X,Y)]$ is

$$n^{-1}\sum_i \hat{r}(X_i, Y_i)\hat{r}(X_i, Y_i)' - \hat{\delta}_n\hat{\delta}_n'.$$

Powell et al. (1989) noted that $E(\hat{\delta}_n) - \delta = o(n^{-1/2})$ by using high-order kernels and assuming enough derivatives of $f(\cdot)$. They also proposed an instrumental variables estimate of $\delta^* = \delta/E[f(X)]$. They noted that

$$\delta^* - \left\{E[f^{(1)}(X)X']\right\}^{-1} F[f^{(1)}(X)Y].$$

Then δ^* is estimated by

$$\hat{D}_n = \hat{\delta}_{xn}^{-1}\hat{\delta}_n$$

where $\hat{\delta}_{xn} = \sum_i f^{(1)}(X_i)X_i'$.

Härdle and Stoker (1989) have obtained semiparametric estimates of $\delta = E[\partial g(X)/\partial X]$, namely $\hat{\delta}_n = -n^{-1}\Sigma_i[Y_i\hat{f}^{(1)}(X_i)/\hat{f}(X_i)]\hat{I}_i$, where $\hat{I}_i$ was defined in the last section. Newey and Stoker (1993) considered efficiency properties of average derivatives estimates. Härdle et al. (1989) have studied the MSE error properties of average derivatives estimates. They found that the bandwidth minimizing the MSE is proportional to $n^{-2/7}$. Stoker (1989) used average derivatives estimates in testing additive derivative constraints. Robinson (1989) used them in testing a variety of hypotheses in parametric and nonparametric time series models. His methods were applied and extended by Lee (1989) in analysis of the 'surprise' consumption function reviewed in section 4.4. Ahn and Manski (1990) used related methods in the analysis of binary choice models with nonparametric estimation of expectations. Samarov (1990) has proposed different tests based on averaged second derivatives.

4.6 Asymptotically efficient estimation in the presence of autocorrelation of unknown form

Consider a linear regression model

$$Y_i = X_i'\beta + U_i \qquad i = 1, \ldots, n$$

where the X_i are time series and the U_i are stationary and nonparametrically autocorrelated. The model can be written in vector form as

$$Y = X\beta + U$$

where $E(UU') = \Gamma$ is an unknown Toeplitz matrix. Then the infeasible generalized least squares estimate

$$\hat{\beta} = (X'\Gamma^{-1}X)^{-1}X'\Gamma^{-1}Y$$

is Gauss–Markov efficient. The problem is to obtain feasible estimates that are as efficient as $\bar{\beta}$. This problem can be solved by pre-multiplying the model by the Fourier matrix which diagonalizes Γ. Then the model becomes a regression model with approximately independent heteroskedastic disturbances. The disturbance variances are proportional to spectral density ordinates of U. If the spectral density were known or correctly parameterized, efficient estimates could be computed in a standard way. Hannan (1963) proposed estimating the spectral density nonparametrically, showing that the corresponding frequency-domain generalized least squares estimate is as efficient as the infeasible one under quite general conditions, and allowing for trending regressors. This idea has been used in other econometric models, such as distributed lags (Hannan, 1965), linear simultaneous equations (Hannan and Terrell, 1973), continuous-time systems (Robinson, 1976) and regression models with conditional heteroskedasticity of unknown form (Hidalgo, 1992a). Robinson (1991b) justified efficiency of the estimates with general data-driven smoothing parameter for the spectral density, justifying the consistency of a particular choice of smoother.

Hidalgo (1992b) has considered the problem of nonlinear autoregressive disturbances, where $U_i = \rho(U_{i-1}) + \varepsilon_i, i = 1, \ldots, n, \rho(\cdot)$ is an unknown function and ε_i is white noise. He proposed a Cochrane–Orcutt type estimate where $\rho(\cdot)$ is estimated nonparametrically.

4.7   Linear regression parameter estimation constructed by nonparametric estimation

Faraldo Roca and González Manteiga (1985), Cristóbal Cristóbal et al. (1987) and Stute and González Manteiga (1990) considered the estimation of the linear regression model $Y = X'\beta^0 + \varepsilon$, where ε is independent of X, $E(\varepsilon) = 0$ and $\text{var}(\varepsilon) = \sigma^2$, by the general class of estimators

$$\hat{\beta} = \underset{\beta}{\text{argmin}} \int [\hat{m}_Y(x) - x'\beta]^2 \, d\Omega_n(x)$$

where $\Omega_n(x)$ is a weighting function and $\hat{m}_Y(x)$ is a nonparametric estimate of $E(Y \mid X = x)$. They propose to use the weighting function

$$\Omega_n(x) = \int_{-\infty}^{x} \hat{f}(t) \, dt$$

where $\hat{f}(x)$ is the nonparametric estimate of the density of X evaluated at x. Faraldo Roca and González Manteiga (1985) and Cristóbal Cristóbal et al. (1987) proved that $\hat{\beta}$ is to first order as efficient as ordinary least squares. They showed good performance of the biased $\hat{\beta}$ with respect to ordinary least squares when MSE is used for comparison. It obviously requires a 'judicious choice' of the smoothing parameter. Faraldo Roca and González Manteiga (1985) calculated the optimal bandwidth using kernels which minimize the MSE of $\hat{\beta}$ in the one-regressor case. For this choice of bandwidth the MSE of $\hat{\beta}$ is smaller than the variance of the ordinary least squares.

A related non-iterative estimation method of a linear regression model with censored data has been proposed by González Manteiga and Cadarso Suárez (1990).

4.8   Testing parametric versus nonparametric hypotheses

The problem of testing a parametric specification is of considerable importance in econometrics, e.g. in testing the adequacy of a linear regression model. Traditionally the approach used in econometrics has been of a parametric character, in that the parametric null hypothesis is nested within a parametric alternative; Lagrange multiplier tests have been particularly popular. However, tests against nonparametric alternatives can also be conducted, problems involving comparison between parametric and nonparametric fits.

The central limit theorem discussed in section 3.2 can be used for testing the hypothesis of a linear regression versus a weakly specified nonparametric alternative, as proposed by Robinson (1983). With X scalar, H_0: $m(x) = \alpha + \beta x$, where α and β are unknown parameters. Then under the null $\Phi m = 0$, where Φ is an $(s-2) \times s$ matrix, $m = (m(x_1), \ldots, m(x_s))'$ and $\{x_1, \ldots, x_s\}$ are distinct fixed points. Then, under the null,

$$\hat{\tau}_n = nh\hat{m}'\Phi'(\Phi\alpha\hat{W}\Phi')^{-1}\Phi\hat{m} \xrightarrow{p} \chi^2_{s-2}$$

where $\hat{m} = (\hat{m}(x_1), \ldots, \hat{m}(x_s))'$ is the kernel estimate of m, and $\hat{W}$ and α were defined in sections 3.1 and 3.2. The statistic $\hat{\tau}_n$ can be used for testing the linearity hypothesis.

Azzalini et al. (1989) have proposed a likelihood ratio test for testing the functional form of the conditional mean in count data models. They considered observations of a count variable Y_i taking values $0, 1, 2, \ldots$ The null hypothesis is H_0: $E(Y \mid X = x) = x'\beta$ versus weakly specified alternatives of the form H_1: $E(Y \mid X = x) = m(x)$, where $m(\cdot)$ is an unknown function. They also assumed that the conditional density of Y given X is such that $f(Y = y \mid X = x) = \mathcal{L}[y, m(x)]$, i.e. conditional density functions which are completely determined by their first conditional moment, e.g. the binomial or the Poisson. The statistic used is

$$\tau_n = \sum_i \left\{ \log \mathcal{L}(Y_i, X_i'\hat{\beta}) - \log \mathcal{L}[Y_i, \hat{m}(X_i)] \right\}$$

where $\hat{\beta}$ is computed by maximum likelihood and $\hat{m}(X_i)$ uses kernel weights. They applied this test to the case that $\mathcal{L}(\cdot)$ is binomial with parameter $p(x) = 1/[1 + \exp(-x'\beta)]$ under the null and parameter of unknown functional form under the alternative. They also applied the method when $\mathcal{L}(\cdot)$ is Poisson with mean $x'\beta$ under the null and with mean of unknown functional form under the alternative. They also discussed the generalization of the method to the case where the conditional distribution is also a function of additional nuisance parameters, η, i.e. $f(Y = y \mid X = x) = \mathcal{L}[y, m(x), \eta]$ and applied the test to an AR(1) model. The implementation of the test is based on bootstrapping in the absence of knowledge of the asymptotic null distribution of the statistic.

Delgado and Stengos (1990a) considered tests for the competing hypothesis

H_0: $E(Y \mid X = x, Z = \mathcal{F}) = x'\beta_0$

versus

H_A: $E(Y \mid X = x, Z = \mathcal{F}) = m(\mathcal{F})$

where $m(\cdot)$ is unknown and X and Z do not completely overlap. That is, the hypotheses are non-nested. They proposed a Davidson and MacKinnon (1981) type test where the two hypotheses are artifically nested by means of the comprehensive regression model

$$Y_i = X_i'\theta_0 + \delta\hat{m}(Z_i) + \text{error}$$

where $\hat{m}(\cdot)$ is a nearest neighbour regression estimate based on the Z regressors, and θ_0 is a parameter vector. Then, the least squares t ratios for δ are asymptotically distributed as a standard normal under the null. The least squares estimate of δ, in the above regression, converges in probability to 1 under the alternative. These t ratios are used for testing H_0 versus H_A. Simulations reported in Delgado and Stengos (1990a) are encouraging. They also consider the case where the model in the null is nonlinear in parameter using J, C and P type tests.

A J test procedure based on estimated residuals has been considered by Wooldridge (1990), using sieve estimates. B. Lee (1991) has also proposed a residual specification test based on the residuals from kernel regression. Cox et al. (1988) considered generalized spline models for regression. They were concerned with testing that the regression function is of a particular parametric form against the alternative that the function is of a partially linear (in the sense of section 4.4). Eubank and Spiegelman (1990) proposed an alternative spline based methodology for testing the goodness of fit of a linear model. Yatchew (1990) and Yatchew and Bos (1991) proposed tests for the difference between two partially linear models. Tests using the average derivative method have been studied by Stoker (1989), Robinson (1989) and Samarov (1990).

5 Software

There is often a tradeoff between computational effort and efficiency. Nonparametric estimates are relatively easy to compute. For instance, in GAUSS or MATLAB a Gaussian kernel estimate for $r = 1$, with a bandwidth h and a data vector stored in the $n \times 1$ array x, is computed at point u by means of the sentence

density = sum(exp($-(u - x)$.*$(u - x)/(2$*h*h$)))/(sqrt(2$*pi)*h*n).

('sum' must be changed by 'sumc' in GAUSS). However, this approach is very inefficient. If we want to obtain estimates at each data point, we can exploit the symmetry of the kernel for reducing the number of computations and the storage size. If we want just to plot the density or regression estimates, we can make use of the Fast Fourier Transform, as suggested by Silverman (1982) and Härdle (1987).

Programs for nonparametric regression are available in abundant supply. The kernel method has been implemented in International Mathematical and Statistical Libraries (IMSL) (1984) as subroutine NDKER and in-IMSL (1987) as subroutine DESKN. In both routines the user provides the kernel function and the bandwidth. The language S (Becker and Chambers, 1984) also provides density estimates. The package CURVDAT provides FORTRAN routines for density, regression, density derivatives and regression derivatives.

The package TIMESLAB (Newton, 1988) provides kernel density estimates using different kernels. The package XploRe (Broich et al., 1990) performs different nonparametric estimation procedures with excellent graphical capabilities (see Ng and Sickles (1990) and Lee (1992) for reviews of this software). The package N-Kernel (see Delgado and Stengos (1990a) and Lee (1992) for reviews of this software) implements a particular method based on local kernel weights which is very useful in investigating departures from linearity in regression. Delgado (1990b) provided a number of FOR-TRAN routines using kernels and nearest neighbours and discusses their application in solving semiparametric problems using standard econometric software.

Note

This article is based on research funded by the Economic and Social Research Council (ESRC) reference number R000231441.

References

Abramson, I. S. (1982) On bandwidth variation in kernel estimates – a square root law. *Annals of Statistics*, 10, 1217–23.

Ahn, H. and Manski, C. F. (1990) Distribution theory for the analysis of binary choice under uncertainty with nonparametric estimation of expectations. Preprint.

—— and Powell, J. L. (1990) Semiparametric estimation of censored selection models with a nonparametric selection mechanism. Preprint.

Akaike, H. (1970) Statistical predictor information. *Annals of the Institute of Statistical Mathematics*, 22, 203–17.

—— (1974) A new look at the statistical model identification. *IEEE Transactions of Automatic Control*, AC-19, 716–23.

Amemiya, T. (1977) The maximum likelihood and the nonlinear three-stage least squares estimator in the nonlinear simultaneous equation model. *Econometrica*, 45, 955–68.

Anderson, T. W. (1965) Some nonparametric multivariate procedures based on statistically equivalent blocks. In P. R. Krishnaiah (ed.), *Multivariate Analysis I*.

Andrews, D. W. K. (1990) Asymptotics for semiparametric econometric models: I estimation and testing. Preprint.

—— (1991a) Asymptotic optimality of generalized C_L, cross-validation and generalized cross-validation in regression with heteroskedastic errors. *Journal of Econometrics*, 47, 359–77.

——(1991b) Asymptotic normality of series estimators for various nonparametric and semi-parametric models, *Econometrica*, 59, 302–46.

Azzalini, A., Bowman, A. and Härdle, W. (1989) On the use of nonparametric regression for model checking. *Biometrika*, 76, 1–12.

Bartlett, M. S. (1963) Statistical estimation of density functions. *Sankhya A* 25, 145–54.

Bean, S. J. and Tsokos, C. P. (1980) Developments in nonparametric density estimation. *International Statistical Review*, 48, 267–87.

Becker, R. A. and Chambers, J. M. (1984) *S: An Interactive Environment for Data Analysis and Graphics*. Belmont, CA: Wadsworth.

Begun, J. M., Hall, W. J., Huang, W. M. and Wellner, J. A. (1983) Information and asymptotic efficiency in parametric–nonparametric models. *Annals of Statistics*, 11, 432–52.

Bertrand-Retali, M. (1978) Convergence uniforme d'un estimateur de la densité par la méthode de noyau, *Revue Roumaine de Mathematiques Pures et Appliquées*, 23, 361–85.

Bickel, P. (1982) On adaptive estimation. *Annals of Statistics*, 447–71.

Bierens, H. J. (1990) Model free asymptotically best forecasting of stationary economic time series. *Econometric Theory*, 6, 348–83.

—— and Pott-Buter, H. A. (1991) Specification of household Engle curves by nonparametric regression. *Econometric Reviews*, 9, 123–84.

Bochner, S. (1955) *Harmonic Analysis and the Theory of Probability*. Chicago, IL: University of Chicago Press.

Boente, G. and Fraiman, R. (1989) Robust nonparametric estimation for dependent observations. *Annals of Statistics*, 17, 1242–56.

—— (1990) Asymptotic distribution of robust estimators for nonparametric models from mixing processes. *Annals of Statistics*, 18, 891–906.

Bosq, D. (1980) Une méthode nonparamétrique de prédiction d'un processus stationnaire. Prédictions d'une mesure aléatoire. *C. R. Acad. Sci. Paris, Sér. A.*, 290, 711–13.

Bowman, A. W. (1985) A comparative study of some kernel-based nonparametric density estimators. *Journal of Statistical Computation and Simulation*, 21, 313–27.

Breiman, L., Meisel, W. and Purcell, E. (1977) Variable kernel estimates of multivariate densities. *Technometrics* 19, 135–44.

Broich, T., Härdle, W. and Krause, A. (1990) *XploRe – a Computing Environment for Exploratory Regression and Analysis*. Springer: New York.

Cacoullos, T. (1966) Estimation of a multivariate density. *Annals of the Institute of Statistical Mathematics*, 18, 178–89.

Carroll, R. J. (1982) Adapting for heteroskedasticity in linear models. *Annals of Statistics*, 10, 1224–33.

—— and Härdle, W. (1989) A note on second-order effects in a semiparametric-context. *Statistics*, 20, 179–86.

Chamberlain, G. (1986) Asymptotic efficiency in semiparametric models with censoring. *Journal of Econometrics*, 32, 189–218.

—— (1990) Efficiency bounds for semiparametric regression. Preprint.

Chan, N. H. and Tran, L. T. (1992) Nonparametric tests for serial dependence. *Journal of Time Series Analysis*, 13, 19–28.

Cheng, K. F. and Lin, P. E. (1981) Nonparametric estimation of a regression function. *Zeitschrift für Wahrsheinlichkeitstheorie und verwandte Gebiete*, 57, 223–33.

Chow, Y. S., Geman, S. and Wu, L. D. (1983) Consistent cross- validated density estimation. *Annals of Statistics*, 11, 25–38.

Clark, R. M. (1975) A calibration curve for radiocarbon dates. *Antiquity*, 49, 251–66.

Cleveland, W. S. (1979) Robust locally weighted regression and smoothing scatterplots. *Journal of the American Statistical Association*, 74, 829–36.

—— and Devlin, S. J. (1988) Locally weighted regression: an approach to regression analysis by local fitting. *Journal of the American Statistical Association*, 83, 596–610.

——, —— and Grosse, E. (1988) Regression by local fitting: methods, properties and computational algorithms. *Journal of Econometrics*, 37, 87–114.

Collomb, G. (1980) Estimation de la régression par la méthode des *k* points les plus proches avec noyau: quelques propriétés de convergence ponctuelle. *Lecture Notes in Mathematics*, 831, 159–75.

—— (1981) Estimation non-paramétrique de la régression: revue bibliographique. *International Statistical Review*, 49, 75–93.

——(1984) Propriétés de convergence presque complète du prédicteur à noyau. *Zeitschrift für Wahrsheinlichkeitstheorie und verwandte Gebiete*, 66, 441–60.

——(1985) Non-parametric regression: an up-to-date bibliography. *Statistics*, 16, 309–24.

Cosslett, S. J. (1987) Efficiency bounds for distribution-free estimators of the binary choice and censored models. *Econometrica*, 55, 559–85.

Cover, T. M. (1968) Estimation by the nearest neighbor rule. *IEEE Transactions on Information Theory*, IT-14, 50–5.

——and Hart, P. E. (1967) Nearest neighbor pattern classification. *IEEE Transactions on Information Theory*, IT-13, 21–7.

Craig, B. (1991) A semiparametric test of fixed costs of labor adjustment. Preprint.

Craven, P. and Wahba, G. (1979) Smoothing noisy data with spline functions: estimating the correct degree of smoothing by the method of generalized cross-validation. *Numerische Mathematik*, 31, 377–403.

Cristóbal Cristóbal, J. A., Faraldo Roca, P. and González Manteiga, W. (1987) A class of linear regression parameter estimators constructed by nonparametric estimation. *Annals of Statistics*, 15, 603–9.

CURVDAT: STATCOM; Institut für Statistic Computing; Walter Köhler; Am Mühlrain 24 B D-6903; Neckargemünd.

Davidson, R. and MacKinnon, J. (1981) Several model specification tests in the presence of alternative hypotheses. *Econometrica*, 49, 781–93.

Deheuvels, P. (1977) Estimation non paramétrique de la densité par histogrammes généralisés. *Revue de Statistique Appliquée*, 25, 5–42.

——and Hominal, P. (1980) Estimation automatiquée de la densité. *Revue de Statistique Appliquée*, 28, 25–55.

Delgado, M. A. (1989) Asymptotically efficient fully iterative nonlinear weighted least squares in the presence of heteroskedasticity of unknown form. Preprint.

——(1992) Semiparametric generalised least squares estimation in the multivariate nonlinear regression model. *Econometric Theory*, 8, 203–22.

——(1990a) Bounded influence regression in the presence of heteroskedasticity of unknown form. In G. Roussas (ed.), *Nonparametric Functional Estimation and Related Topics*, Dordrecht: Kluwer Academic.

——(1990b) Computing nonparametric functional estimates in semiparametric problems. Print.

——and Kniesner, T. (1990) Semiparametric versus parametric models for count data: modeling the causes of sickness spells. Preprint.

——and Stengos, T. (1990a) Semiparametric specification testing of non-nested econometric models. *Review of Economic Studies*, forthcoming.

——and —— (1990b) N-Kernel: a review. *Journal of Applied Econometrics*, 5, 299–304.

Devroye, L. (1978) The uniform convergence of nearest neighbor regression function estimators and their application in optimization. *IEEE Transactions on Information Theory*, IT-24, 142–51.

——(1982) Necessary and sufficient conditions for the pointwise convergence of nearest neighbor regression estimates. *Zeitschrift fur Wahrsheinlichkeitstheorie und verwandte Gebiete*, 61, 467–81.

——(1987) *A Course in Density Estimation*. Boston, MA: Birkhauser.

——and Györfi, L. (1985) *Nonparametric Density Estimation: The L_1 View*. New York: Wiley.

——and Penrod, C. S. (1986) The strong uniform consistency of multivariate variable kernel estimates. *Canadian Journal of Statistics*, 14, 211–19.

——and Wagner, T. J. (1980) Distribution-free consistency results in nonparametric discrimination and regression function estimation. *Annals of Statistics*, 8, 231–9.

Diebold, F. X. and Nason, J. A. (1990) Nonparametric exchange rate prediction? *Journal of International Economics*, 28, 315–32.

Doukhan, P. and Ghindès, M. (1980) Estimations dans le processus '$x_{n+1} = f(x_n) + \varepsilon_n$'. *C. R. Acad. Sci. Paris, Sèr. A.*, 290, 921–3.

——— and ——— (1983) Estimation de la transition de probabilité d'une chaîne de Markov Doeblin-racurrente. *Stochastic Processes and their Applications*, 15, 271–93.

Duin, R. P. W. (1976) On the choice of smoothing parameters for Parzen estimators of probability density functions. *IEEE Transactions on Computers*, C-25, 1175–9.

Engle, R. F. and González-Rivera, G. (1991) Semiparametric ARCH models. *Journal of Business and Economic Statistics*, 9, 345–60.

———, Granger, W. J., Rice, J. A. and Weiss, A. (1986) Semiparametric estimates of the relationship between weather and electricity sales. *Journal of the American Statistical Association*, 81, 310–20.

Epanechnikov, V. A. (1969) Nonparametric estimation of a multivariate probability density. *Theory of Probability and its Applications*, 14, 153–8.

Eubank, R. and Spiegelman, S. (1990) Testing the goodness-of-fit of linear models via regression techniques. *Journal of the American Statistical Association*, 85, 387–97.

Faraldo Roca, P. and González Manteiga, W. (1985) On efficiency of a new class of linear regression estimates obtained by preliminary non-parametric regression. In M. Puri et al. (eds), *New Perspectives in Theoretical and Applied Statistics*, New York: Wiley.

Fix, E. and Hodges, J. L. (1951) Discriminatory analysis, nonparametric estimation: consistency properties. *Report Number 4, Project 21-49-004*, USAF School of Aviation Medicine, Randoph Field, Texas.

Freedman, D. and Diaconis, P. (1981a) On the maximum deviation between the histogram and the underlying density. *Zeitschrift für Wahrsheinlichkeitstheorie und verwandte Gebiete*, 58, 139–67.

——— and ——— (1981b) On the histogram as a density estimator: L_2 theory. *Zeitschrift für Wahrsheinlichkeitstheorie und verwandte Gebiete*, 58, 139–57.

Friedman, J. H., Baskett, F. and Shustek, L. J. (1975) An algorithm for finding nearest neighbors. *IEEE Transactions on Computers*, C-24, 1149–58.

Fryer, M. J. (1977) A review of some nonparametric methods of density estimation. *Journal of the Institute of Mathematics and its Applications*, 20, 335–54.

Fukunaga, K. (1972) *Introduction to Statistical Pattern Recognition*. New York: Academic Press.

Gasser, T. and Müller, H. G. (1979) Kernel estimation of regression functions. In T. Gasser and M. Rosenblatt (eds), *Smoothing Techniques for Curve Estimation*, Lecture Notes in Mathematics 757, Heidelberg: Springer, 23–68.

GAUSS: *Aptech Systems Inc.*, Kent, WA.

Gessaman, M. P. (1970) A consistent nonparametric multivariate density estimator based on statistically equivalent blocks. *Annals of Mathematical Statistics*, 41, 1344–6.

González Manteiga, W. and Cadarso Suárez, C. M. (1990) Linear regression with randomly right-censored data using prior nonparametric estimation. In G. Roussas (ed.), *Nonparametric Functional Estimation and Related Topics*, Dordrecht: Kluwer Academic.

Green, P., Jennison, C. and Seheult, A. (1985) Analysis of field experiments by least squares smoothing. *Journal of the Royal Statistical Society, Series B*, 47, 299–315.

Györfi, L. (1987) Density estimation from dependent sample. In Y. Dodge (ed.) *Statistical Data Analysis based on the L_1 Norm and Related Methods*, Amsterdam: North Holland.

——— (1991) Universal consistencies of a regression estimate for unbounded regression functions. In G. Roussas (ed.), *Nonparametric Functional Estimation and Related Topics*, Dordrecht: Kluwer Academic.

Habbema, J. D. F., Hermans, J. and Remme, J. (1978) Variable kernel density estimation in discriminant analysis. *Compstat 1978, Proceedings in Computational Statistics*, Vienna: Physica.

Hall, P. (1983a) Large sample optimality of least squares cross-validation in density estimation. *Annals of Statistics*, 11, 1156–74.

—— (1983b) Asymptotic theory of minimum integrated square error for multivariate density estimation. *Proceedings of the Sixth International Symposium on Multivariate Analysis*, Pittsburgh.

—— and Hart, J. D. (1989a) Convergence rates in density estimation for data from infinite-order moving average processes. Preprint.

—— and —— (1989b) Nonparametric estimation with long-range dependence. Preprint.

—— and —— (1990) Bootstrap tests for the difference between means in nonparametric regression. *Journal of the American Statistical Association*, 85, 1039–49.

Hand, D. J. (1982) *Kernel Discriminant Analysis*. Chichester: Research Studies Press.

Hannan, E. J. (1963) Regression for time series. In M. Rosenblatt (ed.) *Time Series Analysis*, New York: Wiley.

—— (1965) The estimation of relationships involving distributed lags. *Econometrica*, 33, 206–24.

—— and Terrell, R. D. (1973) Multiple equation systems with stationary errors. *Econometrica*, 41, 299–320.

Härdle, W. (1984) Robust regression function estimation. *Journal of Multivariate Analysis*, 14, 169–80.

—— (1987) Resistant smoothing using the fast Fourier transform, Statistical Algorithm 222. *Applied Statistics*, 36, 104–11.

—— (1990) *Applied Nonparametric Regression*. Cambridge: Cambridge University Press, Econometric Society Monographs.

—— and Jerison, M. (1988) Evolution of Engle curves over time. Technical Report, University of Bonn.

—— and Marron, J. S. (1985a) Asymptotic nonequivalence of some bandwidth selectors in nonparametric regression. *Biometrika*, 72, 481–4.

—— and —— (1985b) Optimal bandwidth selection in nonparametric function estimation. *Annals of Statistics*, 13, 1465–81.

—— and —— (1990) Comparing nonparametric versus parametric regression fits. Preprint.

—— and Stoker, T. (1989) Investigating smooth multiple regression by the method of average derivatives. *Journal of the American Statistical Association*, 84, 986–95.

—— and Tsybakov, A. B. (1990) Robust nonparametric regression with simultaneous scale curve estimation. *Annals of Statistics*, 16, 120–35.

—— and Vieu, P. (1989) Nonparametric prediction by the kernel method. Preprint.

—— Hart, J., Marron, I. S. and Tsybakov, A. B. (1989) Bandwidth choice for average derivative estimation. Preprint.

Hart, J. D. and Vieu, P. (1990) Data driven bandwidth choice for density estimation based on dependent data. *Annals of Statistics*, 18, 873–90.

Hartigan, J. A. and Hartigan, P. M. (1985) The dip test of unimodality. *Annals of Statistics*, 13, 70–84.

Harvey, A. C. and Robinson, P. M. (1988) Efficient estimation of nonstationary time series regression. *Journal of Time Series Analysis*, 9, 201–14.

Hassani, S., Sarda, P. and Vieu, P. (1986) Approche non paramétrique en théorie de la fiabilité. *Revue de Statistique Appliquée*, 35.

Heckman, N. E. (1986) Spline smoothing in a partly linear model. *Journal of the Royal Statistical Society, Series B*, 48, 244–8.

Hidalgo, F. J. (1992a) Adaptive estimation in time series regression models with heteroskedasticity of unknown form. *Journal of Time Series Analysis*, (2b).

—— (1992b) Adaptive semiparametric estimation in the presence of autocorrelation of unknown form, *Econometric Theory*, 8, 161–87.

Hildenbrand, K. and Hildenbrand, W. (1980) On the mean income effect: a data analysis of the U. K. family expenditure family. In W. Hildenbrand and A. Mas-Colell (eds), *Contributions to Mathematical Economics*, New York: North-Holland.

Hill, J. D. (1969) A search technique for multimodal surfaces. *IEEE Transactions on Systems, Science and Cybernetics*, SSC-5, 2–8.

Hsieh, D. and Manski, C. (1987) Monte Carlo evidence on adaptive maximum likelihood estimation. *Annals of Statistics*, 15, 541–51.

International Mathematical and Statistical Libraries (IMSL) (1984) *IMSL Library: FORTRAN Subroutines for Mathematics and Statistics* (ed. 9.2).

—— (1987) STAT/LIBRARY (Version 1.0).

Izenman, A. J. (1991) Recent developments in nonparametric density estimation. *Journal of the American Statistical Association*, 86, 205–24.

Jarvis, R. A. (1970) Adaptive global search in a time-variant environment using a probabilistic automaton with pattern recognition supervision. *IEEE Transactions on Systems, Science and Cybernetics*, SSC-6, 209–16.

Johnston, G. J. (1982) Probabilities of maximal deviations for nonparametric regression function estimates. *Journal of Multivariate Analysis*, 12, 402–14.

King, E. C. (1989) A test for the equality of two regression curves, Ph.D. Thesis, Department of Statistics, Texas A & M University.

Kogure, A. (1987) Asymptotically optimal cells for a histogram. *Annals of Statistics*, 15, 1023–30.

Kreiss, J. P. (1987) On adaptive estimation of stationary ARMA processes. *Annals of Statistics*, 15, 112–33.

Lecoutre, J. P. (1986) The histogram with random partition. In M. Puri et al. (eds), *New Perspectives in Theoretical and Applied Statistics*, Wiley: New York.

Lee, B.-J. (1991) A nonparametric specification test using a kernel estimation method. Preprint.

Lee, D. K. C. (1989) Semiparametric analysis of the 'surprise' consumption function. Preprint.

—— (1990a) Elasticity, fuel efficiency and attribute demand: a semiparametric hedonic approach. Preprint.

—— (1990b) Consumption, growth, interest rates, inflation and ARCH effect on an unknown form. Preprint.

—— (1990c) Cross-validation in semiparametric models: some Monte Carlo results. *Journal of Statistical Simulation and Computation*, 37, 171–87.

—— (1992) N-Kernel and XploRe. *Journal of Economic Surveys*, 6, 89–105.

Lee, L. F. (1990) Efficient semiparametric scoring estimation of sample selection models. Preprint.

—— (1992) Semiparametric nonlinear least squares estimation of truncated regression models. *Econometric Theory*, 8, 52–94.

Leonard, T. (1978) Density estimation, stochastic processes, and prior information (with discussion). *Journal of the Royal Statistical Society, Series B*, 40, 113–46.

Li, K. C. (1984) Consistency of nearest neighbor estimates in non-parametric regression. *Annals of Statistics*, 12, 230–40.

—— (1985) From Stein's unbiased risk estimates to the method of generalized cross-validation. *Annals of Statistics*, 13, 1352–77.

—— (1987) Asymptotic optimality for C_p, C_L cross-validation and generalized cross-validation: discrete index set. *Annals of Statistics*, 15, 958–75.

Loftsgaarden, D. O. and Quesenberry, C. P. (1965) A nonparametric estimate of a multivariate density function. *Annals of Mathematical Statistics*, 36, 1049–51.

Mack, Y. P. (1981) Local properties of *k-NN* regression estimates. *SIAM Journal of Algebraic Discrete Methods*, 2, 311–23.

—— and Rosenblatt, M. (1979) Multivariate *k*-nearest neighbor density estimates. *Journal of Multivariate Analysis*, 9, 1–15.

Manski, C. F. (1984) Adaptive estimation of non-linear regression models. *Econometric Reviews*, 3, 145–94.

MATLAB: *The MATH WORKS Inc.*, 21 Eliot Street, South Natick, MA 01760.

McMurtry, G. J. and Fu, K. S. (1966) A variable structure automaton used as a multi-modal searching technique. *IEEE Transactions in Automatic Control*, AC-11, 379–87.

McQueen, J. B. (1990) *N-Kernel*. Non-standard Statistical Software, Santa Monica, CA.

Moore, D. S. and Yackel, J. W. (1977) Consistency properties of nearest neighbor density function estimates. *Annals of Statistics*, 15, 610–25.

Nadaraya, E. A. (1964) On estimating regression. *Theory of Probability and its Applications*, 9, 141–2.

Newey, W. K. (1989) Locally efficient, residual-based estimation of nonlinear simultaneous equations. Preprint.

—— (1990a) Efficient instrumental variable estimation of nonlinear models. *Econometrica*, 58, 809–37.

—— (1990b) Semiparametric efficiency bounds. *Journal of Applied Econometrics*, 5, 99–135.

—— (1990c) Efficient estimation of semiparametric models via moment restrictions. Preprint.

—— (1991) Series estimators of regression functionals. Preprint.

—— and Powell, J. L. (1987a) Efficient estimation of type I censored regression models under conditional quantile and symmetry restrictions. Preprint.

—— and —— (1987b) Efficient estimation of Tobit models under conditional quantile and symmetry restrictions. Preprint.

—— and Stoker, T. M. (1993) Efficiency on average derivatives estimators and index models. *Econometrica*, 61, 1199–1224.

—— Powell, J. L. and Walker, J. R. (1990) Semiparametric estimation of selection models. *American Economic Review, Papers and Proceedings*, 80, 324–8.

Newton, H. J. (1988) *TIMESLAB: A Time Series Analysis Laboratory*. Belmont, CA: Wadsworth.

Ng, P. T. and Sickles, R. C. (1990) 'XploRe'-ing the world of nonparametric analysis. *Journal of Applied Econometrics*, 5, 293–8.

Pagan, A. R. and Ullah, A. (1988) The econometric analysis of models with risk terms. *Journal of Applied Econometrics*, 3, 87–105.

—— and Schwert, G. W. (1990) Alternative models for conditional stock volatility. *Journal of Econometrics*, 45, 267–90.

Parzen, E. (1962) On estimation of a probability density function and mode. *Annals of Mathematical Statistics*, 33, 1065–76.

Powell, J. L. (1989) Semiparametric estimation of censored regression models. Preprint.

——, Stock, J. H. and Stoker, T. M. (1989) Semiparametric estimation of index coefficients. *Econometrica*, 57, 1403–30.

Prakasa Rao, B. L. S. (1983) *Nonparametric Functional Estimation*. Orlando FL: Academic Press.

Prescott, D. M. and Stengos, T. (1988) Do asset markets overlook exploitable nonlinearities? The case of gold. Preprint.

Priestley, M. B. and Chao, M. T. (1972) Nonparametric function fitting. *Journal of the Royal Statistical Society, Series B*, 34, 385–92.

Rèvèsz, P. (1972) On empirical density function. *Periodica Mathematica Hungarica*, 2, 85–110.

Rice, J. A. (1984) Bandwidth choice for nonparametric regression. *Annals of Statistics*, 12, 1215–30.

—— (1986) Convergence rates for partially splined models. *Statistics and Probability Letters*, 4, 203–8.

Robinson, P. M. (1976) The estimation of linear differential equations with constant coefficients, *Econometrica*, 44, 751–64.

—— (1983) Nonparametric estimators for time series. *Journal of Time Series Analysis*, 4, 185–207.

—— (1984) Robust nonparametric autoregression. *Lecture Notes in Statistics*, 26, 247–55.

—— (1986) Nonparametric estimation of time-varying parameters. In P. Hackl (ed.), *Analysis and Forecasting of Economic Structural Change*, Amsterdam: North-Holland.

—— (1987a) Asymptotically efficient estimation in the presence of heteroskedasticity of unknown form. *Econometrica*, 55, 531–48.

—— (1987b) Time series residuals with application to probability density estimation. *Journal of Time Series Analysis*, 8, 329–44.

—— (1987c) Adaptive estimation of heteroskedastic regression models. *Revista de Econometria*, 7, 5–28.

—— (1987d) Nonparametric function estimates for long-memory memory time series. In W. Barnett et al. (eds), *Nonparametric and Semiparametric Methods in Econometrics and Statistics*, New York: Cambridge University Press.

—— (1988a) Root-n-consistent semiparametric regression. *Econometrica*, 56, 931–54.

—— (1988b) Semiparametric econometrics: a survey. *Journal of Applied Econometrics*, 3, 35–51.

—— (1989) Hypothesis testing in semiparametric and nonparametric models for econometric time series. *Review of Economic Studies*, 56, 511–34.

—— (1991a) Best nonlinear three-stage least squares of certain econometric models. *Econometrica*, 59, 755–86.

—— (1991b) Automatic frequency-domain inference on semiparametric and nonparametric models. *Econometrica*, 59, 1329–63.

—— (1991c) Consistent nonparametric entropy-based testing. *Review of Economic Studies*, 58, 437–53.

Rose, R. L. (1978) Nonparametric estimation of weights in least- squares regression analysis. Thesis, University of California at Davis.

Rosenblatt, M. (1956) Remarks on some nonparametric estimates of a density function. *Annals of Mathematical Statistics*, 27, 832–7.

—— (1969) Conditional probability density and regression estimators. In P. R. Krishnaiah (ed.), *Multivariate Analysis II*, New York: Academic Press, 25–31.

—— (1971) Curve estimates. *Annals of Statistics*, 42, 1815–42.

—— (1979) Global measures of deviation for kernels and nearest neighbor density estimates. In T. Gasser and M. Rosenblatt (eds), *Smoothing Techniques for Curve Estimation*, Lecture Notes in Mathematics 757, Berlin: Springer, 181–90.

Roussas, G. G. (1969) Nonparametric estimation of the transition distribution of a Markov process. *Annals of Mathematical Statistics*, 40, 1386–1400.

—— (1988) Nonparametric estimation in mixing sequences of random variables. *Journal of Statistical Planning and Inference*, 18, 135–49.

Royall, R. M. (1966) *A class of nonparametric estimators of a smooth regression function.* Thesis, Stanford University, California.

Rudemo, M. (1982) Empirical choice of histogram and kernel density estimators. *Scandinavian Journal of Statistics*, 9, 65–78.

Samarov, A. M. (1990) Exploring regression structure using nonparametric functional estimation. Preprint.

Schick, A. (1986) On asymptotically efficient estimation in semiparametric models. *Annals of Statistics*, 14, 1139–51.

Schuster, E. F. (1972) Joint asymptotic distribution of the estimated regression function at a finite number of distinct points. *Annals of Mathematical Statistics*, 43, 84–8.

—— and Gregory, C. G. (1981) On the nonconsistency of maximum likelihood nonparametric density estimators. In W. F. Eddy, (ed.) *Computer Science and Statistics: Proceedings of the 13th Symposium on the Interface*, New York: Springer.

Scott, D. W. (1979) On optimal and data based histograms. *Biometrika*, 66, 605–10.

—— (1985a) Average shifted histograms: effective nonparametric density estimators in several dimensions. *Annals of Statistics*, 13, 1024–40.

—— (1985b) Frequency polygons: theory and applications. *Journal of the American Statistical Association*, 80, 348–54.

—— and Factor, L. E. (1981) Monte Casto study of three data-based nonparametric density estimators. *Journal of the American Statistics Association*, 76, 9–15.

—— Tapia, R. A. and Thompson, J. R. (1977) Kernel density estimation revisited. *Nonlinear Analysis*, 1, 339–72.

Silveira, G. (1990) L_1-strong consistency for density estimates in dependent samples. in G. Roussas (ed.), *Nonparametric Functional Estimation and Related Topics*, Dordrecht: Kluwer Academic.

Silverman, B. W. (1981) Using kernel density estimates to investigate multimodality. *Journal of the Royal Statistics Society, Series B*, 43, 97–9.

—— (1982) Kernel density estimation using the fast Fourier transform, Statistical Algorithm 175. *Applied Statistics*, 31, 93–7.

—— (1983) Some properties of a test for multimodality based on kernel density estimates. In J. F. C. Kingman and G. E. H. Reuter (eds), *Probability, Statistics and Analysis*, Cambridge: Cambridge University Press, 248–59.

—— (1986) *Density Estimation for Statistics and Data Analysis*. London: Chapman and Hall.

Singpurwalla, N. D. and Wong, Y. (1983) Estimation of the failure rate: a survey of nonparametric methods. Part I: non Bayesian methods. *Communications in Statistical Theory and Mathematics*, 12, 559–88.

Speckman, P. (1988) Kernel smoothing in partially linear models. *Journal of the Royal Statistical Society, Series B*, 50, 413–46.

Spiegelman, C. H. (1976) *Two techniques for estimating treatment effects in the presence of hidden variables: adaptive regression and a solution to Riersol's problem*. Thesis, Northwestern University.

—— and Sacks, J. (1980) Consistent window estimation in nonparametric regression. *Annals of Statistics*, 8, 240–6.

Steigerwald, D. (1990) Adaptive estimation in time series models. Preprint.

Stein, C. (1956) Efficient nonparametric testing and estimation. In *Proceedings of the Third Berkeley Symposium on Mathematical Statistics and Probability*, Berkeley, CA: University of California Press.

Stock, J. H. (1989) Nonparametric policy analysis. *Journal of the American Statistical Association*, 84, 567–77.

—— (1991) Nonparametric policy analysis: an application to estimating hazardous waste cleanup benefits. In W. Barnett, J. Powell and G. Tanchen (eds), *Nonparametric and Semiparametric Methods in Econometrics and Statistics*, New York: Cambridge University Press.

Stoker, T. M. (1989) Tests of additive derivative constraints. *Review of Economic Studies*, 56, 535–52.

Stone, C. J. (1975) Adaptive maximum likelihood estimation of a location parameter. *Annals of Statistics*, 3, 267–84.

—— (1977) Consistent nonparametric regression (with discussion). *Annals of Statistics*, 5, 595–645.

—— (1980) Optimal rates of convergence for nonparametric estimators. *Annals of Statistics*, 8, 1348–60.

—— (1982) Optimal rates of convergence for nonparametric regression. *Annals of Statistics*, 10, 1040–53.

—— (1984) An asymptotically optimal window selection rule for kernel density estimates. *Annals of Statistics*, 12, 1285–97.

Stute, W. (1984) Asymptotic normality of nearest neighbor regression function estimates. *Annals of Statistics*, 12, 917–26.

—— and Gonzàlez Mantegia (1990) Nearest neighbor smoothing in linear regression. *Journal of Multivariate Analysis*, 34, 61–74.

Tapia, R. A. and Thompson, J. R. (1978) *Nonparametric Probability Density Estimation*. Baltimore, MD: Johns Hopkins University Press.

Tarter, M. E. and Kronmal, R. A. (1976) An introduction to the implementation and theory of nonparametric density estimation. *American Statistician*, 30, 105–12.

Tran, L. T. (1989) The L_1 convergence of kernel density estimates under dependence. *Canadian Journal of Statistics*, 17, 197–208.

Tsybakov, A. B. (1982) Robust estimates of a function. *Problems, Information and Transmission*, 18, 190–201.

Van Ryzin, J. (1973) A histogram method of density estimation. *Communications in Statistics*, 2, 493–506.

Watson, G. S. (1964) Smooth regression analysis. *Sankhya A*, 26, 359–72.

Wegman, E. J. (1982) Density estimation. In S. Kotz and N. L. Johnson (eds), *Encyclopedia of Statistical Sciences*, vol. 2, New York: Wiley, 309–15.

Wertz, W. and Schneider, B. (1979) Statistical density estimation: a bibliography. *International Statistical Review*, 47, 155–75.

Whistler, D. (1989) Semi-parametric ARCH estimation of intra-daily exchange volatility. Preprint.

Whittle, P. (1958) On smoothing of probability densities. *Journal of the Royal Statistical Society*, 20, 334–43.

Woodroofe, M. (1970) On choosing a delta sequence. *Annals of Mathematical Statistics*, 41, 1665–71.

Wooldridge, J. (1990) A test for functional form against nonparametric alternatives. Preprint.

Yakowitz, S. (1985) Nonparametric density estimation, prediction and regression for Markov's sequences. *Journal of the American Statistical Association*, 80, 215–21.

—— (1987) Nearest neighbor methods for time series analysis. *Journal of Time Series Analysis*, 8, 235–47.

Yang, S. (1981) Linear functions of concomitants of order statistics with application to nonparametric estimation of a regression function. *Journal of the American Statistical Association*, 76, 658–62.

Yatchew, A. (1990) Nonparametric regression tests based on least squares. Preprint.

—— and Bos, L. (1991) Nonparametric regression model tests. Preprint.

Author index

Subject index

Printed and bound by CPI Group (UK) Ltd, Croydon, CR0 4YY

17/04/2025